TROUBLED
- TIMES -

TROUBLED
- TIMES -

Fortnight Magazine and the Troubles in Northern Ireland 1970–91

edited by
Robert Johnstone and Robin Wilson

with a
Chronology of Events, 1970–90
edited by
Robert Bell

THE
BLACKSTAFF PRESS
BELFAST

ACKNOWLEDGEMENTS

Grateful acknowledgement is made to the contributors for permission
to reprint their articles, stories and poems; to Gallery Press for
permission to reprint "Darkies" and "I Stepped on a Small
Landmine" from *A Northern Spring* (1986) by Frank Ormsby; and to
Salmon Publishing for permission to reprint "The Origins of the
Farset—For My Father" from *Song at the Edge of the World* (1988)
by Fred Johnston; illustrative material has been provided by Blotski,
Ralph Dobson, Rita Duffy, Rowel Friers, Gault, Mark Hamilton,
Rosemary Jack, Martyn Turner and Julian Watson.

First published in 1991 by
The Blackstaff Press Limited
3 Galway Park, Dundonald, Belfast BT16 0AN, Northern Ireland

This book has received financial assistance under the Cultural Traditions
Programme which aims to encourage acceptance and understanding of
cultural diversity.

Typeset by Textflow Services Limited

Printed by the Guernsey Press Company Limited

British Library Cataloguing in Publication Data
Troubled times:Fortnight magazine and the troubles
in Northern Ireland 1970–91.
I. Bell, Robert, *1953–* II. Johnstone, Robert, *1951–*
III. Wilson, Robin IV. Fortnight
941.60824
ISBN 0-85640-462-4

CONTENTS

Foreword   ROBIN WILSON   vii

PART ONE
Introduction
Celebrating a long march?   TOM HADDEN   3
The early struggles of a mad little magazine   MARTYN TURNER   7
Oddballs and oracles   ANDY POLLAK   9

PART TWO
Politics and current affairs
The new parties: the SDLP   BARRY WHITE   13
Discrimination: jobs   KATHLEEN BOEHRINGER   16
Steps towards reconciliation   GARRET FITZGERALD   20
Internment   TOM HADDEN   24
Living with bombs   MARTYN TURNER   26
Towards an autonomous Ulster   TOM HADDEN   29
The army in Ulster: why the policy of total control of the Catholic
    community has failed   TOM HADDEN   34
Andy Tyrie   SARAH NELSON   36
A criminal lack of politics   SARAH NELSON   39
The blanket brigade   TOM HADDEN   41
Save the Shankill?   JONATHAN STEPHENSON   43
Editorial: The outer limits of prison reform   45
Where are the Provos going?   ED MOLONEY   46
The brave new voice of southern Protestants   MARY HOLLAND   49
Abuse and failure in security policies   KEVIN BOYLE, TOM HADDEN and
    DERMOT WALSH   52
Sidelines: Assembly politician of the year competition
    JAMES McKNIGHT   56
A city of wise women hidden from history   NELL McCAFFERTY   58
A positive proposal for a new Anglo-Irish treaty on Northern Ireland
    KEVIN BOYLE and TOM HADDEN   60
Young and well-heeled in boomtown Belfast   LESLIE VAN SLYKE   64
Unionism: Jim leads on   PAUL BEW and HENRY PATTERSON   66
Uniting Ireland   FRANK WRIGHT and JOHN LAMPEN   68
The new Ireland finds its voice   DICK WALSH   71

PART THREE
The cultural world
Is that a fax?   ROBERT JOHNSTONE   75
A man's world   JOHN MONTAGUE   77
Ulster '71   ANON.   78
The new Ulster Museum   RAY ROSENFIELD   79
Green fool   MAURICE LEITCH   81
Kinsella's craft   JAMES SIMMONS   82
Orange drums, Tyrone, 1966   SEAMUS HEANEY   83
Gut ta   84

Safe as houses: the Great Belfast Urban Motorway Show
   STEWART PARKER   86
Tree   AUGUSTUS YOUNG   91
The bull with the hard hat   BERNARD MacLAVERTY   91
He is coming   JOHN MORROW   93
Rocky   ROBERT JOHNSTONE   95
The life of Jamesie Coyle (extracts)   MICHAEL FOLEY   96
Armistice Day 1938   ROY McFADDEN   100
Home ground   MICHAEL LONGLEY   100
The truth   DOUGLAS DUNN   101
Place   PATRICK WILLIAMS   101
The Boundary Commission   PAUL MULDOON   101
Honeymoon on a motorbike   KERRY CAMPBELL   102
Gentians   MEDBH McGUCKIAN   102
Beautiful lofty things   MICHAEL FOLEY   102
The flower clock   MEDBH McGUCKIAN   103
Signing the treaty   TOM PAULIN   103
Suicide in fridge bid fails   JAMES SIMMONS   103
The frog   PAUL MULDOON   103
Thin Orange line   SIOBHÁN KILFEATHER   104
Letter to the editor   BOB RODWELL   106
Hard nights: Van Morrison's first band   JIM CUSACK   107
Southern comfort   PATRICK GALVIN   109
A wild Sabbath disorder   JOHN MORROW   111
Forked tongues, céilís and incubators   SEAMUS HEANEY   113
Growing up in the cradle of the cherry-picker   GRAHAM REID   117
The fairy tale   ANDREW ELLIOTT   119
A boy on a sleeping volcano   MICHAEL LONGLEY   121
Traditional music as ideology   SEÁN CORCORAN   122
Colonel Despard and the wind-dog   TOM PAULIN   125
Darkies   FRANK ORMSBY   126
I stepped on a small landmine   FRANK ORMSBY   126
Hiding out in the triangle   GERALD DAWE   127
Inquisition   CIARAN O'DRISCOLL   129
Hercules, Antaeus and Paddy   ROBIN GLENDINNING   130
Mother Superiors   JOHN MONTAGUE   131
A message from the "Big Doc"   G.U.B.U.   134
An Ulster songbook   G.U.B.U.   136
The act   TONY HARRISON   138
The origins of the Farset—for my father   FRED JOHNSTON   140
A wedding picture   KERRY CAMPBELL   140
Opening up: a new pluralism   EDNA LONGLEY   141
The Dublin–Belfast railway line   PAUL DURCAN   144
29/12   GLENN PATTERSON   145

PART FOUR
Chronology of events 1970–90   147

Notes on contributors   222

FOREWORD

E DITORS are well used to issuing disclaimers. (Editors of *Fortnight* are particularly versed in disclaiming any ability to pay contributors.) And this foreword to our 21st-anniversary anthology of material from the magazine is mostly by way of disclaimer.

This anthology is not the *best* material that has appeared in *Fortnight* since it first appeared on the streets of Belfast in September 1970. (It's also, of course, not the worst.) Rather, it is an attempt to give a flavour of how *Fortnight* responded to the evolution of Ulster's "troubles" and the wider cultural milieu in which it found itself.

This book has four sections. First, Tom Hadden—the founder, first editor and supporter of the project throughout—gives an overview of the trials and tribulations of a magazine that has always struggled to survive. And two other editorial mainstays, Martyn Turner and Andy Pollak, describe their experience, with varying degrees of wry humour.

Second is a selection by Jonathan Stephenson, another former editor, and myself from the current affairs part of the magazine. This is in no way comprehensive (and is certainly not a substitute for a set of back issues). Instead, it addresses key moments, such as internment or the Anglo-Irish Agreement, to which *Fortnight* has reacted—or indeed which it has anticipated—and gives some indication of the range of the magazine's interests.

Third comes Robert Johnstone's selection of material from the books and arts section of the magazine—which few figures in Ireland's cultural, especially literary, firmament, have failed to grace at one stage or another. This section has provided an essential counterweight to *Fortnight'*s ever-present tendency to be, well, *worthy*.

The fourth section is a boiled-down version, laboriously compiled by Robert Bell of Belfast's Linen Hall Library, of the chronology of the "troubles" that *Fortnight* has supplied from the outset. This compression has inevitably involved a grisly calculus—many single deaths have been left out, for example. But it is still a vastly more detailed day-by-day account than any other to date and will prove invaluable to researchers.

One final disclaimer: there is relatively little in the book from my own period as editor. This is not false modesty nor a reflection on the quality of the contributions over the past few years (or, if it is, I should be told). Rather, it seemed to us to make sense to prioritise material that was not so recent, which readers would be less likely to have read or retained.

ROBIN WILSON
EDITOR
FORTNIGHT

PART ONE

INTRODUCTION

No. 241   50p (70p in Republic)   23 June–6 July '86

FORTNIGHT

AN INDEPENDENT REVIEW FOR NORTHERN IRELAND

CELEBRATING A LONG MARCH?

TOM HADDEN

"1. ON RETURNING FROM MOSCOW NAPOLEON REACHES FOR HIS CHEQUE-BOOK TO RENEW HIS SUBSCRIPTION."

Fortnight has never been short of an excuse to celebrate. Regular celebration is good for publicity and at times for the bank balance. With a bit of careful management we can fit in several anniversaries and milestone issues a year. In that sense there is nothing special about a 21st anniversary. But a book of the celebration is a bit more serious. It makes it hard to avoid the question, what exactly is it that we are celebrating?

One thing that we are clearly not celebrating is *Fortnight'*s contribution to the resolution of the Northern Ireland problem. If that had been the only or main objective of the magazine when we set it up in 1970 we would have little cause for celebration. Two decades of preaching the middle way to two communities passionately committed to other creeds without making a breakthrough is not a great record. The hard truth is that *Fortnight*, like all the other groups and parties committed to reasonable and peaceful approaches to our problems, has little to celebrate. At times it seems as if the situation is as bad is it ever was.

But there have always been other and more sober objectives. Even in 1970 we were realistic enough not to expect any instant solutions. In the dummy issue dated 31 September 1970—a real collector's item now available at £10 to complete your set—we set ourselves lesser and more attainable goals.

One was to give space to contributors from all sides, with the aim of recognising and then working to accommodate our differences by rational discussion rather than military—or media—confrontations. That has been and is being achieved. The list of contributors to *Fortnight*—with one big self-imposed exception (the DUP leader Ian Paisley)—could serve as a *Who's Who* for Northern Ireland.

Another was to explain the realities and complexities of life here to those at home and abroad who thought they knew all about everything and could provide an instant solution. That, too, has been and is being achieved. *Fortnight* reaches those interested in our little problems all over the world—not just in government circles in London and Dublin and Washington but in major universities in more than 20 countries and even such unlikely places as the British Club in Khartoum. The underlying objective in this context has been to get across to people out there—and to remind ourselves—of the balance between the "troubles" and ordinary life and culture. We liked what they said about us in 1973 when we were given a *Hibernia* Press Award (remember the old *Hibernia*? it went under about 10 years ago). Their citation praised us for managing "to keep our cool while the passions of conflict raged all round". The mention in the citation for the Ewart-Biggs Award, which we were given in 1983, of our contribution to

MARTYN TURNER

Nº 2. NUREMBERG. A. HITLER ORDERS 5 MORE COPIES (TO BE BURNT). THOUSANDS CHEER....

Nº 3. NELSON FAILING IN HIS ATTEMPT TO READ SOMEONE ELSE'S COPY, GROPES FOR HIS WALLET.

peace and reconciliation was perhaps a little unFortnightly. But the cash accompaniment was not unwelcome.

None of these objectives needed or needs now a mass readership. So we have never been discouraged by our relatively small circulation. In fact it has often been relatively large. At the best of times, when Martyn Turner and I set out in the 1970s and under Andy Pollak in the early 1980s and now under Robin Wilson, *Fortnight* has been selling more copies per head of population than the *New Statesman*, *New Society* and the *Spectator* put together.

That level of circulation of course has never been enough to make ends meet. But making ends meet has never been a major objective either. It is encouraging to read from time to time of all the other historically significant magazines that have lived on in perpetual financial crisis. We keep telling our bankers about them. And they too may be beginning to realise that there is more to some enterprises than showing a profit.

Some of us who have been closely involved in the magazine over the years might raise a small cheer for the mere fact of survival. Even that has sometimes been a pretty close run thing, both physically and financially. One way of telling the story of *Fortnight* over the years is to tell about the succession of crises and disasters that we have been through.

We started off in a little office in 61 Great Victoria Street in mid-1970. It is still there, behind the pillar over the car showroom, and we are thinking of putting up a little plaque sometime. The first couple of issues were a big disappointment in visual terms. But despite the amateur initial appearance, we managed to establish a solid circulation from the start. In those days there were a lot more people like us looking for new approaches.

The first major crisis was just after internment in September 1971 when we were put out on the street by our printer with only a few days' notice. The main reason seemed to be the reaction of his workforce to what we insisted on saying about internment, though it must be admitted that we were not paying as promptly as we should have been. That meant several weeks of night-driving in the editorial Lea Francis—not unlike an aluminium tank—up and down to the *Irish Times* in Dublin before a grant from our friends in the Joseph Rowntree Social Service Trust enabled us to buy our own printing machine. We eventually found a suitably cheap Rotaprint in Co Derry.

We moved then to 15 James Street South and for the next few weeks the editors had to serve their time as printers and platemakers. Martyn Turner mastered the beautifully polished mahogany studio camera on three or four yards of brass rails and survived the dangers of being burned alive by the acetylene arc lamps. I spent every other Tuesday night minding the printing machine. And on Wednesdays we would round up half a dozen students from the Queen's Union to do some very poorly paid collating. Some of our most committed readers can still trace their connection with the magazine back to those frantic mornings in the attic unravelling wire from the stapling machine and trying to get enough copies out on time.

We kept up the best part of 10 years of really independent production in that way. But not without more crises. The *Fortnight* office in James Street South was blown up in 1973 when someone—some say the IRA, others the British secret service—put a car bomb bang outside our door. One of the editors narrowly missed serious injury or worse when the intended warning went astray. The next couple of weeks were spent picking glass out of the printing machine and other unexpected places.

Experiences like that have been a commonplace for many business enterprises

No 4. HAROLD RECEIVES A FINAL REMINDER FROM THE SUBSCRIPTIONS DEPARTMENT (MILITARY WING).

No 5. NEVILLE CHAMBERLAIN DISPLAYS THE FIRST COPY TO ARRIVE IN LONDON BY AIR MAIL.

throughout the "troubles'. The more serious and persistent threat to *Fortnight* has been of financial ruin. Fortnight Publications Ltd, it can now safely be revealed, has been technically insolvent for almost the whole of its operating life. And from time to time there have been financial crises that could have put us out of business for ever. But in the early 1970s the fact that we did almost everything ourselves shielded us a little from that kind of threat. We even pioneered the new printing technology by setting up one of the first photo-typesetting units in Belfast. And in 1974 we took advantage of rock-bottom property prices, and an absurd government plan to knock down Lower Crescent to build a road, to buy our present premises at No. 7.

Some years later, in 1976, the operation was handed over on a co-operative basis to a new team of editors, a typesetter and Noel Murphy as printer. But, like most of the fashionable workers' co-operatives of the Benn years, it did not prove particularly successful. After a couple of years of declining sales a decision was made, from a mixture of penury and exhaustion, in November 1978 to cease publication, a decision that incidentally left the serialised version of Michael Foley's *The Passion of Jamesie Coyle* in suspense. It took the best part of nine months for the original editors to find the resources and energy to start all over again, which we did in September 1978. Those were the days of the *Fortnight*, published every two months, much loved by Irish jokers.

Eventually, in 1981, Andy Pollak appeared on the scene and began one of the most successful periods of publication both editorially and financially. In December 1982 we moved from being a wholly part-time and more or less voluntary operation to full-time employment and doubled the schedule to monthly publication. But paradoxically it was that very success that led to one of the most serious financial crises. We had taken advantage of one of the few sets of accounts that showed the company to be both solvent and profitable to make an application for development support to the Local Enterprise Development Unit. But LEDU insisted as a condition of any grant aid on an unrealistic increase in the number of employees, which in turn involved an unwise decision to return to fortnightly publication. It may have boosted their job creation figures but it cost *Fortnight* the best part of £10,000. When Andy Pollak moved to the *Irish Times* his successor, Leslie Van Slyke, was left with the impossible task of trying to keep going on a fortnightly schedule. We're glad to hear that job creation for the sake of the statistics is now less of a priority at LEDU and the IDB, and that productivity is the new name of the game.

It was just when the LEDU-induced crisis was coming to a head in May 1986 that we suffered the ultimate indignity of being burned down by a local wino whom we had been supplying with tea and sympathy for too long. The assistant editor had to jump for his life out of a first-floor window and we were left with a scarcely habitable building. But that may have been a blessing in disguise. The need to refurbish the building gave us an opportunity to rethink our longer-term strategy and to take proper advantage of the office space in Lower Crescent, which was now a prime location in the Queen's Conservation Area. The result was the complete refinancing of the company with the support of the Rowntree Reform Trust and many other loyal supporters.

During this period of Thatcherite economic miracle/mirage we were even targeted by some speculative takeover bidders. With the usual *Fortnight* cynicism we suspected those involved of being more interested in asset-stripping and in taking tax advantage of our accumulated losses than in developing or even preserving the magazine, and we decided to retain our independence.

It remains to be seen whether the latest recession will prove to be the magazine's last financial crisis. It would be a fitting finale to Mrs Thatcher's record on the suppression of press freedom to succeed in eliminating *Fortnight* where the IRA and so many others have failed. But to prevent that at least will be a real reason for soldiering on. So will the continuing faith of so many loyal supporters who have helped us over the years.

All in all we prefer to focus any celebrations on the future than on the past. There are some encouraging signs. Some of us used to say that for *Fortnight* to endorse any politician was the kiss of death. But Mary Robinson has broken that jinx. So let's raise a few cheers for the prospect of the 90s rather than the memory of tribulations in the 70s and 80s: for the revival of the mixed economy rather than the greed and inequity of the untrammelled market; for the rebirth of regionalism in a greater Europe rather than the sterile and dangerous mirage of national state sovereignty; and for an Ireland in which we can all do our things without giving exclusive allegiance to anyone.

THE EARLY STRUGGLES OF A MAD LITTLE MAGAZINE

MARTYN TURNER, one of *Fortnight*'s first editors and now Ireland's leading cartoonist, looks back at the struggles, tribulations and occasional lighter moments of the magazine's earliest days.

The cut and thrust of debate, the philosophical wrangles that went on and on into the night, the terse notes left to a fellow editor putting him back on the straight and narrow—I remember none of that, I don't think such things ever happened. My fellow editor and I would both run many a mile to avoid an argument and we both were of the school which says don't delegate if you can do it yourself.

The nearest we ever came to an argument was the fortnightly ritual dance around the work to be done to see who would crack first and get on with it. The system worked well and we eventually arrived at a modus operandi which left Mr Hadden writing the ponderous political stuff and me leavening the dough with the occasional joke. He will deny this. (*I deny everything!*)

Most of the memorable events in the early years were physical; copy and contributors were never a problem—we were always willing to fill any space with an article or a cartoon that we had lurking on a metaphysical stockpile somewhere.

No, it was the physical and mechanical things. Around the time of internment our printers decided that our brand of politics was too hot to handle and that the colour of our money was wrong. We were left with the choice of printing the magazine ourselves or giving up.

We decided to keep the show on the road—literally. The *Irish Times* agreed to typeset the next issue at a day's notice. But then the Irish Customs impounded the copy at Amiens Street Station—Connolly to you youngsters. Mr Hadden set off at midnight in his Lea Francis, managed to extract the stuff from a sleeping porter in the wee small hours, and got back in time for pasting up and printing. We always got it out on time—well, almost always. Eventually we bought a printing machine from the estate of a deceased German in Co Derry and I carefully drove it down in the back of a van with my companion of the time, an Irish setter called Genghis, riding shotgun.

All went well until we got to Sandy Row, when a child of the loyalist persuasion decided to throw itself in front of the van in an attempt to stop the presses before we had even got them started. A quick thrust of the brake and Genghis avoided decapitation by a whisker as the print machine unshackled itself and lurched horribly around the van.

We learnt who would help in a crisis and who made an excuse and left.

This was our excuse for all the bad printing that was to follow. I became the platemaker, Mr Hadden learnt how to print. I collated the pages, Mr Hadden wrapped the wrappers and licked the stamps.

We had visitors from a trust in England who had offered us money to keep the magazine going. They could see that at that time we wrote, drew, printed and distributed the magazine ourselves; two men and a dog; but when they got back to England they none the less proceeded to write a letter to "The Subscription Department".

We got calls from visiting journalists looking for a "stuck somewhere in the middle point of view".

"We are worried," said an Editorial Executive from the *Daily Mirror*, "that with a power vacuum here the Libyans might move in." I thought that terribly funny, and still do, so much so that I repeated the story to a Northern Irish politician not more than two months ago. He, an SDLP man, agreed with the *Daily Mirror*.

We had a distinctly uncommercial attitude to advertising, cutting the occasional half page ad to a quarter page because we thought something else more interesting. One of our occasional advertisers—a bank with a conscience—stopped because we insisted on printing lists of the number of people killed. But it wasn't always our fault. In a burst of liberal enthusiasm a gent from a brewing concern promised enough ads to keep us going for a year. Delight all round. And then a letter arrived asking us out to lunch at the Europa. Over a hugely expensive meal the advertising manager told us that he was afraid our editorial policy might lose him customers on both the Falls and the Shankill. We would gladly have accepted the lunch cheque, but it was too late.

And mainly, we found out who our friends were. We learnt which Belfast journalists worked for money and which worked for principle (and less money). We learnt who would help in a crisis and who made an excuse and left. To the nice, helpful people, thank you.

ODDBALLS AND ORACLES

One of Fortnight's longest-serving—or long-suffering—stalwarts is ANDY POLLAK, editor of the magazine from 1981 to 1985. Here he recalls some of the high and low moments on *Fortnight*'s rocky road.

"**F**ortnight editor wanted: misfits and oddballs, preferably with foreign blood and left-wing or at the very least anti-establishment tendencies, are particularly encouraged to apply; a healthy scepticism about all forms of organised religion an advantage; should be able to mix with and enjoy the company of rascals and villains of all political persuasions, notably extreme loyalists and republicans; must be prepared to work in Dickensian slum conditions and earn a subsistence wage for a 60 to 70 hour week. The successful applicant will have the time of his or her life."

That was the wording I would have liked to have used in the advertisement seeking someone to run the magazine in my place in the autumn of 1985. For *Fortnight* editors have been an extremely odd bunch by the straitlaced standards of Northern Ireland. The magazine was started by that now virtually extinct phenomenon, an Ulster liberal of Protestant stock, who insisted on believing that guaranteeing civil liberties was more important than the murderous shenanigans of Orange and Green politicians and paramilitaries. He was joined by a gangling, golf-playing English socialist cartoonist, later to make his name as the scourge of conservative Ireland in the illustrious pages of the *Irish Times*.

After the founders came a ragbag of lesser mortals to try their hand at running an iconoclastic wee magazine in range of the guns of both sectarian armies. There was the journalist who tried to turn it into an organ of the Peace People; the Scottish researcher who was the world expert on the internal workings of the UVF; and the nationalist schoolteacher who was the world expert on how many people had been killed, wounded, exploded and otherwise violently classified in the late 20th-century Northern Ireland.

Then there was the "British-Israelite" UDR officer who believed that he would be called to play a special role in the future of "our wee Ulster" . . .

A triumvirate led by a dreamy anarchist poet and the trade unionist brother of the future editor of the *New Statesman* then moved in. In 1981 it was the turn of this writer, son of a Czech Jewish socialist father and a Ballymena Presbyterian mother. I was succeeded by a former Canadian radio producer of Dutch antecedents, and the current editor is, I believe, a County Antrim-born sometime car worker and CND activist. In short, a bunch of weirdos.

Weirdness is what it takes. Everyday problems for a *Fortnight* editor in my time included such delights as lengthy visits from the secretary of the Lord's Day Observance Society—a particular fan of the magazine for some reason—which were usually terminated by polite brush-offs when he suggested an evangelical Protestant analysis of the Irish imbroglio based on readings from the Old Testament prophets. Then there was the "British-Israelite" UDR officer who believed that he would be called to play a special role in the future of "our wee Ulster" at the "second coming" of Christ. Or there might be an invitation-cum-summons from someone unrefusable like John McMichael who was unhappy with the way he was being portrayed in our columns.

On the other side there was a public accusation from a well-known playwright, stung by a mildly critical mention from Columbanus Macnee in the course of a piece on the Belfast Festival, that the magazine was run by supporters of the INLA. And long negotiations with harassed newsagents—those paradigms of petit-bourgeois timidity and small-mindedness—who were afraid to put *Fortnight* openly on the counter because it featured such dangerous revolutionaries as Seamus Mallon and Garret FitzGerald. At least one south Belfast newsagent kept it under the counter like a pornographic magazine only to be produced when specifically requested, although his window was full of garish girlie publications.

At least one south Belfast newsagent kept it under the counter like a pornographic magazine . . .

Then there were the interminable correspondences with officials about why *Fortnight* was not allowed into the jails. Sometime around 1983 it took over from *Magill* as the favourite reading matter of prisoners—both loyalist and republican—in the Maze. I lost count of the number of complaints from relatives about it not being allowed in. The screws at the Crumlin Road jail, in their wisdom, once stopped the magazine being brought in by a visitor, but allowed in *The Art of Revolutionary Warfare*, a handbook of guerrilla fighting by that master of the art, leader of Ho Chi Minh's Vietnamese armies, General Giap.

Our Augean stables of an office in Lower Crescent also became something of a nerve centre for Belfast's "counter-culture". Indigent artists and poets, ageing hippies who had once been something in the music business, and dope-smoking devotees of Krishna and Carlos Castaneda mingled over coffee and chat with former republican prisoners out on parole and loyalist "minders" dropping in articles from their paramilitary bosses. In the middle of this noisy conviviality, the three or four working members of the organisation tried to write articles, sell advertising,

lay out pages and hang out of phones at the other end of which were tetchy typesetters, unpaid contributors, angry creditors or just plain "Disgusted from Banbridge".

Our proudest moment was perhaps the purchase of a small blue mini-van with the *Fortnight* logo emblazoned on its side. This became a favourite object of harassment by UDR patrols on its fortnightly runs to deliver the magazine in Dublin, with assistant editor and driver Martin O'Hagan handing out copies all round—explaining to the bemused and belligerent part-timers that, no, it wasn't a "Taig" magazine despite the occasional picture of John Hume or Gerry Adams on the cover, nor was it a "Prod" publication even though Andy Tyrie or Ian Paisley might occasionally feature. And Professor Kevin Boyle, despite his "Fenian" name and the fact that he was writing about the cross-border security forces, was not a reason to impound the whole delivery.

My four years at *Fortnight* were the happiest and most satisfying of my journalistic career. A dabbler by nature, I was quite prepared to learn some of the skills of being an office manager, a lay-out artist, an advertising salesman and a circulation manager. I was able to indulge myself as an editorial-writer, a pseudonymous gossip columnist (named after James McKnight, the radical 19th-century Presbyterian minister, "tenant right" activist and journalist), a political commentator (the occasional Columbanus Macnee), a "lonely hearts" columnist (most of the Moving Hearts column was written in the office) and an impresario (organising the first of the now annual *Fortnight* parties).

I was also grateful for the privilege of being able to get to know, like and even sometimes admire some of the main characters in what many would see as the rogues' gallery of Northern Ireland politics. They were a disparate bunch: John Hume and Paddy Devlin and John Cushnahan and Frank Millar and Gusty Spence and Andy Tyrie don't have too much in common except for their attempts, sometimes through the pages of *Fortnight*, to grope their way towards a more open-minded definition of Ulster's fettered ideologies.

That small, mad band of utterly different people whom I would call the "radical peacemakers" were also an inspiration: Canon Bill Arlow, John Robb, a couple of hard-working left-wingers in the trade unions, Fr Des Wilson, Rev Ray Davey of Corrymeela, Peter Emerson with his "preferendum"; even the anti-sectarian utopians of the Workers' party, despite their paranoia about criticism and their occasional unnecessary hostility to *Fortnight*.

Finally, I must thank my colleagues, Martin O'Hagan, Moya Henry, Mary Maxwell and Robert Johnstone. I think we can say that for a few years we let loose a little light and fun and understanding in the ugly, violent, lovable old shitheap that is Belfast. That can't be bad.

PART TWO

POLITICS AND CURRENT
AFFAIRS

A child's guide to Ulster politicians

The grand old Duke of Dock

THE NEW PARTIES: THE SDLP

BARRY WHITE

It started with an article in the *Irish Times* on Monday; Radio Éireann helped it along, the *Belfast Telegraph* proclaimed its imminent arrival and before the week was out the Social Democratic and Labour party was born. It is probably the only political party in history to which the media acted as midwife, and time will tell whether the premature delivery has left any scars.

August 21st 1970 was the date of birth, but the exact time of conception and the identity of the parents is decidedly obscure. It probably goes back to 1960 when National Unity, "a para-political pressure group to educate nationalist opinion", was founded. That led to the Maghery conference, at which all shades of green agreed to bury the hatchet in favour of a united front.

Negotiations began between the various Stormont factions, and out of this came the Nationalists' 39 articles of policy in 1964, a vague document, but sufficiently leftish to encourage hopes of a radical alliance. But it wasn't to be, and it took the O'Neill–Lemass meetings of 1965 to begin to break the pattern of the monolithic, sectarian parties and open up differences of class and political outlook which had been submerged before.

For a time, middle-of-the-road parties like the National Democrats and the Northern Ireland Labour party prospered. But by 1968, Catholics were ready for more radical solutions, and the civil rights campaign was timed to perfection. The Nationalist MPs failed to rise to the occasion, and in their place a succession of better-educated, politically aware independents rose to the top, having won their spurs in the streets and on television. Within five months, in February 1969, four of them found themselves in Parliament, John Hume, Ivan Cooper, Paddy Devlin (still nominally NILP) and Paddy O'Hanlon. All were elected on civil rights tickets, and all considered they had a mandate to join a left-of-centre party fighting for civil rights ideals.

They soon found two kindred spirits on the opposition benches, Austin Currie and Gerry Fitt, who had a large hand in the success of civil rights agitation, and since then, it has been a question of wearing down personality with the native Ulster temperament to operate as a lone wolf in politics. In a party, constituency associations have to be kept informed and happy and party lines must be toed. It also costs money and time to set up an organisation and events have moved so fast in the past 18 months that it was easy to postpone the inevitable.

But the pressure has been mounting steadily, and particularly since the events of August 1969. In those dark days, the Unionists were able to present a fairly united front to British observers, while the opposition spoke with several conflicting voices. In October 1969, shortly after Mr Callaghan's second coming, an attempt was made by interested Labour MPs at Westminster to forge some kind of opposition unity, embracing the NILP, the trade unionists and the more radical Stormont MPs. But the NILP was unenthusiastic, and the plan was dropped in favour of a proposed merger between the NILP and the British Labour party intended to establish a viable "British" alternative to unionism. This in turn has been conveniently pigeon-holed by London.

Armagh and Dublin were obviously interested in seeing a new party emerge to challenge the growing influence of the IRA militants . . .

Next followed the short-lived Opposition Alliance, yet another attempt to present the appearance of a unified front with which the British government could do business. Shadow ministers were appointed to give credibility to the façade, but like an earlier Nationalist enterprise along the same lines, it existed only in the columns of the newspapers. The old gentlemen's agreement to lend support to any criticism of the government was unaffected, and the MPs went their several ways as usual.

By Easter of this year, it was apparent that a much more rigid structure was needed, and that only a new party could provide it. The well-planned riots in Ballymurphy confirmed what everyone had suspected, that the supporters of the breakaway Provisional Council of the IRA were stepping up their campaign of confrontation with the British army and that it was time for the elected representatives to assert themselves.

Long discussions between the civil rights MPs took place in Belfast, and the policy document which was drawn up and approved was that which was to be released five months later. Even the name was settled—Hume had long favoured a Social Democratic party, and Fitt insisted that "Labour" must be added to safeguard his lifelong political interests.

All was prepared, and even a provisional date chosen—May 8th—for the launching of the new party. But the gun-running crisis in the south intervened two days before, and thereafter the Westminster election, the Belfast riots and the Orange and Apprentice Boys days led to successive postponements.

Throughout this period, the MPs were subject to direct and indirect pressure from friends of anti-unionism in London, Dublin and even Armagh to declare their hands. But Austin Currie in particular knew the dangers of allowing a publicity campaign to be swamped by better news. If the first civil rights march in 1968 had not coincided with the Russian invasion of Czechoslovakia, Dungannon and not Derry might be remembered as the birthplace of the movement.

The secret was kept, and reports that the go-ahead was advanced because of the dispatch of two emissaries from Cardinal Conway to John Hume's holiday home in Bunbeg are vigorously denied. Armagh and Dublin were obviously interested in seeing a new party emerge to challenge the growing influence of the IRA militants, but there could be no overt indications of support for fear of branding it as sectarian and nationalist.

On the Unionist side, Major Chichester-Clark was going through one of his worst patches. The ban on parades, the riots and the bombings had severely weakened his claim to be in control of events and Mr Maudling was moved to warn that Stormont could be suspended if the policies of "reconciliation and impartiality" were overthrown. A right-wing takeover looked imminent and all the arguments for uniting radical opposition MPs under one banner, so that they would be in a better position to negotiate terms with Westminster, rapidly were becoming irresistible.

Finally, with August 12th safely past, John Hume broke his holiday to do an RTE interview with Michael McInerney, the *Irish Times* political correspondent, on Saturday August 15th. They talked over the general situation, and McInerney, as one of a small group interested in exploring avenues for political co-operation between north and south, put the case for opposition unity.

Hume gave nothing away, but when a leader was being written in Monday's *Irish Times* about this unity theme, McInerney decided to float the idea of a new party in the same issue. The story, only five paragraphs long, appeared on an inside page, and there was nothing to suggest particularly deep inside knowledge. He wrote: "A new form of organisation may be started in the North during the coming week and, in time, could hope to represent, broadly, non-Unionist, or even all progressive peace voices in the North." He mentioned that moves to form a Social Democrat party might also be pushed ahead, but didn't draw any connection between it and the "new organisation"

and seemed to include all 13 MPs in the new alliance.

Such is McInerney's reputation that RTE duly followed it up with a telephoned interview with Austin Currie, which they carried in their lunchtime news. Yes, he said, the possibilities for a new party were very good. No, it wasn't being held up because of the leadership question. For him there could be only one leader. Gerry Fitt.

It was that remark which lit the fuse. The men behind the new party had more or less agreed that Fitt should be leader, but no final decision had been taken. Now Currie had taken the plunge, and Hume was asked how he felt. If he had said no to Fitt, the party might never have got off the ground. He said Fitt was all right with him, and the SDLP was in business.

Fitt himself arrived back from holidays in Cushendun to a barrage of press enquiries. But he didn't know about the Currie interview until Radio Éireann played it over to him during a live broadcast. He had to make up his mind there and then whether to refuse the nomination, and precipitate a leadership crisis, or accept. He accepted.

All that remained was to book a hotel room for the following Friday for the official launching. There, Fitt gave the game away when he admitted that the press "sort of compelled us into a position where we could not say we would have further meetings". That had meant that all the ends hadn't been tied up. "Don't inter or intern us without trial," he pleaded.

But most people already had their minds made up. The NILP attacked it as not being a socialist party, and gave notice that it would oppose SDLP attempts to join the all-Ireland Council of Labour. Sinn Féin described it as a "neo-Redmondite" organisation which would lead the way to tripartite talks between Dublin, London and Belfast, and a federal solution. Eddie McAteer, leader of the Nationalists, complained, with some justification, that he had not been consulted. The Alliance party said the new party would only harden the present religious divide, and did not and could not break through sectarian barriers. The PD looked at the new membership and saw green Tories.

Already shades of green and degrees of leftness can be detected within the present grouping . . .

Only the National Democratic party gave it a qualified welcome, glad perhaps, of the chance to disband in favour of the united party it had long sought. The London *Times* saw merit in attempts to unite the opposition, since "the fragmentary and quarrelsome nature of anti-Unionist

A child's guide to Ulster politicians

MARCH 1971

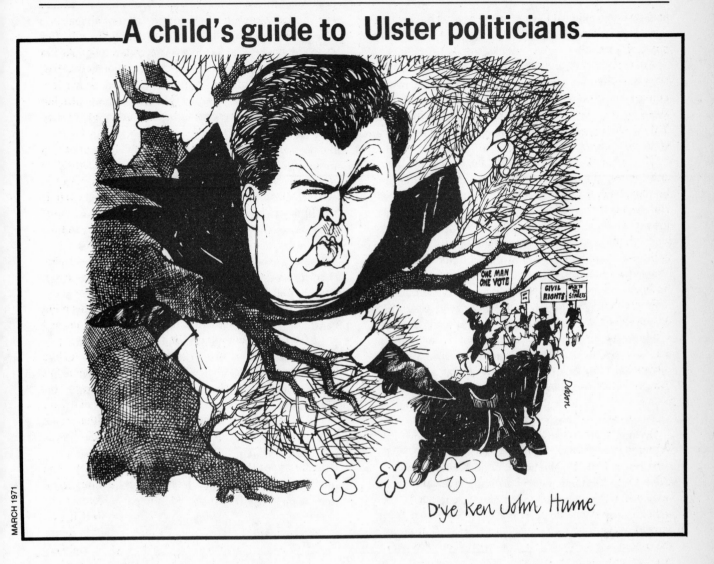

D'ye ken John Hume

politics" was making the province ungovernable.

The Republican Labour party reacted angrily to the sudden defection of two leading lights, Fitt and Senator Paddy Wilson, and promptly threw them out. Former colleague Paddy Kennedy emerged as their most vehement opponent, and his suggestion that the party was receiving money from sectarian sources—the PD named Fianna Fáil—was strenuously denied.

"The only money we have is what we have put into it," said Currie. "Even if we could get money from the south, we wouldn't want it."

So far all that is known about the party's policies is contained in its 12-point statement of aims, and its claim to be based on "radical left of centre principles". These turn out to be very much in line with standard Labour party policy on fair distribution of wealth, a minimum wage, encouragement of co-operatives and civil rights. The extras are support for the re-introduction of PR—something which members regard as essential to Stormont's survival—and a commitment to re-unification by consent of the majority. This realistic "soft line" on the border is in many ways the biggest gamble of the lot, since it invites the kind of criticism from republicans which few Catholic politicians have previously been prepared to face.

But the party will be judged by what it does, rather than what it says, and the only hint of things to come has been the decision to send the new Minister of State at Home Affairs, John Taylor, to a parliamentary Coventry. Pressmen report that hour by hour the statements from the new party on the appointment became more extreme, perhaps reflecting the well-known animosity between Currie and Taylor, until finally recall of Parliament was demanded. If this is typical of the new party's militancy, it is feared that Stormont's reputation as a debating chamber is not likely to be enhanced, nor will sectarianism decline.

Clearly the jibes at the "so-called Socialism" of some of its members, Hume in particular, hit home, and before long the party manifesto was expanded to include public ownership of Irish banks, shipyards, insurance and all credit corporations, as well as the taking over of large estates in town and country to provide farms and cheaper housing. This, it must have been felt, would demonstrate its anti-sectarianism and freedom from any safety-first clerical influence. It also emphasised its working-class base.

Has the SDLP—already nicknamed the LSD party—a future? Certainly it has done what its members did not want it to do, and gone off at half cock, thanks partly to the efforts of the media. But what makes this attempt to draw opposition forces together different from all the others is the mental and political calibre of its members. The "magnificent seven" as they have been called are truly the brains of the opposition, and they have thought long and hard before acting. They know the risks they are taking and the face they would lose if the party failed, but they have invested in all the trappings of a six-county party—including permanent offices in Belfast—in a way that only Labour has done before.

But the proof of its viability must be in the numbers who are willing to put down 10 shillings to join, and it won't be possible to assess the response until the party starts making meaningful political noises at Stormont next month. If all goes well the hope is to establish constituency associations capable of fighting and winning control in the new local government units, post reorganisation. With a firm local government base, it would begin to be a really credible long-term opposition party.

So long as it stays together—and there are none of the perks of power to bind it—no one can afford to ignore the SDLP as both the biggest and most impressive opposition grouping at Stormont. Up to now its members have made their reputations as independents, responsible to no one but themselves, and it remains to be seen if they can discipline their tongues sufficiently to present a unified front. Already shades of green and degrees of leftness can be detected within the present grouping, and these differences are bound to be exploited by their opponents.

For all the expressions of ideological solidarity the feeling remains that the SDLP was formed, like the Alliance party, to meet a very special set of circumstances—the possible takeover of Stormont—and not because like minds have come together. Fitt, as its grossly overworked leader, has yet to prove himself anything other than a good constituency MP, and Hume has still to live down that ill-fated alliance with Eddie McAteer only four months ago. Devlin and Cooper both lost their taste for the party of their first choice, and may do so again.

Events shape those caught up in them, and new qualities of maturity, selflessness and consistent political thought may surface in the months ahead. At this stage, despite Ivan Cooper's presence, it is a Catholic party, and can fairly be regarded by all who have followed recent political history as republican-inclined. As such it can hardly appeal to the Protestant masses, but it does have a chance to prove the significant point that Catholics are ready to abandon their traditional conservatism for a kind of socialism.

Even if it hangs together only long enough to represent an important section of public opinion when Westminster is actively considering direct rule, many people will feel it will have served its purpose. After a takeover—by Westminster or the right wing—all Ulster politics will go back into the melting pot anyway.

FORTNIGHT 17, MAY 14TH 1971

DISCRIMINATION: JOBS

KATHLEEN BOEHRINGER

"Discrimination" is a word which precipitates a host of euphemisms in almost every society: "lack of impartiality", "favouritism", "selectivity", and "unfairness" seem to be the descriptive terms preferrred. Ulster is no exception to this general condition, and the Commissioner for Complaints has taken deliberate pains to spell out a definition of discrimination in his Annual Report for 1970, just published: "The term signifies the taking of a decision in favour of, or against, a person which is motivated by consideration of the person's religious beliefs or political opinions."

Parenthetically, we may note the Commissioner's evidence of pressure put upon him to euphemise another unflattering term: "At the stage of informing the body concerned of the terms of an adverse report which I intended to make, I have several times been pressed to avoid the use of the term 'maladministration' and asked to substitute some less damaging form of words." Thankfully, he has resisted this pressure, although some watering-down of the concept has occurred—distinctions are made between serious and not so serious maladministration. In the same way, one supposes we can look forward to the day when distraught parents can find solace in their daughter's declamation that she is just a little bit pregnant.

"Degree" cannot be the issue in cases of maladministration or discrimination; both are pernicious to the extent that they exist at all. And discrimination not only exists but is both comprehensive and widespread throughout the fabric of Ulster life. Much, as in housing and public employment, is a legacy of the past. Much, as in education, is voluntary. Only some is still actively pursued. But it does exist, and the man in the street has no illusions about it. However, in his official capacity as employer, personnel manager, trade unionist or politician, many Ulstermen will (1) declare it doesn't exist (2) say it's just one of those things you learn to live with (3) state that although they know it exists, there is no way they can combat it in their particular job, place of work, residential area, etc. The result is that any attempt to analyse discrimination becomes a wrestling bout with a very slippery customer indeed, and one is tempted to throw up one's hands, cry simply "unfair", and declare it to be a function of collusive myopia in which those who discriminate and those who are discriminated against join together in clouding the actual situation.

PRIVATE FIRMS

Employment in the private sector provides a good case study of this will o' the wisp quality. Private employment is, as the phrase has it, "well-known" to contain blatant examples of discrimination. Yet the difficulties in ascertaining hard facts, unless one goes in for the rifling-the-personnel-files type of guerrilla research, are enormous. The dimensions of the problem of getting employment facts at all, even from public bodies by a public official, can be seen from the Commissioner for Complaints' Second Report (November 3rd 1970):

"I have found it difficult in almost every case of this kind so far to obtain factual information about the numbers of Protestants and Roman Catholics employed by the bodies concerned. Indeed the initial response to a request from me for information tends to be 'We do not know how many Protestants and how many Catholics we employ. We never ask questions of this kind. And we do not think that we should be asked to find out.' It is, however, to my mind unconvincing in the Northern Ireland situation for the head of a small office or other group of workers to claim not to know pretty accurately how many of his staff are Protestants and how many are Roman Catholics, and correspondingly for a chief officer to claim that he has no means of finding this out."

If he can't obtain such information from public bodies, what do we in unexalted positions of neither influence nor access do, slogging away in the private sector?

SOME FACTS

What we seem to do is to rub along on hearsay and

anecdote, and construct our analysis on rumour, isolated facts which somehow escape the web of silence, and on "what everybody knows".

MAY 1971

"Biased!! How dare you, you long haired Fenian agitator."

In Ulster, discrimination in private employment is usually given in religious terms, and knowledgeable trade unionists may even give figures: in Belfast—and this is a partial list of only the most talked about cases—

Harland and Wolff: out of 9,000 manual workers, there were an estimated 500 Roman Catholics employed, although since the Christmas brouhaha, this later figure may be something nearer 300;

Mackies: out of 8,500 employees, some 120 Catholics (a startling 1 in every 73 or 1.4 per cent);

Sirocco: of 400 employees, no Catholics;

Ormeau Bakery: of some 300 employees, until recently no Catholics (rumour has it that four Catholic roundsmen have been appointed to service appropriate areas);

Hugh J. Scott: no Catholics;

Shorts: at the Christmas pay-out, in a section of 450 employees of whom 14 were Catholics, 10 Catholics were paid off.

A final, perhaps apocryphal, story has it that discrimination has been carried to its ludicrous extreme by a demolition company on the Falls Road which employs only ex-internees!

Three points must be emphasised here. The first is that nobody knows anything for sure, except of course the individual who has experienced either rejection or dismissal. The numbers stated above have either appeared in newspapers or have been let slip by ex-employees . . . or have been vouchsafed as "common knowledge". The second is that even if the statistics are true, discrimination may be worse than it appears because applicants of the opposing persuasion simply don't apply to be taken on at firms known or thought to be known to discriminate. In many cases this impression is given because known vacancies are never even advertised—relatives of current employees get the jobs—or, in the case of school-leavers,

. . . no wand-waving can dispel discontent, frustration and a deep-seated sense of grievance.

firms bypass the Youth Employment Service and contact the "right" school direct to meet their manpower needs. Additionally, since the recent "troubles" many firms are located in a high-risk area for certain prospective employees—no one wants to risk his neck merely getting to work, let alone confront hostility once he gets there.

SELF-PRESERVATION

There must be, of course, an element of sheer self-preservation and avoidance of bother that enters an employer's mind when he contemplates a mixed workforce. It is simply easier, and probably cheaper, not to advertise vacancies in his factory, and to rely on employees to bring in their relatives and friends. If in effect this is discriminatory, the employer will reply "anything for a quiet life" and point to the troubles of adventurous colleagues whose production is disrupted by rival shows of strength on the factory floor—Catholic employees downing tools for two minutes of silence on a Provisional's funeral day, and Protestant employees doing the same on the day of the funeral of the three Scottish soldiers.

But this is not to gainsay that there is a good deal of uncharted iceberg lurking under the tip of the "jobs for the boys" syndrome. One hires one's co-religionists not merely because there's not much economic advantage to go round so you might as well favour your own kind and because it penalises the other side (reinforcing, incidentally, your feelings that "they" are all lazy, dole-collecting, good-for-nothings) but also because you feel "they" are your political enemies who would be assisted at your expense in their bid for power by becoming wage or salary earners. For political reasons of solidarity and continued confidence in leaders, the majority must be seen to focus its benefits on the majority.

Whether the rumour is true or not that there is an unwritten clause in agreements bringing new industry to Ulster whereby an undertaking exists to try to maintain a

60 per cent (Protestant)–40 per cent (Catholic) employment ratio, the fact is that the story is trotted out with satisfaction by Protestants as an example of how the Unionists are looking after their own as a matter of political policy.

The political assumption in all of this is that to the extent Catholics are synonymous with non-unionists they are the political enemy. Therefore discrimination—except for the odd ultra-Orange employer whose constituents would run him out of town on a slippery rail should he allow a Fenian to darken his doorway—in addition to being a product of distrust, fear, and habit, is reinforced and in fact given a lead by political considerations which have an inchoate Unionist imprimatur.

THE US SYSTEM

A similar long-standing and comprehensive system of discrimination exists in the United States with regard to blacks, and the government there, cognisant of its divisive effects and fearful of the exhortations of militants, was moved to enact Title VII of the Civil Rights Act of 1964, "Equal Employment Opportunity". This established the Equal Employment Opportunity Commission which is concerned with discrimination by four major groups—employers, public and private employment agencies, labour organisations and joint labour–management apprenticeship programmes—and its job is (1) to investigate complaints of discrimination and if it finds they are justified, to seek a full remedy by the process of conciliation and (2) to promote programmes of voluntary compliance by employers, unions and community organisations to put the idea of equal employment opportunity into actual operation.

Title VII aids the work of the EEOC by making it unlawful for any employer to discriminate: in hiring or firing; wages, terms, conditions or privileges of employment; classifying, assigning or promoting employees or extending or assigning use of facilities; and training, retraining or apprenticeships. It has a similar range of provisions with regard to employment agencies and labour organisations. Data is gathered through forms which employers, labour unions and employment agencies are required to file covering minority representation, and in the United States this has revealed covert as well as overt techniques of exclusion—techniques which range from outright refusal to consider certain applicants, through the operation of unseen and arbitrary criteria (reminiscent of the prospective postman turned down for a Belfast position, although he had passed the written examination with flying colours, because the interviewing board didn't like his "attitude"; his address at Unity Flats presumably had no bearing on his rejection), to forms of circumstantial exclusion where no specific company policy operates against the minority candidate, but the total effect of company action is to discourage his application and to maintain an all-majority workforce.

A LEGAL ANSWER

This pattern is something we are all familiar with in the Northern Ireland context, and we too are in need of such legislation. There is always a problem, of course, in attempting to legislate for morality, but anti-discriminating legislation in the United States and in Britain, where a similar system was introduced in 1968, has shown that even if you can't make discriminators feel differently, you certainly can make them act differently—and this is what is needed here if Unionist policies are to become credible within the minority community.

> **... anti-discriminating legislation in the United States and in Britain ... has shown that even if you can't make discriminators feel differently, you certainly can make them act differently ...**

In the public sector—after all, a quarter of the insured population of Ulster are employed in local and central government—moves along these lines have begun. Two "watchdogs" have been appointed, the Parliamentary Commissioner and the Commissioner for Complaints,

and Maurice Hayes of the Community Relations Commission has hailed their appearance as helping to create confidence that blatant acts of discrimination can be appealed against, and to educate "other institutions in the community both public and private how and in what ways they can re-examine their procedures and improve their efficiency and impartiality". The most recent CRC report goes on to say, ominously, "What has yet to be tackled and what is much more difficult is the manifestation of discrimination in the private sector", and suggests the most direct avenue to take to this end: "Central to the range of strategies employed to tackle the community relations problem are the acts of government itself; without active support from the legislators, no programme of development and no other strategy can be any more than partially successful."

So there it is, in a nutshell, though in these Tory-ridden days private enterprise is a delicate area in which to inject anything as idealistic as fundamental human rights. It just might—given a modicum of caustic common sense on the part of Stormont—be considered churlish of private employers to accept whacking great government grants without agreeing to some sort of fair employment practices, as, in fact, was suggested in the August 1969 Downing Street statement. If politicians are concerned about lack of public confidence in a whole range of aspects of public and private life, discrimination must be legislated against. It cannot be made to go away by pious promises, reforms too little and too late, or exhortations to brotherhood. "The people" experience discrimination and no wand-waving can dispel discontent, frustration and a deep-seated sense of grievance.

JOB DISCRIMINATION:
Will Legislation Work?

VACANCIES

APRIL 1976

STEPS TOWARDS RECONCILIATION

GARRET FITZGERALD, Fine Gael TD, writes on the changing roles of republic and province since partition.

When the Anglo-Irish Treaty of 1921 was debated in Dáil Éireann, very little of the discussion centred on partition. Most of the debate was on issues such as the Oath of Allegiance. It may seem strange that the proposed division of Ireland should have aroused so little vocal concern at that point in time, but part at least of the explanation probably lies in the fact that to the inhabitants of a country that has never been divided a partition of this kind seems less than real—until some time after it has happened. Partition was certainly envisaged in the south as being temporary in character—and this was probably true also in the north, to a much greater extent than unionists will now admit. (Certainly as a child growing up in the 30s, in continuous contact with my northern Protestant cousins, I had no feeling that they regarded partition as permanent—until the War.)

What all concerned, on both sides of the border, failed to grasp in 1921 was the extent to which any division of this kind automatically leads to a "growing apart". Once the two sundered parts of a country start to live their own lives, these fall into new patterns, governed by the specific needs and aspirations of the people living in the two areas. Curiously enough, this process of growing apart has, arguably, been more evident in the republic than in Northern Ireland. Northern Ireland, indeed, stood virtually still for almost 50 years, until 1968. It was in the republic that the major changes took place—culturally, socially and economically.

The emphasis placed in the south on the Irish language, its introduction as an essential subject for entrance to the public service and for school examination purposes, have had a very marked effect on life in the republic, and, from the viewpoint of the average northern Protestant, have made the south much more "foreign" than it was half a century ago.

The extent to which the implications of this policy for north–south relations have been ignored in the republic is remarkable. On the only occasion when I have had occasion to address a Fianna Fáil meeting (in the early 1960s, before I entered politics, I was asked to speak at a meeting on Irish language policy), I tried to make the point that our language policy has been deeply divisive as between north and south. I was met with the interesting reaction from the spokesmen of two of the study groups into which the meeting broke up for discussion purposes, that I must be some kind of an Orangeman—a curious fate for one concerned to minimise the partitionist effects of policies in the republic!

Again, in social matters, the decade from the late 1920s to the late 1930s saw the introduction of both legislation

The paradox that it was the south which, after 1921, chose to grow apart from the north, and thus to copper-fasten partition, is one which needs to be emphasised at this stage.

and constitutional provisions inspired by specifically Roman Catholic attitudes to such matters as divorce, contraception and censorship of books. By any possible standards this legislation was legislation for one part of Ireland which ignored completely the implications of these provisions for north–south relations. Yet this aspect of the

10p

FRIDAY, 9th JULY, 1971

FORTNIGHT

An independent review for Northern Ireland

50 YEARS OF PARTITION

with

Capt. L. P. S. Orr

Gerry Fitt

Garret FitzGerald

Bernadette Devlin

Happy Birthday Stormont

matter does not seem to have been paid much attention at the time.

In economic matters, too, the south went its own separate way, most notably by introducing industrial protection. This, I think, is easier to justify than the partitionist developments in cultural and social matters, for the one intellectually respectable argument for a period of separation between north and south in 1921 was the need of the south to have the benefit of a generation or so of industrial protection with a view to building up an industrial sector, most of which would within 40 years become strong enough to withstand free trade. This industrial protection policy being inappropriate to the conditions of Northern Ireland, there *was* an argument for separate development for such a period—but only, of course, if steps had been taken to ensure that the two areas did not in other respects grow apart during these decades.

The paradox that it was the south which, after 1921, chose to grow apart from the north, and thus to copper-fasten partition, is one which needs to be emphasised at this stage. For, when this is taken in conjunction with the fact that it is the south that is seeking re-union with the north, and not vice versa, this places the main onus for bridge-building on the republic.

In saying this—and in developing this theme further in later paragraphs—I do not for a moment want to detract from the responsibility of the northern majority to reform radically the society they have misruled for half a century.

The backlog of work to be done in restoring the confidence of the northern minority in the system of government in that part of Ireland is enormous, and will require more imaginative and more sustained efforts than the reform programme enacted to date. Mr Faulkner's most recent proposals, if open to further development, could provide a basis for real progress in this direction. But these are necessary *internal* reforms within Northern Ireland and differ in kind from the sort of changes that are needed in the republic to provide some basis for ultimate unity. It is, therefore, towards the changes required in the republic that I devote the remainder of this article.

To northerners it may seem curious that the people of the republic have been so unconscious of, and so apparently unconcerned about, the partitionist effects of many of the policies they have been pursuing since independence. This attitude contrasts markedly with the strong anti-partitionist sentiments expressed, often vociferously, by the people of the republic. But a clear distinction must be made between how loudly people shout and how strongly they feel. One of the most striking features of a major public opinion poll, carried out by Gallup, which involved the interviewing of a sample of 2,100 people in the republic in April 1969 (*after* Derry and *after* Burntollet) was that when asked: What do you think are the most important national problems (in the plural) facing the country today? only 1 per cent mentioned Northern Ireland–partition amongst these problems!

Of course, this southern lack of interest in the north in April 1969 does not mean that events in the north, such as those of August 1969, do not arouse at the time they happen very strong and deep—and dangerous—emotions in the republic; moreover the Dáil debates on the north in the aftermath of August 1969, while uniformly moderate and constructive in tone—to a degree not, I think, fully appreciated in the north—showed a willingness to look afresh at many aspects of life in the republic to see how we could change our laws or practices so as to create in the south a society with which the northern majority could reasonably be asked to identify themselves in time to come. But these sentiments—generous though they were—reflected the traumatic impact in the republic of the events of August 1969. Emotions of this kind, suddenly aroused, can, however, be dissipated again with the passage of time. And the events of recent months in the republic suggest that this process of dissipation may already have started.

This is suggested by the strength of the reaction against changes in the law on contraception, and by the government's hasty shying away from this issue, as well as by its inept and ham-fisted handling of the Community Schools affair, where the views of the Protestant community were wrongly taken for granted, and the Protestant ecclesiastical interests concerned not consulted before the publication of the government's proposals. These developments cannot easily be reconciled with the sentiments expressed in Dáil Éireann by all parties between October 1969 and October 1970.

Nevertheless, belief in a pluralist society is growing in the republic. Since the presidential campaign of 1966, which Tom O'Higgins of Fine Gael fought largely on this platform, the need to accept the logic of a pluralist society has been vigorously pressed in and outside the Dáil. Moreover in May of last year this concept, hitherto something of an opposition monopoly, was taken up and developed in striking terms by one member of the government, the Minister for Foreign Affairs, Dr Hillery—who is frequently named as the likely successor to Jack Lynch as leader of Fianna Fáil. This concept finds special favour amongst the young, many of whom react strongly against the old inward-looking nationalism which propounds as its ideal the creation of an exclusive neo-Gaelic society that would find little acceptance not alone in Northern Ireland, but amongst many people in the south whose own traditions are not those of a rather remote Gaelic Ireland.

The logic of this pluralist society concept is that legislation in the republic should treat all traditions as having equal rights while, of course, giving due honour to a Gaelic tradition which alone is uniquely Irish, and which incorporates so much of the past history of our country. This concept excludes the kind of provisions that limit the award of school examination certificates to those who pass that examination in Irish, or that keep out of the public service of the republic those who cannot pass tests in Irish; it would exclude also legislation that makes it a

'If we can just wait a few years all our problems will be Europe's.'

criminal offence for a married couple to secure for themselves means of contraception other than the pill; and it would, of course, exclude the dismantling of the multi-denominational state vocational schools and their transfer to trustees appointed by the Roman Catholic hierarchy, as was recently proposed by the Minister for Education.

This concept would also require a genuine effort to incorporate all traditions, including that of northern unionism, into the national life. Logically RTE should for example give to the representatives of northern unionism an appropriate voice in discussion programmes on matters of policy in the republic that have possible implications for ultimate re-union—as I suggested five years ago in the Senate. Equally logically, references to the minority in the north as "our people" should be dropped—for the unionists are "our people" too—although it must be said that this kind of identification with the northern "underdog" minority will inevitably tend to continue until that minority is given fair treatment in all respects and is fully integrated into the northern community. As the people of the republic gradually move towards a fuller—and deeper—acceptance of the concept of a pluralist society, it will be appropriate to seek to place relations between the two parts of Ireland on a better footing. The breakdown in inter-ministerial relations that has been such a sad feature of the past few years must be put right, and the process of frequent inter-governmental consultation must be restored.

Membership of the EEC will make this even more urgent, for on many EEC issues an identity of interest between the two parts of Ireland will emerge—with both parts of Ireland having interests divergent from that of Britain. This will for example be one effect of the implementation of the Common Agricultural Policy. I doubt if northern opinion has yet appreciated the significance of EEC membership from this point of view. In the Council of Ministers Britain's 10 votes will be cast by the British Minister in the interests of Britain—they can't and won't be split so as to give Northern Ireland a share in this voting. More frequently than the north now appreciates it will be the representative of the republic in the Council of Ministers who will be using his three votes to support policies in the interest of Northern Ireland as well as of the republic—and the north's chances of having its case put by the republic will often be much greater than its chances of having its viewpoint adequately represented by the UK minister present.

This will also be true within the European Commission, where the Irish staff members will be much more likely to be familiar with northern problems, and concerned to take them into account, than the British members of the staff.

Again in the European Parliament, Northern Ireland's proportionate share of British representation will be one member in a parliament of 208. The republic, on the other hand, because of the weighting of the system in favour of small countries, will have 10 members—with a population only twice that of Northern Ireland, and a national output only one and a half times as great. If Northern Ireland's views are to be adequately represented in the parliament, it will frequently need the voices of members from the

MAY 1971

'... et maintenant ... les problemes D'Irlande du Nord ...'

'What do I do with it? Eat it or play a tune on it?'

Republic of Ireland to supplement what is likely to be a solitary northern voice.

Another important consequence of EEC membership will be the impact of the EEC's regional policy, which especially favours joint action by member governments, together with the European Commission, to solve the problems of frontier regions. A new initiative will be possible here, under the neutral auspices of the commission, to develop areas such as Derry–Donegal, whose interests can be served only by joint action.

The development of north–south relations within the context of the EEC must involve closer contacts between people in north and south at all levels—not alone at ministerial level, but at parliamentary level, and as between the different interest groups in the two parts of Ireland. The EEC works by a process of intensive consultation with interest groups, whose role in the preparation of decisions is often much greater than we have been accustomed to in this country, with our very centralised and often very bureaucratic administrations in both parts of the country.

With Irish interest groups from north and south frequently sharing common concerns and continuing consultation with the authorities in Brussels, much closer relations between these groups in the two parts of the country must surely follow. I am not, of course, suggesting that the process of bringing the two parts of Ireland closer together in the common interest of the island as a whole should be confined to whatever new contacts may flow from EEC membership. There is room for an imaginative effort to initiate new links between the two areas independently of membership of the EEC. The problem here, of course, is the extreme sensitivity of much of northern majority opinion to what it fears may be possible political implications of closer links between the two parts of the country. This sensitivity must be recognised in the republic, and serious thought must be given to how to arrange such closer relations so that they will not be open to suspicions that they are part of an attempt to achieve re-union by stealth, or against the wishes of the northern majority.

Here the position taken up by the opposition parties in the republic in the wake of the events of August 1969 should be a valuable element in the situation. Fine Gael's firm commitment in September 1969 to the proposition that the re-union of the country can and should come about only with the consent of a majority in the north, and the subsequent endorsement of this by the Labour party, are rocks upon which genuine north–south co-operation could be built—although this would be a good deal easier if Fianna Fáil found it possible to join in this unequivocal statement instead of hedging with a view to satisfying its more extreme supporters, who are in any event drifting away from it towards Kevin Boland's new party. Various methods could be employed to link the two parts of Ireland more closely without prejudice to the northern majority's commitment to continued participation in the United Kingdom. A first step would be the creation of an Irish inter-parliamentary union—possibly informally organised at first until both sides got to know each other well enough eventually to put it on a more formal footing. This could evolve eventually into a Council of Ireland, with a well-defined consultative role.

Plain but courteous speaking at such meetings could engender a good deal of pressure for the changes in each part of the country that are needed in order to eliminate unnecessary obstacles to understanding. Certainly TDs in the republic would be much more likely to grasp nettles like the contraceptive legislation if they were confronted with the arguments of northern MPs—Catholic as well as Protestant—on such an issue, and the Community Schools blunder would never have been committed if it had been preceded by consultations with a north–south body of parliamentarians.

Similarly, in Northern Ireland features of political life such as the involvement of the Orange Order in politics might be modified somewhat more quickly if northern MPs, confronting their counterparts in the republic with allegations about the role of the Roman Catholic Church in its legislation, found themselves faced with requests to justify the Orange Order's involvement in the affairs of the Unionist party on the basis of the criteria they were applying to the Catholic Church in the republic.

Some in the republic and among the northern minority may object that this is a long, circuitous and uncertain road towards what a majority of Irishmen conceive as an ultimate goal of re-union; to them the answer must be given that there is not any other road apart from that of anarchy and bloodshed. If enough people on both sides of the border commit themselves to this proposition, and if both sides can drop the instinctive self-righteousness which is about the most striking—and depressing—common feature of Irishmen both north and south, Catholic and Protestant, we should at least be on the right path and travelling hopefully.

INTERNMENT

TOM HADDEN

It does not take much skill to observe that the intern-ment gamble has not come off. No matter how many times the army or Mr Faulkner or Lord Balniel tell us that the IRA is on its last legs and that time will tell, we all know that there has been no improvement. Quite apart from the awful holocaust which the move sparked off, which in any other country would have been enough to shock some sanity into the authorities, there has been no let-up in the explosions or the attacks on the army.

The simple story of the fiasco runs something like this. Brian Faulkner knew all along that internment was the only way to beat the IRA. After all that was how he did it in the last campaign. So he persuaded Mr Heath to allow him to bring it in against the advice of the army, who wanted nothing of it, in exchange for the ban on the Apprentice Boys parade which the army did want. But the actual operation was badly bungled. Most of the big fish got away, and the inevitable brutality, both in picking the people up and after, made the outburst against the whole business much worse than anyone expected. And so the bombings and the shootings go on without any noticeable effect whatever. Much of the Catholic population is up in arms. The outlook is bleaker than ever. But we must soldier on.

That is how things look from London. From Dublin there is much more emphasis on the brutality and the alleged tortures. The whole operation is seen as an attempt to suppress the northern Catholic population, the last fling of an old-style Unionist government, aided and abetted by the credulous Mr Heath. And so the old anti-Unionist feeling is now being extended to include Britain as well. The reform programme is at last shown up for the sham it always was.

Neither of these accounts will really do. The army preparations for internment started long before the London meeting between Faulkner and Heath, and even General Tuzo's earlier interviews showed quite clearly that in-ternment was very much on the agenda. The internment policy was not a Unionist political effort, but the next inexorable step in the army's drive against the terrorists. The republican claims that the reform programme means nothing and that Mr Faulkner cannot possibly mean his offer of participation are no better. They forget that the IRA campaign of shooting and bombing started long before the participation initiative, and that it was designed precisely to prevent the possibility of any progress along these lines. The two deaths in Derry before internment were the direct result of a sustained campaign of shooting and stoning geared to provoke the army into overreaction, not of any change in policy by the army.

The only thing in common between the two accounts in fact is that neither suggests any acceptable way forward.

> ## The proper policy to follow was thus to sit out the campaign as best we could, and press on with the participation policies.

There is no reason at all to suppose that a release of those Provisionals who are held would make them any the more keen to permit a settlement within a six-county frame-work, or that for the British army to soldier on with the present policy will allow any progress on those lines either, given the strength of Catholic feeling against in-ternment. Yet only a lunatic, or a masochist, would argue for a reunification settlement now with feelings in Belfast as they are.

A deeper analysis of what really went wrong with the internment plan, however, does suggest some possibility of a way out of the impasse.

In the first place the Provisionals were and are far too loosely organised for an internment swoop to have any immediate impact. It was clear that bombs were not only being planted by what might be termed full-timers, but by sympathisers and adherents as well, especially in central Belfast. The gradual build-up in tension against the Brit-ish army since last summer had strengthened the grassroots support for the Provisionsals to a level far beyond that of the traditional terrorist cell. Nor is there any reason to suppose that the supply of gelignite, if not of arms and ammunition, is in any way centralised. A much better analogy would be with the supply of drugs which filter in through all kinds of channels, so that they are available more or less anywhere to anyone who wants them. The number and the nature of the dumps which have been found bear this out. The Provisionals have no hard and fast chain of command. Theirs is grassroots terrorism at its most worrying. General Tuzo's own assessment that some 100,000 Catholics sympathised with them, and some 25,000 might be prepared to help, was probably not all that far out.

The only possible deduction from this assessment is that internment should never have been adopted, as so many central groups and parties, *Fortnight* among them, consistently argued. It was bound to strengthen not weaken the movement, as it has in fact done. Any comparison with the 1956–62 campaign would be quite wrong, since then it was a question of incursions from across the border, without any general support from northern Catholics. In any case it is questionable whether internment had any real impact on that campaign, at least in the north. The move that mattered was internment by the authorities in the south. But the real cause of failure was lack of public support.

The proper policy to follow was thus to sit out the campaign as best we could, and press on with the participation policies. And when the army was forced into mistakes, as in the Derry shootings or the Harry Thompson case, to admit them, or at least to set up impartial investigations to show that there was nothing to hide. But that was not to be.

. . . action must be taken to render the continued detention of proven terrorists acceptable.

Then when internment was introduced, it was bungled, not by too few people but by far too many being pulled in. Instead of a selective and cumulative picking up of those with a proved involvement in violence, the authorities decided after their series of dawn raids to pull in the political side as well, presumably in an attempt to reduce the strength of the organised protest movement which must have been forecast. This was the real blunder which destroyed any beneficial effect which the move might have had. Internment, instead of being an unwise but acceptable tactic against the Provisionals, was turned into an unacceptable political instrument against the minority. The arrest and detention of leading members of the People's Democracy and Republican Clubs could not on any grounds be supported as a necessary part of a move against terrorism. Nor was any overt move made against the UVF. The prospects of supporting action from the south was thus immediately ruled out, and with it the prospects of any real pay off from internment. Added to this the unnecessary brutality by troops and police, in so far as can be assessed from independent witnesses, played into the hands of the extremists who have not been slow to foster the circulation of much more serious allegations about which it is not yet possible to make any final

judgement. Anyone who has had any dealings with the northern crisis knows only too well how reports and rumours grow out of all proportion in the telling. Only a speedy and open investigation of these allegations, and disciplining of offenders, can restore any degree of acceptability to the army and police as peace-keeping forces.

If this analysis is correct, two things follow. First the "political" detainees must be released immediately, in so far as any remain in custody. Those against whom there is no evidence of involvement in violence should be compensated. This is the only way to render any form of detention acceptable to the minority who have a perfect right to campaign peacefully for a united republican Ireland if they wish to.

And secondly action must be taken to render the continued detention of proven terrorists acceptable. The release of those Provisionals and others who have been pulled in is clearly not a practical possibility either on political or security grounds now that internment has been introduced. But it has now to be shown beyond all reasonable doubt that those who are held are terrorists. That is the penalty of having thrown the net too wide in the first place.

There are a number of ways in which this might be done. The best is probably to make use of the existing Special Powers legislation to create new regulations banning specifically and only those organisations openly committed to violence, notably the IRAs and the UVF, and to bring formal charges under those regulations against those known to be active members of such organisations. Where there is evidence of involvement in specific violent activities that would of course be preferable, but in the climate of intimidation and tacit support which persists,

OCTOBER 1971

'I refuse to recognise the inside of this cell'

such evidence is unlikely to be forthcoming. For similar reasons it is probably impractical to rely on ordinary courts and juries for this purpose. The difficulty in bringing home political charges in Belfast without securing an all-Protestant or all-Catholic jury are well known. Hence it would probably be necessary to establish a special tribunal to hear the charges and determine on the balance of probabilities whether detention is justified.

All this may seem to be unnecessarily complex and legalistic in a situation where the objectives are quite simple. But that ignores the extent to which the weapon of internment has been devalued by its indiscriminate use. If it is to remain an acceptable instrument of policy, active steps must be taken to establish that it is being fairly and independently applied. Only then is there any real prospect of the reciprocal action which we need in the republic to put an end to IRA and Provisional incursions.

"and this little piggy stayed at home and threw stones at the hired assassins of British Imperialism."

FORTNIGHT 25, OCTOBER 1ST 1971

LIVING WITH BOMBS

MARTYN TURNER

After eight months of daily explosions of varying intensity and at varying locations there are no indications as to when an end may come. Every time a particular variety of explosion becomes commonplace the population is re-awoken either by an increase in activity or a readjustment in the main direction of attack. A month ago it was the daylight attack on the Electricity Board of Northern Ireland, in recent weeks it has been the blatant use of anti-personnel devices. It is disturbing to know that bystanders or anyone connected with the security forces (or "hazards of war" as Sinn Féin refer to them) are now directly in the firing line. Indeed the only visible pattern which can be seen from the explosions is their irregularity and the ever-widening scope of their targets. The inefficiency and supposed disorganisation of the IRA works to their advantage in these circumstances as it never permits anyone to know where the next explosion may occur.

Loyalist Action Man

No...No...No...No

ULSTER SAYS NO

✳ No Moving Him ✳ Says Only One Word
✳ Easy To Wind Up

DECEMBER 1989

at newspaper offices highlight the diversity of application of such attacks. On August 17th masked men placed 50lb of gelignite in the *Daily Mirror* offices in Suffolk. The *Daily Mirror* had been no more offensive to the IRA than any other newspaper. However, since it is the only UK national paper to be printed locally it might be assumed that the attack was directed at newspapers in general rather than the *Mirror* specifically.

. . . explosions aimed at the business community . . . probably can be considered the most effective in achieving the basic aim of the IRA . . .

The bombs were planted with such expertise that the modern and expensive machinery which makes the Irish edition of the *Daily Mirror* the only newspaper to appear daily in colour was almost completely destroyed. On August the 17th the *Lurgan Mail* office received a parcel of 10lb of gelignite through its front door. The bombing had been announced on the phone prior to its accomplishment following a front-page *Mail* story which obviously was found offensive in some quarters.

Internment hasn't put an end to the explosions. It seems to have had no effect at all. As a recent cover of *Private Eye* put it: "If the IRA are all in prison why are they still fighting?" In the two weeks prior to August 8th there were 31 explosions. In the two weeks following internment there were 27 explosions. Considering the number of bombs which don't go off or which are defused the difference between these two figures is insignificant. In terms of poundage per week there has been a significant increase since the first weeks in August. If one were to assume that internment had been effective then one would expect, if not a decrease in terms of explosions, a decrease in terms of expertise as the result of a loss in personnel. This is clearly not the case. The booby trap which killed Captain Stewardson last month was not the only recent example of a more sophisticated form of device.

The terrorist campaign seems to have a number of different aims. Basic to these must be the complete cessation of normal life in Northern Ireland. This is achieved firstly through destroying, or attempting to destroy, the fabric of government in the six counties through attacks on the necessary institutions which make up the framework of any state. Approximately one third of all explosions are aimed at such targets. For example between July 22nd and August 22nd there were seven explosions at electricity transformers, three at customs posts plus a power station, a sewage plant, a couple of ministry buildings and the Armagh telephone exchange.

There are also those explosions which can be related to some idea of reprisal or revenge. Attacks on the army and police can be categorised thus. Two recent efforts aimed

The latest Crazy Pastime PROVO TRAIN SET

Includes:
✳ Telephone and code words
✳ Oil drums and wires ✳
✳ Bus

✳ BATTERIES NOT INCLUDED

DECEMBER 1989

The success of these and other explosions permits bomb scares to be so plausible that they can cause as much damage as the real thing. The *News Letter*, for example, is so well guarded that the only possible way for the presses to be destroyed would be for the IRA to employ a team of suicide mice to infiltrate the building through the skirting boards with TNT strapped to their backs. None the less, the *News Letter* offices are completely cleared, on average, once or twice a day following bomb threats.

This leaves, as the third main group, those explosions aimed at the business community. Seemingly motiveless, other than the likelihood that the victims are British or Protestant, they probably can be considered the most effective in achieving the basic aim of the IRA—to force some sort of withdrawal of the British army, and ultimately the Westminster government, from Northern Ireland. It is clear that in the last few weeks the continual sound of exploding gelignite has been having its required effect psychologically. This is manifested in many ways.

Firstly, for the politicians, it has resulted in an upsurge of activity, albeit futile activity, with talks following talks following talks. Secondly there is the effect on the public in general. The continual front-page news which Ulster attracts every day inevitably leads to a disillusionment of the British public which will lead to eventual pressure on the Westminster government to withdraw from their present heavy commitments. The population of Ulster, with its usual divisiveness, reacts in a number of ways. To the extreme (and maybe nowadays not so extreme) Protestant the continued terrorism only brings closer the day when the solution will be taken into his own hands. To the "minority", again with the exception of the extremists, the thought of antagonising the "Protestant backlash" must be terrifying indeed. Despite all the talk of the hostility of the minority they must know, obviously, there's only going to be one kind of blood spilled, theirs. To the majority of the population, with no particular political axe to grind, the continued campaign of violence can only sap their confidence and lead to a general depression, in terms of both mental anguish and economic viability.

. . . while we manage to keep the world's news desks busy there is no likelihood of attracting foreign firms to set up shop here.

It has only been in the last three weeks that the business community has been affected considerably. According to a statement issued by the Chamber of Trade on August 25th, trading figures for the first seven months of the year were 1 per cent up on last year. In view of an anticipated yearly growth of 10 per cent this in fact represents a drop in trade of 9 per cent. Not a particularly spectacular loss. However, in the three weeks following that statement the same organisation has been assessing the decrease in city-centre trade as running as high as 30 per cent. This obviously correlates with the introduction of daylight city-centre explosions into the situation.

On a larger commercial scale the Chamber of Commerce feels the main effect to be "loss of business confidence" with both suppliers and markets across the water. The effect in terms of hours lost, etc., in the larger companies is small in terms of the direct effect of bombings. The civil disobedience campaign is obviously a greater factor in this part of the economy. Similarly, while we manage to keep the world's news desks busy there is no likelihood of attracting foreign firms to set up shop here.

The regrettable thing is that the security forces do not seem to be making any progress in stemming the tide. While it remains a relatively simple task for gelignite to be obtained in Dublin (one unexploded device last week consisted simply of a packet of gelignite with a Dublin firm's markings and a fuse) or across the water to be carried across the border and used in the province then there is going to be continued agitation for further security measures. The favourite at this time seems to be the "third force" freely talked of by the Unionist Alliance and Mr John Taylor, and which all the B Specials are waiting to join. Clearly, the onus is on the security forces for something to be seen to be done to prevent a further escalation of the trouble and a further polarisation of the already divided population. It is unbelievable that intelligence units whose contemporaries can get the "angry Brigade" behind bars in a couple of months can do nothing in a situation where evidence and suspects are so thick on the ground.

FEBRUARY 1974

"THERE'S A MUCH BIGGER SELECTION OF INNOCENT VICTIMS OVER THERE."

TOWARDS AN AUTONOMOUS ULSTER

TOM HADDEN

The Ulster Workers' Council strike has not changed anything very much in Ulster. But it has made a number of things a good deal clearer. The first is that no relatively painless solution to the Northern Ireland problem can be found by playing on the Irish dimension. Ulstermen, which for this purpose means Protestant Ulstermen, are not Irish in the same sense as other (Catholic) Ulstermen. Attempts to make them so by political and economic pressures are more likely to have the effect of making them feel even less Irish. For a long time the Ulster Protestants asserted their unIrishness by saying loudly to themselves and the world at large that they were British. Now that is clearly no longer the case they are falling back on the assertion of a kind of Ulster nationalism.

The implication of this is that they should be permitted to rule themselves. The danger is that they will seek to revert to a one-party state in which justice and participation is continually denied to the Catholic minority. But this need not be so. The British government still wields enough influence, if only through the purse strings, to assist in the creation of a new constitution in which the rights of the minority are fairly guaranteed through entrenched constitutional provisions, proportional representation and a bill of rights on the American rather than the British model. There are also strong arguments against attempting to build in a formal requirement of intercommunal power-sharing, as opposed to dynamic power-sharing in a coalition situation. This new constitution should be battled out in a constituent assembly in the autumn, when everyone has had time to cool off a little.

The alternative is for the British government to opt for "unilateral" withdrawal. The effects of this are likely to be unpleasant for everyone, even if it did not lead to a civil war. It would also be an example to the Scots and the Welsh which the British government may not wish to encourage. A better prospect for everyone in London, Dublin and Belfast is to pursue the goal of setting up an autonomous British Ulster within the EEC, and gradually transferring the burden of social and economic subsidisation to the wider forum of the European common market.

MR WHITELAW'S PACKAGE

Before the civil rights campaign Northern Ireland was, like many other countries, an unjust but relatively stable state. The injustice was of a sectarian rather than a class nature, but for a long period it was mutually acceptable to both sides. Catholics preferred to keep themselves apart, even at the cost of fewer opportunities and less prosperity. As a result of their abstention the Unionists built a state which could continue to operate, both politically and economically, without them. The civil rights campaign was in effect a demand by the Catholics to be admitted to that state on equal terms, both politically and economically. When it was rejected, the campaign naturally turned to violence and terrorism. This development was aided and abetted by a number of serious tactical and strategic blunders by the security forces, both the RUC and the British army, culminating in the disastrous internment operation and the Bloody Sunday shootings.

It was only at this point that the British government really decided to take an active hand in promoting a new Ulster settlement. Until then the policy had been to play along with the unionists, putting pressure for reforms

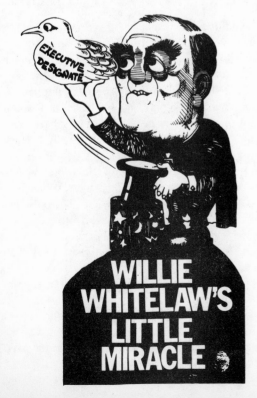

NOVEMBER 1973

WILLIE WHITELAW'S LITTLE MIRACLE

MARCH 1974

THERE CAN BE NO QUESTION OF RENEGOTIATION

SUNNINGDALE

BRUSSELS

wherever and whenever possible. Mr Heath and Mr Whitelaw, however, were determined to look for a new kind of stability in which the Irish aspirations of the Catholic minority were explicitly recognised. The unionists were informed, not explicitly but the message was very clearly expressed between the lines, that they must accept an Irish dimension if they wished to remain British. There were two elements in this: first they must share power with the representatives of the Catholic community, and secondly they must accept a new set of institutions for co-operation with the republic which could in time develop into a kind of Irish federalism or even unity. Initially the British probably hoped that Catholic representation could be ensured through a pro-British Alliance-type party rather than an explicitly pro-republican party,

A better prospect for everyone . . . is to pursue the goal of . . . an autonomous British Ulster within the EEC . . .

but what was seen by the minority as a promise by the British of progress towards Irish unity by consent if they repudiated the IRA ensured a massive vote for the SDLP, whose commitment to an all-Ireland solution became more and more confident as the London/Dublin accord grew in strength. The peculiar nature of the guarantee of continued membership of the United Kingdom as long as the majority wanted it, which was continually and loudly proclaimed as part of the package, was made even clearer by the obstinate refusal of the British government, Tory and Labour alike, to contemplate either an increase in Ulster MPs at Westminster or any form of total integration of Ulster within the UK.

WHY IT FAILED

This package was not doomed to failure. It was enthusiastically adopted by many liberal unionists, not least the Alliance party and Roy Bradford, both of whom for a time

nailed their colours to the Irish dimension. But the combined efforts of the SDLP and the Cosgrave administration to press home their unaccustomed accord with the British government turned the Irish dimension into something much stronger and, for the Protestant community, something to be avoided at all costs. The Sunningdale agreement was proclaimed both in the republic and by the SDLP as the means by which the ultimate dream of Irish unity would be peacefully achieved. And to make the point quite clear the Cosgrave government refused to make any concessions on their constitutional claim to jurisdiction over the north or, which amounted to the same thing, to agree to the extradition of terrorists—a matter which to northern Protestants had become a symbol of the reality of Dublin's claim to have recognised the existence of the north. Firm and decisive action in Dublin by way of a constitutional referendum and an agreement to extradite terrorists might just have saved Mr Faulkner's executive. But Dublin, like London, reckoned that if they stood firm they could win the jackpot.

(The cartoon intended for this space is held up in Dublin. Negotiations for its extradition are pending..)

MAY 1974

The second major reason for the failure of the package was the inability of the Faulkner/Fitt executive to establish and exert their authority in the north. Instead of showing themselves to be a vigorous and reforming government, they spent the first months of their administration in continuous maneouvring and debate on the implementation of the Sunningdale package. The business of administration went on much as usual—it has long been recognised that Northern Ireland can be as effectively governed on a parity basis by civil servants as by politicians—but from the point of view of the working-class voter, whether Catholic or Protestant, it was clear that there were to be no substantial changes from the old regime. The only institution which promised a transfer of effective decision-making to local groups, the Community Relations Commission, was to be scrapped and there was no sign of any substantial change in government attitudes to housing and redevelopment. In simple terms the new-style assembly offered no more to the vast majority of working-class voters, who are the vast majority of voters, than the old Stormont system. When they got the unexpected chance in the February general election, and later in the UWC strike to overturn it, they were happy to accept it.

Finally there was the mishandling of the strike, when it

eventually came. Instead of recognising it for what it was—the expression of the ultimate rejection of the basis of the Sunningdale package as a whole—the new Labour government and the executive alike sought first to ignore it and then to suppress it by force. The executive might possibly have been saved if the ditching of the Council of Ireland, which was finally forced on the SDLP, had been used as a bargaining counter with the Ulster Workers' Council. Instead it was produced, like Mr Heath's new deal for the miners, as if the strike had never been heard of. Faced with a complete refusal to negotiate, the demands of the UWC were gradually increased and when it became clear that the army was both reluctant and probably unable to run essential services, the return to direct rule was inevitable. In all this there were of course elements of bigotry and reaction to the continuing IRA campaign, but the major factor was the brute fact that the power-sharers had ceased to command the general support of the community. It is a nice irony that this precise condition had been written in to the 1973 Constitution Act to protect the principle of power-sharing.

THE IMPLICATIONS

The most important lesson in all this is that there can be no peaceful settlement of the Northern Ireland problem without the active, or at least passive consent of the Protestant majority. It is incredible that this simple fact was lost sight of in the skilful manoeuvring surrounding the Whitelaw constitution and the Sunningdale agreement. The state can just be run without the assent of the Catholic community, though at a heavy cost in justice and violence. Without the consent of the Protestant working class it can only grind to a halt. The fact that this is not in the best economic interests of anyone is neither here nor there. Democracy is not just a matter of occasional voting exercises. It also means consent by the people as a whole to the policies which are being pursued by the government.

On the other hand the past five years of strife have shown equally forcefully the need for consent on the part of the Catholic community as well, if Northern Ireland is to have any kind of peace and stability. The Catholic community cannot bring the economic life of the country to a halt. If they could have done so the SDLP would have had no more hesitation than the UWC in organising the operation at the time of internment. But they can make life unpleasant for everyone by affording that measure of support to the IRA which allows them to continue their operations.

Putting these two requirements together it is clear that a peaceful and stable constitution requires the assent of both communities. One way which this could be encouraged is by requiring a positive vote by referendum for any new arrangement which may emerge from the current round of talks. The use of referendums for constitutional matters is not just a political manoeuvre; it is also a means

of conferring some measure of legitimacy on the new scheme. In Northern Ireland a vote of at least 75 per cent would be needed to achieve this.

THE OPTIONS

Whether popular consent of this degree can be achieved for any of the options currently being considered is another matter. The consensus appears to be that there are five broad lines of action open:

(i) total integration with Britain;
(ii) a fairly rapid withdrawal of British troops to meet the wishes of the British electorate, leaving the locals to sort themselves out;
(iii) a repartition settlement;
(iv) a new power-sharing settlement within Northern Ireland without the disruptive Irish dimension; and
(v) British declaration of support for Irish unification.

The first and last of these options are best ruled out immediately, since neither would meet the essential requirement of consent, either in Britain for total integration or in Ulster for reunification. The effect of a British declaration for Irish unification would in effect be similar to a policy of complete withdrawal, given that the British are not in a position to put any such declaration into effect. The practical choice for Britain is thus between a phased "unilateral" withdrawal regardless of progress towards a political settlement, and a commitment to maintain the troops in Ulster until such a settlement is agreed and implemented.

1. A "unilateral" British withdrawal

The effects of pulling out the British army and leaving the situation more or less as it is now cannot be accurately predicted. But it seems likely that there would be a serious escalation of violence while the two hard-line factions sought to establish military superiority. The mass of the existing forces of law and order would be likely to side with the Protestant cause, with a rapid recruitment of a semi-official militia dedicated to stamping out all forms of militant republicanism. On the other side the IRA would regain much of its lost support as defenders of the Catholic enclaves. Neither of these groups would be in a position to win an immediately victory, unless as seems highly unlikely the Catholic minority were completely deserted by their southern colleagues.

2. Repartition

The longer-term result of such a conflict would almost inevitably be a redrawing of the boundaries of the Protestant and Catholic states of Ireland, with a mass exodus of Catholics from Belfast towards Derry, Newry and the south and a less abrupt process of population movement in the rural counties until some kind of stability was reached. If the British intention is to pull out unilaterally, therefore, it would be kinder to all concerned to embark now on a process of relatively orderly population movement and resettlement, having first indicated the broad lines of the new boundaries which would be adopted. This is not an attractive policy, and is not one which would gain Britain any support in Ireland or much in the world at large. But it would at least be preferable to a unilateral withdrawal which left an unresolved power struggle to be fought out in the streets of Belfast. Nor would it solve the problem of the future of a truncated Protestant Ulster. Would such a state be permitted to remain in the United Kingdom, or be pushed out to fend for itself as a permanent memorial to the failure of British diplomacy in Ireland? It would also serve as an uncomfortable example to the Scots and the Welsh of what can be achieved by a determined working class.

3. Another attempt at power-sharing

This leaves only the remaining option of trying again to reach a settlement which leaves the state of Northern Ireland roughly as it is in physical terms and which seeks some measure of stability by seeking consent from the Catholic community. The policy of imposed power-sharing—under the benevolent eye of an all-powerful secretary of state for Northern Ireland—has not itself been totally discredited, and might be put together again by a man of greater stature than Merlyn Rees or Stan Orme.

The aim ... should be ... a constitution which leads to power-sharing by its own internal dynamic.

William Whitelaw, or Jim Callaghan, or even Henry Kissinger might manage to bring together a new executive within the existing Constitution Act, but the process would be hampered by the emotional objections to the Whitelaw package which the loyalists have stirred up over the past few months. A completely fresh start following an autumn election, as the loyalists have suggested, seems more likely to produce a satisfactory long-term result.

TOWARDS AN AUTONOMOUS ULSTER

The basis of this suggestion is that following a brief period of a few months in which passions might be encouraged to subside a little, a new set of assembly elections be held, on the existing PR voting system, to elect a new set of representatives who would then meet in a constituent assembly with a view to drawing up a new constitution

for an autonomous Ulster. This draft constitution would be drawn up under a neutral (probably British) chairman, and then presented to the people for ratification, by whatever special majority—two thirds or three quarters—was written into the draft. Then once the constitution had been settled the business of normal government could be resumed.

The term "autonomous" for the new Ulster has been carefully chosen to reflect the spirit of Ulster nationalism which has been engendered both by the strike and the British reaction to it. It falls short of independence, but promises a greater degree of freedom of action than is envisaged for Scotland or Wales, and might mean the ending of Ulster representation at Westminster. Ulster on these terms would still be British, but only in the sense that Malta or Gibraltar or the Channel Isles are British. The ties of history and sentiment and loyalty to the Crown, such as they are, would remain but the relationship between Britain and Ulster would be one of direct negotiation rather than devolution under which the ultimate responsibility remained at Westminster.

Whether such an autonomous Ulster could survive and prosper, of course, would be dependent on satisfactory answers being found to the short-term security problem, the position of the Catholic minority, and the financing of the new statelet. The first of these is perhaps the least problematical, since the British involvement in the whole operation would necessarily imply a degree of continuing army presence until stability was attained, though with a phased handing over of control to local security forces. The other two will require more detailed negotiation.

1. The position of the minority

Continued insistence by the representatives of the minority on progress towards unification would rule out any chance of success for a new Ulster state without substantial movement of population. This is the real meaning of the slogan "no power-sharing with republicans". It does not follow that some accord on methods of involving the minority in government cannot be reached. The initial temptation in matters of this kind is to write a degree of formal power-sharing into the constitution as in the 1973 Act. The objection to this is that it has not worked—either here, to date, or in other countries like Cyprus. The aim should rather be to draft a constitution which leads to power-sharing by its own internal dynamic. The first requisite for this is a guarantee of proportional representation, linked to entrenched articles in the constitution which cannot be altered without a two-thirds or three-quarters majority. In the Ulster situation, where the Protestant vote has rarely been solid except in times of "national" emergency, this should ensure periods in office on a coalition basis to any progressive Catholic party. Whether this will be enough for the SDLP remains to be seen. Initially it might be possible to reach tacit agreement on a "constitutional convention" which would ensure full Catholic participation on all official bodies, and at least an initial period in a coalition government. Holland, Belgium and Switzerland have all developed along these lines, from similar conditions of national and religious strife.

The second essential element would be agreement on an entrenched bill of rights, which would cover not only normal but also emergency conditions. It seems likely with almost equal distaste on either side for internment that agreement could be reached on this without too much difficulty.

2. Finance

The second major problem will be the economics of an autonomous Ulster. At present Northern Ireland is in receipt of some £250–£300 million a year from Britain, omitting the special costs of the present emergency and of compensation. Clearly if this were cut off immediately, the results could be as disruptive as a sudden withdrawal of British troops. But a phased programme could be drawn up which might meet all the requirements. Even such enthusiastic supporters of the British subsidy as Professor Gibson of the New University have admitted that given a period of five or ten years the Ulster economy could be made self-sufficient, though doubtless at a lower level of prosperity than the rest of the UK. If an example is required, the speed with which the republic has achieved parity or near parity with Northern Ireland is as good as any. The close tie with British economic policy may in fact on occasions have operated against the interest of Ulster. The continuation of the British subsidy over a period of years might also be used as a kind of sanction against any breaches of the terms of the new settlement by the majority at the expense of the minority.

THE EUROPEAN DIMENSION

In addition it may be assumed that an autonomous Ulster would remain a member of the EEC along with Britain and Ireland. In the longer term this could mean that the present British support for Ulster agriculture and industry could be replaced by a degree of EEC support through the regional and social funds and whatever new form of Common Agricultural Policy is worked out. The sums which Ulster could expect from Brussels would not be of the same order as Northern Ireland now receives from Britain—perhaps a maximum net profit of £50 million a year on the assumption of a substantial regional fund. But the transfer of support for outlying regions from national to EEC sources is an integral part of the whole European philosophy. Explicit guarantees of this kind could serve to sugar the pill of progressive British disengagement. It could also serve to encourage greater co-operation between north and south in Ireland in pursuit of the same economic advantages. Good relations in Ireland are more likely to arise out of genuine common interests than any kind of forced integration.

THE ARMY IN ULSTER: WHY THE POLICY OF TOTAL CONTROL OF THE CATHOLIC COMMUNITY HAS FAILED

TOM HADDEN explains how the army's policy of permanent and total screening of the Catholic population in troubled areas is dependent on the Northern Ireland Emergency Provisions Act, and how its ill-effects might be removed.

L ast month the local representative of the London *Telegraph* got into very hot water for muddling his quotations. He reported that an army spokesman had said that they were waiting for a date to be set for withdrawal of the troops as the only possible end to the Ulster campaign. In fact the quotation came from a Provisional IRA source. The irony of the affair is that despite the muddle the *Telegraph* was accurately reporting what the army really does think. There are not many officers left now who think that the whole thing could be cleared up in a month of so if the army was given a free hand. Two or three years of continued Provisional activity, in spite of the huge numbers of leading officers arrested and interned, has convinced most top army strategists that the battle cannot be won. Some may even be prepared to admit that they have lost the war and should begin now to cut their losses.

THE ARMY STRATEGY

This gradual change in army thinking—observers have noticed how the flow of confident predictions of the defeat of the IRA have dried up lately—comes at a time when the Emergency Provisions Act, introduced in 1973 to replace the notorious Special Powers Act, comes up for renewal. It came into force early in August last year, and lapses at the same date this year unless an order is introduced at Westminster for its continuance. Merlyn Rees has already stated that it will be renewed until the Gardiner committee has had time to review the operation of the new trial procedures recommended by Lord Diplock and also contained in the Act. Rees has also stated that while no amendments will be made to the Act, some of its

provisions may not be renewed. But for the moment these are likely to be unimportant deletions of provisions which have not been widely used, as for instance the power to admit confessions obtained by an inducement short of cruel or inhuman treatment. The more important issue is how long the army should be permitted to use the powers provided under the Act to continue its policy of total screening in Catholic areas.

> **The total number of terrorists in custody . . . increased from 1,033 in May 1973 to 1,501 in May 1974; this figure included 290 convicted loyalists.**

The basis of army thinking since the failure of Mr Whitelaw's truce moves and Operation Motorman in the summer of 1972 has been that the Provisionals could be beaten if enough of the top men could be put safely behind bars. The full weight of army power has thus been deployed in Catholic areas. In contrast the army has clearly been content with a policy of containment in so far as Protestant paramilitary forces are concerned, presumably on the grounds that Protestant violence is essentially a reaction to Provisional violence. Many others would share this approach. But few are fully aware of the implications of the army strategy in practical terms.

TOTAL SCREENING

The army, unlike the RUC, does not think in legal terms. There is no special need from their point of view to prove that a particular suspect has been guilty of any specific criminal activity. The object of the exercise is to identify the terrorists and to put them behind bars. In pursuit of this objective the army has deliberately built up a system for the total screening of the population in all militant

to four hours. But then they must hand them over to the RUC who will decide whether there is any evidence of a criminal charge against them. If there is, the suspect will be processed through the usual legal channels. But if there is not, the army has a second string to its bow, by way of a direct application to the secretary of state for an interim custody order. The rules for this were established late in 1972 by Mr Whitelaw, and require that before a man can be detained at least six "traces" must be established against him. There is no statutory basis for this rule, but it clearly dictates the nature of army operations. Until they have six traces—which can range from an anonymous phone call to a sighting with a suspicious associate—they have no hope of holding a man, otherwise than through the RUC and the criminal courts. The main object of the screening process is in the search for traces; so too for army intelligence and undercover operations. The black marks rule is also applied on an ad hoc basis at the Commissioners' hearings at Long Kesh.

By treating all active members of the Catholic community as potential terrorists . . . the army has succeeded in building up a deep sense of communal antagonism . . .

The result of this system, as will be obvious, is that different rules are applied in Catholic and Protestant areas, where the army has never attempted to build up such comprehensive files. The total number of terrorists in custody, both under detention and convicted, increased from 1,033 in May 1973 to 1,501 in May 1974; this figure included 290 convicted loyalists. Catholics are dealt with primarily through the detention system, though they will be charged with specific crimes if evidence is available. Loyalists, on the other hand, are more likely to be picked up as a result of specific incidents, and dealt with through the RUC and the courts. This simple fact goes a long way to explain the huge imbalance in numbers of republican and loyalist detainees at Long Kesh.

WHY THE SYSTEM HAS FAILED

This imbalance and the resulting feeling of injustice is perhaps the major cause of the failure of the army strategy. By treating all active members of the Catholic community as potential terrorists and by regularly arresting and screening them, the army has succeeded in building up a deep sense of communal antagonism even among those who wish to have nothing to do with the IRA. It has

Catholic areas. What happens is essentially simple. Every person in the area must be identified and identifiable. This is achieved by what is called screening, which in practice means the arrest and questioning of as many inhabitants as possible at periodic intervals. There are even reports that the army operates to a rule of thumb that every potential terrorist should be picked up and screened once every nine months. This is the explanation of the periodic army swoops on whole streets, or estates. Last month, for instance, there were complaints that 71 persons had been arrested and questioned in the Creggan, many of whom were inevitably completely innocent of terrorist activity.

The next element in the system is the maintenance of a complete filing system on the Catholic population in army-occupied areas. The basic record cards are kept in local army posts, and passed on from regiment to regiment. But there is also a central filing system at army HQ in Lisburn. Some observers reckon that up to 40 per cent of the population of Northern Ireland is on record there. The files do not just contain formal names and addresses, but detailed descriptions and assessments of movements and associates. It is highly efficient. Many of those who have been briefly stopped and questioned at airports have probably been picked up on the basis of a Lisburn listing. But all this data is clearly marked "for UK eyes only", a rule which has led to considerable friction with the RUC.

THE BLACK MARKS RULE

The filing system is closely tied to the detention procedures used by the army. Under the Emergency Provisions Act they are permitted to arrest and question any person for up also maintained the easy recruiting platform for the Provisionals which was started by the brutal treatment of some of those detained and interrogated in August 1971.

The conclusion must be that it is not the details of the Emergency Provisions Act which call for parliamentary scrutiny later this month. A study of the operation of the Diplock courts, which is being prepared for the Gardiner committee and is to be published soon from the Law

Faculty at Queen's, suggests that the new court procedures are working reasonably well, though there are still some doubts over the system by which the choice of charges is made. The real issue is whether the army should be permitted to continue its policy of total screening, which is authorised and operated under the part of the Act which provides for detention without trial.

FEBRUARY 1971

"It's Sergeant Goliath, sir, hit by a pebble passing the Primary School."

FORTNIGHT 123, MARCH 19TH 1976

ANDY TYRIE

SARAH NELSON

Andy Tyrie, supreme commander of the UDA—Ulster's largest paramilitary grouping—has been described as one of the most powerful men in Northern Ireland. He excites attention and questioning because of his enigmatic and apparently contradictory characteristics, rather than from any conformity to popular stereotypes of paramilitants. The *Sunday Times* labelled him "a bespectacled, Zapata moustachioed, wise-cracking, nonsmoking, milk-drinking man whose appearance and manner belie his reputation"—for ruthlessness, and unspectacular but effective control over people and events. Though Tyrie is modest and approachable he gives few people the opportunity to discover what he really believes about anything. He shuns TV and newspaper interviews and remains almost silent at conferences (he was at Holland and Amherst) while exerting obvious censorship powers over the other UDA speakers present.

Under his leadership the UDA has been welded together and "cleaned up" financially. It has increasingly diverted its energies into community projects, notably the successful Ulster Community Action Group. UDA members have been consistent attenders at conferences on matters from housing to co-ops, sitting down with such traditional enemies as Provisional Sinn Féin. Yet some of those with the hardest reputations also support him and occupy prominent positions in the UDA: men like ex-internee David Payne, or John Orchin, once allegedly linked with the notorious Ginger Baker. The UDA still issues occasional joint statements with the banned Ulster Freedom Fighters while its members still pass sporadically, if less frequently, through the courts on sectarian murder charges. Informed sources now tend to suspect UDA rather than UVF involvement in the Dublin massacre of May 1974. At this time Tyrie was playing a leading role in the UWC strike, which would probably never have got off the ground without mass UDA involvement.

There have also been political contradictions under his leadership. In April 1974 the UDA made a conditional offer of talks with the IRA and four months later they held abortive discussions with the SDLP. In August 1975 they rejected an Official IRA offer of round-table talks on sectarian killings, threatening "indiscriminate and ruthless action against the enemy and their supporters, whether active or passive" if IRA violence continued. More recently, the UDA appeared to back down from support originally given to William Craig's voluntary coalition proposals.

If these contradictions can be partly explained by reference to Tyrie himself, they also have roots in the structure and situation of the organisation he inherited and within which he must operate.

Tyrie, like Payne, is an ex-UVF man and one-time associate of Gusty Spence. He assumed overall control of the UDA after Charles Harding Smith's enforced flight to England in 1973. Though their respective factions split over the Feakle talks issue, the dispute was not primarily a political one. Rivalry between east and west Belfast factions had long existed in the UDA. There were dissatisfactions about the style of Smith's leadership and about pocket-lining activities within the organisation which had brought the UDA into growing public disrepute since Tommy Herron's time.

OCTOBER 1985

Tyrie's great achievement has been to hold together an amorphous, sprawling organisation, which contains several differently-motivated elements, and which has lost an immediate military role. Apart from any force of personality, he has done this through perceptively identifying

the problems it faced, and through his willingness to experiment with pragmatic solutions to them. This has made for substantial and unprecedented internal coherence, at the cost of an often inconsistent public image.

The most pressing problem he faced was loss of public confidence in areas from which UDA support traditionally came. About 400 sentenced loyalist prisoners are UDA men, and they cost the organisation upwards of £3,500 per week. Racketeering and extortion had at least to be contained, for without regular public contributions the UDA simply could not meet this financial commitment. Under Tyrie, the UDA has also attempted to place the premises it controls on a legitimate footing, and has branched out into legal business enterprises.

Tyrie also appreciated and shared popular loyalist feeling about the killing of fellow Protestants. The UDA exercised what many felt a surprising degree of restraint in its recent feud with the UVF, especially over the McVeigh–Douglas case. This attitude has also improved the UDA's standing with other Protestant paramilitary groups, particularly within the Ulster Army Council (an umbrella co-ordinating body established early in 1975).

Tyrie's support for community projects has pragmatic

He neither sees himself as a politician, nor gives the impression of holding coherent political opinions . . .

roots. As a result of civil disorders the UDA has had community functions almost thrust upon it, which have demanded organisation and expertise. Softer—or less committed—UDA men have gladly diverted into it, while unruly elements have at least had the opportunity to do so. Public credibility is enhanced and a strong rationalisation found for the continued existence of the organisation.

Tyrie's "strong man" image disguises the fact that he has only been able to survive as leader by permitting a degree of internal democracy which some before him did not. But the price of this can be enforced retraction of positions, as over the voluntary coalition issue. The UDA remains basically a military organisation with an influential hard core of men who do not necessarily make a distinction between different categories of the Catholic "enemy". Tyrie's real views on anti-Catholic military activity are hard to establish reliably, but the price of hardline support is that this element be given some freedom at least to pursue its hobbies. Its dissatisfactions must also be noted and responded to.

UDA members must also be reassured that they do have a useful military role. Even if Tyrie shuns the thought of civil war—as he sincerely means to do—he must plan a detailed strategy for it and present it to others. The UDA has done precisely that. But groups like themselves have also made belligerent "civil war" noises for tactical reasons: to frighten loyalist politicians into a renewed search for a political settlement. This is a point often and understandably missed by frightened Catholics.

That the UDA under Tyrie has usually refrained from adopting open political positions reflects his awareness that this would split the organisation and compromise it both with politicians and with the public. He has taken to heart the lessons taught to the UVF's political wing. It also reflects his own attitudes to political–paramilitary relationships. He neither sees himself as a politician, nor gives the impression of holding coherent political opinions, beyond attraction to the idea of a future independent Ulster in which Catholics and Protestants might find common identity. Despite his working-class background, as a machine setter in Rolls Royce, he adopts no socialist positions. The thought that a community convention might produce "a bricklayer running the country" does not appeal to him. For Tyrie governing is the duty of politicians: as he told one reporter "paramilitary groups should never be allowed to gain political power. It would only lead to carnage." It follows that a round-table settlement by all paramilitants could achieve little: "What would we do

next? Go into the streets and tell everyone to agree with it or be shot?"

These views may console politicians and disappoint those who want to see the UDA develop as a working-class political vehicle. But the freedom of action Tyrie has allowed to UDA elements in community work may result in a momentum among them for increased political involvement. On the other hand the latitude given to other, harder factions may prevent the UDA from developing any durable coherent or constructive role. An organisation which plants bombs in the republic one week and organises community ventures with southerners the next needs to ask itself what it is really trying to achieve either in political or military terms. Like the Provos, the UDA has shown that diversification of activity has not produced an ideological coherence which can justify its continued existence to critics, as well as to supporters.

Tyrie cannot provide the impetus towards such coherence until he develops his own political thinking to a level he has not yet attempted or believed to be necessary. Whether or not the "strong man" of Protestant paramilitary politics would then be strong enough to win acceptance throughout the UDA for a unified political strategy must remain an open question.

A CRIMINAL LACK OF POLITICS

SARAH NELSON

Nineteen seventy-six was the year when politics disappeared from Ulster. There were no elections, no assemblies, no conventions, no settlements and—for our politicians—no jobs. People flocked to support a movement which appeared non-political to the point of obsession. Most astonishingly of all, paramilitary groups lost their political content at the drop of a hat and a blast of hot air from the Northern Ireland Office. Miraculously transformed into mafiosi, gangsters and criminals, the Al Capones and Godfathers of terrorism raced their flash cars through our streets and rammed Chicago typewriters against our heads. Now Provos shoot policemen, loyalists kill Catholics, for money or badness—but never for politics.

No evidence has been offered that the criminal element known to exist in paramilitary groups is bigger than it was in 1975, 1974, or 1690. (The Hadden/Boyle study [*Fortnight* 126] actually found that in a sample of 467 Diplock defendants, 47 per cent had no previous criminal record and 33 per cent "non serious" records.) But evidence is irrelevant, since the new revelations are British propaganda weapons rather than statements of truth. As Hadden/Boyle recorded, their introduction by Merlyn Rees was related to "current official policy of relying on the police rather than the army, and to phasing out special category status . . . (and was) part of a wider strategy to deny any possible political legitimacy to the IRA and its loyalist counterparts".

> ### . . . the implication that small bands . . . of outlaws are causing all the trouble exempts everyone else from blame and from responsibility . . .

The strategy has appeared strikingly successful. The press has jumped at the gangster-Mafia image, which has figured more and more in the speeches of local politicians. British ones, to judge from the more lurid rhetorical flights of Roy Mason or Airey Neave, have long since come to believe their own propaganda. Peace Movement leaders have spoken of paramilitants as if they were outlaws beyond the community, rather than integral if unpalatable parts of it. The low support given to militants over retention of political status suggests that the policy has also affected wider public attitudes. It has only failed to diminish the level of paramilitary violence.

Two reasons lie behind its successes. First of all, many people always believed, or wanted to believe, that gunmen were just criminals: they only needed reassurance. Secondly, the myth happens to suit groups right across the spectrum, who have colluded for different reasons in perpetuating it. Both factors contribute to the attitude of the "pop press" journalist who explained: "Al Capone's a good tag for us, the readers like it . . . besides . . . that's what they are anyway, really, isn't it?"

Political centrists in Ulster only received confirmation of what most already believed, while the SDLP found the new line a useful weapon in its constant battle to distinguish itself unequivocally from the Provos, and win Catholic support away from them. Even the Offical republicans have used it as a stick with which to beat the Provos. Again, relations between most loyalist politicians and Protestant paramilitants have long been at best uneasy, at

NOVEMBER 1975

"Am I being intimidated by a revolutionary opportunist or merely redirected by the self-appointed guardian of law and order?"

worst openly hostile. They may want obedient armies opposing direct rule or marching into Poleglass, but only on their terms. When political–paramilitary conflict and mutual name-calling erupts, the IRA "gangster" brush may be used effectively for tarring Protestant gunmen. Meanwhile, the British use it as a mask for their total lack of political initiative, in the apparent belief that depoliticising the conflict will somehow help to solve it.

Two particular aspects of the "criminals" line make it widely attractive. They also make it dangerous and ultimately counter-productive, and explain its inability to affect the actual level of violence.

The "criminals" line is counter-productive just because it helps people postpone facing up to reality.

First, the implication that small bands of outlaws are causing all the trouble exempts everyone else from blame and from responsibility—for past violence and political deadlock, and future political settlements. It also suggests that if all the gunmen were caught and sentenced, conflict would suddenly cease. Secondly, deliberate depoliticisation of the issues marvellously simplifies complex problems or pushes them from sight. At one time, definition of the conflict as a simple law-and-order problem was confined to loyalists: today, those who most strongly opposed that view now join in promulgating it. Westminster's use of the new propaganda to encourage acceptance of the RUC and UDR illustrates the way it is being used to side-step fundamentally *political* political problems—in

this case, widespread Catholic distrust of local security forces, which no propaganda blasts can blow away.

The trouble is that political deadlock has been reached, not by small bands of outlaws but by politicians elected by the population as a whole. There is an integral link between the public and the gunmen—not because they agree with the often bestial acts the militants commit, for most certainly do not. But gunmen who shoot Catholics, soldiers or UDR simply represent the logical extreme of community *political* "no compromise" attitudes, and will neither disappear nor be defeated until these change.

People do not tolerate paramilitary groups from mere intimidation or a dislike of informing. They do so because, when all the gangsters, thugs and criminals have been stripped away, such groups will represent feelings held by very many people in Northern Ireland. Fear of being overrun by the other side; aspirations for political dominance; moral equivocation about the value of their own group's lives compared with others. If Mason or anyone else locked up every gunman in Ulster, these problems would remain unsolved. To imply that things are otherwise is as ridiculous and deluding as the assertion that shooting a soldier is not a political act.

Nor will gunmen disappear until there is a political settlement. The reason people are fighting is because nothing has been solved. They will go on doing so, and victims will be killed day after day, until the two communities reach a compromise settlement based on genuine mutual respect. If the killers get younger and more "mindless", that is itself a reflection of the continuing political void and social chaos, not the iniquity of mysterious Godfathers. The "criminals" line is counter-productive just because it helps people postpone facing up to reality. It is both a symptom and promoter of political backruptcy, and the time is overdue for people to stand up and say so.

"As from the first of January, lads, in accordance with the Discrimination Act, we are obliged to assassinate innocent women in equal numbers to innocent men."

JANUARY 1976

"He said —…'urk?'…"

JUNE 1974

THE BLANKET BRIGADE

Almost a year since the first IRA prisoners were denied special category status, TOM HADDEN argues that Roy Mason's sanctions are probably a breach of the Prison Rules, and almost certainly an infringement of Britain's international commitments. It is time, he writes, for a change in tactics.

The fact that more than 100 men are now being held in cells in the Maze Prison with only blankets to clothe them and without regular daily exercise has made surprisingly little impact. The Provisionals have made some rather ineffectual attempts to publicise the issue by parading blanket-clad women here and there. But the general uninterest in all aspects of the continuing IRA campaign, even in their own areas, has made it impossible for them to raise much public sympathy.

The state should be prepared to treat even those who rebel against it with reasonable humanity.

This will be some comfort to Roy Mason and his advisers in the Northern Ireland Office. Since it was decided to accept the recommendation of the Gardiner committee to phase out special category status, the official policy has been to take a tough line with those IRA prisoners who have been duly convicted and refuse to accept ordinary prison discipline—that is, to wear prison clothes and to work.

NAKED EXERCISE

Those who refuse to comply with the new regime not only lose the chance of gaining remission of half their sentences, they are being regularly deprived of additional privileges such as parcels and letters and association with other prisoners out of working hours. They are also being denied their statutory rights to a regular monthly visit unless they are prepared to put on prison uniform for the purpose. A similar attitude is taken to the right of every prisoner to one hour's exercise each day: facilities for outdoor exercise are offered to the prisoners, but they are not permitted to take their blankets with them outside their cells, nor provided with any alternative to wearing prison clothes. That means in practice that exercise can only be taken virtually naked.

GROWING NUMBERS

The Northern Ireland Office must be less comforted by the knowledge that the number of prisoners being subjected to this treatment is growing. Official figures show that of those who have been convicted of terrorist offences committed since March 1976 (to whom the new policy applies) the majority have accepted prison clothes and work, and that between sixty and seventy have agreed to give up their protest, presumably as a result of the "effectiveness" of the sanctions imposed on them.

But the numbers of those "on the blanket" is not declining. There are now just over 100 protesters in the new H-block at the Maze, and another handful of women at Armagh prison. The women are not subjected to the full indignity of the blanket treatment. Since women prisoners are not required to wear prison clothes, they are permitted to wear their own clothes both in their cells and for exercise, and are not currently being deprived of association with other convicted prisoners. With a new batch of convicted prisoners beginning to flow in from the courts the problem of the blanket brigade in the Maze and their supporters in Armagh is likely to become more rather than less acute.

LEGALITY?

The arguments on the legality of the sanctions which are being imposed on these protesters are not cut and dried. The official position is that the rights of *all* prisoners (even those being subjected to sanctions for failure to comply with prison rules) to daily exercise and a monthly visit can only be exercised by those who agree to wear prison uniform. It is equally arguable that the policies of the NIO are effectively denying the protesters these rights, since it is hardly reasonable to expect anyone to take daily exercise without any clothes on, and that the authorities are thus in breach of their obligation to give daily exercise. This is quite apart from the ill-effects which could well be expected to result from lengthy solitary confinement in cells in conditions of considerable discomfort. The men are not being denied medical treatment and food on the grounds that they refuse to wear prison uniform while being sick or while eating. Why must they be denied reasonable living conditions in their cells and reasonable facilities for exercise without uniforms? The fact that the women in Armagh are in fact granted these rights makes it clear that NIO policy is to force the protesters into submission through sheer discomfort.

THE INTERNATIONAL DIMENSION

Even if the authorities' interpretation of the prison rules were accepted, there are other grounds on which their policies could be declared unlawful. It is highly unlikely that the IRA or their UVF or UDA counterparts could establish that they have a right to prisoner-of-war status under the Geneva Conventions, despite the new protocols drawn up this year to cover guerrilla "freedom fighters" (see panel). But even if they are not entitled to be treated as prisoners-of-war, there are other international obligations which Britain has accepted and which are probably being breached by the authorities at the Maze. The 1949 Geneva Conventions imposed on all signatory states a duty to grant to all persons involved in both international and internal conflicts, including those convicted as rebels, certain basic rights, including the right not to be "subjected to outrages upon personal dignity, in particular humiliating and degrading treatment" (Geneva Convention 1949, Art. 3[1][c]). It is difficult to see how the way in which the blanket men are being treated does not constitute humiliating and degrading treatment. Even if it were not accepted that IRA prisoners are entitled to protection under this convention, there are similar provisions in the European Convention on Human Rights which are specifically designed to protect the rights of all convicted prisoners. Article 3 of that convention, which the British government has already admitted applies to terrorist suspects and was infringed in 1971, states that "no-one shall be subjected . . . to inhuman or degrading treatment or punishment". Since the denial of clothing and exercise to the protesters at the Maze is in effect a punishment for their breach of prison rules, this provision is directly applicable.

HUMANE TREATMENT

It needs to be said that to argue against the legality and humanity of the way in which the blanket brigade are being treated does not imply any sympathy whatever with the aims and methods of the IRA. The state should be prepared to treat even those who rebel against it with reasonable humanity. The same arguments which are now being raised by the authorities in favour of their policies were continually raised in 1971 and 1972 in favour of the need to deal harshly with terrorist suspects, both by internment and interrogation in depth. Those arguments are now generally accepted to have been wrong and counter-productive. The same approach should be taken to the tough line on the treatment of the blanket men. It is perfectly legitimate for them to be denied remission on their sentences for their refusal to accept prison discipline as in Armagh prison. It is neither legitimate nor likely to bring about an end to the IRA campaign to subject them to the inhuman and degrading treatment which they are now suffering in the Maze.

POLITICAL STATUS

Have the Provisionals a legitimate claim to political status?

The claim of the Provisionals and other paramilitary groups to special treatment in prison cannot be based on the concept of a *political prisoner* who is locked up for his political opinions but who has not committed any criminal act other than the expression of those opinions. Political prisoners of that kind are indirectly recognised and protected by the European Convention on Human Rights which grants explicit protection to the expression of all political opinions.

The IRA have a better claim to status as *political offenders* whose crimes have been committed with a political motivation. Under the Extradition Act of 1870 and the European Convention on Extradition of 1957 political offenders are entitled to seek political asylum and to be exempted from extradition. But this status was removed by the European Convention on the Suppression of Terrorism of 1977 from all offenders whose crimes involve the use of "cruel or vicious means" or which create "A COLLECTIVE DANGER TO HUMAN LIFE". The republic has refused to sign this convention, but most other European states including Britain have signed, and thus implicitly removed any right to special treatment in international law from *terrorist offenders*, whatever their political motivation. Such offenders can properly be tried, convicted and imprisoned like ordinary criminals.

The final possibility is the claim to *prisoner-of-war* status under the Geneva Convention. This would give protection from punishment during detention, and a right to release on the cessation of hostilities. Until this year this status could only be claimed by those involved in an international war, or possibly in an internal conflict, if they wore an identifiable uniform and carried an identifying mark as combatants; the rules for recognition for prisoners-of-war have been extended by a new protocol agreed at Geneva in June 1977 to cover all guerrillas or freedom fighters who need only distinguish themselves from civilians by producing their weapons immediately before going into action, and submitting to effective military discipline. But it is highly unlikely that Britain and other Western states will ratify this new protocol which was insisted on by Third World countries.

SAVE THE SHANKILL?

JONATHAN STEPHENSON

Redevelopment is a dirty word in Belfast. It shouldn't be, of course. It ought to mean Renewal, Re-creation, the Revitalising of our inner city, New homes, New shops, a New environment. More often it has been a question of demolition, partial and patchy rehabilitation, blight, mass exodus. That is certainly the way it has been on the Shankill.

The Save the Shankill campaign, partly because of its catchy and emotive title, but mainly because it articulates what a lot of people in all areas feel about the impersonal planning processes of government, has become one of the most successful and prominent community pressure groups of recent years.

... they baldly accuse the government of a "plot to wipe out the Shankill".

The campaign was started in 1974 to combat the Belfast Ring Road proposals, to fight for the restoration and construction of houses instead of the building of flats, and to try to do something to preserve the neighbourhood shopping in the area against the post-development threat of the monopoly chain stores.

GRASSROOTS SUPPORT

It was immediately supported by most of the organisations active in the area, both community and political. Its supporters list sounds like a roll call of the loyalist grassroots—UWC, UDA, UVF, Orange Volunteers, local political parties, local churches, Women's Action, Shankill Community Council. That breadth of support, plus moral support from groups and individuals of quite different political persuasions from outside the Shankill, has helped the campaign to some impressive achievements over the past three years—mostly if not entirely due to its pressure. An end to flat-building on the Shankill; an end to plans to build a huge international chainstore monopoly at Agnes Street; an interruption to the demolition of a whole series of shops on the Shankill, between Townsend Street–Percy Street and Spiers Place–Conway Street; also an end to the demolition of a whole series of shops in the Malvern Street–Forster Street and Blaney Street–Glenfarne Street areas—these houses will instead be improved and have bathrooms added; the gradual re-opening of bricked up houses and the establishment of the Woodvale and Shankill Housing Association to accelerate that process.

MAJOR CHALLENGE

But the basic impact of the campaign, as its secretary, Jackie Redpath, is fully aware, is a negative one. It has blocked the construction of a multinational shopping centre, but it hasn't got a commitment to neighbourhood ribbon-shopping instead. It has prevented the demolition of bricked-up houses and shops, but has not succeeded in getting the government to renovate and rebuild. This is a major challenge for the campaign because "redevelopment" should be viewed comprehensively to include re-development of an area's industry, its education facilities and its social life. Save the Shankill has become deeply sceptical of the government's intentions to do anything of the kind for the Shankill Road.

EXTERMINATION

In fact they baldly accuse the government of a "plot to wipe out the Shankill". Jackie Redpath points out that within the past two years 4,000 jobs have been lost in the area, and the campaign claims that the Northern Ireland Office deliberately allows factories on the Shankill Road, like the Ladybird factory, to close (200 jobs) even though they could have continued to be economically viable.

It claims that plans for a community school have been scrapped because of the government's expectation that the local population level will plummet. It claims that a report from the Northern Ireland Office has gone before the Housing Executive Board recommending, in relation to the Shankill,"the curtailment if not the complete abandonment of further new house building", which would, if true, leave vast areas of the Shankill completely blank. It claims that Ray Carter's proposals to extend the redevelopment line up the road are "a blueprint for destroying the Shankill", that prior consultation with local people has been meagre and illusory, and that promises made previously to rebuild in redevelopment areas have been flatly broken. The campaign is urgently asking people to stay put, not to move out in the expectation of getting back later when the new houses are up because, they say, there aren't going to be any; the Shankill is being exterminated.

APARTHEID

But why? The simplest and most obvious assumption is also the most explosive: that the British government, totally bereft of any coherent or novel policy for dealing with the unruly Irish, has resorted to a very old and shop-worn policy indeed—apartheid. The bulldozer, after all, is as much a political instrument as any other kind—ask the former residents of the black shanty towns that used to stand outside Cape Town. The theory is that, just as Derry's Catholic Bogside and Protestant Waterside are separated by the wide Foyle and linked only by Craigavon Bridge, so the planners can create a Protestant east Belfast and a Catholic west, kept safely apart by the dirty Lagan. The government has repeatedly denied this but there are disturbing indications of a grand plan.

Apart from the depleted Shankill there seems little effort to stop a drift in population away from other Protestant areas on the West Bank, combined with a policy of concentrating housing resources in the Catholic areas. There is plenty of open space for building in the lower Oldpark, but no new houses going up. No new youth club going up either, despite a pressing need for one. The Shankill is being redeveloped wholesale which necessitates the (in theory temporary) displacement of the population.

The Markets on the other hand has been going through a process of gradual renewal, street by street. There the residents have been able to stay in the area, with minimum dislocation, while the work has been done around them. Why the inconsistency? And will the Department of the Environment's road plans pluck the heart out of the Catholic Short Strand in east Belfast?

Hard evidence is slender and Save the Shankill has never made, and does not make now, allegations that there is a firm sectarian strategy. But difficult questions remain to be answered by the government planners to explain their strategy and to demonstrate that their policy is not in fact both short-sighted and retrogressive. In the months to come the Save the Shankill Campaign will surely be around to ask them.

FORTNIGHT, OR THE BELFAST CHARIVARI. — DEC.

DECEMBER 1981

THE RIGHT LOYAL-PEST

HIBERNIA "O MY DEAR SISTER, WHAT *ARE* WE TO DO WITH THESE TROUBLESOME PEOPLE?"
BRITANNIA "TRY ISOLATION FIRST, MY DEAR, AND THEN ——"

EDITORIAL: THE OUTER LIMITS OF PRISON REFORM

We make no apologies for devoting so much of this issue to the H-Block prison crisis. It has done more to polarise the two communities here than any other element in 13 years of "troubles". And until it is resolved, it is ludicrous even to think of new political initiatives of any kind.

Once again the British government has shown its age-old misunderstanding of the Irish nationalist mind. The use of the hunger strike as a weapon of a defenceless prisoner against an arbitrary and unyielding oppressor has a long and respectable history. In Ireland in particular it is a potent symbol of selfless courage, patriotism and martyrdom. Its use by the IRA and INLA prisoners in the Maze has legitimised their cause, so long tarnished by vicious bloodletting, in a way not even their ablest strategist could have dreamt of.

The mood of Belfast's Catholic ghettoes . . . gives good reason for believing that a Provisional candidate would take at least the West Belfast seat in any forthcoming general election.

Now the principal strategist of the IRA's political wing, Gerry Adams, has persuaded his paramilitary colleagues of the usefulness of becoming involved in mainstream electoral politics. He now says that in future Provisional Sinn Féin candidates will contest elections in order to defeat the SDLP and emerge as the undisputed leaders of the nationalist community in Northern Ireland.

The mood of Belfast's Catholic ghettoes, as articulated in this issue by Fr Des Wilson, gives good reason for believing that a Provisional candidate would take at least the West Belfast seat in any forthcoming general election. And it is not only as an electoral force that the IRA has found a new lease of life—as a BBC *Panorama* programme by Peter Taylor, the best-informed of the English television reporters on Ireland, showed at the end of September, the organisation's military wing is now in the happy position of being able to turn away dozens of prospective new recruits.

JULY-AUGUST 1981

"They still haven't achieved political status."

Is this the cost we have to pay for the maintenance of Mrs Thatcher's image as the indomitable foe of international terrorism? There is something terrible happening here in Northern Ireland at the moment, and the action, or rather inaction, of the government on the hunger strike has contributed greatly to it. Its stance has ruled out all mediation efforts by the Irish political and religious establishment, north or south of the border, whether it be SDLP, Catholic Church or Irish government. It has cleared the decks for the simple struggle the IRA thrives on, Provos versus Brits, with no Protestants or moderate nationalists around to confuse the issue.

Inevitably, the result has been the final collapse of any pretence at middle ground and the end of any hope of halting the slide towards total polarisation between the two communities here. There are some who go so far as to say that the events of this spring and summer finally brought home to them how real the prospect of civil war is.

Certainly there are now groups of Protestant vigilantes drilling regularly all over the six counties, and respectable God-fearing Protestant farmers in the border areas have

46

What is needed is a government prepared to risk going to the outer limits of liberal prison reform . . .

NOVEMBER 1988

I WOULD LIKE TO PROTEST ABOUT THE CONDITIONS INSIDE MY COFFIN...

VICTIMS 1969-19

...BUT YOU CAN'T.

thrown off their dislike of the working-class bully boys of the UDA and have been in contact with them for military advice. It is also known that men high in the military leadership of the IRA have been discussing how they would deal with a violent and recalcitrant loyalist population in the event of a British withdrawal.

It would take an enormous leap of political imagination and statemanship to reverse this trend. One doubts whether Margaret Thatcher is the person to do it. One wonders whether Jim Prior, with his justly earned reputation as a conciliator between unions and Tory ideologues, will be given the freedom to do it.

In these pages a number of contributors argue in favour of granting generous concessions to conforming prisoners as a step to solving the hunger strike. That might be one way, though it is doubtful whether it would be enough to satisfy the hunger strikers. What is needed is a government prepared to risk going to the outer limits of liberal prison reform—so as to turn the Maze into something not seen in

Europe outside the Scandinavian countries. That would mean granting some package of concessions similar to those worked out by the Irish Commission for Justice and Peace in July, and which reliable sources reported the protesting republican prisoners were close to accepting. Then, and only then, can we start thinking about repairing some of the damage done to our community by the deaths of the 10 hunger strikers.

FORTNIGHT 194, MAY 1983

WHERE ARE THE PROVOS GOING?

ED MOLONEY

Any journalist—and there have been few of them—who has taken the trouble to observe Sinn Féin since last October's assembly elections can hardly have escaped noticing the air of confidence which pervades that organisation these days. Five years ago Roy Mason had their paramilitary colleagues on the rack and Sinn Féin itself seemed nothing more than a useful and lawful flag of convenience for IRA leaders. Now all has changed—changed utterly, one might say.

Sinn Féin itself, thanks primarily to one Bobby Sands MP, has become a political force in the land. As its fortunes have prospered so, it seems, those of the SDLP have dwindled. After securing a dramatic 35 per cent

share of the nationalist vote, Sinn Féin has become election hungry. It plans to take on the SDLP in 14 of the 17 new seats in the next general election, will probably stand Gerry Adams in next year's European election, and plans a major electoral offensive in the local government elections in the republic the autumn after next, and in the north in 1985.

The Sinn Féin headquarters on Belfast's Falls Road is neatly symbolic of the new mood. Once a rundown, dilapidated building, it now sports an aggressive, brightly painted wall mural outside. Inside, a fresh coat of paint has smartened up the once dirty walls and where prisoners' relatives used to wait amid bits of engines and bald tyres

JUNE 1983

for a trip to Long Kesh there is now a waiting room fit to grace a doctor's surgery.

Upstairs, where Gerry Adams has his office, is a bustle of activity. Sinn Féin activists, like junior executives in a fast-growing corporation, answer phone calls from constituents looking to get rehoused or windows and roofs repaired. Their complaints are dutifully added to a register which eventually makes its way to Adams. They scurry around busily making sure the right calls have been made to the right people in the Housing Executive or the Department of Environment. They arrange Adams's day for him—a tenants' meeting here, a housing protest there, and regular visits to keep in touch with the four outlying advice centres run in west Belfast.

After half an hour of this it's time for a double-take: are these, one wonders, the same people who scorned electoral politics such a short time ago, who seemed to have embraced the revolution of Trotsky? Are these the same people who such a short time ago were more interested in removing roof tiles with gelignite and blasting window panes into fragments?

The answer is a very puzzled "yes". The truth is that, like poachers turned gamekeepers, Sinn Féin has taken to electoral politics and constituency activity with the energy and enthusiasm that only newly won converts can display. Bobby Sands and Margaret Thatcher between them have managed to accomplish what years of intrigue by the Northern Ireland Office failed to do. The hopes of Willie Whitelaw and Merlyn Rees have finally born fruit, in circumstances they could never have imagined: the Provos are going political.

Or at least partly political. Gerry Adams's enemies in the Provos suspect—and of course the Northern Ireland Office hopes—that the logic of the Provos' present course is that Sinn Féin will be inexorably sucked into the world of realpolitik, the world of compromise and double-dealing and that, equally inexorably, the ballot box will ultimately prevail over the Armalite.

But how well grounded in reality is this scenario? The underlying assumption is that Sinn Féin is directly in competition with the SDLP for the electoral allegiance of nationalists. If it wants to grow and eat into the SDLP vote, it is argued, Sinn Féin, or rather the IRA, will have to clean up its act. Viewing the nationalist political scene during the last nine months, it is easy to see how and why people are thinking this way. Everywhere the SDLP are compared, most unfavourably, with Sinn Féin. Sinn Féin's youthful workers, sense of purpose, enthusiasm and roots in working-class areas do indeed contrast sharply with the tired men (and a few women) of the SDLP.

In one way the difference between them almost looks the same as the difference 15 years ago between the bright young things of the civil rights movement and the irrelevant antediluvian old men of the Nationalist party. Little wonder then that people think it possible that in the same way that John Hume, Ivan Cooper and Paddy O'Hanlon swept those old Nationalists into the dustbin, so will the Provos do to them.

Curiously enough, the Sinn Féin leadership are about the only people not carried away by this sort of thinking. They do of course hope that their constituency politics will reveal enough deficiencies in the SDLP's track record to win over a few hundred voters here or there. But the thrust of Sinn Féin political activity since last October has been to maximise the potential republican vote.

That vote or support has of course always been there

48

and helps to explain why the IRA has survived for so long. And the purpose of the advice centres and the constituency politics is primarily to convince that vote that it is worthwhile *continuing* to support Sinn Féin—that it is not just a passing phenomenon which provides a once-off emotional outlet.

In pursuit of this, most of Sinn Féin's political activity has gone unnoticed by a local media which shrinks from contact with ordinary people. It has taken the form of a vote registration drive that would have done Martin Luther King proud. And by all accounts that drive has paid off—hundreds and thousands of people in west Belfast, Derry, Mid-Ulster and Armagh (Fermanagh/South Tyrone is the one major exception—people there imbibe electoral

---

The campaign of violence and the campaign to win votes go hand in hand. The one keeps the pot boiling and the other provides it with legitimacy.

---

arithmetic with their mothers' milk) who had never bothered to cast a vote before have now been dragooned into registration by Sinn Féin.

The Sinn Féin aim, according to the leadership, is to reach an electoral ceiling of 100,000 votes, a position that would put them on a par, more or less, with the SDLP. The bulk of that vote—and the low level of SDLP to Sinn Féin transfers in the assembly vote supports this—can't all come from the SDLP. Eventually, if the vote does come out, it will be, like the bulk of Sinn Féin's 64,000 assembly total, a new vote.

So where are the Provos going? Ultimately of course, Sinn Féin wants a seat at the negotiating table. But given British resistance to talking to them about anything more substantial than broken windows, and the fierce opposition of the current coalition government and civil service in the republic, Sinn Féin needs to win friends in high places.

In the south the one potential friend is Charlie Haughey's Fianna Fáil. Haughey reacted—in private, of course—with something not unlike enthusiasm to Sinn Féin's assembly performance. He saw the vote as the first evidence of nationalists in the north maximising their influence—in other words the Sinn Féin vote measurably increased leverage on the British, a leverage which before took only a violent identity and therefore could be easily dismissed.

Haughey's strategy, of course, is to apply pressure on the British to apply pressure on the unionists to get them

to the negotiating conference which will lead to Irish unity. The Provos are an important element in exerting that pressure.

Sinn Féin's other potential friends are in the British Labour party. Since last October the Provos have openly courted the Livingstone–Bennite left in the Labour party in the hope, almost the expectation, that this element will eventually emerge triumphant from Labour's current internecine conflicts.

This scenario is dependent on Mrs Thatcher winning the next general election. If this happens, so the theory goes, two things will follow: firstly Mrs Thatcher will continue to display the same lack of sensitivity to Irish nationalism which made the hunger strikes a watershed in Provo fortunes—that will ensure the continued impotence of the SDLP and possibly even strengthen Sinn Féin.

In her second term Mrs Thatcher will also embark on the real Tory revolution and will dismantle and reverse all the gains made by the British working class since 1945. In six years' time, the general election after next in other words, the British will react against her and vote in the Labour party. By that time the Healeyite–Foot wing of the party will be in retreat and the Tony Benns and Ken Livingstones in the ascendancy. If it all works out according to plan, then the Provos could indeed end up with friends in high places in both London and Dublin in six or ten years' time.

The Provisional IRA has an important part to play in this ambitious game plan because its violent campaign is the ultimate form of pressure politics. It caused the fall of Stormont and created Sunningdale, and if the Provos have any hope of utilising those friends in high places it can only be by keeping the north unstable in the same way. So, far from it fading away, IRA leaders in Belfast now talk confidently of creating a more professional organisation armed with the most modern weaponry, like helicopter-seeking missiles. The IRA's campaign, including the sectarian headhunting of off-duty UDR and police personnel, will, they hope, continue, as will the occasional "spectacular" act of violence capable of bringing the north to the very brink.

The campaign of violence and the campaign to win votes go hand in hand. The one keeps the pot boiling and the other provides it with legitimacy. The Provos really mean it when they talk about the Armalite and the ballot box.

It is an ambitious plan but one which is dependent on a number of assumptions. The most fragile of these is the belief that the Bennite left will ever be able to win influence in a future Labour cabinet. But one assumption does not seem far-fetched. Margaret Thatcher, as she has been for the past four years, could, if re-elected, prove to be the best, if most unwitting, friend the Provos could ever have dreamt of.

Issue Number: 195   40p (50p in Republic)   JUNE '83

FORTNIGHT

AN INDEPENDENT REVIEW FOR NORTHERN IRELAND

WHAT NEXT FOR NORTHERN IRELAND UNDER THE TORIES?

Plus: Inside the INLA
Poverty – the brutal facts

Blotski after LURIE

FORTNIGHT 194, MAY 1983

THE BRAVE NEW VOICE OF SOUTHERN PROTESTANTS

MARY HOLLAND

The way things are shaping up it now seems that the early meetings of the Forum for a New Ireland will coincide with the start of the campaign on the constitutional referendum to make abortion twice as criminal as it is already. The buzz in the ante-rooms of power is that Garret FitzGerald would like, ideally, to have the poll on the same day as the British general election. That way it's reckoned it will get the minimum of media attention abroad and, you're right, in the north.

It would be comic if it weren't so offensive. There they'll all be inside Dublin Castle talking about how this is a major breakthrough designed to show northern unionists how

much everyone cares about "The Protestant Tradition", while outside they are ramming through an amendment to the constitution which every Protestant church in Ireland has said, again and again, that they don't want.

There's a slightly disorienting sense of déjà vu about the whole debate, at least for this writer. "It's not sectarian," the politicians keep shouting, "it's about fundamental human rights." "But we don't want it," the Protestants reply; "if we don't want it and we've got to have it just because the majority says so, isn't that sectarian?" Back in 1968 Unionist politicians used to argue in just the same way. "There's no discrimination," they would insist. "But we can't get jobs because we're Catholics, isn't that discrimination?" the Catholic minority protested, unanswerably, as it turned out.

A man who's seen all this before is Victor Griffin, Dean of St Patrick's Cathedral. In the early 1960s Dean Griffin was attached to the Church of Ireland cathedral in Derry, where he was a trenchant critic of the Unionist establishment. Twenty years later he's still getting flak, but this time from the likes of Oliver Flanagan, Papal Knight extraordinary, for his outspoken opposition to the abortion referendum.

One is tempted to say that things don't change much in

Ireland, whatever side of the border you're on. There has however been one unusually heartening aspect to the referendum debacle—the consistent and vocal opposition of the Protestant community. As their northern fellow churchmen have been fond of pointing out, Protestants in the republic have never been too keen on shouting the odds about their rights. Since the founding of the Free State it is hard to think of a single issue on which they have been prepared to get involved to the extent of engaging in public controversy. Some people argue that this is because Protestants are a cowed minority in the republic, others reply that they are pretty comfortably off and have no real reason to rock the boat. A third view is that they have never really identified with the southern state and for that reason have not got seriously involved in its politics.

Whatever the reasons, the republic's Protestants have put such considerations aside this time—hopefully for good. It is they who have made the running in opposing the constitutional referendum, who have caused the major embarrassments to politicians of all shades of green.

The Protestant church leaders have stood firm in the face of pressures that have sent supposedly liberal politicians running for cover. They remain opposed to abortion and have understood very well the danger that they will be labelled as "baby murderers" if they oppose the amendment. In doing so they have often found themselves in what must be strange and probably rather uncomfortable company—speaking on platforms with republicans, radicals, feminists and the like.

. . . Protestants have shouted loud and clear that they want the value they place on the individual conscience to be respected. No Irish political leader has shown the slightest sign that he begins to understand . . .

What has been most remarkable, however, has been the tenor of much of the opposition expressed by Protestant churchmen. They have demanded to be heard precisely because they are Irish and reject the idea that the country in which they live should be forever characterised as Catholic. "Do not define my Irishness by your moral code," pleaded the Methodist Desmond Gilliland, speaking to a large hushed audience at Dublin's Mansion House.

In a draughty church hall a couple of weeks ago I listened while a Church of Ireland canon invoked the ideals of Tone and Davis in urging us to build the republic together. The office of the anti-amendment campaign is run, very efficiently too, by a 23-year-old Presbyterian, Jill Nesbitt.

In recent months Charles Haughey, Garret FitzGerald and John Hume have all talked of the importance of the Protestant tradition in Ireland and have, in their various ways, emphasised that the first aim of their Forum will be to demonstrate how that tradition will be cherished in their New Ireland. Hume at least has emphasised that he wants politicians and people in the south to face up to the realities of their state and the practical price that will have to be paid, in terms of political and cultural change, if any accommodation with northern unionists is to be contemplated.

The Protestant tradition has been more visible in the politics of the republic in recent months than at any time in the past 60 years. As individual citizens and through their churches, Protestants have shouted loud and clear that they want the value they place on the individual conscience to be respected. No Irish political leader has shown the slightest sign that he begins to understand what they are talking about, and why. In the light of this it is rather difficult to feel much optimism about the deliberations of the Forum.

ABUSE AND FAILURE IN SECURITY POLICIES

KEVIN BOYLE, TOM HADDEN and DERMOT WALSH analyse the failure of successive governments to get the right balance in security policies and to deal effectively with abuses and disputed shootings.

I t would be absurd to deny that the level of communal strife and terrorism in Northern Ireland since 1969 constitutes an emergency. But none of the policies which have been adopted so far has succeeded in doing more than contain the level of terrorism. In practice security policies and emergency legislation must be seen as only a part, however essential, of a broader attempt to find a way of achieving political and economic stability and communal peace in Northern Ireland. The alternative view, that it is possible to resolve the problems in Northern Ireland by what is variously called "all-out war" or "no-holds-barred" tactics, has been rightly rejected by every administration on the grounds that such tactics would not be acceptable to the public in Britain or either part of Ireland, that it would cause serious problems in international relations and under human rights law, and that it would not resolve the problems.

FUNDAMENTAL PRINCIPLES

There are two fundamental principles in the use of emergency powers in this context: the *minimum derogation* principle—that only those emergency powers and procedures which can be shown to be strictly necessary should be authorised or used—and the *maximum safeguard* principle—that the introduction of emergency powers or the suspension of ordinary legal safeguards should be accompanied by special controls to ensure that any abuses are rapidly identified and effectively dealt with. Both of these principles are built into the various conventions on human rights to which the UK is a party. Both have been asserted in the succession of reports and inquiries into security policy in Northern Ireland. But they have not been adhered to in practice. Emergency powers have typically been enacted in very broad terms and implemented without effective controls. There has also been a lack of will to deal promptly and justly with those cases of abuse which have occurred. This is of special importance in Northern Ireland. Communal support for and the commitment of those involved in terrorist activities, particularly on the republican side, is directly linked to the sense of alienation which the abuse of power by the security forces and the judicial system creates.

ONE THING AFTER ANOTHER

All this can be demonstrated by looking at the succession of abuses which have been allowed to develop in the operation of security policy in Northern Ireland over the years, as shown in the summary chart.

In the initial period the main problem was a sectarian approach to civil rights marches and demonstrations and some incidents of indiscipline by the police and the B Specials. After the intervention of the army in 1969 there was increasing harassment in republican areas, particularly as a result of the implementation of the doubtfully legal system of mass screening by the army. There were also continuing complaints of abuses during interrogation, notably the use of the "five techniques" after the initial internment operation and the use of physical violence by the RUC at Holywood Barracks, both of which were condemned by the European Commission at Strasbourg.

After the ending of internment in 1975 the main focus of security policy shifted to the securing of confessions in the newly built interrogation centres in Belfast and Armagh, and there were renewed complaints of the systematic use of physical violence. This was established by the Amnesty report in 1978 and eventually controlled by the reforms recommended by the Bennett report. Since 1980 there has been increasing reliance on the evidence of so-called "reformed terrorists" and increasing complaints about the bribery of supergrasses. There have also been periods during which both the army, notably in 1978–79, and the police, notably since November 1982, appear to have resorted to a "shoot-to-kill" policy in their frustration at the difficulty of obtaining admissible evidence against "known" terrorists.

DISPUTED SHOOTINGS

Throughout the period of the emergency there have also been large numbers of disputed shootings by the security

AN OVERVIEW OF SECURITY POLICIES AND THEIR OPERATION 1968–83

Dates	Period	Official policy	Actual operation	Abuses
1968–69	Civil rights demonstrations	Policing by RUC and B Specials	Sectarian approach to marches and demonstrations	Attacks on Catholic areas
1969–71	From riots to terrorism	Joint control by army and RUC; B Specials replaced by UDR	Main army presence in Catholic areas	Increasing harassment; Falls curfew; Beattie/ Cusack deaths
1971–72	Initial internment operation	Elimination of IRA by arrest and internment of all leaders and activists	Selection by RUC Special Branch; implementation by army; no-go areas established	Indiscriminate arrest and internment of republicans; five techniques and general ill-treatment; Bloody Sunday
1972–75	Internment and Diplock courts	Putting all terrorists behind bars, where possible by trial, if not by internment	Catholic areas policed by army; RUC limited to Protestant areas; granting of special category status	Mass screenings and harassment in Catholic areas
1976–1980	Criminalisation and Ulsterisation	Trial of all terrorists as criminals in Diplock courts; phasing out of special category status; increasing control by RUC; undercover operations by army and SAS	Beatings during interrogation; disputed army shootings	Interrogation centres in Castlereagh and Armagh; widespread arrests of both republican and loyalist suspects for interrogation and intelligence gathering
1980–81	Hunger strikes	Front-line riot control by RUC; no concessions to political prisoners	Huge increase in use of plastic bullets	Disputed plastic bullet deaths
1981–·	Supergrasses	Use of reformed terrorists to secure arrest of terrorist leadership; transfer of undercover operations to RUC	Use of arrest and interrogation in search for informers	Bribery of suspects; disputed RUC/UDR shootings

forces. Some of these are tabulated in the accompanying table. Though this does not purport to be exhaustive and though the inclusion of some individual cases might be argued about, it indicates that there have been more than 80 disputed shootings. In almost every one there have been repeated demands for a public inquiry. But the response of the authorities has typically been to assert that the matter is being investigated by the police and that criminal proceedings will be considered in due course by the wholly independent Director of Public Prosecutions. In almost every case nothing more is heard until an inquest is held, usually more than a year later.

These procedures are often referred to in official assertions that the security forces are subject to the rule of law in the same way as anyone else. The reality is rather different. In the first place members of the security forces are not subject to the same interrogation procedures as others and there is bound to be suspicion of a lack of impartiality and persistence in the investigations. In the second place the DPP is not independent, since he is formally subject to the attorney general and since it has been admitted that "difficult cases", like those involving

the security forces, are regularly discussed with the attorney general. Since reasons for decisions by the DPP not to prosecute are never given, despite the recommendation to the contrary by the Bennett report in respect of interrogation cases, the possibility that political considerations prevail over purely legal ones cannot be dismissed. In the cases listed in the table, only a handful have led to prosecutions: those of Kevin Heatley, Patrick McElhone, John Boyle—all of which led to acquittals—and more recently those of Eamonn Bradley, Roderick Carroll and Thomas O'Reilly—which have yet to be heard.

All this lends support to the view, which is widely held among the minority community in Northern Ireland and by many foreign observers, that the security forces are not in reality subject to the rule of law, whatever may be claimed to the contrary. In focusing attention on this, rather than on the terrible toll in loss of life and destruction of property caused by terrorists on both sides, there is an obvious risk of giving an unbalanced picture of events since 1969. But there is an equal risk in focusing almost exclusively on the incidence of terrorism, the problems and dangers faced by soldiers and policemen and the very

SOME DISPUTED KILLINGS BY SECURITY FORCES

Classification	Date	Name	Incident
Riot control	13 Jul. 1969	F. McCloskey	RUC baton charge in Dungiven.
Riot control	14 Aug. 1969	J. Gallagher	B Specials opened fire on crowd.
Riot control	15 Aug. 1969	M. Lynch	All four were held by the Scarman Tribunal to have
		S. McLarnon	been innocent victims of police shooting in the Falls
		P. Rooney	area of Belfast.
		H. McCabe	
Falls curfew	3 July 1970	P. Elliman	All three shot by army during curfew as alleged
		W. Burns	gunmen but were apparently innocent.
		Z. Uglik	
		C. O'Neil	Run down by army saracen.
Riot Control	4 July 1970	S. Cusack	Both shot by army in Derry as alleged gunmen.
		D. Beattie	
Shoot to kill	23 Oct. 1971	J. McLaughlin	Shot by army marksmen in robbery at bank in
		and two others	Newry.
Miscellaneous	9 Nov. 1971	K. Thompson	Shot by army marksman in her garden.
Bloody Sunday	30 Jan. 1972	J. Duddy	All 13 were shot by army during and after anti-
		P. Doherty	internment rally in Derry; army claimed all were
		H. Gilmore	gunmen or had nail bombs; Widgery tribunal
		B. McGuigan	concluded that it could not be proved any had been
		J. Young	holding guns or bombs and that some of the shootings
		M. McDaid	were reckless.
		W. Nash	
		M. Kelly	
		K. McElhinney	
		J. Wray	
		G. Donaghy	
		G. McKinney	
		W. McKinney	
Shoot to kill	1 Mar. 1972	J. Maughan	Both shot by RUC in car which failed to stop.
		M. Connors	
Shoot to kill	4 Mar. 1972	A. Kavanagh	Shot by RUC while escaping from bombing attempt.
Rubber bullet	20 Apr. 1972	F. Rowntree	Small boy killed during riot.
Undercover squad	12 May 1972	P. McVeigh	Shot in Belfast from unmarked army car.
Rubber bullet	16 July 1972	T. Molloy	Shot during riot in Strabane.
Undercover squad	27 Sep. 1972	D. Rooney	Shot in Belfast from unmarked army car.
Shoot to kill	1 Oct. 1972	M. Hayes	Shot as alleged gunman in Belfast.
Miscellaneous*	23 Feb. 1973	K. Heatley	Shot as alleged gunman in Newry.
Rubber bullet	17 May 1973	T. Friel	Shot by army during alleged riot.
Shoot to kill*	7 Aug. 1974	P. McElhone	Shot by army while running away after questioning.
Plastic bullet	28 Aug. 1975	S. Geddis	Shot during riot in Belfast.
Shoot to kill	13 Sep. 1975	L. Norney	Shot as alleged gunman in Belfast.
Shoot to kill	13 Sep. 1975	J. Cleary	Shot by SAS patrol in south Armagh while allegedly escaping.

great bravery and commitment to duty which most have displayed.

The most difficult question which faces the current review of emergency laws by Sir George Baker is whether the right balance has been struck in the formulation of the law and in its administration. For this purpose the degree of success which has been attained by the security forces in arresting and convicting terrorists must be set against the fact that any abuse of human and civil rights contributes directly to the flow of recruits to and communal support for terrorist organisations within the minority community. The account above indicates that wholly insufficient attention has been paid throughout the emergency to the provision and operation of safeguards to control abuses. The principle that those who commit offences on behalf of the state should be brought to justice has been subordinated to the notion that it is undesirable to interfere with the operations of the security forces when they are operating in such difficult conditions. The effect of this has been to prolong the emergency, to increase the

Classification	Date	Name	Incident
Shoot to kill	12 June 1976	L. Prince	Shot at army checkpoint in Co Armagh.
Miscellaneous	14 Aug. 1976	M. O'Hare	Shot by army patrol in alleged crossfire in south Armagh.
Plastic bullet	4 Oct. 1976	B. Stewart	Shot during alleged riot in Belfast.
Miscellaneous	4 Aug. 1977	J. McCartan	Shot in disputed circumstances in Belfast.
Undercover squad	12 Dec. 1977	C. McNutt	Shot from unmarked army car.
Shoot to kill	26 Feb. 1978	P. Duffy	Shot at arms dump in Co Tyrone.
Shoot to kill	10 June 1978	D. Heaney	Shot during alleged hijack in Derry.
Shoot to kill	21 June 1978	J. Mulvenna	Three IRA men and passer-by shot by undercover
		D. Brown	army patrol lying in wait at bombing target in
		J. Mealy	Belfast.
		B. Hanna	
Shoot to kill*	11 July 1978	J. Boyle	Innocent teenager shot at arms dump in cemetery.
Shoot to kill	30 Sep. 1978	J. Taylor	Wildfowler shot in Co Tyrone.
Shoot to kill	25 Nov. 1978	P. Duffy	Shot at arms dump in Derry.
Miscellaneous	23 July 1980	M. McCartan	Shot by RUC while painting slogan.
Miscellaneous	9 Aug. 1980	J. McCarron	Shot in disputed circumstances in Belfast.
Plastic bullet	10 Aug. 1980	M. Donnelly	Shot during riot in Belfast.
Plastic bullet	15 Apr. 1980	P. Whitters	Shot during riot in Derry.
Plastic bullet	12 May 1981	J. Livingstone	Shot from army vehicle in Belfast.
Plastic bullet	19 May 1981	C. Kelly	Shot during alleged riot in Belfast.
Plastic bullet	22 May 1981	H. Duffy	Shot during riot in Derry.
Plastic bullet	8 July 1981	N. McCabe	Shot during alleged riot in Belfast.
Shoot to kill	9 July 1981	D. Barrett	Shot from army post in Ardoyne.
Plastic bullet	24 July 1981	P. Doherty	Shot while allegedly throwing missiles.
Plastic bullet	9 Aug. 1981	P. McGuinness	Shot during riot in Belfast.
Plastic bullet	16 Apr. 1982	S. McConomy	Shot during riot in Derry.
Shoot to kill*	25 Aug. 1982	E. Bradley	Shot by army in Derry after arrest.
Shoot to kill	29 Oct. 1982	R. Brennan	Shot by RUC during robbery.
Shoot to kill	11 Nov. 1982	G. McKerr	All three shot by RUC at roadblock while allegedly escaping
		E. Toman	in Lurgan.
		S. Burns	
Shoot to kill	24 Nov. 1982	M. Tighe	Shot by RUC at alleged arms dump near Lurgan.
Shoot to kill*	12 Dec. 1982	S. Grew	Both INLA members shot after chase in Co Armagh.
		R. Carroll	
Shoot to kill	27 Dec. 1982	P. Elliott	Shot during robbery in Belfast.
Shoot to kill	19 Jan. 1983	F. McColgan	Shot by RUC after robbery in Belfast.
Shoot to kill	3 Feb. 1983	E. McGonagle	Shot by plainclothes army patrol.
Shoot to kill	16 Mar. 1983	W. Millar	Shot by RUC in stolen car with guns.
Shoot to kill	26 July 1983	J. O'Hare	Shot by RUC after robbery in Lurgan.
Miscellaneous	30 July 1983	M. Malone	Shot by UDR patrol after scuffle in Armagh.
Miscellaneous*	9 Aug. 1983	T. O'Reilly	Shot by army after stop and search.

*Prosecutions initiated

toll of death and destruction, and to make more difficult the task of finding a stable political settlement. The need to act now to help create confidence in the system of justice is all the greater.

To help achieve this a number of specific reforms in emergency powers are urgently required. Some of the most important are:

1. The security forces should not be permitted to make arrests for intelligence gathering but only to interrogate suspects in respect of specific crimes.

2. There should be a statutory code of interrogation practice and no confession or statement should be admitted in court unless the code has been adhered to and a tape-recording is produced.

3. Trials in Diplock courts should be restricted to cases in which it is certified that a serious terrorist offence has been carried out by a terrorist organisation likely to intimidate witnesses or jurors.

4. Judges in Diplock courts should be accompanied by two lay assessors representative of each community

and unanimity should be required for conviction.

5. Corroboration of confessions obtained during interrogations and of the evidence of supergrasses should be required.

In addition, more effective procedures must be provided to help maintain public confidence in the operation of emergency powers and the security forces generally. In particular the procedures for dealing with disputed incidents should be reformed so that a public investigation is held quickly unless criminal proceedings have been initiated. This could be achieved by the following measures:

1. The law on cororners' inquests should be changed to require an inquest to be held within a month unless criminal charges have already been preferred, and to permit coroners' juries to make recommendations as to future civil or criminal proceedings in addition to specific findings of fact; alternatively a standing judicial commission should be set up with similar powers and duties.
2. The formal subordination of the DPP to the attorney general should be removed and the DPP should be required to give reasons for a decision not to prosecute in any case in which a coroners' jury recommends a prosecution.
3. A statutory code of practice should be introduced stating that lethal force may be used only where there is immediate danger to life, that it may not be used to prevent escape, and that a breach of the code should itself constitute an offence.

(This article is a summary of a submission to the review by Sir George Baker of the Northern Ireland [Emergency Provisions] Act.)

NOVEMBER 1984

FORTNIGHT 200, DECEMBER 1983

Sidelines: Assembly Politician of the Year Competition

James McKnight

Being in a festive mood in the run-up to Christmas, I thought I would take a leaf out of Michael White's book at the *Guardian*, and organise a poll among those of my esteemed fellow hacks who have been condemned to a term of hard covering of the Northern Ireland Assembly to find out who they thought were the most (and least) impressive participants in that less than august forum. After overcoming an initial reluctance to find any individual worthy of merit, I was able to break the competition down into eight categories: the assembly's best and worst speakers, hardest-working and laziest members, most likeable and dislikeable human beings and, finally, its most effective and least effective politicians of the past year.

There was, not surprisingly, some fierce competition to win the prize as the House's worst speaker.

Those 60-odd politicians doomed to become participants in this Christmas charade will, I hope, treat it with the levity and (relative) lack of malice with which it is intended, always bearing in mind that there is no one more jaundiced and less objective than a journalist who knows he can express his most extreme views about politicians without being found out.

All I can disclose is that the panel of judges in this competition consisted of Brian Walker and Ray Hayden of the BBC, Norman Stockton of UTV, Eamonn Mallie of Downtown, Jim Dougal of RTE, Mervyn Pauley and Ann Purdy of the *News Letter*, William Graham of the *Irish News*, Ed Moloney of the *Irish Times* and Andrew Pollak of the *Irish Times* and *Fortnight*. Virtually the whole press gallery, in fact, with the notable exception of the gentlemen from the *Belfast Telegraph*, who were instructed by their singularly humourless editors not to take part.

Strange Tales from Ulster No. 1982
the ASSEMBLY MONSTER!!
WILL PRIOR'S UNLOVELY CREATION DESTROY ITSELF AT BIRTH? SEE THE NEXT EXPLOSIVE ISSUE... BACK to the BARRICADES!
OCTOBER 1982

BEST/WORST SPEAKER

Despite his custom of always speaking from a script, the magisterial **Robert McCartney** won the best speaker prize by a neck from his DUP arch enemies **Ian Paisley** and **Peter Robinson**. As one journalist put it: "By dint of the fact that he speaks so rarely, the sense of occasion holds the audience as much as his appreciation of his own oratorical wizardry."

There was, not surprisingly, some fierce competition to win the prize as the House's worst speaker. There were no fewer than seven nominations: **Billy Bleakes**—"for fulfilling the traditional role of the 'dinner gong' so that when he gets to his feet everyone rushes for the bar, or rather in the assembly, the tea-room"; **Dorothy Dunlop**, another of the press gallery's favourite signals to disappear; **Clifford Forsythe**; **Robert McCartney** (?); **Gregory Campbell**, for his splendidly inarticulate line in bigotry; **James McClure** and **Jack McKee**. In the end it was a dead heat between **Dorothy Dunlop** and **McKee**, the latter perhaps just shading it because of the atavistic ignorance (in the Ulster sense) of his interruptions.

HARDEST-WORKING/LAZIEST MEMBER

John Cushnahan was the clear winner in the hardest-working category, with only **Paisley** anywhere near him. Others to feature were **Peter Robinson, Jim Allister, Will Glendinning** and a lone Official Unionist, **Edgar Graham**.

Unsurprisingly, the Official Unionists swept the board in the laziness stakes, with **Robert McCartney** (there's certainly no ignoring him, that's for sure) winning by a short head from the pompous **Jeremy Burchill**, the absent **Harold McCusker** ("He only turns up for every 16th or 17th session and only then to provoke a row") and the unknown **William Brown**.

NICEST/NASTIEST HUMAN BEING

Again readers will not be amazed to learn that the prize for the "nice guy" of the House went jointly to **John Carson** (who invented the immortal concept of "shower-paring") and **John Cushnahan** (although there must be a slight suspicion that the vote for the latter has more to do with the Alliance man's penchant for journalistic chat and company than any particular commitment to virtuousness). Others who figured well in this category were **Gordon Mawhinney, Lord Dunleath** ("for his witty and entertaining speeches, utterly devoid of personality-bashing or point-scoring") and **Jim Molyneaux** for his old-world courtesy.

The fourth estate's distaste for the bigoted ranting of the DUP back benches was only too evident in the votes for the assembly's most unpleasant human being. All the cat-callers and hatemongers were there, plus a couple of Paisley's sidekicks from the front bench: **Rev Ivan Foster** ("because he shouts louder than Seawright"), **Rev William McCrea** ("all blood and thunder vindictiveness re the minority community—not a sliver of an olive branch anywhere"), **Alan Kane** ("anyone who talks about shooting rats in sewers must get this vote"), **Rev William Beattie, George Seawright** himself, **Wesley Pentland** and **Jim Allister**. But the prize went to wee **David Calvert** from Craigavon as the rudest and nastiest of the whole dreadful shebang.

> **"Paisley in effect has run the assembly over the past year," said one journalist.**

It had to be **Ian Paisley**, although **John Cushnahan** and **Peter Robinson** also polled well, and **Jim Molyneaux** got an honourable mention for "making a pattern of such intricate detail that everyone is too bored to see it until it is actually smothering them". "Paisley in effect has run the assembly over the past year," said one journalist. "He's run the Speaker, he's run the business committee, he's run agriculture, and he has kept the assembly right by acting as father of the House."

The winner here came as something of a surprise to me. I expected someone like Jack McKee to go forward to represent Ulster in the European eliminators for the "General Galtieri Perpetual Trophy" for the world's worst politician.

It was not to be: the hacks voted once again—and somewhat unfairly, I can't help thinking—for **Robert McCartney**. As one said, he is "evidence of the fact that Moses can't hand down the tablets of stone these days, he just drops them on his feet".

MAY 1987

FORTNIGHT 215, MARCH 3RD 1985

A CITY OF WISE WOMEN HIDDEN FROM HISTORY

NELL McCAFFERTY

"**D**erry is the mother of us all," John Hume once intoned solemnly in a little television film about civil rights. Derry is also the Maiden City, never having been taken, men proudly announce.

The supposition that a city, invested with the female gender, can be at once a mother and a virgin comes as no surprise given Derry's religious majority. Roman Catholics have been peddling that belief, about a real woman, for nearly two thousand years.

As with the Mother of God, so it is with Derry women—all pedestal, no power. The city council is run by men, as are the banks, the trade unions, the credit union, the churches, the chamber of commerce, the football club, the greyhound track, the GAA, the school management boards, the tenants' organisations, the drama clubs, and of course the RUC, the British army, the IRA, the UVF, the UDR and all political groups.

It's not even true that men on the dole play a mother's role, feed the children and then walk the dogs. They feed the dogs and send the children out to play, so's they can get a bit of head peace, for Chrissake.

This writer will give a free copy of *John Hume: statesman of the troubles* to any reader who sends in a photograph of any of the following famous Derry men feeding a child or strolling with it down a street (all of them have been photographed a million times each since 1968): John Hume, Paddy Doherty, Eamonn McCann, Seamus Deane, Eddie "Bish" Daly, Glenn Barr, any member of the RUC, Martin McGuinness, Raymond Gilmour, John Tierney (not so famous, but he's mayor), Jobbie Crossan (football) or Charlie Nash.

Talk about the Maiden City, mother of us all, and it's hard to find a woman behind the wall-to-wall façade of men.

Enough of the men, what about the women? That's the trouble, you see. Talk about the Maiden City, mother of us all, and it's hard to find a woman behind the wall-to-wall façade of men. The women have been written out of history.

I know, dear reader: I am one of those women. I was Eamonn McCann's election manager when he ran against Eddie McAteer and John Hume for a seat in Stormont. I know I was, because there is, in the files of the *Derry Journal*, a photograph of me, and Eamonn McCann declaring me as such. Also, the feet were run off me. Eamonn's book *War in an Irish Town* declares one Seamus O'Kane to have been his election manager at that time.

Brigid Bond was chairwoman of the Derry Civil Rights Association. Ever hear of her? Of course not. Her last public appearance was on Bloody Sunday, and we all know who got publicity and promotion out of that little tragedy.

Cathy Harkin was secretary of the Derry Labour party

"Went for that job." *"What happened?"* "They said I wouldn't be able to manage the heavy weights."

when it decided to take part in the historic October 5th 1968 march. You'll find her described in Mr McCann's book as a "general dogsbody".

Enough of this slagging of men and their monopoly of temporal power, attitudes to which are best summed up by the women of Sinn Féin, who have been begged by their leaders to stand in May's local government elections. The Sinn Féin women have pointed out that they are all employed in well-paid satisfying jobs, thank you, which they have no intention of giving up for the sake of having their photograph taken as they preside over the latest council clean-up of some godforsaken back alley.

It is the function of women in Derry—as it is the function of women the world over, until the boys abandon their toys—to preserve the family unit, however loosely that unit is defined. Human relationships are all that matter, in the final analysis, and Derry women know all there is to know about affairs of the heart.

The knowledge has been acquired and refined through generations of suffering and joy, jealously guarded and shared only when the women have decided that the person to whom it should be imparted is of an age to appreciate and benefit from it.

Sometimes it is not shared. Often men are not included in the rite of passage and wisdom. Certainly not men who babble on about virgin motherhood.

It is doubtful if men would be able to bear the burden of truth. It is certain that they have often avoided it.

There are terrible truths in Derry on a Friday night, for example. That is the night when the women have to face the butcher, the baker, and the candlestick maker. The little they have has to be eked out among the men who come claiming it. This entails untruths, pleas, evasions, and sheer bloody cheek. It requires courage and humility. Derry women have both in abundance.

The men walk the dogs. Very far. Very fast.

There is the terrible truth of the bedroom. No man in power has called for birth control facilities, although the city abounds in accidental teenage pregnancies, and the granny functions as mother while the young mother answers the call of the factory horn.

There is the beautiful truth of words, passed in comfort from one woman to another, from one group of women to another, and silence, indicated by one woman to another, and one group of women to another, about who is in trouble and needing help, or discretion.

It is an extraordinary phenomenon in that city how a woman knows when to knock at a door or pass on. There is no need to draw the curtains, or hang out a black bow, or leave the front hall wide open to the four winds. Derry women know when they are wanted, and when it is better to withdraw.

They are tactful, furtive, outspoken, warm and cold as the occasion demands. Diplomacy is their art, home rule their demesne, because they have had little else.

Matriarchy, it is called.

One day it will seep out into the streets, and the corridors of temporal power, and a proper balance will be restored between Derry women and Derry men. And then we can all stop talking about bloody maiden mothers, and snowdrops and daffodils and all kinds of silly nonsense like that.

FORTNIGHT 224, SEPTEMBER 9TH 1985

A POSITIVE PROPOSAL FOR A NEW ANGLO-IRISH TREATY ON NORTHERN IRELAND

Many of the proposals for Northern Ireland being discussed by the British and Irish governments over the past 16 months are believed to have been based on ideas outlined by KEVIN BOYLE and TOM HADDEN, published this week in book form as *Ireland: a positive proposal* (Penguin £2.95). Below we reprint one of the key chapters, with additional footnotes of our own.

The first requirement for resolving the Northern Ireland problem is a decision by the British and Irish states to realign their relationship over a territory that was once in dispute between them so as to emphasise current realities rather than historic enmities.

The only effective method of doing this would be the signing of a new Anglo-Irish treaty setting out the essentials of the approach that both states now accept.

To begin with, such a treaty should record the basic facts about the partition of Ireland and the creation of Northern Ireland . . . It should then commit both states to the same fundamental principles in dealing with the resulting problem: first, that the state to which Northern Ireland belongs must be determined by a free and fair exercise in self-determination by all the people of Northern Ireland; and, second, that the rights, aspirations and interests of both communities within it must be guaranteed and monitored by both states with whatever international assistance may appropriately be sought.

In one sense this would not be a new departure. In the Sunningdale communiqué of December 1973 both states recited their acceptance of the first of these basic principles in the following parallel declarations:

OCTOBER 1983

The Irish Government fully accepted and solemnly declared that there could be no change in the status of Northern Ireland until a majority of the people of Northern Ireland desired a change in that status.

The British Government solemnly declared that it was, and would remain, their policy to support the wishes of the majority of the people of Northern Ireland. The present status of Northern Ireland is that it is part of the United Kingdom. If in future, the majority of the people of Northern Ireland should indicate a wish to become part of a united Ireland the British Government would support that wish.

> ## The exercise of authority by joint agencies on either side of the border on a reciprocal basis . . . emphasises the equal legitimacy of both Northern Ireland and the republic.

These commitments have been repeated at successive Anglo-Irish summits by governments headed both by Garret FitzGerald and by Charles Haughey. The British government for its part has added a more general acceptance of the validity of both the unionist and the nationalist identity in Northern Ireland, notably in the White Paper *A Framework for Devolution*, presented by Jim Prior in 1982 in preparation for the re-establishment of the Northern Ireland Assembly. A corresponding recognition of the validity of the unionist tradition was made in the New Ireland Forum report.

Despite some preliminary studies under the auspices of the so-called Anglo-Irish Intergovernmental Council, established at the summit of 1980, however, little has been done to give practical or legal effect to these declarations. Successive governments in both countries have preferred to work informally on matters of practical day-to-day concern rather than to face the more difficult issues. Neither state has yet been prepared to enter into a binding international agreement or to pass internal legislation to establish beyond all doubt the legitimacy of Northern Ireland and to clarify the respective rights and obligations of the two communities.

The registration of a new Anglo-Irish treaty at the United Nations, as was envisaged for the Sunningdale agreement in 1973, would confirm its status as an agreement between two equal and sovereign states acting in concord with none of the undertones of inequality, duress

and discord that characterised the initial Anglo-Irish treaties. Such a treaty might also provide for some form of international supervision of its performance, notably through its incorporation in the respective constitutional and legal systems of the two states. In so far as the republic is concerned, this would involve the reformation of articles two and three of the Irish Constitution. In so far as Britain is concerned, it would involve the enactment of a new Northern Ireland Constitution Act. In each case it would clearly be desirable that the basic principles should be expressed in identical words, so that the risk of future arguments on interpretation would be minimised.

Agreement by both Britain and the republic on the fundamental principles of their approach to Northern Ireland, as indicated in the draft heads of treaty set out below, would remove one of the major barriers to creating a new relationship between the two communities in Northern Ireland, in that each is currently reluctant to make any concession that might prejudice its position in any future negotiations. It would facilitate the adoption of a series of measures designed to permit nationalists in Northern Ireland to express their Irish identity in ways that do not conflict with the status of Northern Ireland as part of the United Kingdom. This in its turn might facilitate the acceptance by both sides of a form of local administration in which both communities could play a part without requiring the highly unrealistic degree of consensus on all matters built into the power-sharing model that was tried but failed in 1974.

Acceptance of the legitimacy of Northern Ireland on the part of the republic and the acknowledgement by Britain of the existence of an Irish community within Northern Ireland would also facilitate the creation of new formal structures for co-operation between Northern Ireland and the republic. This might include the exercise of joint authority on specified matters on either side of the border on a reciprocal basis, thus avoiding some of the objections to the proposals in the forum report and the Kilbrandon report for the imposition of joint authority by Britain and Ireland on all aspects of the government of Northern Ireland.

The exercise of any authority over Northern Ireland by the republic on a unilateral basis is inherently objectionable to unionists, since it implies that the republic has a right to intervene. The exercise of authority by joint agencies on either side of the border on a reciprocal basis . . . has no such implications and emphasises the equal legitimacy of both Northern Ireland and the republic. Acceptance of a new co-operative relationship between Britain and the republic would likewise make it possible to develop new formal structures to reflect that relationship. The need to monitor progress in the implementation of the more detailed provisions of a new treaty and to supervise the exercise of joint authority on a reciprocal basis would provide an obvious and essential function for the parliamentary tier of the Anglo-Irish Intergovernmental Council that has often been proposed.

. . . It must be stressed that action will have to be taken at each of these three different levels to reflect new relationships between the two communities in Northern Ire-

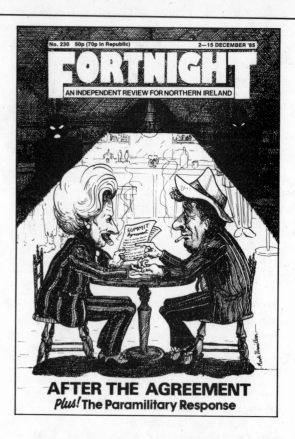

AFTER THE AGREEMENT
Plus! The Paramilitary Response

land, new relationships between Northern Ireland and the republic and new relationships between Britain and the republic. It is for this reason that talk of an "internal settlement" within Northern Ireland without reference to a prior "external settlement" between Britain and Ireland is so unhelpful. It does not follow that progress at each of these levels will be equally easy to achieve or that all the elements of a new settlement are likely to be agreed and implemented within the same timescale. But there can be no question of seeking an internal settlement within Northern Ireland until the relations between Britain and the republic have been put on a sound basis. Nor can there be much progress with respect to relations between Northern Ireland and the republic until appropriate and workable structures for government within Northern Ireland have been established.

> ### . . . there can be no question of seeking an internal settlement within Northern Ireland until the relations between Britain and the republic have been put on a sound basis.

DRAFT HEADS OF A TREATY BETWEEN THE UNITED KINGDOM AND THE REPUBLIC OF IRELAND

The Governments of the United Kingdom and of the Republic of Ireland

recognising their commitments and responsibilities under the Charter of the United Nations, within the European Communities and within the Council of Europe, in particular under the European Convention on Human Rights and Fundamental Freedoms, *recognising* the special relationships which exist between their peoples, and the steps already taken to express those relationships in the Anglo-Irish Intergovernmental Council and other institutions,

recognising that Northern Ireland is a territory in which there are two communities with divided loyalties and in which special arrangements are required to ensure that those loyalties can be fully expressed,

recognising that the conflict in Northern Ireland has caused and continues to cause untold suffering to both its communities and that it poses a grave threat to the prosperity and to the democratic institutions of both countries,

recognising that there is no democratic manner of determining which state the territory of Northern Ireland shall belong to other than by a plebiscite of its people,

recognising that the two communities are entitled to equal respect and to equal treatment before the law,

recognising that the arrangements adopted in 1920 and thereafter failed to give adequate respect and equal treatment to one of those communities,

JULY–AUGUST 1990

BELFAST-DUBLIN-BELFAST-DUBLIN-BELFAST

Have therefore resolved

(1) to take further measures to secure the common concerns of their peoples, and to ensure co-operation and harmony in future relations without prejudice to the independence or the sovereign rights of both states;

(2) that there shall be no change in the constitutional status of Northern Ireland as part of the United Kingdom until a majority of the people of Northern Ireland desire a change;

(3) that appropriate measures[1] shall be taken by both states to guarantee the rights and interests of both communities in Northern Ireland and that if at any time in the future a majority of the people in Northern Ireland should vote to join a united Ireland, corresponding measures shall be taken by both states to guarantee the rights and interests of both communities within a unitary Irish state;

(4) that appropriate measures[2] shall be taken to develop co-operation between Northern Ireland and the republic on matters of social, economic and cultural policy;

(5) that appropriate measures[3] shall be taken by both states to deal more effectively with terrorism;

(6) that appropriate measures shall be taken to give effect to this agreement in the domestic laws and constitutions of both states.

[1] As discussed elsewhere in the book. They include: the right to Irish citizenship; the ending of the bar on joint membership of the Parliament of Britain and the Irish republic; the repeal of the Flags and Emblems Act, which prevents the flying of the Irish tricolour; the opening of Irish consular offices in Belfast and Derry; the election of representatives from Northern Ireland to the Irish parliament; the right of appeal to the United Nations Human Rights Committee; the right to use the Irish language and Irish symbols; a bill of rights to outlaw discrimination against both individuals and communities; and weighted majorities in a new Northern Ireland assembly.

[2] These include: the replacement of articles two and three of the Irish constitution, claiming jurisdiction over Northern Ireland, with a statement of aspiration to unity achieved through agreement and in peace; cross-border co-operation in industry, agriculture and higher education; joint North–South agencies for tourism and industrial development and promotion.

[3] These include: a more representative and powerful Northern Ireland Police Authority and a network of local police liaison committees with statutory powers of consultation and scrutiny, and representation from both Britain and the republic; mutual links between the RUC and the Garda Síochána, with both forces recruiting throughout Ireland; the winding-down of the UDR, to be replaced by an expanded RUC with a higher proportion of Catholic recruits; a statutory code of interrogation practice and restrictions on the powers of arrest and interrogation to prevent "screening"; the limitation of non-jury Diplock courts to those cases where there is a real risk of the intimidation of jurors; provision for a judge or legal assessor from the other Irish jurisdiction to sit as a member of the Special Criminal Court for terrorist offences in Dublin and of the Diplock courts in Belfast; the eventual setting-up of a cross-border court to deal with terrorist offences; and the creation of a cross-border zone in which security force members from either side could operate.

Young and Well-Heeled in Boomtown Belfast

Leslie Van Slyke

Judging by appearances, anyone who has recently returned to Belfast after a lengthy absence could be forgiven for being genuinely impressed by the transformation that has taken place over the last few years in Belfast's city centre. Visible security around the central shopping district has been relaxed, with shoppers no longer being subjected to searches when entering the area. Civilian cars are being allowed through the security gates for the first time and, in some cases, the barriers themselves have come down.

A city once bereft of nightlife has come alive again with trendy, upmarket pubs and discos catering to the Yuppie (Young Urban Professional) set. Restaurants too are serving up a wider choice of fare, and it's becoming as difficult to get a table at the many new "in" eateries as it is to find a parking space.

The Great Victoria Street–Dublin Road–Botanic Avenue triangle is where Belfast's facelift is especially evident. Rundown buildings are being renovated and turned into galleries, gift shops, cafés and expensive clothing stores.

A city once bereft of nightlife has come alive again . . .

A year ago, Joanne Stewart moved her two-year-old business, the Beauty Shop, from Chichester Street to brand-new premises adjoining the Elbow Room pub-cum-nightclub complex on the Dublin Road. "It's very much an up-and-coming area and it's got a lot of passing traffic and lots of people just passing by." Next door, Alison Vance Interiors offers design and decoration for the homes of the well-heeled. "There is a lot of money in the province and in the past these people have tended to shop in London," says Ms Vance. "Belfast has been hibernating for about 10 years, but now with the new shops opening, people are prepared to shop around the north of Ireland, thus giving us a chance."

One of the boldest examples of a retail venture is Zazz on Donegall Pass, which opened in June. Zazz is actually three separate but adjoining businesses all operating under the one name. The café has become so popular that there is standing room only at lunchtimes. Next door is a gift shop where such unusual items as hand-made paper and bottled sand designs are sold.

The main business is a store specialising in modern, Japanese-style furniture. "Modern furniture has never really been pushed here, so you have people who are totally into it or people who have old, traditional interiors and they really can't start putting new stuff into it," says Brian McManus, one of the owners. He is confident that tastes here have become sufficiently diverse that young, first-time home owners can be convinced to switch from, say, traditional bedding to futon mattresses.

Naturally, government officials are eager to claim that the number of new businesses is a sign that the present economic situation, however bad, is really not as grim as the experts would have us believe. At the Conservative party conference in Blackpool last month, Secretary of State Tom King pointed to the rapid growth of new, small industries as an example of the bright spots in an otherwise gloomy economic picture.

But small business growth can also be viewed as an indication of just how bad things are—at least in terms of unemployment. According to Anna Crane, president of the Belfast Chamber of Trade, the small business "boom" in the city began about five years ago. "The economy had worsened, there were many redundancies and many people who had money in their pockets because they had been paid off decided to invest it in a business of their own." Mrs Crane says this is still the case and for many it's the only option left before the dole queue.

At around the same time, Mrs Crane says, city-centre traders became concerned about the growth of large shopping complexes outside Belfast, in dormitory towns such as Newtownabbey, Bangor and Lisburn. That was when the traders, the Department of Environment and City Hall banded together and decided to try and attract shoppers back into the city. Mrs Crane says their aim was to make Belfast the "biggest and brightest place to shop" and it's a campaign which has proved highly successful.

According to figures from the Belfast Development Office, more than £86 million of private-sector investments have poured into the city's commercial heartland over the past two years. And this amount represents investments in the city-centre core alone, and does not include the millions which have gone into investments in the Great Victoria Street, university and Stranmillis areas.

Among the major projects are the John Laing development on Royal Avenue on the site of the old post office and Grand Central Hotel, and the multi-storey car park and shopping complex on High Street. The £86 million also includes the Robinson and Cleaver conversion as well as the extensions and improvements to Marks and Spencer, British Home Stores, C&A, Boots and Littlewoods—among many others.

Public money is also being made available in the form of urban development grants. Some of the retailers mentioned above have applied for the grant, which is aimed at bridging the gap between a viable and non-viable project. The size of the grant varies but a maximum of 30 per cent is available. And an official with the BDO estimates that every public sector pound generates up to £8 from the private sector.

For many business people Belfast's commercial revitalisation is not so much a sign that normality is returning as an indication that people . . . are prepared to carry on regardless.

For Mrs Crane a city's performance is based on its small businesses, but she also notes that measuring real growth can be tricky. A distinction, she says, must be drawn between business growth and business change. A city-centre shop, for example, might close down but will be replaced with another. That does not represent a new business, Mrs Crane argues, it represents a change in business. And since small businesses, especially in the retail trade, traditionally change hands faster than those in the rest of the market, real growth is perhaps lower than many people assume.

Mrs Crane estimates that between 20 and 25 per cent of small businesses fail mainly, she says, because many people don't realise that there is a support network available to those in trouble. The University of Ulster offers courses on how to manage your own business and help is also available from small business clubs and the Chamber of Trade. The Local Enterprise Development Unit—which provides grants for small businesses in the manufacturing and service sectors, but not the retail trade—also offers "hand holding" services, as does the Belfast Enterprise Zone.

One word Mrs Crane makes a conscious effort to avoid is "normality". Such caution is understandable, and many traders wish political leaders would exercise equal restraint. In July, the then secretary of state Douglas Hurd declared the Provisional IRA to be a "dwindling force of a few hundred killers" who, he said, were on the defensive and would eventually be eradicated. The response from the IRA came a few days later in the form of a 500lb bomb which exploded in Ballynahinch, Co Down, devastating much of that town's commercial centre. In the immediate aftermath business people directed as much anger against Mr Hurd as they did against the bombers.

Summing up their feelings, Joy Campbell, president of the Ballynahinch Chamber of Commerce, said: "What particularly annoys us is that after successive statements by successive secretaries of state that the IRA is on the decline, the lesson has yet to be learned. The terrorists always hit back with a sharp lesson."

IRA bombings of Belfast's commercial centre have become a comparative rarity since the late 1970s—a lull which many observers suspected had a great deal to do with Sinn Féin's electoral interventions. In mid-June, just under a month after the local government elections, the IRA launched what it described as the "biggest bomb attack ever seen in Belfast". A 1000lb device exploded just off Chichester Street, causing extensive property damage. Later the Provisionals said in a statement that economic investment in Belfast had provided "the Brits with a propaganda platform from which they have been consciously proclaiming the return of normality".

Six weeks later the IRA launched another massive bomb attack in the same area, which again caused widespread damage. Many feared the attacks signalled the beginning of a new city-centre offensive. They didn't—for a variety of reasons depending on which side one chooses to believe. The authorities claim they have the security situation increasingly under control—through the use of improved intelligence and surveillance and the effects on the IRA and INLA of the supergrass system—while the IRA says it is deliberately waging a more selective campaign of violence.

However, the explosions were potent reminders of the devastation the IRA is still capable of inflicting—and of how fragile the government's "normality" is. Between 1968 and August of this year the government has paid out £474 million in compensation claims. And the recent city-centre bomb blast in Derry alone will push that figure up by another million at least.

For many business people Belfast's commercial revitalisation is not so much a sign that normality is returning as an indication that people are adapting to an abnormal situation and are prepared to carry on regardless. "You just never know, the whole place could literally blow up overnight," says Brian McManus of Zazz. "So you try not to worry too far ahead."

UNIONISM: JIM LEADS ON

PAUL BEW AND HENRY PATTERSON

NOVEMBER 1987

I s unionism in crisis? If so, is this one of the beneficial effects of the Hillsborough agreement? Will this crisis lead eventually to the emergence of a new and more flexible leadership? Such questions have been in the air as the campaign against the agreement has continued to go nowhere. However, much of the questioning stems from wishful thinking by constitutional nationalists and the Northern Ireland Office.

If the agreement is to fulfil its much-puffed "historic" significance then John Hume's claim that being tough with the Protestants strengthens the forces for accommodation in unionist politics must soon begin to look at least a possibility. The bathetic disappearance of the Task Force report (*Fortnight* 254), the outward social mobility of its main Official Unionist author, Frank Millar, and the resignations of several other political "men of reason" do not augur well. More important, though, are certain fundamental structural changes which predated the New Ireland Forum report and the Hillsborough accord.

Crucial among these is the virtual disappearance of an independent base, in either economic structures or political institutions, for a credible unionist strategy. Classical unionism (1885–1920) was built around two major social classes—the industrial bourgeoisie and the proletariat. Although the reproduction of these classes took place within United Kingdom and imperial markets, they were not directly dependent on the British state for their well-being. After partition, the fundamental weakening of their competitive positions was offset by the Protestant bourgeoisie's possession of local state power. Although increasingly dependent on transfer payments from Westminster, especially after 1945, this apparatus of Protestant rule provided the main mechanism by which a ramshackle unionist unity was maintained.

Since the imposition of direct rule in 1972, the earlier trend towards the weakening of the Protestant bourgeoisie has been fulfilled—with no direct access to local political institutions to compensate. It might appear that this creates just the basis for ultimate accommodation, since the only way any leverage over local political institutions can be obtained is through some deal with the SDLP. However, this begs the question of what purpose a share of local state power within these restraints would serve for unionists. The experience of the few months of power-sharing in 1974 demonstrated the massive difficulties of reconciling the opposed dynamics of two communal blocs—and this was with an SDLP leadership more concerned than now about unionist susceptibilities.

In more recent times, the notion of devolved power-sharing with security powers—pioneered by Frank Millar and others—has stretched the bounds of credibility. It has never been convincingly explained why the SDLP should give up its views on the UDR, for example, or voluntarily backtrack on the "Irish dimension". Still less has it been explained why the Haughey government should smile on anything which could be presented as an essentially internal solution.

A powerful devolutionist current persists in unionism—in the DUP and particularly amongst Official Unionists west of the Bann. However its appeal to this constituency is based on a mixture of hankerings for the "good old days", distrust of Britain and a reactionary "little Ulsterism". It is, in other words, the unionist current most unlikely to be able to make the compromises necessary to obtain movement on devolution.

Opposed to this is a broad strand of opinion which it is probably better to label "minimalist" rather than "integrationist". The minimalists doubt whether devolution on terms realistically likely to be available is worth the candle, and they are deeply suspicious of a Paisleyite devolutionism which has at times appeared overly willing to contemplate the ultimate confrontation with the British state. Much more aware than a sizeable section of the DUP of the unwillingness of the Protestant working class readily to contemplate any action which could endanger British financial support, they are painfully aware of their very narrow room for manoeuvre. Hence the decision to expel Robert McCartney, though the president of the Campaign for Equal Citizenship was always likely to prove himself an independent political force.

Although the disarray of the DUP since Hillsborough has, despite the apolitical analysis of sociologists of religion, illustrated yet again the less than hegemonic capacity of Paisleyism, the minimalists have their problems. The central one—and the one which will always make full-blooded integrationism unlikely—is that, for all the moulds of ruling-class consensus which Thatcher is supposed to have broken, she has continued the main lines of policy on the north established in the early 1920s. These were the insulation of the conflict from "the mainland" and where possible encouraging Protestants to see that,

whatever their future in Ireland, their position in the UK was a less than cherished one.

Thus the two serious strategic options for unionism appear to be closed off. This does not mean collapse, but it does mean a politics that is condemned to the largely reactive repetition of Protestant non-compliance with the main elements of the Hillsborough scheme. This can of course be proclaimed as having effects on the pace at which changes are introduced. However, by becoming little more than a pressure group for Protestant interests within a framework of direct rule with a greenish penumbra, unionism in the sense in which it existed from the 1880s to the 1960s will effectively disappear.

All of this does not mean that minimalist unionism may not have a certain future. Jim Molyneaux has cast himself as the Kutuzov of unionist resistance—like Tolstoy's general in *War and Peace* he has been immobile but tenacious, adhering to the now legendary "steady course". In the longer term, it may well be that the agreement can only evolve towards some bastard form of joint authority, but Molyneaux, John Taylor and Co clearly calculate that in the short term this is less likely. They have obviously rejected the thesis of "every day that passes the unionist negotiating position weakens" associated with the supporters of the Task Force. They suspect too that there is little popular enthusiasm for devolution—even perhaps if the terms available were rather better than under the Anglo-Irish Agreement. As few expect Molyneaux to get rid of the agreement anyway, it might be surprisingly popular if he managed to extract improvements in the way Northern Ireland business is handled at Westminster.

Even within the guidelines the British government set for itself in November 1985 there are plenty of things, both symbolic and practical, it could do to protect the fundamental interests of the unionists—if it had a mind to or, more seriously, if it had any interest in doing so. Whatever moves the government makes, or does not make, Jim Molyneaux intends to sit it out for the foreseeable future.

THE DEFIANT DINOSAUR AT ITS DAM

UNITING IRELAND

MAY 1989

FRANK WRIGHT and **JOHN LAMPEN** present an imaginary dialogue which explores whether and how Sinn Féin's demands could actually be met.

British minister: Could you clarify the IRA's position about a ceasefire?

Sinn Féin spokesperson: The terms for a ceasefire are a British declaration of withdrawal from the six counties within a reasonable period.

British minister: Is that military or governmental?

SF spokesperson: Both. And there must be an all-Ireland constitutional conference, the disbanding and disarming of the RUC and UDR, and a loosening of British economic domination.

British minister: It's quite unreasonable to make all these preconditions before a ceasefire. Who would provide essential police services in the interim period before the conference completed its work? Why risk a collapse of the Northern Ireland economy at such a sensitive period?

SF spokesperson: I'm sorry, I didn't make myself clear. Once there is a declaration of intent to withdraw, the IRA is pledged to declare a ceasefire, but if there is no move to meet the other demands the IRA will recommence hostilities.

British minister: But if the other processes are honestly set in motion, the IRA will lay down its arms permanently?

SF spokesperson: Yes, except for defence in the case of a violent loyalist backlash against the nationalist community.

British minister: And is the IRA to be the sole judge of whether reasonable steps are being taken to meet its demands? However hard we try, there may be very great problems.

Republican supporter: Don't worry about that. We support the aims of the IRA, but we're sick to death of all the carry-on. We're the ones who suffer most. Once there's a ceasefire, we'll see the IRA make it stick if you are all doing your best.

British minister (*to Irish minister*): We've come to the conclusion that the time has come for us to leave Northern Ireland. We have our interests at heart, of course, but we're also increasingly convinced that this is the only way to bring the conflict to an end.

Irish minister: To be honest, this is rather a shock. When do you propose to take this step?

British minister: We are considering a statement in the next few days announcing our total withdrawal within five years, and calling on the IRA to declare a ceasefire.

Irish minister: I hope you won't make such a statement till we've had time to prepare our own response. What steps are you taking to make it acceptable to the locally recruited security forces?

British minister: Funny, I thought you would ask first about placating unionist opinion. Do you really think there's going to be trouble with the RUC and UDR? What do you think, general?

British general: You have to realise, minister, that their ultimate commitment will be to their own people, not to the British crown. Do you really intend to disarm and disband them as the IRA wants?

British minister: Well, it will have to happen if the ceasefire is to turn into peace.

General: Then, with about 20,000 of them, I reckon we'll need at least 50,000 British troops to do the job. And they'll have to stay on here for a long time . . .

British minister: But this is meant to be a British withdrawal!

General: . . . And even so you can't count on it succeeding.

British minister: Do you mean mutiny?

General: Orders would keep being returned for clarification. You would be asked to define more and more closely what enforcement measures you allowed. There would be delays and mistakes. And huge numbers of RUC and UDR weapons would just disappear.

SF spokesperson: If you're right, the IRA would have every reason to resume hostilities.

British Minister (*to him, angrily*): And what would that achieve? Do *you* have any suggestions as to how we're supposed to carry out your so-called demands?

Irish minister: If you don't want a confrontation with the local forces, it's going to depend on just what you are going to offer the unionists.

British minister: What *all of us* are going to offer, you mean. Don't forget that your claim to the place is what caused all this trouble! (*American observer intervenes to quieten the ensuing argument.*) Suppose we tell the unionists that we are going to invite a wholly impartial group of international lawyers and statesmen, like our American friend here, to run the conference, listen to everyone and adjudicate on the best constitution for Northern Ireland?

Backbench TD: Did you say *Northern* Ireland?

Irish minister (*whispers to him*): It might be the best answer. We're not able at present for taking on the government of the north!

TD (*whispers*): But if an international group of lawyers sets up an independent Ulster, once it's registered at the United Nations that's the end of the nationalist claim. We can't agree to that!

British minister: I don't know what you're whispering about, but I should like to point out that our aim is simply to disengage. It's up to the people of Northern Ireland and yourselves to tell us what the best arrangements would be.

SF spokesperson: Do I have to remind you that unless the future is discussed on an all-Ireland basis, we shall end our ceasefire?

Unionist spokesperson (*loudly, in the distance*): Though nothing would persuade us to take a place at your table, we can hear enough to know what's going on. We cannot prevent the treacherous British from withdrawing. But if they do we would only co-operate with a decision which recognises the independence of Ulster. And there is no way that anyone can force a million people into something they totally repudiate.

MARCH 1989

Irish minister (*to British minister*): Lower your voice a bit. Our government will agree to an all-Ireland conference, though I must admit there's a bit of hesitation. We've decided that if we are generous enough we just might offer enough for the unionists to bite on and at the same time enough to pin Sinn Féin to their ceasefire. But it must be clear beyond doubt that you can't be blackmailed into staying.

British minister: What do you mean by "generous"?

Irish minister: Well, we aren't ready to make detailed proposals, and it'll all be negotiable anyway; but, by way of example, a large measure of local autonomy for Ulster (including Donegal, but not Monaghan or Cavan), with local taxation and spending systems, no reduction in state benefit levels, a regional assembly, and personal measures such as the right to hold a British passport and nationality. I assume you'll be willing to stand the costs of making the thing work?

British minister: I think you can take it for granted that we'll pay what's necessary to stop hundreds of thousands of unionists from emigrating to Great Britain. But do you think we can get the unionists to the conference?

American observer: That's what I wanted to ask. We're willing to help see fair play at the conference, but we want to see everyone there. Who *will* attend?

British minister: Well, the British and Irish governments, of course, though I would stress again that our own aim is to disengage. We're not there to control the future, only to be as helpful as possible. Then the SDLP will be there . . .

American observer: What about Sinn Féin?

Irish minister: Well, that could be helpful in preventing violence breaking out again, though it goes against the grain. It might be done on the basis of their electoral support.

British minister: It wouldn't be easy for us to agree to, and it would ensure that the unionists aren't there.

Irish minister: That needs thinking about. But what if

Sinn Féin had to earn its place by maintaining the cease-fire? That would be a big bonus all round.

SF spokesperson: But that means you're asking the IRA not just to control its own units, but all republican sources of violence!

Irish minister: Frankly, yes. Who else is able to do it?

SF spokesperson: We can't be held responsible for the INLA or Republican Sinn Féin. It will be a delicate enough business holding our own people together through all this.

British minister: Once the peace process has started, it will be up to you to control *or totally disown* any violence from republican sources.

American observer: If you can't deliver, where is your credibility as representatives of the republican movement? Remember, this discussion is about satisfying your aspirations! (*thoughtful pause*) I'm still waiting to hear about the unionist presence at the conference table. The Alliance party will be there, I hope, but that's not enough.

Unionist spokesperson: We refuse absolutely to take part in such discussions. We would prefer to declare our independence unilaterally.

British minister: All right, but such a step means the immediate cessation of all funding from the British government and the EEC. And I imagine there would be no American support for you either.

American observer: Quite right. No president could consider it.

Unionist spokesperson: What about your duty to the people of Ulster?

British minister: Your UDI would cancel all obligations. (*To the others*) Suppose we invite the Protestant church leaders to represent their community?

Church of Ireland bishop: I do not see an appropriate role for us at such a conference. We have indeed urged our politicians to enter into dialogue, but it is for them, not us, to judge whether an all-Ireland conference can possibly meet our people's aspirations.

British general: Minister, it seems to me essential to look at the question of *where the power is going to lie in the next stage*. We need an interim authority which won't provoke immediate civil war. It therefore needs some legitimacy in the eyes of the unionists. If their elected representatives won't come in, you must call in those people who can be *required* to come: the clerks of the district councils, the chief officers of the health and education boards and, most of all, the chief constable and the o/c of the UDR.

British minister: Can they speak for the unionists?

General: They can speak for a lot of people who want stability and protection. And personally they'll be opposed to UDI: they don't want chaos.

Irish minister: Wait a minute, you're going too fast! We must first do our utmost to get the unionists in.

Unionist spokesperson (*quietly, in his ear*): I don't mind telling you, off the record, that I should like to take part. But the moment I did I'd lose all credibility with my constituents. I've no choice but to stay away.

SDLP spokesperson (*in his other ear*): You must do it the other way round. First let them see that they can't halt the process. Then make sure your offer is more attractive to them than any alternative.

Irish minister: My government agrees that, if we can't get the unionists to the conference, then we should go ahead and involve the civil servants and security forces who will have to take responsibility in the interim. We shall keep open the prospect of involving the unionists: in the meantime we must liaise with the people who represent them—as far as anybody can—at the conference.

SF spokesperson: That won't do. The unionists—or whatever they call themselves when they know the British are withdrawing—can come as elected representatives of part of the Irish people. The apparatus of the British statelet has no place at a conference on the future of Ireland: it has to be dismantled. Otherwise the conference is just a trick to perpetuate the British presence, and the IRA will respond accordingly.

Irish minister: To be honest, my friend, that wouldn't bother me at all. It seems that we've got to the stage of an all-Ireland constitutional conference, with the RUC , the

UDR, the Garda Síochána and the Irish army recognised as the legitimate forces of state to guarantee the decision for some form of united Ireland. We still have the problem of selling the decision to the unionists. But it won't make any difference to the outcome whether you come in or stay out, agree or disagree. Your main demand has already been met.

SF spokesperson: I think I can see what you're trying to do. You want us to carry the can for everybody else. We've forced you to the conference table. So you make your little agreement together and we have to accept it—not just accept it but enforce it on the republican movement—or else the Brits move in and wipe us out. Literally. Even if it's the INLA and not us who break the ceasefire.

General: That's the logic of the position you've chosen.

American observer: Why not get out of it now? You've heard that the British want to go. Give up all your violence and join the normal political process *before* you're forced into the corner.

SF spokesperson: And become no-hopers like the Workers' party? Many of us could never agree to that, after all we've sacrificed.

American observer: You seem to be saying that you need the policy of armed struggle to give you a rationale for existing. If you give it up, you'd fall apart.

C of I bishop: And if you don't give it up, you'll be the scapegoats whom everyone else will turn on to cement the peace.

FORTNIGHT 290, DECEMBER 1990

THE NEW IRELAND FINDS ITS VOICE

Women had rocked the system instead of the cradle, she said. DICK WALSH records the continuing seismic shocks to the republic's political system from Mary Robinson's historic presidential election win.

Mary Robinson will be the seventh president of the republic, the first woman to have held the office, the only presidential candidate to have beaten Fianna Fáil. Had it stopped at that, hers would have been a stunning victory.

But the campaign was crowded with incident. Her main opponent, Brian Lenihan, became embroiled in controversy over attempts to ensure a transfer of power to Fianna Fáil without an election in 1982. His friend of 30 years, Charles Haughey, dismissed him as his deputy and minister for defence. The stability of Fianna Fáil's coalition partnership with the Progressive Democrats was undermined.

Ms Robinson came under attack, personal and political, for her liberal attitude to social issues. There was a whiff of the referenda on divorce and abortion, and older echoes in the red scare raised by her support from Labour and the Workers' party. Partitionism took a more direct form when the northern origins of the Fine Gael candidate, Austin Currie, were called into question.

For once simplification is justified: it was a case of competing visions of the republic. The main protagonists, Mr Lenihan and Ms Robinson, personified differences which were not only of style but of a depth many had thought unlikely, even impossible in a campaign for a non-executive office with strictly limited constitutional functions.

If anyone doubts that, they have only to look at the immediate political consequences of Ms Robinson's victory. The drama did not end with the campaign.

Fine Gael, beaten into third place for the first time in a national election, peremptorily dismissed its leader, Alan Dukes. John Bruton promised a more vigorous style and a move to the central, social-democratic front where the Robinson campaign had such decisive impact.

She had been an advocate of social change for 20 years. Mr Bruton restored divorce to the Fine Gael agenda. She had left the Labour party because she disagreed with unionist exclusion from the Anglo-Irish Agreement and in the presidential campaign favoured the inclusion of a consent clause in articles two and three of the republic's constitution. Mr Bruton made it part of his reconstructed Fine Gael platform.

She has a long record of support for and appeal to European institutions. Mr Bruton's first leadership address spoke of involvement in European defence, implying radical change if not abandonment of neutrality.

The left had united behind Ms Robinson. Within days of Mr Bruton's election, the Labour leader, Dick Spring, also laid claim to the social-democratic middle ground. He called for consolidation of the unity the left had demonstrated and asked his own supporters, "How can we continue to make history?"

The left, he said, should not delude itself: "The election of Mary Robinson does not mean that we will automatically increase our support. We will have to earn it . . . that means, frankly, that we have to change—to modernise our structures, to enhance our capacity to campaign and to refresh and update our policies."

He began by revamping his front bench and promising a more detailed programme of change within weeks. He even envisaged greater co-operation leading eventually to unity with the Workers' party. "I would think it's something to aspire to," he told the *Sunday Business Post*.

In Labour, also, there are hints of change on attitudes to the north—one of the policy areas on which the party differs from the WP. As Mr Spring sees it, a referendum on people's desires for a united Ireland might produce some surprising results: "I think [it] would throw up some very funny attitudes as opposed to what are commonly perceived attitudes. The outcome might well prove embarrassing for politicians on both sides of the border."

Ms Robinson's victory was a triumph for what Mr Lenihan called a rainbow coalition—of the left, of women, of minorities who, as Ms Robinson said, had no voice or whose voice was weak.

There was a coincidence of the right candidate, whose record was undeniable, and a degree of grotesque, unbelievable, bizarre and unprecedented bungling by her opponents. There was a sense in which her poorly funded but enthusiastic campaign was enhanced by the contrast with Fianna Fáil's organisational and financial superiority—the hoopla of the National Sleaze.

Ms Robinson's victory was a triumph for . . . a rainbow coalition—of the left, of women, of minorities . . .

There was also evidence of a restlessness which was apparent in the referenda of the 80s but which had its origins 10 years earlier. The 1969 election was the last in which a government was returned unfettered for another term. The Fianna Fáil administration of the late 70s was the last single-party government. In the elections of 1987 and 1989, between one in six and one in four voters changed their allegiances.

So if Ms Robinson's victory was part of a pattern, did it also suggest the emergence of a new liberal constituency? In the referenda of the 80s strong resistance to the national trends was evident only in Dublin. This year Robinson (or Robinson–Currie) majorities formed a broken U-shape on the map of the republic.

She held Dublin and took areas to the south and west: Kildare and Carlow–Kilkenny, Wicklow, Wexford,

Waterford and Cork, north Kerry, east Limerick, west Galway and Mayo. They included all of the state's cities, many of its big towns—and some predominantly rural areas as well. The midlands, from Tipperary to the border, remained loyal to Fianna Fáil, though polls taken for the *Irish Times* in the last months of the campaign showed Robinson gains in every area, social category and age group.

The left, which failed to show comparable gains, is pinning its hopes on the emergence of a new constituency—the rainbow coalition made permanent. So in its own fashion is Fine Gael. The Progressive Democrats, which threatened to leave the government over the Lenihan affair, have always claimed a liberal role; while the party took no decision to join the Robinson campaign its members clearly supported her.

Which leaves Fianna Fáil, still with 44 per cent of the votes but with a sixth successive failure to win a national majority. The party's rank and file is bitterly divided over Mr Lenihan's dismissal, between those who see it as a betrayal and those who believe it was the price paid for avoiding a general election—and, given their experiences since 1981, general elections are to be avoided at all costs.

But, while every other party in the state has responded with a flurry of activity, Charles Haughey insisted in the aftermath that Fianna Fáil's problems were limited to questions of perception and presentation. A day-long meeting was due as we went to press to survey the results, and there were signs that it might mark the start of a more fundamental stocktaking. Mr Haughey says the party is still capable of winning an overall majority, but only his most loyal supporters believe him.

The party's core support is built on working-class and rural areas, on the middle-aged and the elderly. The middle classes on whom the new constituency depends are reluctant to commit themselves. But they are becoming more numerous, more influential, and more determined to make up their minds on the merits of an argument rather than on its provenance.

Charles Haughey, like Margaret Thatcher, has a fundamentalist appeal. And hers, it is now clear, failed in the long run because while it satisfied the faithful it made no converts in the middle ground.

PART THREE

THE CULTURAL WORLD

No. 223   50p (70p in Republic)   8 JULY—8 SEPT. '85

FORTNIGHT

AN INDEPENDENT REVIEW FOR NORTHERN IRELAND

Summer Issue

JULIAN WATSON 85

**Martin Smyth interview ● Seawright and the Ulster Protestant League ●
Female Exploitation ● Shoot to Kill report ● Longley on Yeats**

IS THAT A FAX?

ROBERT JOHNSTONE

Twelve years before the masthead, man and boy, that's me, a galley-slave in the bowels of the gracious quinquereme that is *Fortnight*. These tyros nowadays can have no conception—*no conception*—what it was like in the dark days before Peter Brooke. Before Humphrey Atkins, for dear sake. Days when publishing, or anything mildly progressive culturally, was a novelty in strife-stricken, bomb-blasted, war-weary Belfast. When I walked into the renovated offices recently for the first time since 1986, I couldn't believe my eyes: photocopier, desks, doors that shut properly . . . There was an odd-looking machine by the door. "Is that a fax?" I queried. "That's right," said young Wilson, cool as you like.

Now they have glossy paper, *supplements*, and they pay contributors. When I started, we carved each individual letter from a block of metal retrieved from the debris of the latest car bomb. Hence the interesting typographical errors, for which the magazine had become justly famous. I remember an early example, in issue 15: on the very same page there were reviews of books by the distinguished Gaelic scholar "Robin Skeleton" and the celebrated woman novelist–philosopher "Irish Murdoch". As in one of my more memorable film reviews, which discussed the career of someone called "Sam Peckinpath", the new names completely supplanted the old, and seemed, in some surrealistic way, to take on a life of their own. I will always cherish the information, in an early article on John Hewitt, that the venerable poet had been penning verses "since 1691".

Such, I'm afraid, are my most incisive conclusions after leafing through the arts pages. In May 1973 Stewart Parker complains that there's nothing to see, apart from *The Godfather*, in Belfast's 12 cinemas. Eating out at Blades in Limavady in 1971 costs the *Fortnight* gastronomes £2.35 each, including wine. In early issues the critics poignantly express gratitude that anything at all is going on, and that more than three brave souls have ventured beyond their front doors to join them at the concert or the play—despite the fact that it probably only cost 20p to get in.

In selecting "The Best of " the back pages, I wanted to include all the regular columnists, to show the cultural landmarks since 1970, to suggest how artistic life has improved, to illustrate how diverse and eclectic *Fortnight* has been. I've failed at each of these. There is so much material that it would be impossible to represent all or even some aspects fairly. One could, for example, put together a full-length anthology of poems that have appeared in *Fortnight* that would stun the publishing world.

I regret not being able to include even one tenth of the contributors to the arts pages. Many were good friends. I read their copy every issue with surprise and delight. And they were all engaged in a common, worthwhile enterprise that usually was more suited to the optimist of India-rubber resilience than the ambitious littérateur. Co-editing the *Honest Ulsterman* confirms my belief that small magazine publishing is for those who don't know the meaning of the word "frustration", for those who are able to cope when their star reviewer absconds to Finland with *the* important book of the season, or when bookshops too far away to threaten refuse to cough up what they owe. It is for people who think all this represents good fun.

I'm glad to see *Fortnight* doing so well, but after looking through the back issues I feel nostalgic for the bad times, when we hand-knitted the pages out of old copies of the *News Letter* and the *Irish News*. How can you compare those piffling plastic computer terminals with the huge brass and mahogany reprographic camera that lurked in the loft in James Street South? It had its own railway track, I swear to God.

A MAN'S WORLD

JOHN MONTAGUE

THOMAS KINSELLA (trans.), *The Tain*
(Dolmen in association with Oxford University Press, cloth 63s, paper 22s)

Thomas Kinsella's struggle with the Tain, the early Irish epic, began fifteen years ago, when he came on the oldest version of the Deirdriu legend. There, free of all medieval or later Celtic Twilight embroidery, was the stark and simple story of a headstrong young couple who court in the earthy terms of a rural civilisation. "That's a fine heifer going by," says Noisi; one can almost hear him slap Deirdriu's plump flanks.

Although it has invariably been given separate romantic billing, the Deirdriu story is also one of the prefatory tales to the Great Tain. It is the murder of the sons of Uislvi by Conchobor, the jealous king of Ulster, which leads to the exile of Fergus and his men at the court of Connaught. They leave Emain Macha in flames, and "for sixteen years they made sure that weeping and trembling never died away in Ulster".

The great confrontation between Ulster and Connaught comes, however, not because of a woman's beauty but a bull's power. In a pastoral society, animals represent power, and many of the early Irish tales are about Tains, or cattle-raids. But there is more to it than that: the only thing Ailill, the king of Connaught, has over his wife is a bull which has deserted her herd "refusing to be led by a woman".

The phallic implications are obvious and when Queen Medb sets out to take the Brown Bull from Ulster and is opposed by the great lover and warrior Cuchulainn, we find ourselves involved in a war not only between provinces, but between the female and male principles, between an older matriarchal and a Mithraic cult. The rest of the men of Ulster are in hibernation, suffering the pangs of childbirth because of an insult to a pregnant woman, Macha, whom they forced to race against their king's horses.

The great strength of Kinsella's translation is that by restoring the coarse detail which even Lady Gregory ignored and his general organisational power he enables us to take an honest look at the story and the civilisation which produced it. The idealised hero of Yeats's poetry is revealed as a right bastard. Cuchulainn always cheats under pressure, whether against his equals, his own seven-year-old son, or the warrior woman Aife, whom he grips by the breasts. He has no respect even for his own word: no sooner has he promised fidelity to his future wife, Emer, than he sleeps with someone else. Indeed, he spends nearly as much time in bed as on the battlefield.

But then the morals of the Tain are as low as the morale. Medb is as generous in her sexual appetites as Cuchulainn; it is part of their contract that her husband should be content to be cuckolded. Their daughter Finnabair is used as a sort of royal whore to entice men to fight Cuchulainn, while the semi-impotence of Medb's chief lover, Fergus (who lost the throne of Ulster because he was in bed with Conchobar's mother) is the subject of a great deal of phallic joking. When he grumbles at the end, "we followed the rump of a misguiding woman", the message of the Tain is repeated: the real world is where males, glittering as peacocks, match each other in samurai frenzy.

TRAUMAS AND TRADITIONS

Every Irishman, especially every Ulsterman, should read this book, for it sends shafts deep into our history and psyche. Is Ulster really under a curse, for example? When I was editing a recent issue of *Threshold* on the northern situation, this passage of the Tain suggested itself as the inevitable beginning. And in "A New Siege", I found myself seeing Ian Paisley in terms of another, earlier defender of Ulster as "a Black Cuchulainn bellowing against the Scarlet Whore". Certainly he is capable of the warp-spasm, the psychological change which strikes terror into the enemies of Cuchulainn:

> On his head the temple-sinews stretched to the nape
> of his neck, each mighty, immense, measureless knob
> as big as the head of a month-old child. His face
> and features became a red bow . . . His mouth weirdly
>   distorted.

The ironical thing is, though, that the Iron Age warriors of the Tain were part of the international Celtic or La Tène civilisation. The article on Navan Fort in *Current Archaeology* bears this out, even detailing that the "outer wall" seems to have been deliberately destroyed by fire in the third century BC. So these early Celtic Ulstermen are responsible for the anti-feminine prejudice which still rules us, one way or another, whether we go to Croke, or Lansdowne or Linfield Park!

ULSTER '71

ANON.

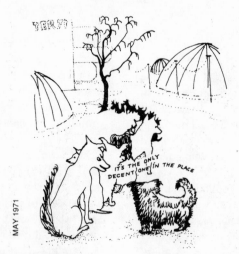

MAY 1971

ITS THE ONLY DECENT ONE IN THE PLACE

A visit to Ulster '71 is like watching a Twelfth of July Orange parade. You know that its existence will offend many people. Yet its gaiety and colour form a temporary victory over the permanent and surrounding drabness of a depressing industrial city. Despite your reservations, you smile.

I had seen Ulster '71 during the press previews but not as a member of the public when it was in full swing. The festival has overbearing tones of neutrality. The flags flapping on poles along the Stranmillis Embankment give the game away immediately. They are a red and white variation on the kind of motif that some firms use to sell tractors or fertiliser. The organisers strenuously avoided any suggestion that Ulster '71 was political, even though it is inconceivable that it would suddenly have happened if 1971 had not been a conventional milestone in the Unionist story. Nevertheless, the flags on the embankment are a tribute to political emasculation. There are no international flags, no tricolours—either French or Irish—to confuse the faithful. Neutrality is all.

The exhibition in the Queen's University gymnasium is also overshadowed by neutrality. But once the point is taken that only certain parts of the story can be told, the designers have been clever and at times brilliant. It starts on a good Irish note with a picture of St Patrick at the entrance to greet those from both sides who claim him as their own. Further along there is a picture of Churchill with the immortal words about Northern Ireland's contribution to the war effort. Lord Brookeborough, unnamed of course, is on the left of the picture. It is one of the rare, perhaps accidental, political moments. But in an exhibition which sets out to show the achievements of Northern Ireland, credentials are impeccable.

The Hall of Fame is a gem of compromise. It depends what they mean by Ulster. Is it to be the nine counties of history or the six of compromise? Lord Montgomery had some tenuous connections with Moville in Donegal. He is in. Sir Tyrone Guthrie had deep roots in Co Monaghan, and was the Chancellor of Queen's for good measure. He is out. Perhaps his speech in 1964 about the border in men's minds was still too radical for a nice neutral exhibition. Georgie Best was there, looking like D. H. Lawrence. So too was Siobhan McKenna, and Paddy Dougherty and Greer Garson. And the "Father of the Suez Canal". I have forgotten his name again but I am assured that he is famous. The two most famous Ulster characters of recent times are out. Paisley and Bernadette have more in common than integrated education.

The "Tunnel" of hate is also a compromise. The slogans to Her Majesty and His Holiness which have taxed the ingenuity of Ulster's generations are conspicuous by their absence. Instead there are worthy niceties like "Down With Poverty" and "Save The Countryside" which look more akin to Sussex or Surbiton. They are weak substitutes for the real slogans of a politically virile province where offspring from the ghettoes make their mark early in life on the nearest gable end. The sounds in the tunnel start like a rowdy football match. But they work up to a pathetic and horrible scream of distress. It was all too familiar, but maybe I am a sensitive soul. Despite the compromise the tunnel makes its point.

The last part of the exhibition consists of a lecture by David Dunseith or Miss Adrienne on three or four screens about the Northern Ireland of the future. It is cleverly presented but the sounds and lights clash. The effect is like chasing shadows down the corridors of a dream.

I have seen the exhibition three times now and the overall impression has this dream-like quality. It is warm, quite pleasant, there are shapes, there are colours. There are no nightmares. You emerge at the other end feeling slightly better. You have shared with others in A Good Thing. But I doubt if many of the hard facts of Ulster life which are presented so ingeniously remain in the mind. It is rather like the man who read *War and Peace* in one night. When he was asked to describe the book he said, "It's about Russia." The exhibition is about Ulster but don't ask me how many houses we have built since the war.

THE NEW ULSTER MUSEUM

RAY ROSENFIELD

The superlatives came quite thick. "The best museum in the British Isles outside London"; "quite the most ambitious display project in the British Isles, something to be compared with the Smithsonian in Washington"; "the special exhibition area is one of the largest to be found outside London". The description came from the Director, Mr Alan Warhurst and his staff.

They were, so far as one not fully conversant with the scope and the style of all the museums in these islands could judge, fully justified. The extended Ulster Museum is truly splendid and every step made in the circuit of the building made by the representatives of the press confirmed the impression made when visiting the Laurens exhibition. It will not be fully operational, so to speak, until the spring of next year; some departments are only sketchily indicated as yet, but even so there is plenty of evidence of an imaginative purpose at work. The building itself is something of which we can justly feel very proud; Francis

The extended Ulster Museum is truly splendid . . .

Pym's design has effected a fine marriage of the old with the new and Mr Harlison of the architects' branch of the Ministry of Finance, who carried on with the work on Mr

Pym's resignation from the project, has achieved his concept of a series of spaces related to the size of the exhibits rising gradually from the entrance in a succession of different levels and linking with the levels of the old building. The stonework of the old building is knitted into the fairfaced concrete of the new; there are terraces on all floors and on one of them there is an open-air terrace extension to the café, overlooking the Botanic Gardens. Offices and workshop accommodation are situated to the side of the spiral, the offices directly related to the display section in each case.

In conformity with sophisticated modern ideas the art department is entirely artificially lighted.

For the first time for many years it is now possible to see such treasures as the Fuseli drawings that are in the possession of the museum and the painting "The Dawn of Christianity" by J. M. W. Turner. Mr James Ford Smith, Keeper of Art, was at pains to point out that Belfast really had an art collection of major importance; it was indeed more highly regarded abroad than locally, borrowings being made frequently by New York, Washington, Paris, Helsinki and even Venice for the Biennale. Belfast can boast one of the largest and best collections of post-war European and American paintings outside London.

Belfast can boast one of the largest and best collections of post-war European and American paintings outside London.

For the first time the museum has a gallery devoted entirely to watercolours. Of equal importance with the collections is the research that is being undertaken by the specialist staff. For example, the first historical survey of Irish painting from 1720 to the present day has been done by the Ulster Museum, and with the aid of the paintings in its possession it is possible for the interested student to follow the history with examples clearly before him.

Mr Ford Smith indicated, moreover, that it is agreed that further research will be carried out, that there will be continuing scholarship practised. It about a year's time,

too, an art workshop should be opened and it will be possible probably, as he put it, "to see art happening".

A special display area is being prepared for the Girona Treasure and the Ulster Museum is expected to become one of the leading centres in the world for the study of Armada material. Exciting display techniques enliven the natural history department already and more are promised, like a large-scale diorama which will show animals and plants as they are in nature. It will be possible for one to press a button and hear the song of the selected bird, and another device will enable the visitor to follow the flight of migratory birds.

Mr Alan Warhurst, Director of the museum, indicated that he saw the Ulster Museum as more than a magnificent building in Belfast with exciting collections, excellently displayed. It would be a base for a regional museum service. Already the Ulster Museum had made history by being the first museum in the British Isles actually to establish mini museums, as it were, away from its base. This had taken place at Tollymore and at Gortin. But more was in prospect—service to the province with material, lectures and assistance to societies and small local museums throughout the province. It was a place from which a real museum service could and would be developed from the whole of Northern Ireland. And in the museum itself it was intended to continue and expand the old scheme of films and lectures and to have music recitals as well.

With regard to major exhibitions in the near future Mr Warhurst said there would be an exhibition on the Ethiopian tradition on loan from the Victoria and Albert Museum, the centenary exhibition of Jack Yeats would come from Dublin before going to New York, as well as a loan exhibition from Amsterdam.

Only two qualms. As yet there is no handy catalogue to aid visitors in their perambulations—the long loose sheets are comprehensive, but very clumsy to consult. The other qualm is over the shadow that looms over all galleries— the threat of imposed entrance fee. The Duke of Abercorn, chairman of the Trustees of the Ulster Museum, told me in answer to my direct question on the matter that he and all members of the board had unanimously voted against the idea of making a charge. However, he said with a sigh, if the powers that be across the water introduced entrance charges he expected that we would have to follow suit.

GREEN FOOL

MAURICE LEITCH

PATRICK KAVANAGH, *The Green Fool*
(Martin, Brian & O'Keefe, £3.00)

I only met Patrick Kavanagh once and it was in a London pub a little while before he died. He was a very sick man and he wheezed heavily, making no effort to moderate his painful gasping for breath. He was also gruff to the point of boorishness but, looking back on that afternoon, it's easier for me to understand now the need a dying man has to conserve his last precious energies—especially from the debilitating inroads made by literary hangers-on.

When the pub closed we shared a taxi. It was a terrifying ordeal sitting in that cab beside one of the most formidable of dying Irish poets, for not a single word was spoken and I was as incapable of speech as he seemed to be. By that time I had been completely demoralised, not only by the brooding presence of the man himself but by the nervousness of his friends.

The taxi drew up to the house in which he was staying and he prepared to get out. Still nothing had been said. I think I mustered a "Goodbye", but he hesitated only slightly. He said, "I liked your book", grunted, and closed the door. It was the only time he had spoken directly to me that day. I hadn't even known he knew my name. The taxi drove off. And that is *my* Kavanagh story—my only one—and is as it stands, as it happened, no loving embellishments have touched it up over the years. . .

It still means a lot to me although I've a deal more cynicism now but the pleasure I felt riding away in that taxi alone came back when I was reading *The Green Fool*, his second book, first published in 1938, now a handsome reissue. Towards its end he describes his first forays into the literary worlds of Dublin and then London and of how sensitive he was at that time to kindness or any form of recognition by his peers, so perhaps he never did forget, even when he was a giant himself, what it felt like to be another young writing "green fool". I like to think of it in that way anyway.

At the same time Kavanagh could be excused, I feel, any residue of bitterness towards writing and other writers because of the way he was treated when *The Green Fool* was first published. Oliver St John Gogarty, in a libel action, forced the book to be withdrawn because of two sentences. Describing what happened at Gogarty's house in Dublin the first time he travelled there on foot on a naively romantic pilgrimage from his native Inniskeen in Monaghan, Kavanagh wrote: "I mistook Gogarty's white-robed maid for his wife—or his mistress. I expected every poet to have a spare wife."

In the book, Kavanagh, after sniffing out the littérateurs and their haunts, returns to his own quieter, more enduring landscape of small fields and farms around the townland of his birth. He had seen the great world of letters his imagination had fed upon when he was a country cobbler and had satisfied himself finally that it was not for him. "Among my own little hills and poplar-lined roads was all romance. For there my imagination had planted in childhood the seeds of whimsical poetry."

In reality of course he returned to literary Dublin which he believed along with F. R. Higgins held more dishonesty than any other quarter of the globe, and his bitterness, alas, flourished among the St John Gogartys of that tiny world of spiteful minds. What saved Kavanagh from the others' sterility was the rich and romantic associations with which *The Green Fool* is densely packed. It is an amazing catalogue of observation on rural Ireland, an unbroken stream of detail, sharply bright and poetic. As he says in the book: "I have little memory for anything save the quaint and bizarre", and it was this storehouse which he drew upon constantly throughout his later writing life and which supplied his genius.

The period stretches from ten years or so before the First World War up until the Coronation of George VI. Wakes, weddings, ploughing and sowing, country politics and characters, fairs and superstitions are noted with an almost overwhelming bright-eyed recall. The sentences are short, almost staccato, but the imagery blazes in almost every one of them. The world recaptured here in the first publishing venture from the newest and, what promises to be, brightest young imprint has vanished in its detail but the spirit of rural Ireland remains total and unmoved in the pages of a truly great book. The greatness lies, I believe, in Kavanagh's acute perception at all times of the balance and continuous interaction between the gross realities of country life and the romance kept alive by the poetry of living speech. "We were all poets, dreamers, and no man was old." No country is ever as black or as green, either, as it's painted.

KINSELLA'S CRAFT

JAMES SIMMONS reacts to Kinsella, then tries
a few lines himself.

At first our poets offered reasons why they weren't
likely to produce poems on the "troubles" . . . a
few years later the most famous names have all
had a go. Montague in his "New Siege", John Hewitt in
his "Ulster Reckoning" and now Thomas Kinsella in
"Butcher's Dozen". The last is the worst. Montague's
long poem didn't really get off the ground. But it was a
serious attempt. He didn't fall into vulgar prejudices.
John Hewitt worried away at the problem with genuine
integrity and modest inspiration. Thomas Kinsella has
considerable sophistication and fluency and a certain lyric
flair, a good critical mind and serious ambitions . . . his
work on *The Tain* could not have been done by a small
man, I think, but this "Butcher's Dozen" is a nasty bit of
work.

But the sort of hate that Kinsella is whipping up here . . . is unforgivable in a man of his education.

At the centre is a well-written attack on imperialism. It
is perfectly true that imperialism was evil and that every
country from which England withdraws suffers and will
go on suffering from the effects of English exploitation:

All your errors heaped behind you,
Promises that do not bind you,
Hopes in conflict, cramped
    commissions,
Faiths exploited, and traditions.

But the sort of hate that Kinsella is whipping up here,
which is understandable evil in the ignorant authors of
street ballads, is unforgivable in a man of his education.
The sons of imperialists are as much saddled with their
burden as the sons of the corrupt and incompetent Irish
leaders who could not defend their country and who
botched their rebellions. The Irish are not traditionally
against war and so on. They are just not very good at it. So
how can any sane Irish man feel morally indignant? The
English behave badly in power as the Germans do and the
Americans and the Irish. If you believe in progress you
work for reform, not to destroy some enemy; but this is
the great Irish flaw (and I find it sickening). John Hewitt
hits it off very nicely in his "An Irishman in Coventry"
talking of his people's "ready wit":

to hit and run and howl when it is hit.

Kinsella is striking this traditional pose when he makes
one of his Derry ghosts say:

Here lies one in blood and bones,
Who lost his life for throwing stones.

It reminds me of "young Albert" who poked his stick in
the old lion's ear and got swallowed . . . "and him in his
Sunday clothes too".
The English soldiers first came to Derry to defend the
threatened Catholics. It was part of the great achievement
of the civil rights martyrs. Kinsella ignores this and betrays
the good work.

The milder forms of violence,
Earn nothing but polite neglect.

A lie. The civil rights movement drew brave and straight-
thinking Ulster men of all denominations together against
prejudice and ignorance. As soon as the IRA were allowed to take over, the condition and hopes of the country
regressed to the old vicious squabbles of the 1920s. The
energies that worked for a better England, a better Ulster
and a better Republic of Ireland are disintegrated, and the
pressure is on us to fight for some nationalist nonsense or
a daydream Socialist Republic that even in dreams could
only be imposed by an ignorant violent minority. With
vile ingenuity Kinsella defends the IRA:

We rap for order with the gun,
The issues simplify to one
—Then your democracy insists
You mustn't talk with terrorists!

and of course the tenor of the passage is fair enough in
blaming the English government:

Divide and ruin, muddle through,
Not principled, but politic.

Tom Paine put it far better: "Policy and interest, therefore,
will, but perhaps too late, dictate in England, what reason

and justice could not." The crime of course is connecting moral indignation with national character. He even sneers at the notion of forgetting old harms and "nursing the living, not the dead".

The failure is bound to be artistic too. Kinsella is using the form used by Joyce in "Gas from a Burner", four-beat couplets. Joyce too is vicious, prejudiced and over-simplified, but the diction warns you that here is a reckless angry man letting himself go:

This lovely land that always sent
Her writers and artists to banishment
And in a spirit of Irish fun
Betrayed her leaders, one by one.

O Ireland my first and only love
Where Christ and Caesar are hand in glove!

The whole thing is open, energetic and funny, and since it is dramatically poised and placed, more profound.

Kinsella mixes uneasily, attempts to be rough and satirical, with implications of more subtlety and solemnity, and even allows himself to drift off on the lyric touch:

I stood like a ghost. My fingers strayed
Along the fatal barricade.
The gentle rainfall drifting down
Over Colmcille's town . . .

The Dolmen Press, without a doubt
Will turn another pamphlet out,
With lyric grace fomenting hate,
And at the end (perhaps too late)
Some pious hopes that Orangemen
And patriots may live again
In peace, a great religious nation!
That ought to boost my reputation
In England and the USA
Where all the cash is anyway.

FORTNIGHT 43, JULY 1972

ORANGE DRUMS, TYRONE, 1966
Seamus Heaney

The Lambeg balloons at his belly, weighs
Him back on his haunches, lodging thunder
Grossly there between his chin and his knees.
He is raised up by what he buckles under.

Each arm extended by a seasoned rod,
He parades behind it. And though the drummers
Are granted passage through the nodding crowd,
It is the drums preside like giant tumours.

Each cocked ear gloating, expert in its greed,
His battered signature subscribes, "No Pope".
The pigskin's scourged until his knuckles bleed.
The air is pounding like a stethoscope.

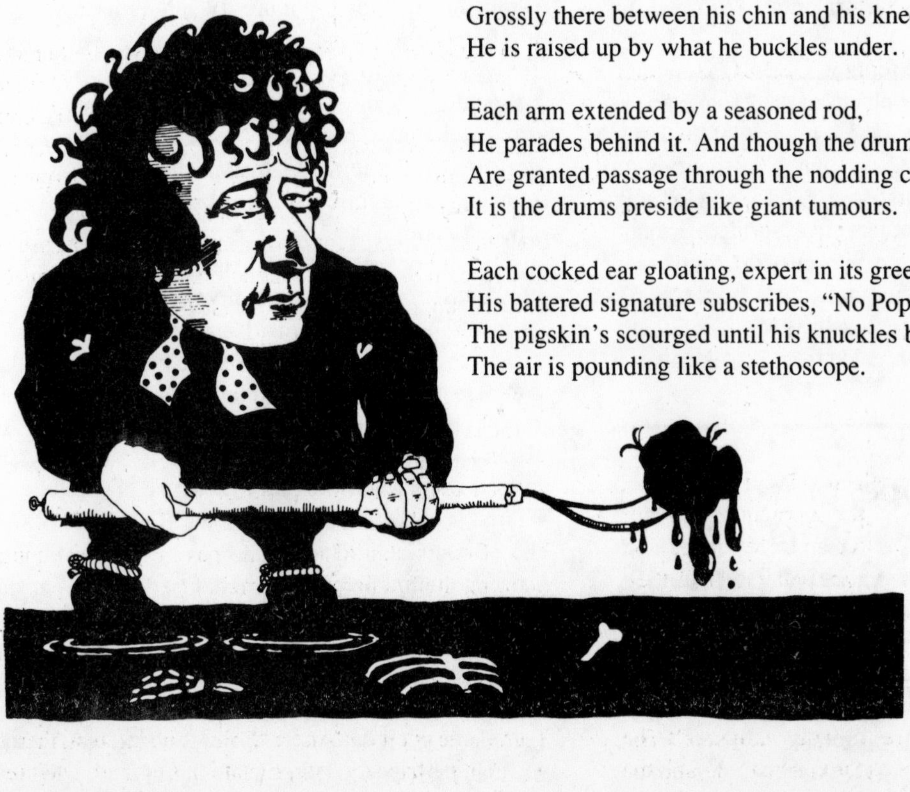

OCTOBER 1976

Gut talk

Jack Foster

JUNE 1985

PÁDRAIG Ó SNÓDAIGH, *Hidden Ulster*
(Dublin, 20p)

Since Irish was not on the curriculum at my particular grammar school, I can't tell you by whom this particular pamphlet is published—indeed, only a familiarity with Dublin postmarks permits me to fathom the city of publication—which is an instructive irony in a booklet that seeks to recall Protestant Ulstermen to their Gaelic heritage.

In thirty pages and 172 footnotes, Mr O Snodaigh strives to demolish one of the planks of the "Two Nations Theory"—"that the Irish language is not part of the heritage of the 'Ulster Protestant Community'", a theory with whose resuscitation he credits British and Irish Communists, the New Ulster Movement, the Northern Ireland Labour party, and—party unto himself—the victimised Conor Cruise O'Brien, that thorn in unthinking flesh. We are all one in our Gaelic heritage, asserts Mr Ó Snódaigh, and for that heritage to be concealed from Protestants is a violation of their civil rights.

O Snodaigh's hope, presumably, is that if Protestants are awakened to their Gaelic heritage, they won't oppose political unity.

On Mondays I agree with him, feel assuredly if not aggressively Irish, regret that I cannot understand the gutturine vocables that rattle out at me from RTE radio and television. Tuesdays, on the other hand, I feel very British, an inseparable part of Anglo-Saxon culture and civilisation. On Wednesdays I feel kinship with neither the English nor the Irish and sense the emotional if never the political logic of an independent Ulster. Thursdays I cast a fond eye once more on the Irish language and the Gaeltacht, this time as a would-be world citizen earnestly sympathising with any minority culture trying to survive the homogenising influence of today's geocultures. On Fridays I say to hell with roots, traditions, heritages, nationalities, glorious memories and the rest of the sexually sublimative, proto-fascist crap. Over the weekend I get drunk. In short, my response to Mr Ó Snódaigh's booklet is as ambivalent, or should I say multivalent, as my nationality.

The author makes a good summary case for a hypothesis whose historical probability is refuted by the feelings of most Ulster Protestants. It appeals to the debunker of received truth in me to learn that many of the planters were Gaelic-speakers, that planters and natives intermarried, that Protestant and Nonconformist clerics were active in keeping the language alive (when the Catholic clergy were openly hostile), and that the driving force behind such seminal bodies as the Belfast Harp Society, the Ulster Gaelic Society and even the Gaelic League came from middle-class Protestants. As a current student of Ulster fiction, I wish Mr Ó Snódaigh would give us a full-blown study of the career of the Irish language in the north, particularly in Belfast, and particularly in "the radical Belfast of the seventeen nineties". I for one would be greatly in his debt were he to raise this pamphlet to the stature of genuine scholarship.

And now for the bad news. So many wingshots have been got off at Cruise O'Brien—the cleverest man in Ireland by several gaelic leagues—that I wonder how he manages to flutter over to Brussels. But O'Brien alone amongst southern politicians has had the logic, honesty and courage to admit the inescapability of what he would call the basic data of the problem—the rejection of Irishness (as it is traditionally and currently defined) and

But . . . sympathy does not lead automatically to a desire for unification.

of unification by a majority of people in the north. Mr Ó Snódaigh and others can show Protestants the extent of their Gaelic heritage without, I believe, fear of much political static; indeed, Protestants like myself feel curiously flattered when our Irishness is asserted for us.

But the flattery is the sugar on the pill, the pill being the historical justification for political unification. Ó Snódaigh's hope, presumably, is that if Protestants are awakened to their Gaelic heritage, they won't oppose

political unity. But the Protestants in sympathy with the Gaelic language and culture whom the author pays tribute to (including LOL 1303 whose banner adorns the booklet's cover) demonstrate that sympathy does not lead automatically to a desire for unification.

Besides, it is too late. If history, as fond of order as the next man, had meant Protestants to retain their putative Gaelic heritage, they would have done so. All that could be done now would be inculcation, which nobody should want.

If it is too late, it is partly due, as Ó Snódaigh says, to the historical opposition to the language of the English government, the Established Church, and societies like the SPCK. But is it not also due to the gross perversion of Gaelic language and culture into nationalist propaganda, making it impossible for many Protestants to begin or continue an interest in them? In this, both sides are the losers.

Unharnessed from the political chariot, Gaelic culture has my best will, now and in the technocratic days to come. I'm pleased and a little proud to learn of my Gaelic heritage from Mr Ó Snódaigh. But I know it's in my head only. Like Lawrence faced with proof of evolutionary theory, I can only press my solar plexus and say regretfully, "I don't feel it *here.*"

SAFE AS HOUSES:
THE GREAT BELFAST URBAN
MOTORWAY SHOW

STEWART
PARKER

NARRATOR The year: 1912. The place: the Atlantic Ocean. The date: April 14th; a Night to Remember . . .

JACK Hey Eddie.

EDDIE What?

JACK Why did they call this ship the *Titanic* anyway?

EDDIE Because it's like one of the Titans of olden days— a giant, the biggest ship ever built and one of the costliest.

JACK The cost was gigantic, true enough.

EDDIE But wasn't it worth it? Isn't it one of the greatest inventions of civilisation?

JACK As far as you or me is concerned, mate, washing the dishes on this tub is the same as washing them on any other.

EDDIE That's no way to look at it. The point is, it's modern, it's got speed plus luxury, it's the modern way to travel.

JACK What are you trying to do, sell me it?

EDDIE I'm just telling you, you're standing in a miracle of modern engineering, an unsinkable mammoth. That's the latest thinking, Jackie boy, that's progress for you— Progress! [*Pause*] What's the matter?

JACK I thought I heard a bump.

NARRATOR Which brings us to three comments on the Belfast Ring Road proposals. First, a man whose house was threatened with demolition.

MAN I own this house and I'm pretty happy the way things are, but I wouldn't have objected to it coming down, because you can't stop progress.

NARRATOR Now, a local MP.

MP We all know that road development is inevitable. . . You cannot stand in the way of progress.

NARRATOR And thirdly, a member of the old Corporation.

MCKEE I hate the thought of the ring road as much as anyone. It is ugly, contemporary and soulless. It marches through the city like a great tank, crushing 5,000 houses and many small businesses. But this is progress. It is inevitable and the sooner we tackle it the better.

NARRATOR What does the Belfast Urban Motorway—or B.U.M., as it's often referred to—mean for the quality of life in central Belfast? When did it start? Where will it end? We hope to suggest few if any answers to these questions by means of a single case history, the case history of an average Belfast working-class couple, Bertie and Bridget Polarity. So here is life with the Polarities; Phase 1, which runs from 1946 till 1967.

1946

BERTIE As I've always said to Bridget, so long as we have a roof over our heads and the price of a packet of fags, we won't go far wrong. But then roads have always been a special interest of mine, you see. Not that we got much time for contemplation in the war against Hitler. Still, all good things must come to an end . . .

BRIDGET   Ach Bertie, isn't it great that you're back from the war and we've got married and settled down in our own wee house in one of the areas of old Victorian housing fringing the city centre? . . . Here we are as happy as the flowers in May in 1946, the year of food rationing and heavy power cuts. But tell me, dear, what's that book you're holding there?

BERTIE   Excuse me, Bridget, I was just browsing through the Report of the Departmental Committee set up by the Minister of War Transport to study the Design and Layout of Roads in Built-Up Areas.

BRIDGET   Oh, you mean the report on which the Belfast Corporation is basing their Outline Advisory Plan, proposing the construction of three ring roads, described as the Inner, Intermediate and Outer Ring Roads?

BERTIE   That's the one, aye.

BRIDGET   What do you mean by ring road, Bertie?

BERTIE   A ring road is a road that goes in a ring, dear, like the old Circular Road was supposed to, instead of going straight, like the Ormeau Road or the Shore Road. It cuts across the other roads in a big wide circle, you see.

BRIDGET   And why does Belfast need ring roads?

BERTIE   Why, to cope with the ever-increasing volume of private cars and lorries—moving about the city and cluttering up the streets.

BRIDGET   Just think, Bertie . . . maybe by 1956, the year of Suez and Elvis Presley, we'll be able to go for a ride on the bus round the new Belfast Inner Ring Road!

1956

BERTIE   1956, that was the year Stormont passed a Housing Act that allowed for Belfast Corporation to redevelop all the old housing areas in and around the city centre. Never you mind, I says to Bridget; so long as we have an umbrella over our heads and the price of a packet of aspirins, we won't go far wrong. Of course, this Housing Act got the Corporation more excited than ever about the ring road idea, since it could be put through the redevelopment areas. In the lightning space of five years, they had produced a detailed ring road scheme. . .

BRIDGET   Tell me this, Bertie, is there anything at all in that oul' paper of yours?

BERTIE   There's a bit of a barney going on between Fidel Castro and President Kennedy and the Corporation Improvement Committee has approved the City Surveyor's Grade Separated Road Scheme.

BRIDGET   I see—so the ring road is to have dual two-lane carriageways running independently of each other?

BERTIE   As you say, Bridget, it'll be a grade separated road going right round the city centre.

BRIDGET   Just imagine, Bertie—maybe by 1963, the year of the Liverpool Sound, it'll run right through our own wee house that we've been living in now for fifteen years—isn't it exciting?

1963

BERTIE   Well, time flew by till December 1963 arrived and by this time the plan was for a multimillion pound six-lane overhead road. We were all agog to hear that they were speeding it up to get it completely finished by 1973. It was to be built on stilts 30 feet above the ground, and it was going to connect the M1, the Sydenham Bypass and the two other motorway approaches to the city. Ach well, Bridget, says I, so long as we have a motorway over our heads and the price of a bottle of tranquillisers, we won't go far wrong. And that was when they called in the English traffic consultants to do a really professional plan. . .

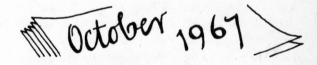

October 1967

BRIDGET   Bertie, there's only half your wages in the pay packet this week.

BERTIE   That's because I stopped off at the City Hall on my way home from work and got you a wee surprise. And there it is.

BRIDGET   Ach, isn't it lovely . . . "Report on the Belfast Urban Motorway, R. Travers Morgan and Partners, Consulting Engineers to the Belfast Corporation and the Ministry of Development: February 1967". You shouldn't have done it, Bertie, really you shouldn't.

BERTIE   Sure it only cost six guineas.

BRIDGET   But February was eight months ago, would it not be out of date by now?

BERTIE   Not at all, the City Council gave approval to the plan only today. It was held up for a while, you see, on account of eighteen councillors having a financial interest in the road plans.

BRIDGET   I suppose the law wouldn't allow them to vote.

BERTIE   That's right, it wouldn't, but the Ministry of

Development waived the law especially for them and the vote was carried by 29 to 11.

BRIDGET 29 to 11? Sure that only adds up to forty altogether. I thought there were sixty councillors.

BERTIE So there is dear, but the other twenty didn't manage to get along to the meeting.

BRIDGET Anyway—the ring road's finally going to be built after all this time.

BERTIE Indeed it is, it'll be started in 1969 and completed in 1976. And guess what—there's to be a big interchange right here in our neighbourhood, wiping out the whole area. Look, do you see that big black circle on the map there?

BRIDGET Isn't that just beautiful?

BERTIE We're right in the middle of that.

BRIDGET Do you think they'll offer us another house?

BERTIE Certainly they will, this isn't just any oul' back street you know. This is Redevelopment Zone 27 scheduled for the major motorway interchange of phases 2 and 3.

BRIDGET Would you credit that? You know, Bertie, we'll look back on today and say—1967—that was the year the traffic engineers put us on the map.

BERTIE And maybe 1973'll be the year they take us off it again!

NARRATOR That ends Phase 1 of Life with the Polarities; however, phase 1 of the urban motorway has not yet started. As to phases 2 and 3, when last heard of they had been postponed indefinitely. Meanwhile, the traffic situation in the centre of Belfast has eased somewhat due to the demolition work carried out by squads of freelance volunteers over the last few years. But how much cash will the motorway cost the taxpayer and ratepayer when it is finally built? The estimate has changed a little over the years.

ANNOUNCER June 1961: The Grade Separated Road system, it was stated today, will cost something of the order of £10 million, exclusive of property acquisition costs. . .

August 1964: The City Surveyor estimated today that the cost of his Urban Motorway Scheme will certainly be in the region of £25 to £30 million. . .

February 1967: The Travers Morgan Report on the Belfast Urban Motorway estimates the cost at £77.4 million, exclusive of legal and engineering fees, supervision and all other professional costs. At an annual increase of only 5 per cent, that would make the cost today, in 1973, over £100 million. But if you add in those legal and engineering fees, supervision, and all other professional costs, as well as the costs of relocating families, businesses and factories, obtaining new jobs for heads of households, possible rent and factory subsidies and unemployment payments . . . not to mention the cost of further delays . . . that would make the total about . . . ah . . . roughly . . . um . . . well, nobody really knows, actually.

NARRATOR It is scarcely possible to place too great an emphasis on the social, physical and visual impact that such a road will make on the city.

BERTIE D'ye know, Bridget, we're very fortunate in this city. You can stand in any part of town you like, look down to the bottom end of the street, and what do you see rising up every time?

BRIDGET The green mountains?

BERTIE Not at all, the ring road, you fathead.

ANNOUNCER The commonly accepted unit of measurement for noise due to moving traffic is decibels of the A scale—dBA—typical noise level at the edge of a motorway being 83 dBA, with peak levels reaching 95 dBA. These levels are above the 65 dBA recommended as a maximum background noise for conversation.

BERTIE There's a soot smudge on your cheek, Bridget.

BRIDGET What did you say?

BERTIE There's a smudge of soot on your cheek.

BRIDGET What's cheap? You want to buy a cheap suit?

BERTIE CHEEK! SOOT ON YOUR CHEEK!

BRIDGET Who has? You have?

BERTIE YOU HAVE!

BRIDGET Oh, I have. That's them big lorries for you.

ANNOUNCER The noise climate due to traffic on an *elevated* motorway, if unimpeded, spreads significantly farther than a similar sound at ground level.

BERTIE You're standing on my sore foot.

BRIDGET Pardon?

BERTIE My foot. You're standing on my foot!

BRIDGET Speak up, I can't hear you.

BERTIE YOU'RE DAMN WELL STANDING ON MY FOOT!

ANNOUNCER   Effects on people: the motorway will have to pass close to a considerable amount of noise-sensitive activity carried out by people. Housing, educational and hospital functions all need a reasonably low background noise climate to be comfortable . . . It has been recorded by the Building Research Station that one of the principal causes of discomfort attributable to noise is overheating and poor ventilation, due to the impracticability of opening windows. The solution in un-airconditioned buildings is to provide double-glazed windows and acoustical baffle ventilators.

BERTIE   Well dear, here it is—our new home—our very own flat in our own barrier-form six-storey linear block running parallel to the motorway.

BRIDGET   Why do they call it a barrier-form block, Bertie?

BERTIE   Because it's designed to act as a barrier to the traffic noise coming from the motorway.

BRIDGET   I'm glad we're just on the second floor, sure I would have got dizzy looking down from six storeys.

BERTIE   There you are, there's your kitchenette.

BRIDGET   Ach, we'll be able to sit here of an evening at our tea, looking through our double-glazed windows at the baffles, or 10-foot high lightweight rigid sound-reducing screens erected along the motorway edge.

BERTIE   It's a wee bit warm with that sun streaming in, I'll adjust the acoustical baffle ventilator.

BRIDGET   There's childer down there clodding stones at one another. I just hope they don't do any damage.

ANNOUNCER   One of the quieter areas in the vicinity of an elevated motorway is underneath it. However, this space is limited in its use by lack of daylight. The residential areas which will remain within the urban motorway should be related to the larger housing areas immediately outside the urban motorway by the provision of *social facilities* beneath it.

BRIDGET   I'm away to visit my sister now, Bertie. Your tea's sitting there on top of the infra-red broiler.

BERTIE   Right you are, love. Will you be back in time to go to the Darby and Joan Club?

BRIDGET   I will indeed. D'ye want to meet me off the bus?

BERTIE   Sure you never know when those buses are going to arrive. Especially now, when there's only the six of them left. No, I'll just see you about half-seven underneath the motorway.

ANNOUNCER   No plant material will survive under the motorway through lack of water and light and probably severe wind conditions, but grass might succeed under some of the intersections if irrigation is provided. Recreational open space under the motorway must therefore be hard surfaced and this limits the type of recreational use acceptable in this location mainly to children's play.

CHILDREN [*singing*]   *Ring a ring a roads*
Thousands of abodes
Beep beep crash crash
All fall down.

[*They all cry.*]

BRIDGET   Did you hear about poor wee Willie Hughes?

BERTIE   No, what happened to him?

BRIDGET   He was playing under the motorway and the wind blew him into the Lagan.

ANNOUNCER   Apart from the large housing areas such as those at Upper Library Street, Cromac, Sandy Row and Donegall Pass, which are within the motorway ring, in nine small areas there are approximately 1,000 to 1,100 houses, the largest single area being less than 300 houses. In these twilight areas "facial cosmetics" of buildings beside the motorway which are left may be necessary so that a good front is presented to the motorway.

BERTIE   Well, Bridget, we finally managed to get our own wee car, even if it is on the never-never.

BRIDGET   At our age, Bertie, it definitely will be never never. But sure you have to have a car these days or starve. Do you think you're going a bit fast, dear?

BERTIE   Not at all, the motorway is specially designed for a 50 mile an hour traffic flow. Ach look, isn't it lovely the way they've camouflaged the back of the slaughterhouse to make it look like a garden centre?

BRIDGET   It's a pity those youngsters have written all over it.

ANNOUNCER   Penetration by the motorway into the city, skirting or cutting through many redevelopment areas, provides unusual opportunities for presenting selected views of the city and surrounding landscape now seldom seen from ground level.

BERTIE   Look Bridget—there's Progressive House.

BRIDGET   So it is dear, that's beautiful.

BERTIE   And there's Chamber of Commerce House.

BRIDGET   Watch that lorry, Bertie.

BERTIE   That's the Europa farther up, do you see it?

BRIDGET   I do indeed, but maybe you should keep your eyes on the road, love.

BERTIE   And miss the unusual opportunities for seeing selected views of the city? Look, that's Fanum House . . . and there's that office block in Shaftesbury Square, Carlton House . . . and that's the City Hospital on our right . . . it's very close, isn't it? . . .

NARRATOR   That ends life with the Polarities. We had planned to conclude by showing them back on a bus again, after private cars have at last been banned from the city—due to the dangerous levels of pollution, the running-out of the world's oil reserves, and the enormous build-up of traffic in the city centre stimulated by the ring road. Instead, for phase 3 of their story, we must follow them into the afterlife.

BERTIE [*echo*]   So I says to Bridget, so long as we've got a halo over our heads and the price of a packet of harp strings, we can't go far wrong. It was a bit of a change from the car, drifting along on this big soft cloud, with a fellow dressed up in a sheet sitting beside us. . .

BRIDGET   Are you rightly, Bertie?

BERTIE   Grand thanks, Bridget. It's very quiet up here, isn't it?

BRIDGET   Aye, and all fluffy and white.

BERTIE   Just like Christmas with the family, eh?

BRIDGET   Who's this other fellow beside us?

GHOST [*sepulchral voice*]   I am the ghost of motorways past.

BERTIE   He says he's the ghost of motorways past.

GHOST   I have a tale to tell of many cities.

BERTIE   Fire away, oul' hand, we're all ears.

GHOST   First, I am forced to speak of Nottingham which abandoned its plans for a ring road system in 1972. These are the words of the city council's Transport Policy.

ANNOUNCER   "No new major motorways shall be constructed nor major improvements to existing highways carried out . . . public transport shall be greatly expanded and improved so as to provide a really attractive alternative to the private motor car."

BRIDGET   Hear, hear!

GHOST   Now I must relate the case of Oxford. These are the words of its Transport Policy.

ANNOUNCER   "Consideration of the problems and the measures possible shows that improvement may be obtained without resorting to large scale road construction . . . the measures which it is proposed should be given immediate priority are intended to reduce the proportion of private car travel to, from and within the city by making specific provision for public transport as the major mode of transport for access to the central area."

BERTIE   He means there'll be a better bus service.

GHOST   Oh, my perturbed spirit!

BRIDGET   Has something disagreed with you?

GHOST   I must turn now to April 1973, the moment of my greatest defeat. For it was then that the newly elected Greater London Council cancelled previous plans to build Ringway One and Ringway Two round the inner city area. How can I forget those stinging words from GLC's new transport consultant?

ANNOUNCER   "We are now in a better position than anyone else to show how to handle the problem of the car in the big city."

BERTIE   Here, we're on the move!

BRIDGET   What's that down below us?

BERTIE   I don't know—it looks like a big long field up in the air.

GHOST   That is the urban motorway in Toronto, abandoned after five miles of it had been built, because of public protest. Alas, it is now grown over with grass.

BRIDGET   Look, there's youngsters playing football on it.

BERTIE   At least it's of some use to somebody.

GHOST   Oh, woe! Even the present Conservative government at Westminster has now set its face against urban motorways.

NARRATOR   Mr Geoffrey Rippon . . . Mr Anthony Barber . . . and ring road proposals have been turned down in Boston . . . San Francisco . . . New York . . . Chicago . . .

BERTIE   He's disappeared.

BRIDGET   I can't say I'm sorry. He wasn't the best of company that fellow.

BERTIE   All the same—if what he says is true, it looks as if motorways have reached the end of the road.

BRIDGET   In that case, we must be in heaven.

(*Safe as Houses* was broadcast on Radio 4 (Northern Ireland) on October 2nd 1973)

Tree
Augustus Young

I am a beech
an elm or an oak.
The sky is beyond reach.
My top branch broke

when a blackbird
threw his voice to the sun
with such ease it was heard
by everyone.

FORTNIGHT 139, DECEMBER 17TH 1976

THE BULL WITH THE HARD HAT

BERNARD MACLAVERTY

It was one of those rare moments when Dick was conscious of driving. He loved the feeling of the car being completely under his control. The road twisted and turned on its way to the top of the mountain. At each bend he moved his weight in the seat as he turned the wheel—"and now Emerson Fittipaldi is a full half minute in front". He crossed the finishing line a minute ahead of the others and pulled in at the lay-by on the mountain top. With the engine switched off, the only sound was the sighing and buffeting of the wind outside the car. He marked up his book. He had done 24 calls that morning. Not bad by anybody's standards—that is if they all worked.

He looked at himself in the driving mirror. He was grey completely—"Emerson Fitt-ee-pal-di, how this man at 45 manages to keep his place in the world championship table . . . nay . . . , not keep his place . . . but LEAD". He reached over the back seat for his lunch. A flask of tea and plastic box of sandwiches. He opened the box—cheese again. Why couldn't Margaret use a bit of imagination about sandwiches. She had work to do—yes—anybody with eight children had their hands full, but it wasn't unreasonable to ask for an occasional change from cheese. The other lads on the job turned up with roast beef and pickle, egg and tomato, and onion, one even boasted of cucumber and cod's roe. But he never got anything except eternal pan bread and processed cheese. Once in a while he would throw these out the window for the birds and

treat himself to a fish supper in one of the small towns he passed through. He rolled down both windows of the car for a bit of air and began to eat.

His call book lay on the seat beside him. He picked it up and began to read as he chewed his way through the plasticy cheese and bread, so dry that it stuck to the roof of his mouth. There were still too many repeats, indicated by a red X. Far too many. He had hit a very bad patch. The voice of the instructor at the Artificial Insemination school came to him. "There are three main reasons for failure. Firstly you may not get to the cow at the right time, secondly the quality of the animal and the sperm used, and lastly the skill of the inseminator himself." Dick counted the number of red Xs he had in his book. They were away above average. Everybody expected to get to the cows at the wrong time now and again. By the time some of these stupid farmers got to the phone and got the cow into the barn the heat was off them. Everybody expected to meet up with heifers who didn't produce results the first time. Dick saw more and more that it was himself to blame. He couldn't figure out what was going wrong. The ultimate insult was when the boss decided you needed to go back to the school for a refresher course. It was a nice way of putting it but it really meant you were no good at your job. It had happened to him twice in 10 years and if his present record continued it would happen him again very soon. He flung the book down on the seat beside him. His tea tasted of flask. On a good day it was said you could see five counties from the mountain top but today it was dull and windy. Some spits of rain began to fall and blow through his open window and he rolled it up. The mist of the coming rain blotted out the far hills at the other side of the valley.

With Carmel it would have been so different. They could have had two nice children and she would be there crisp and clean for him when he came home . . .

He was surprised to see another car pull in to the lay-by. There was a man and a woman in it and immediately they stopped, they started. Their heads seemed to meet and form one. Gradually their car steamed up and when he could see no more he lost interest. It was a bit much at one o'clock in the day. He was bad enough himself but not that bad.

But it wasn't his fault. He had put the thing fairly and squarely to Margaret and she point blank refused to take the Pill or any other precaution. "On your own head be it" was his attitude now . . . and sure enough six months later she was pregnant again. Her answer was always the same— "But it's a sin, it's there in black and white, the Pope says so." If his job was as good as his home record . . . or vice versa everything would be all right, but now more than ever with a ninth child on the way he couldn't afford to lose his job. He settled back in his seat and put his knee up on the steering wheel, eating a chocolate biscuit for dessert. He could dimly see the dark shapes struggling in the other car. Then they stopped. The driver polished a circle for himself in the windscren and they drove off leaving Dick on his own again.

It would serve Margaret right if he did take one of the girls out of the office up here for a lunchtime snack. He had fancied Carmel this long time. She was young and bright, always clean and smelt beautiful. If she wore anything white it was only for the one day, starched, crisp, white. Her tight mini-skirts, tight enough to see the line of her pants, her long graceful legs nearly drove him to distraction. She was good fun too and would allow most of the men occasionally to squeeze her bottom. She would slap their hands away saying, "I'll tell your mammy on you", but she was never seriously angry. Of course Dick knew that it would take more than a squeeze behind the filing cabinets . . . he would have to take her out to dinner some night, somewhere as far away as Fermanagh . . . but even there he knew a lot of people and a lot of people knew him. Carmel, he knew, would cost more than a hot dinner and a few drinks but it would be nice to see how

much. While he had been thinking he found that the chocolate biscuit had melted in his hand. He put the remainder of it into his mouth and licked his fingers. He thought that Carmel liked him more than any of the other men. Any time they happened to be in the office on their own she had told him private things, nice things about herself. Even when the office was full of people he liked to watch her writing and her long yellowy hair trailing the page. She handled the phone beautifully, as well. She would tilt her head quickly so that the hair would fall away from her ear. Her fingers with the long polished nails held it delicately, the other hand jotting quick notes. Best of all was the way she would look at Dick, speaking to the farmers in her best Civil Service voice, and winking and screwing her pretty face into awful shapes. Every time he used the phone in the office he could smell the delicate perfume that she left on the mouthpiece.

He looked at himself in the driving mirror. He thought he was fairly handsome for his age . . . except that he hadn't had time to shave that morning . . . he thought he would be attractive to any young girl. Not a seedy middle-aged man but a lover, like Rossano Brazzi. The bull with the hard hat—that's what he was known as on most of the farms or just simply the bull man. It was stupid and it annoyed him slightly. He had never worn a hard hat in his life, besides it was just a job like any other when you got used to the more disgusting aspects of it. The long rubber glove, the cow's hot insides, the constant prevailing smell of dung, the muck and clabber yards he had to tramp through. It was either that or home, he didn't know which was worse. It was the noise at home that got him more than anything else. Eight children, the eldest 12, the youngest a year, all of whom seemed to fight over the slightest thing. A rag doll, a triangle of cheese, whose turn it was to open the potato crisps, who was to be into the bath first—all could end up in a screaming fight with children rolling about the floor, biting and pulling the hair out of one another. Dick had to scream and yell louder than the rest to get it stopped. It would stop and the only sound was the TV which was always too loud. The children would sit about sullen and whoever Dick had got to with his hand, smacking the first leg he could see, would snuffle quietly in the corner.

"Will somebody turn town that TV."

"It's MY turn."

"NO, it's MY turn. You got turning it off last night."

"Daddy, say it isn't her turn." And it would all start once again.

On the top of the mountain he was surrounded by quiet. The small bleating of sheep carried for miles, the wind moaning past his window. He could build a hut up here and live like a monk. He threw his crusts out the window and screwed the cup back onto the flask.

With Carmel it would have been so different. They could have had two nice children and she would be there crisp and clean for him when he came home, the house immaculate, the toys tidied away. Instead he knew Margaret would be lying on the sofa, her feet up in the air because of her veins—it was like this when he would come home. The floor, from the doorway in, would be covered with treacherous trucks and wheeled things, dolls without limbs, pieces of jigsaws.

"Dick, I'm absolutely done out. Could you get the children their bread and jam . . . and whatever you like yourself. Don't bother about me, I couldn't face food at the minute" and they would all gather round the lino-covered table and he would butter what seemed endless pan loaves of bread, spread with blackcurrant jam. Some of them would always drop their piece, jam side down on the floor, and screech their head off, because they knew it would be a long time before their turn would come again.

"There's a tin of spaghetti there if you would like it," Margaret would shout from the other room, "and while you're there would you heat up the baby's bottle for me." Dick hated spaghetti and the tin had sat in the larder for about three months but Margaret continued to offer it to him every night. Invariably he ended up with a boiled egg and the remains of the children's bread and jam. He hoped that this, their ninth, would be their last. She couldn't go

on producing for ever. She was 43 now . . . and it showed.

He looked at his watch. It was time he was phoning in to the office to get his afternoon calls. There would probably be hundreds . . . enough to sicken him anyway. He knew he could get through them quickly. If there was one thing he *did* know it was his area, every lane, dirt track and byway . . . he was good at getting the order of his calls right so that he never had to cover the same ground twice. Once when he'd been sick for a fortnight, just for something to do, he'd drawn a map of his area, labelling all the roads and farms over an area of some 20 square miles.

The nearest phone was about three miles away. He hoped it would be Carmel who would answer. It might brighten his afternoon a bit. He switched on the engine shattering the silence and edged out onto the main road, looking both ways, then raced through the gears, ". . . and after that prolonged pit-stop Emerson Fittipaldi is a good two minutes behind the leaders. Is it possible that this man can make up the deficit???" He swung the car into a bend and heard the tyres squealing beneath him.

After he left, the lay-by was silent until two hooded crows landed and began to fight over the crusts he had left lying on the gravel.

FORTNIGHT 149, JUNE 10TH 1977

HE IS COMING

JOHN MORROW

JANUARY 1980

He came at the same time every year, halfway between Easter and the Twelfth of July, in the middle of the peerie and hopscotch season. Weeks beforehand his big tent would appear on the waste

ground opposite the park gates on the Ballynafeigh side of the Ormeau Bridge. After school we would cross the bridge and linger with droves of like-minded youngsters, the most daring darting in between the guy ropes to raise

94

the flaps and peep inside the vast canvas dome with its rows of backless benches radiating out from the high lectern.

As an event in those drab between-war days His coming had an interest value equal to Hallowe'en or the last Saturday in August, and I think even Father looked forward to the Big Day—though you'd never have guessed it . . . Looking up from the evening newspaper he would wink at me and say: "I see the Messiah's on his way back from Australia. His feet'll be a bit damp by the time he gets this length."

"May God strike you dead," Mother would say.

"It says here, 'He made such an impact on the aboriginals that they raised idols in his name.' "

"Shut up, you!"

"It's the God's truth: there's a photo here of him helping the Abos to mix the plaster . . ."

On the Big Day the Ormeau Road would be chock-a-block with charabancs and farm carts bearing in the faithful from all arts and parts of the country.

Mother always insisted that we make an early start up the road before the country ones took all the seats. And always, before we had left our own street she and my aunt would be out-distancing Father and me, and by the time we reached the road they would have disappeared into the great throng of people moving towards the bridge. To her credit, Mother never even suggested that we accompany her into the tent—probably fearing an outbreak of political heckling from Father of the sort that had earned him the nickname "Red Ruin". An ex-navyman, he had served in the Home Fleet in that near mutinous period following the Great War when even the chaplains were going a mild pink. The one on his ship had been drummed out of the service for announcing "Land of Hope and Glory" as "our national anthem of the future".

The warm-up sing-song inside had reached a crescendo at His entrance, and now the famous voice began to throb.

The crowd that blocked the bridge and packed the waste ground around the tent was mostly men and boys, their women, like ours, having run on to grab the seats inside: countrymen in bowler hats, hard white collars and brown boots; city men in best double-breasted blues and breadserver's hats; and the majority, like Father, in muffler and duncher, some still wearing the patched remains of the khaki greatcoats they'd worn in Flanders—the unemployed.

The first year I went, Father and I got no further than the centre of the bridge when the word went round that He

was coming. The crowd froze and a narrow lane opened down the roadway. The Great Man came in an open Morris tourer which stopped on the County Antrim side. He then descended and began His now traditional promenade across the bridge. The lane through the crowd was very narrow and Father and I were in the front row, so I had a good view as He passed. Tall and broad-shouldered, He wore a black, three-quarter-length coat, striped trousers and a white bow-tie and winged collar. He was hatless and His long grey hair fell in waves down over His collar, covering His ears (there was a legend that He wore it like this because His ears had been cut off by cannibals in the mission field). He carried a silver-topped stick and His face was the colour of Cousin Billy's when he had the

jaundice, only more evenly spread. But the thing I remember most vividly is the smell that hung in the air in His wake—like Cousin Lily on a Saturday night, on her way to the jig in the Ormeau band hall. I looked up in puzzlement at Father. He grinned down at me, holding his nose between finger and thumb.

We followed in the Great Man's perfumed train and found ourselves a clear spot on the grass near the tent door, where we were joined by a couple of Father's cronies. The warm-up sing-song inside had reached a crescendo at His entrance, and now the famous voice began to throb. I couldn't make out the words, but I remember it as being like the sea, advancing and receding, now soft and soporific, now crashing and thundering—and, like the sea, each wave rising higher, straining for a mark. . .

It seemed to go on for hours. Then I heard Father say to the cronies: "The first one should be out anytime now. . . " And indeed, the very next wave was marked by a piercing shriek from inside the tent. Four St John Ambulance men ran in, nicking fags hurriedly. They emerged holding the four corners of a woman who struggled and screeched, eyes bulging glassily and teeth gnashing as they laid her out on the grass. Of course, everyone crowded round as they do on occasions like this, and most of them seemed to be shouting: "Catch her tongue! . . . Don't let her tongue go!"—in case she swallowed it, I learnt later . . . But they needn't have worried about this first one, who promptly anchored that organ between her foam-flecked teeth and subsided into a coma.

There were others, seven in all, but I didn't witness their ecstatic exits, Father having decided that we should take a walk up the boulevard. When we returned an hour later he surveyed the bodies on the grass and said to a crony: "Not a bad crop."

"Nothin' like 1926," replied the crony sourly: "Fourteen laid out before the second hymn an' one of the ambulance men got his nose broke. 1926 was all their daddies."

The last thing I remember of that year was a little man in brown boots, his bowler hat tipped back, clay pipe fuming, squatting on his heels and holding the purple tongue of his comatose wife. Then Mother and Auntie came out, red-eyed and trembling, clutching sodden handkerchiefs.

In our house that day always ended in a religious argument. I'd lie in bed listening to the barracking voices of Father, Mother and Aunt in the kitchen below. I can't be sure if it was that first year or not, but the parting shot I remember came from Father as Mother and Aunt were on the stairs to bed and he on his way down the hall to bar the door for the night.

"Well, I'll stay an atheist," he said, "if the Odour of Sanctity means smellin' like the backroom in a Bombay kip-house."

"May you drop dead this minnit," screeched Auntie.

FORTNIGHT 149, JUNE 10TH 1977

ROCKY

ROBERT JOHNSTONE

Click click, whirr, buzz buzz, buzz, buzz, buzz.
—Yeah?
—Uh, hullo?
—Nelstein Promotions. Whaddaya want?
—Uh yeah. Hullo Harry. Dis is uh, Bob Johnstone speakin'.
—How ya doin', Bob. Long time.
—Uh yeah. Absolutely. Actually I'm doin' great Harry. I'm uh, keepin' in shape ya know.
—Nice to hear from ya. What can I do for ya?
—Well actually Harry I was uh tinkin' there, uh, that uh maybe I could do sumpin for you Harry.
—Oh yeah?
—Well yeah. Actually, uh, I went to the movies last night Harry.
—Ya don't say. It's great to hear you're keepin' in touch wit what's goin' on.
—Keepin' in touch, absolutely. Listen Harry, I went to the uh Odeon ya know, only they call it the Noo Vic these days, ya know what I mean?
—Yeah yeah, sure, the Noo Vic.
—Yeah, well, listen, I uh, I saw this noo movie called *Rocky*.
—*Rocky*, huh? Ain't that the one wit the three Oscars, one for the best film of '76, an' it's about a down and out boxer called the Italian Stallion an' he gets a shot at the

world title an' the champ's called Apollo Creed an' he acts a bit like Muhammad Ali?
—Uh yeah, that's right. Hey, have you seen it?
—Naw, I just read the papers, Bob.
—Oh yeah. Well listen Harry, this movie's about America being the Land of Opportunity, ya know what I mean? Like, it fits wit bein' the bicentennial year an' like that. See, this no hoper gets a million to one shot to make good.
—Yeah I heard. An' it was in the papers about Sylvester Stallone bein' this unknown who gets a million to one shot at bein' the star an' the writer an' makin' a successful movie an' it comes off with the Oscars. What are ya tryin' to tell me Bob?
—Yeah well actually Harry, I was uh sitting there in the Noo Vic an' watchin' this movie ya know, an' I was thinkin', maybe I could get a chance at makin' a comeback, ya know what I mean? See, I been in trainin' ya know. I got up at six this mornin' an' I fixed myself a five-egg flip an' I started at the old typewriter.
—Ya never did learn to touch type, did ya Bob?
—Yeah well, I been usin' my thumbs for the space bar, an' I got both my index fingers workin' real good—the old one–two, ya know what I mean?
—That last review wit *Network*, that really shook you up. I mean, it was painful to watch, Bob. That heavy stuff is way out of your class. Maybe you should lay off for a

while, give yourself time to recover, ya know what I mean? Like, if you want my advice Bob, all those movies have got you a bit punchy.

—Listen Harry, I really need this chance. I been layin' off the booze, an' I just met this little girl down at the petshop ya know, where I get my turtle food, an' when she takes off her glasses Harry, she's a real knockout. She's given me the confidence to go for the big one.

—How do ya mean, the big one?

—The big one, absolutely. Like, if I could only get the chance to write a review of *Rocky* ya know, goin' the full 750 words, I could really break into the big time . . .

—Listen Bob, frankly, this *Rocky* thing sounds a bit familiar, ya know what I mean? Like, it's all been done before. What about *Somebody Up There Likes Me, The Square Ring, Kid Galahad, The Harder They Fall, Fat City* . . .

—Yeah, yeah sure Harry, but this *Rocky*'s a really good movie. I thought I could, ya know, point out Stallone's humour, an' how he makes the character of Rocky sympathetic. An' another good word I thought of is *authenticity*. See, the movie gives a very *authentic* picture of the poor in Philadelphia. An' I was goin' to say how it's an *ambivalent* view of the *American Dream*, ya know, both *satire* and *sentiment*, like a sort of *hardbitten* version of them old movies. Them are great words Harry. Wit words like that I could make the Tiger look like an amateur. I could beat him at his own game.

—The Tiger?

—Yeah, the Tiger, absolutely. I know I could beat the Tiger Harry, if you give me the chance. The last time I slipped an' knocked myself out on the typewriter. It wasn't my fault I missed the deadline. I been trainin' hard ya know, an' . . .

—Listen Bob, take my advice and forget the whole thing.

—Forget it? But Harry, I mean why?

—Bob, you *are* the Tiger.

—Uh, oh yeah. I forgot about that. Listen Harry, uh, maybe I'll think about it an' give you a call, okay?

—Good thinkin' Bob. Take your time. So long. Click. Burrrrr.

Bob "The Tiger" Johnstone

FORTNIGHT 153, SEPTEMBER 16TH 1977

THE LIFE OF JAMESIE COYLE

MICHAEL FOLEY

These are the opening chapters of a novel by MICHAEL FOLEY that may be described as a burlesque of the Christ story.

CHAPTER ONE

Although a joiner all his life and as such respected for his skill and dependability, Joe Coyle in late middle age, when he might have expected his career to close in comfort and honour, found himself instead going through a sticky patch. This was due to a new breed of workmate, young apprentices of an entirely different generation who had no respect for his craft and dedication or his need to appear well turned out in public. From the moment of his arrival in the morning with his lunch-box and neatly folded raincoat Joe was the object of constant abuse. Even when they were not attacking him personally, the coarseness of their behaviour was an insult to him. Once, on entering a half-finished house, he had come upon a group of them gathered round a girlie magazine open at the centre pages. One of them was hunched over it, violently abusing himself, and the rest were shouting encouragement.

"Go on ahead, John."

"Give it tay her, John."

On another occasion they had removed a brick from a wall in order to spy on a woman undressing in a nearby house, though their boisterous jostling for position made this almost impossible.

"Give us room or Ah'll bate the head off ye."

"Ye couldn't bate snow off a rope."

"Look at her prancin' around," the eventual victor cried, "it's bitin' the leg off her."

Scenes like this could occur at any time during the day—but the lunch break was always an ordeal. This was due to the excellence of Joe's lunches for, although a bachelor of long standing, he was not short of female help, living as he did with his sister and two aunts. Thus the sandwiches, which contained tasty fillings like salmon or roast beef, were always neatly decrusted and quartered and there would be several dessert items such as apple or rhubarb tart, peach flan or chocolate cake.

The apprentices did their best to put him off, displaying their own crude productions, coarse chunks of bread with cheap sticky fillings.

"What do ye think that is, Joe? Have a guess. What does it look like? It's the squeezing of a jam-rag, Joe."

Then there was the after-lunch problem. As always on building sites the arrangements were crude and hazardous, a focal point for practical jokes. On the site at this time there was only one bucket served by a plank with a circular hole. On one occasion the apprentices sawed through the plank so that it would not bear a man's weight and although Joe was not the victim the horror of it shook him to the core. He began to sneak away after lunch and make use of an unfinished house at the end of the site. This continued for several weeks until one night the peace of the Coyle's house was destroyed by a terrible shriek from the kitchen. Joe rushed into the room to find his Aunt Minnie in hysterics before his lunch-box which contained the large stool he had deposited in the empty house that afternoon.

Yet in spite of the provocation Joe himself maintained an amazing, almost superhuman, calm. It seemed nothing could affect him and this exasperated the apprentices further. On the day after the lunch-box incident Joe encountered a hostile silence instead of the usual banter at lunch. It seemed that some outright confrontation was bound to occur. Towards the end of the meal there was a

sighting from the loose brick but, instead of rushing off themselves in the usual way, the apprentices suddenly laid hold of Joe.

"You're gonnay see somethin' now, Joe." And they carried him, struggling, towards the vantage point. "Ye ought tay see this, Joe—a big mush the size of yer han'."

Joe protested with increasing vehemence. "No. No. No . . . No!"

"Why not, Joe?" His tormentors had brought his face almost to the aperture and in desperation he revealed the bizarre truth.

"Because . . . because . . . because *I'm engaged.*"

At once his captors let go in sheer amazement. "Engaged?"

"Engaged," Joe repeated, smoothing down his hair and adjusting his clothes.

"At your age, Joe?"

"Who's the lucky girl, Joe?"

"I'm engaged to marry Mary O'Doherty of Doughal." Somebody from the country . . . a *munchie.*"

"Mary is no munchie."

"And what age is she?"

"She'll be twenty next September."

Now their amazement was complete.

"Ye mean she's still in her teens. Talk about baby snatchin'."

The information took some digesting and they were distracted for quite a while. It was good in another way for Joe no longer had to keep the liaison secret and could now bring Mary to town rather than pursuing his courtship in Doughal. To everyone's amazement the engagement appeared to be a happy one and the couple were often seen together, usually on the way from Coyle's to the Doughal bus, less often enjoying a quiet meal in the San Remo Fish Restaurant and, very occasionally, emerging from a famous musical in the City Picture House.

But of course, once assimilated, the idea provided a rich new field for the apprentices.

"Did you get any last night, Joe?"

"Were ye droppin' the han' in the City, Joe? Ah hear they had tay flash the torch on ye."

As always Joe refused to be drawn and the relationship was eventually accepted. It was then that the first whisper was heard. It began in Cannibal Island, as the council estate where the Coyles lived was known, and from here it

spread rapidly into the town and through the building sites. At first no one believed such a story for although the Coyles lived in Cannibal Island the family had a longstanding reputation for decency and were often cited as an example of what could be achieved, even in such surroundings, by industry and thrift. Then there was Joe Coyle's personal honour, which he had often gone to ridiculous lengths to preserve. Was he not, even yet, paying back a debt incurred by signing an order for a disreputable builder who had instantly gone bankrupt?

Yet the rumour persisted and grew and was in time confirmed by physical evidence. In an odd way the apprentices were more outraged by this than by Joe's conservatism. One morning he found them waiting for him in a body.

Again Joe remained remarkably calm. "Mary is indeed expecting a child but I know for a fact that she has never been with a man."

"We know ye now, Joe."

"We know what kind of a boy you are."

"What do you mean?"

"What do you mean, he says. Ye'd think butter wouldn't melt in his mouth. We mean what d'ye think ye're doin', gettin' some wee country girl up the skite?"

Again Joe remained remarkably calm. "Mary is indeed expecting a child but I know for a fact that she has never been with a man."

The audacity of this ploy deprived them of speech. They had known Joe as an earnest man, not given to flippancy.

"Are ye kiddin', Joe?"

"I am not. Several months ago Mary received a visitation from an angel. He appeared to her and told her to rejoice for in nine months' time she would give birth to a boy, the redeemer of his people."

"An *angel*, Joe?"

"An angel."

There was a long pause.

"And tell us this—is the angel in England now? Did the angel get the Liverpool boat by any chance?"

"The angel went back above in the usual way."

The apprentices looked at each other in wonder.

"God," said one at last, "maybe that wee girl wasn't so soft after all." They looked at Joe again. "Where do you fit in, Joe?"

Joe drew himself up to his full height and as he played his trump his voice lost the calm his secret knowledge had helped him preserve all these months.

"I didn't tell you all the angel said. He said she was

going to have a boy but he also said go and seek out Joe Coyle who shall act as the father of the child. Yese may laugh at wee Joe Coyle but the name still stands for decency in this town. It was Joe Coyle that was picked to be the father and not one of your sort . . . *ye pack of ignorant blaggards.*"

Chapter Two

After a few months Joe and Mary were married in the quiet country church at Doughal and a week later a boy was born and christened Jamesie Coyle. There was the usual malicious whispering and the story of the angel was passed around with a great deal of derisory laughter. Joe avoided some of the talk by moving out of Cannibal Island and acquiring a tiny terraced house in one of the little streets near the town centre. And by and by the talk turned to other subjects, for the Coyles were a quiet family and provided no further basis for gossip.

Jamesie grew up and prospered in an atmosphere of decency and love and there were no unusual occurrences until he was three years old. At this time he was attending a nursery school known as "the wee nuns" and one afternoon, due to a most untypical mix-up, neither of the parents came to collect him. Since the Coyles were normally so reliable no one thought to check on the child and he was left on his own in the empty school. After wandering round there for some time Jamesie became bored and crossed the street to the big school, a place of great fascination to the children.

The big school was also empty but, as luck would have it, Father Patten the parish priest was on his way to visit the head and came upon Jamesie standing in the main hall.

"Well well well," he cried out jovially, "are ye thinking of taking up night classes, ah?"

"No Father," the child replied, shy in such awesome company.

"Ye wouldn't be lost by any chance?"

"Yes, Father."

"Well come on with me." And together they made their way upstairs towards the headmaster's office. "Did ye get any slaps today?"

"No, Father—but Sister Annunciata hit me across the knuckles with a ruler."

"Talking in class," cried the priest with a triumphant smile.

"No, Father—she said she was tired of me daydreaming."

"Oh." He seemed slightly surprised. "Well I hope ye took your oil like a good soldier. We all have to be good soldiers, don't we?" He ushered the child into the office and exchanged cordial greetings with the head. "A stray sheep, John."

"Ah-ha," John Deeny replied, coming from behind his desk to inspect the child, "do ye know your name?"

"Jamesie Coyle, sir."

"Ah suppose you're at the junior school."

"Yes, sir."

"Do they teach you anything there at all?" He exchanged a humorous glance with Father Patten. "Do they teach ye anything at all or is it all playin' around with sand and plasticine? Ah? Do they teach ye your catechism?"

"Yes, sir."

"Alright then. Who is God?"

"God is the creator of heaven and earth and of all things." There was a satisfying rapidity about this reply.

"Good man. Good man. How many persons are in God?"

"There are three—God the Father, God the Son and God the Holy Ghost." Again the answer came pat—but in a sense these apparently innocent questions had been building towards an attack in the manner of a clever opening in chess. Having set the trap John Deeny fell back and allowed the priest to spring it.

"How many Gods are there?" Father Patten posed the question casually, as though it were superfluous—but there was a look of cunning in his half-closed eyes and his head was bent forward to catch the reply. The child curled his lip as though in contempt for such an obvious ploy.

"There is but one God." The two men looked at each other. The boy was no more than three and yet it was a contest. Father Patten dropped his humorous pose.

"Right," he said firmly, plunging straight into the abstruse depths, "are we obliged to keep the commandments of the church?"

"Yes we are. He that will not hear the church (says Christ) let him be to thee as a heathen and a publican."

"Say the commandments of the church."

"One: Sundays and holy days Mass thou shalt hear.
Two: And holy days sanctify through all the year.
Three: Lent, ember days and vigils thou shalt fast.
Four: And on Fridays flesh thou shalt not taste.
Five: In Lent and Advent nuptial feasts forbear.
Six: Confess your sins at least once every year.''

"Stop. Stop." Father Patten could take no more, waving the child to a halt, his face screwed up in agony at the speed and sureness of it. John Deeny tried to come in, failed, cleared his throat, tried again, his voice a mere whisper.

"What persons are exempt from fast days?"

"Heavy manual labourers, nurses, the elderly, those of languishing constitution."

They were beaten and they knew it. The child knew it. There was silence. The parish priest paced the room and as he passed John Deeny spoke out of the corner of his mouth.

"Who's the father, John?"

"I don't think you'll believe this—but it's wee Joe Coyle." They stared in amazement at Joe's unlikely progeny—who was the first to speak.

"Can I ask a question?" Taking their silence as acquiescence he carried on. "A baby is dying—an unbaptised baby. There is no water. There is a deep well—but the well has no bucket. What should one do? If one dropped the baby into the well while pronouncing the words of the sacrament would this constitute a valid baptism? Or would the baby's soul go to Limbo?"

There was a long, profound and deeply troubled silence.

Then the mother burst upon them, distraught and violent.

> ". . . How dare you speak back to your mother." Nothing could justify disobedience before two such important men.
> "I have things to do," the child answered sullenly.

"Thanks be to God," she cried. "I've been searchin' high and low." She dashed across the room towards the child and drawing a handkerchief from her bag licked it and began to wash his face with extreme vehemence. He pulled away, partly in annoyance at the interruption, partly in alarm at her violence—but she seized him even more tightly, running her fingers through his hair and explaining in great disgust to the two men, "I wanted them to leave a bit for combing at the front—but they chopped it all off. I sent him with Joe, ye see, and Joe's that bird-mouthed he wouldn't say anything. He just sat there like a clift and let them cut it all off." Although her husband was to blame she shook the boy by the shoulders.

"Leave go." He pulled away completely this time.

"What? . . . What? . . . How dare you speak back to your mother.'' Nothing could justify disobedience before two such important men.

"I have things to do," the child answered sullenly.

"I don't care what you have to do. As long as you live, look see, never do anything like that again. *Never*.''

And with many snorts of displeasure at him and strained laughs of apology at the men the child was furiously bundled out of the building.

ARMISTICE DAY 1938
Roy McFadden

Every year in the Assembly Hall
We would exhume the dead
Protagonists of the Great War.
With marbled eyes McKelvey prayed
For unknown uncles killed at Passchendaele.

The blood-roll of the drums, the bugle's cry,
The curt succeeding hush
For masochistic memory,
Insinuated a death-wish;
And history sugared to mythology.

In my last year, the radio relayed
A nation's fading grief
Live from the London Cenotaph;
But my suspended disbelief
Was shattered with the silence when a loud

Dissident voice charged puppet-masters with
Rigging another war.
McKelvey broke ranks also, and
Came out against more murder for
Conflicting emblems cut from the same cloth.

FORTNIGHT 170, DECEMBER 1980–JANUARY 1981

HOME GROUND
Michael Longley

I

for S.H.

This was your home ground, comings and goings
When the sand martins collected in flight
Feathers and straw for untidy chambers
Or swooped up to kiss each tiny darkness,
Five white eggs changing to five white chins:

Childhood, and your townland poor enough
For gentians, fairy flax, wild strawberries
And the anxious lapwing that settled there,
Its vocal chords a grass blade stretched
Between your thumbs and blown to tatters.

II

for P.M.

When they landed the first man on the moon
You were picking strawberries in a field,
Straggly fuses, lamps that stained the ground
And lips and fingers with reflected light,
For you were living then from hand to mouth.

Re-entering that atmosphere, you take
The dangerous bend outside the graveyard
Where your mother falls like a meteor
From clouds of may and damson blossom:
There the moon-rocks ripen in your hand.

THE TRUTH
Douglas Dunn

I

I always knew where truth lived.
It was in the empty pockets
Of weary men coming home from work
To their poor houses by the railway bridge.
It lived in the clean slums in their pockets.
Truth is small change, the suspicion
Of a few coppers short, pennies, *sous*,
When you turn them over in your hand.
It was in the eyes of my mother
Who walks in everyone's multitude
With her string-bag, her cabbages,
Her flowers in a wet dusk growing cold.
It was in nothing else I could see.
I did not have it, ever. I knew it,
Lived it; it walked away from me.
I know now where it lives.
In my wallet, on the back of a bill,
I have written down its address.
So many little things soothe me.
Events of such paltry gladdening
Postpone my inevitable visit.

II

It matters less now that I understand
The *who*, the *where*, the place I came here from.
I have a key that unlocks dreams and land
So I can see more clearly where I am
Whatever this town is or where it is
Where milk-floats whisper to the leafy street,
Mist fades above the trees with promises
Of place and clarity where all things meet
In an ungrudging handshake far away
Above, beneath, north, south, or in the head.
At school, a teacher said, 'Speak *properly*!'
Words sounded best on paper when I read,
Though when I read aloud it made him grin.
My mouth was lies to him. My place was lies.
I pleased one with my disinfected Latin,
A tongue not dead but dumb as a surmise
Of mute walked-over helpless countryside.
The shapes of space, informing on my tongue
That had not spoken, therefore had not lied.
It was the truth that teacher thought was wrong.

PLACE
Patrick Williams

Because it teaches us to die
We love and hate where we were born.
Death is when we bow to it.
More and more we feel the pull,
In the end we need that ground.

Many leave when they are young,
Coming home still young and strong.
Restlessly they settle in,
An inflection, turn of phrase
To remind you they were gone.

Some leave later in a fright,
Praying for rejuvenation—
Born again! That clean break.
Mostly though it doesn't take.
The soul rejects? They come home, shamed.

Of the few who leave for good
Nearly all get back to die,
Just as others take a 'plane
For a first or last look,
A little trip to—Paris? Rome?

However wonderful the place
They've no illusions then of staying.
Soon forgetting all the leaving
And returning, seldom knowing
Who it was they travelled in.

THE BOUNDARY COMMISSION
Paul Muldoon

You remember that village where the border ran
Down the middle of the street,
With the butcher and baker in different states?
Well, today I remarked how a shower of rain

Had stopped so cleanly across Golightly's lane
It might have been a pane of glass
That had toppled over. I stood there for ages,
Wondering which side, if any, I should be on.

HONEYMOON ON A MOTORBIKE
Kerry Campbell

Riding down—
Sweeping and bouncing down
The flung back bolt of road,
Rolled over round green hills.
The sky plain blue—
The road baked black.
Low in the dips clear oily air
Slurs liquid on the tar.

I am married!
Plunging forward into shouting
Sun-gulped air.
At each hill crest
My head flies off.

FORTNIGHT 178, OCTOBER–NOVEMBER 1980

GENTIANS
Medbh McGuckian

In my alpine house, the slavery I pay
My wilful gentians! exploring all their pleats
And tucks as though they had something precious
Deep inside, that beard of camel-hair
In the throat. I watch them
Ease their heads so slowly
Through their thumbhole necklines till they sit
Like tailors in their earth shoes,
Their watery husbands' knots—no insects
Visit them, nor do their ovaries swell,
Yet every night in Tibet their seeds
Are membraned by the snow, their roots
Are bathed by the passage of melt-water,
They tease like sullen spinsters
The dewfall of summer limes.

BEAUTIFUL LOFTY THINGS
Michael Foley

The celebration drink for
Una, Eileen, May and Joan
down to their target weights
after weeks of Unislim.

From her bathing suit's
tight gusset-edge
individual, irrepressible
springy hairs.

Returning from seeing
the babysitter home
the old street transmuted
important and rare.

Talk waning, the shy wife
bearing it in—warm, golden,
highpiled, moist—a loaded plate
of freshly toasted sliced pan.

THE FLOWER CLOCK
Medbh McGuckian

I am one room deep with the juice
Of some man resetting like an April day
My body winterised by the valleys
And hills of sleep: I sit to have it
Full of shadows, dreaming of the falling-down
Of houses, though I know that gold
Awakes in nature promptly as a robin,
Paying itself out to her so accurately,
She might buy it back. I would prefer
To be able to run with the leaves loose
Within me so that time would pass

Again; but when those hands merge
At midnight, shortening my days, and
Lengthening my life, I just bump into them.
In no month of no year, a windowless shed
In time with itself keeps trace of the moon's
Foxing, the anatomy of lightning. On a
Flower clock, where each bed is an hour,
The childing pink, the evening primrose,
Chime religiously, yet princess discontent
Claps for the chivalry of leap year,
Or the bashful age of consent.

FORTNIGHT 190, JANUARY 1983

SIGNING THE TREATY
Tom Paulin

A haircrack in bone china
or an eider duck's olive egg
clecking in the squeezed light:
there's a wet mildness now
like that turned earth
or the juices between your legs.

SUICIDE IN FRIDGE BID FAILS
James Simmons

A man was rescued yesterday
twenty-nine hours after
wedging himself into a fridge
in a suicide bid.

Randy Scott (21) was saved
after a maid heard noises
coming from the fridge in his
motel room at Ogden, Utah.

Scott, a US marine,
told police he was absent
without leave and had not
eaten for four days.

A police spokesman said:
He has sore knees and can't walk
well, but he's come away from this
with a new outlook on life.

THE FROG
Paul Muldoon

Comes to mind as another small upheaval
amongst the rubble.
His eye matches exactly the bubble
in my spirit-level.
I set aside hammer and chisel
and take him on the trowel.

The entire population of Ireland
springs from a pair left to stand
overnight in a pond
in the gardens of Trinity College,
two bottles of wine left there to chill
after the Act of Union.

There is, surely, in this story
a moral. A moral for our times.
What if I put him to my head
and squeezed it out of him,
like the juice of freshly squeezed limes,
or a lemon sorbet?

THIN ORANGE LINE

SIOBHÁN KILFEATHER

ROY BRADFORD, *The Last Ditch*
(Blackstaff Press, £3.95)

"Despite his provincial background, he had always regarded himself as something of an intellectual." *The Last Ditch* is a treasure trove of clichés and non sequiturs, mainly running through the mind of its hero, Desmond Carson. While he is congratulating himself on his intellectual *savoir-faire* he is reflecting "with enormous pleasure" on his intimacy with Frank Kitson who, as an English army officer, is presumably "the real thing".

> ... there is a revelation—not altogether intentional, I imagine— of the paranoia and sense of inferiority of the unionist population.

This would be a very bad book were it not for the illumination it sheds on the way that dishonest politicians cannot so much as offer a cup of tea without obfuscating their meaning to themselves and everyone else. Beyond the politicians who once ran this country there is a revelation—not altogether intentional, I imagine—of the paranoia and sense of inferiority of the unionist population. Luxurious interiors are dwelt on lovingly, in marked contrast to the streets of Belfast, which never materialise in any vivid pictures. A knowledge of fine arts and fine wine is affected by the hero, despite his provincial background. There is a hilarious association of sex with food:

> The cotton shirt came down to just above the incipient horizontal crease in her bare buttocks. She replaced the spoon on the bench and smacked her lips. "Hmm . . . I really am a good cook! . . . Oh! what are you *doing*?"

Later on Josephine confesses: "I love you. Come on. Food."
Although the food metaphor may be obvious, it is a salvation in the love scenes, allowing one to retain a slender hope that Desmond Carson will ruin his political career by eating a Catholic.

On the whole Catholics do not feature largely in the novel, for which their politicians are probably on their knees offering thanks at the moment. Not that unionist politicians are exposed as being corrupt—in that respect the novel rather fails as a *roman-à-clef*—but they are shown to be even more stupid than the put-upon Gerry Hacker, and some of them are almost as engaging. The most interesting scenes are those of the cabinet in discussion, portraying men speaking as they imagine (without much imagination) that their roles dictate. Here one witnesses the effects of a total misuse of language. In the second chapter, at the first of these meetings, not a single sentence of either narration or dialogue is in clear, untroubled, saying-what-it-means English—which is alright. The ministers play their games in the spirit and language of the Ewing boardroom in *Dallas*, just as the UDF charge around town murdering people in the way that teenagers kick in a phone box. This is how things happen.

Whether the particular thinly disguised portraits that we all know from the news actually behaved in this way as ministers we do not know, and I would be wary of accepting Bradford's descriptions, even had he the ability to describe. If he is not a charlatan, then where is he in the book? There is an ugly, vicious, sensational description of a kneecapping in chapter one—I did not feel that he was there. Perhaps at one point, when Carson is speaking to the Prime Minister, and for once something is said:

> It was a good question, and the rhetoric of the Cabinet room would provide no hiding place. "Frankly, at this moment, no. I've thought about it. If we defy them, there's only one way we could survive . . . and that's a deal with the South." It was a foolish thing to have said, and the incredulity that registered in Packham's face made Carson swiftly add, smiling to underline the point . . . " That's the kind of lunatic logic we'd end up with."
>
> The Prime Minister's face relaxed. That kind of talk, even in jest, shared the nature of obscenity.
>
> Carson pressed on, at a loss to understand why the idea had occurred to him, out of the blue, intuitively, as a realistic option. It was so alien to his normal thinking.

Some hints for DEFIANT UNIONIST LEADERS who wish to regain the confidence of the electorate through acts of GLORIOUS MARTYRDOM

① SIT UP ALL NIGHT WATCHING T.V. AFTER STATIONS HAVE CLOSED DOWN

② REFUSE TO LET COUNCIL WORKMEN EMPTY YOUR BIN FOR ONE MONTH

③ AFTER A WEEK'S VOLUNTARY EXILE IN PORTRUSH ARRANGE TO BE WELCOMED BY CHEERING CROWDS AT GLENGALL ST. BUS STATION & CARRIED SHOULDER HIGH ALONG SANDY ROW.

④ IF THESE STUNTS DON'T WORK, HANG YOURSELF FROM A NON-ENGINEER CERTIFIED ORANGE ARCH.

Blotski

DOG COLLARS

IN A BELFAST SLUM IN THE SHADOWS OF THE GANTRIES SITS THE **TABERNACLE** OF THE **MASSACRED MASONIC MARTYRS**

NEARBYE IS THE HEADQUARTERS OF A HERETICAL JESUITICAL CONSPIRACY, THE **CHAPEL OF OUR LADY OF THE IMMACULATE CONTRACEPTION**

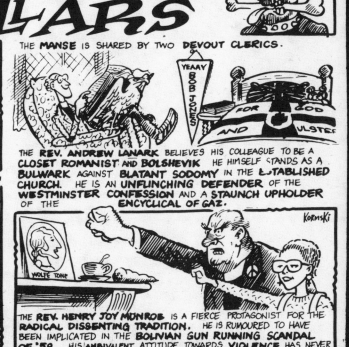

THE **MANSE** IS SHARED BY TWO **DEVOUT CLERICS**.

THE **REV. ANDREW LANARK** BELIEVES HIS COLLEAGUE TO BE A **CLOSET ROMANIST** AND **BOLSHEVIK** HE HIMSELF STANDS AS A **BULWARK** AGAINST BLATANT **SODOMY** IN THE ESTABLISHED CHURCH. HE IS AN **UNFLINCHING DEFENDER** OF THE **WESTMINSTER CONFESSION** AND A **STAUNCH UPHOLDER** OF THE **ENCYCLICAL OF GAZ.**

Kormski

THE **REV. HENRY JOY MUNROE** IS A FIERCE PROTAGONIST FOR THE **RADICAL DISSENTING TRADITION.** HE IS RUMOURED TO HAVE BEEN IMPLICATED IN THE **BOLIVIAN GUN RUNNING SCANDAL OF '58.** HIS AMBIVALENT ATTITUDE TOWARDS **VIOLENCE** HAS NEVER AFFECTED HIS **IMPLACABLE VEGETARIANISM.** HIS UNBEARABLE TOLERATION FOR ALL FORMS OF **BIGOTRY** IS RELIEVED BY HIS LONG HELD CONVICTION THAT HIS COLLEAGUE SHOULD BE **TAKEN AWAY AND SHOT.** HIS ATTITUDES ARE SHARED BY HIS 24 YEAR OLD FRIEND, **MS BRID O'CHOLMONDELY**, A YOUTH LIASON OFFICER FOR **GHETTO MEDIA WORKSHOPS.**

APRIL 1974

FORTNIGHT 191, FEBRUARY 1983

LETTER TO THE EDITOR

Sir,
I wonder what it is
that qualifies something
for the pages you head New Poems.
James Simmons' work on a man
who tried to freeze himself to
death reads just like the news
stories I write every day
except that usually
I don't split sentences up so much.
Try my new work
called SDLP to fight
all 17 seats
Ulster's Social Democratic and
Labour Party decided
yesterday to fight all 17
Northern Ireland seats in the
next general election.
There are several more
stanzas I wrote it yesterday
for this morning's *Guardian*.
It's all right as it goes but
I wouldn't call it poetry as
I'm not
that pretentious.
          Yours, etc.,

                    Bob Rodwell
              63 Sandown Road
                   Belfast 5

Hard nights: van Morrison's first band

JIM CUSACK tells the story of the Monarchs, Van Morrison's first band, who played in Belfast, Scotland and Germany in the early 1960s before breaking up in the face of promoters' and producers' indifference to their rhythm and blues style.

The Monarchs were hot in Heidelberg. All the way from Belfast, from local dance halls, clubs and Orange halls to the Odeon Keller, full of black GIs and fast German girls, strong beer, pot and purple hearts. Ray Charles was their inspiration.

Van Morrison's father was mad keen on black music . . .

The band was Billy McAllen from Knockbreda on lead guitar; Wesley Black from Bloomfield on piano; Geordie Jones, also from Bloomfield on bass; Harry Megahey from Cregagh Road on baritone sax; Van Morrison from Bloomfield on tenor sax; Larry McQueen from Glasgow on drums; and his friend George Hetherington from Glasgow on vocals. They had one mohair band suit apiece, pointed Italian shoes and Rab Maguire's bee-bop or Tony Curtis hairstyles. They went there in a Morris J2 van.

From playing three or four nights a week in Northern Ireland the Monarchs had to turn it up to 9pm to 3am performances with 10-minute breaks on the hour each night, matinees from 4pm to 6pm on Saturdays and Sundays and then from 8pm to 3am after matinees.

They went down a storm for the month-long residency in the Odeon, despite the strain. They were on 70 or 80 quid a week plus digs. They played so long and so hard that they could almost turn their minds off and let the instruments play themselves. It became that automatic.

Before Germany they had toured Scotland and the north of England and they had signed to the Ruby Ward Agency in London. She handled some of the more popular "temperance" and skiffle bands around then, and this rhythm and blues outfit was a departure for her.

The idea, as Harry Megahey remembers it, was that they should play the residency in the Odeon Keller, get their act fully together and then come back to bigger and better things in London. It didn't happen that way.

STRAIN TELLS

After the Odeon Keller, there came another month in the Odeon in Hamburg. Apparently Ruby thought they had done so well in their first month that they might make a name and some money in Hamburg. But the strain began to tell.

After Hamburg there was another residency at the Storyville Club in Frankfurt, in the British-occupied sector. The scene, without the hip Americans, was less attractive, and the band began to come apart at the seams. The drummer went wild and pulled out a wire flex and a whole load of plaster down on top of him on stage one night. The strong beer and ferocious hours led to arguments and depression. George Hetherington and his friend Larry left. The others sent to Belfast for two of their former friends, Roy Kane, who played drums, and Oliver Trimble, who used to run the King Oliver Showband.

They held together for a while and even cut a single on which Geordie Jones led on vocals. It is remembered as an embarrassing effort, although the musicians surpassed themselves with some good backing lines. The "A" side had a song called "Singy Baby" and there was another repetitive song, "Boo Sue, Hully Gully", on the flip. It was aimed at the German teenage market and apparently did quite well. The band, however, received only a single £60 recording fee.

After that there was little hope left in Germany and they headed home. They managed to get some low-key dates in London, and Harry got a job as a mechanic with the Rootes group and a flat in Shepherd's Bush. Harry, Van and some of the others stayed around for a while. Parents sent over some money, but Ruby Ward had lost interest in the band when George Hetherington left. He was regarded as a great white hope of the R & B scene in Britain and the band was to have been a sort of vehicle for his talents.

R & B ORIGINS

The Monarchs had originally come together in 1961 in Belfast from various showbands and small R & B groups.

The British music scene was then dominated by squeaky-clean pop and ballad singers. Elvis had come on the national scene, but his early hard R & B material had been reduced to a mixture of sugar and water to meet tastes that record companies regarded as suitable for teenage consumers. Petula Clarke, Shirley Bassey (a less sleazy version in those days) and the Temperance Seven were in the British charts.

The dark and dangerous rhythms of black Americans were kept well in the background. R & B was possibly at its high point at the time and the US music market was at last beginning to recognise the popularity of black singers. Ray Charles had recorded "What'd I Say" in 1959 and a year before that Chuck Berry had done "Johnny B. Goode".

In Northern Ireland only a very limited number of people had by that time been exposed to the soul rays of black R & B, blues and jazz. Van Morrison's father, George, was mad keen on black music and the boy had been exposed to these musical influences from a very young age. There was almost no modern music on what there was of television and only those with the right connections and the cleanest image made it onto radio.

... at Orange halls ... contracts occasionally bore the legend: "It must be understood that all members of the band are Protestant."

Morrison had shown an early aptitude for playing musical instruments and by the time he was 15 or so he was a good saxophone player. He played with Harry Megahey at some gigs in The Hut, which was a hall at the bottom of Templemore Avenue. Harry had his own band, the Harry Mac Showband, and had picked up his basic musicianship with the Ormeau Military Band.

ORANGE HALLS

The Monarchs were formed, somehow or other, and built up a reputation playing around Belfast and anywhere else where they could get the £30 or £40 fee for a night's work. They played at Carrickfergus town hall, and at the Calypso in Lurgan, which was then regarded as having absolutely the last word in decor. They had to behave themselves at Catholic parochial halls and at Orange halls where contracts occasionally bore the legend: "It must be understood that all members of the band are Protestant." At Thompson's Restaurant in Arthur Street, however, they had a more hip Belfast following and the Ray Charles/ R & B influence came over in a bigger way there.

The big dates in those days were almost still the pre-serve of the big pop/country showbands. Bands like the Royals could earn a couple of hundred pounds a night. The predominance was still the "Irish Pop" sound, and it was a bit unnatural to the R & B enthusiasts in the Monarchs. Morrison and Megahey idolised Ray Charles, John Lee Hooker, Muddy Waters and Miles Davis.

Early in 1963 the Monarchs had, however, developed a steady following and were joined by Hetherington and his friend from Glasgow. Hetherington was already something of a name and was a friend of Alex Harvey and Lord Sutch. His contacts in Scotland helped to get a few dates there and they toured the R & B club circuit, at one stage backing the now-forgotten Don Charles, who had some chart success with his songs "Walk With Me My Angel" and "Windy Mountain".

The skiffle/ballad period of the pop charts was now giving way to the even sweeter nonsense of Cliff Richard and Frank Ifield. The Beatles would soon be capturing the hearts of those from five years up with the refrain, "She loves you, yeah, yeah, yeah. She loves you, yeah, yeah."

However, the Monarchs were still promising material in any agent's eyes, even if a couple of its members did have this aversion towards that heavy-duty black American material. They moved down to the north of England and from there they were picked up by Ruby Ward and packed off to the Odeon Keller.

ONE-WEEK PEAK

Harry Megahey, who is now a heating products manufacturer in Ballinamore, Co Leitrim, remembers that the band actually peaked after about one week in the Odeon Keller. He says: "The arrangement with Ruby was that we would go to Germany for one month and prepare ourselves for recording in London. But, owing to the fact that they were such a tremendous success every night Ruby decided that she would keep them there while they were making money. It ended up as three months. Working those long hours was bad enough, but the band peaked off after one week.

"You could play without thinking you were playing the notes. It was nearly all modern jazz and R & B. Things deteriorated over the second and third months—drinking, long hours, women, the wrong food—we never had a decent cup of tea."

He remembers that Stu Sutcliffe, who with his girlfriend devised The Beatles' image, died because of such conditions in Germany. The Monarchs wore themselves into the ground before packed audiences in the Odeon each night. Their beat was fast enough for the imported black Americans, but too fast for the British pop industry, which was then enraptured with its sweet boy idols. When they returned to London and received no support, the end was in sight.

Harry got work in London and later joined the Royal

Safari Showband in Manchester, where he met and married Briege Sweeney. They later returned to Belfast and then moved to Leitrim, where Harry set up in business.

Billy McAllen and Geordie Jones continued playing music in Belfast and Geordie more recently had a successful career with Clubsound and then as a solo performer.

George Hetherington and Larry McQueen returned to Glasgow and had little further contact with the other band members.

Wesley Black was shot dead on February 28th 1975, as he was walking along Belfast's West Circular Road by a republican gunman who had earlier attempted to assassinate another man in a nearby house. It is believed the gunman thought that Wesley could have identified him, and killed him because of this.

Van Morrison, who had only been 15 years old when he joined the band, relentlessly pursued his musical ambitions and, despite nearly a decade of problems with the music business, eventually emerged as one of the world's great contemporary white singers.

FORTNIGHT 192, MARCH 1983

SOUTHERN COMFORT

PATRICK GALVIN

Doctor—you may not believe this—but I woke up this morning and discovered that I was no longer a man. I'm a woman now—and I'm pregnant.

It suits you.

But I don't want to be a woman. And I sure as hell don't relish the idea of being pregnant.

Have you tried falling down the stairs?

I beg your pardon?

I always recommend that in cases of unwanted pregnancies. Failing that—I suggest acid in the bath or a broom handle up your vagina.

Isn't that dangerous?

Well, you may lose your life—but you won't be pregnant anymore.

I think I'd prefer a proper abortion.

Ah, sorry about that. Abortion is illegal in this country. Immoral too, if I may say so. Goes against everything we stand for.

What about up north?

Don't talk to me about them. They've made a bollox of our tourist industry. You could go to England, of course— but you'll need the fare and a few extra quid in your pocket. Is that feasible?

Can't afford it.

Then I suggest that you have your baby. It is, after all, what the Good Lord created you for. I learned that at school. In fact I learned everything about women at school. A fuck a day and she won't go astray. Isn't that good?

Hilarious.

And wear a longer skirt next time you come in here. You're inciting rape sitting there like that.

Like what?

You know. Now that you're a woman you'll have to bear things like that in mind. Men are weak. They can't be expected to resist temptation all the time. By the way— have you started fantasising about being a prostitute yet?

No.

You will. That's another thing I learned at school. All women fantasise about being prostitutes. And gang-bang rapes. That's another one. They love dreaming about things like that.

Are you sure?

Positive. You have a lot to look forward to.

I can't wait.

One other thing—you'll say no when you mean yes. Remember that. Anything else?

I was only saying to the wife the other day—the Irish male is a very intelligent human being.

I suppose I'd better get myself a job.

Good idea—but don't expect to be offered anything requiring brains. You're less intelligent now—and there's no point in training you for anything complicated. You'll get married in no time. You're bound to become pregnant again and naturally you'll wish to stay at home and look after your husband.

I hadn't thought about that.

That's where intelligence comes in. If you were a man now you'd have thought about that straight away. Is that a bra you're wearing under that blouse?

No.

You should always wear a bra. You only distract people wobbling about like that. Where was I?

You were talking about intelligence.

So I was. I was only saying to the wife the other day—the Irish male is a very intelligent human being. It's a pity he has to be lumbered with the stupidity of women.

Do I have to get married?

No. It's a free country and our politicians are wonderful—but you don't want to be dubbed a lesbian all your life. You're only wasting a good fanny. What you need is a man—someone to look after you—protect you from the rigours of the world.

I thought you said men were weak?

Did I? I like that perfume you're wearing. What's the name of it?

I have no idea.

It's exciting.

Piss off!

You'll learn to handle it properly in time. My wife knows. She's a very happy woman—and she knows how progressive I am.

In what way?

I do the washing-up once a month. I like to be fair. And I talk to her occasionally. That's most important. Nothing too demanding, of course, but you know what I mean.

I think so. Is there any chance of an operation to change me back into a man?

Afraid not. If I was you I should relax and enjoy it. And learn to pray. That's always a good thing. I learned that at school. A religious upbringing has many advantages.

Especially if you're a man.

Quite. Anything else I can do for you?

Not at the moment.

A WILD SABBATH DISORDER

JOHN MORROW

Yesterday's meeting of the Ballyturdeen District Council was again the occasion for scenes of wild disorder when the age-old hare of Lord's Day Observance was raised by Councillor Winston McFetridge of the FTP party.

Councillor McFetridge said that the good people of Ballyturdeen had stood by long enough and watched with heavy hearts the increasing desecration of their Sabbath by greedy profiteers who had twisted the lax laws governing hotels and restaurants to mean that anyone could drink himself footless so long as he had a greasy plate at his elbow.

The town's most notorious offender in this respect, Councillor McFetridge alleged, was the Ballyturdeen Hibernian Motel, Discorama and Hot Food Carry-out, owned by Councillor O'Bannion of the RIP party. Amid uproar, while Councillor O'Bannion was being restrained

by the sergeant-at-arms, Councillor McFetridge declared that last Sunday had been the last straw. Never again should the orgy of alcoholic licentiousness that had marked the visit of a certain Belfast punk rock group—whose name he forbore to mention—be allowed to mar a Ballyturdeen Sabbath.

At this point, Councillor O'Bannion was heard to shout "Thick Boke!" and was evicted from the chamber by order of the mayor, 84-year-old Colonel Yates-Gregory. But when RIP members pointed out that Councillor O'Bannion had merely supplied the name of the punk group in question, he was allowed to return.

Answering the allegation, Councillor O'Bannion said that the visit of Thick Boke to the Hibernian had been a huge and profitable success, thanks to the efforts of Mr Billy Jo Clegg, Councillor McFetridge's son-in-law, who had managed to swing a cheap package deal with the mutual agent of Thick Boke and Mr Tex de Winter, the well-known country and western evangelist who had appeared in Councillor McFetridge's tabernacle that same evening.

Amid cries of "Shame!" from the FTP members, Councillor O'Bannion admitted that some young punk groupies from Belfast had broken into the nearby municipal playground and had picked the locks on the swings. A case, he said, of youthful high spirits.

Councillor McFetridge retorted that a gallon of old rough cider would be more like it, and said that he himself had witnessed acrobatic indecencies being performed on the swings by people with green hair.

This revelation was greeted with cries of "Fairies! Fairies!" from the RIP members. This was countered by cries of "Banioli, Banioli!" from the FTP after Councillor McFetridge had read out an extract from court proceedings in July 1912, when a Signor Enrico Banioli, an ice-cream hawker, had been fined for disturbing the peace of the Sabbath with his bugle.

Stung by this reference to his family's beginnings in the catering trade, Councillor O'Bannion shouted, "My great-granda blew the charge for Liberty and Garibaldi!" At which point the mayor, 84-year-old Colonel Yates-Gregory, in a unique interjection, exclaimed, "That takes the biscuit!" and appeared to laugh himself into a mild seizure amid the stunned silence of both parties.

Councillor O'Bannion then stormed from the chamber to the adjoining car park, followed by his fellow members of the RIP. There, in a gesture of protest, they let down the tyres of Yates-Gregory's private ambulance. Members of the FTP objected strongly to this and the now traditional scenes of grave disorder got underway, but were soon quelled by the resident platoon of Grenadiers camped nearby.

FORKED TONGUES, CÉILÍS AND INCUBATORS

This article is based on the second annual John Malone Memorial Lecture, "Among Schoolchildren", given by SEAMUS HEANEY at Queen's University, Belfast.
John Malone, who died on February 14th 1982, was Director of the School Support Service. A lifelong supporter of comprehensive education, he was formerly a lecturer in education at QUB, a director of the Schools Curriculum Project, and headmaster of Orangefield Secondary School.

What I am involved in here is more autobiography than argument, carried on in the faith that the educational process is a matter of sympathetic recognition. The learning experience is both challenge and liberation so I hope you will bear with me if I adduce myself as an example of the bewilderments and attempts at resolution which the sensibility can undergo in this country as it tries to grow into a coherent personality. I want to muse on my own experience and the experience and writings of others in order to arrive at some clarification of what our attitudes should be as people who practice the responsible and influential arts of teaching in Ireland today.

The national schools were not long established here when a great-great aunt of mine, one Catherine Bradley from the townland of Dreenan, in the parish of Lavey, Co Derry, learned "to cut and sew, be neat in everything in the best modern way". The best modern way for 1843, that is. I have an example of her school needlework, a sampler upon which she embroidered the alphabet, first in lower-case letters, then in capitals; then the numbers 1 to 10; and then, below these neat try-outs, there is this verse:

Ireland as she ought to be
Great glorious and free
First flower of the earth
First gem of the sea.

Girlhood's fire was in her blood. And it was symbolised by another embroidery, beneath the verse, of a shamrock. All very coherent so far, all part of a common culture and attitude, one that flowers in the wild earth of Dreenan to this day. But there are four more words on the sampler that force us to remember other attitudes. Squeezed in to the right of the verse, unbalancing the symmetry of the design and complicating the sentiments of the poem, there are the words "God Save the Queen". The dominant system was making itself felt and the common culture squeezed itself a bit to the side to allow it in. And so, in that sampler sewn by a 19th-century schoolgirl, two value systems which now explode daily are lodged like dormant munitions on one piece of, no doubt, Ulster linen.

Another emblem there, as Yeats would say. Ulster linen. Linen, Huguenots, bleaching greens, Belfast, industrial power, curse the Pope, God save the Queen. Linen stands for "independent, rattling, non-transcendent Ulster", for all that is better and worse in the planter tradition, and when it goes with Ulster, it effects a semantic change in that ancient word. Ulster shrinks to a six-county region, its hero is not Cuchulainn but Carson, and its Great O'Neill is not a rebellious chieftain from 16th-century Tyrone but a unionist Guards officer from Co Antrim.

The official British culture, if you like, was at odds with the anthropological culture.

Yet it was a large map of this younger, smaller Ulster that hung in different shades of greens and blues and fawns in the first classroom I knew, with the border emphasised by a thick red selvedge all the way from Lough Foyle to Carlingford Lough. That vestigially bloody marking halted the eye travelling south and west; but travelling east, on slender dotted lines that curled fluently from Larne to Stranraer, from Derry to Glasgow, from Belfast to Liverpool and Belfast to Heysham, small black steamships lured the eye across the blue wash of the North Channel. Another emblem there, all of a piece with the reading book where we learned off "Oh to be in England" and the singing lesson where we belted out "The Lincolnshire Poacher", good enough stuff in itself, conscientiously and innocently taught and learned, but unconsciously transmitting attitudes and customs and habits of feeling that were at variance with the common hearth feelings of the pupils of that particular school. The official British culture, if you like, was at odds with the anthropological culture; they tended to exist side by side in the mind rather as Catherine Bradley's warring slogans lay contiguous but antithetical inside her dainty sampler.

Moving from primary school to university, when I think back on those years I can see a similar tension. I was studying English, reading Shakespeare and Oscar Wilde and Chaucer and Dickens, considering the rhythms of the Authorised Version of the Bible and their effect on English prose, considering the tradition of courtly love, learning to find my way among the ironies and niceties of Jane Austen's vicarages, discussing Tennyson's loss of faith and Lawrence's phallic consciousness, learning of the rituals of club life in India by reading E. M. Forster and learning the rituals of the sherry party by attending receptions at the house of our Oxford professor, a man who was alleged to have once confessed that he was the first of his family to go into a trade.

Meanwhile, at the weekends and during the holidays, far from the sherry parties of Malone Road, the secretary of the local Pioneer Total Abstinence Association was enrolling me as a probationer in the society; far from the elegances of Oscar Wilde and the profundities of Shakespeare, I was acting with the Bellaghy Dramatic Society in plays about 1798, now playing a United Irishman, a blacksmith forging pikes on a real anvil fetched from Devlin's forge at Hillhead, now playing Robert Emmet in a one-act melodrama and having my performance hailed in the crowded columns of the *Mid-Ulster Mail*. Far from discussing the Victorian loss of faith, I was driving my mother to evening devotions in the "chapel", or looking for my name in a list of "adorers" at the exposition of the Blessed Sacrament. Far from the melodies of courtly love, I was acting as *fear a' tigh* at the GAA *céilí*, crying "*Ballaí Luimní*" or "*cor Seisiúr Déag*" and trying to master a way of coaxing a training college student into the back seat of our Austin 16. And far, far from Lawrence's phallic candour, finding myself subsequently confessing sins of immodest and immoderate embraces.

What had seemed disabling and provincial is suddenly found to be corroborating and fundamental and potentially universal.

Was I two persons or one? Was I extending myself or breaking myself apart? Was I being led out or led away? Was I failing to live up to the aspiring literary intellectual

effort when I was at home, or was I betraying the culture of the parish when I was at the university? Obviously, such tensions and confusions were not the unique affliction of a Northern Ireland Catholic country teenager in the 1950s. In all kinds of ways the experience can be paralleled, notably in English novels of the same period, by poets such as Philip Larkin and Kingsley Amis, scholarship boys who wrote autobiographical fictions about the bruises they suffered, when, as lower-middle-class provincial students, they found themselves among the higher incomes and higher pretensions of an Oxford college or a redbrick common room.

What came to fill the gap between the parish and the academy, between the culture of the GAA hall and the culture of Shakespeare, what realigned my sense of belonging to a place with the attendant sense of displacement, was, first of all, Daniel Corkery and his potent monocular vision of *The Hidden Ireland*. Corkery's message was succinct. "We were robbed," he said. We lost what made us what we are. We had lost the indigenous Gaelic civilisation and he evoked that civilisation in its decline with elegiac nostalgia as he wrote lovingly and romantically about the poets of Munster in the 17th century, poets of a people whom the parliament in Dublin regarded as "the common enemy". Eoghan Rua O Suilleabhain, Aodhgan O Rathaille, the poets of the Maighe, even Brian Merriman. At that time I was also reading in Irish the poems of northerners like Cathal Bui Mac Giolla Gunna and Art MacCooey, finding Tyrone and the O'Neills reflected in a poetry that belonged to the home landscape as truly as Browning's wise thrust belonged to his young summer weather across the water. And it was around this time that I had a small experience which ratified this sense of a relationship to a hidden Ulster in a memorable and intimate way, and ratified Corkery's notion of loss and deprivation.

I came across, in the Dineen's Irish dictionary, a word with the letters *Doir* in brackets after it, a word which was thereby defined as being peculiar to the Irish spoken at one time in my own English-speaking County Derry. The word was "lachtar", meaning a flock of young chickens. Suddenly I was alive to the fact of loss which Corkery had described. The word had survived in our district as a common and, as far as I had known until then, an English word, but now I realised that it lived upon our tongues like a capillary stretching back to a time when Irish was the *lingua franca* of the whole place. Suddenly the resentful nationalism of my Catholic minority experience was fused with a concept of identity that was enlarging and releasing and would eventually help me to relate my literary education with the heritage of the home ground.

But however much Corkery helped, the integration would not have been possible without Joyce, and specifically the Joyce who wrote about Stephen Dedalus's linguistic self-consciousness in *Portrait of the Artist as a Young Man*. Stephen, in that famous passage, feels inadequate when he hears the English Jesuit speaking English, and contact with the English accent itself leaves him smarting. He thought:

> The language in which we are speaking is his before it is mine. How different are the words home, Christ, ale, master, on his lips and on mine ... His language, so familiar and so foreign, will always be for me an acquired speech.

But that was Stephen's view and not necessarily the view of his creator, James Joyce himself. If Stephen, the character, looks with envy at the unity of culture and possession of a shared language and a unified myth which ratifies English identity, Joyce, the writer, did not necessarily look with the same envy at this state of affairs. He accepted the universe of Ireland as a different if also a desperate state with its own integrities and destinies which had to be defined and resolved in accordance with their own structures and idioms.

If, at the point in the book I have just quoted from, Stephen is allowed to express a nostalgia for the more civil and coherent English world, and allowed to feel that his Drumcondra word "tundish", his "lachtar" as it were, is an embarrassment, a kind of Firbolg birthmark rebuked by the Milesian superiority of the standard English "funnel", at a later point Joyce allows a different perspective to enter. Stephen, like many another Irishman and Ulsterman, had felt himself deprived of his full human inheritance just by reason of his cultural and geographical placing. "It wounded him to think," Joyce writes, "that he would never be but a shy guest at the feast of the world's culture and that the monkish learning, in terms of which he was striving to forge out an aesthetic philosophy, was held no higher by the age he lived in than the subtle and curious jargons of heraldry and falconry." But as Stephen comes to a sense of the complex reality of the world he inhabits, this unease drops away. Against his previous linguistic inferiority complex, we must set this later diary entry at the end of *Portrait*:

> That tundish has been on my mind for a long time. I looked it up and find it English and good old blunt English too. Damn the dean of studies and his funnel! What did he come here for to teach us our own language or to learn it from us? Damn him one way or another.

What had seemed disabling and provincial is suddenly found to be corroborating and fundamental and potentially universal. To belong to Ireland and to speak its dialect is not necessarily to be cut off from the world's banquet because that banquet is eaten at the table of one's own life, savoured by the tongue one speaks. Stephen now trusts what he calls "our own language" and in that trust he will go on to encounter what he calls "the reality of experience". But it will be his own specific Dublin experience, with all its religious and historical freight, so different from the English experience to which he had

heretofore stood in a subservient relationship.

And if Joyce is exemplary in revealing that the conceptions, loyalties and ideals of cross-channel culture are not necessarily to be shared by our insular imagination, he is also exemplary in refusing to replace that myth of alien superiority by the myth of native superiority. If the coherence of English culture is a fruitless aspiration, equally fruitless is the dream of a Gaelic order restored. Joyce is against all such alibis. What Stephen called in the diary entry "our own language" is, after all, the English language modified by its residence in Ireland. If he has gone to the trouble of freeing his mind from the net of the English myth, he is also intent on deconstructing the prescriptive myth of Irishness which was burgeoning in his youth and which survives in various sympathetic and unsympathetic forms to this day.

If the coherence of English culture is a fruitless aspiration, equally fruitless is the dream of a Gaelic order restored.

Consider, for example, some lines from a poem by the late Sean O'Riordáin, a significant voice in modern Irish writing, a poet who lived in Cork city but whose dream home was among the native speakers of Dunquin in Co Kerry. I have translated the title as "Come Back Again", and these are the opening verses:

> Leave the Glen of the Mad in the east,
> Drain the spirit of age out of your blood,
> Close your mind to all that happened
> Since the battle of Kinsale was fought,
> Since the load started to weigh heavy
> And the road got longer. Unshackle your mind
>
> Of its civil English tackling,
> Shelley, Keats and Shakespeare.
> Get back to what is your own.
> Wash your mind and wash your tongue
> That was spancelled in a syntax
> Putting you out of step with yourself.

By a curious coincidence, I worked on this translation while I was on a bus trip to Lady Gregory's demesne at Coole Park; and it seemed to me as I journeyed towards the walled garden with its autograph tree carved with initials of W.B. Yeats, AE, George Moore, Sean O'Casey and others, it seemed that I was heading for a head-on collision, spiritually and linguistically, if not geographically, with those who would follow O'Riordáin's advice to find their destination in "Dunquin in the evening light".

As somebody whose sense of poetic form derived not

only from Yeats and Patrick Kavanagh, but also from Keats and Shakespeare, I found the advice to ditch all that impossible, since I do not find that the syntax of my speech puts me out of touch with myself. And I also found the advice to ignore history since Kinsale impossible to accept since it is that history which has made us all what we are. But I did respond to a sense of homecoming at the end of the poem, a sense of release and repose when the poet goes on to describe his destination: for as well as being polemic, this is a poem, an expression of the writer's inner division and of his repining for that universal, paradisiacal place where our conflicts will be resolved. Nevertheless, while the curve of the feeling is true, for me the line of the argument had to be untrue.

That Irish is a fortification and an enrichment I hope I have made clear, but I also hope I have made clear that as a teacher and writer, I do not yield to the notion that my identity is disabled and falsified and somehow slightly traitorous if I conduct my casual and imaginative transactions in the speech I was born to. Both languages are part of the landscape and mention of landscape reminds me of a line in Brian Friel's *Translations* which is entirely pertinent. "It can happen in a civilization," says the schoolmaster in that play, "that the contours of a language no longer match the landscape of fact." The schoolmaster was recognising that in the social and economic landscape of 19th-century Ireland, Irish would necessarily give way to English. But the landscape of fact also includes the cultural and political contours, and those contours have been changed by the retrieval of political independence for twenty-six counties. So that now English can properly give way to the return of Irish to match some parts of the new map—say, Dunquin. But what of Finaghy on a July afternoon?

There we find the obverse of the O'Riordáin position. If he would obliterate history since Kinsale, the loyalist imagination at its most enthusiastic would obliterate history before Kinsale. If O'Riordáin needs to unshackle his tongue of its English harness in order to create a secure and true spiritual home, the anti-O'Riordáin would exclude all taint and acquaintance with the Irish dimension of his experience in order to ratify the purity and liberty of his stand. As with O'Riordáin's poem, the loyalist's fidelity is capable of a double application. It can, on the one hand, be a holding, grounding, utterly necessary exercise in self-definition and self-respect, an insistence on dwelling within conceptions and ideals which animate a certain community and the individuals within that community. It can say, we prefer the dream of a mainland home, we shall remember ancestry and maintain solidarity with our traditional values, and it has in fact strenuously maintained its right to say and do this. But the very strenuousness of this maintained effort constitutes its negative aspect. Just as the O'Riordáin poem, in its sectarian application, would refuse to recognise history and language other than its own espoused versions of them, just as it would turn a

vision of fulfilment into an instrument of coercion, the same neurotic intensity is in danger of turning conceptions and loyalties within the unionist tradition into refusals and paranoias. And hence it is of paramount importance that all who work among schoolchildren, as educators, are clear-headed, sure-footed, nimble and accurate, open and aware of the psychic and historical realm within which they operate so casually and so potently.

Catherine Bradley's sampler, with its ambivalent if not duplicitous texts, still hangs in the balance, and more precariously than ever. It has great allegorical force as a representation of divisions within the country, but I would like to supplement it with another parable.

The myths of identity are only one domain of reality. The facts of lived experience are equally important . . .

To go back to "lachtar". To discover its root was one stage of growth and grounding, a contrary but essential discovery of ancestry and loyalty. But ancestry and loyalty are not everything. The myths of identity are only one domain of reality. The facts of lived experience are equally important, though, oddly enough, sometimes they are harder to establish. But a few years ago, long after the thrill of finding links in "lachtar" with an Irish-speaking Ulster, I remembered with equal affection a different word, one without any particular historical or cultural charge, a 20th-century word, technological, without affiliation, as unattached on the South Downs as in south Derry, but also a word associated with the brooding world of chickens. This was "incubator", and as I write it, its neuter syllables are alive with warmth and cheepings and musty smells, for the incubator was part of the idiom of chicken farming too. It summons the whole secret world of the child in the outhouse, the world of wonder and tenderness. And these deeply lodged intimacies, this phenomenological conditioning of the personal life, is as crucial to the salvation of our human souls as the conditionings we undergo from our myths of identity. And it is the educator's and the artist's special task to reveal to himself and to others the vitality of this inner personal world, and to testify to its fundamental value. The life that the word incubator lives in me has little to do with historical affections and group bonding; it lives in the ground of pre-reflective being and if I were to prepare my own sampler to remind myself of the complex recognitions we are all capable of and which we should all live up to, I could do worse than embroider it and its enigmatic cousin "lachtar" on the pallid but durable texture of some old remnant of linen.

GROWING UP IN THE CRADLE OF THE CHERRY-PICKER

Playwright GRAHAM REID writes about the Donegall Road area of Belfast where his plays are set and where he was born and grew up.

I stood in the cradle of the "cherry-picker", as it rose above the rooftops of Coolderry Street, the street where I was born. Seeing it from above, looking down on it, and wondering if that wasn't really the way I saw it nowadays, even from ground level. My post-production depression was beginning. The actors and actresses had gone. Gone to prepare themselves for the farewell party. The technicians were packing up. On the street the small knots of spectators were breaking up. The last *Billy* play was finished. The last time I'd be in Coolderry Street for a long time, perhaps for ever. It had once seemed a long street, especially when I was a kid ... racing up it after dark, waiting for the "bogey-men" to spring from doorways. It had once been a street where every face was a familiar face. Now it looked small, most of the people were strangers.

The shop at the top corner of Coolbeg Street was deserted, abandoned. It had once been owned by the Turners. They were an old English couple. Their son had lost part of one arm. Some said he caught it in a bicycle chain. The more likely story was that he had picked up an incendiary bomb during the war. They had fled Coolbeg Street and Belfast as the result of another war—threatened for foiling an arson attack on a laundry that adjoined their premises. Self-defence, the protection of two very old crippled parents, was no excuse. Did they take all the little red and blue books with them? How often I'd gone there and had stuff "put in the book".

When we ran out of credit there, we could go to Spooner's. It stood on the top corner of Coolfin Street. It still traded ... an outpost, as such small shops are fast becoming. There had also been a shop at the top of Coolderry Street, but no one ever seemed able to make a go of it. How would we all have survived if those corner shops had displayed that heartless sign: "Please do not ask for credit, as a refusal often offends." It would have offended. It would also have visited severe hardship on many families in those little back streets. We all seemed to survive on "tick", and sharpened our wits learning to dodge the "tickmen".

Three times I'd returned to this little street to make television plays. There would be few enough reasons to return now. On each occasion, despite the friendliness shown to me, I'd felt more and more of a stranger. My mother had been born in number 3, and lived most of her life in number 67. It had been her grandparents' house, the house where I was born. For most of my life it was the place to which I always returned knowing there would always be a welcome, a warm fire, a meal, whatever I required. There was no indication that it was going to change suddenly and totally, all in one June day. It did though—in 1981, just a few months before the making of the first *Billy* play. Since that day, and with the exception of the time spent making the three plays, I have tried to think of that street as just another Belfast street. In my imagination I can re-create the old days; I can re-people that street with ghosts. In a way, and as a result of television plays and changes of fortune, I have become one of those ghosts.

In the old days few people seemed to leave the street. There were few new estates to go to, and seemingly little social mobility. The first television set arrived in the early 50s. The first car shortly afterwards. On a Friday we would crowd into the house with the television and watch *The Cisco Kid*. Those were the days when the hero never lost his hat. He could fall off a stampeding horse or topple down a mountainside, but the hat always remained firmly in place. There was the night the lady who owned that first television set was knocked down and killed at the bottom of the street. Those were the days when we were invited into houses to gaze at the corpse in the open coffin. In the case of the first television lady, though, there was no invitation. The adults took it badly; they mumbled about a sealed, leaded coffin.

One memory calls forth yet another. Newspapers would be tied around the shaft of a brush and set on fire. This flaming torch would then be pushed up the chimney and the soot burned out—it saved the expense of a sweep. One lady just across the road from us specialised in this service. Perhaps a few pence changed hands. The same lady laid out corpses. She also collected for wreaths and coronation parties. The latter did not occupy much of her time. She did door-to-door canvassing during elections. During election campaigns the candidate would appear on a union-jack-bestrewn coal lorry. He would then be accompanied by an "orange" band playing "orange" tunes, whilst the candidate played his "orange" card.

. . . it is different, or perhaps I want to believe it's different—that we had fewer social workers, because we had more "neighbours".

The *Belfast Telegraph* carried pictures of bridges blown up by the IRA and pictures of the Russian tanks entering Budapest. Anthony Eden was well thought of during the Suez War, Nasser was roundly condemned. My father cried when Joe Stalin died. They weren't really the good old days. They were the days when life's biggest disappointment was to lose your favourite marble. The RUC and the B Specials spent a great deal of their time chasing us for playing football on the street, or for trespassing on the railway.

We did make the pages of the *News of the World*—misdemeanours involving girls from the neighbourhood and RUC men. Apart from that, we boasted two real prostitutes in our heyday. The American and Canadian fleets used to pay regular courtesy calls to Belfast. In one house the visiting sailors' caps used to be piled in front of the window. For a brief priod, "The Yanks Are Coming" became an obscene ditty . . . but some of us never caught on.

The corner of the street on the main road was the great meeting-place. A large semi-circle of spittle glistening in the lamplight marked the spot. In plush times there would be minuscule cigarette butts discarded. Often the tips were blackened, evidence of someone enjoying the last grain of tobacco. We went to the public baths in Ormeau Avenue, the washers, on Saturday mornings. This was for a bath, not for swimming. The nearest cinema, the Windsor, provided romance and adventure on screen, and sex and violence in the stalls. The Sandro in Sandy Row was cheap, but it was said you went in at half-eight and came out half-ate! There was the Coliseum on the other side of the Boyne Bridge. For a touch of class, or to impress "the bird", it would be the Majestic on the Lisburn Road.

In our teenage years drinking pints and putting a few bob on the "gee-gees" was a Saturday ritual. Das would discard their "shipyard scoops" and don a good one over Brylcreemed hair. The two smells that dominated my childhood and teenage Saturdays: the smell of Brylcreem and the smell of an Ulster fry. It seemed just about everything was delivered on carts: coal, coalbrick, milk, buttermilk, bread, minerals, herrings, bleach, pine disinfectant. Rags were collected: balloons, or a few coins, given in exchange.

Message boys delivered meat and vegetables and other groceries on large basketed bicycles, delivery bikes. My brother rode one for Ford's of Bradbury Place, a grocery shop. One 11th of July afternoon, he was home for his lunch and I went for a ride on it. It was a wet day. The bonfire wood was all stacked and ready. As I reached the corner I pulled hard on the back brake and remember very little of the rest of that day. I spent it lying on the sofa concussed, missing the bonfire celebrations. It was, according to the doctor, important that I stayed awake. To this end my elder, slightly tipsy, brother, kept pouring lemonade over me.

I never thought girls would take the place of football . . . but they did, and the back entries were the places for "lumbering". Many of us fumbled and stumbled our way to "manhood" in those entries. We all lost our virginity at a very early age, or so we said, often enough to still believe it was true. The more serious among us lumbered in our own front halls. I always thought kissing was overrated, until I discovered that you didn't have to hold your breath for the duration of the kiss. A good-looking cousin, who worked in a local tobacco factory, taught me to French-kiss during her lunch break.

There used to be two piggeries in the area, around Utility Street. We could earn a few shillings after school by collecting "refuse" for the pigs. We would take a bucket, a cart or an old pram and tramp up and down the entries, calling in indecipherable language for "any ra-fee-use" or some such thing. A large bucket filled could mean sixpence. A cart or pram as much as a shilling, or one-and-a-tanner! Payment was at the discretion of the pigman, and he often inspected the quality of the refuse. It was all boiled up in a huge cauldron and fed to the pigs. It could take hours and miles of tramping to fill a cart or pram. The money earned was usually spent on sweets, though in my own case it was often a useful addition to the family budget. Toffee was the favourite purchase,

Highland Toffee, threepence for a substantial plain bar, fourpence for a chocolate-coated one.

The streets look much the same. Behind Coolbeg Street was the perimeter wall of the City Hospital, and a useless bank of mud—we called it the clay-banks. It was a favourite place for playing or for stone-throwing gang fights. Now it has been turned into little gardens. The youngsters who play around these streets are more serious about their stone-throwing. It looks similar, but it is different, or perhaps I want to believe it's different—that we had fewer social workers, because we had more "neighbours".

As I reach the ground again and walk towards my car old neighbours approach me. They smile and congratulate me; they say I've put Coolderry Street on the map. Do they know why I've put Coolderry Street on the map—do they see what I see, hear what I hear, when I watch my "Plays for Today" . . . that are all about yesterday?

THE FAIRY TALE
Andrew Elliott

Because she forfeited her voice to come here
The little mermaid is used to talking in silence—
A wet-dream with hair they all think is just peroxide white
And a skirt that is seaweed—not leather at all.
Her fishnet stockings are the real thing.

Even now she still combs her hair with a scallop shell
And can't understand why it is becoming tatty.
After being picked up each time under the sodium lamps
She lies on her back in the shadowy bedroom
And listens to the light in her eyes rippling on the ceiling.

A BOY ON A SLEEPING VOLCANO

MICHAEL LONGLEY

My childhood home stood in a comfortable middle-class street midway between Belfast's most salubrious thoroughfare, the Malone Road, and the more complex ambience of the Lisburn Road. The self-containment of the large houses on the Malone Road did not excite my young imagination. But the Lisburn Road proved to be an education in itself.

Before the days of the M1 motorway, it was the main route south to Dublin. The section which I explored gradually through my childhood presents with a diagrammatic neatness a miniature version of Ulster's class structure. To the left, as you travel south towards Lisburn, the drawing rooms of dentists, doctors, solicitors enjoy a view, through rhododendrons and rose bushes, of working-class two-up-and-two-down houses packed into the shadowy, gardenless streets which branch off the main road to the right. To move house from the right-hand side to the left, simply to cross the Lisburn Road, would, socially, be an uphill struggle. The financial incline is very steep indeed. As a boy zigzagging backwards and forwards, I soon discovered that the Lisburn Road resembles the side of a sleeping volcano.

My parents came from London to live in Belfast in 1927; and I was born here in 1939, two months before the outbreak of the Second World War. My father, who had survived the Trenches, enlisted again. Because it took him some time after the war to re-establish himself as a commercial traveller, there was not enough money to send my twin brother and me to one of the posher preparatory schools. We attended the local public elementary school where, out of a large class of nearly 40 pupils, we were almost the only middle-class children. Most of the others lived on "the wrong side" of the Lisburn Road.

Tea at Herbie's house was fried bread sprinkled with salt. Herbie came to my home, and gasped when he saw the size of our back garden.

Their clothes were different from ours—woollen balaclavas, laced boots with studs in the soles rather than shoes or sandals. Beside them my twin and I must have appeared chubby and well-scrubbed. I recall skinny knees and snotty noses, but most of all the accent—as abrasive and raucous as a football rattle. This I soon acquired in order to make myself less unacceptable. "Len' us a mey-ek"—"Lend me a make" (a ha'penny). At home I would try to remember to ask for "a slice of cake" and not "a slice of a cey-ek", to refer to the "door" and the "floor" rather than "doo-er" and "floo-er". By the age of six or seven I was beginning to lead a double life, learning how to re-create myself twice daily, acquiring a toe-hold on the side of the volcano.

I made friends with the other pupils and visited their homes: the lavatory outside in the yard, stairs ascending steeply as soon as you entered, low ceilings and no elbow-room at all. Tea at Herbie's house was fried bread sprinkled with salt. Herbie came to my home, and gasped when he saw the size of our back garden. For the first time I felt ashamed of our relative affluence. Our separate drawing and dining rooms, the hall with its wooden panelling, the lavatory upstairs were all novelties to Herbie. He seemed curious rather than envious. Every corner of the home I had taken for granted was illuminated by his gaze as by wintry sunlight.

Another pupil, John McGlinchey, was often caned for being late. He delivered papers for Younger the newsagent. If the *Belfast News-Letter* was delayed or the newsagent slow, poor John, without complaint or explanation, would be standing at 9.30 in front of the class, his expression resigned, his hand presented to the whistling cane and then hugged under his armpit as he stumbled over schoolbags to his desk. Should I have told the teacher that he delivered papers to *our* house? When no one was looking and as though to drown his sorrows, John would swig the blue-grey sludge from all the small white inkwells within easy reach.

Every December my father gave me half-a-crown as a Christmas box for the paper boy, as he called him. I never told my father that the paper boy was in *my* class. On the doorstep John and I behaved like strangers and avoided each other's eyes as the half-crown changed hands. Somehow I understood even then that his dignity was at stake, and, for different reasons, my own. Later, in class, the transaction would not be mentioned.

John and Herbie shared with me their mythology, most of which was centred on Roman Catholics. Did I know why Taigs crossed themselves? What dark practices lurked behind confession and mass? Didn't the nuns kidnap little girls and imprison them behind the suspiciously high walls of the big convent at the top of the Ormeau Road? The Orange Order and the B Specials marched through our conversations. Distorted echoes of sectarian atrocities in the 1920s and 1930s confused me further. I was reluctant to believe such black narratives, but I craved the bond of shared fears and superstitions.

With its dozens of little shops—newsagent's, confectioner's, haberdasher's, ironmonger's—with the Regal cinema where entrance to the front stalls cost all of three-pence, the Lisburn Road had become my hinterland. The cinema was demolished not so long ago, and many of the shops have now been transformed into Chinese restaurants and fast food take-aways. But the rows of back-to-back houses remain, peopled still in my mind by Herbie and John, by Norman Hamilton, Sally Patterson, Alan Gray, Helen Ferguson, Norma Gamble. Recent history will have multiplied the fears and superstitions of our shared childhood. If the volcano rumbles at all, it will do so for the wrong reasons. The big houses on the other side of the Lisburn Road will register hardly a tremor.

FORTNIGHT 210, DECEMBER 3RD 1984

TRADITIONAL MUSIC AS IDEOLOGY

SEÁN CORCORAN

Since this is my first folk column for *Fortnight*, I thought I would take the opportunity to trot out some of my own pet notions (and hopefully initiate a discussion) as to why this type of music is so important and indeed why the necessity for such a column in the first place?

For a start, I must admit that I am not terribly fond of the term "folk music", smacking as it does of a Germanic romanticism and an English naivety—a longing for a mythical past society where there were no football hooligans, TV personalities or Arthur Scargills. The term is essentially an ideological one and has the effect of "back-dating" what in reality is a living cultural phenomenon, seeing it as a survival from a rural past and opposing it to "popular" urban-produced songs.

This approach therefore involves a process of selection from the repertoires of traditional singers only of those songs which reinforce this theory. This is despite the fact that some of our greatest singers (for example, the bilingual Elizabeth Cronin of west Cork) had repertoires which consisted not only of Gaelic songs crammed with medieval motifs, but also included sea-shanties, English music-hall songs, and even songs from the visiting American "black-faced minstrel" troupes of the 1890s.

Perpetrators of this theory of "folk music" also actually refer to the performers as "transmitters" of some ancient tradition rather than as creative artists who constantly refashion their material, who are conscious of the complexity of their musical idiom and who have their own distinct critical aesthetic.

The term "folk music" is particularly ideological when it is used in opposition to "art music", the implication being that the former is "artless". However, if "folk" is used in a purely sociological sense (defining a type of music according to who plays it rather than what one thinks of it) then the proper term for the kind of music played by symphony orchestras and opera companies, largely funded by state grants, and patronised by a small section of the middle and upper classes, should be "Western European Elite Music" (WEEM for short). This was the approach adopted in medieval Ireland and Wales and currently adopted in Asia to distinguish the sung poetry of the folk from the highly mannered verse and music of the aristocracy.

I do not mean to belittle the richness and nobility of the European elite tradition but to emphasise that it is not the *only* musical language in the world. The great civilisations of the East, for example, have their own elite musical traditions which are just as rich and complex yet have totally different concepts of intonation, scale, timbre, rhythm and harmony. Each musical tradition in the world, be it "folk", "popular" or "elite" is artistically valid in itself for its performers and audiences and can only be properly evaluated according to its *own* musical criteria.

Here is a nice wee story to illustrate this: to the average Western European ear the pipe music of Albania sounds decidedly unattractive. The range (number of notes used) seems small and constrained, the melodies repetitive and inconclusive, the timbre (tone) harsh and raucous, and, above all, the rhythms odd and ungainly. The great German musicologist Curt Sachs once took a fine Albanian piper to hear Beethoven's Ninth Symphony. The piper's comment afterwards was, "Fine—but very, very plain."

Sachs explains this reaction: "The Albanian was neither arrogant nor incompetent. He just had a different standard. The unified, over-simplified rhythm could not possibly satisfy his eastern ears—exactly as to an illiterate African, the crotchets and quavers of Western music would appear dull."

To my mind, one of the healthiest developments in the field of modern orchestral music is the fact that many present-day composers are steeping themselves in other musical languages—jazz, folk, Asian and African—and injecting a whole new range of concepts into the WEEM tradition so that nowadays our Albanian piper might not be quite so bored.

Do I hear a protesting voice saying, "Why all this heavy analysis? Surely folk singers just open their mouths and gulder, pipers and fiddlers just hammer away like the dickens and simply enjoy themselves?" Of course they do. One of the most attractive aspects of folk music is its spontaneity and liveliness.

Yet all musical traditions have their own avenues and modes of criticism and anybody who spends half an hour in the company of traditional musicians or singers rapidly becomes aware that here is a level of criticism and re-evaluation just as incisive and debative as anything in the music columns of *The Times* or *Guardian* or of such journals as *Sound Post* or *Downbeat*.

. . . the term "folk music" . . . has the effect of "back-dating" what in reality is a living cultural phenomenon . . .

Another aspect which I believe deserves closer examination and which is sadly neglected by most commentators is the way in which folk music, especially in Ireland, is used in the construction of ideologies. This has been going on since the time of our first great folk song collector, Edward Bunting, whose work was used by Wolfe Tone and the Society of United Irishmen. Since then folk music has been exploited by all the various divisions of Irish political and social life. At times it has been seen as a symbol of national identity: at others, such as during the puritanical reaction of the 1920s and 1930s, as a licentious weakness in Irish society which had to be suppressed by pulpit denunciations and roving bands of police and priests armed with blackthorn sticks. (Needless to say, the musicians, singers and dancers themselves, whether Catholic, Protestant, Dissenter or just plain licentious, were never consulted for *their* opinions.)

Consider the famous Harp lager advertisement on TV (this was brought to my attention by an astute musician friend, Ian Robinson, bodhran-player and drummer): handsome man in desert, apparently making a fortune working on pipelines, purporting to be Irish, dreams of having a pint in snug pub back home while awaiting the chance to chat up the fabulous Sally O'Brien, Irish super-colleen, played by an English actress called Vicky something-or-other. The background music to the pub scene in the RTE version is straighforward Irish traditional music. However in versions broadcast in Northern Ireland the music has been changed to American banjo-and-fiddle traditional. Now, in the north both Catholic and Protestant musicians share a common musical tradition which is a blend of Irish and Scottish elements and this, in turn, is precisely the musical bedrock on which the American tradition is based. Talk about wheels within wheels! It would take an entire book to unravel the symbolic complexity of that few seconds of TV jingling.

DOG COLLARS

COLONEL DESPARD AND
THE WIND-DOG

TOM PAULIN introduces his philologist hero, Colonel Despard, who in the coming months will be traipsing the highways and byways of the north of Ireland in search of stray unpoetic words, rebellious couplets, proud independent phrases and other uncomfortable inhabitants of the linguistic landscape this side of the Black Pig's Dyke.

The colonel was in Belfast lately, talking to a salty hallion in the Crown. In the next snug two literary gents were discussing the difference between a ganch and a glype. The air was thick with smoke and spoof glossaries when a critic with a suitcase pushed the door open and started laying down the law. Both words were good for nothing, said the critic, because neither one was "poetic". The literary gents were left gawping while the colonel sloped off to engage his sensibilities with the Dover Street murals. Some kids were playing about on the road. One of them looked very miserable. "Is there something wrong with her?" asked the colonel. "She's feeling a granne," answered another kid. "What's that mean?" asked Despard. "She feels wick." Consulting the ex-convent girl he hangs around with, the colonel discovered that in Irish there's a word which sounds familiar and means "weak"—or "wick".

. . . the Newfoundland day is divided into morning, evening, night. It is "an afternoonless country" where people munch colcannon and use words like *slob* . . .

After that the colonel slipped off on his own to muse on lost causes and the nature of the poetic word. The streets of the city were pitted like old teeth, a helicopter batted across, a skiff of rain blew in from the lough. Then the colonel resolved to write to the editor of *Fortnight* and ask

could he please imitate John Pepper? He could trawl a few columns through the deep and see what came thrashing on board.

Alternatively, he should maybe consider setting up a home for stray dogs—where all the unpoetic words that scour the streets of Belfast could be cared for and given shelter. After seven days the scruffy waifs would get handed over to the critic for disposal. But the colonel, like a forgotten footnote, would have his hands clean. Like the terrific Michael Traynor MA, who compiled a Donegal glossary far away in Tasmania several decades back, he would bring a scholarly purity to the enterprise. Memories of Oscar Wilde's Australia might be reactivated and that obsolete Australian phrase "cultural cringe" could be considered again.

The colonel, who dips of an evening into a novel by Douglas Hurd or *A Dictionary of Newfoundland English*, is much exercised by unread books and unwritten words. He has discovered that on Newfoundland the first of July is a day of national mourning (many Newfoundlanders died in the Battle of the Somme), and he has also learnt that the Newfoundland day is divided into morning, evening, night. It is "an afternoonless country" where people munch colcannon and use words like *slob, slub, slatch, sluff*. They're lucky people becuse there is a new dictionary on Newfoundland which contains the word *grum*—it means "morose" and is a cross between *grim* and *glum*. A waif of a word, *grum*, and Despard is glad it has found a home.

D for Dog, then, and for Despard. Let's begin with this letter. First of all there's a *wind-dog*, a creature of the sky not the streets. The wind-dog is a rainbow, maybe a broken bit of a rainbow, the end not the arc. He must be a relative of MacDiarmid's "chittering licht o' the watergaw". The colonel used to go out mackerel-fishing with Captain Crabbe and it was the captain first drew his attention to this watery phenomenon. A nautical term, then, like *garboard strake*.

Some other rain words are these ones:

Dag: Fog, mist. Drizzly rain. A sudden heavy shower, a *plump*. Father Hopkins liked this word and he began the poem "Inversnaid" with this alliterative skirl: "Degged with dew, dappled with dew/Are the banks of the braes that the brook treads through". Dryden would have been displeased and have said that "our old Teuton monosyllables" were barking away here. Matthew Arnold would have dismissed these lines as "Scotch" and therefore most unpoetic. The colonel likes their rough texture, a cross between usquebaugh and Georges Braque. They have the scorch-marks of Rabbie Burns, the taste of a Tartan gang or a Jacobite clan pouring down a mountainside. Hopkins used to send Joseph Wright slips of paper on which he had recorded spoken words and phrases. These words eventually found their way into *The English Dialect Dictionary*. And at last that excellent scholar of Belfast English, James Milroy, wrote a study of Hopkins's·language, his fascination with non-standard forms. Sadly, Milroy's book doesn't get looked at much, though some months back Despard met an ex-marine munching popcorn under a catalpa tree and singing its praises.

Dissle: To drizzle, rain mistily. A slight shower, drizzle. It makes a change from drizzle, monotony tinged with the faintest surprise.

Dog in the Sky: Rainbow end, a version of wind-dog.

Draby: Of weather, cold and wet.

Drachie, Drackie, Draghy: Damp, misty, murky, dull, dreary, rainy.

Drawk: To soak, drench. *Drawky*, rainy, drizzly.

Dreep: Drip, drop slowly.

Dribble: To rain slightly, drizzle.

Drouk, drook: To drench, soak.

These raindreeps make the world glisten with another shade. They set it at a different angle, like an Eskimo listing all the words for snow. These ones could do with being looked at too:

Dub: Mud, dirt. Why were the Dub Stores and the Dub Airport so dubbed?

Duff: Soft, spongy surface in bog. Spongy inferior stuff. A duff can-opener is one that doesn't work.

Dwamy: Giddy. *Dwam* is a swoon, faint, weak turn, sudden feeling of faintness, fit of sickness. *Dwamish, Dwamy*, adjectives for feeling sick. *Dwamly*, delicate. A dwamly child. Another Teuton monosyllable with a certain thrummy or twangy quality. Some place its origins in Lurgan, others on the coast of Donegal.

Other words, or some of them, that begin with D, and which the colonel thinks are dead good, flick out like this:

Dote: A foolish man. Term of endearment for a child.

Douce: Gentle, kind, sedate, quiet, grave, tidy, neat, prosperous. A sweet word this, mild and decorous.

Dozed: Of wood, decayed, unsound. Of people, stupid with drink or age. Well-known as the noun *dozer* and its opposite *no dozer*.

Drog: Slow, heavy swell in the sea.

Duskies, Duskiss: Dusk, twilight.

It could be that *Fortnight* readers believe that in 1984 it's pointless hoking up all these aged, half-forgotten or local words. What we may use in speech we must not set down on paper. Between the vernacular and the printed word there is a high wall plastered with signs like *Verboten*. And perhaps sometime far in the future a student of these times will examine this partitioned language? While Despard was talking to the Dover Street kids he saw an open book painted on a gable end—among other things it symbolised the vernacular, the honest and sacred current of the real world. Old Despard waits in hopes that people will float some stray words his way. He is hard at work compiling a list of words for "fool". Suggestions to Despard, c/o *Fortnight*, please.

FORTNIGHT 222, JUNE 24TH 1985

Frank Ormsby

DARKIES

They called themselves the North Fermanagh Branch
of the Brotherhood of Sleeping Car Porters:
Ben Champion, Lester Coleman, Burton Bazanne
escaped for the day from the Quartermaster Corps
to cycle the backroads,
the first "darkies" anyone could remember
in this part of the world.

In May they disappeared, their blood perhaps
acceptable at last to spill in France
or fill a Red Cross bottle. Long after, I recall
their voices raised in bitterness in Ma Kerr's
unsegregated tea-shop, their mock harmonies
on *Ole Man River*, the *Chocolate Soldiers* song.

I STEPPED ON A SMALL LANDMINE

I stepped on a small landmine in the *bocage*
and was spread, with three others, over a field
of burnt lucerne.
The bits they shipped to Georgia at the request
of my two sisters were not entirely me.
If dead men laughed, I would have laughed the day
the committee for white heroes honoured me,
and honoured too the mangled testicles
of Leroy Earl Johnson.

HIDING OUT IN THE TRIANGLE

GERALD DAWE

It was a choice between Art History in England or English in Northern Ireland. Queen's was too much like home and when a friend said he was going to NUU, that was it. We headed off from Belfast one September morning in 1971 and moved into the same B&B for the first term. The house was run by a businesslike woman who took good care of us and her house. Everything was in its place, put there with a kind of brisk love.

Going to university was not the logical thing to do. Most of my friends either hadn't bothered or didn't get the chance. We were, after all, children of the 1960s, full of grace, and it took some time to settle into the failed world that the 1970s brought. For some it meant a struggle; for others it felt like a defeat. Anyway, Coleraine in 1971 was a compromise. The campus looked like an airport, but behind it the Bann curved its way towards the coast and the magnificent sea along whose shoreline holiday resorts clung, full of three- and four-storeyed guest houses with great bay windows like puffed-out bellies, and a wind that would cut right through you.

It wasn't long before a few of us had banded together—mostly from Glasgow and Belfast—and joined the Labour Club. NUU's political birth had been uppermost in many minds but accepting the fact that it was there to stay, we sat in seminar rooms and discussed the Law of the Diminishing Returns of Profit and held a radical stall outside the Refectory every week. When things were looking bad, some of us formed the James Larkin Defence Committee and planned to get threatened Catholics out of isolated places into safety. And we went on marches to meetings and watched steadfastly as everything went from bad to worse. But we lived in a triangle that was symbolic in a way—between Coleraine, Portstewart and Portrush, the lines of experience were open and you could live freely, if experimentally, across the divides. Politics grew into Irish culture and back again into literature. We mixed into traditional music and some of the traditional musicians mixed into politics.

I started to play in a band called Fir Uladh and we performed at various venues from anti-internment rallies to folk concerts. It was blissful. And because I had written some poems that were published and broadcast, the Irish Dramatic Society asked me for a play. I wrote one, a short incoherent thing, the idea of which I'd lifted from Robin Flower's *The Irish Tradition*, and called it *The Skull*. It was duly translated into Irish, and travelling with it, I was proudly introduced once as "Our Belfast Protestant" to a smiling group of anxious Dublin *Gaeilgeoirs*.

We shared a year or two of confusion, mostly of my making, living within that strange triangle. The people who lived there were mostly hospitable to these students in their midst. Even though our lifestyle was, on the face of it, a challenge to their own, I never heard a bad word said against us and only ever in Coleraine did I hear the bigot come out in a person. He was drunk and on his way out of the bar. The group of us, from all over the north, Scotland and England, and from every "side", gazed at his ignorance and smiled sagely that this was the ugly old world shuffling off its mortal coil.

The three years did not last long. They were intense though. Everything was—sitting in the campus listening to the news about the Abercorn blast, watching the slow dismantling of Belfast and the places where we used to meet *back home*. Throwing darts in the university bar, while Walter Allen held court, sipping pink gins and smoking his endless untipped cigarettes, or ensconced in the Anchor Bar, nestled beneath the convent in Portstewart, there was an air of unreality about the whole time and place.

> **. . . between Coleraine, Portstewart and Portrush, the lines of experience were open and you could live freely, if experimentally, across the divides.**

The people of the triangle, however, lived their lives with a keen knowledge we did not have. They were wise before the event and had an almost stoical single-mindedness about what was happening around them as if it were a bad season they just had to thole. And us? The lectures went on as usual for those who cared to attend.

I remember, for instance, in one linguistics class, the distinguished lecturer, noted for his abstract convoluted manner and celestial gaze, talked us through the derivation of Cornish placenames while three ex-Oxfordians sat midway up the lecture hall regaled as Red Indians, warpaint and head-dresses, as a bet to show how oblivious the lecturer was of what went on before him!

Such frivolity disappeared with time. The atmosphere became more obsessive, nervous, shaky. We held together, a generation at sea, but slowly being roped back in by the past. Some returned home more often to discover brothers had been lifted by the police, badly beaten, interned; or a man down the road was murdered, or another Provie bomb had scorched the life out of this street or that, and the inevitable retaliation. Every day was becoming an aftermath of the wreckage from the night before.

The people grew suspicious, distant and hardened. Resentment spiked conversations. Still we walked the coastline, travelled further north, west and south, discovering "Ireland", and finally rented a fine house, five of us, overlooking the Atlantic. My last year was spent there mostly. The white surf from the sea staining the windows, the damp of that big bedroom with its awkward wardrobes, and the endless talk gripped by anger, uncertainty and the curse of everything that looked like going wrong.

The previous summer had shown up how fragile life actually was. Two of us were going to work June, July and August in the north of Scotland, building, of all things, an oil rig. We called down to Coleraine to book our flights and, wandering back to the little station, I could smell something acrid burning. In split seconds a bomb exploded some way behind us. People came slowly walking towards us, bewildered looks on their faces, calling out of shops to other people in doorways, and all the while streaming by us. They just kept coming and we called out to stay back, pointing at a solitary car in the road. But they kept coming and we turned into the railway station, stunned a little, disbelieving. In the train, there was no one but the two of us, so that when the second bomb went up it felt like somebody had shouted out in the eerie silence of the carriage. We gaped at each other as the train pulled out. "Jesus Christ," Joe said, "let's get the fuck out of here." Within a year all of us had left that part of the country.

Three years does not necessarily tell you much about a place. The triangle, within which NUU was, retains its wonder for me because of all that happened there. But sifting through those years I recall a craggy bit of the coast down below the High Road when all you could see was the white spume of a turbulent sea and a rake of gulls thrown up in the wind screeching to their hearts' content. There was something exhilarating and disquieting about it, the dilapidated hotel on down from where I was, its broken windows with curtains flying out of them and all those tall houses closed in on themselves, as if the people were hiding. Maybe they were. Maybe we all were.

APRIL 1975

INQUISITION
Ciaran O'Driscoll

The merest pocket book, its cover
a deeper pink than cherry blossom,
inside it was all newsprint,
the transcript of an interview
with God's press officer, a man
not given to wasting words.

"Who made the world?" "God."
"What is a sacrament?"
"An outward sign of inward grace."

With such accessible doctrine stored
in a small head-space, there was room
for extra-curricular imagination,
and those were years
of staring out the window,
green calling green
over the playground wall.

But then my father crossed
the diocesan boundary,
changing schools only three months
from my confirmation test,

and there was a different book,
full-sized, with a green cover,
illustrated—no compensation
for the new spokesman's verbosity.

Even the first, simplest response
had grown a grammatical tail—
"Who made the world?" "God made the world."
And Dr Butler's shrubbery
was now a bramble-thicket
where subordinate clauses choked
the outward sign, the inward grace.

Time contracted; the window
became a puzzle of straying geese,

an inquisition of green fields.

Note: Dr Butler's Catechism, used in Catholic schools in the
early 1950s, was remarkable for the brevity of its answers.

HERCULES, ANTAEUS AND PADDY

ROBIN GLENDINNING

I think it was the language that did it. The words "traitor", "shame", "ignominy", "enemy" and "betrayal" sounded so overblown as they reached me via the car radio. The venom with which they were uttered appeared melodramatic as did the imagery about "vipers" and "bosoms", and the suggestion that politics has been "prostituted".

It happened to my feet first. It felt as if my shoes were slowly turning into boots and the boots were growing into the large clumsy, mountainy variety of a time long past. The colourful rhetoric of the Ulster members as they questioned the Prime Minister on the Anglo-Irish Agreement in the House of Commons continued and I could detect the chuckles of other honourable members at its quaint biblical flavour.

When Mrs Thatcher raises them off the ground over in Westminster they are enfeebled, pathetic and defeated. But once back in Royal Avenue, Belfast . . .

My hands were now becoming lumpy, bulbous red and raw, as if from severe weather and much grubbing up of roots. On the radio, the desperate earnestness of a rural Ulster member was greeted with mock "ohhs" and "ahhhs" by sophisticates amused at his hyperbole. Ignoring this he continued, raising the volume and the dramatic timbre of his voice in the unmistakable rhythm of an evangelical

sermon. "The honourable gentleman is working himself up," said the Prime Minister with languid confidence and her 600-odd supporters laughed.

At that, the hat came down on my head covering my ears with its floppy brim. It was one of those semi-conical hats that 19th-century *Punch* cartoonists used to draw on their version of the archetypal Paddy. Under it my jaw thickened into a lantern shape and I scowled from beneath beetle brows. The metamorphosis was complete. I had been Paddy-ised.

I recalled this transformation in school the next day when my sixth formers successfully drew me off the subject in hand, *The Comedy of Errors*, to a free-ranging discussion of the Hillsborough agreement.

One of them put his studies in English literature to good use by quoting from a Seamus Heaney poem, "The Act of Union". Something about "parasitical and ignorant little fists beating at the borders of the tall kingdom". He then mentioned "Hercules and Antaeus"—another Heaney poem in which Hercules is England and Antaeus Ireland. Hercules is a civilising power who can defeat Antaeus when he raises him off the ground. But every time he is thrown down, Antaeus redoubles his strength. Heaney describes Antaeus as the "mould hugger". His power lies in "river veins", "secret gullies" and the "cradling dark"— in his language, his myths and his heritage.

The poem cleverly analyses the relationship between native and imperial power. "Supposing we see Mrs Thatcher as Hercules and the Ulster Unionists as Antaeus," I said. Ulster could well rank as the next labour of Hercules after the miner's strike. When Mrs Thatcher raises them off the ground over in Westminster they are enfeebled, pathetic and defeated. But once back in Royal Avenue,

Belfast, appealing to their heritage, their roots and their traditions, their power increases dramatically. The river veins and secret exit gullies are theirs too. Some of the class seemed to agree with me.

I am aware that a great many Ulster unionists have, rather arrogantly, seen themselves as the civilisers in this part of the world. They think *they* are Hercules. Indeed I can remember a rather embarrassing interview on a

Channel 4 documentary when a titled unionist, seated beside his baronial fireside, said exactly that in a most patronising manner. We came and planted and built and worked and civilised. The Irish were by implication savages. I didn't care for his arrogance but I suspect that the shock of my recent metamorphosis into Antaeus meant that I had unconsciously seen myself as a Hercules too. Now I know I am not.

FORTNIGHT 233, FEBRUARY 10TH, 1986

MOTHER SUPERIORS

JOHN MONTAGUE

Josie Mellon left the village early in the morning by the first train. The stationmaster was surprised to see her, dressed up to the nines, as he explained later to a large audience in the Dew Drop Inn. She wore a wide-brimmed floppy hat that might have belonged to a film star, an old-fashioned coat with padded shoulders, still crimped from its long wait in some cupboard or drawer, and a pair of platform shoes. In one hand she clutched a heavy snakeskin handbag, in the other her youngest daughter, startled and silent. Neither had ever been in the railway station before.

The journey to the county capital did not take long, the little train waving its plume of black smoke over the rushy fields. Brushing past the ticket barrier, Josie ignored the taxis, but marched, her daughter on the inside, down towards the distant, spired centre of the town. Once or twice people looked curiously at the pair, but she ignored them also, intent as a terrier.

Josie halted before a pair of wrought iron gates, carrying an elaborate inscription in blue lettering. A handyman working on a flowerbed looked up but did not move to help her as she lifted, pushed and pulled at the heavy gates. Finally she managed to open one, and herself and her daughter set off up the gravelled driveway.

It was a long walk for the child, especially as her mother kept tugging her by the hand. But there were bright flowerbeds and bushes to look at before they found themselves at the massive front door to which, the child thought, everything seemed to lead, like an ogre's castle. There was a brass knocker, higher than her head, and after drawing a deep breath, her mother gave it a sudden, smart bang.

When the huge door opened, a starched figure, all black and white, or black up to the neck and then white above,

looked questioningly down at the two strange waiting figures. But Josie did not falter. "I want to see your boss," she said, in her sharp, nasal Ulster accent. "I want the Mother Superior. As soon as you can, please."

It was the nun's turn to look out of place, flustered almost. "The Mother Superior,'" she repeated, in a puzzled tone, "do you—" but began to retreat before Josie's steady gaze and insistent demand. "Aye, the Mother Superior, I need t'll see her," said Josie, advancing. The nun backed, between two rows of religious pictures, down the bright corridor. "I'll try to find Mother," she flung back, "but she is usually quite busy. You must wait where you are."

The child found the size of the hall dazzling, like something out of a fairy tale, an empty ballroom in a palace. Everything was so clean and shining, and the holy pictures looked lovely, with pedestalled statues in the corners, big as in a church. And the black and white tiles looked as if you could slide on them, which she began to try. Her mother stood still, pointed, waiting.

**The nun's face was a mask beneath which incredulity simmered.
"You know how it is, sister, there's always a lot of lonely fellas in any town . . ."**

The Mother Superior did not take long, bustling through a glass door, rosary beads rattling at her waist, to confront her unplanned visitor. She also was a smallish woman, face scrubbed clean as a new pin, except for the thin, dark shadow of a moustache; as the child sang, or skipped by herself in the unaccustomed spaces of the hall, the two women stood face to face, not speaking. The Mother Superior did not offer her hand, looking uneasily towards the door before she frostily enquired:

"You wished to see me?"

"Right, sister," said Josie. "I do indeed. It's about me poor daughters."

"About your daughters?"

"Aye. I have five, you know. And I'd like you to take the two eldest."

"Take them—?"

"Aye, take them in here. Everyone speaks about the fine place you've got and the great job you do. I'd like my two to become young ladies too, not like me."

"And what do you do, Mrs . . .?"

"Josephine Mellon's the name, but they call me Josie, wee Josie after me father, Big Joe. I was reared hard. Mammy and Daddy both died when I wasn't much more than a cutie. Da was in the Fusiliers and he had a pension but he drank it. I had no chance at all till the War came."

The Mother Superior waited, at sea, but casting desperately for a sign. "You were in the War?" she managed, baffled. Who could this strange, scrawny little woman be, with her beady eyes, and old-fashioned getup, her funny clothes that smelt of the mothball?

"Ach no," said her visitor, impatiently. "Not officially. We'd be Nationalists, like yourself, I suppose: Da was only an accident, the only job he could find. But the troops were very good to me. I'd known fellas before but never fellas like yon."

The nun's face was a mask beneath which incredulity simmered.

"You know how it is, Sister, there's always a lot of lonely fellas in any town. But they have no money, our boys, only hit and run. Not like the Yanks, the doughboys as they called them. They were wild kind."

The little girl had temporarily exhausted the pleasures of sliding and then staring at a statue of the Immaculate Conception, blue-veiled on its polished pedestal. She came over and stood meekly near her mother, inspecting the strange, serious-looking lady talking to her, with her stiff, dark clothes and severe look. She touched the swinging Christ figure at the end of the Rosary with the tip of her finger, wonderingly.

"Stop, child. Biddy here's the youngest. I'd like to keep her with me till she grows up a bit. She's great wee company. But I'll send her along too if you treat the others well and give them the chance I never got. There's Teresa, and Bernie, and Maria and Agnes. I always tried to give them holy names, to call them after saints. Considering how they came into this world, it was the nearest to a good start I could give them."

The Mother Superior's face coloured a little; could this be genuine piety or was she being mocked?

"And what does the father think?" she managed, eventually.

"God look to your wit, Sister. Which father? Two of them died in that dirty old War; poor boys, I often pray for them lying so far away from home, without maybe even a cross over them. And before the Yanks came there was one Englishman but he never wrote to me. I believe he was married. The eldest is Irish though, one of our own. I know her daddy well."

Slowly the Mother Superior mastered herself, all kinds of emotion, from indignation to pity, were running riot through her bloodsteam. But how had this apparition, so shabby and out of place, yet so defiant, ever conceived the idea of coming to her, and to the convent door?

"And who advised you to come here?"

"Everybody in the town told me, all the corner boys. They said you were great, and would surely understand my case. Go to the convent, they said, that's where they'll be sure to take you in." She paused. "I thought they were only having me on, like, but then I asked the Blessed Virgin. After all, she was a mother herself, like me, though she only had the one boy. And God knows where we live in the Back Lane is not much better nor a stable."

A bell rang and the Mother Superior looked down at her watch. Her whole face had flushed and her eyes no longer faced those of her visitor.

"I'm afraid I shall have to go now," she said, ducking her forehead. "But I'll see you out. Perhaps you'll leave your name and address so that I can look into your case, Mrs . . ."

"Miss," said Josie emphatically, "I never caught one of them. Miss Josephine Mellon: everybody knows me." Her hand fumbled for the door knob. "I'm away now, anyway. We'll have to go straight back home. I have to make a bite to eat for the rest of them. You know how it is, at that age, you have so many of them. Mouths gaping wide as scaldies. Come on, now, Biddy dear. I'll get someone to write to ye and then they can read me back the answer when it comes. Goodday to you now, Mam. It was very kind of you to talk t'll us."

The Mother Superior stood watching as the pair dwindled down the avenue. Little Brigid ran over to gaze at a flowerbed once and then looked expectantly over towards her mother. But the mother called the child over just as she was bending down to pluck a blossom. Then they rounded the corner, out of sight, and in the distance she heard the insistent whistle of an approaching train.

KORMSKI

THE REV. **ANDREW LANARK** IS ON THE RUN FROM THE FORCES OF **LAW AND ORDER**.

HE IS BEING SHELTERED BY **REPUBLICANS** WHO THINK HE IS ONE OF THEM.

HE BELIEVES HIS NEWFOUND FRIENDS ARE **LOYALISTS**.

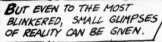

BUT EVEN TO THE MOST BLINKERED, SMALL GLIMPSES OF REALITY CAN BE GIVEN.

UP THE PROVOS! BRITS OUT

ER.. EXCUSE ME, I THINK I NEED TO GO TO THE **TOILET**.

ANDREW LANARK WAS AN OUTRAGEOUS BIGOT, WITH UNTENABLE VIEWS OF THE WORLD AND SOCIETY, BUT-HE WAS A **NICE GUY**. AND WE ALL KNOW WHAT HAPPENS TO NICE GUYS BOTH HERE AND ELSEWHERE. (CONSIDER THE FATE OF **MICHAEL FOOT**).

ACCIDENTALY MANGLED IN A TURNSTILE!

LATER..

POLICE ARE INVESTIGATING THE MYSTERIOUS DEATH OF THE REV. ANDREW LANARK, THE LOYALIST LEADER, WHOSE BODY WAS FOUND IN A MUTILATED CONDITION IN A NATIONALIST AREA..

THAT'S DISGUSTING HENRY! IT WAS AN UNFORTUNATE ACCIDENT AND THEY'RE MAKING IT SOUND AS IF..

POOR ANDREW! HE STOOD IN THE WAY OF **PROGRESS**

WHERE ARE YOU GOING HENRY?

TO CONSTRUCT THE **NEW ORDER!**

SO

THE SABBATH WAS MADE FOR MAN, NOT MAN FOR THE SABBATH.

DING! KLANG! BONG! DING DONG!

SWIMING POOL

REMEMBER TO KEEP IT HOLY.

LATER.. PERHAPS ITS TIME TO RE-ORGANISE THE **SCHOOLS MANAGEMENT COMMITEE..**

DARWIN JOYCE PLATO'S REPUBLIC CRACKLE! D.H. LAWRENCE NEW MATH

THEY SAY THAT IF YOU BEGIN BY BURNING BOOKS YOU WILL END BY BURNING PEOPLE.

FIRST THINGS FIRST HENRY! LETS DEAL WITH THIS FILTH FIRST, THEN WE'LL TALK ABOUT CAPITAL PUNISHMENT!

EVOLUTION

BACK AT THE MANSE.

WELL HENRY, HAS THE MILLENUM BEGUN?

REPORT

IT'S GOING TO BE A LONG STRUGGLE BRID, BUT THE WORD FROM THE DUBLIN ASSEMBLY IS THAT THE FINANCIAL SITUATION MAKES THE APPOINTMENT OF A **SUCESSOR** TO **ANDREW UNLIKELY..**

PRESBYTERIAN GENERAL ASSEMBLY REPORT

SO PERHAPS I CAN RE-OPEN THE DIALOGUE WITH MY COLLEAGUE ON THE OTHER SIDE OF THE SECTARIAN DIVIDE...

KNOCK! KNOCK! KNOCK!

HOT LINE

I'LL GET IT!

FOSTER'S THE NAME. REFORMATION'S THE GAME!

IF YOU THOUGHT THAT **ANDREW LANARK** WAS A **BIGOT** YOU HAVEN'T MET THE **REAL THING!**

A MESSAGE FROM THE "BIG DOC"

G. U. B. U.

It is with a deep sense of honour and humility that *Fortnight* presents the full text of the State of the Province speech delivered by His Excellency "Big Doc", Reverend Ian Paisley, President for Life (DV) of the Independent Republic of Ulster, broadcast on IRUTV yesterday.

"My friends and fellow Ulstermen, most of you will remember those tumultuous days, 10 years ago, in July 1986, when I, as leader of our glorious Unionist Movement, signed the Declaration of Independence which saved our fair province from the clutches of Dublin, Rome and Moscow. Do you recall how the Jeremiahs scoffed and the Weeping Willies threw up their hands, as the hated British oppressors finally over-ran our Provisional headquarters in Marks and Spencers?

"Who can forget the scenes as they led our young men across Donegall Square to be summarily executed outside the City Hall, underneath the traitorous banner erected by the rump of the City Council, with the help of the damned turncoats of the RUC, claiming that 'Belfast Says Yes'? Even they should have known that Belfast never says yes.

"They all thought we were finished. And I don't mind admitting that for a few brief moments I feared we were. The loss of so many fine men—my deputy, Field Marshal Robinson, Commander of our First Army Group, and of course James Molyneaux who, contrary to the wicked rumours that he had only entered Marks to negotiate a surrender, in fact impetuously rushed to join in the armed struggle. The loss of these and all the others was a heavy blow.

"But God was on our side. For, almost as the sad news was arriving at my bunker in Ravenhill, I also received a request for political asylum from Jean-Claude Duvalier, a world statesman who had chosen our small country, in preference to all others, in which to make his home. Only posterity will know the debt we owe to him, to his vast resources—made freely available to me—and to his generous loan of the Tontons Macoute, that fine body of men who have ensured stability, security and peace in our once strife-torn fatherland. Considering all he did during the Civil War against the miserable Cushnahanites and renegade McCusker, it was indeed a bitter irony that he should have passed away last Wednesday in a hunting accident, only a few short days before the tenth anniversary of Ulster independence. And may I add here that scurrilous suggestions of government complicity in this unfortunate incident have been proved absolutely unfounded by an impartial inquiry headed by myself.

"So our celebrations this year must be tinged with a little sorrow. Nevertheless, men of Ulster—and women too, for you also have your role to play—we can justifiably look back with pride upon the first decade of Ulster independence, which will last for a thousand years, or at least until the end of the world.

"There are inevitably some birth-pangs in the creation of any state and ours was no exception. The abolition of unemployment and supplementary benefits, made necessary by the economic warfare waged on us by the perfidious Lundys of Westminster, was of course a difficult hurdle. But I think you will agree that it has made us leaner, fitter and more dynamic.

"And our policy of selective assisted emigration has made us a more homogeneous society. For the implementation of this plan, I am indebted to another great statesmen

MARCH 1986

Blotski

who sought asylum here in 1986, former President P. W. Botha. The 'Bantustans' as he calls them, in Fermanagh, Tyrone, Derry and south Armagh, will soon be granted full, though guided, autonomy within the Provincial Federation. Romanists will then be free to practise their Satanic rites in their own countries to their hearts' content.

"I am aware that some of you are finding it hard to get used to the design of the Ulster Housing Council's award-winning Vernacular Dwelling. Research has shown that thatched roofs and earth walls are the most energy-efficient form of domestic building and use materials which are available to all. So successful has this design been, that I hear it is being copied in northern England, where it is called 'the Thatcher House'! Once the Sperrins uranium mine comes into production, I can assure you that we will seriously consider providing loans towards the purchase of roofing thatch and sods of earth.

"I recently had the pleasure of opening the Rhonda Paisley Arts Complex on the site of the former Whiterock Leisure Centre . . ."

"Things are also looking up on the economic front. Harland, Wolff and Paisley recently announced orders for two tugs and a dredger from Saudi Arabia. Once again, our low wage costs have allowed us to undercut shipyards in Korea and Calcutta. And Short Brothers, Duvalier & Co. have found a new market in Peru for their world-beating hot-air balloons.

"Tourism has again this year been a mainstay of our economy. The casinos in Bangor—or Duvalierville, as it will be known from now on—have proved a great success, and Nico 'The Knife' Corleone richly deserves the Red Hand Medal which I shall present to him at Scarva tomorrow.

"Less obvious, but no less important, is the contribution of 'invisible' exports. Ulster now has 25,000 offshore companies, mainly in the financial and banking sectors, and one adult in five is a director of at least one foreign-owned company. The advantages of liberal tax, banking and company laws mean that more and more entrepreneurs are considering setting up an office in Ulster. The contribution of all those ex-London brokers, forced out of the former financial capital of the world by so-called anti-corruption laws, cannot be overestimated.

"In the field of the arts, Ulster leads the world. I recently had the pleasure of opening the Rhonda Paisley Arts Complex on the site of the former Whiterock Leisure Centre. And I and my good lady wife finally managed to find time to see *A Great Victory for King Billy* by Graham Reid, now entering its third stupendous year at the Grand Opera House. In the music world, our own Rev William McCrea is at the top of the Ulster charts and who among us has not shed a silent tear as the steel guitar wailed on his poignant record, 'My Wee Vernacular Home'?

"Law and order, of course, is one of our highest priorities. We still have isolated outbreaks of criminality around the border areas, but I am confident that our policy of separate development, the erection of the Martin Smyth Line and germ warfare will soon put a stop to that. The Diplock witch trials continue apace in Ballymena and I can assure you that no ducking-stool will be idle in the months to come.

"So, to sum up, I feel I can fairly claim that the year since 12 July 1995 has been one of achievement and consolidation. The way has not been easy in the world for our beloved province. We have had to weather many storms but the sou'wester of faith and the oilskins of loyalty have kept us dry. Wrapped in the weatherproof gear of God's Holy Word, who can say us nay?

"My friends and fellow men of Ulster, Happy Twelfth, Ulster for Ever, Kick the Pope. I thank you."

AN ULSTER SONGBOOK

G. U. B. U.

Country-and-western music, as we know from the career of Rev William McCrea, is the authentic voice of the Ulster people. However, its transatlantic origins mean that few of its songs are strictly relevant to the particular circumstances of our own favourite recording stars. Therefore, as a contribution to the cultural reassessments encouraged by the Anglo-Irish Treaty, and to the continuing artistic renaissance of the province, *Fortnight* offers a selection of new, relevant, Irish-and-Northeastern songs, to be sung by our leading public figures.

For James Molyneaux

WHY DON'T YOU LOVE US?
(to the tune of "Like You Used to Do", as recorded by Hank Williams)

1
Why don't you love us like you used to do?
Not all of us are scrounging on the broo.
Our hearts are still loyal and we're red, white and blue,
So why don't you love us like you used to do?

(*Chorus*)
Ain't had no Stormont with majority rule
In a long, long time.
Can't even run our own wee country
And that's a crime.

2
You were a Unionist in days of yore,
Now you see faults which you ignored before.
Somebody's changed, and it isn't us Prods,
You're a Republican, and we think it's odd.

(*Chorus*)

3
Why don't you say the things you used to say?
Why do you treat us in this off-hand way?
You ran off to Dublin, didn't give us a clue:
Why don't you love us like you used to do?

For Rev Ian Paisley

UDI Now
(to the tune of "Jambalaya", as recorded by Hank Williams)

1
Goodbye Brits
Because it's
UDI now.
Gonna fight
Day and night
For UDI now.
As a Prod
I swear to God
It's UDI now.
Won't have Rome:
It's gonna come—
UDI now.

2

You tried before
By the back door
To have power-sharing.
Stopped it then,
Will again:
No power-sharing!
It's gotta stay
The British way:
No power-sharing!
Because Hume's
In league with Rome,
No power-sharing!

For John Hume

ME AND GARRET FITZ-G

(to the tune of "Me and Bobby McGee", as recorded by Kris Kristofferson)

1

Marchin' up in Derry town,
Waitin' for a change,
Feelin' as hard-done-by as could be;
Charlie helped us out sometimes
But things still stayed the same,
The Unionists wouldn't talk to the SDLP.
Then I got together
With Garret and and Ronald Reagan,
And said I needed help to stop Sinn Féin;
With money from America
The Anglo-Irish process then began,
And things will never be the same again.

(*Chorus*)

Irish is another word for nothin' left to lose,
The Republic ain't worth nothin' but it's free,
The Dublin way was easy, Lord, when it came to choose,
The Anglo-Irish Treaty's down to me,
The whole thing's down to me and Garret Fitz-G.

2

From the Parliament at Strasbourg
To the White House, Washington,
Garret shared the secrets of my plan.
We exposed the Unionists
And everything they'd done,
And people told us, "We'll do what we can."
But Garret's in big trouble now,
And Dessie's on his way,
Says he wants to break free from the past:
Goodbye to twenties attitudes
That plagued us yesterday;
When you break the mould the world starts changin' fast.

(*Chorus*)

For Peter Robinson

TAKE THESE TAIGS

(to the tune of "Take These Chains From My Heart", as recorded by Ray Charles)

1

Take these Taigs from our land and let us keep
Our own cosy wee province, half-asleep.
All our trust in you is gone,
But we're loyal, every one;
Take these Taigs from our land and let us sleep.

2

Take this Treaty, scratch it out and tear it up;
Garret's nice, but we fear you've bought a pup.
He says he'll stop the IRA,
But just think what you've thrown away;
Take this Treaty, scratch it out and tear it up.

3

If you think that Big Ian's a hard man,
Think again, 'cos I'm here with my own plan.
Let Jim Molyneaux be your pet,
For you ain't seen nothin' yet
If you think that Big Ian's a hard man.

For Gerry Adams

YOU CAN NEVER TRUST THE BRITS

(to the tune of "Help Me Make It Through the Night", as
recorded by Kris Kristofferson)

1

Take the Treaty you have signed,
Tear it into little bits.
Do you think we've lost our minds?
You can never trust the Brits.

2

It's a ploy to help John Hume
Fight the challenge from Sinn Féin.
We don't dance to Maggie's tune:
Never trust the Brits again.

(*Chorus*)
We will never sell you out,
We will go on with the war.
Dublin is as bad as Downing Street,
As we've pointed out before.

3

It's because of what we've done
With ballot-box and Armalite.
If we go on killing Brits
Things eventually will turn out right.

Coda
We will take power in this land:
Things eventually will turn out right.

FORTNIGHT 250, APRIL 1987

THE ACT

FOR MICHAEL LONGLEY AND JAMES SIMMONS

TONY HARRISON

Newcastle Airport and scarcely 7 am
yet they foot the white line out towards the plane
still reeling (or as if) from last night's FED
or macho marathons in someone's bed.
They scorn the breakfast croissants and drink beer
and who am I to censure or condemn?
I know oblivion's a balm for man's poor brain
and once roistered in male packs as bad as them.
These brews stoke their bravado, numb their fear
but anaesthetise all joy along with pain.

To show they had a weekend cunt or two
they walked as if they'd shagged the whole world stiff.
The squaddies' favourite and much-bandied words
for describing what they'd done on leave to birds
as if it were pub-brawl or DIY
seem to be, I quote, "bang", "bash", or "screw",
if they did anything (a biggish if!)
more than the banter boomed now at the crew
as our plane levels off in a blue sky
along with half-scared cracks on catching syph.

They've lit Full Strengths on DA 141
despite NO SMOKING signs and cabin crew's
polite requests; they want to disobey
because they bow to orders every day.
The soldiers travel pretty light and free
as if they left Newcastle for the sun,
in winter with bare arms that show tattoos.
The stewardesses clearly hate this run,
the squaddies' continuous crude repartee
and constant button pushing for more booze.

I've heard the same crude words and smutty cracks
and seen the same lads on excursion trains
going back via ferry from Stranraer
queuing at breakfast at the BR bar,
cleaning it out of Tartan and Brown Ale.
With numbered kitbags piled on luggage racks
just after breakfast bombed out of their brains,
they balance their empty cans in wobbly stacks.
An old woman, with indulgence for things male,
smiles at them and says: "They're nobbut wains!"

Kids, mostly cocky Geordies and rough Jocks
with voices coming straight out of their boots,
the voices heard in newsreels about coal
or dockers newly dumped onto the dole
after which the army's the next stop.
One who's breakfasted on Brown Ale cocks
a nail-bitten, nicotined right thumb, and shoots
with loud saliva salvos a red fox
parting the clean green blades of some new crop
planted by farm families with old roots.

A card! The stewardesses almost throw it
into our laps not wanting to come near
to groping soldiers. We write each fact
we're required to enter by "The Act":
profession; place of birth; purpose of visit.
The rowdy squaddy, though he doesn't know it
(and if he did he'd brand the freak as "queer")
is sitting next to one who enters "poet"
where he puts "Forces". But what is it?
My purpose? His? *What* are we doing here?

Being a photographer seems bad enough.
God knows the catcalls that a poet would get!
Newcastle-bound for leave the soldiers rag
the press photographer about his bag
and call him Gert or Daisy, and all laugh.
They shout at him in accents they'd dub "pouf"
Yoo hoo, hinny! Like your handbag pet!
Though what he's snapped has made him just as tough
and his handbag hardware could well photograph
these laughing features when they're cold and set.

I don't like the thought of these lads manning blocks
but saw them as you drove me to my flight,
now khakied up, not kaylied but alert,
their minds on something else than Scotch or skirt,
their elbows bending now to cradle guns.
The road's through deep green fields and wheeling flocks
of lapwings soaring, not the sort of sight
the sentry looks for in his narrow box.
"Cursed by dullards whom no cannon stuns"
I quote. They won't read what we three write.

They occupy NO SMOKING seats and smoke,
commandos free a few days from command
which cries for licence and I watch them cram
anything boozeable, Brown Ale to Babycham,
into their hardened innards, and they drain
whisky/lemonade, Bacardi/Coke,
double after double, one in either hand,
boys' drinks spirit-spiked for the real *bloke*!
Neither passengers nor cabin crew complain
as the squaddies keep on smoking as we land.

And as the morning Belfast plane descends
on Newcastle and one soldier looks,
with tears, on what he greets as "Geordie grass"
and rakes the airport terrace for "wor lass"
and another hollers to his noisy mates
he's going to have before their short leave ends
"firkins of fucking FED, fantastic fucks!"
I wish for you, my Ulster poet friends,
pleasures with no rough strife, no iron gates,
and letter boxes wide enough for books.

THE ORIGINS OF THE FARSET—
FOR MY FATHER
Fred Johnston

My true guide into this old territory
is your informal love:
then there is the rediscovery of language
a texture of steel and poverty, yet
from Shaw's Bridge the view is still of two
lovers under a canopy of sun and memory
invoking each other's assurances:
the gantries splay-legged in a rusty horizon
my aunt's telephone-voice, her inquiry,
the sudden violence of that Easter fife-
and-drum and all the lost little empires
of your childhood and mine:

in a pub we speculated on the origins
of the Farset, knowing it flowed now
under streets flagged in red, white and blue
and for the first time in years I felt home-
sick for the redbrick and bakery smells,
the only air I can breathe guiltless and
without anticipation:

the starlings around the City Hall still
call out of nights full of Land Rovers and
teenagers in love, but I've come back to it
and reaffirmed it for ever, and halfway down
the motorway I want to get off the 'bus and
hitch back into its terraced heartlands and
take in a lungful of the gasworks air when the
shipyard has spilled its day-shift mobs over
the bridges and all the sleekit wee pantomimes
of the pubs and betting-shops are fused
into homely night

the iron gateways of Royal Avenue swinging
closed
on lovers scurrying for taxis.

A WEDDING PICTURE
Kerry Campbell

The air above the lawn is flecked with gold insects
and contained by sycamore, cypress and yew.
Beyond their tops and the abbey ruins,
the September sky is blue.

The bride and solid bridegroom stand at the angle
on what remains of the monks' high-stair.
She smiles, her veil flutters, her hand is in his hand,
posed for the photographer.

The young photographer has kept the party happy,
preened aunts, restless cousins, all looking their best
in group shots behind the airy refectory,
with bridesmaids, pageboys and the rest.

The lumpy bridegroom now shifts from the picture,
leaving the white bride upon the stair,
ready, for her special solo portrait,
to obey the photographer . . .

who, touching her arm like a flower or a bird's wing,
apart from groom and guests, intent on her,
with gentle authority suggests her image,
a butterfly hand upon her hair.

The big groom, backslapping a jolly cousin,
plays up to the relatives' Polaroid band.
The photographer helps the bride from the night-stair,
with a last touch of his gentle hand.

FORTNIGHT 256, NOVEMBER 1987

OPENING UP: A NEW PLURALISM

The north, as a province in two contexts, is like a cultural corridor, suggests EDNA LONGLEY. Unionists and nationalists seek to close it off at either end—it can't be done.

Since the early 1980s literary critics have been arguing about relations between literature and politics in Northern Ireland. Who cares? I hear you ask. But arguments about culture, like arguments about ideology, ultimately affect people's material situation. One reason why unionism finds itself in its current abject state is that it has allowed nationalism to monopolise cultural politics. This blind spot can be disarming—even preferable to the spectacle of Charles Haughey draping himself in any available artistic flag. However, a belated attempt to promote "Ulster British Heritage and Culture" (of which more anon) confirms that a potentially dangerous vacuum exists.

Ireland's binary politics have consistently misrepresented its cultural plurality. Nor is it only the border that divides what is linked or links what is divided. In what follows I will be concentrating on *literary* culture: a narrowing of focus perhaps more excusable here than elsewhere. "This tiny stage", to quote Louis MacNeice, pulls literature towards the general orbit of society, and other media have only recently disputed the primacy of the word.

Few would deny that, over the last 20 years, Ulster's literary output has improved in quality as well as quantity. (Those who deny it are mostly diehards from a Dublin-centred universe.) Whether or not this phenomenon continues, it needs to be thoroughly absorbed and examined. And not merely by the transatlantic and continental academics now converging on "the northern play" and "the northern poem". The creative spark has had repercussions in publishing ventures, the dissemination of local history, reprints, community arts, regional arts centres, school and university syllabuses. But this fall-out still only touches the surfaces of the community in which the writing originated, and which—however obliquely—it defines. Indeed, the overall dynamic must be bound in with processes of communal self-definition, with the felt inadequacy of rigid political categorisation.

Among works published or performed during the last year are: Paul Muldoon's *Meeting the British*, James Simmons's *Poems 1956–1986*, Seamus Heaney's *The Haw Lantern*, Sam Hanna Bell's *Across the Narrow Sea*, Anne Devlin's *The Venus de Milo Instead*, Stewart Parker's *Pentecost, Ancestral Voices: Selected Prose of John Hewitt*, Ciaran Carson's *The Irish for No*. It cannot be repeated too often that the cross-sectarian interaction of such expressions complicates the *political* cliché of "two traditions". At the same time, of course, a writer may draw on the resources of Gaelic literature, or follow Hewitt's interest in Rhyming Weavers, or discover affinity as well as difference in Anglo-Ireland, or "owe his soul" (as Yeats confessed he did) to Shakespeare and Spenser—or to Philip Larkin. The point is that one of these influences cannot operate by itself alone. (Nor do I believe that by taking thought a writer can become exclusively receptive to models from the USA or Eastern Europe.) It is sad that Northern Ireland as a whole does not enjoy the plural possibilities explored by its writers, or by such conjunctions as the Belfast Folk Festival.

The Irish for No, indebted on the one hand to the shanachie, on the other to a galaxy of Eng Lit, both amalgamates and ironically observes the various literary and linguistic claims staked in this territory:

> It was time to turn into the dog's-leg short-cut from
>   Chlorine Gardens
> Into Cloreen Park, where you might see an *Ulster Says No*
>   scrawled on the side
> Of the power-block—which immediately reminds me of
>   the Eglantine Inn
> Just on the corner: on the missing *h* of Cloreen, you might
>   say. We were debating,
> Bacchus and the pards and me, how to render *The Ulster
>   Bank—the Bank*
> *That Likes to Say Yes* into Irish, and whether eglantine was
>   alien to Ireland.

Historically, unionists have distrusted literary culture—not only because of Calvinism, the business ethic, the fear of free speech (hence the Sam Thompson trauma), but because it might be latently "Irish". The Irish Literary Revival remains nationalist in unionist folk-memory, whatever latter-day critics of its "colonialism" may say. The suspicion lingers that the only safe artistic occasion is one blessed by the Queen Mother. It is high time that the political connotations of "Irish" ceased to sabotage its cultural uses (as has happened long since within literature itself). Nationalism still sometimes claims Ulster Protestants as Irish, sometimes not, according to the rhetorical

tack being pursued. Since Protestants divine in this inconsistency the unacceptable alternatives of assimilation and expulsion, they tread warily around "Irish" unless preceded by "Northern". The more subtle manifestation of "the siege mentality" is a sense of being excluded, rather than self-excluded, from political Irishness.

All this signifies not a Protestant "identity crisis"—another cliché ripe for the shredder—but the identification crisis which requires a secure guarantor of who they are. "Are you British or Irish?" is a meaningless question, since "Irish" may be at once an identity and an allegiance, "British" only an allegiance, equally open to the Scots and Welsh. *The Crack*, Sally Belfrage's book of Belfast reportage and interviews, quotes some well-intentioned remarks from a priest which exemplify the unconscious exclusions underlying apparent inclusion: "The unionist people . . . are Irish in a lot of ways, much more Irish than they'd admit, and would be much more Irish if they didn't feel threatened or didn't feel it would be misunderstood." This notion that Irishness is some quantifiable state of grace illustrates the need to break down the term.

The concept of "Ulster British culture" . . . is a misconceived antithesis to an earlier misconception: the dying ideology of primordial Irishness . . .

Of course northern Catholic understandings of Irishness are inevitably more atavistic than attitudes in the Republic: a hotbed of literary as well as historical revisionism. There, for instance, Paul Durcan recently became so enraged with the application of political boundaries to poetry—north as well as south—that he declared himself a *British* poet too: "I refuse to let Margaret Thatcher come between me and John Dryden." Vice versa no Ulster Protestant should let Charles Haughey or Gerry Adams come between him and Nuala ní Dhómhnaill. When Gerald Dawe and I edited a book of critical esssays, *Across a Roaring Hill: The Protestant Imagination in Modern Ireland*, we were accused of colluding in sectarian categories. "Declare your unionist/nationalist colours" cried reviewers (Declan Kiberd, Enoch Powell), insisting on political categories instead. In fact the book's emphasis contended that religious denomination is the basic cultural determinant; that "Irish literature" can more usefully be regarded as the diversified construction of Catholics and Protestants than as a "national" chat-show with peculiar guest-artists; that it is as much the work of Louis MacNeice in London as of James Joyce in Paris.

However, neither Joyce nor MacNeice owe it all to Ireland. In *Irish Review* (no.2) Peter McDonald warned:

> That MacNeice's work has relevance, particularly for contemporary writers in the north, has become obvious, but it is important not to ignore certain problems involved in admitting the poet to an Irish pantheon. Whatever his exemplary status for contemporary poetry, MacNeice's standing as "Irish", considered in a more historical light is problematic, and begs as many questions as does his inclusion in an "Auden generation"; its problematic nature may itself yet turn out to be exemplary, forcing as it does a confrontation with those differences on which an "Irish" culture will have to be built.

The extent to which 20th-century Irish writing meshes with English writing remains an area troubled by politics (hence Durcan's outburst). For instance, Yeats's soul-debts either tend to be over-stressed—when he is called "unionist"—or overlooked. Because Anglo-Ireland has vanished, some of its positive implications for Northern Ireland are forgotten. And the multiple ties between the republic and Britain have been largely inadmissible to political rhetoric.

In my view the Field Day cultural project, with its initial anti-colonial thrust, unduly suppressed these ties (it was Seamus Deane who called Yeats unionist). However, Field Day's horizons have widened, and the following prospectus for its forthcoming *Anthology of Irish Writing* stresses pluralism:

> Field Day sees the anthology as an important act of definition which will show how the various groups, sects and races which have intermingled in Ireland have produced a literature which is unique to them and an achievement which makes manifest what they have in common.

Yet the anthology might just as interestingly manifest what they *don't* have in common. Unitary preconceptions or assimilative impulses ("unique to them") pre-empt the reader's own judgement. Nor can the anthology itself—since anthologies exclude as well as include—be an "act of definition". That belongs to the sum total of relevant texts. And the definition *of* literature, as well as definition *through* literature, is a still-volcanic process. A welcome feature of the Field Day anthology will be Tom Paulin's attention to the Ulster Protestant oratorical tradition in its preacherly and political guises. This is certainly a first for any canon. Nevertheless, the anthology's format, especially when beamed at North America (why not at Ulster?) tends to make the literary pieces fit a prescribed jigsaw shape—the map of Ireland—instead of investigating the shape they make by themselves.

When unionism, as opposed to the individual Protestant, notices literature, it lunges in its two characteristically self-defeating directions. First, it takes the high road, the lofty "citizen of the world" or at least "equal citizenship"

road: "In Finaghy as in Finchley I can read Iris Murdoch and I'm really looking forward to the RSC at the Festival." There's something in this, and proponents of local culture must face the levelling effect of paperbacks and TV. Yet those who live by imported culture increase their chances of getting exported (cf the Anglo-Irish). The planter's root "struck into the soil" (John Mitchel) goes deeper than this. Such abdication to the metropolis also travesties MacNeice's complex tracing of his cultural co-ordinates, let alone Yeats owing his soul to Shakespeare.

Certainly we are witnessing the last spasms of the Green and Orange state-ideologies which literature long ago found unworkable.

The second unionist road is the low road: retreat into a UDI bunker where Cuchulainn is forced to cohabit with Amanda McKittrick Ros. The study of Orange artefacts (if divorced from their triumphalist flaunting) contributes to self- and mutual-awareness, as does appreciation of the townland bards. But John Hewitt did it all so much better 40 years ago, without shutting off Ulster's other cultural dimensions, without propaganda. The selective appropriation of Samuel Ferguson, for instance, shows "Ulster British culture" to be a jigsaw with many missing pieces. Ferguson as epic bard does not escape rebuke for putting Cuchulainn on the wrong map: "In his political innocence, Ferguson provided Gaelic nationalists with material for propagating the mythical notion of a sovereign Gaelic nation beyond the mists of time." Ferguson's complex career, which cannot be subsumed into today's simplicities, dramatises all the confusions and possible fusions. It is a good thing that creative innocence rushes in where political caution fears to tread.

The concept of "Ulster British culture" (as distinct from Ulster's participation in British culture) is a misconceived antithesis to an earlier misconception: the dying ideology of primordial Irishness, which only Sinn Féin and unionist demonising keep on the life-support system. Daniel Corkery and the politicisation of the Gaelic League still have much to answer for. Conscripting Cuchulainn and the questionable Cruthin is of course principally a means of saying "No, *we* were here first." It corresponds to a trope which recurs within the less crudely territorial consciousness of Ulster poetry: here a dolmen, there an omphalos symbolising ancient title. I feel that Paul Durcan's satirical poem "Before the Celtic Yoke", in which Ireland wistfully recalls the days before anyone turned up, should be the last word on all these misty

144

matters, unless it is Ciaran Carson's joke as to "whether eglantine was alien to Ireland". Perhaps we should take note of the controversy about when certain snails got here.

The literature produced by Ulster people suggests that, instead of brooding on Celtic and Orange dawns, its inhabitants might accept this province-in-two-contexts as a cultural corridor. Unionists want to block the corridor at one end, republicans at the other. Culture, like common sense, insists it can't be done. Ulster Irishness and Ulster Britishness are bound to each other and to Britain and Ireland. And the republic will have to come cleaner about its own *de facto* connections with Britain. Only by promoting circulation within and through Ulster will the place ever be part of a healthy system.

And cultural regionalism, again within two further contexts, seems the only possible underpinning of the only rational political outcome—devolution, power-sharing. As Bob Purdie showed in his article on Scotland (*Fortnight* 255), unitary ideas of Britain as well as of Ireland are now being challenged. (John Hewitt took his original regionalist cue from Scotland and Wales.) Certainly we are witnessing the last spasms of the Green and Orange state-ideologies which literature long ago found unworkable. There are two failed *conceptual* entities on this island—hence the agonised self-scrutiny now going on in the south. But unionism must catch the revisionist tide. It might catch up on its reading too.

FEBRUARY 1987

Blotski

FORTNIGHT 279, DECEMBER 1989

THE DUBLIN–BELFAST RAILWAY LINE
Paul Durcan

What I want is free travel
For the heroic democrats of the IRA.
What I want is to put them aboard
The Dublin–Belfast train for six months;
Have them travel up and down the line
Six times a day for six months.
I want them to get to know
All about trains, all about train travel.
I want them to get to know
Every embankment on the line,
Every landscape they have not deflowered,
Every bridge they have not groped,
Every wild hedgerow they have not
Buggered a virgin under.
I want the townspeople of every town

On the line to come out
At the stations and applaud our heroes
Go up and down the line,
Up the down line and down the up line.
I want the heroic democrats of the IRA
To enjoy the benefits of train travel:
The tenacity of luggage racks;
The cups of coffee at sixty miles per hour.
At the end of six months
On the platform at Belfast Central
I want to hear each of them
Swear an oath on a copy of *Mein Kampf*
To the unification of Ireland
With or without trains,
With or without passengers.

$\underline{29}$
12

1690, in this tercentenary year, is one thing. But the organisation founded in 1795 to resist the United Irishmen is quite another. Recalling memories of Twelfths past, GLENN PATTERSON reminds us that, two centuries on, the Orange Walk is no folk festival.

Huge gobs of yellowness spatter the quivering window of blue-white on the living-room wall, then gradually dissolve into the close-up smiling faces of two toddlers, who sit, side by side on a kerb, waving plastic Union Jacks. Behind them are two rows of adults (one seated, one standing), more flags, a dense privet and a pair of pre-war semis backing on to a valley. In front of them is a broad road which is beginning to fill with marching men, some with flutes, some with drums (though the only sound in the room is the whirr of the projector), others carrying swords and wearing fringed sashes. And, bobbing along in their wake, an orange ribbon ("sash" would be overstating it) draped from collarbone to hip-bone, is me, aged 13. Twelfthing.

At the very moment that I (as was) arrive centre frame, I hesitate slightly and glance over my shoulder and I (as am) freeze the film, looking back at myself looking back.

Thirteen, therefore my 14th Twelfth, though only the sixth that I can attach a year to with confidence, for it was not until a month after my eighth that I heard gunfire in the night and became rooted in time. A couple of miles away, at the source of that sound, people were dying, among them a boy not much older than I was, shot while sheltering in his bedroom. I read of their deaths the following day in the *Belfast Telegraph*—my first recollection too of seeing the name of my city.

The next Twelfth, my ninth, the army was on duty along the route of the Belfast parade. One soldier lifted me up into his ferret car, parked at the bottom of Finaghy Road South, and I watched from behind its protective armour as the bands and lodges wheeled right, off the Lisburn Road, over the railway bridge to Finaghy field. Being eight and new to the subject, I not unnaturally ascribed historical significance to the choice of destination and thought Finaghy must be a very important place. The year after that, though, the parade went instead to Edenderry and all future thoughts of "over the bridge" were dominated by what lay at the top of Finaghy Road North, Andersonstown. (The old field was eventually converted into sports grounds, or, as it was indignantly reported south of the bridge, *Gaelic pitches*.)

Shortly after my 13th birthday, I caught the train home to Finaghy from Lisburn baths. The station name had been obliterated by graffiti: "Fuck the Queen", "Up the Provos". Half a dozen boys my own age or slightly older watched from the top of the bridge as I climbed the steps from the platform. I was so scared I couldn't speak when they asked me what I was. Very considerately they asked me just to point where I lived. I pointed south. They lived north. They kicked my lights in.

"If you aren't walking with us," the looks said, "you must be against us" . . .

"It'll harden you," my friends said, "taking the train."

The next Eleventh night, drunk on lager stockpiled through June ("Mister, mister, go into the offie for us. Aw, mister, go on, just one can. Thanks, mister . . ."), I cruised the bonfires looking for Twelfth kisses. The Eleventh night exceeded even New Year's Eve in its potential for licence. I succeeded in lumbering (a long-forgotten word that captures the technique perfectly) one girl who let me squeeze my hand down the front of her high-waister trousers. I kept it there, motionless, for five minutes before finally withdrawing it. I don't know which of us was more relieved.

Needless to say my hand didn't stay still when I bragged about it to my friends the next day, the day I walked with the men for the first time.

My father was standing with his home-movie camera at the roundabout below Barnett's Park. He filmed two toddlers grinning and waving plastic Union Jacks while he waited for the procession to appear. And he filmed me as I passed by, looking back over my shoulder.

I have caught up with myself. The projector whirrs on, my head jerks round again and I continue across the living room wall, facing forward.

146

I never did walk with a lodge again, though in subsequent years I followed this band or that—the more "kick-the-Pope" the better—to the field. On my 17th Twelfth, which was not, in fact, on the 12th at all, I followed one band I knew as it made its way between skyscrapers and shopping malls to a pedestrian precinct in downtown Toronto. (There are at least three Twelfths that I know of besides the *Twelfth* Twelfth: the Wee, the Scottish and the Canadian—something to do, perhaps, with the *Twelfth* Twelfth's own migration from 1st July. Indeed I would not be surprised to learn that there are as many different *Twelfth* dates as there are countries with Orange lodges to observe them.)

I had sat my "O" levels the previous June and was in Canada visiting relatives. I attended socials in a Rangers' Club-cum-bandhall west of Toronto and heard "The Protestant Boys" sung in the bug-crackling darkness of late-night poolside parties. One *emigré* Orangeman I met told me how he'd laid out some dumbfuck Canadian with the mace for attempting to cross the road during a parade:

"Bastard nearly broke the ranks," he said.

I suppose it was the vastness of Canada that made this belligerence over a matter of feet sound so absurd, so irrelevant. But, of course, I was wrong. Nothing could have been more relevant. For if the essence of the Twelfth is not contained in the destination of the march (take your pick: Belmont, Finaghy, Edenderry, Toronto), nor, ultimately, in the date, then it can only lie in the act of marching itself. The Twelfth is the march and the march is the demonstration of nothing so much as the ability to march when and where the marchers please. The medium is the message and must remain inviolate.

Though I trace the roots of my disaffection back to that summer in Canada, I did not formulate these thoughts until a couple of Twelfths later, my 20th (held on the 13th, a Monday, as if to prove the point about date, though ostensibly to keep the Sabbath holy). Trying to reach a friend's house in the university area of Belfast, I found myself walking down the Lisburn Road away from town as the parade and its followers were walking up. It was the summer of the hunger strike (indeed a prisoner had died that very morning) and the ranks were even closer than usual. I had never before felt myself to be so conspicuously out of step, nor experienced such hostility in my own city.

"If you aren't walking with us," the looks said, "you must be against us," and I understood then something of the psychological threat Catholic friends had talked of feeling when they heard the pounding of Orange drums. (Green drums are equally terrifying, but of course they are kept well away from the city centre.) When I finally reached my friend's house I was shaking with fear.

The next Twelfth I spent with my girlfriend in a cinema in Dublin and the Twelfth after that I was in England—for good, or so I told myself.

Yet here I am, back in Belfast, running home movies of Twelfths past. A band crosses the living room wall. Friends

MARCH 1984

of mine half a lifetime ago. I would have been walking beside them that day if I hadn't been such a tube on the flute, for despite months of practice I only ever mastered two tunes: "The Queen" and "The Billy Boys".

There has been much talk lately of emphasising the folk-festival aspect of the Twelfth, restoring the carnival atmosphere of "the old days before the troubles"—a reference, no doubt, to the fun-filled folk festivals of 1857, 1864, 1872 etc., or the famous York St carnival of 1935. The suspicion of the minority community, this argument runs, is based on a misunderstanding of what is really being celebrated.

But there is no ambiguity in a song like "The Billy Boys": "We're up to our necks in Fenian blood, surrender or you'll die." The truth of the matter is, of course, that the Twelfth has never aspired to ecumenism and no amount of tercentennial revisionism can disguise the fact that the Orange Order has its origins not in the 1690s but in the bitter sectarian warfare of a century later. The Twelfth is by its nature divisive and, in its embolic, intrinsically militaristic progress through the streets of Northern Ireland, it is an annual reminder of the power of the past to mobilise and paralyse in one.

Coda: Sunday afternoon. Two lodges shuffle, rather than march, into view behind the bandsmen whose shoulders dance a decoy lambada while their feet do little more than mark time.

They pass, eventually, but the bald-brake screech of the flutes lingers in the air, mocking the traffic backed up in their wake. Fiestas, Novas, 205s and a Daihatsu 4WD idle past my flat. (It seems that wherever I see a flute band these days I see a Daihatsu 4WD crawling along forlornly behind it.) Someone's engine, tired of just ticking over, cuts out completely. The whole line comes to a standstill. An Escort XR3i stops below my window, sunroof down, radio up, blasting out this year's ubiquitous summer sound, the Ter(se-)centenary Rap:

> No Surrender
> No Pope Here
> NOT AN INCH

The Lambeg-drum-machine, programmed to the boom of an IRA railway bomb, thunders on, accentuating the negative.

PART FOUR

CHRONOLOGY OF EVENTS
1970–90

PREFACE

TO CHRONOLOGY OF EVENTS
1970–90

I would like to apologise for certain omissions in this chronology that were forced by shortage of space. The first and most important is that very, very many of the deaths arising from the "troubles", all of which were recorded in the pages of *Fortnight*, are not included, not to mention the enormous number of injuries incurred. In particular, single deaths are far from fully represented. It is very important to bear in mind that the "troubles", at almost any time, have occurred against a background of sectarian murders which, apart from the early 70s, have been directed much more heavily against the Catholic community. At the same time murders of individual RUC officers, British soldiers and members of the UDR have been similarly omnipresent over the past 21 years and, equally, here go largely unrecorded.

Other areas which the *Fortnight* diary of events covers well—the economy, government spending and employment issues—are, in this editing, included only when of particular significance.

No attempt has been made systematically to check the accuracy of each entry—this would, besides being a Herculean task, be ultimately impossible, so many incidents being subject to conflicting witness accounts and interpretations. That said, obvious anomalies and inconsistencies have been checked and resolved as far as they could be. With regard to these I would like to thank Bern Kane, John Rainey and Marion Duffy, of the Northern Ireland Political Collection at the Linen Hall Library, for all their help.

Lastly I would like to express thanks to all those who have, over the last 21 years, laboured with a largely thankless task—the writing of the diary of events. Everyone who, on any level, studies the politics and history of this place uses the diary regularly. All are grateful to its compilers for its brevity and at the same time its objectivity and depth.

As *Fortnight* began publishing in September 1970, this chronology does not cover the preceding events from 1968 onwards. For these, readers should turn to volume one of Richard Deutsch and Vivien Magowan's *Northern Ireland 1968-73: a chronology of events*.

ROBERT BELL
BELFAST
FEBRUARY 1991

LIST OF ABBREVIATIONS

ACE	Action for Community Employment
AOH	Ancient Order of Hibernians
BBC	British Broadcasting Corporation
CCDC	Central Citizens Defence Committee
CIA	Central Intelligence Agency (USA)
CIE	Coras Iompair Éireann (republic's public transport company)
DPP	director of public prosecutions
DUP	Democratic Unionist party
EC	European Community
FBI	Federal Bureau of Investigation (USA)
FEA	Fair Employment Agency
GAA	Gaelic Athletic Association
GLC	Greater London Council
GOC	general officer commanding
ICJP	Irish Commission for Justice and Peace
INLA	Irish National Liberation Army
IPLO	Irish People's Liberation Organisation
IRA	Irish Republican Army (Provisional/Official)
IRSP	Irish Republican Socialist party
ITN	Independent Television News
LAW	Loyalist Association of Workers
LPAF	Loyalist Prisoners Action Force
NCCL	National Council for Civil Liberties
NICRA	Northern Ireland Civil Rights Association
NILP	Northern Ireland Labour party
NIO	Northern Ireland Office
Noraid	Irish Northern Aid (republican support group in the USA)
NUJ	National Union of Journalists
PAF	Protestant Action Force
PD	People's Democracy
PDs	Progressive Democrats
PLO	Palestine Liberation Organisation
PR	proportional representation
RTE	Radio Telefis Éireann
RUC	Royal Ulster Constabulary
RVH	Royal Victoria Hospital
SARAF	South Armagh Republican Action Force
SAS	Special Air Service
SDLP	Social Democratic and Labour party
TD	Teachta Dála (member of the Dáil)
TUC	Trades Union Congress
UDA	Ulster Defence Association
UDI	unilateral declaration of independence
UDR	Ulster Defence Regiment
UFF	Ulster Freedom Fighters
ULCCC	Ulster Loyalist Central Co-ordinating Committee
UN	United Nations
UP	Unionist party
UPNI	Unionist Party of Northern Ireland
UPUP	Ulster Popular Unionist party
USC	Ulster Service Corps
UUAC	United Unionist Action Council
UUAP	Ulster Unionist Assembly party
UUP	Ulster Unionist party
UUUC	United Ulster Unionist Council
UUUM	United Ulster Unionist Movement
UUUP	United Ulster Unionist party
UVF	Ulster Volunteer Force
UWC	Ulster Workers' Council
VPP	Volunteer Political party
VUPP	Vanguard Unionist Progressive party

1970

Fri. 4.9.70: One Provisional IRA member was killed and another seriously injured while trying to plant a bomb at New Forge Lane, Belfast.

Tues. 15.9.70: Members of the Royal Ulster Constabulary (RUC) voted by a narrow majority to remain unarmed. Three hundred and twenty Protestant families left the Ballymurphy/Springfield area of Belfast.

Tues. 22.9.70: The trial began in Dublin of Charles Haughey, Neil Blaney, and two others on charges of conspiracy to import ammunition and arms into the Irish republic.

Thur. 24.9.70: Derry's Nationalist party announced it would join the Social Democratic and Labour party (SDLP).

Sat. 26.9.70: Following an incident when Linfield football club supporters were passing Unity Flats in Belfast, there was a night of serious rioting on the Shankill, which continued the next day with many injuries to police, army and civilians.

Sat. 10.10.70: Serious rioting broke out in Derry and lasted until the following Monday.

Wed. 21.10.70: Bernadette Devlin was released from Armagh prison after serving four months of a six-month sentence for her role in the Bogside riots in Derry in August 1969.

Fri. 23.10.70: The Dublin arms conspiracy trial ended with all four defendants found not guilty.

Thur. 29.10.70: Two days of serious rioting began in the Ardoyne area of Belfast.

Wed. 4.11.70: The RUC chief constable, Sir Arthur Young, admitted a "conspiracy of silence" among RUC men about the identity of the officers involved in the fatal assault on Samuel Devenny in Derry in April 1969.

Tues. 17.11.70: The new RUC chief constable, Graham Shillington, was sworn in.

Sat. 28.11.70: A Northern Ireland Civil Rights Association (NICRA) rally in Enniskillen, Co Fermanagh, met a counter-demonstration led by Rev Ivan Foster, but there were no clashes.

Tues. 1.12.70: For the first time in 40 years an award (of £75) was made under the Special Powers Act for damage caused during an army search (of a house in the Lower Falls in Belfast in July).

Thur. 17.12.70: The Stormont prime minister, James Chichester-Clarke, announced the government's acceptance of the MacRory report on local government reform.

Wed. 23.12.70: Fr Robert Murphy of Newtownards, Co Down, was nominated as the first Catholic chaplain at Stormont.

Thur. 31.12.70: Local authority elections were postponed until March 1st 1971 to allow time to implement reforms including "one man, one vote".

1971

Sun. 10.1.71: Troops and police began searches in the Ballymurphy area of Belfast that were to last all week, giving rise to continuous rioting.

Sun. 17.1.71: The Stormont prime minister, James Chichester-Clarke, postponed a visit to the USA because of the new outbreak of violence.

Mon. 18.1.71: Frank McManus, Westminster MP for Fermanagh/South Tyrone, was jailed for six months for taking part in the banned NICRA march in Enniskillen on November 28th.

Sat. 23.1.71: Clashes between returning Linfield football club supporters and police at Unity Flats in Belfast led to rioting on the Shankill, which spread to the Crumlin Road and continued the following day.

Sun. 31.1.71: A six-month ban on processions expired at midnight, with Paisleyite, civil rights and Apprentice Boys parades scheduled for the following week.

Wed. 3.2.71: Local women and girls objected to house searches in the Kashmir Road and Clonard areas of Belfast. This later escalated into "defensive" rioting, the setting up of barricades, and the burning of vehicles. There were machine-gun attacks on army posts on the Crumlin and Malone roads.

Thur. 4.2.71: The new army general officer commanding (GOC), Lieut-Gen Erskine Crum, arrived in Northern Ireland. The commander-in-chief, land operations, Maj-Gen Anthony Farrar-Hockley, blamed rioting on the Provisional IRA and named five of its alleged members.

Fri. 5.2.71: Beginning with stone-throwing between schoolchildren in the Crumlin Road area of Belfast, rioting and gun battles were reported in many areas of the city and in Derry.

Mon. 8.2.71: There were riots and shots were fired in the Ardoyne and New Lodge areas of Belfast after the death of a child involved in an accident with an army scout car.

Tues. 9.2.71: Three construction workers and two British Broadcasting Corporation (BBC) engineers were killed when a mine exploded under their Land Rover near the transmitter on top of Brougher Mountain, Co Tyrone.

Sat. 13.2.71: The wearing of military-style uniforms by the IRA or other "subversive organisations" was banned.

Thur. 18.2.71: Lieut-Gen Harry Tuzo was appointed army GOC. Lieut-Gen Erskine Crum had suffered a heart attack.

Sun. 21.2.71: Six women in combat uniforms protested against the "internment by remand" of three men held for the previous two weeks for wearing military-style uniforms at the funeral of a man shot during street violence.

Tues. 23.2.71: A bill amending the Firearms Act was published making the offence of discharging a firearm in a public place, including churchyards and cemeteries, punishable by a mandatory six-month sentence.

Thur. 25.2.71: The Stormont prime minister, James Chichester-Clarke, had a private meeting with the Catholic primate, Cardinal Conway, reported to be the first of its kind in 50 years.

Fri. 26.2.71: Women in military-style uniforms protested outside the Custody Court in Chichester Street, Belfast. Thirty women and six men were arrested. It was claimed that no action was taken against Protestant counter-demonstrators.

Sat. 27.2.71: There was a night of rioting in the Markets area of Belfast. Two policemen were shot dead by gunmen in Alliance Avenue in Ardoyne, and troops returning fire claimed two hits. Other policemen were injured by gunshots in the Glen Road area and by a bomb at Ligoniel police station. In total, explosions were reported in seven parts of the city.

Sun. 28.2.71: The RUC was issued with flak jackets and bullet-proof vests.

Mon. 1.3.71: In the Bogside area of Derry a military policeman died when his Land Rover was attacked and set on fire in the early hours.

Thurs. 4.3.71: The home secretary, Reginald Maudling, visited Northern Ireland.

Fri. 5.3.71: Rioting broke out in the Leeson Street area of Belfast after searches by police and soldiers. It was to last several days. An explosion damaged the RUC station at Roden Street.

Mon. 8.3.71: The Leeson Street area of Belfast was again barricaded with hijacked buses. Gun battles followed between the Official and Provisional IRAs, in which one man died and several were wounded. A truce was negotiated that night.

Wed. 10.3.71: The bodies of three young soldiers of the Royal Highland Fusiliers were found in the Ligoniel area of Belfast. The killings, eventually ascribed to members of the Provisional IRA, were widely condemned.

Fri. 12.3.71: Four thousand shipyard workers marched to the Unionist party headquarters in Belfast demanding immediate internment of IRA leaders.

Tues. 16.3.71: The Stormont prime minister, James Chichester-Clarke, flew to London for talks with the British prime minister, home secretary and defence secretary, and the army GOC.

Sat. 20.3.71: The defence minister, Lord Carrington, and the chief of staff, Sir Geoffrey Baker, flew in to Aldergrove for a day of talks with security chiefs and the Northern Ireland cabinet. James Chichester-Clarke resigned as prime minister.

Tues. 23.3.71: Brian Faulkner was elected prime minister by the Unionist parliamentary party, by a majority of 26–4 over William Craig.

Thur. 25.3.71: The new Stormont cabinet was announced. It included David Bleakley of the Northern Ireland Labour party (NILP) as minister of community relations and Harry West, Unionist MP for Enniskillen, as minister of agriculture.

Tues. 30.3.71: The Stormont prime minister, Brian Faulkner, announced an amnesty for unlicensed arms until April 8th. More than 1,000 weapons and nearly 100,000 rounds of ammunition were handed in.

Sat. 3.4.71: There was an extensive search for arms in Ballymurphy in Belfast, drawing crowds and stone-throwing.

Tues. 6.4.71: Uniformed Provisional IRA men were amongst hundreds who formed a guard of honour in Belfast to meet the cortege of a Provisional IRA man who had been killed in a shooting accident at an IRA training camp in the republic. Intensified activity by security forces in the Falls area of Belfast provoked protests from opposition Stormont MPs and community leaders.

Tues. 13.4.71: Followers of a junior Orange parade in east Belfast broke through a police cordon and entered Catholic streets. The army opened fire and later said that four people, including a 12-year-old, were admitted to hospital. Rioting followed in the Newtownards Road district. Rev Ian Paisley condemned the "brutal actions" of the troops.

Sun 18.4.71: The Republican Clubs, political wing of the Official IRA in the north, called for republicans to refuse to fill in their census forms in protest against repressive legislation.

Mon. 26.4.71: More than 40 priests and the Stormont Nationalist MP James O'Reilly said they would refuse to fill in their census forms.

Mon. 3.5.71: There were five explosions in Belfast during the night, two at the homes of senior officers of the RUC Special Branch.

Tues. 4.5.71: The Stormont prime minister, Brian Faulkner, said intelligence reports showed no evidence of any group "other than one with republican aims" being responsible at this time for explosions.

Sat. 8.5.71: The mother of John McKeague, chair of the Shankill Defence Association, died in her flat above a hardware shop in east Belfast when an explosion set fire to the premises.

Wed. 12.5.71: An attempt to introduce a bill of rights for Northern Ireland in the Commons at Westminster was defeated by 175 votes to 135.

Thur. 13.5.71: The Northern Ireland Housing Executive held its first meeting in Belfast.

Fri. 14.5.71: An Ulster '71 exhibition was opened in Belfast by the lord mayor of London, Sir Peter Studd.

Tues. 18.5.71: Frank McManus, Westminster MP for Fermanagh/South Tyrone, was released from prison, having served four months of his six-month sentence.

Wed. 19.5.71: The Stormont prime minister, Brian Faulkner, said that the Orange Order had agreed to hold fewer parades in the coming season.

Fri. 21.5.71: Troops made charges and searches in the New Lodge Road in Belfast, after a second day of trouble between workers at the Gallaher tobacco factory. Later, in a raid on the Starry Plough bar, 30 men, including prominent Catholic politicians, were taken to Glenravel RUC station.

Sat. 22.5.71: At a crowded British Legion hall in the Suffolk area of Belfast, several people were injured by a bomb thrown through a window.

Sun. 23.5.71: A meeting of more than 1,000 people in the New Lodge Road condemned the "brutality" of the soldiers in their recent actions there.

Mon. 24.5.71: The Mountain View Tavern on the Shankill Road in Belfast was wrecked by a blast bomb which caused several injuries.

Tues. 25.5.71: A suitcase bomb thrown into the reception area of the Springfield Road barracks in Belfast killed an army sergeant who threw himself on the bomb, trying to protect children.

Wed. 2.6.71: For the first time in Northern Ireland a man was charged under the Incitement to Disaffection Act for handing out leaflets to soldiers urging them to desert.

Thur. 3.6.71: John McKeague and two other committee members of the Ulster Loyalist Association, who had become the first to be charged under the Incitement to Hatred Act, appeared before Belfast magistrates' court. John Taylor, minister of home affairs, said it had not been possible to establish how confidential RUC information had come into the hands of Rev Ian Paisley, but he accepted it was deplorable.

Tues. 8.6.71: In a television interview, the army GOC, Harry Tuzo, said a permanent solution could not be achieved by military means.

Sun. 13.6.71: At a banned Orange procession in Dungiven, Co Derry, Orangemen broke through a police cordon and tried to rush an army barrier. Some 300 engaged the army in stone-throwing and hand-to-hand fighting, before being dispersed by rubber bullets and CS gas.

Wed. 16.6.71: The Ancient Order of Hibernians (AOH) decided to call off its August parades in order to reduce the burden on the security forces.

Sat. 19.6.71: The Ministry of Defence announced that the army would in future spray coloured dye on rioters.

Sun. 20.6.71: Incendiary devices left in Belfast shops the previous evening caused several fires—a camping store in High Street was destroyed. Two explosions later damaged city-centre premises.

Tues. 22.6.71: In a major speech, the Stormont prime minister, Brian Faulkner, outlined proposals for participation by members of the opposition as chairs of parliamentary committees.

Mon. 28.6.71: Brian Faulkner, along with five senior ministers of state and their parliamentary secretaries, travelled to the headquarters of the Royal Black Institution in Lurgan for talks with the Orange and Black orders and the Apprentice Boys about forthcoming parades.

Tues. 29.6.71: Harry West, minister of agriculture, resigned from the West Ulster Unionist Council.

Wed. 7.7.71: An unprecedented inter-party meeting was held at Stormont, attended by representatives of the Unionist party, the SDLP, the Nationalist party and the NILP.

Thur. 8.7.71: During the fourth successive night of rioting in Derry, a man was shot dead by the army. After mourning processions and demonstrations, another was shot dead.

Mon 12.7.71: Shortly after midnight, 10 explosions caused extensive damage and injured nine pedestrians along the route of that day's Orange procession to Finaghy in Belfast. The march went off peacefully.

Fri. 16.7.71: After the previous day's announcement that there would be no inquiry into the deaths of the two Derry men killed on July 8th, SDLP MPs announced a boycott of Stormont and the setting up of their own "non-sectarian, non-unionist assembly".

Sat. 17.7.71: The *Daily Mirror* printing plant in the Suffolk area of Belfast was severely damaged by a large bomb.

Fri. 23.7.71: In joint army/RUC dawn raids, 48 people were taken in for questioning. Maire Drumm was found guilty on IRA charges and sentenced to six months' imprisonment.

Wed. 28.7.71: The home secretary, Reginald Maudling, said there was a state of war between the army and the IRA and he was prepared to introduce internment.

Mon. 2.8.71: The army carried out further dawn searches across Northern Ireland.

Sat. 7.8.71: Widespread rioting and shooting followed the shooting dead of a civilian whose van had backfired outside Springfield Road RUC station in Belfast.

Sun. 8.8.71: In the early hours a soldier was shot dead in the Ardoyne area of Belfast. Rioting spread throughout the city. Six other soldiers and four civilians were injured by gunfire.

Mon. 9.8.71: The Stormont government introduced internment. In dawn raids throughout Northern Ireland 342 men were arrested. A six-month ban on processions was also announced. There was extensive rioting in Belfast, which spread to Newry, Strabane, Armagh and Derry. By the end of the day two soldiers and eight civilians were dead. Meanwhile, in the Ardoyne area of Belfast, some 100 Protestants, claiming intimidation, left and set fire to their homes.

Tues. 10.8.71: Rioting on a scale not seen since 1969 broke out in Belfast and Derry. Thirteen people were reported killed in shooting incidents. In widespread burning of houses by both Protestants and Catholics, approximately 240 homes were destroyed.

Wed. 11.8.71: Violence and shooting continued, the death toll since the introduction of internment rising to 23. Seventy of those interned were released, detention orders being served on the remainder.

Thur. 12.8.71: More than 7,000 refugees from Belfast were reported to have arrived in army camps in the republic. The taoiseach, Jack Lynch, called for the abolition of Stormont.

Sat. 14.8.71: After a meeting of nine Stormont opposition MPs, the SDLP leader, Gerry Fitt, announced a non-violent civil disobedience campaign.

Wed. 18.8.71: A man who was said to be a deaf mute was shot by the army after a meeting in Strabane, Co Tyrone, addressed by the Mid-Ulster MP, Bernadette Devlin. The army claimed he had been armed. In Derry, security forces broke up a sit-down demonstration with water cannon, rubber bullets, CS gas and batons and arrested the SDLP Stormont MPs John Hume and Ivan Cooper, though both were later released. The prime minister, Brian Faulkner, travelled to Chequers for talks with the British prime minister, Edward Heath.

Tues. 24.8.71: The GOC, Gen Tuzo, announced an independent inquiry into allegations of ill-treatment of internees. But it was later announced that this would not be public, bringing calls for a boycott.

Wed. 25.8.71: A bomb exploded at the Electricity Board office on the Malone Road in Belfast, killing one employee and injuring 16.

Thur. 26.8.71: A one-day strike against internment was observed in various towns in Northern Ireland.

Sun. 29.8.71: Two army scout cars strayed across the border into Co Louth and were surrounded by a hostile crowd who set fire to one of them. After the patrol returned north, one of the soldiers was shot dead.

Wed. 1.9.71: There were explosions in Belfast, Bessbrook, Derry, Dungannon and Newry.

Thur. 2.9.71: Joseph Cahill, a leading Provisional IRA figure, was refused entry into the United States. There were three large explosions in Belfast city centre, including one at the Unionist party headquarters. Forty civilians were injured, eight seriously.

Mon. 6.9.71: At a mass rally in Victoria Park, Belfast, attended by 15,000–20,000 people and addressed by the former home affairs minister, William Craig, and Rev Ian Paisley, a "third force" was demanded.

Sun. 12.9.71: Bernadette Devlin, MP for Mid-Ulster, was amongst the speakers at a mass anti-internment rally in west Belfast, attended by about 15,000 people.

Mon. 13.9.71: Desmond Boal, Stormont MP for Shankill, announced his resignation from the Unionist party over Brian Faulkner's decision to attend tripartite talks with the republic's and Britain's prime ministers.

Tues. 14.9.71: Twelve internees were released, including Michael Farrell and Kevin McCorry of People's Democracy (PD).

Sun. 19.9.71: The 219 people still interned were ferried in helicopters to a new camp at Long Kesh, Co Antrim.

Mon. 20.9.71: Twenty-five people were injured by a bomb in the Bluebell bar on Sandy Row in Belfast.

Sun. 26.9.71: David Bleakley, minister of community relations, resigned from the government in protest against internment and the lack of political initiatives.

Tues. 28.9.71: A communiqué issued at the end of the tripartite talks at Chequers said only that all three prime ministers had agreed that violence and emergency measures should be brought to an end as soon as possible.

Thur. 30.9.71: An explosion at the Four Step Inn on the Shankill Road in Belfast killed two men and injured 20, bringing sectarian clashes in the city the following day.

Sun. 10.10.71: One woman was killed and nine people wounded in an explosion in the Fiddler's House, a bar in Durham Street in Belfast. More than 5,000 people attended a peace rally in the Botanic Gardens.

Thur. 14.10.71: There were gun battles between IRA men and the army in east and north Belfast, the Creggan in Derry, and near Forkhill, Co Armagh.

Fri. 15.10.71: Two RUC men were shot dead at the junction of the Woodvale and Crumlin roads in Belfast.

Sun. 17.10.71: Seven hundred shots were estimated to have been fired in a protracted gun battle between the IRA and the army in the Short Strand area of Belfast.

Mon. 18.10.71: Labour leaders met the British prime minister, Edward Heath, to discuss allegations of brainwashing and torture of internees at Palace Barracks, Holywood.

Tues. 19.10.71: Students at Queen's University prevented the arrest of Tomás Mac Giolla, president of Official Sinn Féin, by barricading the Students' Union and keeping him overnight. The following day Mr Mac Giolla was allowed to drive back over the border unmolested.

Thur. 21.10.71: The Payments for Debt (Emergency Provisions) Act was passed to counter the rent and rates strike against internment. It allowed for deductions from wages or state benefits.

Sat. 23.10.71: Soldiers shot dead two women in a car in the Falls area of Belfast, claiming they had been fired upon. Witnesses disputed this.

Sun. 24.10.71: The army shot and killed three youths attempting to rob a man lodging money at a night safe in Newry, Co Down, causing extensive rioting. In Belfast police shot and killed a man planting a bomb in Donegall Place and seriously wounded his woman companion. The bomb exploded just after midnight.

Tues. 26.10.71: A riot in one of the compounds at Long Kesh was brought under control by troop reinforcements.

Wed. 27.10.71: Two soldiers were killed in a bomb attack in Derry and an RUC man was shot dead in Toomebridge, Co Antrim.

Fri. 29.10.71: An explosion demolished Chichester Park RUC station in Belfast, killing an inspector.

Sat. 30.10.71: The Democratic Unionist party (DUP) was launched by Rev Ian Paisley at a rally in the Ulster Hall in Belfast.

Mon. 1.11.71: A statement, signed by 387 priests, alleging brutality and torture against internees, was distributed internationally. Two RUC detectives were shot dead in the Andersonstown area of Belfast while investigating a burglary.

Tues. 2.11.71: The Red Lion, a bar on the Ormeau Road in Belfast, was destroyed when gunmen planted a bomb and gave only a 10-second warning. Three people were killed and 36 injured.

Tues. 9.11.71: Amnesty International called for an independent inquiry into "serious and apparently substantiated allegations of ill-treatment of internees". The Woodbourne House Hotel in the Suffolk area of Belfast and the Toddle Inn in York Street were destroyed by bombs.

Thur. 11.11.71: Two RUC men were shot dead in a bar while making routine inquiries in north Belfast. Twenty thousand workers downed tools and marched in Belfast protesting at the visit of James Callaghan, Labour's shadow home secretary.

Sun. 14.11.71: All Remembrance Day parades were banned to ease the burden on the security forces.

Mon. 15.11.71: Frank McManus, Westminster MP for Fermanagh/South Tyrone, was amongst those arrested in incidents involving the filling-in of cratered roads on the border on this and previous days.

Tues. 16.11.71: The report was published of the inquiry, under Sir Edmund Compton, into the treatment of internees. It found no evidence of brutality but found that ill-treatment had taken

place during interrogations. Nine men escaped from Crumlin Road prison in Belfast. Three more escaped the following Thursday.

Sat. 4.12.71: Fifteen people were killed and eight injured when a no-warning bomb exploded in McGurk's bar in Belfast.

Wed. 8.12.71: An Ulster Defence Regiment (UDR) private was shot dead in his home in Caledon, Co Tyrone, and another the following day in New Barnsley in Belfast.

Sat. 11.12.71: Four people, including two young children, were killed in an explosion in a furniture store on the Shankill Road in Belfast.

Sun. 12.12.71: A Unionist senator, Jack Barnhill, was shot dead and his house in Strabane, Co Tyrone, was partly demolished by a bomb. The attack, claimed by the Official IRA, was widely condemned.

Wed. 15.12.71: The home secretary, Reginald Maudling, said he could foresee a time when IRA violence could be reduced to an "acceptable level".

Thur. 16.12.71: The republic's government filed a complaint at Strasbourg against the British government, alleging infringement of six articles of the European Convention on Human Rights.

Sat. 18.12.71: Three men were killed when a bomb they were transporting in a car went off in Magherafelt, Co Derry. A 16-year-old barman was killed when a bar in Mayo Street in Belfast was destroyed by a bomb.

Thur. 23.12.71: The British prime minister, Edward Heath, visited troops in Armagh, Belfast and Derry and met the Stormont premier, Brian Faulkner.

Sat. 25.12.71: In Belfast about 1,000 marchers defied the ban on parades and marched along the M1 motorway to protest against internment.

1972

Mon. 3.1.72: Sixty-two people were seriously injured when a no-warning bomb went off in Callender Street, Belfast, while it was full of shoppers.

Thur. 6.1.72: It was announced that a second internment camp would be opened at Magilligan, Co Derry. Fifty internees from HMS *Maidstone* were transferred there by helicopter 10 days later.

Mon. 17.1.72: Seven internees escaped from HMS *Maidstone,* swam the Musgrave Channel, hijacked a bus and disappeared into the Market area of Belfast.

Tues. 18.1.72: A bus driver, Sidney Agnew, who was to appear as a witness in a case involving the hijacking and burning of his bus, was shot dead at his home. The Stormont prime minister, Brian Faulkner, announced that the ban on parades would be extended for another year, bringing angry reaction from Orange leaders.

Sat. 22.1.72: Civil rights marchers defied the ban on parades in Armagh and Magilligan, where there was hand-to-hand fighting with troops on the beach.

Wed. 26.1.72: There were 14 bombs throughout Northern Ireland including two in Belfast,

154

several in Newry and four in Castlewellan, where a bomb-planter was killed. William Craig announced a series of rallies in defiance of the government ban.

Sat. 29.1.72: Several thousand troops kept civil rights marchers off the streets in Dungannon, Co Tyrone.

Sun. 30.1.72: Bloody Sunday—13 protesters were shot dead in Derry by British paratroopers following violence which broke out at the end of a civil rights rally in which 20,000 people took part.

Mon. 31.1.72: There were protests in towns throughout Northern Ireland about the killings in Derry. In Andersonstown, west Belfast, vehicles, shops and the offices of Bass Charrington were burned. There were two explosions in central Belfast. Petrol bombs were thrown at the British embassy in Dublin and the republic's ambassador to Britain was recalled. Bernadette Devlin physically attacked the home secretary, Reginald Maudling, in the Commons.

Tues. 1.2.72: The British prime minister, Edward Heath, announced the setting up of a tribunal of inquiry, under Lord Chief Justice Widgery, into the shootings in Derry. Violence continued in Belfast and there were outbreaks in Strabane, Dungannon, Armagh and Lurgan. A bomb was thrown at the British embassy in Dublin.

Wed. 2.2.72: A crowd of 20,000–30,000 attacked the British embassy in Dublin, burning it down. Catholic-owned premises throughout Northern Ireland were closed and 20,000 people attended the funerals in Derry of those shot on Bloody Sunday.

Thur. 3.2.72: There were explosions in Derry and Armagh and troops came under fire in several incidents in Belfast.

Sat. 5.2.72: There were demonstrations over the Derry shootings in Glasgow, Cardiff, Birmingham and London.

Sun. 6.2.72: A civil rights rally in Newry attended by about 20,000 people passed off without incident, but the following day 26 summonses were issued—recipients included several MPs—for breaking the ban on marches.

Wed. 9.2.72: Maurice Hayes resigned as chair of the Community Relations Commission, claiming security policies were alienating almost the entire Catholic community.

Sun. 13.2.72: A new loyalist movement, Ulster Vanguard, led by William Craig, held its first rally in Lisburn, Co Antrim. At Enniskillen, Co Fermanagh, about 7,000 supporters of the Northern Resistance Movement held an anti-internment march. A rally in support of the IRA at the GPO in O'Connell Street in Dublin was addressed by Francis McGuigan, a recent escaper from Long Kesh.

Mon. 14.2.72: At the Widgery inquiry's preliminary hearing in Coleraine, Co Derry, there were complaints that its terms of reference were too narrow.

Fri. 18.2.72: An independent MP, an independent unionist MP and a Unionist MP announced they were joining the Alliance party. The MPs Frank McManus and Ivan Cooper were sentenced to six months' imprisonment for taking part in an anti-internment march on the

M1 on Christmas Day. Bombs exploded in Belfast, Newry, Dungannon and Derry.

Mon. 21.2.72: Four men were killed when a bomb exploded in a car in which they were travelling at Castlereagh, Co Down. At the opening day of the Widgery inquiry at Coleraine, Lord Widgery refused a request to sit in Derry for the convenience of witnesses.

Tues. 22.2.72: The Official IRA claimed responsibility for a massive explosion in the officers' mess of the Parachute Regiment in Aldershot, Surrey. Five women canteen workers, a Catholic padre and a gardener were killed and several people injured.

Wed. 23.2.72: In the High Court in Belfast, five people, including the SDLP MPs John Hume and Ivan Cooper, won their appeal against conviction for remaining in an assembly after it had been ordered to disperse. The judges found that the government of Northern Ireland was not empowered to order the armed forces of the Crown to take actions. An act so to empower it and retrospectively to cover the army for such actions was rushed through Westminster, receiving the royal assent within hours. In Dublin 18 IRA leaders, including Cathal Goulding of the Official IRA, were arrested. At Stormont, the DUP became the official opposition.

Fri. 25.2.72: The Official IRA claimed responsibility for the attempted assassination of John Taylor, minister of state for home affairs, who was seriously wounded as he got into his car in Armagh.

Sun. 27.2.72: In Dublin, 14 of the 18 IRA men arrested earlier were released. The others, including Cathal Goulding, were charged with membership of an illegal organisation. The charges were dropped a fortnight later.

Mon. 28.2.72: Prominent unionists and nationalists were in Washington to give evidence to the foreign affairs sub-committee of the House of Representatives in a three-day sitting to determine US policy.

Thur. 2.3.72: The findings of the Parker inquiry into interrogation methods were announced. The committee had not been unanimous: the majority report said the methods were justified in extreme circumstances, the minority that they were not. The British prime minister, Edward Heath, announced that the methods—including hooding, wall-standing, and sensory deprivation—would no longer be employed.

Sat. 4.3.72: A no-warning bomb exploded in the Abercorn restaurant in central Belfast. Two women were killed and 130 people were injured, some extremely seriously.

Thur. 9.3.72: Four Provisional IRA men were killed in an explosion in a house in Clonard Street in Belfast.

Fri. 10.3.72: The Provisional IRA announced a 72-hour truce, to begin at midnight.

Sat. 11.3.72: Ten thousand people attended an Ulster Vanguard rally in Portadown, Co Armagh.

Mon. 13.3.72: An Amnesty International report into treatment of internees found that "ill-treatment used amounted to brutality". The end of the Provisional IRA truce was marked by bombs in Lisburn, Belfast and Derry.

Sat. 18.3.72: Around 70,000 people attended an Ulster Vanguard rally in south Belfast.

Sun. 19.3.72: About 20,000 people attended an anti-internment rally in west Belfast.

Mon. 20.3.72: A 100lb no-warning car bomb exploded in Donegall Street, Belfast. It was later claimed by the Provisional IRA. Two RUC men and four civilians were killed, and more than 100 people injured, 19 seriously. Several IRA leaders, including Seán Mac Stíofáin, received parcel bombs in the post.

Fri. 24.3.72: British government proposals including the transfer of security responsibility from Stormont to Westminster provoked the resignation of the Northern Ireland government. It was announced that the republic's ambassador to Britain would return to his post. Parking was banned in many areas of Northern Ireland, mainly town centres.

Sat. 25.3.72: William Whitelaw, first secretary of state for Northern Ireland under the new regime of direct rule, arrived in Belfast.

Mon. 27.3.72: The former Stormont prime minister, Brian Faulkner, told the Ulster Unionist Council that a proposed advisory commission to the secretary of state was a "totally undemocratic sham". A two-day stoppage called by the Ulster Vanguard leader, William Craig, involved some 190,000 workers, though many of them could not work because of power cuts while others claimed intimidation. Mr Craig addressed a crowd of 25,000 at Belfast City Hall.

Tues. 28.3.72: On the second day of the loyalist stoppage, marked by several outbreaks of violence, around 100,000 Vanguard supporters marched to Stormont. They were addressed by the former prime minister, Brian Faulkner, with his cabinet, and by the Vanguard leader, William Craig.

Wed. 29.3.72: The Northern Ireland Bill establishing the framework of direct rule was given its second and third reading in the Lords, received the royal assent and became law.

Mon. 3.4.72: A meeting in west Belfast, called by neighbours of a woman shot in crossfire the previous week and attended by women's peace organisations, was disrupted by women IRA supporters.

Thur. 6.4.72: The inquiry under Lord Scarman into the civil disturbances of 1969 reported that there had been no plot to overthrow the government and that the RUC had not acted as a partisan force – though it was severely faulted.

Fri. 7.4.72: William Whitelaw, the secretary of state, announced the release of 73 internees, and said HMS *Maidstone* would no longer be used to house prisoners.

Fri. 14.4.72: There was almost continuous bombing throughout Northern Ireland.

Sat. 15.4.72: A leader of the Official IRA, Joe McCann, was shot dead in the Markets area of Belfast by a paratroop patrol. Violence broke out in Catholic districts of Belfast and Derry, continuing into the night and in Belfast for the following two days. Two soldiers were shot dead in Derry, as were a soldier and a youth in Belfast.

Tues. 18.4.72: Both wings of the IRA were represented among 5,000 mourners at the funeral of Joe McCann. The MPs Bernadette Devlin and Frank McManus and the PD figure Michael Farrell were sentenced to six months in prison for taking part in a march on February 13th.

Wed. 19.4.72: The Widgery inquiry into the shooting dead of 13 civilians in Derry on Bloody Sunday reported that the army had opened fire after a single shot had been fired at soldiers, but Lord Widgery was unconvinced that those who died had been armed.

Wed. 26.4.72: Tartan gangs of loyalist youths attacked police in east Belfast after a Vanguard rally, the violence continuing for six successive nights and spreading to the north of the city, with widespread sectarian clashes, burnings, stone-throwing, shooting, and erection of barricades.

Fri. 28.4.72: The secretary of state, William Whitelaw, announced the lifting of the ban on marches and an amnesty for those convicted.

Mon. 1.5.72: One man was killed and 15 injured in explosions at Courtauld's factory in Carrickfergus, Co Antrim.

Tues. 2.5.72: It was announced that internees would no longer be held at Magilligan.

Sat. 6.5.72: In Crumlin Road jail in Belfast loyalist and republican prisoners went on strike for recognition as political prisoners.

Wed. 10.5.72: The Co-operative store on York Street, Belfast, was destroyed by fire after a bomb attack later claimed by the Provisional IRA.

Sat. 13.5.72: Kelly's bar in west Belfast was badly damaged by a bomb injuring 60 people. Shooting broke out from the direction of Catholic and Protestant enclaves and four civilians and one soldier were shot dead. Gun battles continued the following day until 400 paratroopers took up positions between (Catholic) Ballymurphy and (Protestant) Springmartin. By the end of the second day the death toll had risen to eight, seven of whom were civilians—six Catholics and one Protestant.

Mon. 15.5.72: The Ulster Defence Association (UDA) set up barricades at Woodvale in west Belfast, in protest at no-go areas in Derry.

Sun. 21.5.72: UDA barricades went up in the Shankill and east Belfast and buses were burned. A car bomb in east Belfast destroyed several Catholic houses. In all, three civilians and one UDR man died in a weekend of violence.

Mon. 22.5.72: All UDA barricades were peacefully demolished. The Official IRA claimed the killing of Ranger William Best, home on leave in the Creggan district of Derry. There was widespread condemnation, including an angry march of 200 women to the Officials' headquarters.

Sat. 27.5.72: During the week several large bombs exploded in Belfast, causing one death, many casualties and extensive damage.

Sun. 28.5.72: Four Provisional IRA men and four civilians were killed and many Catholic houses were destroyed in an explosion in the Short Strand area of Belfast. The army claimed the bomb had been detonated accidentally but the Provisionals claimed it was a sectarian

attack. Three large bombs went off in the evening in Belfast city centre, causing extensive damage.

Mon. 29.5.72: The Official IRA declared a ceasefire but reserved a defensive role in Catholic areas.

Tues. 30.5.72: The Provisional IRA announced that it would continue operations. A large bomb exploded inside Springfield Road barracks in Belfast, killing one soldier and injuring several others. The Provisional IRA disclaimed responsibility.

Wed. 31.5.72: Joseph Cahill, a leading Provisional IRA figure, and Ruairí Ó Brádaigh, president of Provisional Sinn Féin, were arrested in the republic.

Sat. 3.6.72: Thirteen thousand attended a Vanguard rally in Derry. Barricades were set up in many towns by UDA supporters.

Wed. 7.6.72: There was a three-hour gun battle with troops in the New Lodge area of Belfast. One hundred and twenty-five internees were released on this and the following day.

Sun. 11.6.72: Vehicles were hijacked and UDA barricades erected all over Belfast and manned for 24 hours. Three civilians were killed and two soldiers wounded in a gun battle between Protestants and Catholics in the Oldpark area of the city.

Mon. 12.6.72: The Guildhall in Derry was badly damaged by a 200lb bomb.

Tues. 13.6.72: The secretary of state, William Whitelaw, saw a three-man UDA delegation at Stormont. They arrived hooded and wearing sunglasses. Later the UDA announced it would postpone for two weeks the threatened erection of permanent barricades, expecting action against the no-go areas in Derry. At a press conference in Derry Seán Mac Stíofáin, chief of staff of the Provisional IRA, invited Mr Whitelaw to meet the IRA to discuss its three-point peace plan. He offered a seven-day truce. Mr Whitelaw rejected the proposal.

Wed. 14.6.72: The 13-man council of the UDA met William Whitelaw for an hour.

Fri. 16.6.72: William Whitelaw announced that the local government elections scheduled for the autumn would be held on the basis of proportional representation. Vanguard said it would attempt to disrupt the elections.

Sat. 17.6.72: William Whitelaw declared that the border would not be changed against the will of the majority in Northern Ireland, that Catholics would have a fair deal on jobs and that he did not respond to ultimatums. He called for a ceasefire. The Guildhall in Derry was further damaged by a 100lb bomb. A bar on the Shankill Road in Belfast and one on the Springfield Road were destroyed by bombs.

Sun. 18.6.72: A Northern Resistance Movement march in support of a hunger strike at Crumlin Road jail in Belfast was prevented from marching down Royal Avenue in Belfast. The marchers complained that non-unionists were "kept out of the city centre at all costs".

Mon. 19.6.72: After meeting John Hume and Paddy Devlin of the SDLP, the secretary of state, William Whitelaw, announced special steps to relieve the tension in Crumlin Road jail. Prisoners who had been on hunger strike, some

for 30 days, ended their strike the following day. The Association for Legal Justice welcomed the *de facto* granting of political status.

Wed. 21.6.72: In Dublin, Joseph Cahill, a former Belfast commander of the Provisional IRA, was found not guilty of incitement to join an illegal organisation. Bombs exploded in Donemana, Strabane, Armagh and Dungannon.

Thur. 22.6.72: The Provisional IRA announced that it would suspend offensive operations from midnight on June 26th. Gun battles began in the Suffolk area of Belfast and continued for three days.

Sat. 24.6.72: Three soldiers were killed when mines exploded under their Land Rover on the Glenshane Pass in Co Derry. The action was claimed by the Provisional IRA.

Mon. 26.6.72: The Provisional IRA, in many actions before its midnight ceasefire deadline, killed two soldiers and one policeman, caused numerous explosions throughout Northern Ireland and undertook many armed robberies.

Wed. 28.6.72: The Provisional IRA outlined its peace proposals, entitled *Eire Nua*. Hooded members of the UDA announced after a meeting with the secretary of state, William Whitelaw, that they would erect permanent barricades in Northern Ireland at the weekend.

Fri. 30.6.72: Retailers in central Belfast reported a significant increase in trade in the absence of bombing. Three barricades in the Bogside in Derry were removed and the Brandywell army post was dismantled, but the inner rings of barricades remained in Bogside and Creggan. The UDA said this was too little, too late, and set up its own barricades and hijacked vehicles in the Shankill, Woodvale and Oldpark areas of Belfast.

Sun. 2.7.72: Gusty Spence, Ulster Volunteer Force (UVF) commander in Crumlin Road jail in Belfast, was kidnapped at Springmartin while on parole. The following week the UVF issued photographs proving that it was holding him until the arrest of two named IRA men.

Mon. 3.7.72: Several thousand UDA men, armed with bars and clubs, were prevented by troops from setting up another no-go area, in west Belfast.

Fri. 7.7.72: The Central Citizens Defence Committee (CCDC) said that it would be moving Catholic families into 16 houses vacated by Protestants in the Lenadoon area of west Belfast. The secretary of state, William Whitelaw, had discussions with six senior Provisional IRA leaders in London, including Gerry Adams who was released from internment, and heard their demands in return for a continued ceasefire.

Sat. 8.7.72: Tom Cromey, head of the new Public Protection Agency established by the direct rule administration, chaired a meeting to discuss the rehousing of the Catholic families in Lenadoon. The UDA representative said that if the families were moved in it would burn the houses. The Provisional IRA representative demanded that the army implement the Catholic families' tenancy agreements and move them in or else it would. The UDA set up another no-go area, in east Belfast.

Sun. 9.7.72: In Derry, two soldiers were released unharmed by the Provisional IRA after they had walked into the Bogside in plain clothes while off duty. In Belfast a large Catholic demonstration in Lenadoon attempted to rehouse families into their allocated homes but were prevented by the army. Missiles were thrown, the army responding with rubber bullets and CS gas. Seamus Twomey of the Provisional IRA told the army commander that the army had violated the truce. Shooting broke out and the Provisional IRA later announced that the ceasefire was over. Uniformed UDA men watched the confrontation from behind the army line but took no part. Ten people were killed in violence in Belfast during the weekend, many of them murdered with no apparent motive.

Fri. 14.7.72: The army occupied parts of Andersonstown and Divis Flats in west Belfast. Over the ensuing weekend three soldiers, one policeman and three civilians were killed.

Tues. 18.7.72: In London, the Labour leader, Harold Wilson, met the same six senior Provisional IRA leaders who had met the secretary of state, William Whitelaw, the previous week.

Fri. 21.7.72: Bloody Friday—the Provisional IRA set off 26 explosions in Belfast, killing 11 people and injuring 130, many seriously. Seven were killed at Oxford Street bus station and four at a shopping centre on Cavehill Road. Three large bombs were also detonated in Derry. In the first killing by what is thought to have been the Shankill Butchers, led by Lenny Murphy of the UVF, a Catholic, Francis Arthurs, was taken to a social club in the Shankill area of Belfast, beaten until unrecognisable, stabbed repeatedly, shot and dumped.

Sun. 23.7.72: The UDA said that it was breaking its links with Vanguard and would not be supporting the latter's proposed rent and rates strike.

Thur. 27.7.72: It was announced that a further 4,000 troops would be sent to Northern Ireland, bringing the total to 21,000.

Mon. 31.7.72: Operation Motorman—troops cleared barricades with tanks in the Bogside in Derry and occupied positions in all no-go areas. In Claudy, near Derry, three no-warning car bombs exploded, killing eight people and wounding several others, two of whom later died.

Fri. 4.8.72: About 1,000 uniformed and masked UDA men paraded in east Belfast in protest against a statement by the secretary of state, William Whitelaw, that paramilitary uniforms would not be tolerated.

Mon. 7.8.72: Two soldiers were killed by a mine near Lisnaskea, Co Fermanagh.

Tues. 8.8.72: In Armagh a soldier was killed when stone-throwing children caused him to crash his Land Rover.

Wed. 9.8.72: Violent protests took place in Belfast to mark the first anniversary of the introduction of internment.

Fri. 11.8.72: A man and a woman, members of the Provisional IRA, died trying to plant a bomb in a Belfast supermarket—the bomb went off in their van. Six other people were injured, one seriously. The last Official IRA internee in Long Kesh was released. The secretary of state, William Whitelaw, sent invitations to leaders of

the political parties to attend a conference on the political future of Northern Ireland in England on September 25th–27th. The venue was later announced to be in Darlington.

Wed. 16.8.72: The UVF inaugurated a taxi service in the Shankill Road area.

Thur. 17.8.72: The Standard bar on the Shankill Road in Belfast was wrecked by a bomb which injured 55 people. The Provisional IRA claimed responsibility, saying the bar was a base for loyalist assassination groups.

Sat. 19.8.72: About 5,000 unmasked UDA men marched in military style to a rally in east Belfast which was addressed by William Craig of Vanguard and Billy Hull of the Loyalist Association of Workers (LAW).

Tues. 22.8.72: A bomb exploded in a customs clearance station near Newry, Co Down, killing two members of the Provisional IRA, four customs officers and two lorry drivers. The following day another body was found in the rubble.

Fri. 25.8.72: Two UDR soldiers were killed by a bomb near Kesh, Co Fermanagh, and 11 regular soldiers were injured by another in the same area. An army sergeant was killed by a sniper in Derry.

Sat. 26.8.72: Another army sergeant was killed by a sniper in Derry. A bomb exploded as it was being primed at Downpatrick racecourse and three Provisional IRA men were killed. In separate incidents two Catholics and a Protestant were shot dead in north Belfast.

Mon. 28.8.72: A gun battle took place with troops at Broadway in west Belfast. The army claimed to have hit eight gunmen. The Provisional IRA claimed that "heavily armed Protestants" had joined in the attack. In separate incidents two soldiers were shot dead by a Provisional IRA sniper, reported at the time to be a special marksman responsible for the recent spate of single-shot killings of soldiers. Another soldier was killed later in the week by a single shot from a sniper.

Tues. 5.9.72: The Unionist party published its proposals—*Towards the Future*—to be put to the forthcoming political conference at Darlington.

Thur. 7.9.72: After two days of violent incidents in the Shankill area of Belfast, units of the Parachute Regiment were deployed and shot dead two civilians. The army claimed it had come under fire but residents said it had been quiet at the time. Neither of the two dead was a member of the UDA. The Alliance party and the NILP published their Darlington proposals.

Mon. 11.9.72: Fr Denis Faul of Dungannon, Co. Tyrone, said that he was preparing evidence of inhuman treatment of prisoners under the Whitelaw administration. Workers at two power stations in Belfast went on strike demanding a public inquiry into the killings on the Shankill, and the city was subject to intermittent power failures for days. The UDA, Vanguard and LAW announced they would unite under a United Loyalist Front, to be led by William Craig, and claims were made that Northern Ireland could be brought to a standstill. Three soldiers were killed by a 500lb mine near Dungannon.

Fri. 15.9.72: The DUP announced its withdrawal from the proposed political

conference, in protest at the absence of an inquiry into the Shankill killings.

Sun. 17.9.72: A UVF man was shot dead and several Catholic houses were burned in sectarian clashes in Larne, Co Antrim. About 7,000 masked UDA men marched through Belfast city centre to a rally.

Wed. 20.9.72: The SDLP issued a policy document, but later in the week it reiterated its refusal to attend the Darlington conference because internment had not been ended.

Fri. 22.9.72: The Special Powers Act was extended to include those who advocated membership of illegal organisations. The cases of internees would henceforth be reviewed by a tribunal.

Sat. 23.9.72: After a meeting in Dundalk, Co Louth, to protest about the treatment of a member of the Provisional IRA by a special court, a crowd marched to the Garda barracks and rioting broke out.

Sun. 24.9.72: The Darlington conference, which was to last for four days, opened with representatives of the Unionist, Alliance and Northern Ireland Labour parties, as well as the British government, attending.

Mon. 25.9.72: The newly opened Russell Court Hotel in Belfast, owned by the republic's transport company, CIE, was badly damaged by a 500lb bomb. The European Court of Human Rights at Strasbourg began hearing submissions in camera on the claim brought by the republic against Britain for violation of internees' human rights.

Wed. 27.9.72: At the close of the Darlington conference the secretary of state, William Whitelaw, said the government would include the proposals of all parties in a green paper, whether they had attended the conference or not.

Sat. 30.9.72: A Vanguard rally at Stormont attracted what the army said was 15,000 and the organisers 100,000 people. The DUP leader, Rev Ian Paisley, refused to attend, claiming the rally had a unilateral declaration of independence in mind. The Unionist party leader, Brian Faulkner, refused to attend because speakers would be advocating policies at variance with those of his party.

Mon. 2.10.72: An undercover army organisation, operating as the Four Square Laundry, was exposed when the Provisional IRA shot dead a soldier posing as the driver of a laundry van in Twinbrook, west Belfast.

Wed. 4.10.72: The Vanguard leader, William Craig, escaped injury when shots were fired at his car near Lisburn, Co Antrim.

Fri. 6.10.72: The Dublin headquarters of the Provisional IRA was closed by gardaí.

Wed. 11.10.72: William Staunton, a Belfast magistrate, was seriously wounded by gunfire from two motor cyclists as he was driving along the Falls Road in Belfast. Tartan gangs attacked Catholic premises in east Belfast, giving rise to rioting and shooting. Troops raided a social club on the Shankill Road and arrested several men, again sparking clashes.

Mon. 16.10.72: On the second day of extensive rioting in east Belfast, a man and a 15-year-old boy were killed by army vehicles, prompting a UDA statement that the "British army and the

British government are now our enemies". There were also riots and shots fired in the Shankill district.

Tues. 17.10.72: Loyalist gunmen attacked the army in several parts of Belfast. There was rioting in Protestant districts and violence spread to Lisburn, Co Antrim.

Wed. 18.10.72: After talks with senior army officers in Belfast, the UDA announced that it would once more co-operate with the security forces. In the Creggan, in Derry, cars were hijacked and burned and barricades were set up.

Fri. 20.10.72: In a speech to the Westminster Monday Club, the Vanguard leader, William Craig, said he could mobilise 80,000 men who would shoot to kill if the British government tried to impose any edict upon the loyalists of Ulster. The speech was widely condemned by many, including Austin Ardill, vice-chair of Vanguard, and senior Unionist party figures, but it was welcomed by many loyalist organisations.

Fri. 27.10.72: The secretary of state, William Whitelaw, again postponed the local government elections, due to be held on December 6th, until 1973. He announced that the proposed border referendum would be held before the elections.

Sun. 29.10.72: Four firebombs exploded in Dublin hotels and a 12lb bomb was defused in Connolly Station.

Mon. 30.10.72: The British government published its green paper, *The Future of Northern Ireland*. It repeated the guarantee of Northern Ireland's constitutional position but recognised an "Irish dimension".

Tues. 31.10.72: A car bomb exploded outside Benny's bar in Ship Street, Belfast, killing two children playing at a Hallowe'en bonfire.

Sat. 4.11.72: Gusty Spence, a UVF leader "kidnapped" by the organisation, was arrested in the Woodvale area of Belfast as he was about to get into a stolen car.

Sun. 5.11.72: The UDA claimed responsibility for an explosion at a soft drinks factory at Muff, Co Donegal—the second for which it had claimed responsibility in the county that week. It promised to retaliate for every IRA bomb in Northern Ireland. Gardaí arrested Maire Drumm, a vice-president of Provisional Sinn Féin, in Mullingar, Co Westmeath.

Mon. 6.11.72: During the night troops erected 41 steel gates and fences, sealing off many of Belfast's city-centre streets. Under the Detention of Terrorists Order, three commissioners were appointed to hear cases of men in detention.

Thur. 16.11.72: The prime minister, Edward Heath, arrived in Northern Ireland for a two-day visit. The SDLP and the Nationalist party had turned down invitations to meet him.

Fri. 17.11.72: Volleys of shots were fired and effigies of Edward Heath were burned in various parts of Belfast in protest at his refusal to meet the Ulster Loyalist Council. Mr Heath visited Derry, Omagh, Lisburn and Stormont. At a press conference before returning to London he warned that UDI would lead to a bloodbath and the removal of the £200 million subsidy from the government to Northern Ireland. Anita Currie, wife of Austin Currie, the SDLP MP,

was beaten by armed men in their Co Tyrone home and had the letters UVF carved on her chest.

Sun. 19.11.72: Seán Mac Stíofáin, chief of staff of the Provisional IRA, was arrested in the republic after being interviewed by an RTE reporter. He immediately went on hunger and thirst strike. Two days later he was charged with belonging to an illegal organisation.

Mon. 20.11.72: At a press conference Fr Desmond Wilson read a statement signed by 65 priests complaining of army harassment, killings and inhuman treatment of Catholic civilians.

Fri. 24.11.72: The republic's government dismissed the nine-member board of RTE following the interview with Seán Mac Stíofáin.

Sat. 25.11.72: Seán Mac Stíofáin was sentenced in Dublin to six months' imprisonment and transferred to the Mater Hospital. The following day a crowd of over 5,000 marched to the hospital and Provisional IRA men, dressed as priests and orderlies, attempted to free him. This led to a gun battle with Special Branch officers. In Ardoyne, north Belfast, more than 350 shots were fired at an army post.

Fri. 1.12.72: Two people were killed and 80 injured in Dublin when two bombs exploded while the Dáil was debating the Offences Against the State (Amendment) Bill, which would strengthen powers against illegal organisations. The UDA and both IRAs denied responsibility.

Thur. 7.12.72: The secretary of state, William Whitelaw, announced new measures to deal with the increasing number of sectarian assassinations in Belfast. Lord Windlesham, speaking for the government, said of the UDA that the wearing of uniforms was not illegal in the case of an organisation that was not proscribed.

Fri. 8.12.72: A Catholic church in Martinstown, Co Antrim, was destroyed by an explosion before parishioners arrived for morning Mass.

Tues. 12.12.72: In separate meetings with the secretary of state, William Whitelaw, the SDLP proposed joint sovereignty over Northern Ireland between the British and Irish governments and the Unionist party demanded that any form of government for Northern Ireland must have control of the police and administration of the courts.

Wed. 13.12.72: Rev Martin Smyth, deputy leader of Vanguard and a member of the Unionist party, was elected grand master of the Grand Orange Lodge of Ireland. The following day he gave details of the Orange Volunteers, 2,000 strong, who could be called on to assist the security forces.

Wed. 20.12.72: The British government published and accepted the recommendations of the Diplock commission, the most important of which was no-jury trials for terrorist-type offences.

Thur. 21.12.72: A Catholic-owned bar in the Waterside in Derry was attacked and five men—four Catholics and one Protestant—were killed by machine-gun fire.

Fri. 22.12.72: The Provisional IRA declared a three-day truce from midnight.

Fri. 29.12.72: Ruairí Ó Brádaigh, president of Provisional Sinn Féin, was arrested in Dublin.

Sun. 31.12.72: Martin McGuinness and Joseph McCallion of the Provisional IRA were arrested by gardaí near Ballybofey, Co Donegal, when their car was found to contain explosives. Two others escaped.

1973

Mon. 1.1.73: The UK, the Republic of Ireland and Denmark became members of the European Community (EC).

Wed. 3.1.73: The secretary of state, William Whitelaw, announced that the "murder task force" had been increased to combat sectarian assassinations.

Thur. 4.1.73: The UDA warned all those involved in sectarian murders to stop. Later in the week, the SDLP MP Paddy Devlin denounced this as a "smokescreen". But the statement was welcomed by the DUP leader, Rev Ian Paisley, and the Provisional IRA, which offered to meet the UDA.

Sat. 6.1.73: Maire Drumm was appointed temporary president of Provisional Sinn Féin, during the imprisonment of Ruairí Ó Brádaigh.

Sun. 7.1.73: Five hundred women protested in Andersonstown in Belfast against the detention of Elizabeth McKee, the first woman to be detained under the Special Powers Act.

Thur. 11.1.73: There were bombs in Derry and Belfast. The following day a bomb destroyed a building on Royal Avenue in Belfast.

Sat. 13.1.73: Seventeen people were injured, some seriously, by a bomb in a Catholic-owned bar off the Springfield Road, Belfast.

Sun. 14.1.73: Two RUC men were killed in Derry when their car tripped a wire attached to explosives.

Mon. 15.1.73: An auction room on Great Victoria Street in Belfast and a bookshop on Botanic Avenue were destroyed by bombs. The Provisional IRA called on Seán Mac Stíofáin to end his hunger strike, as it was serving "no useful purpose". The following day he came off it, after 58 days.

Sat. 20.1.73: One man was killed and another seriously injured by a car bomb in Dublin. The car had been hijacked on the Shankill Road in Belfast.

Mon. 22.1.73: A joint statement from the UDA, the LAW, the UVF and the Loyalist Defence Volunteers said that representatives of the four organisations had found common purpose. It was the first time the UVF had been included in any statement from the United Loyalist Council, but it later said that the main body of its organisation dissociated itself from the talks.

Tues. 23.1.73: The Republican Labour and Nationalist parties agreed to boycott the border referendum on March 8th. The following day the SDLP also called on its members to boycott the poll.

Sun. 28.1.73: After ceremonies in the Bogside in Derry to mark the first anniversary of Bloody Sunday, rioting broke out and was quelled with CS gas, water cannon and rubber bullets.

Tues. 30.1.73: Rioting broke out in Newry and Strabane after PD meetings to commemorate Bloody Sunday.

Wed. 31.1.73: Two Catholic youths were murdered, the body of one being found at the Giant's Ring, a prehistoric site outside Belfast. In different statements that week the SDLP called for a crackdown on the UDA.

Fri. 2.2.73: There were three sectarian assassinations in Belfast—one Catholic and two Protestants were killed.

Sat. 3.2.73: A loyalist crowd marched to Castlereagh police station in east Belfast to protest about the detention of the first two Protestants held under the Detention of Terrorists Order.

Mon. 5.2.73: The United Loyalist Council called a general strike for the following Wednesday, in protest against the detention of two Protestants.

Wed. 7.2.73: The United Loyalist Council one-day strike brought an electricity black-out. There were widespread reports of intimidation. Police stations in east and south Belfast were attacked by mobs. Lavery's bar in Bradbury Place was burned and many shops were set on fire. While fighting a fire in Sandy Row, a fireman was shot dead. St Anthony's Catholic church was ransacked and a Catholic home for mentally handicapped children near Whiteabbey, Co Antrim, was attacked. In an exchange of fire in east Belfast, the army shot two men dead. A soldier was killed in a rocket attack in the New Lodge. In all five people were killed.

Fri. 9.2.73: A further seven Protestants, including the prominent Belfast loyalist John McKeague, were arrested under the Special Powers Act.

Sat. 10.2.73: John McKeague refused to recognise the court when charged with robbery and possession of a pistol. Volleys were fired at the funerals of a UVF man and a UDA man killed in Wednesday 7th's violence.

Mon. 12.2.73: In a speech in the Ulster Hall, Belfast, the Vanguard leader, William Craig, suggested dominion status for Northern Ireland.

Thur. 15.2.73: After a statement by the SDLP MP John Hume that he saw common ground between William Craig's speech and SDLP policies, the party proposed talks with the United Loyalist Council. Though the invitation was initially welcomed by Mr Craig, the council later declined it. A mandatory death sentence was handed down to a UDA man, Albert Browne, for the murder of a policeman, though it was later to be commuted to life imprisonment by the secretary of state.

Sun. 18.2.73: Two Catholic postmen were shot dead as they left work in Divis Street, Belfast.

Wed. 21.2.73: Three soldiers were killed in two attacks in west Belfast.

Sun. 25.2.73: A 10-year-old boy was killed in the Creggan in Derry when he activated the trip wire of a landmine. There were clashes with troops.

Tues. 27.2.73: A 13-year-old boy, Kevin Heatley, was shot dead when an army patrol passed through the Derrybeg estate in Newry, Co Down. A soldier, L/Cpl Foxford, was later convicted of his unlawful killing and sentenced to three years in prison, the conviction was later overturned at appeal.

Fri. 2.3.73: Following the shooting dead of a Catholic bus driver at the wheel of his bus in the Woodvale area of Belfast, bus drivers went on strike until after his funeral the following Wednesday.

Tues. 6.3.73: Talks were held between Paddy Devlin and Ivan Cooper of the SDLP and William Craig and John Taylor of the Unionist party. The UDA said that Mr Craig attended the talks in a personal capacity but the United Loyalist Council had full confidence in him.

Thur. 8.3.73: On the day of the border poll there were six explosions in Belfast, five in Derry, and two in central London, where one man was killed and 180 people injured. No organisation claimed responsibility for the London bombs. The poll, intended to be the first of a series to be held every 10 years, was boycotted by most nationalists. Nearly 600,000 voted to remain in the UK and just over 6,000 to join with the republic.

Mon. 12.3.73: Seven men and three women, all except one from Belfast, and including Marion and Dolores Price, were charged at Ealing police station with conspiring to cause explosions.

Wed. 14.3.73: The secretary of state, William Whitelaw, announced that the first local elections in Northern Ireland since 1967 would be held on May 30th, under proportional representation.

Mon. 19.3.73: Emily Groves, a 53-year-old mother of 11 from Andersonstown, west Belfast, who was blinded by a rubber bullet fired by a soldier in November 1971, was awarded £35,000 damages by the High Court in Belfast.

Tues. 20.3.73: The British government issued a white paper on Northern Ireland. It proposed an assembly of 80 members, elected by proportional representation, though with the secretary of state remaining in office and control of security remaining at Westminster. The chairs of assembly committees would form an executive. A Council of Ireland would be set up. The DUP leader Rev Ian Paisley was "disappointed". The Vanguard leader, William Craig, called the proposals "absurd". The Unionist party leader, Brian Faulkner, foresaw "no problem" in joining the assembly. The following weeks saw a succession of MPs, senators and councillors defecting from the Unionist party variously to Alliance and the new Vanguard Unionist Progressive party (VUPP). Other parties accepted the proposals in general, though the SDLP withheld comment for 48 hours.

Wed. 21.3.73: A new loyalist group, consisting of William Craig, Rev Ian Paisley, Capt Lawrence Orr, and representatives of the UDA, the LAW and the Orange Order, met at Stormont and announced a campaign against the government's proposals.

Thur. 22.3.73: The SDLP gave the white paper a cautious welcome.

Fri. 23.3.73: The Provisional IRA said the government's proposals were unacceptable and it would continue its campaign in the north. The parliamentary Unionist party (UP) voted to accept the proposals, as did the Republican Labour party and the Nationalist party. In

Belfast, three soldiers were killed and a fourth was seriously wounded by the Provisional IRA after being lured by women to a party on the Antrim Road.

Sat. 24.3.73: A United Loyalist Council rally at Belfast City Hall was attended by only about 2,000 people. The Alliance party conference accepted the white paper as a basis for peace.

Wed. 28.3.73: The republic's government announced the seizure of the *Claudia*, off the coast of Waterford, containing nearly 500 arms as well as mines and explosives. The following day six men were charged, including Joseph Cahill, former Belfast commander of the Provisional IRA.

Thur. 29.3.73: At Westminster, the white paper was approved by 329 votes to 5.

Fri. 30.3.73: Following a meeting with representatives of the UDA, the LAW and the DUP, William Craig announced the formation of the VUPP and his impending resignation from the Unionist party. The VUPP's aims were to win enough representation in the assembly to make the white paper unworkable and to negotiate a new constitution outside the UK.

Thur. 5.4.73: The British government announced that the declaration of allegiance to the Crown by those elected to local government had been abolished.

Sat. 7.4.73: Two soldiers of the Parachute Regiment were killed when a mine exploded beneath their Land Rover near Newtownhamilton, Co Armagh.

Mon. 16.4.73: Seán Mac Stíofáin, previously chief of staff of the Provisional IRA, was released from the Curragh in Co Kildare, having served his six-month sentence. At the unopposed second reading of the Northern Ireland Assembly Bill, it was announced that the first elections to the new assembly would be on June 28th.

Tues. 17.4.73: Letter bombs were used for the first time in Northern Ireland; they were sent to five policemen in Derry.

Wed. 18.4.73: Amid complaints from residents in the Ardoyne area of Belfast, echoed by nationalist politicians and the NILP, the secretary of state, William Whitelaw, denied that the Parachute Regiment was adopting tougher tactics.

Thur. 19.4.73: In Belfast a Ballymurphy man was sentenced to death for the murder of a British soldier in September 1972.

Sat. 21.4.73: Malachy McGurran, chair of the Republican Clubs, northern political wing of the Official IRA, having been released the previous day after 60 hours' interrogation in Derry, was refused entry into Britain at Birmingham airport and flown back to Belfast. The SDLP leader, Gerry Fitt, challenged the constitutional validity of deportation from one part of the UK to another.

Wed. 25.4.73: In the second such attack in a week, the home in Derry of a Creggan Women's Peace Committee member was attacked by a mob. Her house was attacked again the following week.

Sat. 28.4.73: The UDA blocked up to 50 roads in Belfast for an hour in protest at the proposed extradition to the republic of one of its members, Robert Taylor, from Derry.

Sun. 29.4.73: The Orange Order rejected the white paper.

Wed. 2.5.73: The Official IRA claimed responsibility for the death of seven British soldiers and the wounding of several others in "recent retaliatory action".

Sat. 5.5.73: Three soldiers were killed when a booby-trap mine exploded near Crossmaglen in Co Armagh. Wires were found running across the border.

Sat. 12.5.73: Twelve people were injured, some seriously, when a bomb exploded without warning in the doorway of McLaughlin's bar in Smithfield Square, Belfast.

Sun. 13.5.73: On the Falls Road in Belfast, three soldiers were seriously injured, two later dying in hospital, when a booby-trap bomb exploded in a derelict factory.

Mon. 14.5.73: A van driver, later described in death notices as a member of the Provisional IRA, was shot dead by UDR soldiers when he failed to stop at a checkpoint near Coagh, Co Tyrone. In a free vote at Westminster, it was decided to abolish the death penalty for murder in Northern Ireland. It was also decided that the Republican Clubs would no longer be proscribed. Ruairí Ó Brádaigh, president of Provisional Sinn Féin, was released from the Curragh camp in Kildare, having served six months' detention for IRA membership. The following day Martin McGuinness, formerly Provisional IRA commander in Derry, also completed his six-month sentence in the camp.

Thur. 17.5.73: The Provisional IRA announced that Aldergrove airport was now a "legitimate target".

Fri. 18.5.73: Two Belfast railway stations, the Great Victoria Street and the County Down, were damaged, the former severely, by bombs. Four off-duty soldiers were killed instantly when their car was destroyed by an explosion in Omagh, Co Tyrone.

Tues. 22.5.73: Following the death in hospital of a Derry man as a result of injuries received from a rubber bullet, there was rioting in the Creggan and the Bogside. A 300lb car bomb in Belfast city centre caused considerable damage to commercial property.

Thur. 24.5.73: In an explosion claimed by the Provisional IRA, two soldiers were killed in a booby-trapped house at Culloville, Co Armagh.

Fri. 25.5.73: A 600lb van bomb in Dungannon, Co Tyrone, wrecked shops and offices. There were three bombs in Belfast.

Sat. 26.5.73: A four-year-old boy, playing in the garden of his home in west Belfast, was killed in crossfire between the army and unidentified gunmen. Bombs exploded in four bars in Belfast.

Wed. 30.5.73: Polling took place in Northern Ireland for local government seats and in the republic for the presidency. In the north it was the first local government election since 1967, the first under proportional representation since 1925, the first since "one man, one vote" had been introduced and the first for which 18-year-olds were enfranchised. A passer-by was killed and at least 16 people injured in an explosion at McGlade's bar in Donegall Street in Belfast. In the republic Erskine Childers of Fianna Fáil was elected president.

Fri. 1.6.73: The final local government count revealed the following distribution of seats: UP 233, DUP 21, Vanguard Unionist Loyalist Coalition 9, Loyalist Coalition 40, other loyalists 4, Alliance 63, SDLP 83, NILP 4, Republic Clubs 7, Nationalist/Unity 13 and others 49.

Sun. 3.6.73: A Protestant couple were shot dead in their home in the Oldpark area of Belfast. After an anti-internment rally in Derry, crowds attacked troops and were dispersed with rubber bullets.

Mon. 4.6.73: Following the suicide the previous day of a detainee in Long Kesh, the Provisional IRA declared all prison officers "legitimate targets".

Thur. 7.6.73: On succeeding days, the DUP and VUPP issued their election manifestos.

Sat. 9.6.73: The secretary of state, William Whitelaw, had talks with the republic's foreign minister, Garret FitzGerald, in London. In Belfast the UDA announced that "a sudden sharp upheaval in UDA ranks has now led to the removal of four company commanders and 18 other senior officers".

Sun. 10.6.73: A Protestant bus driver was killed in crossfire between the UDA and troops in the Short Strand area of Belfast. After arms and ammunition were discovered at UDA headquarters in east Belfast, 12 UDA men were detained. The following day the Shankill Road was blocked in protest. Troops used rubber bullets to disperse the crowd, later coming under fire for over two hours.

Tues. 12.6.73: After a wrong location was given in a warning, a car bomb exploded in Coleraine, Co Derry, killing six people and injuring 33, 18 seriously. A second car bomb in the town caused severe damage but no casualties.

Wed. 13.6.73: The SDLP issued its election manifesto.

Thur. 14.6.73: An 18-year-old UDA man, Robert Taylor, was extradited to the republic to face murder charges. The UP published its election manifesto and listed the 39 candidates with official backing. Several others, standing under the party name, would not have official backing.

Fri. 15.6.73: Michael Wilson, brother-in-law of Tommy Herron, former vice-chair of the UDA, was shot dead by gunmen at Mr Herron's home while he was away. The NILP published its election manifesto.

Sat. 16.6.73: A 17-year-old Catholic youth was found shot dead in Dunmurry in Belfast. Claiming responsibility for this attack, allegedly in retaliation for the killing of Michael Wilson, and for the killing of a Catholic sailor (whose body was found at the side of the Belfast–Larne road the following day), a new group called the Ulster Freedom Fighters (UFF) said it was a breakaway from the UDA. The Provisional IRA disclaimed responsibility for the Wilson killing and said it did not engage in armed action against the UDA.

Mon. 18.6.73: There were explosions in Derry, Enniskillen, Strabane, and Swatragh, Co Derry.

In Belfast the election headquarters of the Republican Clubs were wrecked by a bomb. The Official IRA claimed responsibility for the blowing up of the car of the managing director of a mill in west Belfast, saying it was a protest against working conditions. A bomb in a bar on Manor Street in north Belfast was claimed by the UFF.

Wed. 20.6.73: In seven explosions in Derry, four civilians were injured, one seriously.

Thur. 21.6.73: A speech by the taoiseach, Liam Cosgrave, offering to meet the new executive and offering talks without preconditions to political groups in the north was welcomed by the Unionist party leader, Brian Faulkner, and by the Alliance party. A mentally handicapped Protestant boy, David Andrews, from south Belfast, was found shot dead in west Belfast. The Provisional IRA later disclaimed responsibility. There were two bombs in Belfast and others in Dungannon, Warrenpoint and Newtownstewart. An army bomb disposal officer was killed and three soldiers were seriously wounded by a bomb in a house in the Brandywell district of Derry. Throughout the night and the following day in Derry there were vehicle burnings, shootings, petrol bombings and explosions.

Sat. 23.6.73: In Derry an army post at Butcher Gate was wrecked by a bomb, the main library was burned down after three bombs had detonated and a shop was demolished by a bomb. The headquarters of Fermanagh Unionist Association in Enniskillen were wrecked by an explosion. There were also explosions in Rosslea, Co Fermanagh, and in Dungannon, Co Tyrone. The Provisional IRA called for the spoiling of votes in the assembly elections.

Mon. 25.6.73: Three Provisional IRA men were killed when a bomb they were transporting went off near Omagh, Co Tyrone.

Tues. 26.6.73: Senator Paddy Wilson of the SDLP, and his passenger, Irene Andrews, were found dead by his car on the Hightown Road in Belfast. They had been stabbed. The UFF claimed responsibility. In Derry a Pakistani civilian canteen operator for the army was shot dead by the Provisional IRA as an "army spy", an RUC man and a civilian girl were wounded in a gun attack on a police Land Rover and a solicitor was injured by a letter bomb. Michael Farrell, leader of PD, was sent to prison for eight months for breach of the peace during a march in Belfast in February.

Thur. 28.6.73: Over 72 per cent of the electorate turned out for the assembly elections. Rita O'Hare, from Andersonstown in Belfast, was arrested in Dublin on an extradition warrant, on a charge of the attempted murder of a soldier in Northern Ireland. She was later discharged.

Fri. 29.6.73: Sean Armstrong, a field officer for International Voluntary Service, was shot dead at his flat in Belfast.

Sat. 30.6.73: The final results in the assembly election left the following distribution of seats: Official Unionists 24, Unionists 8, Loyalist Coalition (DUP and VUPP) 15, other loyalists 3, SDLP 19, Alliance party 8, NILP 1.

Mon. 2.7.73: The secretary of state, William Whitelaw, held talks with the leaders of the assembly parties. Speaking after talks in London with the prime minister, Edward Heath, the taoiseach, Liam Cosgrave, said that to press for a united Ireland now would "dangerously exacerbate tensions and fears" and "double the problem at a stroke." The CCDC made the latest in a series of peace calls to the Provisional IRA.

Tues. 3.7.73: Oliver Napier was appointed leader of the Alliance party.

Wed. 4.7.73: Prisoners at Long Kesh rioted in protest at search regulations. In Belfast, armed men hijacked and burned buses and lorries. In one incident, at Cliftonville Road, five passengers sustained burns.

Fri. 6.7.73: In Crumlin Road jail in Belfast, Michael Farrell and Tony Canavan of PD went on hunger strike, demanding to be treated as political prisoners.

Mon. 9.7.73: In Belfast, a 47-year-old woman who had been injured when a bus was set on fire died in hospital. More buses and lorries were hijacked and burned by armed youths.

Wed. 11.7.73: The secretary of state, William Whitelaw, continued talks with party leaders about power-sharing. At Orange rallies the following day the Unionist MP James Molyneaux said power-sharing was "a political obscenity" and the Unionist party leader, Brian Faulkner, was called "Lundy" by hecklers.

Tues. 17.7.73: Two soldiers were killed by a booby-trap bomb on a landing in Divis Flats in Belfast. One man was killed and 15 injured when a no-warning bomb exploded at a bar in Glenavy, Co Antrim.

Wed. 18.7.73: The Northern Ireland Constitution Bill received royal assent. It formally abolished the Stormont Parliament and the office of governor of Northern Ireland. Northern Ireland would remain part of the UK except by the wish of the majority, it reaffirmed. A border poll would be held every 10 years.

Thur. 19.7.73: Seventeen republican suspects, including Gerry Adams, were arrested in raids in Belfast.

Sat. 21.7.73: On the anniversary of Bloody Friday, and after three bomb attacks on bars in Belfast the previous day, 4,000 troops sealed off parts of the city and controlled traffic for 48 hours. But no arms or explosives were discovered in the associated searches.

Wed. 25.7.73: The Northern Ireland (Emergency Provisions) Bill received royal assent. It provided for trial by a single judge without a jury for "terrorist-type" offences, as recommended by the Diplock report. The Special Powers Act was now repealed.

Sun. 29.7.73: In Belfast, a PD march from the Falls Road, through Royal Avenue to Crumlin Road jail, previously permitted but banned the the night before, was stopped at Castle Street. After stone-throwing, troops attacked the crowd with rubber bullets and water cannon.

Tues. 31.7.73: At the first meeting of the assembly at Stormont, a heated debate broke down in disorder and the meeting was adjourned. Twenty-six DUP, VUPP and unofficial Unionists remained, held an impromptu debate and sang "God Save the Queen".

Fri. 3.8.73: Two Englishmen, Kenneth and Keith Littlejohn, were sentenced to 20 and 15 years' imprisonment at the Special Criminal Court in Dublin for their part in a bank robbery. They claimed to have been working for the British Ministry of Defence. The money had mainly gone to the Official IRA.

Wed. 8.8.73: After a hunger strike of 37 days, Michael Farrell and Tony Canavan of PD were released from prison along with 98 other short-term, non-"terrorist" offenders. The Northern Ireland (Emergency Provisions) Act had come into force at midnight, ending the Special Powers Act and a range of mandatory sentences under public order legislation.

Thur. 9.8.73: In Omagh, Co Tyrone, a bomb damaged 50 houses in an army housing estate. The Provisional IRA said army dwellings and anyone who assisted the army were "legitimate targets".

Sat. 11.8.73: For the first time since 1969, the Apprentice Boys' annual march in Derry was permitted. It was attended by 7,000 members.

Sun. 12.8.73: Seven thousand people attended an anti-internment rally in Andersonstown, west Belfast, but were prevented by troops from reaching the M1 motorway, where they had intended walking to Long Kesh. After stone-throwing, rubber bullets were fired and a water cannon brought in. There were other demonstrations in London and at the Curragh camp in Co Kildare.

Wed. 15.8.73: A no-warning car bomb outside a bar in Great Patrick Street, Belfast, killed one man and injured nine others.

Fri. 17.8.73: The National Council for Civil Liberties (NCCL) called for an independent body to investigate charges against the security forces and to reconstitute the RUC.

Tues. 21.8.73: At the close of the inquest into the deaths of 13 people on Bloody Sunday, the Derry coroner, Maj Hubert O'Neill, said the shootings by the army had been "sheer unadulterated murder". In what were to be the first of a series of such attacks in which many people were maimed, seven letter bombs were received at addresses in London.

Wed. 22.8.73: Two Catholic churches in Co Antrim were destroyed by bombs.

Sun. 26.8.73: A 600–800lb car bomb exploded outside a Catholic church in Ballycastle, Co Antrim, during Mass, injuring 200 people, four seriously. The Provisional IRA said a plain-clothes soldier it had shot and wounded the previous day was a member of the Special Air Service (SAS). This was denied by the army.

Tues. 28.8.73: The prime minister, Edward Heath, began a two-day visit to Northern Ireland, attending a memorial service to Lord Brookeborough. Outside the cathedral a crowd heckled Mr Heath and the Unionist party leader, Brian Faulkner, but cheered the VUPP leader, William Craig, on his arrival. Mr Heath met several political leaders and stressed the urgency of forming an executive.

Fri. 31.8.73: Seamus Twomey, chief of staff of the Provisional IRA, was arrested by gardaí in Co Monaghan. In a gun battle in Ballymurphy in Belfast, Patrick Mulvenna was shot dead by troops and Jim Bryson, a leading figure in the

Provisional IRA, who had earlier escaped from both HMS *Maidstone* and Crumlin Road jail, was seriously wounded. He later died in hospital.

Mon. 10.9.73: Bombs exploded in London at King's Cross and Euston stations, injuring 13 people, several seriously. The trial opened in Winchester of 10 Belfast people accused of planting car bombs in London on March 8th 1973. A bomb exploded at a Catholic church on Holywood Road, Belfast, causing serious damage.

Tues. 11.9.73: James Flanagan was appointed RUC chief constable, the first Catholic to hold the post. He was sworn in on November 1st. Kenneth Newman of the Metropolitan Police was appointed senior deputy chief constable.

Wed. 12.9.73: In London, a Belfast woman collapsed and died at Euston station during a bomb alert, a no-warning bomb exploded in Oxford Street, injuring six people, and a bomb exploded in Lower Sloane Street.

Sun. 16.9.73: The body of Tommy Herron, former vice-chair of the UDA, was found at Drumbo, Belfast. Missing for two days, he had been shot in the head.

Mon. 17.9.73: The prime minister, Edward Heath, visited the republic and talked for nine hours with the taoiseach, Liam Cosgrave. It was the first such visit by a British premier since before the foundation of the state in 1922. A communiqué affirmed their mutual support for a Council of Ireland. A 400lb car bomb, described as a present from "Protestants in protest at Mr Heath's visit to Mr Cosgrave" exploded in Belfast injuring 10 people. An army bomb disposal officer was seriously injured by a bomb in Birmingham, and a bomb exploded at an army camp in Surrey.

Tues. 18.9.73: In a television interview the prime minister, Edward Heath, said that if the parties in the assembly did not form an executive by March 1974 it would be much better to integrate Northern Ireland within the UK than to maintain direct rule indefinitely.

Wed. 19.9.73: About 30,000 people, including 8,000 uniformed members of the UDA, attended Tommy Herron's funeral. Following the recent bomb attacks in Britain, identification forms were introduced to check passengers flying between Ireland and England.

Thur. 20.9.73: The Derry UDA man Robert Taylor, who had been extradited to the republic on a charge of murder, was found not guilty in Dublin.

Sat. 29.9.73: There were several explosions and bomb scares in Belfast.

Sun. 30.9.73: The UFF claimed responsibility for the murder of a young Catholic woman from Andersonstown in Belfast. A taxi in which she was travelling was hijacked and she was shot dead.

Tues. 2.10.73: Ten people were injured, two seriously, when a bomb exploded at a bar near Lurgan, Co Armagh.

Thur. 4.10.73: A protest by the United Loyalist Front in support of loyalist detainees in Long Kesh stopped traffic in Belfast from 4pm to 6pm.

Fri. 5.10.73: The secretary of state, William Whitelaw, chaired seven hours of talks between those Unionists supporting Brian Faulkner and the SDLP and Alliance. The parties agreed in principle to form an executive. There were 60 bomb scares in Belfast.

Tues. 9.10.73: After two and a half hours of talks at Stormont, the Unionist and Alliance parties and the SDLP announced a broad measure of agreement on an economic and social programme.

Mon. 15.10.73: The assembly met for the second time. Traffic in Belfast was again brought to a halt by a loyalist demonstration in support of loyalist prisoners in Long Kesh. The first case was heard by a Diplock no-jury court.

Tues. 16.10.73: Unionist, SDLP and Alliance members met again at Stormont and issued an agreed statement on law and order. A UDR soldier was shot dead in the Suffolk area of Belfast. A regular soldier who disappeared with his rifle was being sought by the army. Some weeks later, Provisional Sinn Féin's Dublin paper, *An Phoblacht*, said he was being assisted by the Provisional IRA to leave the country.

Wed. 17.10.73: The assembly met again at Stormont. In raids in the Andersonstown, Falls, New Lodge, Short Strand and Turf Lodge areas of Belfast, troops arrested 16 men and one woman.

Sat. 20.10.73: A further 12 men were arrested in Catholic areas of Belfast. In Dublin, Dáithí Ó Conaill, chief of staff of the Provisional IRA, slipped through a cordon to give a speech to the Provisional Sinn Féin ard fheis.

Mon. 22.10.73: A man died after an explosion at a bar in east Belfast.

Wed. 24.10.73: The SDLP presented a dossier on loyalist violence to William Van Straubenzee, minister of state, but declared that he had offered only "pious platitudes and unfulfilled promises". In the assembly the DUP leader, Rev Ian Paisley, spoke for over three hours.

Thur. 25.10.73: There were bombs, bomb scares, hijackings and burnings across Northern Ireland.

Wed. 31.10.73: Seamus Twomey, former Belfast commander of the Provisional IRA, and two other Provisional IRA men escaped from the exercise yard of Mountjoy prison in Dublin in a hijacked helicopter.

Thur. 1.11.73: In west Belfast three bombs wrecked the Beehive bar, the Republican Clubs headquarters and the headquarters of the CCDC. There were many injuries from flying glass. James Flanagan was sworn in as RUC chief constable.

Sun. 4.11.73: The republic's government announced that its army was to recruit another 3,500 men, half assuming border duties.

Tues. 6.11.73: Night trains between Belfast and Dublin were suspended after hijackings and bombings along the line.

Fri. 9.11.73: The Catholic primate of Ireland, Cardinal William Conway, asked why official condemnation of the assassinations of Catholics was "so muted".

Mon. 12.11.73: Seven no-warning car bombs exploded outside Catholic-owned bars and premises in Belfast. The following day Catholic bars in Armagh and Dungannon and a hotel in Pomeroy used for SDLP conferences were damaged by car bombs. Two loyalist paramilitary groups, the UFF and the Red Hand Commandos, were proscribed.

Wed. 14.11.73: Despite intensive checks by security forces, three bars were wrecked by no-warning car bombs in Belfast.

Thur. 15.11.73: In Winchester, eight members of the Provisional IRA were sentenced to life imprisonment and one to 15 years in jail for their part in planting car bombs in London. Four, Marion and Dolores Price, Hugh Feeney and Gerard Kelly, went on hunger strike demanding to be allowed to serve their sentences in Northern Ireland.

Sat. 17.11.73: The UVF declared a 43-day ceasefire from midnight on the 18th. It claimed responsibility for 97 per cent of loyalist violence "with the exception of sectarian murders".

Wed. 21.11.73: After 10 hours of talks between the secretary of state, William Whitelaw, and the Unionist party, Alliance and the SDLP, an agreement to form an executive of six Unionist, four SDLP and one Alliance member was announced, with Brian Faulkner (Unionist) as chief executive and Gerry Fitt (SDLP) as deputy chief executive. Rev William Beattie of the DUP called the agreement "the greatest betrayal since Lundy". The Provisional IRA said the SDLP were "arch-collaborators" and the armed struggle would be "pursued and intensified". William Craig of the VUPP said his party would make the executive "unworkable". A Marplan poll the following week showed 75 per cent of those interviewed approved power-sharing and the formation of an executive.

Wed. 28.11.73: An assembly meeting was twice interrupted by "grave disorder" and finally adjourned in the face of loyalist disruption.

Sun. 2.12.73: It was announced that Francis Pym was to replace William Whitelaw as secretary of state. The Unionist party throught it strange that Mr Whitelaw should be replaced only three days before the Sunningdale tripartite talks. The SDLP was "bitterly disappointed". The republic's government was "dismayed".

Mon. 3.12.73: Francis Pym was sworn in as secretary of state. "Unpledged" Unionists established a new political group, the Ulster Unionist Assembly party (UUAP), to be led by Harry West. It would remain part of the Unionist party.

Tues. 4.12.73: Francis Pym arrived in Northern Ireland. The DUP leader, Rev Ian Paisley, walked out of a meeting with Mr Pym after hearing that loyalist representatives would not be invited to attend the Sunningdale conference.

Wed. 5.12.73: During an assembly debate, several DUP and VUPP members physically attacked Unionist members.

Thur. 6.12.73: The prime minister, Edward Heath, opened the tripartite talks at Sunningdale in Berkshire, welcoming the taoiseach, Liam Cosgrave, and members of the executive-designate. At a rally in the Ulster Hall in Belfast, the DUP leader, Rev Ian Paisley, addressed 600 delegates from Unionist associations, the DUP, the VUPP and the Orange Order. The United Ulster Unionist Council (UUUC) was formed to oppose power-sharing.

Sun. 9.12.73: After 50 hours of discussion at Sunningdale, an agreed communiqué said that the republic and the British government supported no change in Northern Ireland without the assent of a majority there.

Mon. 10.12.73: The UVF said it would not break its ceasefire over the Sunningdale agreement but that a new Ulster Army Council had been set up—including the UDA, the Ulster Special Constabulary Association, the Loyalist Defence Volunteers and the Red Hand Commandos—to resist a Council of Ireland.

Thur. 13.12.73: At Westminster the Northern Ireland Constitution (Amendment) Bill and a Devolution Order ending direct rule were passed.

Tues. 18.12.73: Three bombs exploded in London after inadequate warnings. Sixty-three people were injured, three seriously, and a letter bomb injured a brigadier aide-de-camp to the Queen. A further three bombs exploded at midnight on Thursday 20th, injuring two.

Mon. 24.12.73: The UVF announced an indefinite extension of its ceasefire.

Thur. 27.12.73: Thomas Niedermayer, honorary West German consul in Belfast, and chair of Grundig, was kidnapped from his home. His body was found in west Belfast in March 1980.

Sat. 29.12.73: Shots were fired at police in many loyalist areas of Belfast, killing one officer and injuring another.

Mon. 31.12.73: The 11 members of the executive and four other members of the power-sharing administration were sworn in. The executive held its first meeting, called for an end to the killings and said 1974 should be the "year of reconciliation".

1974

Tues. 1.1.74: The executive assumed responsibility for government in Northern Ireland.

Thur. 3.1.74: In Belfast, the Garda commissioner, Patrick Malone, had talks with the RUC chief constable, James Flanagan.

Fri. 4.1.74: At the Ulster Unionist Council meeting in Belfast, a motion put by John Taylor, an "unpledged" Unionist, rejecting the "proposed all-Ireland Council settlement", was supported by a majority of 80.

Mon. 7.1.74: Brian Faulkner "reluctantly" resigned as Unionist leader. A few days later his assembly Unionist group moved its headquarters from the Unionist party office in Glengall Street in Belfast.

Wed. 9.1.74: The RUC said a ransom of £250,000 had been demanded for the return of Thomas Niedermayer, kidnapped on December 27th.

Fri. 11.1.74: In Derry a man and a woman were killed in an explosion at Ebrington barracks, where they were employed as civilian workers.

Tues. 15.1.74: Austin Currie, housing minister in the power-sharing executive, was jostled by crowds in Ballymena and Magherafelt.

Wed. 16.1.74: The chief executive, Brian Faulkner, flew to a military airfield outside Dublin for talks with the taoiseach, Liam Cosgrave. He later said he was reassured about "ambiguities" in the republic's interpretation of the Sunningdale agreement. Earlier, in the Dublin High Court, a case brought by Kevin Boland against the republic's government for agreeing to the Sunningdale pact was dismissed. In Hillsborough, loyalists blocked roads in protest at the visit of judges from the republic to attend a meeting of the Anglo-Irish Law Enforcement Commission. Several thousand loyalists, many of whom had gone on strike for the day, attended a rally at Belfast City Hall.

Thur. 17.1.74: The republic's foreign minister, Garret FitzGerald, had talks in London with the secretary of state, Francis Pym. Also in London, the deputy chief executive, Gerry Fitt, had talks with the prime minister, Edward Heath.

Sat. 19.1.74: After a UDA man was arrested in east Belfast, extensive rioting broke out with vehicles hijacked and shops burned. The UDA blamed Tartan gangs.

Sun. 20.1.74: When security forces tried to stop a protest march in support of the Winchester bomb trial prisoners from reaching Belfast city centre, rioting broke out and Hastings Street RUC station was attacked.

Tues. 22.1.74: At the first meeting of the assembly since the formation of the executive, loyalist members occupied frontbench seats and were removed from the chamber. After 18 members had been removed, proceedings resumed. At a meeting of the Standing Committee of the Unionist party, Harry West defeated James Molyneaux by 42 votes to become the new party leader.

Wed. 23.1.74: In Belfast, shops in Wellington Place and Queen Street were destroyed by fire.

Thur. 24.1.74: Armed men and a woman hijacked a helicopter and its pilot in Donegal, flew to Strabane and attempted to drop milk-churn bombs on the RUC station but missed.

Sat. 26.1.74: Around 3,500 people attended a NICRA Bloody Sunday commemoration in Derry and unveiled a monument to the dead. The following day 6,500 people attended a Provisional IRA commemoration.

Mon. 28.1.74: The Provisional IRA announced that it would no longer kill off-duty UDR men. In response, the following day the UVF called on all loyalist paramilitaries to stop sectarian murders. The UFF declared that it would continue to kill "enemies of our state". The Home Office confirmed a claim by the DUP leader, Rev Ian Paisley, that the Provisional IRA had demanded the return to Northern Ireland of the London car bombers in return for the safe release of Thomas Niedermayer. A leading Republican Clubs figure in Belfast, Jim Sullivan, was awarded £1,000 damages at Belfast High Court for maltreatment following his arrest on October 9th 1971.

Thur. 31.1.74: In Newtownabbey, Co Antrim, gunmen held electricity workers at gunpoint in their hut, stole their pay packets, separated the Protestants and the Catholics and opened fire, killing two Catholics and wounding two others and a Protestant.

Fri.1.2.74: Talks were held at Hillsborough between the chief executive, Brian Faulkner, and seven executive members and the taoiseach, Liam Cosgrave, and seven members of his cabinet. There were loyalist protest walkouts at some factories.

Mon. 4.2.74: Eleven people, including two children and a woman, died in an explosion that wrecked an army coach on the M62 in Yorkshire. The UDA rejected an appeal for "peace and reconciliation" made the previous day by the UVF. The Provisional IRA had welcomed it.

Tues. 5.2.74: In Preston in Lancashire eight UDA men were arrested and arms and ammunition were seized in raids.

Thur. 7.2.74: The prime minister, Edward Heath, announced that a general election would be held on February 28th.

Sat. 9.2.74: In Belfast, UFF gunmen firing from the grounds of the Royal Victoria Hospital killed two men and seriously injured a woman leaving a bar.

Mon. 11.2.74: In a gun attack on a car full of Catholic workers on their way to Whiteabbey, Co Antrim, UFF gunmen killed a youth and wounded four others. One, an 18-year-old woman, later died in hospital. A Protestant youth in a car behind was also wounded. The UFF claimed the action was in retaliation for the coach bomb in Yorkshire. Fr Edward Daly was appointed Catholic bishop of Derry.

Tues. 12.2.74: A bomb at an army staff college in Buckinghamshire injured 10 people, four seriously.

Wed. 13.2.74: One of the detainees who had been arrested in the first internment swoops and subjected to "deep interrogation techniques" was awarded £15,000 at Belfast High Court.

Thur. 14.2.74: In Dungannon, Co Tyrone, a 700lb bomb in a hijacked post office van caused an estimated £1 million damage to property. Two days later another bomb in a post office van caused extensive damage to Omagh town centre.

Sat. 16.2.74: There was rioting in east Belfast and, later, in an exchange of fire between troops and gunmen, a 19-year-old civilian was shot dead and two others seriously wounded. One later died in hospital.

Mon. 18.2.74: In Belfast, troops escorted prisoners to courts when RUC men withdrew this service in protest at a Special Branch detective being charged under the Northern Ireland (Emergency Provisions) Act. Eight hundred members of the Police Federation had voted unanimously for the RUC action the previous day.

Tues. 19.2.74: A no-warning bomb at a bar between Armagh and Moy killed two men, a Protestant and a Catholic. A 500lb bomb in a car hijacked in Andersonstown caused extensive damage and minor injuries in Castle Street in Belfast.

Thur. 21.2.74: An 81-year-old man was killed and a woman seriously wounded in a no-warning bomb in a bar on the New Lodge Road in Belfast.

Fri. 22.2.74: Firebombs badly damaged the Woolworths store on High Street, Belfast. Later a 200lb bomb exploded in Union Street,

damaging several buildings. There were also bombs in Castlewellan, Cookstown and Newcastle. Ivor Bell, commander of the Belfast brigade of the Provisional IRA and one of the delegates to the secret talks in London in June 1972, was arrested by troops in Andersonstown.

Mon. 25.2.74: Following the death in hospital of a youth shot in an exchange of fire between troops and gunmen in east Belfast on February 16th, vehicles were hijacked and burned.

Tues. 26.2.74: A bomb wrecked the headquarters of the Alliance party in Belfast.

Wed. 27.2.74: In Dublin Martin McGuinness, former commander of the Provisional IRA in Derry, was sentenced to 12 months in prison for membership of the IRA.

Thur. 28.2.74: Polling took place in the UK general election. Twelve bombs exploded in Belfast, killing a man, seriously injuring a woman and causing extensive damage. The Provisional IRA claimed responsibility.

Fri. 1.3.74: In a swing of 15.8 per cent, later described as "unprecedented in British politics", results in the UK election showed that the UUUC, supporting anti-Sunningdale policies, had gained 11 out of the 12 Northern Ireland seats. The other, West Belfast, was won by Gerry Fitt of the SDLP. Successful UUUC candidates included Rev Ian Paisley, William Craig, Harry West, Rev Robert Bradford, James Molyneaux, James Kilfedder, William Ross, and Harold McCusker.

Sun. 3.3.74: The newly elected UUUC members decided they would not accept the whip of any of the British parties.

Tues. 5.3.74: In the change of government at Westminster, Labour's Merlyn Rees was appointed secretary of state. Numerous fires and three explosions caused extensive damage to city-centre shops in Belfast. There were car bombs in Coalisland and Downpatrick, the latter damaging 25 shops. The deputy chief executive, Gerry Fitt, flew to London for talks with the new prime minister, Harold Wilson, and Mr Rees. Later Mr Rees flew to Belfast and began talks with the chief executive, Brian Faulkner, and John Hume and Oliver Napier, executive members.

Wed. 6.3.74: The secretary of state, Merlyn Rees, had talks at Stormont with the executive, the GOC and the RUC chief constable. At a press conference he said that he had met the Provisional IRA twice while in opposition but would never do so again.

Thur. 7.3.74: Merlyn Rees had talks in London with the UUUC MPs Harry West, William Craig and Rev Ian Paisley, and later with the republic's foreign minister, Garret FitzGerald. In Belfast the army-occupied Grand Central Hotel was severely damaged by a 500lb bomb.

Sat. 9.3.74: UUUC MPs took part in a march to Stormont, addressing a 2,000-strong rally. Rev Ian Paisley said that the Sunningdale agreement was dead.

Mon. 11.3.74: In Dublin the Littlejohn brothers escaped from Mountjoy prison. Keith was recaptured shortly afterwards.

Tues. 12.3.74: The UFF claimed the assassination of the Seanad member, Billy Fox, near Clones, Co Monaghan. Maire Drumm, vice-president of Provisional Sinn Féin, was arrested in Dublin.

Wed. 13.3.74: A gunman shot dead a soldier from the porch of a Catholic church in Chapel Lane in Belfast, escaping through the church. The bishop of Down and Connor, Dr William Philbin, said it was "murder and sacrilege". After many calls to clarify his position on the constitution of Northern Ireland in the light of Sunningdale, the taoiseach, Liam Cosgrave, told the Dáil that "the factual position of Northern Ireland is that it is within the UK and my government accepts this as a fact".

Fri. 15.3.74: Three people were killed in explosions, two at Dungannon and one at Magherafelt. Incendiary devices caused considerable damage to shops, and traffic was severely disrupted by hoax calls in Belfast.

Sat. 16.3.74: Two soldiers were shot dead in an ambush near Crossmaglen, Co Armagh.

Mon. 18.3.74: The army confirmed that plain-clothes SAS men were now on duty in Northern Ireland.

Wed. 20.3.74: Two men shot dead by the RUC on a country road near Mowhan, Co Armagh, turned out to be soldiers returning from leave. The secretary of state, Merlyn Rees, denied the following day that the soldiers had been part of an undercover unit.

Tues. 26.3.74: A bookshop in central Belfast was badly damaged in the second incendiary attack on it in a week.

Thur. 28.3.74: The Grand Central Hotel in Belfast was again damaged by a large bomb. Fire brigades from four towns were called to deal with fires after a bomb attached to a tanker of liquid gas exploded in Derry.

Sat. 30.3.74: A no-warning bomb exploded in the Crescent bar in Sandy Row, Belfast, killing two men.

Sun. 31.3.74: In Lurgan, Co Armagh, troops found a Russian-made RPG-7 rocket launcher.

Mon. 1.4.74: A senior UVF officer, Jim Hanna, was found shot dead in a car in the Shankill area of Belfast. The prime minister, Harold Wilson, the secretary of state, Merlyn Rees, and the chief executive, Brian Faulkner, met at Downing Street. Later the deputy chief executive, Gerry Fitt, had talks with Mr Wilson.

Tues. 2.4.74: The army announced the capture of three American rifles, Armalite 180s, which had not been seen before in Northern Ireland.

Wed. 3.4.74: The RUC chief constable, James Flanagan, and the Garda commissioner, Patrick Malone, had talks at Garda headquarters in Dublin.

Thur. 4.4.74: In the Commons, the secretary of state, Merlyn Rees, outlined proposals for Northern Ireland which included phased releases of detainees, changes in the RUC and the removal of Provisional Sinn Féin and the UVF from the proscribed list. He expressed the government's support for the Sunningdale agreement and the executive.

Fri. 5.4.74: The taoiseach, Liam Cosgrave, and the prime minister, Harold Wilson, had talks at Downing Street.

Sat. 6.4.74: Fourteen bombs, mainly incendiaries, exploded in London shops, with three in Birmingham and two in Manchester. The chief executive, Brian Faulkner, called for the transfer of law and order powers to the executive.

Tues. 9.4.74: The centre of Armagh was partly destroyed by incendiary bombs, claimed by the Provisional IRA, which burned down 10 shops. Incendiaries also caused fires in Belfast, Newry and Dungannon. Also in Belfast, bombs in Hillman Street, North Queen Street and Botanic Avenue caused widespread damage and injured eight people, one seriously. Vehicles were hijacked and rioting developed in Catholic west Belfast. The defence secretary, Roy Mason, said no members of the SAS were serving in Northern Ireland.

Wed. 10.4.74: The Home Office confirmed that three IRA prisoners in Albany prison, Isle of Wight—Francis Stagg, Michael Gaughan and Paul Holmes—had been on hunger strike since March 30th for the right to serve their sentences in Northern Ireland.

Thur. 11.4.74: The Northern Ireland Office (NIO) confirmed that civilian searchers would replace soldiers at some city-centre security gates.

Fri. 12.4.74: After the last of a three-part interview with Kenneth Littlejohn had been published in *Time Out* magazine, detailing his involvement with British Special Branch officers in the activities which led to his imprisonment in the republic, a warrant for his arrest was issued in Bedfordshire.

Sat. 13.4.74: Rioting broke out after paratroops questioned a man in the Shankill area of Belfast. Troops eventually opened fire, wounding three civilians.

Sun. 14.4.74: After the death in hospital of a youth who had been wounded by troops the previous day, rioting again broke out on the Shankill. In Derry a plain-clothes army officer was shot dead while taking photographs of a Sinn Féin march. The Provisional IRA claimed he was a member of the SAS, but the army denied this.

Mon. 15.4.74: Ivor Bell, former Belfast commander of the Provisional IRA, escaped from the Maze prison. He was found two weeks later in a south Belfast flat.

Thur. 18.4.74: After a series of talks in an eight-hour visit to Northern Ireland, the prime minister, Harold Wilson, said if the power-sharing executive failed "there would be little hope that we could once again reconstruct a fresh political initiative". Speaking in Belfast, the former Conservative MP Enoch Powell called for full integration of Northern Ireland within the UK and said he would consider standing for a Northern Ireland seat at Westminster should one become available. A BBC/RTE opinion poll found that 69 per cent favoured giving the executive and the Sunningdale agreement a chance.

Fri. 19.4.74: Bombs and incendiary devices exploded in Belfast and several towns in Northern Ireland.

Mon. 22.4.74: An 18-year-old Pakistani army canteen attendant was shot dead in Co Armagh by the Provisional IRA, which claimed he was a member of the SAS. An SDLP delegation met members of the republic's cabinet in Dublin.

Wed. 24.4.74: In a speech at Newcastle under Lyme, the defence secretary, Roy Mason, said that pressure was mounting in Britain to set a date for the withdrawal of troops from Northern Ireland. The Ministry of Defence later denied that there had been a change in policy. This was reiterated the following day by the prime minister, Harold Wilson, and the secretary of state for Northern Ireland, Merlyn Rees.

Tues. 30.4.74: Judith Ward was charged with the murder of the 11 victims of the army coach bomb on February 4th. In the assembly, Basil McIvor, minister of education, outlined proposals for gradual integration of schooling.

Thur. 2.5.74: A bomb thrown into the lounge of the Rose and Crown bar in south Belfast killed five Catholics and injured 18 others, some seriously. One of these, the manager, Francis Brennan, later died in hospital. Two bombs exploded inside the Europa Hotel in Belfast.

Sun. 5.5.74: Brian Faulkner's pro-assembly Unionists decided to sever links with the Ulster Unionist party and reform as a new Unionist party. A bomb exploded at the home of William Craig, the VUPP leader.

Tues. 7.5.74: A Catholic couple, Mr and Mrs James Devlin, were shot dead and their daughter was seriously wounded when gunmen opened fire on their car near Coalisland, Co Tyrone. Two Catholic workmen were shot dead and five wounded in a machine-gun attack at Carnmoney, Co Antrim. Smithfield market in Belfast was destroyed by fire.

Fri. 10.5.74: Two RUC men were shot dead in the Finaghy area of Belfast. Police raided a house in the Malone area and arrested Brendan Hughes, who had escaped from the Maze five months earlier and was posing as a stockbroker, and Denis Loughran—both were leading members of the Provisional IRA. Weapons, ammunition, explosives and maps were seized.

Wed. 15.5.74: After a motion supporting the Sunningdale agreement had been passed in the assembly the previous day, the Ulster Workers' Council (UWC) called a "general stoppage". Four-hourly power cuts were imposed throughout Northern Ireland, many factories closed, there were reports of intimidation and buses were hijacked in Belfast. In Larne, Co Antrim, 100 uniformed UDA men, some armed with clubs, sealed off the town with hijacked vehicles and ordered those going to work to return home.

Thur. 16.5.74: Uniformed UDA men stopped vehicles, commandeering cars and buses for barricades. The Citybus fleet in Belfast was withdrawn. The UWC issued a phone number for those who considered their work essential. Bars, hotels and bookmakers were ordered to close by the UWC. There were widespread reports of intimidation. The secretary of state, Merlyn Rees, met loyalist leaders at Stormont and refused to negotiate with representatives of the UWC.

Fri. 17.5.74: No-warning car bombs exploded in the republic, killing five people in Monaghan and, in three blasts, 22 people in Dublin. More than 100 were injured, many seriously. The death toll later rose to 32. Two of the three cars used in Dublin had been hijacked earlier in the day in Protestant areas of Belfast, and the

Monaghan car in Portadown, Co Armagh. The UDA and the UVF both denied responsibility, although the UDA press officer said he was "happy" about the bombings. As the UWC strike continued, petrol supplies began to run low. All major factories and most building sites were closed following massive intimidation.

Sat. 18.5.74: There were long food queues throughout Northern Ireland. The UWC called for an all-out stoppage from Sunday midnight because of the secretary of state's refusal to meet it.

Sun. 19.5.74: A 100lb car bomb exploded in a multi-storey car park at Heathrow airport, causing extensive damage. The secretary of state, Merlyn Rees, announced a state of emergency. It was reported that several hundred Royal Engineers were on standby. The only power station operating was Ballylumford in Co Antrim, producing a quarter of its normal supply, and there were power cuts for up to 12 hours throughout Northern Ireland. Panic buying of food was widespread. In the late evening the UWC announced a shutdown of all industrial and commercial business and public transport, but held back from an all-out stoppage at the power stations.

Mon. 20.5.74: Five hundred additional troops were flown into Northern Ireland, bringing the total to 16,000. In the morning some 100 barricades were erected in Belfast alone. No factories and few petrol stations were open in the city, electricity supply was cut to one-third and buses ran on only three routes, in Catholic areas. In the evening the UDA announced that all major roads would be barricaded the following morning and only doctors, nurses and ambulances would be allowed to pass.

Tues. 21.5.74: A "back-to-work" march, led by Len Murray, general secretary of the British Trades Union Congress, and supported by leading trade union officials, drew only 200 people who were jeered and attacked by a hostile crowd. There was widespread barricading but most access roads to Belfast were kept open by troops and police. Long queues of people looking for passes to go about their business formed outside the UWC headquarters in east Belfast. There were also long queues for food, milk and emergency benefit payments ordered by Paddy Devlin, minister of health and social services. The UWC announced an embargo on oil and petrol supplies.

Wed. 22.5.74: The NIO said the government would not negotiate with the UWC. A further 500 troops arrived. There were loyalist rallies throughout Northern Ireland. The chief executive, Brian Faulkner, in a statement agreed by the executive parties, announced the executive's contention that elements of the Sunningdale agreement should be deferred until after the next election in 1977–78.

Thur. 23.5.74: Security forces removed barricades continually, only to find them reappearing. The deputy chief executive, Gerry Fitt, called for troops to go into the power stations immediately.

Fri. 24.5.74: Brian Faulkner, Gerry Fitt and Oliver Napier flew to London for urgent talks with the prime minister, Harold Wilson. Two

brothers, Sean and Brendan Byrne, were shot dead in their bar in Tannaghmore, Co Antrim.

Sat. 25.5.74: Hundreds of farmers blocked roads throughout Northern Ireland in support of the strike. Around 10,000 people attended an anti-Sunningdale rally in Portadown, Co Armagh. The prime minister, Harold Wilson, broadcast to the country in the evening and called the strike organisers "thugs and bullies" who were "sponging on Westminster and British democracy". Over the following days many people in Protestant districts defiantly wore pieces of sponge in their lapels.

Mon. 27.5.74: Gas supplies in Belfast, Bangor and Carrickfergus had to be withdrawn. The army was ordered to take over 21 petrol stations and control distribution to essential users. The UWC announced that the army could now undertake all essential deliveries of food etc., and that Ballylumford power station would now close. No trains ran from Belfast to Dublin.

Tues. 28.5.74: After a meeting of the executive, Brian Faulkner advised the secretary of state, Merlyn Rees, to open talks with the UWC. When Mr Rees refused, Mr Faulkner and his Unionist colleagues resigned. Mr Rees declared that there was now no statutory basis for the executive. Farmers drove hundreds of tractors to Stormont and lined the drive calling for negotiations with the UWC. After meeting Rev Ian Paisley, William Craig and Harry West, the UWC said the strike was still on as new assembly elections had not been called and it had not officially heard from Merlyn Rees. There were bonfires and parades in many towns and in Protestant areas of Belfast.

Wed. 29.5.74: The UWC announced the end of the strike and a phased return to work. The secretary of state, Merlyn Rees, announced that the assembly would be prorogued for four months. There were loyalist victory rallies in many parts of Northern Ireland.

Thur. 30.5.74: The Northern Ireland Chamber of Commerce said that one and a half million worker days had been lost in the strike and the total cost was £30 million. The secretary of state, Merlyn Rees, had talks with the leaders of the six main political parties.

Fri. 31.5.74: Merlyn Rees said that the "rise of Ulster nationalism" demonstrated during the strike was a major force, which the British government had to take into account.

Sat. 1.6.74: The home secretary, Roy Jenkins, said while it was reasonable that the Price sisters might serve their sentences in Northern Ireland, he would not be pressurised into decisions. After they had been force-fed for 167 days, prison doctors had thought it unsafe to continue and for the previous 14 days the sisters had had water only. Eight thousand people attended a loyalist rally at Stormont to celebrate the fall of the executive.

Mon. 3.6.74: Michael Gaughan, a republican prisoner in Parkhurst prison, Isle of Wight, died after 65 days on hunger strike for political status and the right to serve his sentence in Northern Ireland.

Tues. 4.6.74: Lord and Lady Donoughmore were kidnapped by armed men from their home near Clonmel, Co Tipperary.

Fri. 7.6.74: Dolores and Marion Price, Gerard Kelly and Hugh Feeney, republican prisoners held in English jails for their part in the London car bombings of March 1973, ended their hunger strikes after 206 days, including 167 days of force-feeding.

Sat. 8.6.74: After Frank Stagg was "instructed" by the Provisional IRA to end his 70-day hunger strike, the Home Office announced that all hunger strikers were now taking food.

Sun. 9.6.74: A 13-year-old Catholic girl was killed and 12 people injured, three seriously, in a no-warning car bomb in Hannahstown, outside Belfast, claimed by the UFF. Lord and Lady Donoughmore were released by their captors in Phoenix Park, Dublin, and said they understood that they had been released because of the ending of the Price sisters' hunger strike. Ten thousand people attended the funeral of Michael Gaughan at Ballina, Co Mayo. The oration was read by Dáithí Ó Conaill, chief of staff of the Provisional IRA.

Wed. 12.6.74: Thomas Passmore, Belfast grand master of the Orange Order, said he was "shocked and surprised" that troops had found 50 weapons and 6,000 rounds of ammunition in two Orange halls in Belfast. More weapons were found the following day at a third Orange hall.

Thur. 13.6.74: A 500lb car bomb caused considerable damage to houses and injured a soldier in the Malone area of Belfast.

Sat. 15.6.74: Patrick Cunningham, a 22-year-old Catholic with a reputed mental age of 10, was shot dead by soldiers near Benburb, Co Tyrone. Austin Currie, a former executive member, called for an inquiry. A 200lb bomb caused considerable damage to the BBC headquarters in Belfast.

Mon. 17.6.74: A bomb injured seven people and started a fire which extensively damaged Westminster Great Hall.

Tues. 18.6.74: An RUC man was killed in an explosion in Lurgan, Co Armagh. Nine people were injured by a car bomb which seriously damaged the Europa Hotel in Belfast. Car bombs exploded at seven other locations in Northern Ireland. All were claimed by the Provisional IRA.

Wed. 19.6.74: The Provisional IRA claimed responsibility for several more explosions in towns in Northern Ireland, including four inside the security gates in Derry.

Thur. 20.6.74: Oliver Napier, leader of the Alliance party, called for an end to internment.

Fri. 21.6.74: Clifford Smyth, UUUC candidate in the North Antrim assembly by-election, won the seat easily with almost 30,000 votes. The three-year prison sentence passed on L/Cpl Foxford for "unlawfully killing" a 13-year-old boy in Newry on February 27th 1973 was quashed on appeal.

Sat. 22.6.74: An unarmed Catholic, Hugh Devine, was shot dead by a soldier in Strabane, Co Tyrone. The following day Trooper Alec Fury of the Life Guards became the first soldier to be charged with murder while serving in Northern Ireland. The UVF launched the Volunteer Political party, saying it would seek affiliation to the UUUC.

Sat. 29.6.74: In Lurgan, Co Armagh, the headquarters of the Royal Black Institution was severely damaged by fire.

Sun. 30.6.74: The Ulster Unionist party (UUP) issued its policy manifesto, calling for a strong regional parliament for Northern Ireland and rejecting power-sharing with "republicans". The republic's foreign minister, Garret FitzGerald, began a two-day visit to Belfast.

Tues. 2.7.74: One soldier was killed and another was seriously injured in an explosion in Newtownhamilton, Co Armagh.

Wed. 3.7.74: Nine Lancashire UDA men were jailed for two years for conspiracy with intent to use force and possession of firearms.

Thur. 4.7.74: A British government white paper proposed a 78-seat constitutional convention. It insisted on power-sharing and said the willingness of Britain to aid Northern Ireland economically would "inevitably be affected by the progress of events there".

Sun. 7.7.74: At a seminar in Oxford a statement signed by members of the Faulknerite Unionists, the SDLP and Alliance and by Harry Murray of the UWC called for the ending of internment. Brian Faulkner later distanced himself from the statement. Mr Murray said the UWC was prepared to talk to the IRA in the event of a ceasefire. Maire Drumm of Provisional Sinn Féin said that though it had not been invited to the seminar it was willing to talk to the UWC. The following day Mr Murray's attendance was condemned by the VUPP leader, William Craig.

Mon. 8.7.74: The Provisional IRA repudiated the white paper.

Tues. 9.7.74: In the Commons debate on the white paper the secretary of state, Merlyn Rees, announced a gradual phasing out of internment, despite open army opposition. Harry Murray resigned as chair of the UWC after criticism of his "soft line" on the IRA.

Wed. 10.7.74: Further loyalist divisions emerged, with John Taylor urging a hard line on internment, while the UDA said it would no longer support politicians who did not call for it to be ended.

Fri. 12.7.74: At the Twelfth "field" at Edenderry in Belfast, John Taylor called for the formation of a 20,000-strong armed "home guard", with or without the assent of the government. The call was later welcomed by the Ulster Unionist leader, Harry West, but condemned as "an open incitement to civil war" by Brian Faulkner and as "sedition" by the Alliance leader, Oliver Napier.

Tues. 16.7.74: A Catholic man was killed and six people injured, three seriously, by a no-warning bomb outside the Sunflower bar in Corporation Street in Belfast. In the republic a bill regulating contraception, introduced by the government but voted against by the taoiseach, Liam Cosgrave, was defeated by a small majority. The result was condemned by the Alliance party and the SDLP and greeted with glee by loyalist politicians.

Sun. 21.7.74: The UDA announced its resignation from the co-ordinating committee of loyalist paramilitary groups and from the UWC and invited representatives of the Catholic community to talks. The SDLP and Republican Clubs later contacted the UDA. The Official Republican movement expelled Seamus Costello, a former member of its leadership.

Mon. 22.7.74: The British government announced it was to acquire a major shareholding in Harland and Wolff shipyard to save it from liquidation.

Tues. 23.7.74: A bomb claimed by the Provisional IRA was discovered on a British Airways plane, prompting a British Airline Pilots Association refusal to take cleaners or food on board at Aldergrove.

Thur. 25.7.74: Five proxy car bombs exploded in central Belfast, causing widespread damage and traffic chaos.

Fri. 25.7.74: Following an explosion in a car park at Heathrow airport and two incendiary explosions in a Birmingham factory, the secretary of state, Merlyn Rees, suspended the phasing out of internment.

Sat. 27.7.74: Five bombs caused extensive damage in Portglenone, Co Antrim.

Sun. 28.7.74: Provisional Sinn Féin began a fortnight of anti-internment protest with a rally in Andersonstown in Belfast at which the vice-president, Maire Drumm, announced its willingness to talk to any loyalist organisation.

Mon. 29.7.74: The body of a young woman, Ann Ogilvy, was found beaten to death near the M1 motorway in Belfast. In February of the following year two teenage girls pleaded guilty to her murder in a UDA club in Sandy Row. The Provisional IRA announced a month-long amnesty for informers. An Official Sinn Féin "anti-imperialist" conference opened in Belfast.

Tues. 30.7.74: The defence secretary, Roy Mason, again denied that members of the SAS were serving in Northern Ireland. A soldier was shot dead in the New Lodge area of Belfast.

Thur. 1.8.74: A 400lb bomb caused structural damage to the Belfast Co-operative store and to the *Irish News* office. The SDLP and the UDA met for under two hours but hopes of further talks ended when the UDA laid down a precondition that the SDLP end its aspiration to a united Ireland.

Mon. 5.8.74: During a two-hour gun battle in the Ardoyne area of Belfast, a 66-year-old grandmother was shot dead by a stray bullet and two soldiers received leg wounds.

Tues. 6.8.74: The Provisional IRA announced that electricity installations and employees in the Newry area would be legitimate targets while the army controlled street lighting. Electricity workers went on strike.

Wed. 7.8.74: The secretary of state, Merlyn Rees, broke Labour policy by entering discussions with the co-ordinating committee of the UWC. Patrick McElhone, a 22-year-old Catholic, was shot dead after questioning by British soldiers at his home in Pomeroy, Co Tyrone. The army said the incident was *sub judice*, but the following day, when a soldier was charged with murder, John Taylor, the former minister of home affairs, said this was no excuse for withholding information. Fr Denis Faul of Dungannon called the death "premeditated murder". The soldier was acquitted on March 27th 1975. The Faulknerite

Unionist party issued a policy document abandoning the idea of a Council of Ireland.

Fri. 9.8.74: The third anniversary of internment was marked by hijackings, burnings and barricades on the Falls Road in Belfast. In Pomeroy, 3,000 mourners attended the funeral of Patrick McElhone. The government announced that there was now a blueprint for controlling essential services in the event of another loyalist strike.

Sun. 11.8.74: A march against internment, organised by the Political Hostages Release Committee, attracted 2,000 people who closed the M1 while attempting to march to Long Kesh. Troops fired baton rounds and marchers threw stones.

Mon. 12.8.74: The loyalist Red Hand Commandos, thought responsible for many sectarian killings, declared a ceasefire.

Tues. 13.8.74: A blast bomb, claimed by the Provisional IRA, killed two marines and injured two others near Crossmaglen, Co Armagh.

Thur. 15.8.74: Much of Newry's industry came to a halt because of the strike by electricity workers.

Sun. 18.8.74: Nineteen Provisional IRA prisoners, including Kevin Mallon, Martin McGuinness and Brendan Hughes, blasted their way out of Portlaoise prison in the republic.

Mon. 19.8.74: The UDA came out strongly against loyalist calls for a "third force", claiming it would push the Catholic community "deeper into the grip of the IRA".

Tues. 20.8.74: A mass meeting in Newry called for trade union and business leaders to negotiate with the Provisional IRA and the army about the control of street lighting. The following days saw demonstrations blocking the town's main streets.

Wed. 21.8.74: The NIO announced the winding up of the Community Relations Commission.

Fri. 23.8.74: Det Insp Peter Flanagan, head of the Special Branch in Omagh, Co Tyrone, was shot dead in a bar in the town. The killing was claimed by the Provisional IRA.

Sat. 31.8.74: Five proxy car bombs exploded in Belfast.

Mon. 2.9.74: The secretary of state, Merlyn Rees, announced that the RUC, RUC Reserve and UDR were to be greatly expanded, that a form of community policing was to be tried but that there would be no large-scale withdrawal of troops and no "third force".

Tues. 3.9.74: Enoch Powell was nominated Ulster Unionist candidate for South Down. The following day he dismissed the idea of power-sharing.

Wed. 4.9.74: Following a statement by minister of state, Stan Orme, that control of electricity in Newry would return to the Northern Ireland Electricity Service, the Provisional IRA said electricity workers were free to return to work. The RUC station at Newtownhamilton, Co Armagh, was extensively damaged by a proxy car bomb.

Fri. 6.9.74: An RUC inspector was shot dead attempting to stop bank robbers escaping in Rathcoole, north Belfast. Their car had been hijacked in Catholic west Belfast.

Sat. 7.9.74: A 75lb car bomb caused extensive damage to a shopping centre in south Belfast.

Sun. 8.9.74: Two ex-UWC leaders, Bob Pagles and Harry Murray, were among members of a Peace and Reconciliation Committee formed by 12 Belfast peace groups. The UWC said the following day that Messrs Pagles and Murray had been expelled for consorting "with the enemies of Ulster". Mr Pagles resigned from the peace committee two days later.

Mon. 9.9.74: The first of a series of British government green papers, *Northern Ireland: finance and the economy*, was published. The secretary of state, Merlyn Rees, advised "the UDI brigade" to look very closely at it.

Tues. 10.9.74: After an SDLP delegation met the prime minister, Harold Wilson, a communiqué said any political arrangement must include "some form of power-sharing" and a recognition of the "special relationship of Northern Ireland with the south".

Wed. 11.9.74: After a meeting in London between the prime minister, Harold Wilson, and the taoiseach, Liam Cosgrave, and senior members of their cabinets, a communiqué said that the necessity for power-sharing and recognition of the "special relationship" were agreed.

Thur. 12.9.74: In Belfast there were loyalist and republican demonstrations in support of protests by "special category" prisoners in Long Kesh about food and conditions.

Fri.13.9.74: The republic's foreign minister, Garret FitzGerald, made an unannounced visit to Derry and met representatives of the SDLP and the Faulknerite Unionist party.

Mon. 16.9.74: In Belfast Justice Rory Conaghan and Martin McBirney, a magistrate, were shot dead at their homes by the Provisional IRA. A joint statement from UDA, UVF, Provisional and Official IRA prisoners in Long Kesh rejected improvements proposed by the secretary of state, Merlyn Rees, the previous Sunday.

Sat. 21.9.74: Loyalist prisoners in Long Kesh ended their two-week protest against food standards and conditions. Provisional IRA prisoners said they would continue and if necessary escalate their protest.

Tues. 24.9.74: Bombs in Derry badly damaged four shops.

Wed. 25.9.74: In Long Kesh, republican prisoners continued to throw food over the wire and threatened to burn the camp, along with Magilligan and Armagh prisoners. The *Irish Times* published a leaked report by Conor Cruise O'Brien, minister for posts and telegraphs, which recommended a low profile on the part of the Dublin government to ensure a non-loyalist victory in the coming elections in the north and considered how the republic might respond to a situation where a loyalist majority declared UDI and the British pulled out.

Sun. 29.9.74: Loyalist prisoners in Long Kesh resumed their protest.

Tues. 1.10.74: Rioting broke out among loyalist and republican prisoners in Long Kesh. The SDLP launched its manifesto and said that in the event of a loyalist majority rejecting power-sharing and the "Irish dimension", it would call

on the British government to withdraw its constitutional guarantees. A group of dissident NILP members set up a new Labour party, accusing the NILP of adopting sectarian policies to win Protestant votes.

Wed. 2.10.74: After visitors to Long Kesh had torn down fences and burned huts in the car park, a truce was announced between prisoners and the authorities.

Thur. 3.10.74: The Alliance party manifesto stressed that power-sharing was the only principle on which Northern Ireland could be governed. Enoch Powell, in open contradiction of UUUC policy, called for the British electorate to vote Labour. The following day he denied the right of nationalists to aspire to a united Ireland.

Sat. 5.10.74: Two soldiers and three civilians, two female and one male, were killed and 54 people were injured when bombs exploded without warning in two pubs in Guildford, Surrey.

Sun. 6.10.74: It was disclosed that two UDA leaders had had talks with the taoiseach, Liam Cosgrave, on September 26th.

Tues. 8.10.74: Several bombs exploded in central Belfast without warning, causing extensive damage.

Wed. 9.10.74: It was disclosed that Frank Stagg had resumed his hunger strike at Long Lartin prison against body searches before visits.

Thur. 10.10.74: A sectarian killing of a Catholic in Newtownabbey, Co Antrim, was claimed by the Protestant Action Force (PAF).

Fri. 11.10.74: Labour won the British general election. In Northern Ireland, UUUC candidates won an overwhelming victory, winning 10 of the 12 Westminster seats. The SDLP held West Belfast and an independent, Frank Maguire, took Fermanagh/South Tyrone from Harry West, leader of the UUP. The Faulknerite Unionists, who had formally established the Unionist Party of Northern Ireland in September, polled fewer votes than the Republican Clubs.

Sun. 13.10.74: A 17-year-old Catholic was found beaten and shot dead on the Hightown Road, Belfast, bringing the number of sectarian assassinations in the previous two weeks to 16. The following week saw many attempted killings of Catholics.

Tues. 15.10.74: Republican prisoners in Long Kesh burned down a major part of the camp, including 40 huts. A pitched battle with security forces followed, during which loyalist prisoners set up a field hospital in support. Three hundred republicans eventually sought refuge in the loyalist compounds, whence a safe passage was negotiated by loyalist leaders.

Wed. 16.10.74: Nine prisoners were said officially to have been injured at Long Kesh, but it was reported that over 130 had been treated at the Royal Victoria Hospital (RVH) in Belfast alone. The following day the figure for injured prison officers and troops was given as 37, for prisoners as 29. There were riots in Crumlin Road jail and as many as 100 prisoners received injuries requiring at least stitching. Prisoners at Magilligan rioted and burned huts in solidarity. Women prisoners in Armagh held hostage the

governor and three senior prison officers. There were running battles and barricades on the Falls Road in Belfast and Derry and Strabane saw large demonstrations.

Fri. 18.10.74: Long Kesh chaplains appealed for clothing for the very many prisoners forced to sleep in the open.

Mon. 21.10.74: Two Catholics were shot dead on their way to work on the Falls Road in Belfast. The body of a Protestant was found in the Catholic Glenard estate.

Tues. 22.10.74: A Catholic was killed and six others injured by a bomb in a radio outside a bookmaker's shop in central Belfast. The UUUC parliamentary group unanimously elected the Ulster Unionist James Molyneaux as its leader in the Commons.

Mon. 28.10.74: Two soldiers were killed and 28 injured, along with three civilians, when a 300lb no-warning bomb exploded at a recreational centre outside Ballykinlar military camp in Co Down.

Mon. 4.11.74: At Wakefield Crown Court Judith Ward was sentenced to 20 years in prison for 12 murders in the army coach bombing on the M62 on February 4th. The following day the Provisional IRA denied she was a member or had been involved.

Tues. 5.11.74: The Irish Civil Rights Association announced that Frank Stagg had come off his 34-day hunger strike after the Home Office had met his demands.

Wed. 6.11.74: Thirty-three republican prisoners escaped from Long Kesh through a tunnel, under cover of an attack on the main gate by 300 prisoners. One escaper, Hugh Coney, a detainee later claimed as a lieutenant by the Provisional IRA, was shot dead by a sentry, 29 were recaptured near the camp within hours and the remaining three in Andersonstown, west Belfast, that evening. The Provisional IRA claimed the ambush and killing of two soldiers and injuring of a third, meanwhile, in reprisal for Mr Coney's death. There were demonstrations in Catholic towns and areas all over Northern Ireland.

Thur. 7.11.74: Two bomb-disposal officers were killed and five other soldiers, two RUC men and a civilian were injured by a land mine at an electricity sub-station near Stewartstown, Co Tyrone. The bomb was claimed by the Provisional IRA as another retaliation for Hugh Coney's killing. One soldier and one civilian were killed and 20 others injured by a bomb in a pub frequented by soldiers in Woolwich in London.

Fri. 8.11.74: Six thousand people attended the funeral of Hugh Coney in Coalisland, Co Tyrone, and there were demonstrations, hijackings and burnings in many Catholic areas.

Sat. 9.11.74: In what was thought to be a factional dispute among loyalists, Billy Hull, ex-leader of the LAW, and Jim Anderson, ex-chair of the UDA, were wounded by gunfire on the Crumlin Road in Belfast. In five incidents in or near Belfast, four Catholics were assassinated and one Catholic and one Protestant injured.

Tues. 12.11.74: Two Protestant civilians who had been working in Ebrington Barracks in Derry were shot dead by the Provisional IRA as "spies working with British intelligence". Their bodies were found near a border road. There were three more sectarian assassinations in Belfast and Derry.

Thur. 14.11.74: Both the UDA and the Provisional IRA said they had held separate talks with Libyan authorities in Tripoli in the previous two weeks. A member of the Provisional IRA, James McDade, was killed when a bomb exploded outside a telephone exchange in Coventry. Another man, who ran away, was later charged.

Sat. 16.11.74: The president of the republic, Erskine Childers, collapsed at a function and died the following day.

Sun. 17.11.74: Dáithí Ó Conaill, chief of staff of the Provisional IRA, said in an interview on British television that the campaign in Britain would be escalated.

Wed. 20.11.74: Another British government green paper, *Constitutional Convention Procedure*, was published.

Thur. 21.11.74: After staff in Aldergrove airport refused to handle the body of James McDade, it was flown into Dublin. In the evening, after an inadequate warning, bombs exploded in two public houses in Birmingham, killing 21 people and injuring more than 180. A few hours later, five men from Northern Ireland living in Birmingham were arrested boarding the Heysham–Belfast ferry. A sixth was arrested in Birmingham.

Sun. 24.11.74: Over the weekend four Catholics and three Protestants were killed in sectarian assassinations. The following day two more Protestants were shot dead.

Tues. 26.11.74: At the Special Criminal Court in Dublin Dr Rose Dugdale and two Co Tyrone men were found guilty of hijacking a helicopter and attempting to bomb Strabane RUC station in January 1974. The following day she was sentenced to nine years' imprisonment and the others to three and six years'.

Fri. 29.11.74: In the Commons the Prevention of Terrorism (Temporary Provisions) Act was given the royal assent after a 17-hour sitting. It empowered the Home Office to expel suspected terrorists from Britain or refuse them entry, gave police wide powers of arrest without warrant and the power to hold suspects for seven days without charge and proscribed the Provisional IRA in Great Britain. Following an announcement from the home secretary, Roy Jenkins, the previous day ruling out any transfer of the Price sisters to Northern Ireland in the near future, the sisters resumed their hunger strike.

Sun. 1.12.74: Following the recent spate of sectarian assassinations, two Protestants and 16 Catholics were arrested and served with detention orders. At the Official Sinn Féin ard fheis delegates voted to end the party's abstentionist policy. The Provisional IRA announced that none of the six men charged with the Birmingham bombs was a member of any branch of the republican movement. After a visit from their father, the Price sisters came off their hunger strike.

Mon. 2.12.74: A 20-year-old Irishman was charged at Guildford Magistrates' Court with

the murder of one of the victims of the Guildford pub bombings of October 5th.

Tues. 3.12.74: An explosion caused extensive damage to Omagh town centre in Co Tyrone. Later in the town, Trooper Fury was charged with the manslaughter of Hugh Devine in Strabane in June.

Thur. 5.12.74: Parliament extended the Prevention of Terrorism Act to Northern Ireland, allowing, among other things, detention of suspects for up to seven days, as in Britain.

Sun. 8.12.74: In Dublin 80 delegates of groups which had broken away from Official Sinn Féin met and formed the Irish Republican Socialist party (IRSP).

Mon. 9.12.74: Eleven named persons were charged at Guildford Magistrates' Court with offences arising out of the Guildford pub bombings.

Tues. 10.12.74: A group of four northern Protestant clergymen met senior representatives of Provisional Sinn Féin at Feakle, Co Clare. Following a tip-off, Dáithí Ó Conaill, Seamus Twomey and Kevin Mallon of the Provisional army council slipped away before the premises were raided by the republic's Special Branch. A week later the clergymen reported on the talks and brought Provisional ceasefire terms to the secretary of state, Merlyn Rees.

Thur. 12.12.74: Leaders of the four main churches in Ireland launched a united peace campaign to include prayers for peace in all churches and massive advertising.

Fri. 13.12.74: Three bombs went off at the homes of civil servants in Belfast. Three people were slightly injured. Twenty-eight men were convicted of intimidation in the Ballymena area during the UWC strike.

Sat. 14.12.74: An RUC man and a soldier were killed in an ambush between Forkhill and Newry.

Sun. 15.12.74: Prayers for peace and reconciliation were made in 4,000 Protestant and Catholic churches throughout Ireland.

Tues. 17.12.74: Three small bombs exploded in London, killing one man and injuring several others.

Wed. 18.12.74: Thirteen people were injured when two bombs exploded in the centre of Bristol. Three bombs exploded in Belfast and two in Co Tyrone. The Ministry of Defence agreed to pay sums ranging from £250 to £16,000 to relatives of those killed on Bloody Sunday, as a gesture of "goodwill and conciliation".

Thur. 19.12.74: A 200lb bomb caused substantial damage in Oxford Street in London. Though a warning had been given, five Christmas shoppers were injured. Cearbhall Ó Dálaigh, an agreed candidate, was installed as fifth president of the republic. The home secretary, Roy Jenkins, ordered an investigation into reports that the six Irishmen charged with the Birmingham bombings had been beaten up in custody.

Fri. 20.12.74: In Dublin the Provisional IRA announced an 11-day truce, to operate from midnight on December 22nd. It said its decision had been prompted by the "courageous and

positive action" of the four clergymen. The ceasefire would only continue on the clear understanding that a positive response would be forthcoming from the British government.

Sat. 21.12.74: A bomb exploded in Harrods store in London. A warning had been given. Another bomb was defused in Wiltshire.

Sun. 22.12.74: A bomb thrown at the London flat of the opposition leader, Edward Heath, blew out windows but caused no other damage. Bombs exploded in Belfast, Lurgan and Killyclogher, near Omagh. Dáithí Ó Conaill of the Provisional IRA warned of the devastation of British cities if its peace terms were not accepted. Seven thousand people attended an inter-denominational peace service at Belfast City Hall.

Mon. 23.12.74: Edward Heath began a two-day visit to troops in Northern Ireland.

Sun. 29.12.74: A riot by Provisional prisoners in Portlaoise was quashed when gardaí, backed by 200 troops in riot gear, rushed the main cell block.

Mon. 30.12.74: The leaders of the four main churches met the secretary of state, Merlyn Rees, to urge that he do everything possible to extend the Provisional ceasefire. It was reported that the government had had indirect contact with Provisional Sinn Féin.

Tues. 31.12.74: Merlyn Rees announced his response to the Provisional IRA ceasefire. Seventeen republican and three loyalist detainees were released and early releases were promised for 100 convicted prisoners by exercise of the royal prerogative. There was a hostile response from loyalists.

1975

Wed. 1.1.75: The leaders of the four main churches in Ireland met the prime minister, Harold Wilson. Afterwards they expressed optimism that the Provisional IRA ceasefire would be extended.

Thur. 2.1.75: The Provisional IRA announced a 14-day extension to its Christmas ceasefire, recognising the "minor developments" on prisoner releases but demanding "substantial progress" before considering a permanent ceasefire. An emergency meeting of the UUUC expressed anxiety about the secretive negotiations with the Provisional IRA. Alliance and the SDLP welcomed the extension of the truce.

Fri. 3.1.75: Rev William Arlow, one of those involved in the Feakle talks, said the clergymen were withdrawing from involvement in talks.

Mon. 6.1.75: The secretary of state, Merlyn Rees, requested meetings with all political parties. The west Belfast brigade of the UDA broke away from the UDA inner council. The following day the Londonderry brigade declared its support for the inner council but the Mid-Ulster brigade declared it was going independent until problems were sorted out.

Wed. 8.1.75: The Garda Special Branch recaptured the Provisional IRA prison escaper Kevin Mallon, who had taken part in the Feakle talks.

168

Thur. 9.1.75: The secretary of state, Merlyn Rees, gave an assurance to Harry West of the Ulster Unionists that there would be no negotiations with the Provisional IRA. He also met the Alliance party.

Fri. 10.1.75: Merlyn Rees completed a series of political discussions, meeting delegations from the SDLP and Vanguard. In Dublin the leaders of the four main churches met the taoiseach, Liam Cosgrave. In a killing which the Provisional IRA claimed was the work of a "British execution squad", John Francis Green, a Provisional IRA internee who had escaped from Long Kesh in 1973, was found murdered in a farmhouse in Co Monaghan. It was later alleged that the killing was the work of Capt Robert Nairac, a British intelligence officer. The killing was claimed by the UVF in March of the following year.

Tues. 14.1.75: The leader of the west Belfast brigade of the UDA, Charles Harding Smith, was shot but not seriously injured in the UDA headquarters on the Shankill Road. In the Commons the secretary of state, Merlyn Rees, promised that if there was a permanent ceasefire all detainees would be gradually released and army strength reduced to peacetime levels. The SDLP leader, Gerry Fitt, expressed disappointment that there had been no mention of the immediate release of detainees. Provisional Sinn Féin said that Mr Rees had done nothing to meet the Provisional IRA demands.

Wed. 15.1.75: Merlyn Rees released 20 republican and five loyalist detainees and offered three days' home leave to 50 others. Six UDA men were sentenced to life imprisonment for the murder of a police constable in the Glencairn area of Belfast in December 1973.

Thur. 16.1.75: The Provisional IRA announced the ending of its ceasefire, saying the response from the British government had been insufficient and that troops had not observed the truce. Merlyn Rees said he was still prepared to permit his officials to enter into discussions with representatives of Provisional Sinn Féin.

Sat. 18.1.75: At the SDLP conference the party leader, Gerry Fitt, said he had been authorised by Merlyn Rees to say that if violence ceased all internees would be released.

Sun. 19.1.75: Peace marches in Belfast and Dublin were attended by huge crowds, between 10,000 and 20,000 strong. A meeting was held outside Belfast between representatives of the NIO and Provisional Sinn Féin. A seven-year-old Catholic boy was killed at Forkhill, Co Armagh, when a herd of cows he was driving detonated a land mine.

Tues. 21.1.75: Two Provisional IRA men were killed when a bomb exploded prematurely in a car in Victoria Street, Belfast. Bombs exploded in College Street, Belfast, and in Strabane, Co Tyrone.

Wed. 22.1.75: It was announced that a further meeting had taken place between representatives of the NIO and Provisional Sinn Féin. A government spokesperson emphasised that the meetings were to ensure that the ceasefire had not ended through any misunderstanding of the government's position.

Thur. 23.1.75: The Europa Hotel in Belfast was bombed for the 27th time.

Fri. 24.1.75: Bombs exploded at two supermarkets in south Belfast. The NIO released details of the Criminal Law Jurisdiction Bill, which would allow those suspected of offences committed in the republic to be tried in Northern Ireland. The bill and its counterpart in the republic stemmed from agreements reached at the Sunningdale conference.

Sun. 26.1.75: A 16-year-old air force cadet was killed and five others were injured by a booby-trap bomb on the Cavehill Road in Belfast. In Derry 10,000 and in Newry 3,000 people attended peace rallies.

Mon. 27.1.75: Four bombs exploded in London, one in Manchester, three in Derry and one in Lurgan, Co Armagh. Representatives of the UDA and UVF had discussions with the NIO about a proposed new parole system.

Wed. 29.1.75: In the latest of many such SDLP statements John Hume reiterated that his party would not call for support for the RUC until the establishment of a new power-sharing executive.

Thur. 30.1.75: The report of the Gardiner committee on the control of terrorism in Northern Ireland recommended that detention without trial could be continued only for a short period, was very critical of the introduction of special category status, recommended a streamlined system to review the cases of internees and floated the idea of a bill of rights. Unionists generally welcomed the report, but the SDLP was disappointed. Paramilitaries on both sides were critical of the proposal to do away with special category status. In the republic, Charles Haughey and James Gibbons, who had been dismissed from the cabinet over the gun-running affair in 1970, were reappointed to the Fianna Fáil front bench.

Mon. 3.2.75: The secretary of state, Merlyn Rees, told a UUUC delegation that though there had been two further meetings with Provisional Sinn Féin members the previous week, there would be no discussions with them about the future of Northern Ireland. Seven republicans were interned, the first since before the ceasefire.

Tues. 4.2.75: Two teenage girls pleaded guilty to the murder of Ann Ogilvy, who had been beaten to death in a Sandy Row UDA club in July 1974. Seven other women admitted involvement in the kidnapping and beating.

Wed. 5.2.75: The final government paper on the future of Northern Ireland, *The Government of Northern Ireland: a divided society*, was published in preparation for the constitutional convention elections. Responses were mostly unenthusiastic. It was announced that work would start immediately on cellular accommodation at the Maze prison, to replace the compound system criticised by the Gardiner report. Bombs exploded in the central shopping areas of Belfast and Dungannon.

Thur. 6.2.75: A second assassination attempt was made on Charles Harding Smith, leader of the UDA in west Belfast, but again he was not seriously injured. The Belfast Orange grand master, Thomas Passmore, claimed that traders on the Shankill were being intimidated by racketeers. The following week, Hugh Smyth, a

West Belfast assembly member, denied that the UDA or UVF were involved.

Sun. 9.2.75: The Provisional IRA announced that, in the light of discussions with the British government, there would be an indefinite ceasefire. Two gunmen opened fire on the first people leaving evening Mass at Derryvolgie Avenue in Belfast, killing two men.

Mon. 10.2.75: Two Catholics were shot dead and three others seriously injured in sectarian attacks in Belfast and Pomeroy, Co Tyrone. Explosions in Belfast and Newry, Co Down, preceded the Provisional IRA ceasefire.

Tues. 11.2.75: The secretary of state, Merlyn Rees, announced the setting up of "incident centres" in republican areas. These were to be staffed by civil servants and Provisional Sinn Féin members who would monitor the ceasefire and be in direct contact with his office. The announcement brought criticism from unionist and SDLP politicians.

Thur. 13.2.75: Letter bombs disguised as Valentine's Day cards were sent to Catholic homes in Belfast. Two exploded but caused no injuries.

Fri. 14.2.75: Fred Proctor, a DUP councillor in Belfast who had condemned gangsterism, was shot but not seriously injured by masked men at his home in the Woodvale area.

Sun. 16.2.75: Provisional IRA prisoners ended a protracted hunger strike in Portlaoise after being offered a measure of segregation. It was reported that the split in the UDA between east and west Belfast had been healed and that Charles Harding Smith, the subject of two assassination attempts, had been replaced as west Belfast commander.

Mon. 17.2.75: A UUUC delegation complained to the secretary of state, Merlyn Rees, about the new status afforded to the Provisional IRA by the incident centres.

Tues. 18.2.75: The new Conservative leader at Westminster, Margaret Thatcher, appointed Airey Neave as shadow spokesperson on Northern Ireland. The NIO announced more stringent criteria for renewal of gun licences.

Thur. 20.2.75: A Catholic man was killed and 26 other customers injured by a bomb outside a Catholic bar in Greencastle, Co Antrim. A bomb outside a Catholic bar on the New Lodge Road in Belfast was reported to be the result of a feud between the Official IRA and the IRSP. In another incident the IRSP accused the Official IRA of the murder of Hugh Ferguson, chair of the newly-formed IRSP in the Whiterock area of Belfast.

Fri. 21.2.75: The secretary of state, Merlyn Rees, announced that the lord chief justice, Sir Robert Lowry, would chair the constitutional convention.

Sat. 22.2.75: The UUUC announced that it would be urging supporters not to hand in hitherto legally held firearms. At the Alliance conference, party leader Oliver Napier called for a unifying Ulster identity, with a new Ulster flag and anthem.

Sun. 23.2.75: It was revealed that the republic's government had expressed concern to the British government over the establishment of the incident centres over the heads of local elected representatives.

Mon. 24.2.75: The secretary of state, Merlyn Rees, announced that 80 detainees would be released in coming weeks. A Vanguard delegation complained that the incident centres betrayed both the majority and minority communities.

Tues. 25.2.75: In the Official IRA/IRSP feud a leading Official officer, Sean Fox, was shot dead in Divis Flats in Belfast and two youths were wounded in Ballymurphy. In a sectarian incident, a Catholic was separated from his workmates in the Boucher Road industrial estate, told to kneel down and shot dead.

Wed. 26.2.75: In response to reports in the Sinn Féin newspaper *An Phoblacht* of plans to set up communal policing in Catholic areas, the UDA announced its own vigilante policing in Protestant areas, from which the RUC would be excluded. NIO officials later held secret talks with the UDA to try to persuade it to abandon its plans. Further talks the following day brought no resolution but the next day UDA representatives met the secretary of state, Merlyn Rees, and announced that while UDA patrols would go ahead the RUC would not be ostracised.

Sat. 1.3.75: The directive to the RUC demanding restrictions on the issue of firearms certificates was withdrawn. Some UDA patrols appeared on the streets of east Belfast and in other areas, but fewer than expected.

Sun. 2.3.75: In the Official IRA/IRSP feud an Official organiser, Sean Garland, was attacked by gunmen at his home in Ballymun in Dublin.

Mon. 3.3.75: Shots were fired into houses in the Armagh/Monaghan area, where threatening letters had earlier been received from the UVF. In the Official IRA/IRSP feud one man from each faction was injured in a shooting incident in Turf Lodge in Belfast.

Tues. 4.3.75: In London a deputation from loyalist paramilitary organisations met the secretary of state, Merlyn Rees, and the Conservative and Liberal spokespersons on Northern Ireland to press for the suppression of the incident centres. The following day the UDA said that, as a result of these discussions, its patrols would be withdrawn. The Official IRA claimed that the IRSP had drawn up a detailed assassination list of its members. Bernadette McAliskey, a leading IRSP figure, called for discussions with the Officials to end the feud.

Wed. 5.3.75: In London, the republic's minister for foreign affairs, Garret FitzGerald, met the secretary of state, Merlyn Rees, to express concern that Provisional Sinn Féin might be given some official policing power in minority areas of Northern Ireland.

Thur. 6.3.75: The NILP's manifesto for the convention elections called for regional government by executive committees chosen by PR. The CCDC issued a 10-point plan to make the RUC acceptable to both communities.

Fri. 7.3.75: It was announced that the IRSP had been disbanded and that members would have to reapply to the Dublin headquarters.

Sun. 9.3.75: The Red Hand Commandos in Derry claimed firebomb attacks on fishing boats in Greencastle, Co Donegal.

Mon. 10.3.75: Twelve Provisional IRA suspects escaped from the courthouse in Newry, Co Down. Two were later recaptured. The heads of the EC countries began a two-day summit in Dublin.

Wed. 12.3.75: The secretary of state, Merlyn Rees, announced that 122 detainees had been released since the beginning of the ceasefire on December 22nd and that he hoped to release a further 40 before Easter.

Thur. 13.3.75: Armed men left a bomb in a Catholic bar in Greencastle, Co Antrim, which exploded prematurely injuring one of them, killing a woman, and injuring 13 other people.

Sat. 15.3.75: After meetings in Dublin and Dundalk, a temporary ceasefire was announced between the IRSP and the Official IRA. The UDA said that the UVF, in collaboration with the Officials, was responsible for the murder of two UDA men in a bar on York Road in Belfast. Two days later the UVF admitted the killings, along with four other recent assassinations.

Sun. 16.3.75: A woman RUC constable was killed when a bomb exploded without warning outside a bar in Bangor, Co Down. One IRA prisoner was killed and two others injured in a concerted attempt to escape from Portlaoise in the republic.

Tues. 18.3.75: It was announced that the Price sisters had been transferred from Durham prison to Armagh, where they would serve out their life sentences along with other special-category prisoners. In further feuding between the UDA and the UVF three men were shot in bars in east Belfast. The Ulster Unionist party condemned the "repugnant phenomenon of gun law" and the following day, after shots were fired at the RUC in east Belfast, the DUP leader, Rev Ian Paisley, called for the withdrawal of all Protestant support from loyalist paramilitary groups.

Fri. 21.3.75: It was announced that in the previous 11 days there had been four shooting incidents in the IRSP/Official IRA feud, wounding three men, nine in the UDA/UVF feud, killing two and wounding seven, and nine sectarian incidents in which two had been killed and seven wounded.

Tues. 25.3.75: It was announced that the assembly would be officially dissolved on March 29th and that the elections to the convention would be held on May 1st. The prime minister, Harold Wilson, visited Belfast and met leaders of the UUP, the SDLP, the Unionist Party of Northern Ireland (UPNI) (the Faulknerite unionists), the Alliance party and the Volunteer Political party. The DUP leader, Rev Ian Paisley, refused to attend and the Vanguard leader, William Craig, was abroad. Mr Wilson stressed that there was only an Ulster solution for the Ulster problem.

Wed. 26.3.75: The British government announced the nationalisation of the Harland and Wolff shipyard.

Thur. 27.3.75: L/Cpl Jones was acquitted of the murder of Patrick McElhone during a search of his farm in Co Tyrone in August 1974. The judge ruled that though McElhone had no connection with terrorism, the defendant had sincerely believed he might be dealing with a terrorist trying to escape. The acquittal was strongly criticised by local politicians and residents.

Sat. 29.3.75: The homes of 10 members of the UVF in east Belfast were attacked with pistols and shotguns.

Sun. 30.3.75: The Provisional IRA army council's Easter message called for a planned and orderly withdrawal of the English establishment from Ireland and said there was a limit to its patience in terms of the ceasefire.

Wed. 2.4.75: In Dublin, talks were started by Senator Michael Mullen between representatives of the Official IRA and the IRSP. A bomb and ensuing fire destroyed a travel agent's on Great Victoria Street in Belfast. The Provisional IRA admitted responsibility, saying it was in retaliation for violations of the ceasefire by the army.

Sat. 5.4.75: Two Catholic men were killed when a bomb was thrown into McLaughlin's bar on the New Lodge Road in Belfast. Three hours later five Protestant men were killed by a bomb thrown into the Mountainview Tavern on the Shankill Road. More than 70 people were injured in the two attacks. In the Official IRA/IRSP feud an 18-year-old member of the IRSP was shot dead in Ballymurphy.

Sun. 6.4.75: A 19-year-old Protestant was shot dead outside a UDA club on Alliance Avenue in Belfast. In continuing feuds there were assassination attempts on Sammy Smyth, a former UDA press officer, and Des O'Hagan, a leading Official Sinn Féin spokesperson, and two Official republicans were injured in a shooting incident in Ballymurphy. There were bomb attacks on a Catholic club in Short Strand and a Catholic house on the Ballysillan Road. At its first conference in Dublin, the IRSP decided not to contest the convention elections.

Mon. 7.4.75: It was announced that two UDA men—one of them, Hugh McVeigh, a leading officer—were missing, last seen on the Shankill Road in Belfast. Their bodies, presumed killed in the UDA/UVF feud, were found in a shallow grave near Whitehead, Co Antrim, on September 1st.

Tues. 8.4.75: In what the Provisional IRA again claimed was a retaliation for army violations of the ceasefire, the Bank Buildings in Belfast was destroyed by a firebomb. It was announced that two more of those serving sentences for the London car bombings of 1973 had been transferred to Northern Ireland to finish their sentences, as had a loyalist prisoner in a Scottish prison.

Fri. 11.4.75: Talks were held between the UVF and the UDA in an attempt to settle the feud. Two men seen throwing a bomb into a Catholic bar on the Ormeau Road in Belfast were fired on and pursued by British soldiers to Sandy Row where their car crashed. One had been shot dead and the other injured.

Sat. 12.4.75: At a conference in Nottingham, the army GOC, Gen Sir Frank King, warned that if detainees continued to be released at the present rate they would all be out by October and the IRA would be able to start all over again. In an attack claimed by both the "Young Militants" and the Red Hand Commandos, four Catholic women and two Catholic men were killed and 39 people were injured when a bomb was thrown into a bar in the Short Strand in Belfast. One of those who laid the bomb was shot by local gunmen and died the following day in hospital. In the Official IRA/IRSP feud a Republican Clubs pamphlet seller was shot dead from a passing car on the Falls Road.

Mon. 14.4.75: Nominations closed for the convention elections. Following controversy over Gen Sir Frank King's Nottingham speech, the secretary of state, Merlyn Rees, emphasised that responsibility for security policy rested solely with himself.

Tues. 15.4.75: The SDLP manifesto was published.

Wed. 16.4.75: The UUUC and Alliance manifestos were published.

Thur. 17.4.75: The UPNI and Republican Clubs manifestos were published.

Sun. 20.4.75: An Amnesty International report alleged maltreatment during interrogation in 1973 of female republican detainees in Armagh prison.

Mon. 21.4.75: In Dungannon, Co Tyrone, in what was thought to be a sectarian attack, two Catholic brothers and their married sister were killed in the booby-trap bombing of the empty house they were planning to decorate and occupy. The RUC reported that there had been 54 incidents, including two deaths, in the UDA/UVF feud and 48 incidents, including five deaths, in the Official IRA/IRSP feud. As a result 19 loyalists and 16 republicans had been arrested.

Wed. 23.4.75: A 10-year-old child of an Irish/Italian family lost an arm and an eye when a transistor radio exploded in his father's chip shop on the Springfield Road in Belfast. Three other children were injured. The NICRA published a draft bill of rights. An inter-church working party, meeting in Dundalk, Co Louth, claimed internment had operated mainly against Catholics and should be ended.

Sat. 26.4.75: There was sectarian rioting in central Belfast in the wake of an Orange parade to the opening of new premises for the order on Dublin Road.

Sun. 27.4.75: Three Catholic men were killed and another was seriously wounded when gunmen fired shots into a darts club in Bleary, Lurgan. At election meetings throughout Northern Ireland SDLP candidates stressed that power-sharing and institutionalised recognition of the "Irish dimension" were non-negotiable.

Mon. 28.4.75: The secretary of state, Merlyn Rees, ordered the release of the remaining eight female detainees from Armagh prison. In the Official IRA/IRSP feud, the Officials' leader in Belfast, Billy McMillen, was shot dead in the Falls Road area.

Wed. 30.4.75: The Protestant Action Group claimed it had murdered seven Catholics in the previous 14 days.

Thur. 1.5.75: Despite widespread reports of abstention and intimidation there was a 64 per cent turnout in the convention election. Overnight, bomb attacks had been made on SDLP candidates in north Belfast and Lurgan, Co Armagh. In the republic, a retired judge from the British Colonial Service, Sir Paget Bourke,

was kidnapped and his wife was tied up in their Dublin home. The car in which he was driven north by two gunmen ran into an army/Garda checkpoint near the Fermanagh border, the gunmen escaped and Sir Paget was released.

Fri. 2.5.75: An Ulsterbus inspector, Alex Millar, was shot dead in the Ardoyne depot in Belfast. The following Tuesday he was given a UDA military funeral and 700 Citybus drivers and conductors staged a 24-hour strike in protest at his murder.

Sat. 3.5.75: Results of the convention election indicated that the UUUC's 46 members, along with one independent loyalist, represented a majority of 16 over the combined opposition of 17 SDLP, 8 Alliance, 5 UPNI and 1 NILP members. In renewed UDA/UVF feuding two men were injured in a bar in east Belfast.

Tues. 6.5.75: The Fair Employment (Northern Ireland) Bill, making religious and political discrimination illegal and establishing an independent Fair Employment Agency (FEA), was introduced in the Lords.

Wed. 7.5.75: The secretary of state, Merlyn Rees, said the task of the convention was to fashion a new set of political arrangements that would command widespread acceptance, but ultimately the decision rested with the UK Parliament. Two republican prisoners escaped from Magilligan.

Thurs. 8.5.75: In what was assumed to be part of the Official IRA/IRSP feud, but was denied by the Officials, shots were fired at a car in which the IRSP leader, Seamus Costello, was travelling near Waterford. Des O'Hagan, editor of the Officials' newspaper, claimed an assassination attempt had been made on him the previous day in Dublin. At the opening of the convention, the Ulster Unionist leader, Harry West, said the UUUC would not use its majority position to kick the minority around, but it would not allow those who hoped for a united Ireland to lay a hand on the steering wheel of the state. The Provisional IRA warned that if the UUUC attempted to establish a six-county fascist state it would face the full might of the IRA.

Fri. 9.5.75: In response to a statement from the Conservative Northern Ireland spokesperson, Airey Neave, that power-sharing was not now enforceable, the deputy leader of the party, William Whitelaw, told the party leader, Margaret Thatcher, that he and several other senior Tories would not support a return to unionist one-party rule.

Sat. 10.5.75: In what the Provisional IRA claimed was a retaliation for a breach of the ceasefire by the RUC, an RUC man was ambushed and shot dead in Derry.

Mon. 12.5.75: The DUP leader, Rev Ian Paisley, was elected chair of the convention rules committee.

Tues. 13.5.75: A motion renewing the Prevention of Terrorism (Temporary Provisions) Act for a further six months was passed in the Lords. Following its poor showing in the election, the UPNI laid off most of its full-time staff and moved to smaller premises. Lenny Murphy of the UVF, who it was later to become clear was the leader of the Shankill Butchers, was released from prison.

Wed. 14.5.75: The housing minister, Don Concannon, announced details of a five-year redevelopment plan for Belfast.

Sat. 17.5.75: There was serious disagreement on the rules committee of the convention, the unionist majority wanting a single report to the British government, the SDLP members wishing to include a minority report.

Mon. 19.5.75: An RUC guard claimed to have shot and wounded one of five republican remand prisoners who escaped from their cell at Belfast Magistrates' Court. Three RUC detectives were committed for trial at Cookstown, Co Tyrone, on charges of inflicting grievous bodily harm on an arrested man in January.

Fri. 23.5.75: UUUC leaders tabled three motions at the convention calling for devolved government, majority rule, and a bill of rights for the UK. Two Catholic brothers were shot dead by the PAF in a flat on the Shore Road in Belfast.

Sat. 24.5.75: The Provisional IRA denied responsibility for a booby-trap bomb in a car which killed Const Noel Davis outside a gun club in Maghera, Co Derry.

Sun. 25.5.75: One of the clergymen involved in the Feakle talks, Rev William Arlow, claimed that the British government had given a commitment to the Provisional IRA to withdraw from Northern Ireland and added that this would happen if the convention did not produce an agreed structure for government. The secretary of state, Merlyn Rees, denied any such agreement.

Mon. 26.5.75: Rev Arlow repeated his claim and said that he had two reliable sources, one of which was believed to be a British cabinet minister and the other a leading Provisional. There were demands from politicians on all sides for clarification and the VUPP said that in the event of a withdrawal the only alternative would be for loyalists to set up a provisional government.

Tues. 27.5.75: The secretary of state, Merlyn Rees, repeated there would be no "sell-out" but that there would be a progressive reduction in troops if security improved. A serious situation would arise if the convention failed, however. In the convention, SDLP members contested the legality of the proposed standing orders.

Wed. 28.5.75: Gerard McClenaghan died in hospital from wounds sustained in a shooting incident in March in Leeson Street in Belfast, thought to have been part of the Official IRA/IRSP feud. The convention chair, Sir Robert Lowry, rejected the SDLP contention that the standing orders were illegal but said minority views should be reported to Westminster. In a speech to mark the anniversary of the fall of the executive, Glenn Barr, chair of the Ulster Loyalist Central Co-ordinating Committee (ULCCC), said that plans had been drawn up for a provisional government in the unlikely event of a British withdrawal. The UDA leader, Andy Tyrie, claimed all loyalist paramilitary groups except the UVF had united in the Ulster Army Council in preparation for a doomsday situation.

Thur. 29.5.75: The UUUC said that elected representatives and not paramilitaries would give a lead to the community in the event of a British withdrawal.

Fri. 30.5.75: The UVF confirmed it would not be joining the six other loyalist paramilitary groups on the new Ulster Army Council.

Sat. 31.5.75: It was announced that two loyalist prisoners would be transferred from Scotland to Northern Ireland prisons. Glenn Barr announced that as a result he would now take part in the convention.

Sun. 1.6.75: A 61-year-old Protestant, Margaret Kilfedder, was killed and her husband injured when a bomb exploded in a house near Garrison, Co Fermanagh, which they had rented from a UDR man who had fled after threats to his life. Three men were admitted to hospital in Belfast with gunshot wounds, following incidents in the IRSP/Official IRA feud.

Mon. 2.6.75: The secretary of state, Merlyn Rees, told the Belfast Rotary Club that there would be no sell-out or sudden withdrawal of troops and that those who spoke wildly of UDI, private armies or provisional governments were destructive and disloyal. With the support of two UPNI members, an SDLP councillor was elected chair of Fermanagh District Council.

Tues. 3.6.75: Three Protestants returning home from a dog show in Cork were picked out when they stopped in Dundalk and shot dead on the Dublin–Belfast road at Killeen, Co Armagh.

Wed. 4.6.75: A Catholic man from Jonesborough, Co Armagh, Francis Jordan, was shot dead by the army after throwing a bomb into a Protestant bar in Bessbrook.

Thur. 5.6.75: Voting took place in the UK EC referendum. The SDLP, Alliance, the UPNI and the NILP had called for a "yes" vote. The DUP, Official and Provisional Sinn Féin and many trade unions had called for a "no" vote. The UUP and VUPP had not taken a party line. An informal meeting, the first of a series to avoid confrontation, was held between the UUUC and the SDLP at the convention. Brendan McNamee of the IRSP was shot dead in the Suffolk area of Belfast, in what was thought to be part of the Official IRA/IRSP feud.

Fri. 6.6.75: In what was the lowest turnout in the EC referendum and the lowest vote in favour of membership of any UK region, apart from the Western Isles and Shetland, in Northern Ireland 52 per cent voted for, and 48 per cent voted against.

Sat. 7.6.75: The Shankill and Crumlin roads in Belfast were blocked in UVF protests against the doubling of the sentence of a post office robber, Francis Newell, by the Court of Appeal.

Sun. 8.6.75: Security forces ordered an investigation into allegations in the *Sunday Times* that army and RUC documents on IRA suspects had been given to loyalist paramilitaries. In Co Monaghan there were clashes between mourners and gardaí after shots were fired over the coffin of a prominent Newry republican.

Tues. 10.6.75: Buses were hijacked in the Shankill and Albertbridge Road areas of Belfast over the doubling of Francis Newell's sentence.

Wed. 11.6.75: In the Official IRA/IRSP feud a member of Saor Eire, Larry White, was shot dead in Cork. The grand master of the Orange

Order, Rev Martin Smyth, made a strong attack on terrorism carried out in the name of Protestantism and called for the order to dissociate itself clearly from it.

Thur. 12.6.75: In the convention the final ruling providing for reports to Westminster to be by majority voting was approved. The UUUC assured the SDLP that minority views could be included in any reports made. Two Protestants were killed when a bomb exploded prematurely in the car they were driving on Great Patrick Street in Belfast.

Fri. 13.6.75: A four-year-old Catholic girl was killed and her father was seriously injured when a booby-trap bomb exploded in his car in the Ormeau Road area of Belfast.

Sat. 14.6.75: In what was thought to be a retaliation for the previous day's bombing, a 65-year-old woman and her 28-year-old son were killed when a booby-trap bomb exploded under his car in Castlewellan, Co Down. In Belfast a 58-year-old Catholic woman was killed and five people were wounded when a car containing four gunmen drove down the New Lodge Road spraying bullets at pedestrians. Four Protestants were arrested shortly afterwards at an army checkpoint. Later a Protestant man was shot dead by gunmen in a passing car outside a Protestant bar on Lower Meadow Street.

Mon. 16.6.75: More than 200 weapons were stolen from a UDR armoury in Magherafelt, Co Derry. The SDLP convention member Ivan Cooper alleged collusion by UDR men. A UDR patrol recovered all the weapons the following day in a slurry pit. The secretary of state, Merlyn Rees, said that the Provisional IRA ceasefire had brought into focus the violence within and between the two communities and that on balance more sectarian murders were perpetrated from the majority community. Fr Desmond Wilson, Catholic curate for the Ballymurphy area of Belfast, announced his reluctant resignation from the diocese of Down and Connor because of the treatment of people within and outside the Church. There was no question, he said, of his leaving the Church nor ceasing to be a priest. Later in the week 1,000 people attended a meeting to support his stand and elected a committee which called for the withholding of contributions to the Church. Seventeen priests in the republic declared their support.

Tues. 17.6.75: Bomb hoaxes in Belfast were claimed by the People's Liberation Army, an offshoot of the IRSP.

Tues. 24.6.75: Doctors at the Royal Victoria Hospital in Belfast reported that two people had been killed and 40 seriously injured by the 33,000 rubber bullets fired by the security forces in recent years. In the convention, an all-party motion condemning all violence and committing members to work to devise a system of government commanding widespread acceptance was unanimously carried. The Vanguard leader, William Craig, made a strong attack on the PAF, which had claimed several sectarian attacks in the previous week. In Dublin, Seamus Costello, leader of the IRSP, was arrested under the Offences Against the State Act.

Thur. 26.6.75: The RUC chief constable, Sir

Jamie Flanagan, announced the formation of a special murder squad of detectives.

Sun. 29.6.75: It was reported that the UVF and other loyalist paramilitary groups had established an Ulster Central Intelligence Agency to which information was fed by sympathetic members of the security forces.

Thur. 3.7.75: In the convention, an all-party motion on social and economic problems was carried unanimously and the convention adjourned for the summer. A Provisional Sinn Féin spokesperson was detained under the Prevention of Terrorism Act at London airport.

Sat. 5.7.75: A report in Provisional Sinn Féin's Belfast paper, *Republican News*, warned that unless the British government declared its intent to withdraw there might be further prolonged hostilities. An armed gang raided a chemical plant in Belfast. A UDA member was detained under the Prevention of Terrorism Act in Liverpool.

Sun. 6.7.75: Responding to a statement by the UUP MP Enoch Powell, that Ulster unionists must be loyal to the Crown in Parliament, the DUP and UUP leaders, Rev Ian Paisley and Harry West, said unionists were loyal to the Crown but not necessarily to Parliament.

Mon. 7.7.75: A booby-trap bomb exploded in a school in Lurgan, Co Armagh. It was thought to have been meant for the headmaster, Allister Black, a Vanguard convention member, but it killed an RUC constable and injured two other men. After attempted mediation by unions and local politicians, the Grundig tape recorder factory in south Belfast closed over a dispute in which Catholic workers had objected to the erection of a Vanguard flag by loyalist workers. But after three weeks the dispute was settled with a policy disallowing any flags or emblems.

Wed. 9.7.75: The Northern Ireland Committee at Westminster, set up to deal with Northern Ireland business there, held its first meeting. The UDA halted traffic on the Shankill Road in Belfast for several hours in protest against the detention of a UDA member in Liverpool the previous Saturday. The Provisional IRA claimed responsibility for three bombs which caused serious damage to the Crown Buildings in Derry. It said the action was in retaliation for army harassment. In Dublin the leading Provisional IRA figure Dáithí Ó Conaill was arrested by Special Branch detectives.

Thur. 10.7.75: The UDA member detained in Liverpool the previous Saturday was served with an exclusion order.

Sat. 12.7.75: Tens of thousands of Orangemen marched peacefully to 19 centres throughout Northern Ireland. A young Protestant man was found on the outskirts of Belfast, bound and gagged and shot twice in the head. Charles Irvine, a 16-year-old Catholic boy, was shot dead by the army in the Falls Road area. The army claimed it had been fired on from the car in which the boy was travelling but local people said the car had backfired.

Sun. 13.7.75: In what was thought to be part of the UDA/UVF feud, a Protestant man was shot dead and another man injured as they left a UDA club in south Belfast.

Mon. 14.7.75: Three men, including Sean Kinsella, an IRA man who had escaped from

172

Portlaoise in 1974, were being detained in Liverpool after a shooting incident and the discovery of a large arms cache in a flat in the city.

Thur. 17.7.75: A booby-trap bomb killed four soldiers on patrol near Forkhill, Co Armagh. The Provisional IRA claimed it was in retaliation for the shooting of Francis Jordan on June 4th and Charles Irvine on July 13th.

Fri. 18.7.75: On succeeding days bombs exploded in Catholic bars in Carrickfergus and Portadown.

Sun. 20.7.75: Provisional Sinn Féin said that despite recent incidents there was no immediate danger of the ceasefire ending. A convicted republican prisoner escaped from the Maze prison, Long Kesh, disguised as a priest, after attending Mass.

Mon. 21.7.75: The secretary of state, Merlyn Rees, said that despite recent incidents the policy was still to seek a permanent peace in Northern Ireland.

Thur. 24.7.75: Merlyn Rees said he hoped there would be sufficient progress to allow all detainees to be released by Christmas.

Fri. 25.7.75: In Dublin the leading Provisional IRA figure Dáithí Ó Conaill was sentenced to one years' imprisonment at the Special Criminal Court for IRA membership.

Sat. 26.7.75: Const Robert John McPherson was shot dead and another RUC man seriously wounded in an ambush in Dungiven, Co Derry. The NIO later said it accepted denials of responsibility by both wings of the IRA.

Thur. 31.7.75: Three members of the Miami Showband were shot dead and one seriously injured by UVF men who flagged down their van near Newry, Co Down. Two of the UVF men were killed when a bomb they were placing in the showband's van blew up prematurely. There was prolonged rioting in Derry on the third anniversary of Operation Motorman.

Sat. 2.8.75: Large crowds attended both the funerals of the Miami Showband victims in Dublin and Caledon and the funerals of the UVF men who died in the attack.

Mon. 4.8.75: The VUPP claimed that Seamus Twomey of the Provisional IRA had been arrested in the Whiterock area of Belfast but had been released. The army denied this.

Tues. 5.8.75: The secretary of state, Merlyn Rees, announced that the NIO would now receive deputations from convention members on constituency matters previously reserved for Westminster MPs.

Fri. 8.8.75: Informal talks between the SDLP and UUUC groups in the convention were reported to have started well. Following sectarian clashes on the previous three nights in Lurgan, Co Armagh, local convention members and the security forces held talks to try to mediate.

Sat. 9.8.75: Airey Neave, Conservative spokesperson on Northern Ireland, accused the government of causing fear among the law-abiding people and democratic politicians of Northern Ireland through the release of detainees and the widespread uncertainty as to its intentions. Following rallies throughout Northern Ireland to mark the fourth anniversary

of the introduction of internment, there were widespread disturbances and 46 arrests.

Sun. 10.8.75: An anti-internment rally at Dunville Park in Belfast was followed by exchanges of fire between gunmen and the security forces and rioting in the Falls area. A three-year-old Catholic girl, Siobhan McCabe, was killed in crossfire. A 13-year-old Catholic boy, Patrick Crawford, was killed in the grounds of the Royal Victoria Hospital. Eight other people were injured. In Lurgan, Co Armagh, the Provisional IRA claimed responsibility for a bomb that destroyed the newly built railway station. It said the bombing was in retaliation for security-force harassment. A Lurgan Protestant was charged with the murder of one of the Miami Showband.

Mon. 11.8.75: Following a bank raid on the Shankill Road in Belfast and the arrest of two loyalist gunmen, there were prolonged disturbances and clashes between loyalists and the security forces, with shots fired at RUC and army posts.

Tues. 12.8.75: There were stone-throwing incidents in Derry, following the first Appentice Boys march in some years to be permitted to enter the walled city.

Wed. 13.8.75: Four men and a woman, all Protestants, were killed and 40 others were injured when a bomb exploded in the Bayardo bar on the Shankill Road in Belfast. A Catholic man from the Ardoyne was detained shortly afterwards at a checkpoint. The following week two other Ardoyne men were charged with the murders. The SDLP accused the Provisional IRA of orchestrating violence to prevent the convention reaching agreement.

Thur. 14.8.75: The formal reopening of the convention was postponed to allow informal talks between the parties to continue.

Fri. 15.8.75: The secretary of state, Merlyn Rees, said that if necessary he would revert to detention without trial against any organisation involved in violence, proscribed or not. In a sectarian attack, a car bomb exploded in a side street by Divis Flats in Belfast, injuring 35 people and damaging many houses. Later, Samuel Llewellyn, a Protestant council worker from the Shankill, who was delivering emergency supplies of hardboard to the Divis residents, was dragged from his lorry and shot dead by an angry crowd. One man was killed and 24 injured when a bomb exploded in a Protestant bar in Derriaghy, near Belfast.

Sat. 16.8.75: The body of a travelling grocer, William Meaklim, an ex-RUC reservist, was found on a border road in south Armagh. There were sectarian clashes following an Orange parade in Portadown.

Sun. 17.8.75: A message from priests and people of the Falls area of Belfast was read at the Shankill Mission, deploring the torture and murder of Samuel Llewellyn two days earlier and expressing their shame that the perpetrators had come from the Catholic community. The CCDC announced it was suspending its free bus transport to Long Kesh for relatives of prisoners and detainees in protest at the murder. The Catholic primate of Ireland, Cardinal William Conway, expressed horror and revulsion at the murders of recent weeks and said those guilty would have to answer before God.

Tues. 19.8.75: There were further sectarian clashes between youths in Lurgan and Portadown, Co Armagh. In Belfast, many Catholics attended the funeral of Samuel Llewellyn.

Wed. 20.8.75: The US State Department refused visas to four Provisional Sinn Féin members seeking to attend an all-party forum on the Irish problem. It was reported from the convention inter-party talks that there was disagreement on the structure of executive government but talks would continue.

Fri. 22.8.75: Three people were killed and 20 injured when a bomb exploded in a Catholic bar in Armagh. The UPNI leader, Brian Faulkner, criticised security policies in a speech at York. A deputation from the ULCCC met minister of state Stan Orme to complain of security-force harassment in Protestant areas and an alleged low profile in Catholic areas.

Sat. 23.8.75: A recently completed Catholic church in Larne, Co Antrim, was destroyed by fire.

Sun. 24.8.75: Two young Catholics, Sean Farmer and Colum McCartney, were flagged down and shot dead at a fake military checkpoint in south Armagh, through which an RUC patrol had previously passed. The murders were claimed by the UVF on behalf of the PAF.

Wed. 27.8.75: The secretary of state, Merlyn Rees, issued another statement denying that any deal had been negotiated with the Provisional IRA for Britain to pull out of Northern Ireland. The Provisional IRA denied responsibility for an explosion at a public house in Caterham, Surrey, in which 23 people were injured.

Thur. 28.8.75: Seven people were injured when a bomb exploded in Oxford Street in London. After meeting the secretary of state, Merlyn Rees, the Conservative spokesperson for Northern Ireland, Airey Neave, said that the bipartisan policy was not at risk, despite his recent criticisms of security policy.

Fri. 29.8.75: The former president of the republic, Eamon de Valera, died in Dublin. A bomb disposal officer died trying to defuse a bomb in Kensington, London. A 15-year-old Catholic boy, Jim Templeton, was shot dead by gunmen in a passing car on the Ormeau Road in Belfast. A 10-year-old Catholic boy, Stephen Geddis, died in hospital of a plastic bullet injury sustained the previous day during a riot in the Lower Falls.

Sat. 30.8.75: Two UDR men were shot dead on succeeding days in south Armagh. Responsibility was claimed by the South Armagh Republican Action Force (SARAF), regarded by security forces as a flag of convenience for Provisional IRA units. A Catholic man was killed and a number of others injured by a bomb outside the Harp bar in Belfast. Another Catholic man, one of those injured, died later. The secretary of state, Merlyn Rees, issued a further statement denying that Seamus Twomey, Provisional IRA leader, had been taken off the army's wanted list.

August 1975: There were increasing reports throughout the month that some members of the Provisional IRA, unhappy with the ceasefire, were joining the military wing of the IRSP, later identified as the Irish National Liberation Army (INLA).

Mon. 1.9.75: Seven people in all were killed in sectarian assassinations. Four Orangemen were killed and seven others wounded when members of the SARAF broke into an Orange hall in Newtownhamilton, Co Armagh, and opened fire with a machine gun. In Belfast a Protestant was found shot dead in his shop. Near Ballyclare, Co Antrim, a Protestant man was shot when gunmen attempted to shoot the Catholic owners of a scrapyard, who escaped injury. In Moy, Co Tyrone, a prominent SDLP member, Denis Mullen, was shot dead by gunmen at his home. The bodies of two UDA men, Hugh McVeigh and David Douglas, who disappeared in the Shankill area on April 7th, were found in a shallow grave near Whitehead, Co Antrim.

Tues. 2.9.75: In Belfast a Protestant man was picked out from his Catholic workmates and shot dead. Following widespread loyalist protestations, the secretary of state, Merlyn Rees, announced intensified security activity in south Armagh, the sealing of cross-border roads and increased co-operation with the republic's security forces.

Wed. 3.9.75: The next plenary session of the convention was again postponed to allow more time for informal inter-party talks. Gunmen broke into a family reunion at a farmhouse in north Belfast, shooting dead a Catholic man, William Hamilton, and his daughter, Patricia McGrenaghan.

Thur. 4.9.75: In a statement not agreed with other UUUC leaders, the DUP leader, Rev Ian Paisley, said that if the secretary of state did not take immediate action on security, loyalists would withdraw from the convention. Scotland Yard said that Margaret McKearney (21), from Moy, Co Tyrone, was the most dangerous woman terrorist in Britain. Her parents denied this and claimed she was working in Dublin. The following day it was reported that a TV crew had seen her in Dublin and it was alleged that the statement had been issued by Scotland Yard to embarrass the republic's government over extradition. It was announced that a further 700 troops were to be sent to Northern Ireland. One Catholic man was killed and eight others injured when a bomb exploded outside a Catholic bar in Loughgall, Co Armagh, and it was hit by gunfire.

Fri. 5.9.75: In London, two people were killed and more than 50 injured by a bomb at the Hilton Hotel.

Sun. 7.9.75: The United Unionist Councillors Association announced plans to disrupt council meetings in protest at the "rapidly deteriorating security situation".

Mon. 8.9.75: A meeting of the UUUC convention members voted 37–1 against having any republicans in a future cabinet in Northern Ireland. The VUPP leader, William Craig, voted against: he supported voluntary coalition in times of emergency. A Catholic and a Protestant were killed and many others wounded in several sectarian bombings and shootings.

Tues. 9.9.75: William Craig announced his resignation as leader of the Vanguard convention party, in protest at the UUUC decision to call off talks with the SDLP. He said that what had been under discussion with the SDLP had not been "power-sharing" and that the SDLP had been prepared to consider the UUUC proposal for a return of a Northern Ireland parliament. Glenn Barr supported Mr Craig's stand.

Wed. 10.9.75: William Craig refused to resume the leadership of the Vanguard convention party until its members gave his policies their full support. He threatened to resign from the UUUC if it vetoed any attempt to seek agreement with the SDLP. The UDA supported him. Contradicting previous denials, the army confirmed the authenticity of a document publicised by the DUP leader, Rev Ian Paisley, which indicated that Seamus Twomey of the Provisional IRA was no longer a wanted man. A meeting was consequently arranged between the prime minister, Harold Wilson, and the opposition leader, Margaret Thatcher.

Thur. 11.9.75: The first full meeting of the convention after the summer recess was boycotted by the SDLP, which said it had asked that the convention be wound up, with the chair drafting a final report to Westminster.

Fri. 12.9.75: The UUUC said that the inter-party talks had broken down because of the SDLP's refusal to accept the principles of British parliamentary democracy. It was also reported that the UUP leader, Harry West, had indicated to the convention chair that the UUUC was prepared to resume discussions with the SDLP.

Sat. 13.9.75: Leo Norney, a 17-year-old Catholic, was shot dead by soldiers in the Turf Lodge area of Belfast. The army said he was one of a group of gunmen who had fired on a patrol, but residents said he had no involvement in any group and had merely been walking home.

Mon. 15.9.75: William Craig withdrew his resignation as leader of the Vanguard convention party despite his failure to secure a majority behind further discussion with the SDLP.

Tues. 16.9.75: The United Unionist Councillors Association announced the suspension of its campaign of disruption of councils following a request from the secretary of state, Merlyn Rees.

Wed. 17.9.75: Airey Neave, Conservative spokesperson, visited Northern Ireland and met security chiefs, UUUC leaders and an SDLP deputation. The SDLP deputy leader, John Hume, said that in view of the events of the previous week it would be pointless to resume talks with the UUUC.

Thur. 18.9.75: William Craig announced his intention to resign as deputy leader of the UUUC following the UUUC convention members' rejection, by 35 votes to nil, of his proposal that there be further discussion of an emergency coalition with the SDLP.

Fri. 19.9.75: The SDLP leader, Gerry Fitt, met the prime minister, Harold Wilson, and expressed concern at continued meetings between government and paramilitary groups. The SDLP chief whip, Paddy Devlin, called for the removal of Merlyn Rees as secretary of state.

Sat. 20.9.75: The Belfast brigade of the Provisional IRA said the RUC was excluded from its truce and called for the closure of the interrogation centre at Castlereagh.

Sun. 21.9.75: The army checkpoint on the Newry–Omeath road was destroyed by a proxy lorry bomb.

Mon. 22.9.75: Ten people were injured in 18 explosions, some of which were claimed by the Belfast brigade of the Provisional IRA. One of those injured, an RUC reservist, died the following month. The Alliance party released details of its proposals to the convention.

Tues. 23.9.75: A Provisional IRA statement from Dublin denied that the ceasefire was over. The secretary of state, Merlyn Rees, announced that, in response to the new wave of bombings, selective screening of suspects would be reintroduced, and a number were taken in for questioning throughout Northern Ireland. The SDLP, the UUUC and the UPNI all published their proposals for future government.

Wed. 24.9.75: In what Merlyn Rees described as a "mockery and travesty of any ceasefire", three bombs caused extensive damage to the Strand Road shopping centre in Derry.

Thur. 25.9.75: It was announced that a new £30 million prison would be built on a disused airport at Maghaberry, Co Antrim. The Provisional IRA alleged that there had been a bipartisan truce agreement with the British government which had been breached by harassment and torture of civilians. It said it would retaliate for every such violation.

Fri. 26.9.75: In Belfast two soldiers were injured, one seriously, by a booby-trap bomb in the Whiterock area. In Derry, a soldier was hit by a sniper and died several weeks later in hospital. At a VUPP meeting, William Craig said it would be madness to exclude the SDLP from a voluntary coalition if certain conditions were met. His comments were later repudiated by the UUP and DUP leaders, Harry West and Rev Ian Paisley. Six men with UDA associations were charged in a Glasgow court with conspiracy to obtain arms. The following day eight men were arrested on the Scottish coast as they set out with a cargo of arms and explosives.

Wed. 1.10.75: In the convention, the SDLP introduced its proposals for government.

Thur. 2.10.75: Twelve people were killed and more than 40 injured in bombings and shootings throughout Northern Ireland, many later claimed by the UVF. At Millfield in Belfast two Catholic sisters and two Catholic youths were shot dead by a UVF gang led by Lenny Murphy. On the Antrim Road, a Catholic was killed when a bomb in a duffel bag was thrown into his shop. In east Belfast a Protestant man was shot dead outside his home. In Catholic west Belfast 10 people were injured in a bomb attack on a bar in Leeson Street. In Crumlin, Co Antrim, a man was killed in a bomb attack on a Catholic-owned bar. In Killyleagh, Co Down, a woman was killed when a bomb was thrown into a bar. There were also bomb attacks on Catholic premises in Co Armagh, Co Derry and Co Antrim. Four men, believed to be UVF members on a bombing mission, were killed when their car exploded outside Limavady, Co Derry. In Armagh three people were injured and severe damage was caused to the city centre by

174

three bombs, thought to have been laid by the Provisional IRA. In the convention the Alliance party introduced its government proposals.

Fri. 3.10.75: A Protestant man was found shot through the head in the Markets area of Belfast. A shop owned by the prominent loyalist John McKeague was destroyed by a bomb, killing a Catholic woman and injuring another woman and a youth. Following a UVF statement claiming responsibility for many of the previous day's attacks, the secretary of state, Merlyn Rees, re-proscribed the organisation. He had lifted a previous ban in April 1974. In the republic, a dissident Provisional IRA unit kidnapped the Dutch industrialist Tiede Herrema, managing director of a Limerick steel firm, Ferenka, and later threatened to execute him if three republican prisoners, Rose Dugdale, Kevin Mallon and James Hyland, were not released.

Sat. 4.10.75: The UVF said it had held talks with senior government officials and offered to stand down the UVF in return for a government commitment to defeat the IRA and close the Provisional Sinn Féin incident centres.

Mon. 6.10.75: The Garda Síochána said it was searching for Eddie Gallagher and Marion Coyle, believed to be part of the gang holding Tiede Herrema. The Provisional IRA denied involvement and said it too was searching for the perpetrators.

Wed. 8.10.75: A booklet entitled *Subversion* was issued by the UUUC at the Conservative party conference at Blackpool. It accused not only republicans but also the SDLP, the Catholic Church and the Gaelic Athletic Association (GAA) of attempting to subvert the Northern Ireland state.

Thur. 9.10.75: A Crossmaglen Provisional IRA unit claimed responsibility for a land-mine explosion near the village which killed one soldier and injured three others. Sixteen alleged UVF men appeared in court charged with the murders of two UDA men and two civilians. It was reported that the Ferenka company had contacted Tiede Herrema's kidnappers and verified he was alive.

Sat. 11.10.75: At a VUPP central council meeting William Craig won support for his policy of a voluntary coalition with the SDLP by 128 votes to 79. The nine Vanguard convention members who opposed the policy resigned from the party. Twenty men were detained for questioning in south Armagh.

Sun. 12.10.75: The taoiseach, Liam Cosgrave, and the Catholic primate, Cardinal William Conway, attended the canonisation in Rome of Blessed Oliver Plunket, in whose honour 84 prisoners, none of them of the IRA, were released in the republic.

Mon. 13.10.75: The secretary of state, Merlyn Rees, rejected allegations by a Conservative MP, Jill Knight, that government money was being fed to the IRA through Northern Ireland Housing Executive building schemes in west Belfast.

Tues. 14.10.75: The UUUC suspended William Craig and his supporters from the council, admitting the nine dissident Vanguard convention members. Their leader, Ernest Baird,

took Mr Craig's place as deputy leader of the UUUC.

Tues. 21.10.75: Gardaí laid siege to a council house in Monasterevin, Co Kildare, where they had discovered that the kidnapped Dutch industrialist, Tiede Herrema, was being held. It was reported that a new brigade staff had taken control of the UVF.

Wed. 22.10.75: At the Old Bailey in London three Northern Ireland men, Paul Hill, Patrick Armstrong and Gerard Conlon, and a Londoner, Carole Richardson, were found guilty of the Guildford bombings of October 1974 and sentenced to life imprisonment. Supporters of the Guildford Four, as they became known, campaigned for the following 15 years, protesting that the four were innocent and that their confessions had been beaten out of them. They were finally found not guilty in a retrial in 1990 and released.

Thur. 23.10.75: An elderly Catholic couple were shot dead in their home in Moy, Co Tyrone. In the third day of the siege at Monasterevin, food was given to the kidnappers.

Fri. 24.10.75: A special meeting of the UUUC expelled William Craig and his three Vanguard convention member supporters from the council. Tiede Herrema appealed for help from a window of the house at Monasterevin under siege by gardaí.

Sun. 26.10.75: Three hundred people using bulldozers reopened three border roads between Crossmaglen and Co Monaghan. At the Provisional Sinn Féin ard fheis in Dublin, the president, Ruairí Ó Brádaigh, called for an amnesty for all "Irish political prisoners" and for the release of Tiede Herrema.

Mon. 27.10.75: The Conservative party spokesperson on Northern Ireland, Airey Neave, had discussions in Belfast with representatives of the UUP, the DUP, Alliance, the NILP and ex-members of the VUPP. He distanced himself from an earlier statement by his deputy party leader, William Whitelaw, that so long as the Unionist party remained connected with the Orange Order it was a sectarian organisation with which Conservatives could not be allied.

Tues. 28.10.75: While the convention began a two-day debate on the UUUC report, recommending the return of majority rule to Northern Ireland, SDLP leaders were lobbying British MPs, stressing the need for minority representation in any future administration.

Wed. 29.10.75: In concerted attacks in Belfast on members of the Official republican movement, heralding another republican feud, the Provisional IRA shot one man dead and wounded 17 others. In a major policy change, the opposition party in the republic, Fianna Fáil, demanded a declaration by the British government of its intention to withdraw from Northern Ireland. A no-warning bomb injured 17 people in central London.

Thur. 30.10.75: In the Falls area of Belfast a six-year-old girl was shot dead when Provisional IRA men called at her home looking for her father, believed to have Official republican connections.

Fri. 31.10.75: In the New Lodge area of Belfast a prominent Provisional Sinn Féin member,

Seamus McCusker, was shot dead by the Official IRA. In the Short Strand area a Republican Clubs (Officials) member was shot dead. Five people were wounded in other incidents in the Provisional IRA/Official IRA feud.

Sun. 2.11.75: Women in the Short Strand area of Belfast demonstrated in protest at the latest series of inter-republican shootings.

Mon. 3.11.75: A man with Republican Clubs connections was shot dead by the Provisional IRA in the Whiterock area of Belfast.

Tues. 4.11.75: The secretary of state, Merlyn Rees, announced at Westminster that special-category status for prisoners was to be phased out.

Thur. 6.11.75: In a shooting later claimed by the Provisional IRA, a UDR man was ambushed and shot dead near Newtownhamilton, Co Armagh.

Fri. 7.11.75: After 17 days, the siege at Monasterevin ended when the kidnappers, Eddie Gallagher and Marion Coyle, surrendered and Tiede Herrema was released. At the last sitting of the convention a proposal that the unionist report should be presented to the secretary of state, Merlyn Rees, as the final convention report was passed by 42 votes to 31. A proposal by the Alliance party to extend the convention for three months to allow inter-party talks was defeated by 42 votes to 8.

Sun. 9.11.75: Over the weekend a Republican Clubs member was shot dead and another seriously wounded. A Provisional Sinn Féin member was also seriously wounded.

Mon. 10.11.75: In a shooting later claimed by the Provisional IRA, a part-time UDR man was shot dead near Keady, Co Armagh. Provisional Sinn Féin in Derry closed its incident centre in protest at army activity.

Tues. 11.11.75: The Provisional IRA carried out further attacks on Republican Clubs members, killing three as well as one other man through mistaken identity. The four deaths brought the total number of civilian deaths in the "troubles" to 1,000.

Wed. 12.11.75: Michael Duggan, chair of the Falls Taxi Association, was shot dead in a club in the Falls area of Belfast. The secretary of state, Merlyn Rees, announced that the incident centres set up to monitor the ceasefire were to be closed. Provisional Sinn Féin said that its incident centres would remain open as advice centres. An 18-year-old UDA member was beaten to death in the Shankill area of Belfast. A man was killed when a bomb exploded in a restaurant in Mayfair in London. A republican prisoner escaped from Magilligan by posing as a teacher. Twenty detainees were released from Long Kesh, leaving 123.

Thur. 13.11.75: The Falls Taxi Association threatened to cease work if the Provisional/Official feud did not stop. After two weeks of fighting, costing 11 lives, the two organisations arranged a ceasefire.

Sat. 15.11.75: Following the wrecking of bars in north Belfast the previous night, a UDA man was shot dead in the Park bar in the same area. The incidents were seen as a resurgence of the UDA/UVF feud. A 400lb land mine killed an

RUC man and injured four others when it exploded under their Land Rover near Omagh, Co Tyrone.

Tues. 18.11.75: In another restaurant bombing in London, two people were killed when a bomb packed with bolts and ball bearings was thrown through a window in Chelsea.

Wed. 19.11.75: The MP for South Belfast, Rev Robert Bradford, announced his resignation from the VUPP to join the UUP.

Thur. 20.11.75: The report of the convention was published by the government.

Sat. 22.11.75: The Provisional IRA attacked a secret army observation post near Crossmaglen in south Armagh, killing three soldiers and seriously injuring another. Over the following days, loyalist politicians and Conservative spokespeople strongly criticised security policy in south Armagh.

Mon. 24.11.75: A Catholic man, Francis Crossan, was abducted on the Antrim Road in Belfast by Lenny Murphy of the UVF and others, and in another of the Shankill Butcher killings was tortured in the Shankill with butchers' knives until dead.

Tues. 25.11.75: A UDR man was shot dead outside his home in Derry. Two RUC men were shot dead and two wounded in an ambush near Castlecaulfield, Co Tyrone. A Catholic man was shot dead on the Shankill Road in Belfast. A 250lb bomb in a hijacked van demolished the army checkpoint at Coshquin on the Derry–Buncrana road.

Thur. 27.11.75: Ross McWhirter, writer and TV personality, was shot dead outside his home in Enfield, London. A campaigner for the death penalty for terrorists, he had recently offered a £50,000 reward for the arrest of those responsible for bombs in London.

Fri. 28.11.75: Representatives of loyalist and republican organisations took part in a conference organised by the Irish Council of Churches in Bergen, near Amsterdam.

Sat. 29.11.75: In an attack later claimed by the UDA, two bombs exploded in Dublin airport, killing one man and injuring five other people. In what was thought to be an internal UVF dispute, a man was shot dead in his car in the Shankill area of Belfast.

Sun. 30.11.75: Eleven members of the IRSP national executive, including Bernadette McAliskey and Jim McCorry, said the party's programme was now indistinguishable from either of the other two republican movements in downgrading "the struggle for class politics" and reverting to "sterile nationalism". The following day they resigned.

Mon. 1.12.75: Two Provisional IRA members, Paul Fox and Laura Crawford, died when the hijacked car they were driving exploded in a central Belfast car park.

Tues. 2.12.75: In an attack disclaimed by both wings of the IRA, two Protestant businessmen were picked out in a crowded restaurant in Derry and shot dead. The Conservative spokesperson on Northern Ireland, Airey Neave, criticised the continued release of detainees.

Wed. 3.12.75: The secretary of state, Merlyn Rees, reaffirmed that he would continue to release detainees, whilst retaining the power of detention in case a concerted paramilitary campaign should again swamp the RUC. The ULCCC announced its support for the UUUC convention report.

Thur. 4.12.75: Priests at St Paul's in Belfast refused to allow the body of the Provisional IRA member Paul Fox into the church for requiem Mass.

Fri. 5.12.75: Detention without trial ended with the release of the last 46 detainees from Long Kesh. The secretary of state, Merlyn Rees, said that it had been ended because it was a cause of discontent and it was better to rely on convictions in court. The move was generally condemned by unionist politicians and welcomed by the Provisional IRA, the SDLP and church leaders.

Sat. 6.12.75: A large department store in Lurgan, Co Armagh, was destroyed by firebombs. Two Provisional IRA men died when a land mine they were attempting to lay exploded at the Killeen customs post on the Belfast–Dublin road.

Sun. 7.12.75: Four armed Provisional IRA men were trapped when they took refuge in a flat in central London, holding two hostages, following an attack on a restaurant in Mayfair.

Mon. 8.12.75: The secretary of state, Merlyn Rees, said that the continued shootings and bombings were criminal and not political and that the security forces required the support of everyone. The deputy leader of the SDLP, John Hume, defended his party's policing policy saying agreement on government was necessary before agreement could be reached on policing.

Tues. 9.12.75: In a Gallup Poll for the *Daily Telegraph*, 64 per cent of people in Britain supported withdrawing troops from Northern Ireland—compared with 55 per cent a year previously and 34 per cent in 1972.

Wed. 10.12.75: It was reported that the Police Authority had voted not to renew the appointment of the RUC chief constable, Sir Jamie Flanagan, when his contract expired in 1976. After a 51-day-trial in London, 14 supporters of the British Withdrawal from Northern Ireland Campaign were acquitted of incitement to disaffection.

Thur. 11.12.75: MPs voted by 361 to 232 against the death penalty for terrorists, but renewed the Northern Ireland (Emergency Provisions) Act for a further six months. Army headquarters in Belfast, the Grand Central Hotel, was severely damaged by a bomb in a hijacked post office van.

Fri. 12.12.75: After a six-day siege in Balcombe Street in London, the four trapped Provisional IRA men gave themselves and their hostages up to police.

Sun. 14.12.75: One man was killed and five people injured when a bomb exploded outside a Catholic-owned house outside Portadown, Co Armagh. NICRA called for the retirement of the chief constable, Sir Jamie Flanagan, when his term of office expired.

Mon. 15.12.75: In a parliamentary answer, the secretary of state, Merlyn Rees, identified 14 areas in Northern Ireland where the RUC only operated with army support. Mr Rees held separate talks with UUUC and SDLP leaders at Stormont, following the delivery of the convention report.

Thur. 18.12.75: The prime minister, Harold Wilson, made a brief trip to Northern Ireland to pay a pre-Christmas visit to troops at Ballykinlar and Derry. Two soldiers were killed in a bomb attack on an army post in Derry shortly afterwards. It was announced that the Queen would visit Northern Ireland in 1977 as part of her silver jubilee celebrations.

Fri. 19.12.75: In attacks claimed by the Red Hand Commandos, two men and a boy were killed in an explosion in a bar in Silverbridge, Co Armagh, and one in an explosion outside a bar in Dundalk, Co Louth. Paddy Devlin of the SDLP criticised Housing Executive plans to halve the number of houses to be built at Poleglass in west Belfast, following representations from unionist politicians, and Protestant residents in nearby Dunmurry.

Wed. 31.12.75: In an attack claimed by the Armagh People's Republican Army, two Protestant men and a Protestant woman were killed when a bomb exploded in a bar in Gilford, Co Down.

1976

Fri. 2.1.76: Firebombs caused several million pounds' worth of damage to four city-centre stores in Belfast.

Sun. 4.1.76: Two Catholic brothers were shot dead by masked gunmen in their farmhouse at Whitecross, Co Armagh. And two Catholic brothers and their uncle were shot dead by masked gunmen in their home at Ballydugan, Co Down.

Mon. 5.1.76: In a massacre claimed by the SARAF, a works bus carrying Protestant workers from Newry to their homes in Bessbrook was stopped at Kingsmills, Co Armagh, by 12 gunmen. The Catholic driver was separated from the others, 10 of whom were shot dead by machine-gun fire and the other seriously wounded and left for dead. After a meeting between the secretary of state, Merlyn Rees, and a UUUC delegation, Rev Ian Paisley said that the UUUC would never go back on its convention report. An RUC reservist was shot dead near Castledawson, Co Derry.

Tues. 6.1.76: Following an emergency meeting between Merlyn Rees and the prime minister, Harold Wilson, it was announced that 600 men of the Spearhead battalion were moving immediately into south Armagh. The following day it was announced that units of the SAS were being sent there. The move to employ the SAS was criticised by Alliance and the SDLP but welcomed by unionists.

Fri. 9.1.76: Several thousand workers paraded through Lurgan, Co Armagh, in a silent protest against sectarian murders.

Mon. 12.1.76: In the Commons, the secretary of state, Merlyn Rees, said the convention was to be recalled for four weeks to see if it could agree on proposals that would command widespread acceptance. He said there was no need for an institutionalised Council of Ireland and that all members of a devolved government would have publicly to support the security forces. The former Conservative prime minister, Edward Heath, called for more troops to be sent to Northern Ireland. The UUUC said it would not discuss compulsory power-sharing.

Tues. 13.1.76: Two Provisional IRA members and three civilians were killed and 20 injured when a bomb exploded prematurely in a shopping arcade in central Belfast.

Thur. 15.1.76: At Downing Street, the prime minister, Harold Wilson, presided over the first all-party committee discussion on security in Northern Ireland; both UUUC and SDLP leaders took part.

Sat. 17.1.76: The Provisional IRA claimed responsibility for the shooting dead of a soldier in Derry and a man, Seamus O'Brien, in Belfast, who they said had been spying for British and loyalist forces. Two Catholics were killed and 20 people injured when a no-warning bomb exploded in a bar on the New Lodge Road in Belfast.

Mon. 19.1.76: It was reported that the condition of Frank Stagg, a Provisional IRA prisoner in Wakefield prison, had deteriorated. He had gone on hunger strike in December against the refusal of the Home Office to transfer him to a prison in Northern Ireland. Trade union leaders in Northern Ireland launched a campaign calling for an end to violence and for better economic and social conditions.

Tues. 20.1.76: A firebomb destroyed the Woolworths store in central Belfast, causing an estimated £3 million damage. The Northern Ireland Police Authority announced that it was to interview candidates for the post of chief constable of the RUC, despite the campaign for the reappointment of Sir Jamie Flanagan.

Wed. 21.1.76: The secretary of state, Merlyn Rees, ordered an investigation into a leak to the DUP leader, Rev Ian Paisley, of a document saying that the new head of the Housing Executive, James O'Hara, had been appointed because he would be sympathetic to the minority community and that excessive sums were being paid to IRA-dominated housing repair firms.

Thur. 22.1.76: Insp George Bell and Const Neville Cummings were killed when a booby-trapped shotgun, found after a tip-off, exploded as they were examining it in Donegall Pass RUC station in Belfast. In four separate incidents in Northern Ireland, three Catholics and a Protestant UDR man were shot dead.

Fri. 23.1.76: Vehicles were hijacked and set on fire in the Whiterock area of Belfast in support of the hunger striker Frank Stagg.

Sat. 24.1.76: It was reported that the number of women travelling to Britain from Northern Ireland and the republic for legal abortions was growing; the known figures for 1974 being 1,102 and 1,406 respectively.

Sun. 25.1.76: Two Catholics were killed in a bomb attack on a Hibernian (AOH) club in Lisburn, Co Antrim.

Tues. 27.1.76: The Irish Congress of Trade Unions organised a two-minute silence at Belfast City Hall for the victims of terrorism. In Dunmurry, south Belfast, two Protestants were killed and four injured when gunmen opened fire on a bar.

Wed. 28.1.76: The Home Office said there was no case for the transfer of Frank Stagg to Northern Ireland.

Thur. 29.1.76: Two Catholic men were shot dead in separate incidents in Belfast. In a report unanimously approved by the 147 members of the Council of Europe, strong coalition government was seen as the only way out of Ulster's economic and social crisis.

Fri. 30.1.76: One Protestant was killed and seven injured in a bomb attack on a bar in Sandy Row in Belfast.

Sat. 31.1.76: The army shot dead a man outside a bar on the Shankill Road in Belfast. There was rioting for several hours following the killing.

Sun. 1.2.76: More than 1,000 people attended a Provisional Sinn Féin rally in Derry to commemorate Bloody Sunday. In London more than 1,000 people marched in support of the hunger striker Frank Stagg and called for British withdrawal from Northern Ireland. The European Commission on Human Rights rejected the cases, sponsored by NICRA in 1972, of seven individuals who claimed they had been tortured by the security forces.

Tues. 3.2.76: The constitutional convention was reconvened. Inter-party talks began immediately between the SDLP, Alliance and the UPNI. In Banbridge, Co Down, the DUP leader, Rev Ian Paisley, said that attempts to establish a coalition government were a holding operation for the final victory of the terrorists. He called for the isolation of quislings in unionist ranks.

Wed. 4.2.76: The SDLP took out an advertisement in the *News Letter*, addressed to the loyalist people and saying the party believed in law, order and effective policing. It said that while the SDLP's long-term aspiration was for an agreed Ireland, there could be no change in the status of Northern Ireland without consent. It sought a united government backed by a united people. The statement was welcomed by William Craig of the VUPP. In the convention, inter-party talks took place between the UUUC and Alliance.

Fri. 6.2.76: An RUC sergeant and an inspector were shot dead in the Cliftonville area of Belfast. In another of the Shankill Butcher killings (claimed by the "Young Militants"), Thomas Joseph Quinn, a roadsweeper, was abducted, beaten and killed with knives on waste ground. Four people were injured when the Belfast–Dublin train was derailed by an explosion near Scarva, Co Down.

Sat. 7.2.76: In Portadown, Co Armagh, the body of a 14-year-old boy was found in a derelict house. It was thought he had been killed by a booby-trap bomb some days before. In Cookstown, Co Tyrone, a brother and sister were killed by a booby-trap bomb when they stopped to investigate what they thought was a car accident. In Belfast a Protestant was found shot dead in Glencairn.

Mon. 9.2.76: In a sectarian attack gone wrong, carried out by Lenny Murphy and other UVF men, two Protestant men were shot dead and three others injured when their works bus was ambushed on the Shankill Road in Belfast.

Tues. 10.2.76: The Provisional IRA claimed responsibility for a series of bomb attacks in Belfast, causing serious damage to the Orange Order headquarters and three city-centre businesses. At a UUUC rally in Newtownards, Co Down, the UUP leader, Harry West, called for those who supported a voluntary coalition to contest an election on that platform.

Thur. 12.2.76: The inter-party talks in the convention between the UUUC and the SDLP broke up after one hour—the SDLP said the UUUC was not prepared to discuss power-sharing. The hunger striker Frank Stagg died in Wakefield prison. There was widespread rioting in west Belfast and the security forces came under attack across Northern Ireland. An RUC reservist and a Catholic man were killed, and a man was killed in a petrol-bomb attack on a warehouse next door to the house of the SDLP leader, Gerry Fitt. Over the following days there were explosions in Dublin and widespread bombings and attacks on the security forces in the north. The Police Authority announced that the deputy chief constable, Kenneth Newman, was to succeed Sir Jamie Flanagan as chief constable on April 30th.

Sun. 15.2.76: The Fianna Fáil ard fheis in Dublin called on Britain to declare its commitment to an ordered withdrawal. Three Catholic women were shot dead by gunmen after a robbery at their house at Ligoniel in Belfast.

Mon. 16.2.76: Following reports that soldiers were using forged press cards to gather information at riots and the scenes of explosions, the army said the practice would be stopped.

Sat. 21.2.76: In the republic, 1,500 members of the security forces were on duty when 500 mourners attended the funeral of Frank Stagg in Ballina, Co Mayo. The funeral was boycotted by Provisional Sinn Féin and its supporters, some 5,000 of whom attended a demonstration at the graveyard the following day which ended in clashes with the security forces after pistol shots were fired. In another Shankill Butcher killing in Belfast, a Catholic man was found tortured to death with knife wounds in an entry off the Shankill Road.

Fri. 27.2.76: There were bombs and riots in Protestant areas of Belfast in protest against the announcement two days previously that special-category status was to end. The disturbances continued the following day.

Sat. 28.2.76: Glenn Barr, convention member for Derry, announced that he would be resigning from the UDA over its refusal to back William Craig's call for a voluntary coalition.

Mon. 1.3.76: New prison rules were introduced in Northern Ireland. Special-category status was withdrawn from those convicted of terrorist offences committed after this date but provision was made for half instead of one-third remission of sentence, allowing 450 special-category and 164 ordinary prisoners to be released on licence between March and June. Existing special-category prisoners maintained their privileges and remained in the Maze (Compound). A new complex, the Maze (Cellular), to become famous as the H-blocks, so named because of their shape, was opened to hold new inmates. The UDA said it no longer supported the VUPP policy of voluntary coalition.

Tues. 2.3.76: At the final session of the convention, John Hume of the SDLP said that the DUP leader, Rev Ian Paisley, and Ernest Baird of the VUPP were responsible for its failure. William Craig of Vanguard said that the UUUC was responsible. At Belfast Magistrates' Court, charges of IRA membership against the Derry republican Martin McGuinness were dropped.

Wed. 3.3.76: The convention ended in uproar as the unionist majority voted through its report seeking a return to majority rule.

Thur. 4.3.76: Despite the UUUC's determination that it would reconvene the convention the following Tuesday, it was dissolved by order in council.

Fri. 5.3.76: In London, the taoiseach, Liam Cosgrave, met the prime minister, Harold Wilson, and the opposition leader, Margaret Thatcher, and was informed of Britain's plans in the wake of the convention's failure.

Sat. 6.3.76: The Provisional IRA claimed responsibility for a mortar-bomb attack on Aldergrove airport.

Sun. 7.3.76: A car bomb in Castleblayney, Co Monaghan, killed one man and seriously injured 16 other people.

Tues. 9.3.76: The two Catholic owners of the Golden Pheasant restaurant near Lisburn, Co Antrim, were shot dead and their restaurant was bombed.

Wed. 10.3.76: A UDA spokesperson, Sammy Smyth, was shot dead at a house on Alliance Avenue in Belfast. In what was interpreted as a reprisal for the Golden Pheasant killings, one man was killed and six were wounded when gunmen sprayed the Homestead Inn in Ballyaughlis, Co Down. The republic referred a test case alleging inhuman and degrading treatment of detainees in Northern Ireland to the European Court of Human Rights.

Thur. 11.3.76: At the Special Criminal Court in Dublin, Eddie Gallagher was sentenced to 20 years and Marion Coyle to 15 years in prison for the kidnapping of Tiede Herrema.

Sat. 13.3.76: Lenny Murphy, later exposed as the leader of the Shankill Butchers, was arrested and charged with attempted murder. He was held on remand until his conviction in October 1977.

Mon. 15.3.76: The Russell Court Hotel in Belfast was bombed for the third time, and severely damaged.

Tues. 16.3.76: The Provisional IRA warned that prison staff would have to "bear the consequences" of the ending of special-category status.

Wed. 17.3.76: Four people, including two teenage boys, were killed when a no-warning bomb exploded outside a Catholic bar in Dungannon, Co Tyrone. Provisional IRA prisoners in the Maze announced that they had withdrawn from "all institutional schemes and projects" in protest at the ending of special-category status.

Thur. 18.3.76: A Catholic schoolteacher was found stabbed to death behind a bar in the Cregagh area of Belfast. Three days later another stab victim was found in Sandy Row in Belfast.

Thur. 25.3.76: William Craig of the VUPP

visited Dublin for talks with the taoiseach, Liam Cosgrave, and the minister for foreign affairs, Garret FitzGerald. Two bombs caused extensive damage to office blocks and shops in Great Victoria Street in Belfast. The secretary of state, Merlyn Rees, stated his intention to restore the "primacy" of the RUC in Northern Ireland.

Fri. 26.3.76: Following a similar attack the previous week, there were mortar attacks on two army camps in Derry. The extension of the Prevention of Terrorism Act to Northern Ireland came into effect, making it an offence to withhold information that might prevent an act of terrorism.

Sat. 27.3.76: In what the Provisional IRA described as attacks on the "rich and ruling class", four private houses were bombed in Belfast.

Mon. 29.3.76: UUUC representatives met loyalist paramilitary leaders at the UUP headquarters in Belfast to discuss the formation of a loyalist action council to oppose direct rule. Before the meeting, the Conservative spokesperson on Northern Ireland, Airey Neave, met UUP representatives.

Tues. 30.3.76: A soldier searching Ballygargan Orange hall near Lurgan, Co Armagh, was killed in a booby-trap explosion. NICRA called off its rent and rates strike after nearly five years.

Wed. 31.3.76: Three soldiers were killed and one seriously injured when a land mine exploded under their vehicle at Belleek, Co Fermanagh. A mail train was robbed of £221,000 by armed men at Sallins, Co Kildare.

Thur. 1.4.76: The US ambassador to Britain started a two-day visit to Northern Ireland. He said that US customs officials would be coming to Britain to discuss ways of preventing the flow of arms from the US.

Fri. 2.4.76: The UUP rejected the idea, mooted earlier in the week, of an anti-direct-rule council.

Sun. 4.4.76: A Catholic woman was found stabbed to death in the Antrim Road area of Belfast.

Mon. 5.4.76: Three bombs destroyed the Conway Hotel in Dunmurry, south Belfast, and a bomb badly damaged the Wellington Park Hotel. There were also explosions in Belfast city centre, Omagh, Strabane and Keady. Following the Conway Hotel attack, a Provisional IRA staff officer, Sean McDermott, was shot dead by an RUC reservist. Mairead Farrell, one of five others caught at the scene and who served 10 years in prison for her part in the attack, was one of the victims of the Gibraltar SAS killings in 1988. In south Armagh, a part-time UDR man, Robert McConnell, was shot dead after visiting a neighbour. The prime minister, Harold Wilson, resigned and was succeeded by James Callaghan.

Tues. 6.4.76: Nineteen IRSP members were arrested in Dublin in connection with the mail-train robbery of the previous week.

Wed. 7.4.76: A woman UDR corporal was shot dead in a Land Rover near Middletown, Co Armagh. The driver was wounded. In Dromore, Co Down, three members of the Herron family died in a fire at their drapery shop, thought to have been started by an incendiary device. In

Dublin four IRSP members were charged with the Sallins mail-train robbery.

Thur. 8.4.76: In the first of a series of assassinations following the ending of special-category status, a prison officer at Magilligan, Patrick Dillon, was shot dead by the Provisional IRA at his home near Omagh, Co Tyrone.

Fri. 9.4.76: Two men were killed and 20 injured in bomb attacks on Catholic bars in Armagh and west Belfast.

Tues. 13.4.76: Two Catholic schoolboys were severely burned when a mob of Protestant boys set fire to them in a park in the Oldpark area of Belfast.

Wed. 14.4.76: Prison officers at the Maze refused to grant visits and other privileges to special-category prisoners in protest against the assassination of an officer the previous week. Damage estimated at £3 million was caused by firebombs at an industrial estate in the Sandy Row area of Belfast.

Fri. 16.4.76: The SAS shot dead a wanted IRA suspect, Peter Cleary, after a house search in south Armagh. The army said he had been trying to escape but locals said he had been shot in cold blood. Two men were killed in an explosion at a furniture works in the Falls area of Belfast.

Sun. 18.4.76: More than 10,000 people attended commemorations of the 60th anniversary of the Easter Rising, the largest at Milltown cemetery in Belfast.

Mon. 19.4.76: A prison officer was shot dead at his home in Dunmurry, south Belfast, and another was wounded outside Crumlin Road prison. The following day representatives of prison officers had a meeting with NIO minister Don Conannon, at which the arming of prison officers was raised. The secretary of state, Merlyn Rees, appealed to the officers to end their protest.

Wed. 21.4.76: Prison officers at Magilligan ended their withdrawal of special privileges from Provisional IRA prisoners.

Thur. 22.4.76: The UUP MP for South Down, Enoch Powell, claimed that the UUUC was extinct. The following day the deputy leader of the DUP, Rev William Beattie, called on the UUP to expel him.

Sat. 24.4.76: A Catholic man was killed and 10 people were injured in three bomb attacks on Catholic bars in Hilltown, Warrenpoint and Dunloy.

Sun. 25.4.76: There were scuffles with gardaí when 10,000 people attended a banned Provisional Sinn Féin rally at the GPO in Dublin to commemorate the Easter Rising. The *Sunday Times* claimed that the NIO planned a progressive withdrawal of troops from Northern Ireland and the "Ulsterisation" of security.

Mon. 26.4.76: The Police Authority announced that the RUC was to receive three armoured personnel carriers and have its rifles replaced by more modern self-loading rifles. The Police Federation later denied that the RUC was taking on a paramilitary role.

Wed. 28.4.76: In Dublin the minister for foreign affairs, Garret FitzGerald, advocated changes in the constitution to repeal the ban on divorce, relax the law on contraception and provide for mixed rather than denominational education.

Thur. 29.4.76: A UDR man and his brother were killed by gunmen outside his farm near Dungannon, Co Tyrone.

Fri. 30.4.76: The chief constable of the RUC, Sir Jamie Flanagan, retired and was succeeded by his deputy, Kenneth Newman.

Sat. 1.5.76: There were three separate International Workers' Day marches in Belfast, organised by the Irish Congress of Trade Unions, the NILP, and the PD.

Sun. 2.5.76: Prison officers voted to restore privileges to Provisional IRA prisoners.

Tues. 4.5.76: The secretary of state, Merlyn Rees, announced a troop reduction of 500 and a greater deployment of the RUC and the Royal Military Police in west Belfast.

Wed. 5.5.76: Nine IRSP men escaped from the Maze prison through a tunnel. One was recaptured later in the day.

Thur. 6.5.76: Eight SAS men were apprehended by a Garda patrol 500 yards inside Co Louth. They were taken to Dublin, charged with firearms offences and released on £5,000 bail each. The following day there were two further army incursions into the republic and the patrols were turned back. Also in the republic, the Criminal Law (Jurisdiction) Bill, allowing for the trial of persons in the republic for offences committed elsewhere and vice versa, was signed by the president, after the Supreme Court had ruled that it was constitutional.

Fri. 7.5.76: Two of the IRSP Maze escapers were recaptured in the north and two were being held by gardaí in Monaghan. Extradition orders were granted against them the following week. Two UVF men were jailed for life for the murder of a UDA man during the UVF/UDA feud.

Mon. 10.5.76: William Craig of the VUPP called for renewed talks between all political parties in the hope that the convention would be recalled. Later in the week, the UPNI supported the call. The ULCCC announced that its constituent paramilitary groups, including the UVF and UDA, would not take part in the proposed Loyalist Action Council but that it would initiate a conference on negotiated independence. The following day the Loyalist Action Council denied that it was defunct.

Fri. 14.5.76: The UDA said it had withdrawn from all loyalist co-ordinating groups.

Sat. 15.5.76: Following a Provisional IRA threat of a "long hot summer" for the RUC, three policemen were killed and a fourth was seriously injured in an explosion at Belcoo on the Fermanagh/Cavan border, and an RUC man was killed and two reservists were wounded when their car came under heavy fire at Warrenpoint, Co Down. A duffel-bag bomb was thrown into the Catholic Unity Flats in Belfast, killing two men and injuring 13 people, three seriously. At Charlemont, Co Armagh, gunmen threw a duffel-bag bomb into a Catholic bar, killing four people and seriously injuring one, and then sprayed another Catholic bar with machine-gun fire, seriously wounding three people. No one was injured when a bomb was thrown into a Catholic bar in Stewartstown, Co

Tyrone, but six were injured in another attack at Ardboe.

Sun. 16.5.76: An RUC reservist was shot dead at his home near Benburb, Co Tyrone. Two Protestant men were killed by gunmen outside a social club in Ardoyne in Belfast.

Mon. 17.5.76: A Catholic man was shot dead in a bus outside an army camp in Derry and another man on the bus and a woman pedestrian were wounded. The following day a soldier was charged with manslaughter. At Moy, near Charlemont, Co Armagh, two Protestant brothers were shot dead at their egg-exporting firm. The secretary of state, Merlyn Rees, said he would not replace any of the 1,000 troops recently withdrawn from Northern Ireland and was determined to establish the primacy of the RUC. The Provisional IRA claimed responsibility for the previous day's killings of RUC men and said the campaign would continue against the foisting of the RUC on "the republican community". The UDA said it could test the Provisional IRA's claim to be the protector of the republican people and that "the long hot summer can work both ways". In Portadown, Co Armagh, VUPP leaders including William Craig and Glenn Barr, along with a Conservative MP, were prevented from entering an Orange hall they had hired by what the MP called "Paisleyite louts". The Grand Orange Lodge later denied any involvement.

Tues. 18.5.76: Busmen in Derry stopped work and marched in protest to Fort George army camp on Strand Road, the scene of the previous day's killing.

Thur. 20.5.76: The Conservative spokesperson on Northern Ireland, Airey Neave, said he was disappointed with the government's security policies and repeated a call he had made the previous week for a combined anti-terrorist unit under one command and comprising the army, the RUC and the UDR.

Fri. 21.5.76: A young woman was killed by a bomb on a train at Moira, Co Down.

Sat. 22.5.76: The UVF announced a three-month ceasefire.

Mon. 24.5.76: Ernest Baird and Rev Ian Paisley, joint deputy leaders of the UUUC, said the loyalists of Ulster were about to defend their province.

Wed. 26.5.76: The UUP called on public bodies to snub the secretary of state, Merlyn Rees.

Thur. 27.5.76: Following a claim by a paratrooper that he had been ordered to lie in court, Merlyn Rees ordered the review of the case of Edward McClafferty, serving eight years in the Maze prison for possession of a firearm.

Fri. 28.5.76: Merlyn Rees travelled to Dublin for talks with ministers. Two men were killed when a bomb exploded without warning in the toilets of the Club bar in Belfast.

Wed. 2.6.76: A leading Belfast loyalist paramilitant, Jack Parsons of the Woodvale Defence Association, was shot dead at his home in Cambrai Street. A Special Branch officer was shot dead at the Royal Victoria Hospital. A 19-year-old female RUC reservist, shot in Derry the previous week, died in hospital.

Fri. 4.6.76: A conference of loyalist paramilitary groups, with the exception of the

UDA, met near Portrush, Co. Antrim, to discuss negotiated independence. The DUP alleged that the UUP was holding secret talks with the SDLP. It was stated the following day that despite this premature disclosure the talks would go on.

Sat. 5.6.76: A bomb in a Protestant bar on York Road in Belfast killed two people and injured 18 others. Later three gunmen burst into the Clorane bar near Smithfield market and sprayed it with machine-gun fire, killing four men. A man was killed by a bomb in a bar in Portaferry, Co Down. In several other bombings and shootings in Belfast, one man was killed and three were seriously wounded. The following day it was announced that troop levels were to be increased by 200.

Sun. 6.6.76: Expressing a personal opinion, Paddy Devlin of the SDLP argued that an independent Northern Ireland could prosper and, by getting rid of the British presence, would remove the excuse for paramilitary violence. Later in the week the SDLP chief whip, Austin Currie, gave the go-ahead for discussion of negotiated independence in the party.

Mon. 7.6.76: The UUUC censured the UUP for taking part in talks with the SDLP. The following week it was revealed that the talks were continuing, despite the censure. James Hegarty, a Nationalist alderman, became the first Nationalist mayor of Derry since 1920.

Sat. 12.6.76: A Catholic schoolteacher was killed near Forkhill, Co Armagh, in what the army said was crossfire following a land-mine explosion, an explanation strongly disputed by locals.

Thur. 17.6.76: The Provisional IRA claimed two explosions, which destroyed the Clorane bar and Madden's bar in Smithfield in Belfast, saying they could not protect the largely Catholic clientele from loyalist attack.

Sun. 20.6.76: Two men were found stabbed to death in the same area of north Belfast, it was believed by the same gang.

Tues. 22.6.76: The UDA, reversing an earlier decision, backed the Loyalist Action Council.

Fri. 25.6.76: Three people were shot dead in an attack on a bar near Templepatrick, Co Antrim. Rioting followed an explosion in the Hunting Lodge bar in Andersonstown in Belfast.

Wed. 30.6.76: Charles Eaton, a Territorial Army officer who had recently retired from the Police Authority, was shot dead as he arrived at his office in west Belfast.

Thur. 1.7.76: Six men were killed by UVF gunmen at the Catholic-owned Ramble Inn near Ballymena, Co Antrim.

Fri. 2.7.76: After a shooting incident in Ardoyne in Belfast in which a man and a pregnant woman were seriously injured, the woman gave birth and the baby had to have a bullet removed from its spine.

Sat. 3.7.76: After an advance warning from the UFF, four people were injured in bomb attacks on four hotels in Dublin, Rosslare, Limerick and Killarney in the republic. The UFF also claimed a bomb that exploded later in the week in a hotel in Salthill, Co Galway. In Derry a soldier was killed by gunmen at a checkpoint and widespread damage was caused in the city by two bombs.

Mon. 5.7.76: In his first visit to Northern Ireland as prime minister, James Callaghan said there would be no political, economic or military withdrawal from the north by Britain. He met representatives of the four main churches, visited police and troops at North Queen Street RUC station in Belfast and staged a walk-about in the city centre.

Fri. 9.7.76: In an attack claimed by the UFF, a young couple were shot dead in their home in Newtownabbey, Co Antrim.

Mon. 12.7.76: More than 50,000 Orangemen marched to 19 centres throughout Northern Ireland. At the Broughshane field, William Craig of the VUPP said that the Orange Order was an impotent force and that the UUUC's attitude to the convention had been disastrous.

Tues. 13.7.76: Gardaí claimed that British soldiers had abducted two men in the republic and brought them across the border for interrogation at Bessbrook, Co Armagh. After a man sprayed the interior of the British Legion club in Suffolk in Belfast with machine-gun fire, seriously wounding one man, two dozen Protestant families moved out of homes nearby. The following day a 14-year-old girl evacuee was injured when six shots were fired at the school where her family was staying.

Thur. 15.7.76: Gardaí launched a nationwide search for a Provisional IRA prisoner who escaped from cells in the Special Criminal Court after two explosions.

Fri. 16.7.76: In an attack claimed by the Provisional IRA, two huge bombs destroyed most of the shops in Castledawson, Co Derry, and left many families homeless.

Mon. 19.7.76: The NIO announced the closure of all but one of the approach roads to Aldergrove airport.

Wed. 21.7.76: The British ambassador to the republic, Christopher Ewart-Biggs, and a Stormont civil servant, Judith Cooke, were killed and the permanent under-secretary for Northern Ireland and the driver were seriously injured when a land mine exploded under their car near the ambassador's residence in Sandyford, Co Dublin. Some months later the Provisional IRA claimed the killings. The republic's cabinet went into emergency session and the attack was to give rise to the declaration of a state of emergency in the republic and additional anti-terrorist measures there.

Thur. 22.7.76: The SDLP and UUP announced that after private meetings for several months they had agreed on wide areas of policy but were still divided on the crucial point of a power-sharing executive. Ruairí Ó Brádaigh, president of Provisional Sinn Féin, and Sean Keenan, a prominent Derry republican, were detained by the RUC on their way to a funeral in Maghera, Co Derry. Mr Ó Brádaigh was eventually served with an exclusion order.

Mon. 26.7.76: Provisional IRA, IRSP and UDA prisoners threw meals over the wire of their compounds in the Maze in protest at recently introduced strip-searching and integration of loyalists and republicans.

Tues. 27.7.76: About 200 UDA prisoners broke out of their compound in the Maze in an attempt to attack two arrivals whom they thought were UVF men responsible for the murders of two UDA members. It was reported that talks between the NIO and Provisional Sinn Féin had been going on since early the previous year but had now ended. The secretary of state, Merlyn Rees, later denied that there had been any talks since early 1976.

Thur. 29.7.76: Two men were killed and 30 people were injured when a no-warning bomb exploded in the White Fort Inn in Belfast. For the fourth day running, UDA prisoners at Magilligan threw their meals over the wire of their compound in protest against prison policy.

Fri. 30.7.76: Gunmen raked the crowded bar of the Stag Inn in Belfast with machine-gun fire, killing four men. All Provisional IRA prisoners in the Maze threw their meals over the wire, while 200 UDA prisoners refused all their meals except eggs. In Magilligan meals were thrown over the wire for the fifth day.

Sun. 1.8.76: The NIO announced that 230 long-term prisoners were being offered a week's home leave. The following day Provisional IRA and IRSP prisoners rejected the offer.

Tues. 3.8.76: In an attack claimed by the Provisional IRA, six explosions wrecked the centre of Portrush, Co Antrim, at the height of the holiday season.

Thur. 5.8.76: The UPNI leader, Brian Faulkner, called for the reintroduction of internment.

Fri. 6.8.76: It was announced that the private talks between the SDLP and the UUP were to resume at the end of the month. As protests continued at the Maze and Magilligan prisons, it was revealed that a warder had been strip-searched by republicans in Magilligan in protest at the policy.

Sun. 8.8.76: There were disturbances in the Falls area of Belfast after a Provisional Sinn Féin rally attracted some 3,000 people to mark the fifth anniversary of the introduction of internment.

Mon. 9.8.76: On the fifth anniversary of internment there·was widespread unrest in Catholic areas of Belfast, including 30 shooting incidents and the hijacking and burning of 40 vehicles. Maire Drumm, vice-president of Provisional Sinn Féin, was arrested at her home in Andersonstown in connection with her speech at the previous day's rally. The charge against her was dropped on August 27th. About 30 republicans attacked the Antrim Road home of the SDLP leader, Gerry Fitt, at one stage entering the house and only leaving when Mr Fitt produced a gun.

Tues. 10.8.76: Two children were killed and another fatally injured when a car crushed them and their mother, Anne Maguire, against railings after the driver had been shot by troops involved in a car chase at Finaghy Road North in Belfast. The third child died the following day. The event was to give rise to the Women's Peace Movement, which became the Peace People, both organisations set up and led by Mairead Corrigan, sister of Anne Maguire, Betty Williams and Ciaran McKeown. Widespread rioting and bombings continued in Catholic areas of Belfast. In the wake of the Ewart-Biggs assassination, the Dáil was recalled from its summer recess to pass emergency legislation.

Thur. 12.8.76: More than 1,000 women gathered at the spot in west Belfast where three Maguire children had been killed. Women in Andersonstown collected 6,000 signatures on a peace petition.

Sat. 14.8.76: More than 10,000 people, including several busloads of Protestant women from the Shankill, attended a peace rally at Finaghy Road North in Belfast. Provisional Sinn Féin sympathisers harassed those attending.

Mon. 16.8.76: Two men were killed and 17 people injured, three seriously, when a bomb exploded outside a bar in Keady, Co Armagh. The Conservative spokesperson on Northern Ireland, Airey Neave, arrived in Belfast to press for a tougher security policy.

Tues. 17.8.76: The maximum sentence for possession of firearms was increased from five years to 10.

Wed. 18.8.76: Brian Faulkner, leader of the UPNI, announced his retirement from politics.

Thur. 19.8.76: The father of the county grand master of the Orange Lodge, Thomas Passmore, was shot at his son's home in Belfast and died the following week in hospital. The Provisional IRA blacklisted two BBC journalists and one from the *Irish News* because of their reporting of the internment anniversary events.

Sat. 21.8.76: Around 20,000 people from all over Belfast attended a march for a peace rally in Ormeau Park in Belfast. It was addressed by Mairead Corrigan. There was a similar substantial march in Dublin. Maire Drumm of Provisional Sinn Féin said the rally was illegal as it had not given five days' notice, and was motivated by the British army. The DUP leader, Rev Ian Paisley, said it was a front for the Catholic Church.

Tues. 24.8.76: The republic's government decided to declare a state of emergency and invoke article 28 of the constitution, allowing the introduction of a law to enable suspects to be held for seven days without charge.

Thur. 26.8.76: It was revealed that the European Commission of Human Rights had ruled that the British government had been guilty of using torture after the introduction of internment, but that internment had been justified and had not been discriminatory against the minority.

Fri. 27.8.76: A young couple and their 10-month-old baby were killed when their home in the New Lodge area of Belfast was petrol-bombed.

Sat. 28.8.76: Some 20,000–30,000 people marched up the Shankill Road to Woodvale Park in Belfast as part of the campaign of the Women's Peace Movement. In Dublin some 20,000 people attended a peace rally in Mount Merrion Square and there were marches in Lurgan, Bangor and Strabane.

Wed. 1.9.76: A state of emergency was declared in the republic.

Thur. 2.9.76: The European Commission of Human Rights report, leaked the previous week, was published.

Sat. 4.9.76: About 25,000 people from all over Northern Ireland attended a peace rally at Craigavon Bridge in Derry. About 150 Provisional Sinn Féin supporters staged a counter-protest. There were also peace rallies in Portadown, Limerick, Sligo and Thurles.

Tues. 7.9.76: The UUP announced its withdrawal from talks with the SDLP.

Thur. 9.9.76: The leaders of the four main churches issued a statement praising the Women's Peace Movement.

Fri. 10.9.76: Merlyn Rees became home secretary and his position as secretary of state for Northern Ireland was taken by Roy Mason. The UUUC welcomed the appointment but the SDLP leader, Gerry Fitt, expressed "strong objections". Shane O'Doherty, a 21-year-old Derry man, was sentenced to life imprisonment at the Old Bailey in London after being found guilty of 31 charges of sending letter and parcel bombs. Thirty-two UDA prisoners and six prison officers were injured in rioting at the Maze following a search of the UDA compound.

Sat. 11.9.76: Mairead Corrigan and Betty Williams led 5,000 peace demonstrators through Antrim. There were peace rallies also at Coleraine, Strabane, Craigavon, Dungannon, Newtownards, Ballynahinch, Drogheda, Waterford, Dundalk and Longford. The following day there were further marches in Kilkenny, Ennis, Nenagh and Gorey.

Mon. 13.9.76: A week of UDA disruption began in protest at the treatment of UDA prisoners in the Maze the previous Friday. There were more than 40 bomb hoaxes, 21 hijackings and other bomb and petrol-bomb attacks in Protestant areas of Belfast. The UFF said that unless prison officers stopped working in loyalist compounds they and their families would be considered legitimate targets.

Tues. 14.9.76: After the hijacking of two buses, 150 women supporters of the Peace Movement blocked the Shankill Road in Belfast in protest. They were pelted with eggs and fruit by youths.

Wed. 15.9.76: Kieran Nugent, a Provisional IRA member arrested in May, and the first prisoner not to have benefit of special-category status, entered the H-blocks at the Maze and refused to accept prison uniform. He returned to his cell wrapped only in a blanket—the "blanket" protest had begun. After a third day of hijackings and bomb hoaxes the UDA called a truce when minister of state Don Concannon agreed to discuss the events in the Maze of the previous Friday. Anne Dickson became the first woman to lead an Irish political party when she was elected leader of the UPNI.

Fri. 17.9.76: When the minister of state, Don Concannon, refused to instigate an inquiry into recent disturbances in the Maze, violence again erupted in Protestant areas of Belfast.

Sat. 18.9.76: About 20,000 in Newry and about 4,000 in Liverpool attended peace marches. The following day 3,000 people took part in a peace demonstration in Mullingar.

Mon. 20.9.76: After being told that the Board of Visitors at the Maze had begun an investigation into allegations of ill-treatment of loyalist prisoners, the UDA called off its street protests.

Tues. 21.9.76: There was a reshuffle of responsibilities among NIO ministers. The Derry brigade of the Provisional IRA stated that anyone working in prison camps or army bases,

or for businesses offering facilities to Crown forces, would be considered legitimate targets.

Fri. 24.9.76: The president of the republic, Cearbhall Ó Dálaigh, signed the Criminal Law Bill but referred the controversial Emergency Powers Bill—which would allow suspects to be held for seven days without charge—to the Supreme Court.

Sat. 25.9.76: There were peace rallies of 6,000 people in Dungannon, 2,000 in Glasgow and smaller gatherings at Greenisland, Co Antrim, and at Clonmel, Co. Tipperary. The Belfast brigade of the Provisional IRA warned peace women that they "must be prepared to accept the consequences" if they were to inform on any of its members.

Sun 26.9.76: About 10,000 people, including a large number of men, attended a peace rally at Larne.

Sat. 2.10.76: Peace rallies drew 25,000 people in Cork, 5,000 in Ballymena and 2,000 in Birmingham.

Mon. 4.10.76: There were riots in Turf Lodge in Belfast after a 13-year-old Catholic boy, Brian Stewart, was killed by a plastic bullet fired by a soldier.

Tues. 5.10.76: At the Conservative conference in Brighton, the party spokesperson on Northern Ireland, Airey Neave, said that British withdrawal would mean not only civil war but that "Ulster would be left open to the red menace".

Wed. 6.10.76: A 68-year-old woman and her son-in-law were shot dead in their home at Victoria Gardens in Belfast.

Fri. 8.10.76: A prison officer was shot dead outside his home in Derry. An RUC reservist was killed and five soldiers were injured in a booby-trap bomb at Kilrea, Co Derry.

Sat. 9.10.76: One woman was burned to death in one of 15 firebomb attacks in Ballymena, Co Antrim. Later a Catholic man was found beaten and burned to death in a nearby alley. Peace rallies attracted 4,000 people in Downpatrick, 4,000 in Leeds, 3,000 in Armagh and 2,000 at Shannon airport.

Sun. 10.10.76: Three peace leaders were attacked and two had their cars wrecked when they attended a meeting in Turf Lodge in Belfast to protest against the killing of Brian Stewart by a plastic bullet the previous Monday.

Wed. 13.10.76: The RUC said that the weapon used to kill a Protestant man near his home at Annaghmore, Co Armagh, was a Russian Kalashnikov rifle. In Dublin, Dáithí Ó Conaill, a leading Provisional IRA figure, was jailed for 18 months for IRA membership.

Thur. 14.10.76: Following a bomb attack on a furniture store in south Belfast, police and soldiers surprised the eight attackers. Four others were arrested near the scene and a gun was found in their car. One, jailed for possession of the gun, was Bobby Sands.

Fri. 15.10.76: Two members of the UVF, both ex-UDR men, were sentenced to life imprisonment for the Miami Showband murders of July 1975. A garda was killed and four gardaí were injured in a booby-trap bomb at Garryhinch, Co Laois.

Sat. 16.10.76: Three Provisional IRA members were killed in a bomb attack which started a massive fire in Belfast gasworks.

Sun. 17.10.76: The Variety Club of Great Britain's Woman of the Year award went to Betty Williams, who accepted it on behalf of the whole peace movement.

Mon. 18.10.76: The president of the republic, Cearbhall Ó Dálaigh, was described by the defence minister, Patrick Donegan, as a "thundering disgrace" for referring the Emergency Powers Bill to the Supreme Court. The republic's government ordered RTE to ban publicity, including interviews, for all paramilitary groups, north and south. Five men, past or present soldiers in the Black Watch Regiment, faced 24 charges in Belfast of faking the statements of suspects and falsely detaining them.

Wed. 20.10.76: The funerals of two of the Provisional IRA men killed the previous Saturday were delayed for an hour by security forces at Short Strand in Belfast until tricolours over their coffins were concealed by wreaths.

Fri. 22.10.76: The president of the republic, Cearbhall Ó Dálaigh, resigned "to protect the dignity of the office".

Sat. 23.10.76: A Peace People march on the Falls Road in Belfast came under vicious attack from Provisional Sinn Féin supporters. Sixteen people were taken to hospital and many others were treated on the spot. The rally in Musgrave Park was attended by 15,000 people, while a republican counter-rally in Falls Park attracted 2,000. Seven soldiers were injured in a Provisional IRA mortar attack on the security base in Crossmaglen, Co Armagh.

Sun. 24.10.76: A peace rally in Newcastle upon Tyne drew 10,000 people.

Tues. 26.10.76: As part of the blanket protest, republican remand prisoners appeared in Belfast Magistrates' Court dressed only in their underpants and demanded political status.

Wed. 27.10.76: There were seven hours of rioting in Turf Lodge in Belfast, in protest against army harassment.

Thur. 28.10.76: Maire Drumm, former vice-president of Provisional Sinn Féin, was shot dead by loyalist gunmen in the Mater Hospital where she was being treated for an eye ailment.

Fri. 29.10.76: In the first of another spate of Shankill Butcher killings, a young Catholic man was beaten, stabbed and shot in the head.

Sat. 30.10.76: Two Catholic newspaper delivery men were shot dead, and the 10-year-old son of one was wounded, by the UFF on Crumlin Road in Belfast.

Sun. 31.10.76: Several thousand people followed the coffin of Maire Drumm from her home to St Agnes's Church in Belfast on the eve of her funeral.

Mon. 1.11.76: Maire Drumm was buried in her family grave and not in the republican plot at Milltown cemetery.

Thur. 4.11.76: The SDLP said it was fully behind the Peace People.

Sat. 6.11.76: There were peace rallies in Omagh (3,000 people), Strabane (2,000) and Edinburgh (3,000).

Sun. 7.11.76: At a ceremony organised by Witness for Peace, 1,662 white crosses—one for every death in the "troubles"—were planted in the grounds of Belfast City Hall.

Thur. 11.11.76: The Belfast headquarters of the National Trust, along with 10,000 items of historical interest, was destroyed by a fire which followed two explosions. The ULCCC published a blueprint for an independent Ulster. An informal conference about the idea was held at the Corrymeela Community in Ballycastle the following Sunday.

Wed. 24.11.76: The Provisional IRA and the INLA both claimed the killing of a soldier shot in the neck in Ardoyne in Belfast.

Fri. 26.11.76: The secretary of state, Roy Mason, warned the political parties of Northern Ireland that they were in danger of being "left behind by the tide of devolution". A proxy bomb in a car caused widespread damage to an estate for army officers in Lisburn, Co Antrim. The Provisional IRA said it would give no warnings in future before attacking the homes of soldiers' families in Northern Ireland.

Sat. 27.11.76: A Peace People rally in Trafalgar Square in London drew 15,000 people.

Sun. 28.11.76: The Provisional IRA "apologised" for two booby-trap bombs meant for security forces that killed a 16-year-old Catholic girl in Lurgan, Co Armagh, and a 40-year-old Catholic man in Derry. The UDA rejected a Provisional IRA open letter to loyalist paramilitaries calling for talks.

Tues. 30.11.76: The three leaders of the Peace People, Ciaran McKeown, Mairead Corrigan and Betty Williams, were in Oslo to collect a cheque for £200,000 from the Norwegian people and for an audience with King Olaf.

Wed. 1.12.76: The Fair Employment Act, which made it an offence to discriminate in employment on religious or political grounds, came into effect.

Fri. 3.12.76: Dr Patrick Hillery, who had earlier been selected unopposed, was inaugurated sixth president of the republic.

Sat. 4.12.76: The SDLP conference voted to shelve the "independent Ulster" issue. It rejected by 153 votes to 111 a resolution calling for a declaration of intent by Britain to withdraw.

Sun. 5.12.76: Provisional IRA firebombs destroyed 17 shops in Derry.

Sun. 12.12.76: The ULCCC accused unionist politicans of being "godfathers of terrorism", guilty in the past of gun-running, selecting bomb targets, and promising money to buy arms and explosives.

Mon. 13.12.76: The Provisional IRA, demanding the return of political status for prisoners, unleashed a campaign of bombings, shootings, hijackings and hoaxes, causing one death, several injuries and widespread disruption and traffic chaos throughout Northern Ireland.

Fri. 17.12.76: It was announced that troop levels were to be reduced by 500 to 14,000. At Westminster the SDLP leader, Gerry Fitt, accused the unionist politicians Rev Ian Paisley, Ernest Baird and John Taylor of connection

with loyalist violence in the past. All three denied this.

Sat. 18.12.76: Five thousand people, including the four main church leaders, attended a peace rally in Armagh.

Thur. 23.12.76: The Provisional IRA declared a three-day ceasefire from December 25th to 27th. The secretary of state, Roy Mason, said 1977 would be "the year the net tightens on terrorists".

Fri. 24.12.76: Five-day parole was offered to 94 prisoners in Northern Ireland. It was refused by republicans.

Thur. 30.12.76: Brian Faulkner was awarded a life peerage in the New Year's honours list.

1977

Sat. 1.1.77: Three people were injured and a baby boy was killed when a 200lb bomb exploded after an inadequate warning at a house in Glengormley, Co Antrim. A south Belfast golf club was destroyed by an explosion and fire. The Provisional IRA threatened to "hot things up" in 1977.

Sun. 2.1.77: Dr Cahal Daly, bishop of Ardagh and Clonmacnois, said British policy in Northern Ireland caused a political vacuum and was "unpardonable and disastrous".

Wed. 5.1.77: The UVF was reported to have called off a ceasefire declared in November 1975 and to have claimed responsibility for some recent bomb attacks in its campaign for the return of political status and segregation from republican prisoners. There were riots and shootings in Turf Lodge in Belfast on this and the following day.

Thur. 6.1.77: The Peace People issued a document, *Strategy for Peace*, calling for a non-political assembly of community groups that would elect an executive.

Sat. 8.1.77: The Provisional IRA threatened punishments for burglars, muggers and other "offenders" in west Belfast.

Mon. 10.1.77: The RUC denied torture allegations by the Provisional IRA in north Armagh. The Provisional IRA said families of RUC men in the area would be regarded as "legitimate reprisal targets".

Thur. 13.1.77: The secretary of state, Roy Mason, said the Peace People had helped the security situation and there had been an increase of 12 per cent in the use of the confidential telephone.

Sun. 16.1.77: A Provisional IRA man was shot dead in a gunfight with the SAS in south Armagh.

Thur. 20.1.77: The Provisional IRA said it would remove "the English presence" even if it meant pulling down Belfast brick by brick.

Fri. 21.1.77: Buses were hijacked and burned in west Belfast.

Tues. 25.1.77: The DUP leader, Rev Ian Paisley, said he would contest one of the three Northern Ireland seats in the elections to the European Parliament the following year.

Mon. 31.1.77: The secretary of state, Roy Mason, had talks with an SDLP delegation about ways to fill the "political vacuum".

Wed. 2.2.77: In the first of a series of attacks on businessmen, Jeffrey Agate, manager of Du Pont in Derry, was shot dead by the Provisional IRA.

Fri. 4.2.77: The refusal of the UUP leader, Harry West, to meet the visiting Conservative spokesperson on Northern Ireland, Airey Neave, caused the Conservatives to break off relations with the UUP. Five men, past or present soldiers in the Black Watch Regiment, were jailed for planting evidence during searches in Andersonstown in Belfast in 1975.

Sun. 6.2.77: John McQuade, former MP and assembly member for Woodvale in Belfast, claimed he had a private army of 500 ex-servicemen who would carry the war to the IRA. Shots were fired into his home later in the week.

Mon. 7.2.77: The Peace People accepted an offer to meet the UDA to discuss community work and the investigation of protection rackets. They met the following Tuesday.

Wed. 9.2.77: The four defendants in the Balcombe Street siege trial were found guilty of six murders, including that of Ross McWhirter, and various bombings in London. The following day all were sentenced to life imprisonment.

Mon. 14.2.77: The UUP attacked the Fair Employment Act and said local councils should not consider it binding.

Wed. 16.2.77: The UUP MP for Armagh, Harold McCusker, revealed a copy of a letter from the UFF threatening businesses which supplied the prison service. The following day the UVF threatened the lives of prison staff.

Mon. 21.2.77: The Conservative leader, Margaret Thatcher, visited Belfast and Derry.

Sat. 26.2.77: Robert Mitchell, a justice of the peace and prominent Orangeman, was shot dead in his home in Newry, Co Down. Another JP and Orangeman, Walker Whitten, was shot and seriously wounded in a street in Portadown, Co Armagh, the following Tuesday. He died of his wounds four months later.

Sun. 27.2.77: Two UVF men were killed when a bomb they were carrying exploded in Corporation Street in Belfast.

Mon. 28.2.77: The National Council for Civil Liberties (NCCL) called for the repeal of the Prevention of Terrorism Act.

Tues. 1.3.77: A defence white paper revealed that there was a squadron (100–140 men) of SAS in Northern Ireland. It confirmed the policy of Ulsterisation.

Thur. 3.3.77: Lord Faulkner of Downpatrick, former Stormont prime minister and chief executive in the power-sharing administration, died in a riding accident.

Fri. 4.3.77: Rory O'Kelly, an SDLP election agent, was shot dead in a bar in Bangor, Co Down.

Mon. 7.3.77: Twenty Provisional IRA prisoners in Portlaoise started a hunger strike in protest against conditions.

Tues. 8.3.77: In what was seen as a significant change of policy, the SDLP attacked RUC interrogation methods. Eight SAS men were fined £100 each in a Dublin court for carrying weapons without a certificate when they were arrested the previous year by gardaí.

Fri. 11.3.77: In what, at 76 days, was the longest and costliest trial ever in Northern Ireland, 26 men of the east Antrim brigade of the UVF were sentenced to a total of 700 years' imprisonment for crimes including murder and attempted murder.

Sat. 12.3.77: The secretary of state, Roy Mason, denied allegations in the *Sunday Times* that any of his officials were involved in "black propaganda" or "dirty tricks" by the army.

Sun. 13.3.77: Const William David Brown (18), from Strabane, Co Tyrone, became the 100th RUC victim since 1969.

Mon. 21.3.77: A Police Federation spokesperson accused the secretary of state, Roy Mason, of unwillingness to deal effectively with terrorists and said a Conservative government would be more sympathetic. Rioting, which had begun the previous day in Turf Lodge in Belfast in protest against the army, continued.

Mon. 28.3.77: Following an earlier statement by the Provisional IRA that the immediate families of RUC men were to be "legitimate targets", Hester McMullan, the 63-year-old mother of a reservist, was shot dead in her farmhouse near Toomebridge, Co Antrim.

Tues. 29.3.77: It was revealed that the UUP was boycotting meetings of the UUUC, of which the UUP leader, Harry West, was technically the head, because of disagreements between himself and Ernest Baird of the United Ulster Unionist Movement (UUUM).

Fri. 1.4.77: A government proposal to treat Northern Ireland as a three-seat PR constituency in European Parliament elections was attacked by unionists but welcomed by the SDLP and Alliance.

Sun. 3.4.77: Sixty people, including eight gardaí, were taken to hospital after clashes as 1,000 people demonstrated outside Portlaoise prison in support of Provisional IRA hunger strikers there. The Conservative spokesperson on Northern Ireland, Airey Neave, called for Provisional Sinn Féin to be outlawed and for the creation of a new anti-terrorist brigade of the army.

Mon. 4.4.77: Forty people were injured when two bombs exploded without warning in cafés in Rosemary Street, Belfast.

Wed. 6.4.77: John Higgins, British national organiser for Provisional Sinn Féin, was sentenced at the Old Bailey to 10 years' imprisonment for offences under the Prevention of Terrorism Act.

Fri. 8.4.77: Two RUC men were shot dead and one was injured while chasing a suspect car near Magherafelt, Co Derry. There was a massive hunt for the killers, thought to be members of the South Derry Marxist Republican group responsible for several recent murders of RUC and UDR men. The army announced the impending installation of a computer that would hold information on almost everyone in Northern Ireland. The Provisional IRA announced that civilian searchers would be considered part of the "British occupation forces".

Sun. 10.4.77: As Republican Clubs members were gathering in Beechmount in west Belfast for a march to commemorate the Easter Rising,

a bomb exploded killing a 10-year-old boy and seriously injuring three other people. The boy's uncle was shot dead as he went to inform relatives. The chair of the Republican Clubs, Malachy McGurran, blamed the Provisional IRA. Later, Republican Clubs marchers were attacked by Provisional IRA supporters in Milltown cemetery and a woman was wounded when shots were fired.

Sun. 17.4.77: The Catholic primate, Cardinal William Conway, died in Armagh.

Tues. 19.4.77: One thousand people demonstrated outside the courthouse in Portadown, Co Armagh, where five members of the Ulster Service Corps (USC) were in the dock. They were addressed by the DUP leader, Rev Ian Paisley, and Ernest Baird of the UUUM. The previous day the USC had set up roadblocks around the town. The following day it set up roadblocks from south Derry to Ballymena and from Portadown to Enniskillen.

Wed. 20.4.77: Two youths were killed and 30 people were injured when a car bomb exploded at the funeral of Provisional IRA member, Trevor McKibbin, shot dead by the army the previous Sunday.

Fri. 22.4.77: Following the intervention of Dr James Kavanagh, auxiliary bishop of Dublin, 14 Provisional IRA prisoners ended their 47-day hunger strike in Portlaoise.

Sat. 23.4.77: The United Unionist Action Council (UUAC), which spawned the USC, gave the secretary of state, Roy Mason, seven days to start a new offensive against the IRA and announce steps to implement the convention report. It threatened an immediate general strike. Two days later the UUAC's plans were condemned by the UUP, the VUPP and the Orange Order.

Mon. 25.4.77: The British government decided against introducing a bill of rights for Northern Ireland.

Fri. 29.4.77: The DUP leader, Rev Ian Paisley, called for labour, rent, rates and VAT strikes. But Belfast shipyard workers voted by a large majority not to support strike action. Ballylumford power station workers said they would wait to see how much support the strike received. The secretary of state, Roy Mason, announced that 500 more troops were to be flown to Northern Ireland.

Sat. 30.4.77: Paramilitary groups in the ULCCC said they were supporting the strike reluctantly, to avoid bloodshed in clashes with the British army. The DUP leader, Rev Ian Paisley, said he would quit politics if the strike failed. He refused to meet William Craig of the VUPP, who had hoped to persuade him to call off the stoppage. There was panic buying in the shops.

Sun. 1.5.77: Twelve hundred extra troops arrived in Northern Ireland and police leave was cancelled. The UUP, VUPP, Orange Order, Peace People, trade unions, churchpeople and others called on the UUAC to abandon its strike plans.

Mon. 2.5.77: The UUAC leaders, Rev Ian Paisley and Ernest Baird, met the secretary of state, Roy Mason, but failed to gain concessions. Mr Mason said the extra troops were a "precautionary measure" and were not

for "loyalist bashing". It was also announced that "SAS-type" units had been doubled in Northern Ireland. Mr Paisley denied that the stoppage was a ploy to achieve an independent Ulster.

Tues. 3.5.77: On the first day of the UUAC stoppage the port of Larne closed but many factories remained open. There were many complaints of intimidation.

Wed. 4.5.77: James Molyneaux, parliamentary leader of the UUP, dissolved the UUUC and accused the UUAC of planning a provisional government. Despite attacks on buses, busmen voted to continue working.

Thur. 5.5.77: The RUC said it had removed 300 roadblocks, arrested 23 people and received over 1,000 complaints of intimidation.

Fri. 6.5.77: After 100 men in cars had been prevented by police from approaching Ballylumford power station, workers there voted not to join the strike. The NIO said industry was "near normal", but the DUP leader, Rev Ian Paisley, and the UVF claimed support for the strike was growing.

Sat. 7.5.77: The Peace People held their first rally for several months at Belfast City Hall, to protest about intimidation. There was a three-mile cavalcade of farm vehicles in the Lisburn–Hillsborough–Moira area in protest at security policies, but the demonstrators said they did not support the strike.

Mon. 9.5.77: There were roadblocks, cavalcades of farm vehicles and demonstrations in support of the strike in Ballymena, Belfast, Enniskillen, Larne, Portadown, Tandragee and Newtownards.

Tues. 10.5.77: A busman was shot dead at the wheel of his bus on Crumlin Road in Belfast and a part-time UDR man was killed and 13 people injured when a bomb exploded at the Mountainview filling station, which had remained open during the strike.

Fri. 13.5.77: The UUAC strike was called off. It was widely regarded as a political setback for its leaders. Rev Ian Paisley maintained, however, that it had been a success and said he would not be leaving politics.

Sat. 14.5.77: Capt Robert Nairac was kidnapped by the Provisional IRA from a bar in south Armagh where he had been engaged in "undercover intelligence-gathering" duties. The Provisional IRA later admitted killing him and said he had admitted under interrogation that he was a member of the SAS. Though this was denied by the army, it is now widely accepted.

Sun. 15.5.77: The SDLP leader, Gerry Fitt, called for talks between the anti-strike parties to break the "political logjam".

Mon. 16.5.77: A British TV programme revealed that the Provisional IRA and the UDA had been involved in peace talks, mediated by the Belfast barrister Desmond Boal and the ex-foreign minister of the republic, Sean MacBride. The following day the British and Irish governments denounced the initiative.

Wed. 18.5.77: There was a 58 per cent turnout in district council elections in Northern Ireland. With the dissolution of the UUUC, this was the first time since 1974 that the unionist parties had contested an election independently.

Fri. 20.5.77: Despite the fragmentation of the party system the count in the local elections revealed that four parties dominated. The UUP, the DUP, the SDLP and Alliance between them took over 80 per cent of the seats. Ernest Baird's United Ulster Unionist party (UUUP), derived from the UUUM, did poorly and the VUPP, UPNI, and NILP were virtually eliminated.

Mon. 23.5.77: The secretary of state, Roy Mason, started a new round of talks with the political parties.

Wed. 25.5.77: In a switch of Labour policy, the prime minister, James Callaghan, announced the setting up of an all-party Speaker's conference to consider the possibility of creating more Northern Ireland MPs.

Sat. 28.5.77: The UVF announced an indefinite ceasefire.

Mon. 30.5.77: In the latest of a series of such killings, thought to be the work of the Provisional IRA, a company director was shot dead at his place of work in Belfast.

Thur. 2.6.77: The Provisional IRA shot dead two RUC members and a full-time reservist in a car near Stewartstown, Co Tyrone.

Fri. 3.6.77: Nine UVF men from Coleraine, Co Derry, were sentenced at a Belfast court for a total of 108 years for terrorist offences.

Sat. 4.6.77: The UVF broke its week-long ceasefire, in response to the killing of three policemen on June 2nd.

Wed. 8.6.77: Gerald Tucker, a part-time UDR man, was shot dead as he got into his car at the Royal Victoria Hospital in Belfast, where he worked. The secretary of state, Roy Mason, announced that the Spearhead battalion, brought to Northern Ireland for the UUAC strike, was to leave. But there were to be more specialist troops, engaging in "increased SAS-type activity", police strength was to be increased by a minimum of 1,200, the full-time UDR was to be increased to 2,500, and there would be more "anti-terrorist squads" in the RUC. He also announced plans to increase sentences for a range of conspiracy, membership and explosives offences. The UUP claimed victory for constitutional politics but the UUAC claimed the package was a result of the strike.

Fri. 10.6.77: Five hundred Royal Victoria Hospital staff blocked the gates as a protest against the killing of Gerald Tucker two days earlier. There were claims that an active service unit of the Provisional IRA was operating in the hospital. The Provisional IRA claimed that the RVH was used by the army for "intelligence-gathering" and said it would remain a target.

Sat. 11.6.77: Following an announcement by the secretary of state, Roy Mason, that he would employ 200 civilians to release RUC members from desk jobs, the Provisional IRA threatened to "execute" any civilians working in police stations.

Thur. 16.6.77: Voting took place in a general election in the republic.

Fri. 17.6.77: Fianna Fáil secured a record 20-seat majority in the republic's general election.

Wed. 22.6.77: James Molyneaux, the UUP leader at Westminster, said that if there was to be no devolution Ulster should be integrated into the UK.

Wed. 29.6.77: Two soldiers were shot dead and a padre was seriously injured outside an army camp on the Falls Road in Belfast.

Fri. 1.7.77: Following the resignation of Liam Cosgrave as leader of Fine Gael, in the wake of the republic's election, Garret FitzGerald became party leader. Labour appointed Frank Cluskey as leader, to take over from Brendan Corish.

Tues. 5.7.77: The 21st Dáil assembled and the Fianna Fáil leader, Jack Lynch, was elected taoiseach.

Thur. 7.7.77: A new paramilitary group, the Loyalist Prisoners Action Force (LPAF), thought to consist of members of both the UDA and the UVF, organised a spate of bomb hoaxes in Belfast in pursuit of segregation in the prisons. These continued the following day. And on Saturday the LPAF fired shots into a prison officer's home in the Shankill area.

Tues. 26.7.77: New offences were introduced to deal with bomb hoaxes and threats and maximum sentences for explosives offences and conspiracy to murder were increased.

Wed. 27.7.77: A feud broke out between the Provisional IRA and the Officials. In the first evening's fighting in Belfast four people were killed and 19 injured. The following day a ceasefire was called, but six people were injured in further incidents.

Fri. 29.7.77: It was announced that the security forces were to be rearmed with Armalite rifles, the favourite weapon of the Provisional IRA.

Mon. 1.8.77: The secretary of state, Roy Mason, announced a "flexible" £1,000 million package to assist foreign companies in Northern Ireland. *Republican News* published details of the Queen's forthcoming visit.

Sun. 7.8.77: In what was seen as a move to prevent Provisional IRA disruption during the impending visit by the Queen, security forces detained many republican suspects.

Wed. 10.8.77: The Queen and Prince Philip began a two-day visit to Northern Ireland, visiting Hillsborough, Coleraine, and Portrush. SDLP and other anti-unionist politicians declined invitations to meet her. A 3,000 strong Provisional Sinn Féin march in Belfast protesting against the visit was halted by the army at Castle Street. The following day a small bomb exploded at the New University of Ulster at Coleraine after the Queen had left.

Sat. 13.8.77: The SDLP threatened to "review its long-term policy for the future of Ireland" because of lack of progress towards power-sharing.

Wed. 17.8.77: The RUC chief constable, Kenneth Newman, said that the RUC was now the "front-line force", with the army as back up.

Fri. 19.8.77: Thirty-five incendiaries caused 26 fires in Belfast.

Mon. 22.8.77: Dr Tomás Ó Fiaich was appointed archbishop of Armagh and Catholic primate.

Thur. 25.8.77: Paddy Devlin resigned as chair of the SDLP, attacking its emphasis on the "Irish dimension" and drift away from socialist principles. Six days later he was relieved of all party offices and ceased to be a party spokesperson. He was later expelled.

Tues. 30.8.77: The US president, Jimmy Carter, said he would support investment in Northern Ireland if a solution acceptable to both communities could be found.

Tues. 13.9.77: In a speech marking the end of his first year in office, the secretary of state, Roy Mason, said the myth of British withdrawal from Northern Ireland was now dead for ever.

Tues. 20.9.77: In a reassessment of party policy, the SDLP called on the government to bring about "an agreed Ireland".

Fri. 23.9.77: Two Belfast cinemas were destroyed and a third was damaged by firebomb attacks.

Wed. 28.9.77: The taoiseach, Jack Lynch, met the prime minister, James Callaghan, in London. A statement emphasised the British insistence on power-sharing. The following day he met the leader of the Conservative party, Margaret Thatcher.

Fri. 30.9.77: In the latest of a spate of many such incidents in Belfast, the Provisional IRA kneecapped three young men.

Wed. 5.10.77: Seamus Costello, leader of the IRSP, was shot dead in his car in Dublin. The perpetrators were assumed to be members of the Official IRA.

Fri. 7.10.77: The Irish Independence party, led by Frank McManus and Fergus McAteer, was launched in Belfast.

Mon. 10.10.77: Mairead Corrigan and Betty Williams, two of the leaders of the Peace People, were awarded the Nobel Peace Prize for 1976.

Tues. 11.10.77: In a plea bargain, Lenny Murphy of the UVF, leader of the Shankill Butchers, was found guilty of possession of a firearm and sentenced to 12 years in prison.

Fri. 14.10.77: Provisional IRA incendiary attacks continued, damaging many buildings in Belfast and Holywood, Co Down.

Sun. 6.11.77: At the SDLP annual conference the party rejected a call for British withdrawal and gave the go-ahead for new inter-party talks. The following day it was reported that the secretary of state, Roy Mason, was making arrangements to meet with the major parties.

Mon. 21.11.77: An SDLP delegation met Roy Mason.

Tues. 22.11.77: Roy Mason suggested the setting up of a 78-member assembly, without legislative powers, to run local departments.

Wed. 23.11.77: The Provisional IRA admitted responsibility for the spate of firebombings throughout Northern Ireland.

Fri. 25.11.77: The UUP met the secretary of state, Roy Mason.

Sat. 26.11.77: The VUPP leader, William Craig, said the party was being disbanded and he would be rejoining the UUP.

Fri. 2.12.77: The four main churches expressed concern about allegations of ill-treatment of suspects and prisoners by the RUC.

Sat. 3.12.77: Twenty-three people, including seven RUC men and a soldier, were injured in an explosion at the Wellworths store in Dungannon, Co Tyrone. Seamus Twomey, a former Provisional IRA chief of staff who had escaped by helicopter from Mountjoy prison in 1973, was recaptured by Special Branch detectives in Dublin.

Sat. 10.12.77: Mairead Corrigan and Betty Williams, two of the leaders of the Peace People, received the Nobel Peace Prize in a ceremony at Oslo, Norway.

Sat. 17.12.77: In an atmosphere of controversy following a decision by Belfast City Council not to honour them with a civic reception, Mairead Corrigan and Betty Williams returned from Norway and led a rally through Belfast to the City Hall.

1978

Mon. 9.1.78: The taoiseach, Jack Lynch, reaffirmed his government's commitment to eventual unification, and said that in such circumstances he would offer an amnesty to Provisional IRA prisoners. The unionist parties withdrew from talks with the NIO in response.

Wed. 11.1.78: The FEA published a report indicating that Catholic men were two and a half times as likely to be unemployed as their Protestant counterparts.

Fri. 13.1.78: A bomb caused extensive damage to Derry's Guildhall, only months after it had been reopened following £1 million restoration work.

Mon. 16.1.78: The Catholic primate, Dr Tomás Ó Fiaich, said "the British should withdraw from Ireland . . . I think it's the only way to get things moving."

Wed. 18.1.78: The European Court of Human Rights ruled that interrogation methods used by the security forces on internees had not amounted to torture, although they were "undoubtedly inhuman and degrading".

Sun. 22.1.78: An "anti-repression" conference in Coalisland, Co Tyrone, organised by Bernadette McAliskey and the Tyrone Relatives Action Committee, attracted 1,000 people who voted to organise marches and petitions in support of the prisoners in the H-blocks.

Wed. 1.2.78: The Conservative party spokesperson on Northern Ireland, Airey Neave, said his party no longer supported power-sharing devolution.

Wed. 8.2.78: A UDR man and his 10-year-old daughter were killed by a bomb under their car in Maghera, Co Derry.

Sat. 11.2.78: The Fine Gael leader, Garret FitzGerald, said northern Protestants would be "bloody fools" to join the republic under its present constitution.

Fri. 17.2.78: Twelve people were killed and 23 were injured when a Provisional IRA bomb with cans of petrol attached exploded at a window of the La Mon restaurant in Co Down, causing a fireball that engulfed the function rooms.

Thur. 2.3.78: Gerry Adams, detained by police after the La Mon bombing, appeared in a Belfast court on a charge of IRA membership. He was described in court as the Belfast brigade commander of the Provisional IRA.

Fri. 3.3.78: Norma Spence, a young civilian searcher, and a soldier were shot dead by gunmen posing as Rag Day students at a security gate in Donegall Street, Belfast. Gusty Spence, commander of the UVF in the Maze, resigned from the organisation for health reasons.

Mon. 6.3.78: The UUP turned down an invitation to a meeting on unionist unity organised by the DUP leader, Rev Ian Paisley, and the UUUP leader, Ernest Baird.

Sun. 12.3.78: Comments by the secretary of state, Roy Mason, about the amount of terrorist incidents allegedly launched in the republic brought angry retorts from Dublin politicians.

Mon. 27.3.78: The GAA voted to continue to ban members of the RUC and British forces from membership.

Fri. 7.4.78: The Conservative spokesperson on Northern Ireland, Airey Neave, said in Belfast that power-sharing was no longer "practical politics" and pledged the support of a future Conservative government for the UUP proposal for an upper tier of local government. After discussion at the Copenhagen EC summit, the prime minister, James Callaghan, and the taoiseach, Jack Lynch, announced improvement in recently strained Anglo-Irish relations on security.

Wed. 19.4.78: The prime minister, James Callaghan, said legislation would be introduced to increase representation of Northern Ireland at Westminster from 12 MPs to between 16 and 18.

Thur. 27.4.78: David Payne, former UDA commander for north Belfast, who had recently addressed a Peace People meeting, was wounded in his home in the Shankill by loyalist gunmen. In an operation involving more than 300 policemen, 15 leading Provisional Sinn Féin members were arrested and many files were confiscated at the party headquarters in west Belfast.

Fri. 5.5.78: In Dublin the secretary of state, Roy Mason, along with his senior officials, met ministers from the republic to discuss economic and security matters.

Fri. 12.5.78: Following two nights of rioting in west Belfast after a republican prisoner had been found hanged in his cell in Castlereagh holding centre, the chief constable, Kenneth Newman, announced an investigation into the circumstances of the death. Rioting continued that night.

Tues. 16.5.78: Having been closed to everyone except passengers for five years, Aldergrove airport was reopened to the public.

Thur. 1.6.78: An Alliance councillor, David Cooke, was installed as the first non-unionist mayor of Belfast.

Fri. 2.6.78: Incendiary bombs destroyed the Gas Department headquarters in Ormeau Avenue in Belfast.

Sat. 3.6.78: The Provisional IRA claimed responsibility for explosions that destroyed a freight warehouse in Drumahoe, Derry, causing £5 million worth of damage.

Tues. 13.6.78: An Amnesty International report, previously extensively leaked, was published, indicating several instances of RUC malpractice and ill-treatment of terrorist suspects, particularly in Castlereagh detention centre in Belfast. The secretary of state, Roy Mason, later announced a private inquiry.

Fri. 16.6.78: In a Provisional IRA ambush near Crossmaglen, Co Armagh, a young RUC man was shot dead and another, Const William Turbitt, was kidnapped. His body was found in a derelict house on July 10th.

Sun. 18.6.78: Fr Hugh Murphy, from Ahoghill, Co Antrim, was kidnapped, it was thought by a loyalist gang, in an attempt to gain the release of Const Turbitt. He was released after a plea from the DUP leader, Rev Ian Paisley. In December 1978 three RUC men were charged with the kidnapping and, along with two other policemen, with the murder of an Ahoghill grocer.

Mon. 19.6.78: The Conservative leader, Margaret Thatcher, visited Northern Ireland. In what was seen as a deal with unionists, she promised that a Tory government would form a "regional council structure" in Northern Ireland.

Wed. 21.6.78: Troops shot dead four unarmed men at a post office depot in the Ballysillan area of Belfast. Three were Provisional IRA men attempting to plant a bomb and the fourth was an innocent bystander.

Thur. 6.7.78: Members of the United Troops Out Movement threw horse dung into the Commons chamber, calling for the release of "Irish political prisoners".

Tues. 11.7.78: A 16-year-old Catholic, John Boyle, from Dunloy, Co Antrim, was shot dead by SAS men who claimed he was one of three gunmen surprised taking weapons from a graveyard. In fact the cache had been found by the boy and reported to the police. The killing provoked widespread criticism. Two SAS men were eventually tried for murder but acquitted.

Thur. 27.7.78: Malachy McGurran, vice-president of Sinn Féin the Workers Party (formerly Official Sinn Féin) and a founder member of NICRA, died in a Dublin hospital.

Wed. 2.8.78: Following a visit on July 30th to the H-blocks of the Maze prison, the Catholic primate, Archbishop Tomás Ó Fiaich, described his horror at the conditions in which those on the "dirty protest" were living, saying "one would hardly allow an animal to remain in such conditions, let alone a human being". His statement was welcomed by Provisional Sinn Féin and the SDLP but brought a quick reply from the NIO and criticism from unionists, Alliance and the Conservative party. The secretary of state, Roy Mason, announced that De Lorean Motor Company was to open a sports car factory at Twinbrook in west Belfast. The government was to provide £56 million of the £65 million cost.

Tues. 8.8.78: Three thousand people marched in west Belfast to mark the anniversary of internment and to support the prisoners in the H-block protest. Riots broke out in the early hours of the 9th and continued all day and that night.

Thur. 24.8.78: A report on the operation of the Prevention of Terrorism Act in Britain by Lord Shackleton recommended changes but not repeal.

Sun. 27.8.78: The 10th anniversary of the first civil rights march was marked by another march from Coalisland to Dungannon, attended by 5,000–10,000 people.

Sat. 2.9.78: A report in *Republican News* indicated that Provisional Sinn Féin was now fully behind the broadly-based H-block campaign.

Tues. 5.9.78: The SDLP called for the return of jury trial and repeal of the Emergency Provisions Act.

Wed. 6.9.78: The Provisional IRA shot dead a major in the army cadet force, claiming he was "part of the British war machine". Gerry Adams was released from court in Belfast after the lord chief justice, Lord Lowry, threw out charges against him of IRA membership.

Sun. 17.9.78: The army defused a bomb in west Belfast intended to explode during a 3,000-strong Provisional Sinn Féin protest march about the H-block issue.

Thur. 21.9.78: A Provisional IRA bomb attack on Eglinton airfield in Co Derry destroyed the terminal, two hangars and four planes.

Fri. 22.9.78: The SDLP accused the Provisional IRA of hypocrisy on the H-block issue, but said the NIO was being vindictive and inflexible.

Sat. 30.9.78: At Ballygoney, Co Tyrone, a wildfowler, James Taylor, was killed by plainclothes soldiers who shot him in the back after an argument with him as to why they had let down his car tyres. The director of public prosecutions (DPP) announced on April 19th 1979 that there would be no prosecution.

Thur. 5.10.78: Mairead Corrigan, Betty Williams and Ciaran McKeown announced they would step down as leaders of the Peace People.

Sun. 8.10.78: In Derry, 69 policemen were injured in clashes with loyalists attending a counter-demonstration, organised by the DUP leader, Rev Ian Paisley, against a Provisional Sinn Féin march to commemorate the 10th anniversary of the original civil rights rally in the city. A former Faulknerite assembly member, Peter McLachlan, was elected chair of the Peace People.

Thur. 12.10.78: Letitia McCrory, a 55-year-old Dublin woman, was killed and two other women were injured when a bomb exploded in the Dublin–Belfast train as it approached Central Station in Belfast.

Sat. 14.10.78: Thirty-two RUC men were injured and considerable damage was done to property in Derry at a DUP march to protest about the previous weekend's republican march.

Sun. 15.10.78: Fifteen RUC men, including an assistant chief constable, were injured and plastic bullets were fired for the first time in some years during clashes with republican youths who were attempting to march along the M1 motorway to the Maze in support of the prisoners in the H-blocks.

Sun. 22.10.78: Despite strong opposition from northern delegates, Provisional Sinn Féin agreed at its ard fheis in Dublin to welcome open discussions with loyalists.

Sat. 4.11.78: The SDLP conference voted 700–2 for a British withdrawal from Northern Ireland.

Fri. 10.11.78: After prolonged controversy involving loyalist demonstrations against an expansion of "Catholic" west Belfast, it was announced that work was to begin on the new Poleglass estate in mid-1979.

Tues. 14.11.78: Thirty-seven people were injured by Provisional IRA bombs in Belfast, Armagh, Dungannon, Enniskillen, Cookstown and Castlederg. By Monday 20th, 50 bombs had exploded in a week.

Thur. 16.11.78: A Provisional IRA bomb attack on the Ulster Brewery in west Belfast led to the death of a senior fire officer.

Mon. 27.11.78: Albert Miles, deputy governor of the Maze prison with special responsibility for the H-blocks, was shot dead by the Provisional IRA at his home in north Belfast.

Tues. 28.11.78: In the Commons the Redistribution of Seats Bill, to increase Northern Ireland representation from 12 to 17 MPs, passed its second reading by 350 votes to 49.

Thur. 30.11.78: Admitting setting off bombs in 14 towns and villages that day, the Provisional IRA warned it was "preparing for a long war".

Fri. 1.12.78: The Provisional IRA bombing campaign continued, with explosions in 11 towns across Northern Ireland, injuring two children and two policemen.

Thur. 7.12.78: The SDLP launched a campaign for a "new Ireland".

Tues. 12.12.78: Three prison officers' wives and a postman were injured by parcel bombs in Belfast and Lisburn and seven other parcel bombs were defused.

Sun. 17.12.78: Provisional IRA bombs exploded in Bristol, Manchester, Liverpool, Coventry and Southampton.

Mon. 18.12.78: Two Provisional IRA car bombs went off in central London. In Belfast, five RUC men were charged with the murder of a Catholic shopkeeper and three of them with the kidnapping of a priest after the Provisional IRA had kidnapped a policeman.

Wed. 20.12.78: In further Provisional IRA bomb attacks, six hotels in Northern Ireland were seriously damaged.

Thur. 21.12.78: In Crossmaglen, Co Armagh, three soldiers were shot dead from the back of a van.

1979

Mon. 1.1.79: The year began with a Provisional IRA bomb blitz in several towns across Northern Ireland.

Fri. 5.1.79: Two Provisional IRA bombers were killed by their own bomb in the Ardoyne area of Belfast. Three thousand people took part in a 10th anniversary commemoration of the civil rights march ambushed at Burntollet.

Thur. 18.1.79: Twenty-five buses were destroyed in a firebomb attack at the Citybus depot in Andersonstown, west Belfast. An all-party delegation of Westminster MPs visited the Maze prison. Later in the month the NIO issued details and photographs of conditions in the H-blocks.

Thur. 1.2.79: Following months of controversy, the RUC announced that two SAS men were to be charged with the murder of John Boyle, the 16-year-old shot dead in Dunloy, Co Antrim, in July 1978.

Sun. 4.2.79: Provisional IRA gunmen shot dead Patrick Macken, retired head of training for prison officers, and his wife at their home in Belfast.

Wed. 7.2.79: After the secretary of state, Roy Mason, had described the SDLP as turning "a little green", and described the decline in popularity of the party as a sign of movement towards moderation, the party leader, Gerry Fitt, said Mr Mason was "in the pockets of the unionists" and announced that the party would no longer take part in talks with him.

Tues. 20.2.79: Eleven Protestants, members of the Shankill Butcher gang, were convicted of 112 offences, including 19 murders.

Sat. 24.2.79: In an explosion near Keady, Co Armagh, two youths were killed and three were seriously injured by the Provisional IRA in mistake for soldiers. The Provisional IRA later offered its "deepest sympathy" to their families.

Sun. 11.3.79: Dr Robert Irwin, forensic medical officer and secretary to the Northern Ireland Police Surgeons' Federation, said that 150 people he had seen at Castlereagh interrogation centre in Belfast bore evidence of having been ill-treated by RUC detectives. He was supported by Jack Hassard, who had recently resigned from the Police Authority after making similar allegations. Dr Irwin was supported by his federation but attacked by loyalists and the NIO. Various attempts were made to blacken his name, including a security-force leak that his wife had been raped some years before by soldiers.

Fri. 16.3.79: The pressure of the Irwin affair made the British government publish the long-delayed report by Judge Harry Bennett on police interrogation in Northern Ireland, which concluded that there was "prime facie evidence that ill-treatment had taken place". The report was accepted by the secretary of state, Roy Mason, who promised action.

Thur. 22.3.79: The Provisional IRA shot dead the British ambassador to Holland, Sir Richard Sykes, in the Hague. In renewed Provisional IRA bombing, there were 24 explosions across Northern Ireland. The total number of explosions for the month was 52.

Fri. 23.3.79: Dr Denis Elliot, chief medical officer at Gough Barracks interrogation centre, Armagh, resigned, claiming he could no longer work under the conditions prevailing.

Wed. 28.3.79: The votes of Northern Ireland MPs were decisive in defeating the Labour government by 311 to 310, precipitating a general election. Eight unionists voted with the Conservatives, two with the government. Gerry Fitt of the SDLP and the independent Frank Maguire abstained.

Thur. 29.3.79: The UDA-linked New Ulster Political Research Group published a proposal for an independent Northern Ireland, in a document entitled *Beyond the Religious Divide*.

Fri. 30.3.79: The INLA claimed responsibility for the assassination of the Conservative spokesperson on Northern Ireland, Airey Neave. A bomb had been placed in his car in the underground Commons car park.

Tues. 10.4.79: In the first such tribunal for 14 years, a public inquiry began into allegations by

186

James Rafferty that he had been maltreated by RUC men during questioning at Omagh, Co Tyrone, in November 1976.

Mon. 16.4.79: The Provisional IRA shot dead a prison officer at his sister's wedding in Clogher, Co Tyrone.

Tues. 17.4.79: In Bessbrook, Co Armagh, four RUC men were killed when a 1,000lb bomb in a van exploded as they drove past.

Thur. 19.4.79: A woman prison officer was killed and three others were wounded in a gun and grenade attack outside Armagh prison later claimed by the INLA. April also saw the killings of eight soldiers and three UDR men.

Thur. 3.5.79: The Conservative party returned to power in the UK general election. The DUP took two seats from the UUP.

Sat. 5.5.79: Humphrey Atkins was appointed secretary of state for Northern Ireland.

Thur. 10.5.79: The taoiseach, Jack Lynch, met the new prime minister, Margaret Thatcher, in London. It was reported that a top-security army document, detailing the army's assessment of Provisional IRA strengths and weaknesses, had fallen into the hands of the Provisional IRA.

Fri. 11.5.79: Kieran Nugent, the first prisoner to be refused special-category status and the first to go on the blanket protest, walked free from the Maze, 14 months later than if he had conformed.

Fri. 18.5.79: Bombs exploded in Ballymena, Banbridge, Dungannon and Fivemiletown.

Sun. 27.5.79: It was announced that the Catholic primate, Archbishop Tomás Ó Fiaich, was to be elevated to cardinal.

Sun. 3.6.79: Two RUC men, including Supt Stanley Hanna, the highest-ranking officer to have been killed in the "troubles", died in a booby-trap bomb on the south Armagh border.

Thur. 7.6.79: In the first direct elections to the European Parliament, the three Northern Ireland seats were won by Rev Ian Paisley (DUP), John Taylor (UUP) and John Hume (SDLP).

Tues. 19.6.79: There were explosions in five Northern Ireland hotels.

Wed. 27.6.79: The secretary of state, Humphrey Atkins, had talks in Dublin with the republic's foreign minister, Michael O'Kennedy, and presented a four-point plan to defeat terrorism.

Sat. 30.6.79: Humphrey Atkins told the Commons that of seven people the RUC sought in the republic, the courts had refused to extradite five, one could not be found and another was serving a sentence there. The Catholic primate, Archbishop Tomás Ó Fiaich, was elevated to cardinal in Rome.

Mon. 2.7.79: Humphrey Atkins proscribed the INLA in Northern Ireland. The following day the home secretary, William Whitelaw, banned it in Britain. Mr Atkins also announced that the government accepted the findings of the Bennett report and he outlined reforms. Harry West resigned as leader of the UUP.

Wed. 4.7.79: An organisation called the Loyalist Ex-prisoners Association claimed responsibility for 23 bomb hoaxes in Belfast that caused traffic chaos. It said prison officers and Special Branch detectives would now be

"legitimate targets". The two SAS soldiers accused of murdering John Boyle in July 1978 were acquitted. The judge said he accepted they had thought their lives to be in danger.

Thur. 5.7.79: A political storm followed a BBC television interview with a member of the INLA.

Sun. 15.7.79: Five thousand members of the GAA demonstrated in Crossmaglen, Co Armagh, against the army's takeover of part of a football pitch as a helicopter pad.

Tues. 17.7.79: A woman civilian was killed and six members of the security forces were injured in a bomb attack in Rosslea, Co Fermanagh.

Wed. 18.7.79: At the opening session of the European Parliament at Strasbourg, Rev Ian Paisley complained that the Union flag was flying the wrong way up on the parliament building.

Thur. 19.7.79: Rev Ian Paisley was shouted down in the European Parliament when he attempted to interrupt the European Council president, Jack Lynch.

Sat. 21.7.79: It was announced that Pope John Paul II was to visit Ireland on September 29th. The expressed hope that he would be able to visit Northern Ireland brought warnings from the DUP leader, Rev Ian Paisley, and the Orange Order.

Mon. 23.7.79: The Northern Ireland Police Complaints Board's annual report complained of difficulty in obtaining information from the DPP about cases the board was forwarding to it. In 1978 the RUC received 1,629 complaints, of which 1,318 were referred to the board. The board investigated 834 of these and referred 762 cases to the DPP. The DPP ordered prosecutions in only 23.

Tues. 24.7.79: It was announced that the RUC chief constable, Sir Kenneth Newman, was to leave the force at the end of the year for a post in a police training college in Hampshire.

Thur. 26.7.79: The Provisional IRA claimed responsibility for the bombing of the Belgravia hotel in Belfast, a home for 36 elderly and infirm people.

Wed. 1.8.79: There were angry reactions from RUC spokespersons and unionist MPs following the announcement by the US State Department that it was banning sales of arms to the RUC.

Thur. 2.8.79: The Provisional IRA claimed responsibility for the deaths of two British soldiers, the 300th and 301st to be killed in the "troubles", in a land-mine explosion near Armagh.

Mon. 6.8.79: The governor of New York, Hugh Carey, met the secretary of state, Humphrey Atkins, in London, and later announced on his return to the USA that both Mr Atkins and the republic's foreign minister, Michael O'Kennedy, had agreed to meet him in New York to discuss "peace, security and an end to violence in Northern Ireland". Following protests from unionist MPs, the NIO rejected foreign intervention and said Mr Atkins would not be discussing security matters.

Thur. 9.8.79: The eighth anniversary of the introduction of internment heralded a week of street violence, petrol-bombings and sniper

attacks on the army in Belfast and led to a UDA statement that it would return to a "more positive military role".

Sat. 11.8.79: An Irish National Caucus delegation said in Belfast that it planned to make Northern Ireland a major issue in the 1980 US presidential election.

Sun. 12.8.79: An estimated 8,000 Provisional Sinn Féin supporters marched through Belfast, at one point joined by four masked men and a woman holding guns; the following week saw angry reactions from unionist spokespersons to the low profile adopted by the security forces.

Fri. 24.8.79: Following a meeting with the prime minister, Margaret Thatcher, the secretary of state, Humphrey Atkins, said he would not now be accepting the invitation from the governor of New York, Hugh Carey, to talks about Northern Ireland.

Mon. 27.8.79: In the biggest death toll in a single incident in the north during the "troubles", the Provisional IRA killed 18 soldiers in a land-mine ambush near Warrenpoint, Co Down. In an ensuing gun battle across Carlingford Lough, an English tourist was killed by an army bullet. Lord Mountbatten of Burma was killed when a Provisional IRA radio-triggered bomb destroyed his boat at Mullaghmore, Co Sligo. His 14-year-old grandson, Nicholas, and a crew member, Paul Maxwell, aged 14, also died instantly and the Dowager Lady Brabourne died later from her injuries. The following week saw unionist calls for the resignation of the secretary of state, Humphrey Atkins.

Wed. 29.8.79: The prime minister, Margaret Thatcher, flew to Northern Ireland to discuss the tightening of security. It was announced in Rome that because of the recent Provisional IRA killings the Pope would not now be visiting Northern Ireland.

Thur. 30.8.79: It was announced that the RUC complement was to be increased by 1,000 to 7,500.

Sat. 1.9.79: The Provisional IRA stated that the killing of Lord Mountbatten would not be the last assassination. The British government let it be known that the taoiseach, Jack Lynch, was being summoned to London to explain his government's alleged lack of action.

Sun. 2.9.79: The UFF announced a murder campaign against "known republicans", about whom it said detailed dossiers had been compiled.

Mon. 3.9.79: The secretary of state, Humphrey Atkins, said the security situation "constituted a major stumbling block to any political agreement".

Wed. 5.9.79: The prime minister, Margaret Thatcher, and the taoiseach, Jack Lynch, met in London after the funeral of Lord Mountbatten.

Fri. 7.9.79: James Molyneaux, MP for South Antrim and hitherto leader of the UUP at Westminster, was elected leader of the party.

Sun. 9.9.79: Security experts claimed that the re-grouping of the Provisional IRA into three- and four-person cells was now complete, that it had an annual income of £1.5 million and that it had 5,000 modern weapons.

Fri. 14.9.79: Close to Belfast prison, the Provisional IRA seriously wounded a prison officer and shot dead another, the fourth to be murdered that year and the 12th since prison officers were declared "legitimate targets" in the campaign for political status.

Sat. 15.9.79: The newly elected leader of the UUP, James Molyneaux, said devolved government would be impossible for at least five years and the party should try to improve direct rule.

Wed. 19.9.79: The Provisional IRA shot dead Edward Jones, assistant governor of Belfast prison, outside the prison gates.

Wed. 26.9.79: Less than a quarter of the 410 members were present when the European Parliament held its first debate on terrorism in Northern Ireland.

Sat. 29.9.79: The first papal vist to Ireland began with an open-air Mass in Dublin's Phoenix Park, attended by about one million people. About 250,000 attended a meeting in Drogheda where Pope John Paul II spoke to "all men and women engaged in violence" and said: "On my knees I beg you to turn away from the paths of violence and return to the ways of peace."

Tues. 2.10.79: The Provisional IRA rejected the Pope's plea for an end to violence. The British government announced the appointment of Sir Maurice Oldfield, former MI6 chief, to a new post of security co-ordinator for Northern Ireland. Separate statements named John Hermon as successor, from January 1980, to Sir Kenneth Newman as chief constable of the RUC and Maj-Gen Richard Lawson as the new GOC, in place of Lieut-Gen Sir Timothy Creasey.

Fri. 5.10.79: After seven hours of talks in London, the secretary of state, Humphrey Atkins, the republic's foreign minister, Michael O'Kennedy, and the minister for justice, Gerry Collins, issued a communiqué on cross-border security.

Tues. 9.10.79: Sir Maurice Oldfield arrived in Belfast to take up his post as security co-ordinator. The UUP leader, James Molyneaux, announced party organisational changes and said talks with the secretary of state, Humphrey Atkins, had "wrongly been interpreted as a progress report on negotiations likely to produce a so-called initiative".

Tues. 16.10.79: Nineteen of the 26 district councils met to consider a joint UUP/DUP motion demanding stringent security measures.

Sun. 21.10.79: The National H-block/Armagh Committee launched a new campaign based on five demands for prisoners' rights—to wear their own clothes, refuse prison work, receive one parcel and one visit a week, associate freely and have restored remission lost on the blanket protest.

Thur. 25.10.79: At Westminster, the secretary of state, Humphrey Atkins, proposed a conference of the four major parties to seek agreement on the restoration of local powers. The UUP said it would not take part, although some of the rank-and-file dissented. The SDLP was unenthusiastic. The DUP criticised the proposal but did not rule out participation. Alliance gave the proposal an unqualified welcome.

Mon. 5.11.79: The Provisional IRA claimed responsibility for the killing of a prison officer as he drove away from Belfast prison.

Wed. 7.11.79: The INLA claimed responsibility for the killing of a wages clerk who worked at Belfast prison. Two Catholic men were shot dead by loyalists in the Short Strand area of Belfast.

Sat. 10.11.79: The Provisional IRA launched the first in a new series of firebomb attacks.

Wed. 14.11.79: The prime minister, Margaret Thatcher, met the unionist leaders, James Molyneaux and Rev Ian Paisley, in separate talks on security.

Thur. 15.11.79: The DUP leader, Rev Ian Paisley, said he would attend the constitutional conference if the consultative document contained "no nasty surprises".

Sat. 17.11.79: There were further signs of disagreement within the UUP about whether it should attend the constitutional conference.

Tues. 20.11.79: The British government published its consultative document for the proposed constitutional conference. It was rejected by the UUP but the DUP leader, Rev Ian Paisley, and Gerry Fitt of the SDLP reacted favourably. Mr Fitt, however, was criticised for his comments by SDLP constituency representatives, who rejected the document because it had no "Irish dimension" and "reduced power-sharing to a mere option". The following day the secretary of state, Humphrey Atkins, sent an urgent letter to the SDLP, appealing for it not to boycott the conference.

Thur. 22.11.79: Gerry Fitt announced his resignation from the SDLP, describing its attitude as "disastrous and completely misguided". He said he would stand in the next election as an independent socialist.

Mon. 26.11.79: The Provisional IRA set off 24 bombs in Belfast, and others in Omagh, Strabane, Dungannon, Newry, Armagh, Lurgan and Lisburn.

Wed. 28.11.79: John Hume was elected leader of the SDLP, with Seamus Mallon as deputy.

Thur. 29.11.79: The secretary of state, Humphrey Atkins, told the Commons he was postponing the constitutional conference. He appealed to the SDLP and the UUP to participate.

Mon. 3.12.79: The second in command to the governor of Belfast prison was shot dead outside his home in north Belfast.

Wed. 5.12.79: Jack Lynch announced his resignation as taoiseach and leader of Fianna Fáil.

Fri. 7.12.79: Charles Haughey was elected leader of Fianna Fáil, by 44 votes against 38 for George Colley.

Mon. 10.12.79: Following two meetings between the secretary of state, Humphrey Atkins, and the SDLP leader, John Hume, the NIO said the constitutional conference would be postponed until January 1980.

Tues. 11.12.79: Charles Haughey was elected taoiseach. He said there would be no change in the government's Northern Ireland policy.

Sun. 16.12.79: Four soldiers were killed when a 600–1,000lb land mine exploded under their

Land Rover in Co Tyrone. Another regular soldier was killed in a booby-trap explosion in south Armagh and an ex-UDR man was shot dead in Omagh, Co Tyrone. Following a further meeting the previous day between the secretary of state, Humphrey Atkins, and the SDLP leader, John Hume, the party announced a six-point agreement and its unanimous decision to attend the constitutional conference. This was now scheduled for January 7th.

1980

Tues. 1.1.80: Two soldiers were killed in south Armagh when two army patrols surprised each other in the darkness. Three thousand people marching in support of the H-block campaign were stopped by the RUC when they attempted to leave west Belfast by the Stewartstown Road *en route* for the Maze.

Thur. 3.1.80: The UUP published its proposals for future government, a return to the old-style Stormont.

Fri. 4.1.80: Three UDR men were killed and four were seriously injured when a booby trap set off more than a ton of explosives. The killings brought the death toll since 1969 to 2,000.

Mon. 7.1.80: The constitutional conference began, attended by representatives of the NIO, the DUP, the SDLP and Alliance. The report of the Boundary Commission was published, recommending five new Westminster seats for Northern Ireland, making a total of 17. The Provisional IRA claimed responsibility for the shooting dead of an RUC man inside the Crusaders football ground in Belfast during an Irish League match.

Tues. 8.1.80: In the second and third sessions of the constitutional conference each party presented its position papers. The conference then considered proposals for an agenda.

Wed. 9.1.80: Following disagreement over an agenda, the constitutional conference was adjourned until January 21st. The secretary of state, Humphrey Atkins, said he intended inviting the four main parties to an unscheduled meeting to discuss matters outside the scope of the conference. The UUP said it would not attend any unscheduled talks.

Tues. 15.1.80: Provisional IRA bomb attacks caused explosions in Belfast, and in counties Fermanagh, Tyrone and Derry. It was announced that security forces would be withdrawn from security gates in Belfast city centre. The civilian searchers threatened to strike.

Thur. 17.1.80: Three people were killed and two were seriously injured when a no-warning bomb exploded on a train at Dunmurry, south Belfast. The Provisional IRA claimed the bomb had gone off prematurely and that one of the dead was a member. Following a campaign by residents, it was announced that two blocks of Divis flats were to be demolished. The residents said their campaign would continue until the complex was razed.

Mon. 21.1.80: The constitutional conference reconvened for its fifth session and reached agreement on an agenda. There were to be a

188

further 29 sessions before it was adjourned on March 24th.

Wed. 30.1.80: While still attending the constitutional conference, the SDLP met the secretary of state, Humphrey Atkins, for "parallel talks".

Fri. 8.2.80: The Alliance party decided to have "parallel talks" with the secretary of state. Leonard Kaitcer, a Belfast antiques dealer, was murdered after a kidnap and £1 million ransom demand.

Mon. 11.2.80: A Provisional IRA remote-control bomb killed two RUC men near Lisnaskea, Co Fermanagh. Amid reports of a split in the Peace People, Betty Williams resigned. The Church of Ireland primate, Dr George Otto Simms, retired.

Sat. 16.2.80: The taoiseach, Charles Haughey, urged a joint British–Irish initiative on Northern Ireland.

Mon. 18.2.80: The Provisional IRA claimed responsibility for the death of an army colonel shot dead in Germany at the weekend.

Mon. 25.2.80: Dr John Armstrong was elected Church of Ireland primate.

Mon. 3.3.80: The Catholic primate, Cardinal Tomás Ó Fiaich, making his second visit, and Dr Edward Daly, bishop of Derry, went into the H-blocks of the Maze. They met the secretary of state, Humphrey Atkins, two days later to voice their concern about conditions there.

Wed. 5.3.80: Following the resignation of Betty Williams, Peter McLachlan, former chair of the Peace People, also resigned.

Tues. 11.3.80: The body of the German industrialist Thomas Niedermayer, who had disappeared in December 1973, was found at Colinglen Road in Belfast.

Sat. 15.3.80: A demonstration called by the Orange Order to protest about security policy drew 15,000 Orangemen.

Mon. 24.3.80: The constitutional conference was adjourned indefinitely with no sign of agreement.

Tues. 25.3.80: The Provisional IRA threatened to kill Northern Ireland Electricity Service workmen attempting to disconnect supplies to families in debt.

Wed. 26.3.80: The secretary of state, Humphrey Atkins, offered minor concessions to the protesting prisoners in the H-blocks, including permission to exercise in sports clothing, an extra visit a month and a letter weekly rather than monthly. The concessions were later rejected by the prisoners.

Mon. 31.3.80: A 15-year-old Catholic boy was shot dead by a soldier after crashing through a checkpoint on Glen Road in Belfast. Concern was expressed about the increased incidence of joyriding amongst teenagers.

Tues. 1.4.80: On the 10th anniversary of the UDR's establishment, the freedom of the city of Belfast was conferred on the regiment. The Catholic primate, Cardinal Tomás Ó Fiaich, and the bishop of Derry, Dr Edward Daly, again met the secretary of state, Humphrey Atkins, to discuss the H-block problem.

Thur. 3.4.80: Three staff members were charged with acts of gross indecency against

inmates of Kincora boys' home in east Belfast. As the affair developed, there were repeated allegations that British intelligence had been aware of the situation as early as 1973 but, for political reasons, had done nothing.

Mon. 14.4.80: The secretary of state, Humphrey Atkins, met the taoiseach, Charles Haughey, in Dublin.

Wed. 16.4.80: The UDA-sponsored New Ulster Political Research Group, led by Glenn Barr, held secret talks in Dublin with the taoiseach, Charles Haughey.

Thur. 17.4.80: An ex-UDR man was shot dead in Newtownbutler, the fifth person killed in south Fermanagh since the start of the year.

Fri. 18.4.80: A final session took place of the constitutional conference.

Wed. 30.4.80: Marion Price, who with her sister Dolores had been sentenced to life imprisonment for their part in London car bombings in 1973, was released from prison on humanitarian grounds. She was suffering from anorexia nervosa.

Fri. 2.5.80: A plain-clothes soldier attached to an army patrol was shot dead from a house on the Antrim Road in Belfast. The patrol surrounded the house, those inside surrendered and an M60 machine gun and other weapons were found.

Mon. 5.5.80: The Provisional IRA blew up a pylon near Crossmaglen, Co Armagh, that was integral to the plans of both governments to link the electricity grids north and south.

Tues. 6.5.80: The DUP leader, Rev Ian Paisley, was arrested outside Armagh Church of Ireland cathedral, while protesting about the attendance of the taoiseach, Charles Haughey, at the installation of Dr John Armstrong as primate.

Tues. 13.5.80: The SDLP leader, John Hume, met the prime minister, Margaret Thatcher, urging quadripartite talks about Northern Ireland.

Wed. 21.5.80: In their first major meeting, the taoiseach, Charles Haughey, had talks in London with Margaret Thatcher. The communiqué promised closer political co-operation and referred to the "unique relationship" between the two countries.

Thur. 29.5.80: There was widespread disruption of traffic in Belfast when the Provisional IRA abandoned 18 hijacked vehicles, two of which contained bombs.

Wed. 4.6.80: John Turnly, Protestant joint chair of the Irish Independence party, was shot dead by loyalists at his home near Carnlough, Co Antrim.

Thur. 5.6.80: The Presbyterian general assembly voted by 443 to 322 to take the church out of the World Council of Churches because the WCC supported "terrorist" groups.

Mon. 9.6.80: The taoiseach, Charles Haughey, appealed to Britain on a BBC programme to accept that withdrawal was in the best interests of the UK and Ireland.

Wed. 11.6.80: The Provisional IRA said it would resume attacks on prison officers, suspended since March. Two recent attacks had been by loyalist paramilitaries.

Thur. 12.6.80: The centre of the village of Markethill, Co Armagh, was seriously damaged by a Provisional IRA bomb. Sir Francis Brookes Richards was named as replacement for Sir Maurice Oldfield, who had resigned on grounds of "ill-health" as security co-ordinator for Northern Ireland. There were allegations of a smear campaign against Sir Maurice.

Thur. 19.6.80: The European Commission of Human Rights rejected the case of the protesting H-block prisoners, finding that the "almost sub-human" debasement of the dirty protest was self-inflicted. But it also said the British government was being "inflexible".

Wed. 25.6.80: The US Democratic party adopted Senator Edward Kennedy's policy, calling for "an end to the divisions of the Irish people" and a solution based on consent.

Thur. 26.6.80: Dr Miriam Daly, a prominent republican and member of the National H-block/Armagh Committee, was shot dead by UFF gunmen at her home in Andersonstown in Belfast.

Tues. 1.7.80: The government-sponsored Standing Advisory Commission on Human Rights claimed that the continuation of the Emergency Provisions Act undermined the rule of law.

Wed. 2.7.80: The British government published its long-awaited discussion document on devolution, which contained two options. Unionists rejected the option of a large element of power-sharing and nationalists turned down the option of majority rule.

Fri. 4.7.80: The grand master of the Orange Order, Rev Martin Smyth, suggested Britain should re-annex Donegal, Cavan and Monaghan to ease border security. The DUP leader, Rev Ian Paisley, described this as "dangerous lunacy".

Mon. 7.7.80: In the republic, in the first application of the Criminal Law (Jurisdiction) Act of 1976, three Monaghan men were charged with the murder of a UDR soldier in Northern Ireland.

Wed. 9.7.80: Section 12 of the Emergency Provisions Act, the internment schedule, unused since 1975, was deleted.

Thur. 10.7.80: There were talks between An Bord Gais and private gas companies in Northern Ireland about a possible link with Britain and the republic.

Wed. 23.7.80: Michael McCartan, a 16-year-old Catholic, was shot dead by police while painting "Provos" on a wall by the Ormeau bridge in Belfast. Police claimed he had ignored calls to halt and seemed to be pointing a weapon. Following demonstrations in west Belfast supporting the hunger striker Martin Meehan, a Provisional IRA prisoner in the Maze, lorries were hijacked and burned. Meehan ended his 60-day fast after pleas by the Catholic primate, Cardinal Tomás Ó Fiaich, and an offer by Amnesty International to review his case.

Fri. 8.8.80: Three people were killed and 18 were injured in widespread disturbances on the eve of the ninth anniversary of the introduction of internment.

Fri. 15.8.80: William Younger, an 87-year-old Protestant, and his daughter, Letitia (51), were beaten and shot dead at their home in the mainly Catholic Ligoniel area of Belfast.

Wed. 27.8.80: Two army bases in west Belfast were demolished.

Mon. 1.9.80: Throne Primary School, Belfast, was kept open by redefining itself as the first integrated school. But there were no Catholic pupils on the first day of term.

Tues. 23.9.80: The Catholic primate, Cardinal Tomás Ó Fiaich, stated after talks with the secretary of state, Humphrey Atkins, that he was "hopeful of progress" on the H-block issue. The following day Mr Atkins said he was not willing to negotiate on the principle of special-catetory status.

Wed. 8.10.80: It was announced that the army was to vacate the Grand Central Hotel and Flax Street Mill in Belfast.

Fri. 10.10.80: In the H-block campaign, it was announced that republican prisoners would commence a hunger strike on the 27th.

Wed. 15.10.80: Two IRSP members, Ronnie Bunting, son of the former loyalist leader Maj Ronald Bunting, and Noel Little, were shot dead at Mr Bunting's house in Andersonstown in Belfast by UFF gunmen. Mr Bunting's wife was seriously injured.

Thur. 23.10.80: The NIO announced that prisoners would be allowed to wear "civilian style" clothes provided by the authorities. The concession was rejected by prisoners in the H-blocks as "meaningless" and was condemned by unionist politicians.

Mon. 27.10.80: Seven republican prisoners in the H-blocks of the Maze prison refused meals on the first day of a "fast to the death", saying that each one who died would have his place taken by one of the other 342 prisoners involved in the dirty protest. The following day the prime minister, Margaret Thatcher, repeated that political status would not be granted.

Sun. 2.11.80: At the Provisional Sinn Féin ard fheis in Dublin plans for demonstrations on the H-block issue throughout Northern Ireland were announced. Its president, Ruairí Ó Brádaigh, described the issue as a "showdown with imperialism".

Mon. 3.11.80: The British government issued an eight-page pamphlet setting out its position on the H-blocks.

Wed. 5.11.80: The secretary of state, Humphrey Atkins, said that in the light of recent sectarian killings there was a "case for outlawing the UDA".

Thur. 6.11.80: The seven Maze hunger strikers were moved to new cells in a reserved wing so that their condition could be monitored.

Sat. 8.11.80: The SDLP leader, John Hume, revealed that his party had offered the unionists "partnership" government for 10 years as an "experiment", with the relationship with the republic to be mutually agreed, but that the unionists had refused to share power.

Mon. 10.11.80: In the Commons, the former SDLP leader, Gerry Fitt, warned the government not to grant concessions to the hunger strikers. He criticised the Catholic primate, Cardinal Tomás Ó Fiaich, for allegedly allowing himself to become identified with the strikers.

Thur. 13.11.80: The H-block prisoners repeated that all of their five demands would have to be met.

Sun. 16.11.80: The archbishop of Westminster, Cardinal Basil Hume, called for an end to the hunger strike. The Fine Gael leader, Garret FitzGerald, urged the British government not to concede political status.

Sat. 22.11.80: Twelve thousand people marched in Dublin in support of the hunger strikers.

Thur. 27.11.80: The NIO issued a 12-page booklet claiming to set out "the reality" of the H-blocks. The Catholic primate, Cardinal Tomás Ó Fiaich, and five Irish bishops called on the hunger strikers to stop.

Tues. 2.12.80: Having previously refused to make a categorical statement of his government's position, the taoiseach, Charles Haughey, urged Margaret Thatcher at an EC meeting in Luxembourg to be flexible in dealing with prison protests, to avoid loss of life. Three republican women in Armagh jail commenced a hunger strike in solidarity with the hunger strikers in the Maze.

Thur. 4.12.80: The SDLP leader, John Hume, met the secretary of state, Humphrey Atkins, for talks in London on the prison protests.

Sat. 6.12.80: Three thousand gardaí and 500 troops in riot gear were on duty when 20,000 people marched to the British embassy in Dublin in support of the hunger strikers.

Mon. 8.12.80: In a uniquely high-level meeting, the prime minister, Margaret Thatcher, the foreign secretary, Lord Carrington, the chancellor of the exchequer, Sir Geoffrey Howe, and the secretary of state for Northern Ireland, Humphrey Atkins, had talks in Dublin with the taoiseach, Charles Haughey, and his senior ministers. The meeting agreed to joint studies on a wide range of subjects and Mr Haughey described it as "a historic breakthrough". But the following day there was confusion and controversy over the contrasting attitudes of the British and Irish governments to the summit.

Wed. 10.12.80: An NIO assistant secretary visited the Maze hunger strikers, ostensibly to clarify the government's position. Unionist politicians condemned both the visit and the recent summit. There were H-block demonstrations in Belfast, Derry, Newry, Strabane, and Toomebridge, where 20 people were arrested.

Fri. 12.12.80: Six UDA prisoners in the H-blocks went on hunger strike for political status and segregation from republicans.

Sat. 13.12.80: All RUC leave was cancelled until further notice as tension mounted over the hunger strikes.

Mon. 15.12.80: Twenty-three more republican prisoners joined the hunger strike, a further seven the following day.

Wed. 17.12.80: The six UDA hunger strikers "suspended" their fasts to give the NIO the opportunity to act on their demands. The NIO announced that Sean McKenna, one of the original seven hunger strikers, was "deteriorating rapidly".

Thur. 18.12.80: The seven hunger strikers ended their fast after 53 days, Sean McKenna having previously received the last rites. The

following day, Gerry Adams, deputy leader of Provisional Sinn Féin, said that the blanket protest would end by Christmas and that all five demands had been won.

Sat. 20.12.80: An offer of their own clothes for association, recreation and visits, and "civilian type clothing" for the working day was turned down by the protesting prisoners via Provisional Sinn Féin, which said private assurances of further concessions had been received from the NIO. The NIO denied this.

Sun. 21.12.80: Provisional Sinn Féin said the blanket protest would continue and the hunger strikes would resume if concessions were not forthcoming. The Dungannon priest Fr Denis Faul, having visited the Maze, said prisoners were confused about whether they had gained any concessions and some were anxious to continue the struggle.

Tues. 30.12.80: In separate incidents, an RUC man was shot dead and another was injured by a loyalist group calling itself the Prisoners Action Force. The attacks were condemned by the UDA.

1981

Mon. 5.1.81: The National H-block/Armagh Committee ruled out a further hunger strike for the moment. One of its members, Bernadette McAliskey, alleged that "private assurances" had been reneged on by the NIO.

Fri. 9.1.81: The Provisional IRA admitted a number of operations including recent London bombings, and warned the British: "You are only getting a taste of what is to come."

Fri. 16.1.81: Bernadette McAliskey, a prominent H-block campaigner, and her husband, Michael, were shot and seriously wounded at their home at Derryloughan, Co Tyrone. In confusing circumstances the gunmen were caught by an undercover army patrol keeping watch on the house, who tended the McAliskeys' wounds.

Wed. 21.1.81: The Provisional IRA shot dead Sir Norman Stronge and his son James at their home, Tynan Abbey, near the south Armagh border. The house was also bombed. Sir Norman had been Speaker of the Stormont Parliament and an MP for 24 years. His son James, an RUC reservist, had also been an MP.

Mon. 26.1.81: Twelve people were injured in explosions in Lisnaskea, Newry, Omagh, Portadown, and Meigh, Co Armagh.

Thur. 29.1.81: Ninety-six republican prisoners began fouling their cells again after having smashed furniture the previous day.

Sun. 1.2.81: About 3,000 people marched in Derry to commemorate Bloody Sunday.

Mon. 2.2.81: British and Irish government officials began joint studies of possible "new institutional structures". The studies arose from the summit of December 1980.

Thur. 5.2.81: Provisional Sinn Féin issued a statement from republican prisoners at the Maze announcing another hunger strike, to begin on March 1st.

Fri. 6.2.81: Five journalists were taken at night to a remote hillside in Co Antrim where the DUP leader, Rev Ian Paisley, displayed 500 men waving firearms certificates to show that force would be used if necessary to thwart the talks arising out of the Anglo-Irish summit. The *Nellie M,* a British coal boat, was sunk by Provisional IRA bombs at Moville, Co Donegal.

Mon. 9.2.81: Rev Ian Paisley launched an Ulster Declaration, a Carson-style covenant, in Belfast City Hall, and announced a series of demonstrations against the Anglo-Irish talks, on what he called the Carson Trail.

Thur. 12.2.81: Rev Ian Paisley was suspended from the Commons when he persisted in calling the secretary of state for Northern Ireland, Humphrey Atkins, a "liar".

Fri. 13.2.81: The first of the Carson Trail meetings was held in the Orange hall in Omagh, Co Tyrone.

Wed. 18.2.81: Carson Orange hall in Portadown, Co Armagh, refused the DUP its use for a Carson Trail meeting. The Action for Community Employment (ACE) scheme was announced, to provide 450 temporary jobs for the long-term unemployed.

Thur. 19.2.81: At a Carson Trail rally in Newtownards, Co Down, the DUP leader, Rev Ian Paisley, alleged a plot in the UUP to kill him. The UUP leader, James Molyneaux, described this as "ludicrous".

Sat. 21.2.81: The Provisional IRA damaged eight stores in Belfast and three in Derry with firebombs.

Sun. 1.3.81: A new hunger strike began when Bobby Sands, leader of the Provisional IRA prisoners in the H-blocks, refused food. It was five years to the day since special-category status had ended. Four thousand people marched on the Falls Road in Belfast in support of the five demands, and there were demonstrations in London and New York.

Mon. 2.3.81: Apparently to focus attention on the hunger strike, the dirty protest was called off, although 411 male and 28 female prisoners remained "on the blanket".

Tues. 3.3.81: The secretary of state, Humphrey Atkins, said political status would not be granted.

Thur. 5.3.81: Frank Maguire, independent MP for Fermanagh/South Tyrone, died suddenly of a heart attack. The prime minister, Margaret Thatcher, began a two-day visit to Northern Ireland. There were scuffles at the Europa Hotel in Belfast when DUP members led by Rev Ian Paisley protested about the visit of Dublin's lord mayor, who was physically attacked.

Fri. 6.3.81: The prime minister, Margaret Thatcher, went on a helicopter patrol of the Fermanagh border. She said she would continue to try to reassure unionists about the Anglo-Irish talks.

Wed. 11.3.81: The army began building a permanent brick wall along the "peace line" dividing the Catholic Falls Road from the Protestant Shankill in Belfast.

Fri. 13.3.81: The Fine Gael leader, Garret FitzGerald, claimed there was a "hiatus" in the bipartisan approach to Northern Ireland between his party and Fianna Fáil.

Sun. 15.3.81: Francis Hughes, a Provisional IRA prisoner in the H-blocks, joined the hunger strike.

Sun. 22.3.81: Patsy O'Hara, the leader of the INLA prisoners in the H-blocks, and Raymond McCreesh, a Provisional IRA prisoner, joined the hunger strike. The republic's foreign minister, Brian Lenihan, said the Anglo-Irish talks could lead to Irish unity in 10 years. The secretary of state, Humphrey Atkins, said this was "misleading".

Tues. 24.3.81: A British Leyland executive, Geoffrey Armstrong, addressing a conference in Trinity College, Dublin, was shot three times in the legs by hunger-strike campaign supporters. The incident was disclaimed by the National H-blocks/Armagh Committee and the Provisional IRA.

Wed. 25.3.81: A Belfast councillor and UDA member, Sammy Millar, was shot and seriously wounded by INLA gunmen in his home in the Shankill area.

Thur. 26.3.81: Representatives of the hunger striker Bobby Sands announced his candidature in the Fermanagh/South Tyrone by-election.

Fri. 27.3.81: Austin Currie was selected by the SDLP to stand in Fermanagh/South Tyrone. He said he would not stand down in favour of Noel Maguire, the previous MP's brother.

Sat. 28.3.81: Rev Ian Paisley's Carson Trail rally at Stormont drew a crowd estimated by the RUC at 30,000 people.

Sun. 29.3.81: The day before nominations closed for the Fermanagh/South Tyrone by-election, the SDLP withdrew Austin Currie's nomination.

Mon. 30.3.81: Noel Maguire, the brother of the previous MP, withdrew at the last moment before nominations closed in the Fermanagh/South Tyrone by-election, leaving Bobby Sands as the only anti-unionist candidate, against Harry West of the UUP. There was widespread criticism of the SDLP for withdrawing from the field.

Wed. 1.4.81: The DUP held three late-night rallies on hillsides near Gortin, Newry and Armagh. At Gortin two police vehicles were overturned but no charges were brought.

Sun. 5.4.81: The SDLP asked its supporters to boycott the Fermanagh/South Tyrone by-election rather than vote for Bobby Sands or Harry West. Census forms were burned by H-block protesters in Belfast and Derry.

Tues. 7.4.81: Carol Mathers (26) was shot dead in Derry as she was collecting census forms.

Thur. 9.4.81: There was an 87 per cent poll in the Fermanagh/South Tyrone by-election. In what was seen as a huge boost for the hunger-strike campaign, it was declared the following day that Bobby Sands had been elected to Westminster with 30,492 votes, against Harry West's 29,046.

Sat. 11.4.81: After parades celebrating Bobby Sands's victory, there were riots in Belfast, Lurgan and Cookstown.

Wed. 15.4.81: A boy of 15, Paul Whitters, was seriously injured by a plastic bullet during a riot in Derry. He died 10 days later in hospital.

Sun. 19.4.81: On the fifth successive night of rioting in Derry, two youths were killed by an army Land Rover. Provisional Sinn Féin threatened that the death of a hunger striker

would make earlier violence seem like a "Buckingham Palace tea party".

Mon. 20.4.81: Three Dáil deputies, Neil Blaney, John O'Connell and Sile de Valera, were allowed into the Maze prison to visit Bobby Sands. They later sought urgent talks with the British government. The prime minister, Margaret Thatcher, said: "It is not my custom to meet MPs from a different country about a citizen of the United Kingdom."

Wed. 22.4.81: Dolores Price was released from Armagh Prison on humanitarian grounds. She was suffering from anorexia nervosa (the same illness her sister Marion had been released for the previous year) and her life was in danger. Following the funeral of two 19-year-olds killed three days earlier, there was rioting in Derry for the eighth consecutive night. There were also riots in Lurgan, Portadown, Dungannon, Strabane, Newry and Belfast.

Thur. 23.4.81: The leaders of the four main churches appealed for restraint from all those involved in the hunger strike. The Pope appealed for peace. The Ulster Army Council was reactivated to co-ordinate loyalist paramilitarism.

Sun. 26.4.81: Fifteen thousand people marched in Belfast in support of the hunger strikers.

Mon. 27.4.81: An RUC constable was killed and three others were injured by an INLA booby-trap bomb in west Belfast.

Tues. 28.4.81: In what they described as a "purely defensive mobilisation exercise", 2,500 UDA men assembled on the Shankill Road in Belfast. John Magee, the Pope's private secretary, visited Bobby Sands in the Maze prison. The following day he met the secretary of state for Northern Ireland, Humphrey Atkins, and returned to the Maze to meet the other hunger strikers, McCreesh, O'Hara and Hughes.

Tues. 5.5.81: Bobby Sands died on the 66th day of his hunger strike. There were riots in Derry, Dublin, and Belfast, where a milkman and his 15-year-old son were fatally injured when the float was pelted by bricks. The following day 600 extra troops were sent to Northern Ireland.

Thur. 7.5.81: About 100,000 people attended the funeral in Belfast of Bobby Sands.

Fri. 8.5.81: Joe McDonnell, a Provisional IRA prisoner, went on hunger strike to take Bobby Sands's place.

Tues. 12.5.81: Francis Hughes died on the 59th day of his hunger strike in the Maze prison. Blast- and petrol-bombs were thrown at security forces in Belfast and Derry. The English and Welsh soccer teams and various artists cancelled planned appearances in Northern Ireland.

Wed. 13.5.81: A 14-year-old girl, Julie Livingstone, was killed by a plastic bullet in Lenadoon, west Belfast. The SDLP leader, John Hume, met the prime minister, Margaret Thatcher. He unsuccessfully urged concessions to the hunger strikers on clothing and association.

Thur. 14.5.81: Brendan McLaughlin, a Provisional IRA prisoner, joined the hunger strike in place of Francis Hughes.

Sun. 17.5.81: Amnesty International declared that the hunger strikers were not "prisoners of conscience" and said it would not get involved.

Mon. 18.5.81: The NIO claimed that Raymond McCreesh had said he wanted to end his fast but had been talked into continuing by his family. The family denied this.

Tues. 19.5.81: Five soldiers were killed when their armoured car was destroyed by a Provisional IRA land mine near Bessbrook, Co Armagh. An 11-year-old girl, Carol-Anne Kelly, was hit on the head by a plastic bullet in Twinbrook, west Belfast, dying three days later in hospital.

Wed. 20.5.81: Polling took place in district council elections.

Thur. 21.5.81: Raymond McCreesh and Patsy O'Hara died on the 61st day of their fast. The government repeated that its attitude was unchanged. The Catholic primate, Cardinal Tomás Ó Fiaich, warned that it would face "the wrath of the whole nationalist population" if its "rigid stance" were not modified. His statement was criticised by some leading Catholics.

Fri. 22.5.81: In the Maze, a Provisional IRA prisoner, Kieran Doherty, went on hunger strike. A man was killed by a plastic bullet in Derry and in Belfast 20 people were taken to hospital with injuries caused by the weapon. The results of the local government elections gave the DUP a slight edge over the UUP in votes, though it won fewer seats. The SDLP and Alliance lost seats while the IRSP and PD won seats on Belfast City Council as a result of pro-hunger-strike feeling.

Mon. 25.5.81: The Belfast socialist councillor Paddy Devlin, social security minister in the power-sharing executive, left his home in Andersonstown after intimidation of his children.

Tues. 26.5.81: A Provisional IRA hunger striker, Brendan McLaughlin, accepted limited medical attention for a perforated ulcer and internal bleeding. The following day he was taken off the strike. The RUC found a large quantity of arms and ammunition in UDA headquarters in east Belfast.

Thur. 28.5.81: In Derry two Provisional IRA men were killed and another was seriously injured in a gun battle with the army. The prime minister, Margaret Thatcher, visited Northern Ireland and said the hunger strike might well be the Provisional IRA's final card. Martin Hurson of the Provisional IRA joined the hunger strike in place of Brendan McLaughlin.

Fri. 29.5.81: The Liberal leader, David Steel, visited the hunger strikers in the Maze and found "no room for manoeuvre". Nine men in Northern Ireland prisons, four of them hunger strikers, were announced as candidates in the forthcoming general election in the republic.

Mon. 1.6.81: Grace Bannister of the UUP became the first female mayor of Belfast.

Tues. 2.6.81: The UDA announced the launch of a new political party, the Ulster Loyalist Democratic party, to replace the New Ulster Political Research Group.

Sun. 7.6.81: The Catholic bishop of Derry, Dr Edward Daly, called for serious consideration of proposals on the prison conflict by the Irish Commission for Justice and Peace (ICJP). He reiterated that the hunger strike was not morally justified, but said the government's attitude was "unreasonable" and "inflexible".

Mon. 8.6.81: Tom McElwee of the Provisional IRA joined the hunger strike.

Wed. 10.6.81: The SDLP leader, John Hume, met the secretary of state, Humphrey Atkins, and recommended a solution to the prison dispute based on the ICJP proposals. Five solicitors were detained by the RUC when eight republican remand prisoners escaped from the Crumlin Road court/jail complex in Belfast.

Thur. 11.6.81: Voting took place in the republic's general election.

Fri. 12.6.81: The British government published an amendment to the Representation of the People Act to prevent prisoners standing for Parliament.

Sun. 14.6.81: In the republic's general election, a Fine Gael/Labour coalition took power, with Garret FitzGerald as taoiseach. Two H-block prisoners, Kieran Doherty, a Provisional IRA hunger striker, and Paddy Agnew, previously on the blanket protest, were elected as TDs.

Mon. 15.6.81: To "avoid a breathing space between deaths" for the British government, Provisional Sinn Féin announced that new hunger strikers would join the fast each week. Paddy Quinn became the sixth to do so.

Mon. 22.6.81: Mickey Devine of the INLA became the seventh hunger striker in the Maze.

Tues. 23.6.81: The ICJP said the protesting prisoners were prepared to enter into talks with the authorities.

Fri. 26.6.81: Though the ICJP met the minister of state, Michael Alison, for the second time in a week, seeking "clarification" of points raised, the NIO denied that the organisation was mediating.

Sat. 27.6.81: Thirty-four people, including six city councillors, were arrested at an H-block demonstration in Belfast.

Sun. 28.6.81: A statement by the hunger strikers criticised the ICJP proposals. Several thousand people demonstrated on the Falls Road, west Belfast, in support of their demands.

Mon. 29.6.81: Laurence McKeown of the Provisional IRA joined the hunger strike.

Tues. 30.6.81: Hunger strikers and their families were given a statement by the secretary of state, Humphrey Atkins, telling of conditions available to conforming prisoners. Room for further improvements was promised but only when the fast was over.

Wed. 1.7.81: The IRSP rejected the statement made the previous day by the secretary of state, Humphrey Atkins. The new taoiseach, Garret FitzGerald, met the British ambassador, Sir Leonard Figg, to discuss the hunger strike.

Thur. 2.7.81: The British government proposed a Northern Ireland advisory council of 50 already elected representatives, to be nominated by parties according to their numerical strength. The DUP leader, Rev Ian Paisley, led 1,000 men through Sixmilecross, Co Tyrone. He said the IRA should be "flushed out" and killers killed.

Fri. 3.7.81: Discussions continued for a second day between the ICJP and Michael Alison, the minister of state, and ICJP representatives visited the hunger strikers. A US federal court required Noraid to register as an agent of the IRA.

Sat. 4.7.81: The protesting prisoners appeared to drop their demand for political status and said they would be happy if any concessions granted applied to all prisoners.

Tues. 7.7.81: After a further few days of meetings with relatives, Provisional Sinn Féin and the IRSP, and the NIO, the ICJP seemed to have convinced the NIO to send a senior civil servant into the Maze to talk to the hunger strikers. When this did not happen, it was alleged that the prime minister, Margaret Thatcher, had overruled an undertaking by the minister of state, Michael Alison.

Wed. 8.7.81: Joe McDonnell died on the 61st day of his hunger strike. In the disturbances in Catholic areas that followed the announcement, a 16-year-old was shot dead by the army and a woman died after being hit on the head by a plastic bullet in the Falls district of Belfast. It was announced that Patrick McGeown of the Provisional IRA would replace Joe McDonnell. A statement was read to fasting prisoners by the governor of the Maze, in the company of a senior civil servant.

Thur. 9.7.81: A 15-year-old boy was shot dead by troops under attack on the Crumlin Road in Belfast.

Fri. 10.7.81: Soldiers pursued a Provisional IRA firing party at the funeral of Joe McDonnell in west Belfast. Guns were seized and several people arrested and a riot followed.

Sun. 12.7.81: Following a week of ICJP meetings with the hunger strikers, their families and representatives, the NIO, and the taoiseach, the protesting prisoners in the Maze said there was now no room for intermediaries.

Mon. 13.7.81: Martin Hurson became the sixth hunger striker to die, on the 45th day of his fast. Traditional Orange Order marches took place this day because the Twelfth fell on a Sunday. In a message endorsed by the Catholic primate, Cardinal Tomás Ó Fiaich, the republic's government called for direct contact between the protesting prisoners and the British government.

Tues. 14.7.81: The republic's ambassador to the US, Sean Donlon, appealed to the president, Ronald Reagan, to intervene with the British government in the hunger-strike crisis.

Thur. 16.7.81: In what the prisoners described as "brinkmanship" on the part of the authorities, the International Red Cross was allowed to visit them in the Maze. The following day the three-man team had extensive meetings with the prisoners and with the secretary of state, Humphrey Atkins. But on the Saturday the prisoners asked them to withdraw because the British government was not prepared to enter direct discussions.

Sat. 18.7.81: Clashes when an H-block demonstration tried to reach the British embassy in Dublin left 120 gardaí and more than 80 protesters injured.

Sun. 19.7.81: The prime minister, Margaret Thatcher, discussed Northern Ireland with the US president, Ronald Reagan, at the Ottawa summit of industrial nations. The secretary of state, Humphrey Atkins, said there would be no negotiations in the prison dispute.

Tues. 21.7.81: Two senior government officials visited the Maze but the initiative collapsed when Brendan "Bik" McFarlane, leader of the Provisional IRA prisoners, was not allowed to see them.

Mon. 27.7.81: Brendan "Bik" McFarlane said he would attend any meeting in a "non-negotiating role". The NIO said he had no role to play and it would clarify matters directly to the hunger strikers.

Tues. 28.7.81: Fr Denis Faul held a meeting with the hunger strikers' families at which it was agreed to contact Gerry Adams, vice-president of Provisional Sinn Féin, and ask him to have the strike called off.

Wed. 29.7.81: Provisional Sinn Féin and IRSP delegations visited the eight hunger strikers and Brendan "Bik" McFarlane in the Maze, with a proposal to suspend the fasts for three months to allow monitoring of prison reforms. The prisoners refused to call off the strike.

Thur. 30.7.81: Relatives of the hunger strikers called on the Provisional IRA to order the prisoners to end the strike.

Fri. 31.7.81: The relatives of the hunger striker Paddy Quinn asked doctors to resuscitate him. The taoiseach, Garret FitzGerald, said the Provisional IRA could call off the hunger strike if it wanted.

Sat. 1.8.81: Kevin Lynch of the INLA was the seventh hunger striker to die, on the 71st day of his strike. The bishop of Derry, Dr Edward Daly, urged relatives to ask doctors to resuscitate unconscious hunger strikers.

Sun. 2.8.81: Kieran Doherty, TD for Cavan/Monaghan, was the eighth hunger striker to die, on the 73rd day of his strike. Two RUC men were killed in a land mine explosion in Co Tyrone.

Mon. 3.8.81: Liam McCloskey of the INLA joined the hunger strike, despite his ill-health.

Tues. 4.8.81: Despite the wishes of the local party that John Hume should stand, the SDLP decided for a second time not to contest the Fermanagh/South Tyrone by-election.

Wed. 5.8.81: Provisional IRA car bombs and incendiaries exploded in Belfast, Lisburn, Armagh, Newry, Portadown, and Derry, causing much damage but no serious injuries.

Sat. 8.8.81: Tom McElwee became the ninth hunger striker to die, on the 62nd day of his strike. Following the rejection the previous day of a relatives' call for the government to meet the strikers halfway, the relatives said they supported the hunger strikers.

Sun. 9.8.81: A man died during a riot in Newtownabbey, Co Antrim, struck in the chest by a plastic bullet. A man was shot dead in the street in the Ardoyne area of Belfast and another was injured there in a separate incident. The UFF said it would step up sectarian killings.

Mon. 10.8.81: Patrick Sheehan of the Provisional IRA joined the hunger strike.

Sat. 15.8.81: There were seven punishment shootings by the Provisional IRA in west Belfast.

Sun. 16.8.81: The SDLP said it would not take part in the government's proposed advisory council because there was no "Irish dimension" and it was neither "serious" nor "radical".

Mon. 17.8.81: Jackie McMullan of the Provisional IRA joined the hunger strike.

Tues. 18.8.81: The Alliance party, like the DUP, UUP and SDLP, rejected the advisory council idea.

Thur. 20.8.81: Mickey Devine, leader of the INLA prisoners, became the 10th hunger striker to die, on the 60th day of his strike. There was an 88 per cent turnout in the Fermanagh/South Tyrone by-election. The family of the hunger striker Patrick McGeown agreed to medical intervention to save his life.

Fri. 21.8.81: It was announced that Bobby Sands's election agent, Owen Carron, had won the Fermanagh/South Tyrone by-election, with 31,278 votes against the 29,048 votes cast for Ken Maginnis (UUP).

Sun. 23.8.81: Provisional Sinn Féin said it would contest Northern Ireland elections in future and try to unseat Gerry Fitt (independent socialist) in West Belfast.

Mon. 24.8.81: The newly elected Fermanagh/South Tyrone MP, Owen Carron, asked to meet the prime minister, Margaret Thatcher, to discuss the hunger strike. Bernard Fox of the Provisional IRA joined the strike. The following day the taoiseach, Garret FitzGerald, refused a request for a meeting from Mr Carron. On the Wednesday, Mrs Thatcher refused to meet Mr Carron but suggested he discuss the hunger strike with the minister of state, Michael Alison.

Thur. 27.8.81: The Boundary Commission recommended 17 constituencies for Northern Ireland. The unionists had wanted 18–24, while the SDLP had wanted no increase. Owen Carron met Michael Alison. Three days later the NIO said that Mr Carron would not become a negotiator in the dispute.

Mon. 31.8.81: Hugh Carville of the Provisional IRA joined the strike.

Tues. 1.9.81: Following a meeting with the Fermanagh/South Tyrone MP, Owen Carron, the Fianna Fáil leader, Charles Haughey, called for a settlement of the hunger-strike dispute "on the basis of the five demands". Lagan College, an integrated secondary school set up by All Children Together, opened outside Belfast.

Wed. 2.9.81: The DUP leader, Rev Ian Paisley, called for the formation of a "third force" on the lines of the B Specials.

Fri. 4.9.81: The family of Matthew Devlin, on the 52nd day of his hunger strike, permitted medical intervention to save his life.

Sat. 5.9.81: A soldier was shot dead and another was seriously injured by the Provisional IRA after being lured by two women to a house in Stranmillis in Belfast.

Sun. 6.9.81: The IRSP announced that it would not replace hunger strikers at the same rate as before. (There were 28 INLA and 380 Provisional IRA prisoners at the time.) Laurence McKeown, on the 70th day of his fast, was the fifth hunger striker to be given medical attention at the request of his family.

Mon. 7.9.81: Two teenage RUC men on their first patrol were killed by a Provisional IRA land mine near Pomeroy, Co Tyrone. John Pickering of the Provisional IRA joined the hunger strike.

Mon. 14.9.81: James Prior was appointed secretary of state for Northern Ireland in a cabinet reshuffle. Gerard Hodgkins of the Provisional IRA joined the hunger strike.

Thur. 17.9.81: The first excursion by the new secretary of state, James Prior, was to the Maze prison where he spent three hours and spoke to some of the protesting prisoners. The following day he met UUP, DUP and SDLP delegations.

Mon. 21.9.81: James Devine of the Provisional IRA joined the hunger strike.

Thur. 24.9.81: Bernard Fox ended his hunger strike after 32 days. Provisional Sinn Féin said that, because of medical complications, he "was dying too quickly". The SDLP admitted it had discussed the hunger strike with Provisional Sinn Féin and the UDA.

Sat. 26.9.81: Liam McCloskey, the last INLA hunger striker, ended his 55-day fast after talking to his family.

Sun. 27.9.81: The taoiseach, Garret FitzGerald, launched a "crusade" to alter the republic's constitution and what he called the "sectarian" nature of southern society.

Tues. 29.9.81: The British Labour party voted to "campaign actively" for a united Ireland by consent.

Sat. 3.10.81: The hunger strike was called off. Ten men had died on the strike and a total of 61 people, including 30 members of the security forces, had lost their lives in its seven months' duration.

Tues. 6.10.81: The secretary of state, James Prior, announced that all prisoners were to have their own clothes, 50 per cent of lost remission would be restored, association would be permitted in adjacent wings of the H-blocks and more visits would be allowed.

Thur. 8.10.81: An independent councillor, Laurence Kennedy, was shot dead in a social club in the Ardoyne area of Belfast, apparently by a loyalist.

Sat. 10.10.81: A Provisional IRA remote-control nail bomb in a van at Chelsea Barracks in London killed an elderly woman and a teenager and injured 23 soldiers and 16 civilians, some seriously.

Fri. 16.10.81: William McCullough, a senior UDA member, was shot dead in the Shankill area of Belfast by the INLA, in retaliation, they said, for recent murders of Catholics.

Sat. 17.10.81: Maj-Gen Sir Stewart Pringle, commandant general of the Royal Marines, lost a leg when a Provisional IRA bomb exploded in his car in London.

Thur. 22.10.81: Jeff Dudgeon won his case against Britain when the European Court of Human Rights found that the Northern Ireland law prohibiting male homosexual acts was in breach of the European Convention on Human Rights.

Sat. 24.10.81: The UUP conference rejected the integrationist policy of the party leader, James Molyneaux, in favour of devolution with a Stormont-type assembly. At the DUP conference, Rev Ian Paisley said loyalists should resist by force any British attempt to impose a solution on Northern Ireland.

Sun. 25.10.81: Though prison work was still a matter of disagreement, it was revealed that all but 10 of the 399 protesting prisoners in the Maze were now "off the blanket", and wearing their own clothes.

Mon. 26.10.81: A police bomb disposal officer was killed by a bomb in a restaurant in Oxford Street, London.

Sun. 1.11.81: The Provisional Sinn Féin ard fheis voted to rescind the party's traditional support for a federal Ireland, though the motion did not win the two-thirds majority necessary to make it policy. (It won the necessary majority the following year.) Speaking for a successful motion to allow the party to fight elections and not abstain from taking seats in Northern Ireland local elections, Danny Morrison asked if anyone would object if "with a ballot paper in this hand and an Armalite in this hand, we take power in Ireland?" The conference was also told that the bombing campaign in England would be escalated.

Fri. 6.11.81: The prime minister, Margaret Thatcher, and the taoiseach, Garret FitzGerald, met in London for the second Anglo-Irish summit and, amongst other things, agreed on setting up a British–Irish Intergovernmental Council.

Wed. 11.11.81: All of the joint studies arising from the Anglo-Irish summits, excepting that dealing with security, were published.

Fri. 13.11.81: The 28 INLA prisoners in the Maze decided to end their protest over work and to conform from December 1st. The Provisional IRA prisoners decided to wait and see how conforming prisoners were treated.

Sat. 14.11.81: The UUP MP for South Belfast, Rev Robert Bradford, was shot dead by the Provisional IRA at Finaghy community centre in Belfast. The caretaker was also killed. There was widespread condemnation of the murders.

Mon. 16.11.81: Rev Ian Paisley, Peter Robinson and John McQuade, all of the DUP, were suspended from the Commons after disruptions related to the killing of Rev Robert Bradford. Mr Paisley called for a "day of action" on November 23rd. Six hundred members of Mr Paisley's "third force" marched through Enniskillen. The UUP threatened to set up its own force.

Tues. 17.11.81: At the funeral of Rev Robert Bradford, the secretary of state, James Prior, was abused and the DUP leader, Rev Ian Paisley, threatened to "make the province ungovernable". The RUC cancelled all leave.

Wed. 18.11.81: The UDA said it would not support Rev Ian Paisley's "day of action" or "third force".

Sat. 21.11.81: Handguns were displayed for the first time at a "third force" demonstration, at Newbuildings, Co Derry. Christopher Black of the Provisional IRA was arrested in Belfast for setting up roadblocks. A few days later he was to become the first of the "supergrasses", giving evidence against others in return for immunity from prosecution and resettlement outside Northern Ireland.

Mon. 23.11.81: The day of action was strongly supported by rallies and strikes in Protestant areas. The UUP held a separate demonstration from the DUP at Belfast City Hall. The DUP leader, Rev Ian Paisley, led 5,000 men in a march through Newtownards, Co Down. Andy Tyrie, supreme commander of the UDA, welcomed Garret FitzGerald's "crusade" and criticised Mr Paisley.

Mon. 30.11.81: Several unionist-controlled councils adjourned in protest at the security situation.

Thur. 3.12.81: The DUP leader, Rev Ian Paisley, claimed the "third force" had 15,000–20,000 members. It was revealed that the security forces were investigating alleged RUC and UDR links with it. The secretary of state, James Prior, said "private armies" would not be tolerated.

Sat. 5.12.81: In a smaller than expected demonstration, 500 members of the "third force" marched in Enniskillen, Co Fermanagh.

Wed. 9.12.81: The taoiseach, Garret FitzGerald, said the republic should be prepared to sacrifice its wish for unity in the short term to wait for agreement, and that articles two and three of its constitution should be rewritten.

Mon. 14.12.81: The secretary of state, James Prior, held the first of a series of talks about devolution with UUP representatives.

Wed. 16.12.81: After a long controversy alleging a cover-up by leading unionist politicians, the RUC, the army and the NIO, six men were sentenced for sexual offences against boys aged 11–16 in Kincora Boys' Home between 1960 and 1980.

Mon. 21.12.81: In a meeting boycotted by the UUP and DUP leaders, the secretary of state, James Prior, discussed the economy with five of Northern Ireland's MPs. The DUP leader, Rev Ian Paisley, was refused an entry visa for the USA, preventing him from joining his Operation USA propaganda tour.

Wed. 23.12.81: In the first successful application of the Criminal Law (Jurisdiction) Act of 1976, two men were convicted in Dublin for firearms offences committed while escaping from Crumlin Road prison in Belfast.

Thur. 31.12.81: December was the first month since June 1971 during which there were no deaths due to the "troubles".

1982

Sat. 9.1.82: The UUP executive committee voted to end the local government boycott.

Fri. 15.1.82: The secretary of state, James Prior, announced a committee of inquiry into the Kincora scandal, to be chaired by Stephen McGonagle, chair of the Police Complaints Board in Northern Ireland. There were criticisms of the private nature of the inquiry.

Sat. 16.1.82: Seamus Twomey, former chief of staff of the Provisional IRA, was released from Portlaoise after serving five years.

Sat. 23.1.82: In what was believed to be an internal loyalist assassination, a UDA man and his son were shot dead in their east Belfast home.

Mon. 25.1.82: An organisation called Silent Too Long published a book claiming that the killings of over 600 innocent Catholics had been swept under the carpet by the authorities.

Wed. 27.1.82: The DUP leader, Rev Ian Paisley, admitted that Valerie Shaw, while working for his Free Presbyterian Church, had told him that William McGrath, a prominent member of the church and house parent at Kincora Boys' Home, was a homosexual. But Mr Paisley denied that he had known of Mr McGrath's employment at Kincora. Ms Shaw reiterated that she had told Mr Paisley because of her concern over Mr McGrath's position at Kincora and had resigned from her job because of Mr Paisley's lack of response. It was reported that the RUC had repeatedly blocked attempts to start a major inquiry into the scandal. The coalition government in the republic was defeated by one vote on the budget and resigned. A general election was called for February 18th.

Fri. 29.1.82: John McKeague, the prominent east Belfast loyalist, was shot dead in his shop by the INLA.

Mon. 1.2.82: A UUP delegation told the secretary of state, James Prior, they opposed his rolling devolution plan and would go no further than the 1976 convention report. The Labour leader, Michael Foot, began a three-day visit to Northern Ireland. He said jobs were the priority.

Mon. 8.2.82: Strabane golf club and hotels in Warrenpoint and Derry were badly damaged by Provisional IRA bombs.

Tues. 9.2.82: In the republic, election broadcasts by Provisional Sinn Féin, which had seven candidates, were banned, though a judge was to rule this unconstitutional after polling day in the general election.

Fri. 12.2.82: Three of the five members of the committee of inquiry into the Kincora scandal resigned because the RUC had not dealt with all major criminal aspects as they had been led to believe.

Sat. 13.2.82: Five men were charged in Belfast with offences including murder and INLA membership, making a total of 25 men and women so charged that week.

Thur. 18.2.82: The secretary of state, James Prior, promised a public inquiry into the Kincora scandal. There was a 70 per cent turnout in the republic's general election, which was to return Fianna Fáil to power with the support of Sinn Féin the Workers' party and independent TDs.

Fri. 19.2.82: The De Lorean Motor Company went into receivership. The project had cost the taxpayer £77 million, a loss that was to be described by the Westminster Public Accounts Committee as "one of the gravest cases of the misuse of public money for many years".

Tues. 23.2.82: Provisional IRA gunmen planted bombs which sank the coal boat *St Bedan* in Lough Foyle.

Wed. 24.2.82: Following the European Court of Human Rights decision against the British government, it was announced that homosexual law in Northern Ireland would be brought into line with that of the rest of the UK. The decision was condemned by the DUP and the Catholic bishops.

Tues. 2.3.82: The lord chief justice, Lord Lowry, escaped a murder attempt outside

194

Queen's University, Belfast, but a professor was shot in the leg.

Fri. 5.3.82: The result of the previous day's South Belfast by-election, caused by the murder of the Rev Robert Bradford, was a convincing win by Rev Martin Smyth of the UUP.

Sat. 6.3.82: Gerard Tuite became the first person to be charged in the republic with an offence committed in Britain, when he was charged in Dublin with causing explosions in London.

Mon. 8.3.82: The New Ireland Group was formed by John Robb and others to seek "political reconciliation" and a "new Ireland established by negotiation".

Tues. 9.3.82: The Commons was told that there were 115,940 legally held guns in Northern Ireland. Charles Haughey was elected taoiseach.

Sun. 14.3.82: The SDLP said the secretary of state's rolling devolution plan was "largely unworkable".

Mon. 15.3.82: An 11-year-old boy, Alan McCrum, was killed and 15 people were injured by a bomb in Banbridge, Co Down. The UUP said it would no longer participate in talks on devolution.

Sat. 20.3.82: The Provisional IRA warned it would shoot parents who did not prevent their children's "criminal activities" in "nationalist areas" and admitted already having shot one.

Tues. 23.3.82: Thirteen people had charges of INLA membership against them dropped after an informer withdrew his evidence, but seven were rearrested as they left the court.

Wed. 24.3.82: The RUC chief constable, Sir John Hermon, said the Provisional IRA and INLA informers (to become famous as the first of the supergrasses) had led to terrorist charges against almost 200 people.

Thur. 25.3.82: In a Provisional IRA M60 machine-gun attack on Springfield Road in west Belfast, three soldiers were killed and four passers-by and another soldier were injured. The British cabinet approved the secretary of state's rolling devolution plan.

Sat. 27.3.82: The Provisional IRA offered an "amnesty" to informers who retracted their evidence.

Thur. 1.4.82: Two plain-clothes soldiers were shot dead in a Provisional IRA machine-gun attack in Derry.

Mon. 5.4.82: The British government's white paper on devolution was published. It proposed a 78-member assembly elected by PR, with 70 per cent agreement required for transfer of powers from Westminster.

Wed. 14.4.82: Four leading members of the UDA, including Andy Tyrie and John McMichael, were arrested after ammunition and gun parts had been discovered in a search of UDA headquarters in east Belfast.

Fri. 16.4.82: An 11-year-old boy, Stephen McConomy, was hit on the head by a plastic bullet in Derry and died three days later in hospital. His death brought many calls for the banning of plastic bullets.

Tues. 20.4.82: Provisional IRA bombs in Belfast, Derry, Armagh, Strabane, Ballymena, and Bessbrook killed two people, injured 12 and caused £1 million of damage.

Thur. 22.4.82: Sinn Féin the Workers' party denied allegations in *Magill* magazine that the Official IRA was still active and responsible for murders and armed robberies.

Sun. 25.4.82: Sinn Féin the Workers' party changed its name to the Workers' party.

Tues. 4.5.82: Paddy Power, the republic's defence minister, described Britain as the "aggressor" in the Falklands conflict. Though the statement was disowned by other ministers, the following day the republic's government said it was "appalled" at the sinking of the Argentine warship *General Belgrano*. The Falklands war was to sour Anglo-Irish relations for some time.

Wed. 5.5.82: Following a march to mark the first anniversary of the death of the hunger striker Bobby Sands, there were riots in west Belfast. In the ensuing week, rioting continued sporadically there and in Derry.

Mon. 10.5.82: The secretary of state, James Prior, held out the possibility that the proposed assembly might be allowed powers to discuss security. The taoiseach, Charles Haughey, appointed Seamus Mallon, deputy leader of the SDLP, and John Robb, of the newly formed New Ireland Group, to the Seanad.

Thur. 13.5.82: The European Parliament voted to ban plastic bullets throughout the EEC, though this was not binding on member states.

Thur. 20.5.82: An INLA bomb was defused at the home of Rev William Beattie of the DUP.

Mon. 24.5.82: A soldier was set on fire by a petrol bomb and crushed by a personnel carrier when his patrol was attacked in Derry. It was announced that the De Lorean Motor Company was to close on May 31st with the loss of 1,500 jobs.

Fri. 28.5.82: Six Free Presbyterian ministers were among those arrested at a demonstration in London when the Pope began a six-day visit to Britain.

Sat. 29.5.82: A US Congress Friends of Ireland group arrived in Northern Ireland on a fact-finding tour.

Wed. 2.6.82: A 16-year-old boy was killed and two of his friends were injured when they triggered an INLA booby-trap bomb on a motorcycle in the university area of Belfast.

Fri. 11.6.82: A detective constable was killed and two other RUC men were injured, one seriously, by a Provisional IRA booby-trap bomb in Derry.

Fri. 18.6.82: A retired RUC inspector, Albert White, was shot dead by the Provisional IRA near his home in Newry, Co Down.

Mon. 21.6.82: The FBI revealed it had arrested four men in New York who had allegedly tried to buy Redeye surface-to-air missiles for the Provisional IRA.

Fri. 25.6.82: Twenty-five people, most of them nurses, were injured by a 200lb bomb near the nurses' hostel in Brunswick Street, Belfast. An amendment to the Devolution Bill required that both houses of Parliament be satisfied of "cross-community support" before any transfer of powers.

Mon. 28.6.82: Three hundred houses were damaged and £1 million of damage was caused

by a 1,000lb bomb in Springfield Avenue in Belfast. A 68-year-old Mullaghbawn man was kidnapped and interrogated by the Provisional IRA, which blew up his house. The RUC denied he was an informer.

Thur. 1.7.82: Gardaí discovered a massive cache of bombs in Castlefin, Co Donegal.

Sat. 3.7.82: A joyrider was killed when he crashed a stolen van in west Belfast. Nine joyriders and three pedestrians had been killed in such incidents in the previous three years.

Thur. 8.7.82: The preliminary report of the 1981 census showed that over 130,000 people had left Northern Ireland since 1971, double the rate for the previous decade.

Tues. 13.7.82: Gerard Tuite, the first person to be tried in the republic under the Criminal Law (Jurisdiction) Act of 1976 for offences committed outside the state, was sentenced to 10 years' imprisonment for bombing in London.

Thur. 15.7.82: Fiona Brown, pregnant wife of the supergrass Robert Brown, was kidnapped. The republic's foreign minister, Gerry Collins, accused the British government of breaking the letter and the spirit of the Anglo-Irish understanding because there had been no consultation about the Prior plan, which contained no "Irish dimension" and had retreated from power-sharing.

Tues. 20.7.82: In London, eight soldiers were killed and 51 people were injured, many seriously, by two Provisional IRA nail bombs that exploded without warning, one near the Household Cavalry barracks at Knightsbridge, and the other under an army band playing on a bandstand in Regent's Park. Three more people died later.

Fri. 23.7.82: The Northern Ireland Assembly Bill was given the royal assent. Three days later the date for the assembly election was announced as October 20th.

Tues. 27.7.82: The republic's ambassador to Britain was told that London was under no obligation to consult Dublin about Northern Ireland matters. A week later Dublin rejected this claim, but the prime minister, Margaret Thatcher, reasserted it.

Mon. 2.8.82: A parade led by the DUP leader, Rev Ian Paisley, through Downpatrick, Co Down, provoked a counter-demonstration and disturbances. The following day an RUC constable was shot in the chest in the town.

Sun. 8.8.82: Speakers at the internment anniversary rally in west Belfast included representatives of Noraid and the Palestine Liberation Organisation (PLO).

Sun. 15.8.82: Five policemen were injured, and a civilian was seriously injured by a plastic bullet, when 500 people rioted in Lurgan, Co Armagh. In the USA, the South Belfast UUP MP, Rev Martin Smyth, alleged that the CIA was involved in Northern Ireland.

Tues. 17.8.82: Robert Brown, the supergrass whose pregnant wife Fiona had been kidnapped on July 15th, withdrew his evidence with the result that terrorist charges against five men were dropped. Ms Brown appeared at a Provisional Sinn Féin press conference three days later saying she had been in hiding, afraid of being taken into RUC protective custody.

Wed. 25.8.82: The SDLP decided to contest the assembly election but not to take any seats won. All other constitutional parties in Northern Ireland attacked the decision.

Sat. 28.8.82: The RUC found 1.5 tons of gelignite in a lorry near Banbridge and gardaí seized a smaller quantity of gelignite and 10,000 rounds of ammunition in Glencree, Co Wicklow.

Wed. 1.9.82: Two RUC men were injured, one seriously, by a blast bomb in the Creggan area of Derry. Following the 11th successive day of rioting and bus hijacking in Derry, services to the Creggan and Bogside were suspended. Billy Dickson, a DUP councillor in Belfast, was seriously wounded at his Donegall Road home by members of the INLA. The departments of Commerce and Manpower merged to become the Department of Economic Development.

Thur. 16.9.82: An INLA remote-control booby-trap bomb in Divis Flats in Belfast killed a soldier, a 12-year-old boy and a 14-year-old boy, seriously wounded another soldier and injured three other children. The INLA expressed its "deepest sympathy". Two days later more than 250 women marched to the IRSP offices on the Falls Road in protest.

Mon. 20.9.82: A soldier was killed in a Provisional IRA RPG-7 rocket attack at Springfield Road RUC station in Belfast. The INLA bombed a radar tracking station near Schull, Co Cork.

Tues. 21.9.82: The Fermanagh/South Tyrone MP, Owen Carron, was arrested for assault after a courtroom protest in Belfast about a bill of indictment that was being used to send men for trial without a preliminary hearing, thus avoiding the appearance of a supergrass in court.

Thur. 23.9.82: The RUC chief constable, Sir John Hermon, said that the Provisional IRA and INLA were "reeling" after arrests arising from the evidence of informers.

Fri. 1.10.82: The SDLP leader, John Hume, said there was no way his party would participate in the assembly. It was seeking a "council for a new Ireland". The Labour party conference in Blackpool voted to ban plastic bullets.

Wed. 13.10.82: The Criminal Bar Association in Northern Ireland protested about the use of a bill of indictment to send 39 republicans to trial without a preliminary hearing.

Sun. 17.10.82: At the Fine Gael ard fheis, the party leader, Garret FitzGerald, called for a "republic of pluralism and tolerance" and the dismantling of the "mentality of partition".

Mon. 18.10.82: An INLA gunman wounded a 61-year-old headmaster, who had left the UDR six years previously, in front of his class of 10-year-olds in Newry, Co Down.

Tues. 19.10.82: An INLA bomb damaged the UUP headquarters in Glengall Street, Belfast.

Wed. 20.10.82: There was a 60 per cent turnout in the assembly election. Provisional Sinn Féin did better than expected, taking five seats with 10 per cent of first preferences, at the expense of the SDLP. The UUP remained the largest unionist party, with a 7 per cent lead over the DUP in first preferences. The secretary of state, James Prior, later described the results as a "setback" but said the assembly would go ahead. The car maker John De Lorean was charged in California with drug-smuggling offences.

Fri. 22.10.82: The Provisional IRA kidnapped a part-time UDR man, Thomas Cochrane, near Markethill, Co Armagh. In retaliation the PAF kidnapped a Catholic father of seven, Joseph Donegan, in the Whiterock area of Belfast. The NIO said that 218 of the 300 loyalist prisoners in the Maze were campaigning for segregation.

Sat. 23.10.82: The secretary of state, James Prior, invited all parties except Provisional Sinn Féin to discuss the opening of the assembly.

Mon. 25.10.82: Joseph Donegan, kidnapped three days earlier, was found beaten to death in the Lower Shankill area of Belfast. Peter Corrigan, a Provisional Sinn Féin election agent, was shot dead by the PAF in Armagh. A UDR soldier was convicted of the murder in January 1985. Homosexuality law in Northern Ireland was brought into line with that in Great Britain.

Tues. 26.10.82: The Provisional IRA said it had been unable to prevent the murder of Thomas Cochrane, whom it kidnapped four days earlier, because of tight security in south Armagh.

Wed. 27.10.82: Three RUC constables were killed by a 1,000lb land mine near Lurgan, Co Armagh.

Fri. 29.10.82: The body of Thomas Cochrane was found in south Armagh.

Sat. 30.10.82: At the Provisional Sinn Féin ard fheis, the party deleted the goal of a federal Ireland from its platform and decided to expand its electoral activities.

Tues. 2.11.82: The NIO said 145 republican prisoners in the Maze had abandoned the no-work protest, the final element of the campaign for political status which had culminated in the hunger strikes.

Thur. 4.11.82: It was revealed that Provisional Sinn Féin assembly members would have access to all NIO ministers except the secretary of state.

Tues. 9.11.82: An RUC constable and a woman leisure centre worker were killed by a booby-trap bomb in the policeman's car in Enniskillen, Co Fermanagh:

Thur. 11.11.82: Three unarmed Provisional IRA members were shot dead by the RUC in Lurgan, Co Armagh. The RUC claimed the car had driven through a checkpoint, hitting a policeman. There were calls for an independent inquiry. Three RUC men were charged with the murder of one of the men, Eugene Toman, the following September, but were acquitted in June 1984. The Northern Ireland assembly met for the first time, boycotted by Provisional Sinn Féin and the SDLP. James Kilfedder of the Ulster Popular Unionist party (UPUP) was elected Speaker.

Mon. 15.11.82: The secretary of state, James Prior, began a week-long visit to the USA. The bishop of Down and Connor, Dr Cahal Daly, restored the priestly faculties of saying Mass and preaching to Fr Des Wilson. Fr Wilson's Springhill Community House this month took over a floor in Conway Mill off the Falls Road in Belfast, converting it into an education and discussion centre.

Tues. 16.11.82: The leader of the Shankill Butchers, Lenny Murphy of the UVF, who had recently been released from prison, was shot dead in the Shankill district by the Provisional IRA—in collusion, it was believed, with loyalist paramilitaries. A Catholic man was shot dead at his shop on the Cregagh Road, Belfast. Two RUC reservists were shot dead at a checkpoint in Markethill, Co Armagh.

Wed. 24.11.82: In the latest incident in what was alleged to be a "shoot to kill" policy, an RUC patrol which had staked out a farm near Craigavon, Co Armagh, shot dead Michael Tighe and seriously wounded Martin McCauley. This incident in particular was to spark the inquiry by the deputy chief constable of Greater Manchester, John Stalker. There was a 70 per cent turnout in the republic's general election in which, between them, Fine Gael and the Labour party secured an overall majority, paving the way for a coalition.

Tues. 30.11.82: Addressing the assembly, the secretary of state, James Prior, announced increases in RUC strength.

Sun. 5.12.82: The SDLP leader, John Hume, reiterated his suggestion that political parties in the whole of Ireland should produce a blueprint of the new Ireland they envisaged.

Mon. 6.12.82: Twelve soldiers and five civilians were killed and 66 were injured, some seriously, in the INLA bombing of a disco at the Droppin' Well bar at Ballykelly, Co Derry. The trial opened in Belfast of 38 people on a total of 184 charges including Provisional IRA membership, implicated by the evidence of the supergrass Christopher Black. The Labour leader, Michael Foot, rebuked Ken Livingstone, leader of the Greater London Council (GLC), for inviting a Provisional Sinn Féin delegation to London to be led by Gerry Adams. Two days later the home secretary, William Whitelaw, banned the delegation from entering Britain and on the Thursday Ken Livingstone accepted an invitation from Provisional Sinn Féin to visit Northern Ireland.

Tues. 7.12.82: The assembly called for the reintroduction of capital punishment and internment. The republic's Supreme Court ordered the extradition of Dominic McGlinchey to the north.

Sun. 12.12.82: In the latest incidence of an alleged "shoot to kill" policy, two INLA members, Seamus Grew and Roderick Carroll, were shot dead at an RUC checkpoint on the outskirts of Armagh. A constable was charged with Grew's murder on September 1st 1983. Gerry Adams and Danny Morrison, Provisional Sinn Féin assembly members, took part in a phone-in programme on the independent London radio station LBC.

Thur. 16.12.82: At an Election Petition Court in Armagh, Seamus Mallon, deputy leader of the SDLP, was deprived of his seat in the assembly on the grounds that he was a senator in the republic.

Wed. 22.12.82: The prime minister, Margaret Thatcher, made a seven-hour visit to Northern Ireland. Following the abduction of Patrick Gilmour in Derry, his family were told by the Provisional IRA that they would not see him again if his son, Raymond, did not withdraw his evidence against 40 people. Patrick Gilmour was eventually released in September of the following year.

1983

Wed. 5.1.83: The INLA was proscribed in the republic.

Thur. 6.1.83: Two RUC men, a sergeant and a constable, were shot dead and another constable was injured in a Provisional IRA attack in Rostrevor, Co Down.

Sun. 16.1.83: Judge William Doyle, a Catholic, was shot dead by the Provisional IRA as he left Mass in St Brigid's Church in Derryvolgie Avenue, south Belfast.

Thur. 27.1.83: A large bomb in a van destroyed the RUC station in Sion Mills, Co Tyrone, and badly damaged a Catholic church and many local houses.

Fri. 28.1.83: The republic's government announced that it would give full voting rights to 20,000 British citizens living there.

Tues. 1.2.83: Christopher Black, Provisional IRA supergrass, finished giving evidence at Belfast Crown Court and was flown to England. The republic's foreign minister, Peter Barry, met the secretary of state, James Prior, in London. He expressed doubt that the assembly had a future.

Sun. 6.2.83: More than 2,000 people marched through Lurgan, Co Armagh, in protest against alleged "shoot to kill" tactics by the security forces.

Mon. 7.2.83: The SDLP leader, John Hume, led a party delegation, meeting the secretary of state, James Prior, at Stormont on the economy. Stephen McGonagle, chair of the Police Complaints Board in Northern Ireland, was named as a member of the republic's Seanad. Following strong unionist criticism of his acceptance, Mr McGonagle resigned from the board on February 18th.

Tues. 8.2.83: Around half the UUP members walked out of the assembly after a dispute with the Speaker, James Kilfedder. The racehorse Shergar, worth £10 million, was kidnapped from a stud in Newbridge, Co Kildare.

Thur. 17.2.83: The British Labour party decided to oppose the Prevention of Terrorism Act in its current form.

Wed. 23.2.83: Despite opposition from the British government and Conservative and unionist MEPs, the political committee of the European Parliament voted for an inquiry on whether the EC could help solve Northern Ireland's economic and political problems.

Sat. 26.2.83: The leader of the GLC, Ken Livingstone, began a two-day visit to Northern Ireland at the invitation of Provisional Sinn Féin.

Sun. 27.2.83: At the Fianna Fáil ard fheis in Dublin, the party leader, Charles Haughey, urged the British and Irish governments to organise a constitutional conference as a prelude to British withdrawal.

Wed. 2.3.83: The assembly voted unanimously to urge the British government to halt the proposed European Parliament inquiry on Northern Ireland. It also voted to set up a security and home affairs committee.

Mon. 7.3.83: The home secretary, William Whitelaw, announced a new Prevention of Terrorism Bill with a five-year life, subject to annual renewal.

Fri. 11.3.83: The republic's government announced plans to instigate an all-Ireland forum along the lines suggested by the SDLP.

Mon. 21.3.83: For the first time in 16 months, the prime minister, Margaret Thatcher, met the taoiseach, Garret FitzGerald, at an EC heads of government meeting in Brussels.

Thur. 24.3.83: The unionist parties and Alliance declined the invitation from the taoiseach, Garret FitzGerald, to participate in the New Ireland Forum in Dublin.

Tues. 29.3.83: The Workers' party announced it would not participate in the New Ireland Forum.

Sun. 3.4.83: The Provisional Sinn Féin assembly member Martin McGuinness said that the Provisional IRA had ended its practice of kneecapping.

Mon. 11.4.83: Fourteen UVF men were jailed, two for life, on the evidence of the supergrass Joseph Bennett, a former UVF battalion commander granted immunity from prosecution in respect of two murders and other terrorist crimes.

Wed. 13.4.83: Trevor Elliott, a member of the Territorial Army and DUP activist, was shot dead by the Provisional IRA in Keady, Co Armagh. The leaders of the three main parties in the republic and John Hume, leader of the SDLP, met in Dublin to discuss the setting up of the New Ireland Forum.

Wed. 27.4.83: After a week of controversy about the use of supergrasses, the secretary of state, James Prior, gave the RUC policy his full support.

Thur. 5.5.83: The secretary of state, James Prior, was in Dublin for talks with the republic's government.

Mon. 9.5.83: After months of speculation, the prime minister, Margaret Thatcher, announced a general election for June 9th.

Tues. 10.5.83: Alice Purvis, the wife of a British soldier, was shot dead by the Provisional IRA in her parents' home in Gobnascale, Derry, as she tried to protect her husband, who was on leave from England. Her mother was seriously wounded. The killing was condemned by the bishop of Derry, Edward Daly, who called on Catholics to examine their consciences before voting for candidates associated with violence. The assembly had an all-night sitting but failed to agree on a clear-cut approach to devolution.

Mon. 16.5.83: The INLA said it had kidnapped the wife of the supergrass Harry Kirkpatrick from her home in Ballymurphy in Belfast. The following Saturday 12 men appeared in court in Belfast, implicated by Kirkpatrick's testimony.

Sat. 21.5.83: The RUC came under fire in the Bogside in Derry, during the worst rioting since the hunger strike.

Tues. 24.5.83: Fifteen people were injured and 300 houses were damaged by a 1,000lb Provisional IRA bomb outside Andersonstown RUC station in west Belfast.

Mon. 30.5.83: Three shops were destroyed and several others were damaged by Provisional IRA incendiary devices in Belfast. During the first session of the New Ireland Forum in Dublin, the taoiseach, Garret FitzGerald, said the forum's main task was the reconciling of the two traditions in Ireland. The Fianna Fáil leader, Charles Haughey, by contrast, said peace and stability in Northern Ireland were dependent on a British withdrawal.

Fri. 3.6.83: The INLA supergrass Harry Kirkpatrick was sentenced to life imprisonment for five murders and 72 other offences. It was reported that, as part of his deal, he would serve his sentence in an English prison.

Wed. 8.6.83: The Provisional Sinn Féin candidate in West Belfast, Gerry Adams, along with several of his election workers, was briefly detained during scuffles when the RUC removed tricolours from his cavalcade.

Thur. 9.6.83: There was a turnout of 73 per cent in Northern Ireland in the Westminster general election, the first since the increase in the number of seats. The UUP won 11, the DUP three, SDLP one, and UPUP one. Provisional Sinn Féin won one seat, West Belfast, Gerry Adams defeating the veteran Gerry Fitt. Ken Maginnis (UUP) took Fermanagh/South Tyrone from Owen Carron (Provisional Sinn Féin). The Provisional Sinn Féin vote increased overall to 13.4 per cent. The home secretary, William Whitelaw, lifted the ban excluding Gerry Adams from entering Great Britain.

Tues. 14.6.83: Speaking for the first time since his reappointment after the general election, the secretary of state, James Prior, said he would not speak to Gerry Adams unless he renounced violence.

Tues. 28.6.83: The SDLP leader, John Hume, in his maiden speech at Westminster, having been elected for Foyle, accused the British government of indifference to and "psychological withdrawal" from the problems of Northern Ireland.

Sun. 3.7.83: The unoccupied home of the former West Belfast MP, Gerry Fitt, was set alight by youths.

Mon. 4.7.83: Eight Catholic bishops and three auxiliary bishops condemned the use of plastic bullets and warned against the reintroduction of the death penalty.

Fri. 8.7.83: A motion calling for restoration of the death penalty for terrorist offences was approved by 35 votes to 11 in the assembly.

Sun. 10.7.83: In a letter to his constituency party, the secretary of state, James Prior, said the return of capital punishment would increase terrorism and lead to "violent disorders" in Northern Ireland.

Wed. 13.7.83: Four UDR soldiers were killed by a Provisional IRA land mine near Omagh, Co Tyrone. The bodies of two men, apparently killed by republican paramilitaries, were found in the back of a car in south Armagh. In the Commons, reintroduction of the death penalty for terrorist murders was rejected by a majority of 116.

Sun. 17.7.83: Following a week of rioting in Derry, the Catholic bishop, Edward Daly, condemned sectarian attacks and called for calm. The DUP leader, Rev Ian Paisley, was granted a visa to the USA, provided his visit was of a religious nature. Former secretary of state Merlyn Rees said a cabinet sub-committee had considered withdrawal from Northern Ireland between 1974 and 1976, but no minister had favoured it.

Thur. 21.7.83: In the dissolution honours list the former West Belfast MP, Gerry Fitt, was made a life peer. The UUP leader, James Molyneaux, was appointed a privy councillor.

Tues. 26.7.83: The republic's foreign minister, Peter Barry, told MPs at Westminster that democracy in Northern Ireland was being undermined by the increased Provisional Sinn Féin vote. The Provisional Sinn Féin MP for West Belfast, Gerry Adams, in London on a two-day visit as a guest of the GLC leader, Ken Livingstone, said Britain had erected a "wall of disinformation" around Northern Ireland.

Fri. 29.7.83: Martin Malone (18) was shot dead in Armagh by a UDR patrol, following a scuffle between the patrol and locals. At Mr Malone's funeral on August 1st, the Catholic primate, Cardinal Tomás Ó Fiaich, accused the UDR of murder.

Tues. 2.8.83: Eighty Noraid members arrived in Belfast on a fact-finding tour as guests of Provisional Sinn Féin.

Fri. 5.8.83: The 120-day trial of 38 people implicated by the Provisional IRA supergrass Christopher Black ended at Belfast Crown Court. Twenty-two were jailed, with sentences totalling more than 4,000 years. Of these, 18 were to have their convictions quashed by the Court of Appeal in 1986. Four of the defendants were acquitted and the others mainly received suspended sentences.

Tues. 9.8.83: Thomas "Kidso" Reilly was shot dead by a soldier during a fracas with youths in west Belfast. The following day Pte Ian Thain, of the 1st Light Infantry, was charged with his murder.

Sat. 13.8.83: Two INLA men were shot dead in an exchange of gunfire with the RUC in Dungannon, Co Tyrone.

Sat. 20.8.83: More than 3,000 people marched to a rally in the Shankill area of Belfast demanding segregation of loyalist prisoners.

Thur. 25.8.83: Elizabeth Kirkpatrick, wife of the INLA supergrass Harry, was released by the INLA after being held captive for two months. She called on her husband to retract his evidence.

Sat. 27.8.83: The UDA leaders Andy Tyrie and John McMichael were among 12 men charged with a number of offences, including murder.

Sun. 28.8.83: The GLC leader, Ken Livingstone, drew strong criticism when he alleged that Britain's treatment of the Irish over 800 years had been worse than Hitler's treatment of the Jews.

Thur. 1.9.83: An RUC constable was charged with the murder of the INLA man Seamus Grew in Co Armagh in December 1982.

Thur. 8.9.83: In a referendum in the republic, 67 per cent voted in favour of inserting a "pro-life" (anti-abortion) amendment into the constitution. Unionists claimed this

strengthened the sectarian nature of southern society.

Fri. 9.9.83: Following the arrest of 28 people in west Belfast, Robert Lean emerged as the latest Provisional IRA supergrass. The secretary of state, James Prior, defended the use of supergrasses the following day.

Fri. 16.9.83: Three RUC men were charged with the murder of the Provisional IRA member Eugene Toman in Co Armagh in November 1982.

Fri. 23.9.83: The FEA said it would be monitoring recruitment procedures at the Shorts aerospace factory in Belfast, following allegations of discrimination against Catholics.

Sun. 25.9.83: In the biggest escape in UK prison history, 38 Provisional IRA prisoners escaped from the Maze. Nineteen were recaptured within a few days but the others, including the Provisional IRA leader Brendan "Bik" McFarlane, got away. One warder died.

Mon. 26.9.83: The secretary of state, James Prior, established a committee of inquiry into the Maze escape, to be chaired by Sir James Hennessy, the chief inspector of British prisons. Patrick Gilmour, the father of the Derry supergrass Raymond Gilmour, was released by the Provisional IRA after being held for 10 months. A New Ireland Forum delegation, including the Fianna Fáil TD Brian Lenihan, was attacked by DUP demonstrators in Derry.

Fri. 30.9.83: The secretary of state, James Prior, refused to meet the assembly's unofficial security committee to discuss the Maze escape.

Thur. 6.10.83: Two RUC reservists were shot dead by the Provisional IRA in Downpatrick, Co Down.

Tues. 11.10.83: The secretary of state, James Prior, met the assembly's unofficial security committee and said he would resign if the inquiry into the Maze escape found his policies responsible.

Wed. 19.10.83: After having escaped from RUC custody, the Provisional IRA supergrass Robert Lean appeared at a Provisional Sinn Féin press conference and said he had signed an affidavit retracting his evidence against 28 people. He was immediately rearrested by the RUC. The following day 11 people implicated by him were released. Lean was released on the 25th and immediately went into hiding in the republic.

Mon. 24.10.83: Eight Dungannon men, facing a total of 20 terrorist charges, were freed at Belfast Crown Court after the Provisional IRA supergrass Patrick McGurk withdrew his evidence against them.

Wed. 26.10.83: The former West Belfast MP, Gerry Fitt, was ennobled as Baron Fitt of Bell's Hill. Seven men were convicted and sentenced to terms ranging from two years' to life imprisonment on the uncorroborated evidence of the supergrass Kevin McGrady.

Fri. 28.10.83: Sir George Terry, former chief constable of Sussex, said in his report on the Kincora Boys' Home scandal that he had found no evidence that civil servants, the RUC or British intelligence had been involved in homosexual activities at the home or had tried to suppress information about them.

Wed. 2.11.83: The Criminal Bar Association of Northern Ireland recommended that its members withdraw from all cases involving supergrasses.

Fri. 4.11.83: A Provisional IRA bomb exploded in a lecture room at the Ulster Polytechnic at Jordanstown, Co Antrim, killing an RUC inspector and a sergeant and injuring 33 other officers and civilians, most of them students. Another sergeant was to die nine months later from his wounds.

Tues. 8.11.83: Adrian Carroll, a brother of an INLA member shot dead by the RUC the previous December, was shot dead in Armagh. The killing was claimed by the PAF. In 1986 four UDR men were convicted of his murder, though their guilt was to be sharply contested.

Wed. 9.11.83: The secretary of state, James Prior, said he would be announcing a new inquiry with limited powers into the Kincora affair.

Thur. 10.11.83: James Prior said that Ireland could become another Cuba if Provisional Sinn Féin took over in Northern Ireland. He stressed his pessimism about the SDLP's chances of halting Provisional Sinn Féin's electoral advance.

Sun. 13.11.83: The West Belfast MP, Gerry Adams, was elected president of Provisional Sinn Féin at its ard fheis. The outgoing president, Ruairí Ó Brádaigh, and Dáithí Ó Conaill, two of the party's old guard, resigned from the executive, leaving the leadership in the hands of young northerners.

Mon. 14.11.83: Charles Armstrong, the UUP chair of Armagh District Council and a UDR member, was killed when two Provisional IRA bombs exploded under his car as he left a council meeting. Ten of the 15 men implicated by Provisional IRA supergrass William Skelly were freed at Belfast Crown Court after he retracted his evidence.

Sun. 20.11.83: Three elders of Darkley Pentecostal Church near Keady, Co Armagh, were shot dead and seven other churchgoers were injured when gunmen opened fire on the congregation. The attack was claimed by the previously unheard of Catholic Reaction Force but the RUC said one of the weapons belonged to an INLA group and they were searching for a former Provisional IRA man, Dominic McGlinchey, in connection with the attack.

Tues. 22.11.83: The UUP members of the assembly decided to boycott it until further notice in protest against the lack of security in border areas.

Wed. 23.11.83: The evidence of the INLA supergrass Jackie Grimley against seven men was thrown out at Belfast Crown Court on the grounds that he was a liar and a habitual criminal.

Thur. 24.11.83: A US supermarket executive, Don Tidey, was kidnapped by the Provisional IRA from near his home at Rathfarnham, Co Dublin.

Sun. 27.11.83: Dominic McGlinchey, alleged to be INLA chief of staff, admitted that the INLA had been indirectly involved in the Darkley massacre. The Provisional Sinn Féin president, Gerry Adams, defended the killing of soldiers and RUC members, but condemned the Darkley killings as sectarian.

Mon. 28.11.83: An 80-year-old Catholic woman was shot dead by the RUC in Pomeroy, Co Tyrone, during a shoot-out with gunmen robbing a post office. The secretary of state, James Prior, strongly criticised the UUP, DUP and SDLP for refusing his offer of joint talks on security with the chief constable, the GOC and himself.

Sun. 4.12.83: An SAS undercover unit shot dead two Provisional IRA members near Coalisland, Co Tyrone.

Mon. 5.12.83: An INLA member, Joseph Craven, was shot dead by loyalists in the Bawnmore area of Belfast. Two full-time members of the UDR in Armagh were charged with the murder of Adrian Carroll on November 8th. The following day a third UDR man was charged with the murder and a further four were charged on the Friday.

Wed. 7.12.83: The UUP assembly member and home affairs spokesman, Edgar Graham, was shot dead by the Provisional IRA outside the law faculty of Queen's University in Belfast, where he was a lecturer.

Thur. 8.12.83: The FEA found that Catholics were under-represented at policy-making levels in the Northern Ireland civil service. Fighting broke out at the funeral of the INLA member Joseph Craven in north Belfast, when RUC men forced their way through a crowd to remove a black beret and gloves from his coffin.

Mon. 12.12.83: The European Parliament report on Northern Ireland, prepared by the Danish MEP Niels Haagerup, called on the British and Irish governments to back power-sharing.

Fri. 16.12.83: Following the rescue of Don Tidey, kidnapped in the republic by the Provisional IRA on November 24th, a soldier and a Garda cadet were killed in a gun battle with the kidnappers near Ballinamore, Co Leitrim.

Sat. 17.12.83: Six people were killed and 91 were injured when a Provisional IRA car bomb exploded outside the Harrods store in London. The Provisional IRA said the action had not been authorised by its army council and that it regretted the deaths.

Fri. 23.12.83: The prime minister, Margaret Thatcher, paid a six-hour visit to Northern Ireland, during which she went to Drumadd army headquarters in Armagh, base for those UDR members recently charged with the murder of Adrian Carroll.

1984

Mon. 9.1.84: The secretary of state, James Prior, paid a surprise visit to Dublin to discuss security co-operation. Five DUP assembly members, led by Peter Robinson, returned from a week-long visit to Israel, proposing that the border be sealed with wire fencing and electronic surveillance equipment.

Wed. 11.1.84: The Catholic Reaction Force, a cover name for the INLA, threatened attacks which would send "shock waves" across Europe if action was not taken against UDR members allegedly involved in sectarian murders of Catholics.

Sat. 14.1.84: An accidental fire at Maysfield Leisure Centre in Belfast killed six people, including a mother and her two small children.

Sun. 15.1.84: The Catholic primate, Cardinal Tomás Ó Fiaich, described as "disgusting" the Christmas visit by the prime minister, Margaret Thatcher, to Drumadd barracks in Armagh, where several UDR men accused of sectarian murder were based. He also said that, because of its work on housing and other community issues, it was not morally wrong to join Provisional Sinn Féin. The following day the government of the republic said it could not be identified with the cardinal's remarks, though it was later revealed that a private protest about the visit had been made to the British government.

Tues. 17.1.84: The SDLP leader, John Hume, attacked Margaret Thatcher's recent visit to Drumadd barracks.

Wed. 18.1.84: The secretary of state, James Prior, announced a public inquiry into the Kincora scandal.

Tues. 24.1.84: The British government gave Londonderry City Council the go-ahead to drop "London" from its name. The Church of Ireland bishop of Derry and Raphoe, Dr James Mehaffy, condemned the change and the DUP assembly member Gregory Campbell called for the resignation of the environment minister, Chris Patten.

Thur. 26.1.84: The Hennessy report on the Maze escape of September 1983 was published. It laid most of the blame on prison staff. The governor, Ernest Whittington, resigned. The secretary of state, James Prior, said that as the report showed "no policy failures" there would be no ministerial resignations. The following day, amid unionist calls for resignations, the prime minister, Margaret Thatcher, pledged her full support for Mr Prior and his ministerial team. The Northern Ireland Prison Officers' Association and the Prison Governors' Association claimed that political restraints imposed by the NIO after the hunger strikes had been to blame for the escape.

Mon. 30.1.84: A young Catholic man was shot dead when a soldier opened fire on a stolen car on Springfield Road in Belfast.

Tues. 31.1.84: Two RUC men, a sergeant and a constable, were killed by a 1,000lb Provisional IRA culvert bomb at Dromintee, Co Armagh.

Fri. 3.2.84: The Duke of Edinburgh arrived at Drumadd barracks in Armagh, in what the army described as an "entirely private" visit. The SDLP deputy leader, Seamus Mallon, called the visit a "calculated insult". The following day, the republic's government expressed alarm and concern "at the second high-level visit to the only barracks where eight people have been charged with murder". The DUP welcomed the visit, saying the royal family were free to visit anywhere in the UK.

Mon. 6.2.84: The NIO responded to the republic's protest over the Duke of Edinburgh's visit to Drumadd, saying a visit by a colonel-in-chief to his regiment was an internal matter for the UK. The owners of the kidnapped racehorse Shergar, missing for a year, said they believed it had been killed by the Provisional IRA after ransom negotiations had failed.

Thur. 9.2.84: At the New Ireland Forum, the bishop of Down and Connor, Dr Cahal Daly, speaking on behalf of the Catholic hierarchy, said the bishops did not want a Catholic state for a Catholic people. The SDLP leader, John Hume, discussed the forum and the British government's attitude to it with the prime minister, Margaret Thatcher. Terrorist charges against Andy Tyrie and eight other loyalists were dropped after the UDA supergrass Stanley Smith withdrew his evidence.

Sun. 19.2.84: A large knitwear factory in Armagh was destroyed by Provisional IRA incendiary devices.

Tues. 21.2.84: Two Provisional IRA members and one soldier were killed and another soldier was seriously wounded in a shooting incident at Dunloy, Co Antrim.

Sat. 25.2.84: Two thousand loyalists, led by the DUP leader, Rev Ian Paisley, marched to Stormont to protest against the city council name change in Derry.

Wed. 29.2.84: The assembly voted by 20 votes to 1 against any extension of the 1967 Abortion Act to Northern Ireland.

Tues. 6.3.84: The Maze prison assistant governor, and spokesperson for the Prison Governors' Association in the recent controversy over the escape, William McConnell, was shot dead by the Provisional IRA outside his east Belfast home.

Sat. 10.3.84: Twelve civilians and several RUC men were injured in riots following a 2,000-strong loyalist parade to Derry city centre in protest at the city council name change.

Wed. 14.3.84: The Provisional Sinn Féin president, Gerry Adams, and three other party members where shot and wounded as they drove away from a court appearance in Belfast city centre. Soldiers in plain clothes stopped an escaping car and arrested three men, one of whom was shot in the foot. The attack was claimed by the UFF.

Thur. 15.3.84: The taoiseach, Garret FitzGerald, speaking to the joint houses of Congress, urged US politicians to call for British acceptance of New Ireland Forum proposals.

Sat. 17.3.84: The alleged INLA leader, Dominic McGlinchey, was captured by gardaí after a shoot-out in Co Clare. At an emergency sitting of the Supreme Court, McGlinchey failed to halt his extradition, which had been ordered in 1982. Within hours he was handed over to the RUC at the border, thus becoming the first member of a republican organisation to be extradited to the north to face a terrorist charge. The following day he was charged in Ballymena, Co Antrim, with the murder of Hester McMullan in Toomebridge in 1977.

Thur. 22.3.84: Provisional IRA bombs destroyed three buildings in Belfast city centre.

Thur. 29.3.84: Const John Robinson, on trial for the murder of the INLA man Seamus Grew, claimed that senior RUC officers had ordered him to lie about events leading up to the shooting.

Tues. 3.4.84: Const John Robinson was acquitted of the murder of Seamus Grew, the judge ruling that he had acted in self-defence, adding that allegations of an RUC cover-up did not concern him.

Fri. 6.4.84: A UDR man was charged with the murder of a Catholic youth in Armagh the previous July. An Irish-medium school in west Belfast was granted maintained status by the education minister, Nicholas Scott.

Sat. 7.4.84: The RUC chief constable, Sir John Hermon, denied any cover-up by the RUC over the killings of the INLA men Seamus Grew and Roddy Carroll. But he admitted that two unarmed RUC men had crossed into the republic for observation purposes in December 1982.

Sun. 8.4.84: The Provisional IRA shot dead Mary Travers and wounded her magistrate father, Thomas, as they left Mass at St Brigid's Church off the Malone Road in Belfast.

Tues. 10.4.84: A review of the Emergency Provisions Act by Sir George Baker recommended that Diplock courts be retained, the use of supergrass evidence be continued and the UDA to remain legal.

Wed. 11.4.84: At the funeral of Mary Travers, the bishop of Down and Connor, Dr Cahal Daly, appealed to voters to remember her death when asked to vote for Provisional Sinn Féin.

Thur. 12.4.84: A loyalist bomb attack on a Catholic family in the university area of Belfast killed a mother of eight, Peggy Whyte, and an RUC constable who arrived to give assistance.

Thur. 19.4.84: The chair of the FEA, Bob Cooper, said the Belfast shipyard, Harland and Wolff, had agreed to recruit more Catholics.

Thur. 26.4.84: The UUP proposed that Northern Ireland should have a regional council with purely administrative powers.

Wed. 2.5.84: After 11 months of deliberations, the New Ireland Forum report came out in favour of a united Ireland by consent. But agreement had not been reached. The taoiseach, Garret FitzGerald, said a unitary state was the preferred option but a federal Ireland and joint authority over Northern Ireland were both on the table. The Fianna Fáil leader, Charles Haughey, said, however, that a unitary state was the forum's only choice. The Robert Quigley supergrass trial ended with nine Derry men and a woman being sentenced to a total of 1,000 years' imprisonment.

Sun. 6.5.84: There was rioting in Belfast, Newry, Lurgan, Portadown and Strabane on the third anniversary of the death of the hunger striker Bobby Sands.

Wed. 9.5.84: A Territorial Army corporal was killed and two of his colleagues were seriously injured by a Provisional IRA car bomb in Newry, Co Down. The Provisional IRA said that the Territorial Army now comprised legitimate targets. Pte Ian Thain was charged with the murder of Thomas "Kidso" Reilly in west Belfast on August 9th 1983.

Thur. 17.5.84: The northern editor of the *Sunday World*, Jim Campbell, was shot and seriously wounded at his north Belfast home in what was thought to have been a UVF attack.

Fri. 18.5.84: Two RUC constables were killed and another was seriously injured by a 1,000lb Provisional IRA land mine at Camlough, Co

Armagh. Two off-duty British soldiers were killed and two other soldiers and eight civilians were injured by a Provisional IRA booby-trap bomb after a fishing competition at Enniskillen, Co Fermanagh. A third soldier died of his injuries five months later.

Wed. 23.5.84: The UUP announced the end of its six-month boycott of the assembly.

Fri. 25.5.84: The security forces made large hauls of explosives at Carrickmore, Co Tyrone, and Castlewellan, Co Down. In the first vote by the US Congress on an issue connected with Ireland, both houses unanimously supported the New Ireland Forum report.

Tues. 29.5.84: The trial began in Belfast of three RUC men accused of the murder of Eugene Toman in Co Armagh in November 1982.

Wed. 30.5.84: The DUP assembly member George Seawright said at a Belfast Education and Library Board meeting that Catholics and their priests should be incinerated.

Fri. 1.6.84: The US president, Ronald Reagan, landed at Shannon airport to begin a four-day visit to the republic.

Sun. 3.6.84: Ten thousand people demonstrated against US foreign policy as President Reagan arrived for a banquet at Dublin Castle.

Mon. 4.6.84: Addressing the Dáil and the Seanad, President Reagan said US policy was not to interfere in Irish matters, but he praised the New Ireland Forum and denounced violence.

Tues. 5.6.84: Lord Justice Gibson acquitted three RUC officers of the murder of Eugene Toman in Co Armagh in November 1982. He praised them for their courage and determination in bringing Toman and his two colleagues (all three unarmed Provisional IRA volunteers) to justice—"in this case to the final court of justice". He condemned the DPP for bringing the prosecution, claiming it would deter the security forces from attempting to arrest dangerous persons. The statements were condemned by members of the Northern Ireland Criminal Bar Association and by Cardinal Tomás Ó Fiaich and the northern Catholic bishops. The DUP withdrew the party whip from the assembly member George Seawright over his "incinerate Catholics" remark.

Mon. 11.6.84: George Seawright was voted off Belfast Education and Library Board over his "incinerate Catholics" remark.

Thur. 14.6.84: There was a 65 per cent turnout on polling day for the European elections.

Fri. 15.6.84: An RUC constable and an INLA man were shot dead and two other policemen were injured in a shooting incident in a flat in Lenadoon Avenue in west Belfast.

Mon. 18.6.84: The count for the European elections revealed that Rev Ian Paisley, John Hume and John Taylor had retained their seats.

Wed. 20.6.84: The Labour party leader, Neil Kinnock, gave his support for the New Ireland Forum report and urged the British government to adopt the goal of a united Ireland by consent.

Fri. 22.6.84: Lord Justice Gibson issued an unprecedented statement denying that his remarks in the Toman murder trial meant he would approve of a "shoot to kill" policy.

Thur. 28.6.84: Twenty-nine people were returned for trial on the evidence of the UVF supergrass James Crockard.

Mon. 2.7.84: The secretary of state, James Prior, speaking at Westminster, rejected the unitary state, federal Ireland and joint authority options of the New Ireland Forum report.

Mon. 9.7.84: The Provisional Sinn Féin president, Gerry Adams, was refused a visa to visit the USA because of his support for the Provisional IRA.

Thur. 12.7.84: Resolutions at the Twelfth demonstrations condemned the New Ireland Forum report. Following the parades, Catholic families were attacked in Limavady, Ballymena and Ballynahinch. In Derry, 300 petrol bombs were thrown at police after an Orange parade passed near the Catholic Rossville Flats.

Sat. 14.7.84: The Provisional IRA admitted responsibility for a 200lb land mine which killed two UDR soldiers, one male and one female, at Castlederg, Co Tyrone.

Wed. 18.7.84: The Westminster Public Accounts Committee described the loss of £77 million of taxpayers' money in the De Lorean venture as "one of the gravest cases of the misuse of public resources for many years".

Wed. 25.7.84: The secretary of state, James Prior, confirmed he would be leaving Northern Ireland in the autumn.

Sat. 28.7.84: The loyalist assembly member George Seawright was charged with threatening behaviour in connection with his "incinerate Catholics" remark. The home secretary, Leon Brittan, issued an exclusion order on the Noraid leader, Martin Galvin.

Tues. 31.7.84: Seamus Shannon became the first IRA man to be extradited from the republic to Northern Ireland when the Supreme Court refused to accept that the 1981 murders of Sir Norman Stronge and his son James were political.

Fri. 3.8.84: Dominic Adams (19), brother of the Provisional Sinn Féin president, Gerry, appeared in court on a charge of conspiracy to murder an RUC man and possession of a gun and a bomb.

Wed. 8.8.84: A Provisional IRA man was killed by his own bomb in Newry, Co Down. On the eve of the anniversary of the introduction of internment, rioting flared in Newry, west Belfast, Derry, and Downpatrick.

Thur. 9.8.84: Two UDA members serving life sentences for murder were crushed by machinery in the back of a bin lorry as they tried to escape from the Maze. One died later in hospital. The Noraid leader Martin Galvin defied the exclusion order against himself, appearing at the unveiling of a Provisional IRA plaque in Derry.

Sat. 11.8.84: A 1,000lb Provisional IRA land mine killed an RUC sergeant and seriously injured a constable near Omagh, Co Tyrone.

Sun. 12.8.84: Sean Downes was killed by a plastic bullet and 20 other people were injured when the RUC charged through an internment anniversary rally in an attempt to arrest the banned Noraid leader Martin Galvin when he tried to address a crowd of 2,000 outside Provisional Sinn Féin headquarters in

Andersonstown in Belfast. Sgt William McDonald became the 200th RUC member to be killed in the "troubles" when he died nine months after being injured in a Provisional IRA bomb attack on a police class in the Ulster Polytechnic.

Mon. 13.8.84: The RUC chief constable, Sir John Hermon, denied his officers had used excessive force when attempting to arrest Martin Galvin in west Belfast and said he had evidence that Sean Downes was a rioter. This was denied by Mr Downes's family and journalists present, although film taken by an RTE crew suggested he had attacked a policeman. But it showed another policeman firing a plastic bullet directly at his chest at close range. Unionist politicians backed the RUC action, the NIO blamed Mr Galvin for provoking the violence and the republic's government expressed its concern. Thousands of people took part in a black flag march in west Belfast. Rioting and attacks on RUC patrols followed.

Tues. 14.8.84: The secretary of state, James Prior, admitted that the decision to ban Martin Galvin from the UK had been "a bad mistake". The bishop of Down and Connor, Dr Cahal Daly, called the RUC action "menacing and unjustified". Plastic bullets were fired at a football ground in Belfast when rioting broke out and Cliftonville and Glasgow Celtic supporters attacked the RUC.

Wed. 15.8.84: The first of three nights of rioting on the Shankill Road in Belfast broke out after the UVF supergrass William "Budgie" Allen signed statements implicating 46 people in terrorist offences.

Thur. 16.8.84: John De Lorean was acquitted in a Los Angeles court of drug smuggling after the acceptance of his plea of entrapment.

Fri. 17.8.84: Loyalist rioting spread to north and east Belfast.

Wed. 22.8.84: The Armagh coroner, Gerry Curran, resigned after viewing RUC files on the INLA members Seamus Grew and Roddy Carroll, shot dead by the RUC in 1982. He said he had found "grave irregularities" in the documents and was not prepared to preside over the inquests.

Fri. 24.8.84: The UVF supergrass John Gibson, who had implicated himself and 50 others on 184 terrorist charges, was returned for trial at Belfast Crown Court.

Wed. 29.8.84: The acting Armagh coroner, James Rodgers, who took over from Gerry Curran after his resignation the previous week, said he would not be able to preside over the Grew/Carroll inquests because of "professional commitments". It was announced that the Fermanagh coroner would preside.

Fri. 31.8.84: The secretary of state, James Prior, flew to Dublin for his last talks with the taoiseach, Garret FitzGerald, and the foreign minister, Peter Barry.

Mon. 3.9.84: It was announced that the inquests into the deaths of Seamus Grew and Roddy Carroll would be postponed pending the results of an investigation by officers of the Greater Manchester police into the RUC's investigation of the shooting. The prime minister, Margaret

Thatcher, met the taoiseach, Garret FitzGerald, in London and made arrangements for an Anglo-Irish summit in November.

Tues. 4.9.84: Seventy-one people were injured by a 300lb Provisional IRA car bomb in Newry, Co Down.

Thur. 6.9.84: The British government announced it would not be going ahead with a proposed north–south gas link and would cease to subsidise Northern Ireland's gas industry, causing the loss of 1,000 jobs.

Fri. 7.9.84: A part-time UDR man and his workmate were shot dead by the Provisional IRA in Dungannon, Co Tyrone. The DUP leader, Rev Ian Paisley, held talks with six loyalist hunger strikers seeking segregation from republicans in Magilligan prison. It was announced that a further four loyalists had joined the protest.

Mon. 10.9.84: Douglas Hurd was appointed secretary of state in place of James Prior, who left the government. Four hundred loyalist prisoners in the Crumlin Road and Maze prisons began a three-day fast in support of the hunger strikers in Magilligan.

Wed. 12.9.84: Belfast city centre was brought to a standstill by 23 UVF bomb hoaxes in support of the hunger strikers in Magilligan prison.

Wed. 19.9.84: Following a meeting the previous day between a deputation led by Peter Robinson of the DUP and John Carson of the UUP and the prisons minister, Nicholas Scott, the hunger strikers in Magilligan suspended their fast to allow talks to continue on their demand for segregation.

Thur. 20.9.84: The DUP launched proposals for devolution including majority cabinet government, a role for minorities in departmental committees and a bill of rights.

Fri. 21.9.84: Twenty-two people were returned for trial on the evidence of the INLA supergrass Harry Kirkpatrick.

Sat. 22.9.84: About 2,000 people attended a rally on the Shankill Road in Belfast in support of the campaign for segregation in Magilligan prison.

Mon. 24.9.84: Oliver Napier stepped down after over 11 years as leader of the Alliance party, to be replaced by John Cushnahan.

Thur. 27.9.84: The prisons minister, Nicholas Scott, said the government would not grant segregation to any prisoners. Its aim was total integration, he said.

Sat. 29.9.84: Gardaí and the republic's navy seized the trawler *Marita Ann* off the Co Kerry coast, with seven tons of arms and ammunition on board.

Tues. 2.10.84: Gerry Adams and several other Provisional Sinn Féin leaders were arrested and questioned for several hours about the appearance of the Noraid leader, Martin Galvin, at a rally in west Belfast in August.

Fri. 5.10.84: The Labour party conference in Blackpool voted to ban plastic bullets, Diplock courts, the use of supergrass evidence and strip-searching of prisoners, but it rejected withdrawal of troops.

Sat. 6.10.84: The suspended loyalist hunger strike at Magilligan prison was called off.

Tues. 9.10.84: The 19 prisoners recaptured after the 1983 Maze escape were charged with 45 offences including murder and attempted murder. Sixteen were charged with the murder of a warder who had been stabbed during the escape, but were later acquitted, because of the possibility that the warder had died from natural causes.

Fri. 12.10.84: A Provisional IRA bomb exploded in the Grand Hotel, Brighton, headquarters of the Conservative party conference, in an attempt to kill the prime minister, Margaret Thatcher, and senior members of the cabinet. A total of five people were killed, including Sir Anthony Berry, a senior Tory MP, and Mrs Robert Wakeham, wife of the government chief whip. The Provisional IRA said: "Today we were unlucky, but remember, we only have to be lucky once."

Tues. 16.10.84: The prime minister, Margaret Thatcher, discounted any "sudden new initiative" on Northern Ireland.

Wed. 17.10.84: The trawler *Valhalla* was seized in Boston, suspected of being the mother ship that had transferred seven tons of arms and ammunition to the *Marita Ann* off the Irish coast on September 29th.

Thur. 18.10.84: The loyalist assembly member George Seawright was charged with possession of a gun under suspicious circumstances after he had removed a tricolour from Whiterock Leisure Centre in west Belfast, brandishing his legally held pistol.

Mon. 22.10.84: The European Commission of Human Rights ruled that because the 90,000 plastic and rubber bullets fired since 1969 had caused only 13 deaths, their use in riots was justified.

Thur. 25.10.84: The secretary of state, Douglas Hurd, made his first official visit to Dublin, meeting the foreign minister, Peter Barry, to discuss the agenda for the forthcoming Anglo-Irish summit.

Thur. 1.11.84: The independent Kilbrandon committee, made up of British and Northern Ireland politicians and academics, published its response to the New Ireland Forum report. The majority report suggested the devolution of executive powers to a five-person body, the secretary of state for Northern Ireland, a minister from the republic and three elected representatives from Northern Ireland.

Mon. 5.11.84: The trial began at Belfast Crown Court of Pte Ian Thain, charged with the murder of Thomas "Kidso" Reilly in west Belfast in August 1983.

Tues. 6.11.84: The Queen's Speech promised legislation against personation in Northern Ireland.

Wed. 14.11.84: The UVF supergrass John Gibson was sentenced to life imprisonment for the murder of four Belfast Catholics. Fifty people were meanwhile being held on his word.

Fri. 16.11.84: A Provisional Sinn Féin member was shot dead by the UFF as he arrived at his work on Boucher Road in Belfast.

Mon. 19.11.84: After a two-day Anglo-Irish summit at Chequers, the prime minister, Margaret Thatcher, described it as "the fullest, frankest and most realistic meeting" she had yet had with the taoiseach, Garret FitzGerald, whereas Dublin government sources called it "a very difficult meeting". In what became known as her "Out! Out! Out!" speech, Mrs Thatcher rejected the three options advanced by the New Ireland Forum: a unitary state, a federal Ireland and joint authority. The following day the Fianna Fáil leader, Charles Haughey, accused Dr FitzGerald of being responsible for the republic's "greatest humiliation in recent history" in his "abject capitulation to a new British intransigence". The unionist parties reacted enthusiastically to Mrs Thatcher's outright rejection of the forum report. The Belfast woman Evelyn Glenholmes, whose extradition was being sought by British police for her alleged part in bombing offences, was interviewed in Dublin and said she had not been in England since she was nine years old.

Tues. 20.11.84: The veteran loyalist Johnny McQuade died in hospital.

Wed. 21.11.84: The taoiseach, Garret FitzGerald, was reported as saying that the behaviour of the prime minister, Margaret Thatcher, after the summit had been "gratuitously offensive".

Fri. 23.11.84: In Belfast 46 people were charged with 229 terrorist offences on the word of the UVF supergrass William "Budgie" Allen.

Sat. 24.11.84: At the UUP annual conference in Newcastle, Co Down, the party leader, James Molyneaux, said the prime minister, Margaret Thatcher, had "slapped down the plotters". The South Down MP, Enoch Powell, said she had "broken out of a vicious spiral planned to create an all-Ireland state".

Sun. 25.11.84: The Catholic bishop of Down and Connor, Dr Cahal Daly, warned that the failure of the Anglo-Irish dialogue would be too calamitous to contemplate and would not be the fault of the Irish. Commenting on a statement by the secretary of state, Douglas Hurd, earlier in the week, that Catholic alienation did not exist, Dr Daly said he lived in the middle of it and it was not confined to those who voted for Provisional Sinn Féin. The following day the DUP leader, Rev Ian Paisley, called Dr Daly "the black Pope of republicanism".

Wed. 28.11.84: A deputation of Church of Ireland bishops met the secretary of state, Douglas Hurd. They said they believed alienation did exist in the Catholic community and should be addressed.

Thur. 29.11.84: The loyalist assembly member George Seawright was fined £100 and given a suspended six-month sentence for his "incinerate Catholics" remark.

Sun. 2.12.84: An undercover SAS soldier and a Provisional IRA member died in a shoot-out at Drumrush, Co Fermanagh. A fortnight later, after the Provisional IRA had said that another of its members was still missing after the shoot-out, the body of the Maze escaper Kieran Fleming was found in a river.

Mon. 3.12.84: The prime minister, Margaret Thatcher, arrived in Dublin amid tight security for an EC summit.

Tues. 4.12.84: The secretary of state, Douglas Hurd, told assembly members that if they did not make a significant move to accommodate

nationalists the British government would continue to consult with Dublin over their heads. At the EC summit in Dublin, the taoiseach, Garret FitzGerald, and the prime minister, Margaret Thatcher, met in an apparently successful attempt to heal the rift between their governments. Mrs Thatcher blamed the misunderstandings after the Anglo-Irish summit on her "weakness for giving a direct answer at press conferences to a direct question".

Thur. 6.12.84: Two Provisional IRA members, believed to be on their way to assassinate a member of the security forces at Gransha psychiatric hospital in Derry, were shot dead by undercover SAS soldiers as they rode a motorcycle through the grounds.

Thur. 13.12.84: The Labour party leader, Neil Kinnock, on a visit to Derry Labour party, called for an inquiry into the killings of the two Provisional IRA men at Gransha hospital.

Fri. 14.12.84: Pte Ian Thain became the first British soldier to be convicted of murdering a civilian while on duty in Northern Ireland when he was sentenced to life imprisonment at Belfast Crown Court for the murder of Thomas "Kidso" Reilly in west Belfast in August 1983.

Tues. 18.12.84: After most of the defendants had been held on remand for two and a half years, the Raymond Gilmour supergrass trial of 35 Derry people collapsed when the lord chief justice, Lord Lowry, said Gilmour was "entirely unworthy of belief".

Sun. 23.12.84: In the second massive security operation around a Provisional IRA funeral that week, 30 people were injured in clashes with the RUC at the funeral of Kieran Fleming in Derry. The Catholic primate, Cardinal Tomás Ó Fiaich, said alienation among northern Catholics was at an "unprecedented level". He said the supergrass system was internment under another name.

Mon. 24.12.84: At the Court of Appeal, the lord chief justice, Lord Lowry, quashed the convictions of 14 men jailed on the evidence of the UVF supergrass Joseph Bennett, saying they were "unsafe and unsatisfactory". Dominic McGlinchey, the first republican to be extradited from the republic to the north, was jailed for life for the murder of Hester McMullan in Toomebridge in 1977.

Fri. 28.12.84: The loyalist assembly member George Seawright was expelled from the DUP over his "incinerate Catholics" remark.

1985

Tues. 1.1.85: The bishop of Down and Connor, Dr Cahal Daly, appealed to the Provisional IRA and INLA to renounce violence and "join in the peaceful struggle for the rights of nationalists".

Sat. 5.1.85: St Comgall's Catholic Church in Bangor, Co Down, was badly damaged in an arson attack.

Thur. 10.1.85: It was revealed that the RUC Mobile Support Unit was being equipped with German Heckler and Koch MP5 machine guns and HK33 rifles, to replace outdated British and American weapons.

Fri. 11.1.85: The DUP leader, Rev Ian Paisley,

claimed "divine intervention" had led him to arrive late at his church where the Provisional IRA was waiting to kill him. The INLA later claimed responsibility for the incident. The Presbyterian Church said it accepted the sincerity of Catholic leaders about nationalist alienation and called for "policies, programmes and structures which will enable a pluralistic society to emerge within Northern Ireland".

Tues. 15.1.85: A 17-year-old joyrider, Paul Kelly, was shot dead and four other teenagers in the car were wounded by the UDR at a checkpoint in Andersonstown, west Belfast. The shooting was condemned by nationalist politicians and the republic's government.

Wed. 16.1.85: At the trial in Belfast of Martin McCauley from Lurgan, Co Armagh, for possession of firearms, an RUC sergeant from the anti-terrorist unit involved in the shooting dead of Michael Tighe and the shooting and arrest of McCauley near Lurgan in November 1982 admitted he had made false statements when ordered to do so by senior officers. The following week another RUC man made a similar admission.

Fri. 25.1.85: A UDR soldier was jailed for life for murdering a Provisional Sinn Féin election worker, Peter Corrigan, in October 1982. He had pleaded guilty to 18 other charges, including the attempted murder of six Catholics in the Armagh area. The SDLP annual conference unanimously passed a resolution describing the UDR as "a sectarian and partisan force" which should be disbanded as a matter of urgency. It also called for the ending of strip-searching in Armagh women's prison.

Sun. 27.1.85: Around 5,000 people attended a Provisional Sinn Féin march in Derry to commemorate the 13th anniversary of Bloody Sunday. Petrol and blast bombs were thrown at security forces afterwards.

Wed. 30.1.85: The secretary of state, Douglas Hurd, rejected calls for the disbandment of the UDR.

Thur. 31.1.85: Replying on a radio phone-in programme to an invitation from the Provisional Sinn Féin president, Gerry Adams, to the SDLP to talk to Provisional Sinn Féin about "pan-nationalist interests", the SDLP leader, John Hume, said he would talk to the Provisional IRA army council and ask it to stop the campaign of violence. The following day unionist leaders were outraged when Mr Hume agreed to a Provisional IRA invitation to talks. In the days that followed the SDLP was warned against the meeting by the taoiseach, Garret FitzGerald, the tánaiste and Labour leader, Dick Spring, and the secretary of state, Douglas Hurd. But the Fianna Fáil leader, Charles Haughey, pledged full support.

Thur. 7.2.85: A teenage joyrider was shot dead by the RUC in west Belfast.

Wed. 13.2.85: The RUC denied reports that no country in the world wanted to accept supergrasses from Northern Ireland.

Fri. 15.2.85: Martin McCauley, from Lurgan, Co Armagh, who had been shot and arrested by the RUC when his friend, Michael Tighe, was shot dead near the town in November 1982, was given only a suspended sentence at Belfast Crown Court for possession of firearms after the judge threw out the evidence of three RUC officers.

Sat. 16.2.85: The US State Department refused the Provisional Sinn Féin president, Gerry Adams, a visa to enable him to address a meeting of Congressmen.

Tues. 19.2.85: The republic's government pushed through emergency legislation to freeze cash, believed to be about £1.75 million, held by nominees of the Provisional IRA in an Irish bank. After a legal battle lasting 14 years, Crossmaglen GAA club was awarded £150,000 and costs in an out-of-court settlement over the army's takeover and use of its grounds.

Wed. 20.2.85: The prime minister, Margaret Thatcher, addressing the US Congress, asked Americans not to give money to Noraid.

Thur. 21.2.85: Frank Murphy, an RUC sergeant in community relations, was shot dead in Armagh by the Provisional IRA as he returned children home from an inter-schools quiz. Seventeen men were released by Mr Justice McDermott when he rejected the evidence of the UVF supergrass James Crockard.

Sat. 23.2.85: The SDLP leader, John Hume, met representatives of the Provisional IRA at a secret location, believed to be in the republic, but walked out within a few minutes, refusing a Provisional IRA demand that part of the meeting should be recorded on video. Three Provisional IRA men were ambushed and shot dead by undercover soldiers in Strabane, Co Tyrone.

Wed. 27.2.85: After leaving a bomb near Windsor Park football ground in Belfast, where Northern Ireland were playing England, the INLA warned British sports teams to stay out of Northern Ireland.

Thur. 28.2.85: In the largest death toll inflicted on the RUC in any one incident, a Provisional IRA mortar attack on Newry RUC station in Co Down killed seven male and two female RUC officers and injured 30 others. The following day several hundred members of the Newry branch of Pax Christi, a Catholic peace organisation, held a torchlight procession in protest.

Thur. 14.3.85: Twelve men appeared at Belfast Crown Court on the word of a new Provisional IRA supergrass, Eamon Collins.

Sun. 17.3.85: The first ever joint St Patrick's Day service, involving the leaders of the four main churches, took place in the Church of Ireland cathedral in Downpatrick, Co Down, despite a Free Presbyterian protest.

Mon. 18.3.85: Cecil Maxwell, UUP chair of Down District Council, resigned after criticisms of his attendance at an ecumenical service in Downpatrick.

Fri. 22.3.85: The secretary of state, Douglas Hurd, and the British foreign secretary, Sir Geoffrey Howe, met the taoiseach, Garret FitzGerald, and the republic's foreign minister, Peter Barry, in Dublin, in what was the second top-level meeting in under two months. A total of 12 men were released at Belfast Crown Court when the UVF supergrass John Gibson and the Provisional IRA supergrass Eamon Collins withdrew their evidence.

Sat. 23.3.85: At the DUP annual conference, Rev Ian Paisley claimed the Catholic hierarchy,

the SDLP and the republic's government had a vested interest in Provisional IRA atrocities.

Mon. 25.3.85: A Presbyterian minister in Limavady, Co Derry, Rev David Armstrong, announced his resignation over bigotry both inside and outside his church. He had had rows with his church elders over his exchanging Christmas greetings with a neighbouring Catholic priest and other ecumenical gestures.

Sat. 30.3.85: The prime minister, Margaret Thatcher, and the taoiseach, Garret FitzGerald, had a half-hour meeting on Northern Ireland during the Brussels EC summit.

Mon. 1.4.85: A further 29 people were released when the UVF supergrass John Gibson withdrew his evidence against them at Belfast Crown Court.

Mon. 8.4.85: A Catholic man, Martin Love, was shot dead in Enniskillen, Co Fermanagh. The killing was claimed by the UFF. Later in the week a UDR man and a British soldier were charged with his murder.

Thur. 11.4.85: The secretary of state, Douglas Hurd, announced plans for a new commission to deal with complaints against the RUC.

Fri. 12.4.85: An RUC reservist, Nigel Hegarty, was charged with the manslaughter of Sean Downes, killed by a plastic bullet in August 1984 when RUC officers tried to arrest the banned Noraid leader Martin Galvin at a Provisional Sinn Féin rally in west Belfast.

Sat. 20.4.85: It was reported that four senior Provisional IRA members had been expelled from the organisation after arguing for a return to an all-out campaign of violence.

Tues. 30.4.85: The taoiseach, Garret FitzGerald, flew into Derry on the inaugural flight of a new Dublin–Derry service.

Wed. 15.5.85: There was a 60 per cent turnout in the district council elections, the first contested by Provisional Sinn Féin, which won 11.8 per cent of the vote and 59 seats. The NIO confirmed that the secretary of state, Douglas Hurd, had instructed his ministers to have no dealings with council delegations which included Provisional Sinn Féin councillors.

Mon. 20.5.85: Three RUC men and one RUC woman were killed by a 1,000lb Provisional IRA bomb which destroyed their car on the border at Killeen, Co Armagh, bringing to 14 the number of RUC personnel killed in the area since the end of February. The following days saw a heated dispute between the Garda and the RUC over which side of the border the attack had been launched from.

Sun. 26.5.85: The US Lear Fan aircraft company announced the closure of its Northern Ireland operation, with the loss of £57 million of taxpayers' money.

Tues. 28.5.85: Seamus Kerr of Sinn Féin was elected chair of Omagh District Council, with the support of SDLP and other nationalist councillors.

Mon. 3.6.85: At Belfast council, unionist attempts to exclude Provisional Sinn Féin councillors from committees were declared illegal by the town clerk. The unionist-controlled Craigavon council was forbidden to meet by a High Court injunction sought by two Provisional Sinn Féin councillors who had been

expelled from the previous meeting. That Friday the two were again escorted from the chamber by RUC officers after being expelled by a vote of unionist councillors.

Tues. 4.6.85: Paul Corrigan of Provisional Sinn Féin was elected chair of Fermanagh council, with an SDLP councillor as vice-chair. In Magherafelt, the SDLP councillor Paddy Sweeney was elected chair, with a Provisional Sinn Féin councillor as vice-chair.

Fri. 14.6.85: In the first major bombing in Belfast city centre for two years, a 1,000lb Provisional IRA car bomb caused widespread damage. The former Alliance leader, Oliver Napier, was awarded a knighthood in the Queen's birthday honours list.

Sun. 23.6.85: Following the discovery of a 5lb delayed-action bomb in a hotel in London, Scotland Yard claimed it had uncovered a Provisional IRA plan to bomb English seaside resorts.

Mon. 24.6.85: Britain and the USA signed a treaty preventing suspects from avoiding extradition on political grounds.

Thur. 27.6.85: The secretary of state, Douglas Hurd, announced that government funding would be withheld from certain community groups because of their "close links with paramilitary organisations". The Conway Mill Education Centre off the Falls Road in Belfast was one of the first to fall foul of this "political vetting".

Tues. 2.7.85: The secretary of state, Douglas Hurd, walked out of the assembly security committee after being called "a liar" by a DUP member.

Wed. 3.7.85: An estimated 30,000 Orangemen and their supporters massed in Portadown, Co Armagh, to protest about the rerouting of Orange parades away from a traditional route taking in the Catholic Obins Street.

Fri. 5.7.85: Twenty men were freed when a judge threw out the evidence of the UVF supergrass William "Budgie" Allen at Belfast Crown Court.

Sun. 7.7.85: The RUC gave permission for an Orange parade to march through Obins Street in Portadown, Co Armagh. There were arrests when Catholic protesters clashed with the RUC before the parade began.

Mon. 8.7.85: The Orange Order appealed to its Portadown membership to observe the RUC's rerouting of Twelfth and Thirteenth day parades away from Catholic areas.

Fri. 12.7.85: A large force of RUC men prevented the annual Orange parade from marching through the Obins Street area of Portadown. But 28 RUC men were injured in the clashes.

Sat. 13.7.85: Rioting erupted again in Portadown when the Royal Black Preceptory parade was prevented from marching through Obins Street. Several dozen shops were damaged and 52 RUC men and many civilians were injured.

Mon. 15.7.85: The prime minister, Margaret Thatcher, addressing the American Bar Association in London, said it was necessary to starve terrorists of "the oxygen of publicity".

Sun. 21.7.85: The United Ulster Loyalist Front was formed in Portadown, Co Armagh, to resist the rerouting of Orange parades. The Catholic primate, Cardinal Tomás Ó Fiaich, said in a newspaper interview that 90 per cent of religious bigotry in Northern Ireland was found among Protestants. The Provisional IRA did not kill Protestants because they were Protestants but because they were members of the security forces, he said.

Tues. 30.7.85: The BBC board of governors bowed to government pressure not to screen a documentary, *At the Edge of the Union*, which featured profiles of Derry Provisional Sinn Féin leader Martin McGuinness and Gregory Campbell of the DUP, both assembly members for Derry. The following day the BBC Northern Ireland controller, James Hawthorne, offered his resignation—which he later withdrew—because of the decision.

Wed. 7.8.85: BBC journalists stopped work for 24 hours in Northern Ireland, in support of a UK-wide BBC journalists' strike in protest at the banning of *At the Edge of the Union*.

Thur. 8.8.85: Rioting followed a funeral in Derry at which the banned Noraid leader, Martin Galvin, appeared briefly and posed for photographs carrying the coffin of a local Provisional IRA man, who had been killed attempting an attack on the RUC.

Fri. 9.8.85: Internment day was marked by sporadic rioting in Belfast, Armagh, Downpatrick, Newry and Castlewellan.

Fri. 16.8.85: Shops were looted and burned in Portadown, Co Armagh, following a loyalist band parade through the town.

Fri. 30.8.85: The DUP leader, Rev Ian Paisley, and the leader of the UUP, James Molyneaux, met the prime minister, Margaret Thatcher, at Downing Street to object to the continuing Anglo-Irish talks.

Mon. 2.9.85: The employment secretary, Tom King, replaced Douglas Hurd as secretary of state for Northern Ireland in a cabinet reshuffle.

Wed. 4.9.85: The RUC training depot in Enniskillen, Co Fermanagh, was badly damaged in a Provisional IRA mortar attack. The environment secretary, Chris Patten, was replaced by Richard Needham.

Sun. 8.9.85: The Provisional IRA shot dead a couple in Turf Lodge in Belfast, alleging they were informers.

Tues. 17.9.85: The secretary of state, Tom King, paid a four-hour visit to Dublin, where he met the taoiseach, Garret FitzGerald, and the foreign minister, Peter Barry, to discuss southern proposals for an Anglo-Irish agreement.

Wed. 18.9.85: The initial report of an investigation led by John Stalker, deputy chief constable of Greater Manchester, into RUC operations in Co Armagh in 1982 that resulted in six deaths and allegations of a "shoot to kill" policy, was presented to the RUC chief constable, Sir John Hermon.

Tues. 24.9.85: The secretary of state, Tom King, called for an end to widespread speculation about the intergovernmental talks. Peter Robinson of the DUP said a joint plan had

been organised with the UUP to resist any Anglo-Irish settlement unionists opposed.

Sat. 28.9.85: A Provisional IRA car bomb virtually demolished Shantallow RUC station in Derry.

Tues. 1.10.85: At a joint UUP/DUP press conference in Belfast, unionists stated their intention to resign seats and seek a popular mandate against giving the republic a consultative role in northern affairs.

Sat. 5.10.85: The Fianna Fáil leader, Charles Haughey, said his party would not stand for any departure from the principles of Irish unity set down in the New Ireland Forum report and enshrined in the 1937 constitution.

Mon. 7.10.85: The tánaiste, Dick Spring, and the republic's foreign minister, Peter Barry, met the secretary of state, Tom King, and the foreign secretary, Sir Geoffrey Howe, for three hours in London to discuss unresolved matters in the draft Anglo-Irish agreement.

Tues. 8.10.85: The Court of Appeal in Belfast quashed the conviction for murder against the former INLA leader, Dominic McGlinchey, who was remanded in custody and three days later re-extradited to the republic.

Tues. 15.10.85: Fr Pat Buckley, who had frequently criticised the Catholic hierarchy, was dismissed from his post as a curate in Larne by the bishop of Down and Connor, Dr Cahal Daly.

Fri. 18.10.85: A massive Provisional IRA van bomb caused widespread damage to Derry's city centre and injured 27 people.

Fri. 25.10.85: The Stalker report into the alleged "shoot to kill" policy of the RUC in Co Armagh in 1982 was handed over to the DPP.

Mon. 28.10.85: Granada TV's *World in Action* offered new evidence that suggested that the Birmingham Six had been innocent of the pub bombings of 1974 and had been beaten by police to force confessions.

Wed. 30.10.85: Speaking after an hour-long meeting with the prime minister, Margaret Thatcher, the DUP leader, Rev Ian Paisley, and the UUP leader, James Molyneaux, warned of a Protestant backlash if the republic was given a consultative role in Northern Ireland affairs.

Thur. 31.10.85: The home secretary, Douglas Hurd, told the SDLP leader, John Hume, that he had ordered an investigation into the cases of the Birmingham Six.

Sat. 2.11.85: Around 5,000 United Ulster Loyalist Front supporters marched through Belfast in the launch of a campaign to form Ulster Clubs in each of the 26 council areas to resist any Anglo-Irish deal.

Sun. 3.11.85: The Provisional Sinn Féin ard fheis rejected a motion backed by the northern leadership that the party's policy of abstention from the Dáil should be changed from a principle to a tactic. The Provisional Sinn Féin president, Gerry Adams, claimed the party's electoral gains, along with the Provisional IRA's campaign, had fuelled British and Irish paranoia and led to the Anglo-Irish talks.

Fri. 15.11.85: The Anglo-Irish Agreement was signed at Hillsborough, Co Down, by the prime minister, Margaret Thatcher, and the taoiseach, Garret FitzGerald, amid one of the largest

security operations ever mounted in the north. The agreement gave the republic a consultative role in Northern Ireland through an intergovernmental conference, to be serviced by a secretariat of British and Irish civil servants based at Maryfield in Belfast. The agreement was welcomed by the SDLP, but described as a "sell-out" by unionists, a "disaster" by Provisional Sinn Féin and a "sad day for Irish nationalism" by Fianna Fáil. The UFF said members of the conference and secretariat would be considered legitimate targets. Most party leaders in London reacted favourably but a Treasury minister, Ian Gow, resigned, saying it would "prolong Ulster's agony".

Sat. 16.11.85: Unionist leaders said the 14 UUP and DUP MPs would resign from Westminster and force by-elections if a northern referendum on the Anglo-Irish Agreement was rejected.

Mon. 18.11.85: Senator Mary Robinson of the republic's Labour party resigned because the Anglo-Irish Agreement was "unacceptable to all sections of unionist opinion". Unionist MPs announced plans to challenge the agreement in the High Court. The SDLP rejected a Provisional Sinn Féin invitation for an electoral pact in any by-elections caused by unionist resignations.

Tues. 19.11.85: A three-day Dáil debate on the Anglo-Irish Agreement began with strong hints from the Fianna Fáil leader, Charles Haughey, that in government his party would not feel bound by the deal. The following day he said Fianna Fáil would not oppose developments in the intergovernmental conference that would benefit nationalists.

Wed. 20.11.85: The secretary of state, Tom King, was attacked by loyalists when he arrived for a lunch at Belfast City Hall. The UUP mayor, John Carson, attended the lunch in defiance of a unionist boycott of government ministers.

Thur. 21.11.85: At the end of its three-day debate, the Dáil voted in favour of the Anglo-Irish Agreement by 88 votes to 75.

Sat. 23.11.85: A massive loyalist demonstration against the Anglo-Irish Agreement brought Belfast city centre to a standstill, with crowds estimated variously from 35,000 to 200,000.

Mon. 25.11.85: The High Court in London refused unionists leave to challenge the legality of the Anglo-Irish Agreement.

Tues. 26.11.85: A two-day debate on the agreement began in the Commons, with the prime minister, Margaret Thatcher, warning unionist MPs that the government would not give way to threats or violence.

Wed. 27.11.85: The Commons approved the agreement by 437 votes to 47.

Mon. 2.12.85: The RUC chief constable, Sir John Hermon, and the Garda commissioner, Lawrence Wren, met for the first time in three years at Garda headquarters in Dublin.

Tues. 3.12.85: The secretary of state, Tom King, sparked off a political row when he said the republic's government now accepted there would never be a united Ireland. He later said he regretted the remarks.

Sat. 7.12.85: Two RUC constables were shot dead and three others were injured by a bomb when the Provisional IRA attacked and destroyed Ballygawley RUC station in Co Tyrone.

Wed. 11.12.85: The first session of the Anglo-Irish Intergovernmental Conference was held amid tight security at Stormont. Two thousand workers marched to the site of the proposed secretariat at Maryfield, where a section of the crowd attacked the RUC.

Tues. 17.12.85: All 14 UUP and DUP MPs and Jim Kilfedder of the UPUP resigned from their seats to force by-elections on the agreement.

Wed. 18.12.85: At Belfast Crown Court, 25 of the 27 defendants in the Harry Kirkpatrick INLA supergrass case were convicted.

Sat. 21.12.85: Desmond O'Malley, expelled from Fianna Fáil the previous year for challenging the party line that the unitary state was the only acceptable form of Irish unity, founded the PDs.

Tues. 24.12.85: The former Provisional Sinn Féin MP, Owen Carron, was charged with possessing a rifle and ammunition.

Sat. 28.12.85: Eighteen Provisional Sinn Féin members, including Martin McGuinness and several councillors, were arrested in dawn raids.

Tues. 31.12.85: A five-day loyalist anti-agreement march, to the Maryfield secretariat, began in Derry.

1986

Wed. 1.1.86: Two RUC members were killed by a remote-control bomb in a litter bin in Armagh.

Thur. 2.1.86: Five hundred and fifty soldiers of the Royal Anglian Regiment were ordered to Northern Ireland to provide extra protection for builders engaged in the reconstruction of RUC stations. Some contractors had cancelled contracts after Provisional IRA threats. The following week army engineers began work rebuilding Ballygawley RUC station in Co Tyrone.

Sat. 4.1.86: At the end of the five-day anti-agreement march from Derry, a section of the crowd attacked the RUC and tore down the gates of the secretariat at Maryfield.

Sat. 11.1.86: Unionist members of Belfast City Council erected a 40-foot banner outside the City Hall saying "Belfast Says No". A former mayor, David Cooke of Alliance, began proceedings to have the banner taken down.

Tues. 14.1.86: At a press conference pre-empting the launch of the joint unionist election manifesto, the secretary of state, Tom King, said the unionist campaign against the Anglo-Irish Agreement was misconceived and unduly negative and would not succeed in altering Parliament's support for the accord. The DUP leader, Rev Ian Paisley, said unionists did not only say "no"—they were saying "yes" to the Union. Owen Carron of Provisional Sinn Féin, on remand for firearms offences, was released on bail to contest the Fermanagh/South Tyrone by-election.

Thur. 16.1.86: Dutch police arrested three men, including the Maze escapers Brendan "Bik"

McFarlane and Gerry Kelly, in an Amsterdam flat.

Thur. 23.1.86: There was a 62 per cent turnout in the 15 Westminster by-elections on the agreement. The following day it was revealed that the unionists had increased their vote but had fallen well short of their 500,000 target, and had lost Newry and Armagh to Seamus Mallon of the SDLP. The secretary of state, Tom King, said he was encouraged by a 5 per cent swing of the nationalist vote away from Provisional Sinn Féin.

Sat. 25.1.86: Owen Carron, released on bail to contest the Fermanagh/South Tyrone by-election, failed to report back to Crumlin Road prison.

Tues. 28.1.86: In a parliamentary answer it was stated that one tenth of the RUC were Catholics.

Wed. 29.1.86: Following representations by the republic's foreign affairs minister, Peter Barry, about an incident the previous Sunday in which two young men were wounded by a UDR patrol near Cookstown, Co Tyrone, six UDR men were relieved of duty pending an RUC investigation.

Thur. 30.1.86: Fianna Fáil welcomed a call from UUP MP Harold McCusker for a conference of British, northern and southern politicians to discuss "the totality of relationships" in the two islands.

Fri. 31.1.86: A Provisional IRA van bomb outside the RUC station in Coalisland, Co Tyrone, caused widespread damage.

Wed. 5.2.86: The DUP leader, Rev Ian Paisley, called on the prime minister, Margaret Thatcher, to put the agreement on hold until an alternative could be found.

Thur. 6.2.86: The prime minister, Margaret Thatcher, invited unionist leaders for talks on the Anglo-Irish Agreement. The chair of the Northern Ireland Police Federation, Alan Wright, disputed the legality of an order from the chief constable, Sir John Hermon, that the federation needed clearance from RUC headquarters before talking to the media.

Fri. 7.2.86: In a case brought by the Alliance party, the High Court ordered Belfast City Council to remove its "Belfast Says No" banner and resume normal business.

Tues. 11.2.86: An RUC detective and a barman were shot dead in a Provisional IRA attack on a bar in Maguiresbridge, Co Fermanagh.

Thur. 13.2.86: The republic's justice minister and attorney general met their British counterparts in London to discuss the administration of justice in Northern Ireland.

Mon. 17.2.86: The grand master of the Orange Order, Rev Martin Smyth, said the order would not accept the re-routing of parades in the forthcoming year.

Tues. 18.2.86: The republic's government announced its intention to sign the European Convention on the Suppression of Terrorism, which would restrict the scope for terrorist suspects to claim that their alleged offences were political as a defence against extradition.

Mon. 24.2.86: The UUP leader, James Molyneaux, said he would ask the prime minister, Margaret Thatcher, for a three-month

suspension of the Anglo-Irish Agreement. Speaking on the eve of his meeting with her, he said unionists would consider talks if given an equal voice with the Dublin government.

Tues. 25.2.86: After meeting Margaret Thatcher at Downing Street, the unionist leaders, James Molyneaux and Rev Ian Paisley, responded positively to Mrs Thatcher's pledge to consider their proposals for round-table talks on devolution. But, following their return to Belfast and a heated three-hour meeting with unionist and loyalist workers' representatives, they announced they would discharge their electoral mandates, withdraw consent from the government and take part in no further talks with the prime minister until the agreement was scrapped.

Wed. 26.2.86: The unionist leaders, James Molyneaux and Rev Ian Paisley, announced a 24-hour strike against the agreement for March 3rd, urging a peaceful protest without paramilitary participation.

Thur. 27.2.86: Northern Ireland's 18 unionist-controlled councils, whose business had been adjourned as a protest at the agreement, were given a March 8th deadline for striking a rate by the Department of the Environment.

Mon. 3.3.86: The loyalist day of action against the agreement shut down much of Northern Ireland's industry and commerce, disrupted public services and transport and brought extensive power cuts. Masked loyalists manned barricades in many areas and in the evening there were riots and sniper attacks on the RUC in Protestant areas of Belfast. The NIO and the RUC were widely criticised for failing to keep roads open and for failing to prevent intimidation.

Tues. 4.3.86: The unionist leaders, James Molyneaux and Rev Ian Paisley, condemned the previous day's violence, as did MPs on all sides of the Commons.

Fri. 7.3.86: The taoiseach, Garret FitzGerald, accused the Fianna Fáil leader, Charles Haughey, of trying to sabotage the agreement during his visit to the USA. Mr Haughey had said that the statement by the secretary of state, Tom King, that the agreement meant there would not be a united Ireland had vindicated his opposition to the accord.

Sun. 9.3.86: The chief constable, Sir John Hermon, defended the RUC's conduct during recent protests and confirmed that 15 RUC families had been forced to leave their homes after loyalist attacks.

Mon. 10.3.86: The unionist leaders, James Molyneaux and Rev Ian Paisley, offered to reopen talks if the agreement was suspended, but the secretary of state, Tom King, ruled this out.

Tues. 11.3.86: Three DUP assembly members were arrested trying to cut through the barbed wire surrounding Stormont Castle while the fourth meeting of the Intergovernmental Conference was being held.

Thur. 13.3.86: It was announced that an additional battalion of troops was being brought in to support the RUC.

Mon. 17.3.86: The taoiseach, Garret FitzGerald, told the US president, Ronald Reagan, that unionists opposed to the agreement wished to "get off the hook" and get on with discussions about devolution.

Tues. 18.3.86: The women prisoners in Armagh became the first occupants of the new £30 million prison at Maghaberry, Co Antrim.

Thur. 20.3.86: In a press advertisement, the NIO described unionist criticism of the agreement as a "campaign of lies, deceit, distortions and half truths".

Sat. 22.3.86: Evelyn Glenholmes was released in Dublin when it was ruled that the British extradition warrant against her was invalid. She was rearrested after a car chase through Dublin, was later released and went into hiding.

Mon. 24.3.86: In a letter to unionist leaders, the prime minister, Margaret Thatcher, turned down their demand for a suspension of the agreement during talks on devolution.

Mon. 31.3.86: Despite the banning of an Apprentice Boys parade there, more than 2,000 loyalists showed up in Portadown, Co Armagh, and marched through the Catholic Garvaghy district of the town, provoking serious rioting against the RUC. Loyalist gangs petrol-bombed 11 Catholic homes in Lisburn, Co Antrim.

Tues. 1.4.86: Serious rioting continued in Portadown. A 20-year-old Protestant, Keith White, was shot in the chest with a plastic bullet and went into a coma. He died a fortnight later.

Thur. 3.4.86: The SDLP leader, John Hume, praised the recent RUC action in Portadown.

Fri. 4.4.86: Fourteen RUC homes had been attacked overnight. The main Protestant churches condemned the wave of attacks on Catholic and RUC property.

Sun. 6.4.86: More overnight attacks took place on Catholic and RUC homes.

Tues. 8.4.86: There was serious rioting in loyalist areas of Belfast and there were further attacks on Catholic and RUC homes throughout Northern Ireland.

Thur. 10.4.86: The chair of the Northern Ireland Police Federation, Alan Wright, called on the RUC chief constable, Sir John Hermon, to withdraw from meetings of the Intergovernmental Conference.

Fri. 11.4.86: Brian Keenan, a teacher from Belfast, was kidnapped in Beirut.

Mon. 14.4.86: Keith White became the first Protestant to be killed by a plastic bullet. He died in hospital.

Mon. 21.4.86: Dr Robin Eames was enthroned as Church of Ireland primate and archbishop of Armagh.

Wed. 23.4.86: The unionist leaders, James Molyneaux and Rev Ian Paisley, called for a rates strike as part of a 12-point plan of civil disobedience against the Anglo-Irish Agreement.

Fri. 25.4.86: The UUP severed its historic links with the Conservative party in protest at the agreement.

Tues. 6.5.86: Belfast City Council voted 27–23 to resume normal business, ending the adjournment protests against the agreement.

Sun. 11.5.86: The secretary of state, Tom King, recommended that the UVF supergrass William "Budgie" Allen be released after serving only two years of a 14-year sentence.

Wed. 14.5.86: In the assembly, unionists warned that a sectarian "bloodbath" was inevitable unless the Anglo-Irish Agreement was suspended.

Thur. 15.5.86: The six-month anniversary of the signing of the agreement was marked by a large loyalist demonstration in Hillsborough, Co Down.

Fri. 16.5.86: At a seminar on Northern Ireland in Amsterdam, the Provisional Sinn Féin president, Gerry Adams, said the agreement had copper-fastened partition and insulated the British government from international criticism.

Tues. 20.5.86: It was announced that there had been 368 cases of intimidation against members of the RUC and their families during recent loyalist violence.

Thur. 22.5.86: The Ulster Young Unionist Council advocated complete integration into Britain, with a Northern Ireland grand committee at Westminster.

Thur. 29.5.86: The secretary of state, Tom King, said the assembly was to be dissolved.

Fri. 30.5.86: One of the five UDR members accused of the murder of the Armagh man Adrian Carroll in November 1983 was freed after the judge threw out his alleged confession. The remaining men, known subsequently as the UDR Four, were to become the subject of a prolonged campaign to prove their innocence.

Wed. 4.6.86: British political and media figures sympathetic to the unionist cause launched the Friends of the Union group.

Thur. 5.6.86: The deputy chief constable of Greater Manchester, John Stalker, was removed from the inquiry into the alleged "shoot to kill" policy of the RUC in 1982. He was replaced by the West Yorkshire chief constable, Colin Sampson, who was also to investigate allegations of connections between Mr Stalker and Manchester criminals.

Wed. 11.6.86: Five Irish people were found guilty in London of conspiring to cause explosions in Britain, including the 1984 Brighton bombing.

Mon. 16.6.86: BBC's *Panorama* claimed that the RUC chief constable, Sir John Hermon, had refused to suspend two senior RUC officers on the recommendation of the deputy chief constable of Greater Manchester, John Stalker. It also reported that MI5 had bugged the hayshed in Co Armagh where Michael Tighe was shot dead by the RUC in 1982.

Tues. 17.6.86: The Libyan deputy leader, Ahmed Jalloud, told German MEPs that his country would resume aid to the Provisional IRA.

Fri. 20.6.86: The RUC chief constable, Sir John Hermon, said he was considering legal action against members of the media who had accused him of being involved in the removal of the deputy chief constable of Greater Manchester, John Stalker, from the "shoot to kill" inquiry.

Mon. 23.6.86: The assembly was dissolved. Twenty-two members, mainly DUP, refused to leave the chamber. They were removed by the RUC the following morning. The DUP leader, Rev Ian Paisley, told the officers involved not to come crying to him when their homes were attacked.

Tues. 24.6.86: The DUP leader, Rev Ian Paisley, said Northern Ireland was on the verge of civil war and called on Protestants to mobilise.

Thur. 26.6.86: A proposal to amend the republic's constitution to allow divorce was defeated in a referendum by 935,843 votes to 538,279.

Wed. 2.7.86: Four members of the UDR were sentenced to life imprisonment for the murder of Adrian Carroll in Armagh in 1983.

Thur. 3.7.86: The RUC said an Orange church parade could march through the Catholic Obins Street in Portadown, Co Armagh, the following Sunday but the Twelfth and Thirteenth parades would be banned from the area.

Sun. 6.7.86: Hand-to-hand fighting broke out in Portadown after the RUC tried to prevent the loyalist George Seawright from entering Obins Street as part of the Orange church parade through the area.

Mon. 7.7.86: A report by the NCCL condemned strip-searching in prisons.

Tues. 8.7.86: The UVF supergrass William "Budgie" Allen was released from prison, after serving only two years of a 14-year sentence.

Wed. 9.7.86: Two soldiers were killed by a Provisional IRA land mine near Crossmaglen, Co Armagh.

Thur. 10.7.86: The DUP leader, Rev Ian Paisley, and his deputy, Peter Robinson, were among 4,000 loyalists who took over Hillsborough, Co Down, in an early-morning protest against the Anglo-Irish Agreement.

Fri. 11.7.86: Portadown Orangemen accepted a compromise offer by the RUC, allowing them to march along the town's Garvaghy Road—itself predominantly Catholic—instead of the traditional Obins Street route. The following day the SDLP leader, John Hume, said the decision was a victory for the bullyboys and a breach of the chief constable's undertaking on provocative marches.

Sun.13.7.86: The RUC chief constable, Sir John Hermon, said he was suspending two senior officers as a result of investigations into the alleged "shoot to kill" policy. Weekend violence resulted in 128 RUC men and 66 civilians being injured and 127 people arrested.

Mon. 14.7.86: In Portadown, Co Armagh, the Royal Black Preceptory parade was followed by rioting. In Rasharkin, Co Antrim, 20 Catholic homes were damaged by a loyalist gang and in Castlewellan, Co Down, a loyalist car bomb destroyed a Catholic-owned restaurant.

Tues. 15.7.86: The republic's foreign minister, Peter Barry, said he shared the "deep resentment" of nationalists about the RUC decision to allow an Orange march along Garvaghy Road in Portadown, Co Armagh.

Wed. 16.7.86: Rioting continued for the sixth consecutive night in parts of Belfast and Portadown.

Thur. 17.7.86: The Court of Appeal quashed the convictions of 18 men found guilty in 1983 on the word of the Provisional IRA supergrass

206

Christopher Black but confirmed the convictions of four others.

Mon.21.7.86: Commenting on a spate of sectarian killings of Catholics in north Belfast, the UUP MP Ken Maginnis suggested they had been "provoked by the sectarian nature of Peter Barry's statements" over the previous month.

Sat. 26.7.86: Two RUC constables and a sergeant were shot dead by the Provisional IRA in Newry, Co Down.

Wed. 30.7.86: A local businessman, John Kyle, was shot dead by the Provisional IRA in a bar in Greencastle, Co Tyrone. The Provisional IRA said he had supplied the security forces. The following day, contractors stopped work on the rebuilding of Enniskillen RUC station.

Tues. 5.8.86: The Provisional IRA issued a new threat to contractors providing services to the security forces and extended its list of those considered "legitimate targets". Two days later the UFF announced an expansion of its own list of "legitimate targets" in response.

Thur. 7.8.86: The DUP deputy leader, Peter Robinson, was arrested during an incursion into the republic when 500 loyalists converged on Clontibret, Co Monaghan, beating up two gardaí, daubing slogans on the Garda station and marching through the village in military formation.

Sat. 9.8.86: Rioting by both loyalists and nationalists flared in west Belfast, Derry, Kilkeel and Downpatrick.

Fri. 15.8.86: In a Dundalk court, Peter Robinson was remanded to a further court appearance at Ballybay, Co Monaghan, over the Clontibret incursion. One hundred and fifty loyalists who had accompanied him were stoned and petrol-bombed. For the second night running, Catholic homes in Lisburn, Co Antrim, were petrol-bombed.

Mon. 18.8.86: The Northern Ireland Housing Executive said that more than 300, mainly Catholic, families had fled their homes that year because of intimidation and sectarian attacks. The following day the SDLP accused the RUC of not doing enough to halt intimidation of Catholics in Lisburn.

Fri. 22.8.86: John Stalker was cleared of allegations of misconduct and reinstated in his job as deputy chief constable of Greater Manchester, but not to the Northern Ireland "shoot to kill" inquiry. Management of the Shorts aerospace factory in east Belfast ordered the removal of loyalist flags and emblems from the workplace following intimidation of Catholic workers.

Tues. 2.9.86: The SDLP-controlled Newry and Mourne District Council instructed its employees not to collect refuse from the local RUC station.

Wed. 3.9.86: The UUP MP Harold McCusker called for a new relationship between Britain and Northern Ireland, saying that under the Anglo-Irish Agreement the Union was not worth fighting for.

Sun. 14.9.86: A UVF commander, John Bingham, was shot dead at his north Belfast home by the Provisional IRA, which claimed he had been behind recent sectarian murders. The army shot dead a Provisional IRA man, James

McKernan, in disputed circumstances, in west Belfast.

Tues. 16.9.86: The RUC was criticised for the contrast in its handling of two paramilitary funerals—a low profile at the funeral of the UVF commander John Bingham, which was attended by several unionist politicians, and a massive security operation at the funeral of the Provisional IRA man James McKernan. The secretary of state, Tom King, launched a consultative paper on options for a new fair employment regime for Northern Ireland.

Wed. 24.9.86: The unionist leaders, James Molyneaux and Rev Ian Paisley, advised those who had joined their rates strike against the agreement now to pay arrears in full.

Mon. 29.9.86: Claiming that 18 of the 34 people shot dead by the security forces since 1982 had been unarmed, Amnesty International reiterated its call for a judicial inquiry into disputed killings in Northern Ireland.

Wed. 1.10.86: The former chair of the Housing Executive, Charles Brett, was named as chair of the new International Fund for Ireland, established in the wake of the Anglo-Irish Agreement.

Tues. 2.10.86: The Belfast loyalist councillor George Seawright was given a nine-month sentence for his part in a protest outside Belfast City Hall the previous November, during which the secretary of state, Tom King, came under attack.

Mon. 6.10.86: The Intergovernmental Conference was held in Dublin for the first time. Several unionist politicians protested outside the meeting.

Sun. 12.10.86: The Fianna Fáil leader, Charles Haughey, said the position of the northern minority had "seriously worsened" since the Anglo-Irish Agreement, which his party would seek to renegotiate when it returned to power.

Mon. 13.10.86: In an initiative that the SDLP sought to link to the agreement, the British government agreed to demolish progressively Divis Flats in Belfast and Rossville Flats in Derry.

Wed. 15.10.86: After what it said was its first army convention in 16 years, the Provisional IRA decided to support elected Provisional Sinn Féin members taking their seats in the Dáil.

Thur. 16.10.86: A 76-year-old Catholic woman and her son were shot dead by the UFF at their home near Ballynahinch, Co Down.

Sat. 1.11.86: The unionist leaders, James Molyneaux and Rev Ian Paisley, launched a campaign in Britain against the Anglo-Irish Agreement at a large Orange rally in Glasgow.

Sun. 2.11.86: At the Provisional Sinn Féin ard fheis in Dublin, the party voted to end its abstentionist policy towards Dáil Éireann, which led to a walk-out of 100 delegates led by the former president, Ruairí Ó Brádaigh. The dissidents later set up a rival party, Republican Sinn Féin.

Tues. 4.11.86: In a confidential letter to the taoiseach, Garret FitzGerald, the prime minister, Margaret Thatcher, rejected the republic's demand that the number of judges in Diplock courts be increased to three.

Fri. 7.11.86: The DUP mayor of Belfast,

Sammy Wilson, barred NIO ministers from the wreath-laying Remembrance Day service at the City Hall.

Sat. 8.11.86: The UFF planted four small bombs in Dublin, of which two exploded and two were defused.

Mon. 10.11.86: At a closed meeting in Belfast's Ulster Hall, more than 1,000 loyalists met to form a new force, to be called Ulster Resistance, prepared to "take direct action as and when required" against the Anglo-Irish Agreement. The following day more than 2,000 men, many in military jackets, paraded in Kilkeel, Co Down, in Ulster Resistance's first show of strength.

Wed. 12.11.86: At the opening of Parliament, the Queen's Speech reiterated the government's commitment to the agreement.

Sat. 15.11.86: Following a huge anti-agreement demonstration at Belfast City Hall, a section of the crowd damaged 70 shops, some of which were looted.

Mon. 17.11.86: The RUC reissued a warning that anyone wearing paramilitary uniforms could face prosecution. Two days later the colour party at an Ulster Resistance parade in Portadown, Co Armagh, defied the warning, with the DUP deputy leader, Peter Robinson, and the Ulster Clubs chair, Alan Wright, wearing red berets.

Tues. 18.11.86: The unionist leaders, James Molyneaux and Rev Ian Paisley, met the Labour party leader, Neil Kinnock, in London. Eight Derry men, convicted on the word of the Provisional IRA supergrass Robert Quigley two years previously, were released on appeal in Belfast.

Fri. 21.11.86: The SDLP's annual conference rejected any suspension of the Anglo-Irish Agreement.

Mon. 24.11.86: After a four-day trial, an RUC man, Const Nigel Hegarty, was acquitted of the murder of Sean Downes at an internment anniversary rally in west Belfast in 1984.

Wed. 26.11.86: UUP councillors voted not to resign their seats on the 26 district councils, even though the option was supported by the party leadership. The Standing Advisory Commission on Human Rights recommended the introduction of three judges in Diplock courts but rejected a return to jury trial.

Mon. 1.12.86: The secretary of state, Tom King, announced changes in the law governing demonstrations and incitement and the repeal of the Flags and Emblems Act.

Wed. 3.12.86: The Maze escapers Brendan "Bik" McFarlane and Gerry Kelly were extradited from the Netherlands, appearing in court in Lisburn, Co Antrim, charged with offences connected with the escape in September 1983.

Tues. 9.12.86: The DUP leader, Rev Ian Paisley, was expelled from the European Parliament after repeatedly interrupting an address by the prime minister, Margaret Thatcher, in protest against the Anglo-Irish Agreement. A Catholic man was beaten to death in a bar in Lisburn, Co Antrim, in front of 30 witnesses. Some of these later gave statements to the RUC, leading to the arrest of members of the UDA, but later still the statements were withdrawn and the men were released.

Wed. 10.12.86: The Provisional Sinn Féin president, Gerry Adams, said at the launch of his book *The Politics of Irish Freedom* that he had never been a member of the IRA.

Tues. 16.12.86: Seven hundred homes and scores of businesses were damaged when a Provisional IRA proxy bomb destroyed Lisburn Road RUC station in Belfast.

Wed. 17.12.86: The Dáil passed the Extradition (European Convention on the Suppression of Terrorism) Bill providing for the republic's accession to the convention. But implementation was postponed until December 1st 1987, in the expectation of judicial reform in the north in the interim.

Fri. 19.12.86: The deputy chief constable of Greater Manchester, John Stalker, who had been removed from the investigation into the alleged RUC "shoot to kill" policy, announced he would resign the following spring for "personal and family reasons".

Sun. 21.12.86: The Catholic primate, Cardinal Tomás Ó Fiaich, said nationalist morale had improved since the Anglo-Irish Agreement but that the time was not right to urge Catholics to join the RUC.

Tues. 23.12.86: The prime minister, Margaret Thatcher, paid an eight-hour visit to Northern Ireland and said a change of government in the republic would not alter the agreement. Twenty-four Belfast men, convicted on the word of the INLA supergrass Harry Kirkpatrick, were freed after their convictions were quashed by the Court of Appeal.

1987

Thur. 1.1.87: Unionist leaders launched a petition at Belfast City Hall, to be presented to the Queen, calling for a referendum on the Anglo-Irish Agreement.

Tues. 6.1.87: The Northern Ireland Housing Executive revealed it had dealt with 1,118 cases of intimidation, mainly against Catholics and RUC men, in 1986.

Thur. 8.1.87: The UUP leader, James Molyneaux, warned loyalists against holding another day of action against the agreement.

Wed. 14.1.87: The Catholic primate, Cardinal Tomás Ó Fiaich, said he was "appalled" by Lord Brookeborough's description of him in the Lords as an "evil prelate".

Fri. 16.1.87: After a week-long trial in the Special Criminal Court, the DUP deputy leader, Peter Robinson, pleaded guilty to unlawful assembly in Clontibret, Co Monaghan, the previous August and was freed after paying £17,500 in fines and compensation.

Mon. 19.1.87: The minister of state, Nicholas Scott, denied a suggestion by the Fianna Fáil leader, Charles Haughey, that article one of the Anglo-Irish Agreement could be renegotiated.

Tues. 20.1.87: At the outbreak of an internal feud, two leading members of the INLA were shot dead in a bar in Drogheda. Following the withdrawal of four Labour ministers from his coalition government, the taoiseach, Garret

FitzGerald, dissolved the 24th Dáil. The UUP MEP, John Taylor, left the European Democratic Group and joined the neo-fascist European Right.

Wed. 21.1.87: A statement purportedly from the INLA said it would disband in its present form. Two days later this was denied by the INLA in Belfast, saying it was propaganda by the Irish People's Liberation Organisation (IPLO), one of the factions in the internal feud.

Sat. 24.1.87: The Labour party leader, Neil Kinnock, paid a flying visit to border security bases and defended his party's policy of meeting Provisional Sinn Féin representatives. He said, however, that it would not be "productive" for him to meet them in person.

Sun. 25.1.87: About 3,000 people gathered in Derry to mark the 15th anniversary of Bloody Sunday.

Thur. 29.1.87: The UDA's Ulster Political Research Group published a document, written by John McMichael and others, entitled *Common Sense*, which called for a constitutional conference leading to a devolved assembly and a coalition government based on party strengths.

Fri. 30.1.87: Provisional IRA bombs exploded in Belfast and Lisburn, Co Antrim.

Sat. 31.1.87: Mary McGlinchey, wife of the former INLA leader Dominic, was shot dead in her Dundalk home.

Thur. 5.2.87: Tony McCluskey, the fourth victim of the INLA feud, was shot dead outside Middletown, Co Armagh. *An Phoblacht Republican News* called on the INLA to disband.

Sat. 7.2.87: The UFF planted 18 incendiary devices in Dublin and Co Donegal, in protest against the Anglo-Irish Agreement.

Thur. 12.2.87: Unionist MPs delivered a 400,000-signature petition to Buckingham Palace, calling for a referendum on the agreement.

Thur. 19.2.87: In the republic's general election, Fianna Fáil won 81 seats, three short of a majority. In the INLA feud, a man was shot dead in west Belfast.

Sun. 22.2.87: Armed loyalists stole more than 100 weapons and a large quantity of ammunition from a UDR base in Coleraine, Co Derry.

Mon. 23.2.87: The outgoing Presbyterian moderator, Dr John Thompson, described the unionist campaign against the agreement as "counter-productive and morally questionable". Belfast City Council was fined £25,000 by the High Court for failing to resume normal business. The Department of the Environment appointed a commissioner to strike a rate in the unionist-dominated councils that had failed to do so.

Tues. 24.2.87: The US Police Foundation cancelled an invitation to the RUC chief constable, Sir John Hermon, following protests by the Irish National Caucus.

Mon. 2.3.87: The Ulster Clubs announced a plan to set up an alternative system of government, to be run by unionist political and paramilitary organisations.

Tues. 3.3.87: The home secretary, Douglas Hurd, said he would consider reopening the case of the Guildford Four.

Sat. 7.3.87: In Newry, Co Down, another man was shot dead in the INLA feud, the sixth such victim.

Mon. 9.3.87: Thirty-one RUC women were awarded a total of £240,000 compensation for sex discrimination in their case against the chief constable, Sir John Hermon.

Tues. 10.3.87: After weeks of uncertainty, the Fianna Fáil leader, Charles Haughey, was elected taoiseach on the casting vote of the Ceam Comhairle in the Dáil. The NIO environment minister, Richard Needham, approved a £300 million development plan for Laganside in Belfast.

Wed. 11.3.87: Garret FitzGerald resigned as leader of Fine Gael.

Sat. 14.3.87: In the INLA feud, the leader of the army council of the IPLO faction, Gerard Steenson, and a friend, Anthony McCarthy, were shot dead in Ballymurphy, west Belfast. The body of a Newry IRSP member, Fergus Conlon, was found near the border.

Tues. 17.3.87: The US president, Ronald Reagan, authorised the first $50 million grant for the International Fund for Ireland.

Sat. 21.3.87: Alan Dukes was elected leader of Fine Gael. The killing of an INLA member in a bar on the Ormeau Road in Belfast, and of another in Armagh, brought the death toll in the feud to 12.

Sun. 22.3.87: A former MI5 agent, James Miller, claimed that British Intelligence had helped promote the 1974 UWC strike to destabilise the Labour government of Harold Wilson.

Mon. 23.3.87: A civilian prison instructor, Leslie Jarvis, was shot dead in his car at Magee College, Derry. Forty minutes later two RUC men, Det Insp Austin Wilson and Det Sgt John Bennison, were killed when the car exploded as they investigated it. The Provisional IRA claimed responsibility. A Provisional IRA car bomb exploded at a joint army/RAF base at Rheindalen, West Germany, injuring 31 people, mostly Germans.

Tues. 24.3.87: The unionist leaders, James Molyneaux and Rev Ian Paisley, called for "peaceful" demonstrations on April 11th against the new Public Order Order regulating marches and rallies.

Wed. 25.3.87: The Standing Advisory Commission on Human Rights called for a strengthening of fair employment law, claiming "serious problems of inequality" between Catholics and Protestants.

Thur. 26.3.87: After shots had been fired over a coffin of a Provisional IRA man in church grounds two days before, the Catholic bishop of Derry, Dr Edward Daly, said requiem Mass would not be celebrated at funerals in the city with paramilitary trappings.

Sat. 28.3.87: Two west Belfast priests announced the end of the INLA feud.

Wed. 1.4.87: The RUC suggested that the "provocative" flying of the Union flag could be illegal under the new Public Order Order.

Thur. 2.4.87: A Provisional IRA member, Lawrence Marley, was shot dead by the UVF at his home in Ardoyne in Belfast.

Mon. 6.4.87: Lawrence Marley's funeral was postponed by his family because of the RUC presence outside his home—500 people attended a rally in west Belfast in protest. There were 40 bomb scares in the city and two explosions, while two bombs were defused. There were also gun and blast-bomb attacks on RUC stations.

Tues. 7.4.87: Lawrence Marley's funeral was postponed for the second day after police and mourners clashed outside his home, prompting protest meetings and bomb hoaxes in west Belfast and Derry.

Wed. 8.4.87: Lawrence Marley was buried in the largest republican funeral since the hunger strikes, with 5,000–6,000 mourners. Rioting later continued into the early hours of the morning.

Fri. 10.4.87: Ten unionist MPs, including the party leaders, James Molyneaux and Rev Ian Paisley, took part in an illegal march through Belfast in protest at the new Public Order Order.

Sat. 11.4.87: The Provisional IRA shot dead two RUC constables in Portrush, Co Antrim. There was a low turnout for a loyalist "day of defiance", prompting the UDA to call the following day for the resignation of the unionist leaders, James Molyneaux and Rev Ian Paisley.

Wed. 15.4.87: Provisional IRA letter bombs, franked "Students Union, University of Ulster" were sent to the prime minister's press secretary and senior Cabinet Office civil servants in London. The Libyan leader, Colonel Qaddafi, announced he would open centres for the Provisional IRA and the PLO.

Thur. 16.4.87: The Provisional IRA announced it would no longer fire volleys in church grounds over the coffins of dead members.

Mon. 20.4.87: The anniversary of the Easter Rising in 1916 was celebrated in west Belfast and Derry with several marches that were illegal under the Public Order Order.

Tues. 21.4.87: Eight thousand Apprentice Boys marched through Portadown, Co Armagh, in a parade that was illegal under the Public Order Order.

Thur. 23.4.87: Labour's Northern Ireland spokesperson, Peter Archer, wrote a letter supporting the MacBride fair employment principles to be circulated in the US by the Fair Employment Trust.

Sat. 25.4.87: Lord Justice Maurice Gibson and his wife, Cecily, were killed by a Provisional IRA car bomb in no-man's-land on the border at Killeen, Co Armagh, after leaving their Garda escort and before reaching their RUC escort.

Tues. 28.4.87: The Provisional IRA shot dead William "Frenchy" Marchant on the Shankill Road, claiming he was second-in-command in the Belfast UVF. The trial began of 18 of the Maze escapers, 16 for the murder of a prison officer, James Ferris. Unionists launched a press campaign in Britain against the Anglo-Irish Agreement, with a £15,000 advertisement in *The Times*.

Fri. 1.5.87: Provisional Sinn Féin issued a policy document, *Scenario for Peace*, which demanded a British withdrawal and an all-Ireland constitutional conference.

Tues. 5.5.87: Following reports that a unionist "task force"—comprising Frank Millar and Harold McCusker of the UUP and Peter Robinson of the DUP—might suggest devolution with an executive based on proportions of party support, the DUP leader, Rev Ian Paisley, said his party would have no part in any power-sharing arrangement.

Wed. 6.5.87: The secretary of state, Tom King, announced plans to recruit several hundred full-time RUC reservists.

Fri. 8.5.87: Eight Provisional IRA men and an innocent passer-by were shot dead by the SAS in Loughgall, Co Armagh. The Provisional IRA men had attacked the village RUC station with a bomb in the bucket of a mechanical digger, but the SAS had been lying in wait and a gun battle ensued after the bomb was detonated. No SAS men were wounded in the exchanges, but all the Provisional IRA men involved were killed, leading to speculation that some had been summarily executed by the soldiers. The passer-by was Anthony Hughes of Caledon, Co Tyrone, whose brother Frank was seriously injured. West Belfast saw the worst rioting for years.

Sat. 9.5.87: An RPG-7 rocket launcher was seized in a search of a west Belfast youth club. The RUC chief constable, Sir John Hermon, said the RUC would in future liaise with clergy and relatives of the dead in paramilitary funerals.

Mon. 11.5.87: A British general election was announced for June 11th. Gardaí clashed with mourners following the cortege in Emyvale, Co Monaghan, of one of the Loughgall dead, Jim Lynagh, after a colour party fired shots over the coffin. Over the next two days, Lynagh's funeral and the funerals in the north of the seven other Provisional IRA men passed off quietly.

Wed. 13.5.87: It was announced that Viscount Colville of Culross was to undertake an independent annual review of the Emergency Provisions Act.

Tues. 19.5.87: Two days after being selected as UUP candidate for North Down, Robert McCartney was expelled from the UUP because of his presidency of the Campaign for Equal Citizenship—which sought the extension of British party organisations to Northern Ireland—and comments he had made about the UUP leadership. The following day he launched his campaign as a "Real Unionist".

Thur. 21.5.87: The unionist leaders, James Molyneaux and Rev Ian Paisley, launched a joint manifesto, offering "consent" to a new government in return for a suspension of the Anglo-Irish Agreement.

Fri. 22.5.87: A Provisional Sinn Féin councillor, Alex Maskey, was seriously wounded at his home in Andersonstown, west Belfast, by loyalists. A senior DUP figure and former assembly member, Jim Allister, resigned from the party because of its continued involvement in an electoral pact with the UUP. The following day several DUP figures in his East Antrim constituency also resigned from the party, followed a few days later by 10 DUP councillors.

Thur. 4.6.87: A British soldier was shot dead in Andersonstown, west Belfast. The Presbyterian general assembly called on unionist MPs to return to Westminster.

Fri. 5.6.87: The RUC said there had been more paramilitary, especially loyalist, punishment shootings and beatings in the first four months of 1987 than in all of 1986.

Tues. 9.6.87: The former SDLP MP for West Belfast, Lord Fitt, attacked the party he once led and said that if he had a vote in the election it would go to the Workers' party.

Thur. 11.6.87: There was a 67 per cent turnout in Northern Ireland in the Westminster election.

Fri. 12.6.87: The Conservatives were returned to power with 375 seats. The only change in Northern Ireland was the defeat of the UUP MP, Enoch Powell, by Eddie McGrady of the SDLP.

Mon. 15.6.87: Tom King returned as secretary of state for Northern Ireland.

Thur. 25.6.87: The Queen's Speech at the opening of Parliament expressed a commitment to devolution in Northern Ireland and did not mention the Anglo-Irish Agreement.

Tues. 30.6.87: Three men were jailed in Boston for from four to 10 years for their part in the *Marita Ann* Provisional IRA gun-smuggling affair of 1984.

Wed. 1.7.87: Management at the Shorts aerospace factory in Belfast threatened to close sections of the plant over a row about the display of loyalist flags and bunting. After a walkout by 2,000 workers and a picket of the factory the following day, the company closed three of its main production areas on July 3rd, reopening them on July 6th after discussions with trade unions.

Thur. 2.7.87: The unionist "task force" report urged discussions to secure an acceptable devolved government for Northern Ireland.

Tues. 21.7.87: The newly appointed Labour party spokesperson on Northern Ireland, Kevin McNamara, visited Belfast.

Wed. 22.7.87: An FEA draft inquiry into Derry City Council cleared it of unionist allegations of discrimination against Protestants.

Sat. 1.8.87: Fifty members of Noraid arrived in Northern Ireland on a fact-finding mission.

Tues. 4.8.87: The Planning Appeals Commission refused permission for the "Belfast Says No" banner on the City Hall.

Sat. 8.8.87: There was rioting in Catholic areas of Belfast on the eve of the annual internment rally.

Wed. 12.8.87: The DUP leader, Rev Ian Paisley, rejected an attempt by the Church of Ireland primate, Dr Robin Eames, to set up informal talks between the four main constitutional party leaders.

Fri. 14.8.87: The home secretary, Douglas Hurd, ordered a fresh police inquiry into the Guildford Four case. Unionists called for an end to RUC–Garda intelligence co-operation after a Garda memo fell into the hands of the Provisional IRA.

Wed. 26.8.87: Two off-duty RUC detectives were shot dead and several bystanders were injured by the Provisional IRA in the Liverpool bar in Belfast.

Sun. 30.8.87: In the latest of several such attacks, the Fine Gael leader, Alan Dukes, criticised the Fianna Fáil government for not pursuing the Anglo-Irish Agreement, particularly the demand for three-judge courts, with sufficient vigour.

Mon. 31.8.87: Two men and a woman were detained under the Prevention of Terrorism Act after their arrest the previous day near the Wiltshire home of the secretary of state, Tom King.

Wed. 2.9.87: The UUP MP John Taylor claimed that the Provisional IRA campaign had consolidated the Protestant community and benefited it financially. He urged unionists to accept the challenge of devolution and improved links with Dublin.

Sat. 5.9.87: Two men and a woman, all from the republic, arrested near the Wiltshire home of the secretary of state, Tom King, on August 30th, were charged with conspiracy to murder him. Eleven unionist MPs, including the party leaders, James Molyneaux and Rev Ian Paisley, were summoned under the new public order legislation for taking part in an illegal march through Belfast on April 10th and the loyalist "day of defiance" on April 11th.

Sun. 6.9.87: The Labour MP Chris Mullin claimed to have interviewed the real perpetrators of the Birmingham pub bombings of 1974.

Mon. 7.9.87: John Cushnahan announced he was going to resign as leader of the Alliance party.

Thur. 10.9.87: The US ambassador to the UK, Charles Price, supported the British government's stand against the MacBride fair employment principles.

Sat. 12.9.87: The Workers' party leader, Tomás Mac Giolla, announced his resignation. The Catholic primate, Cardinal Tomás Ó Fiaich, described the Anglo-Irish Agreement as "a shot in the arm for Catholics in the North".

Mon. 14.9.87: Following three rounds of meetings with senior NIO civil servants, the unionist leaders, James Molyneaux and Rev Ian Paisley, ended a 19-month boycott and met the secretary of state, Tom King, for "talks about talks".

Tues. 15.9.87: Tom King launched a fair employment guide for employers, *Religious Equality of Opportunity in Employment,* in the continuing debate about new anti-discrimination measures.

Wed. 16.9.87: The European Commission of Human Rights found that seven-day detention under the Prevention of Terrorism Act breached the requirement in the European Convention on Human Rights that suspects be charged "promptly".

Sun. 27.9.87: In the latest of a series of such demonstrations, several hundred people protested against the siting of an army observation post at Glassdrummond, Co Armagh. The following week the Provisional IRA launched a mortar attack on the post.

Thur. 1.10.87: The FEA said that Catholic males were still two and a half times more likely to be unemployed than Protestant men.

Sat. 3.10.87: Dr John Alderdice was elected leader of the Alliance party.

Sun. 4.10.87: In Denmark, the republic's former foreign minister, Peter Barry, said that the coalition government had been given a British undertaking to reform the Diplock court system. This was denied by the British foreign secretary, Sir Geoffrey Howe.

Wed. 7.10.87: Peter Robinson resigned as deputy leader of the DUP.

Fri. 9.10.87: The RUC chief constable, Sir John Hermon, approved a new RUC code of conduct, denying that the development had stemmed from the Anglo-Irish Agreement.

Sun. 11.10.87: The taoiseach, Charles Haughey, expressed disappointment at the limited progress made under the agreement and cast doubt on the republic's willingness to allow extradition in advance of judicial reform in Northern Ireland.

Thur. 15.10.87: The DPP, Sir Barry Shaw, denied a claim by the Fine Gael leader, Garret FitzGerald, that the ending of supergrass trials was a consequence of the agreement.

Sat. 17.10.87: The tánaiste and foreign minister, Brian Lenihan, met the secretary of state, Tom King, in London for talks before the Intergovernmental Conference.

Tues. 20.10.87: Unionist councillors in Belfast agreed to pay a £25,000 High Court fine and £11,000 costs over their anti-agreement abstention.

Wed. 21.10.87: After a four-hour meeting with the tánaiste and foreign minister, Brian Lenihan, the secretary of state, Tom King, warned of "serious implications" if the republic's Extradition Act did not come into effect on December 1st.

Thur. 22.10.87: The prime minister, Margaret Thatcher, said that "the future of courts in Northern Ireland is a matter for the UK government and is not a bargaining point".

Fri. 23.10.87: Provisional Sinn Féin won Belfast council by-elections for Upper and Lower Falls.

Wed. 28.10.87: Two Provisional IRA men were killed in Derry when a bomb they were carrying in a hijacked car exploded.

Thur. 29.10.87: The Standing Advisory Commission on Human Rights published a report advocating a much tougher fair employment regime, including replacement of the FEA with a more powerful body.

Fri. 30.10.87: The review of the Birmingham Six trial opened at the Court of Appeal in London.

Sun. 1.11.87: One hundred and fifty tons of arms and ammunition, including 20 surface-to-air missiles, bound from Libya for the Provisional IRA, were seized on a coaster, *Eksund,* off the French coast.

Mon. 2.11.87: Requiem Mass was offered in Derry at the funerals of two Provisional IRA men, overturning the earlier ban by the bishop, Dr Edward Daly. Later there were clashes with mourners when the RUC moved in to arrest gunmen who fired a volley over the coffins.

Sun. 8.11.87: Eleven people were killed and 63 injured, 19 very seriously, when a Provisional

IRA bomb exploded at a Remembrance Day ceremony in Enniskillen, Co Fermanagh.

Wed. 11.11.87: The taoiseach, Charles Haughey, met the leader of the British Labour party, Neil Kinnock, to discuss the implementation of the 1986 Extradition Act.

Thur. 12.11.87: More than 2,000 unionists, led by the party leaders, James Molyneaux and Rev Ian Paisley, marched through London to mark the second anniversary of the Anglo-Irish Agreement.

Sun. 15.11.87: A minute's silence was observed across the republic in memory of those killed in the Remembrance Day bombing in Enniskillen.

Mon. 16.11.87: The Intergovernmental Conference in Dublin agreed on the need for a "very positive response" to security following the Enniskillen bombing.

Tues. 17.11.87: The Department of the Environment published the Belfast Urban Area Plan 2001, to widespread criticism.

Thur. 19.11.87: The former loyalist politician George Seawright was shot and fatally injured off the Shankill Road in Belfast by the IPLO.

Sun. 22.11.87: About 7,000 people, including the prime minister, Margaret Thatcher, attended the rearranged Remembrance Day service in Enniskillen, Co Fermanagh.

Mon. 23.11.87: A massive arms search got under way in the republic and Northern Ireland following claims of three successful arms runs from Libya to the Provisional IRA before the *Eksund* seizure. The republic's government published a bill amending the 1965 Extradition Act to require the attorney general to satisfy himself of an intention to prosecute, based on a sufficiency of evidence, before endorsing a warrant for extradition to the UK.

Tues. 24.11.87: Forty Provisional Sinn Féin activists were arrested in dawn raids in Belfast, Derry and the border counties.

Fri. 27.11.87: The "border fox", Dessie O'Hare, a maverick republican paramilitary figure responsible for many serious offences, including the kidnap and maiming of a Dublin dentist, John O'Grady, was seriously injured in a shoot-out with gardaí and soldiers in Kilkenny and eventually arrested.

Mon. 30.11.87: The Extradition Act passed by the Dáil a year earlier, providing for ratification of the European Convention on the Suppression of Terrorism, came into force at midnight.

Tues. 1.12.87: The prime minister, Margaret Thatcher, attacked the republic's insistence on extra safeguards over extradition reflected in the proposed amendments to the 1965 act, saying that Britain was being treated as a "least favoured nation".

Wed. 2.12.87: The unionist leaders, James Molyneaux and Rev Ian Paisley, met the secretary of state, Tom King, for the fifth round of "talks about talks".

Thur. 3.12.87: George Seawright died of wounds sustained in an IPLO attack a fortnight earlier. The Extradition Amendment Bill was passed by the Dáil.

Sat. 5.12.87: The prime minister, Margaret Thatcher, met the taoiseach, Charles Haughey, at the EC summit in Copenhagen and re-established a "working relationship". The funeral of George Seawright in Belfast was attended by unionist politicians and paramilitary figures.

Sun. 13.12.87: The RUC chief constable, Sir John Hermon, confirmed that there had been cross-border co-operation between bomb disposal teams.

Tues. 22.12.87: The UDA deputy leader, John McMichael, was killed by an IRA booby-trap bomb under his car outside his home in Lisburn, Co Antrim.

1988

Fri. 1.1.88: The RUC chief constable, Sir John Hermon, warned that the Provisional IRA might have obtained SAM-7 surface-to-air missiles, in shipments prior to the *Eksund*.

Fri. 8.1.88: In the biggest loyalist arms find ever, 100 guns, along with ammunition, were intercepted in three cars near Portadown, Co Armagh, and three UDA men were arrested. Peter Robinson was re-elected deputy leader of the DUP.

Sat. 9.1.88: The law courts in Chichester Street in Belfast were extensively damaged by a Provisional IRA car bomb.

Mon. 11.1.88: The SDLP leader, John Hume, had the first of a series of meetings with the Provisional Sinn Féin president, Gerry Adams, which involved senior figures from both parties.

Tues. 19.1.88: Following an announcement by the Provisional IRA in Derry that it would no longer fire volleys at the funerals of members, the Catholic bishop of Derry, Dr Edward Daly, rescinded his ban on requiem Mass for paramilitaries.

Wed. 20.1.88: The UK opposed the inclusion of Northern Ireland among the poorest EC countries, entitled to major increases in support from the enhanced structural fund. Northern Ireland's MPs united to back a private member's bill to reduce the time limit for abortion to 18 weeks.

Thur. 21.1.88: The secretary of state, Tom King, announced that the army would have more control over border security.

Sun. 24.1.88: SDLP constituency representatives endorsed the Hume/Adams talks.

Mon. 25.1.88: The attorney general, Sir Patrick Mayhew, announced that 11 RUC officers investigated in the Stalker/Sampson inquiry into the alleged RUC "shoot to kill" policy were not to be prosecuted for alleged perversion of the course of justice, for reasons of "national security". The republic's government expressed "deep dismay".

Tues. 26.1.88: The unionist leaders, James Molyneaux and Rev Ian Paisley, met the secretary of state, Tom King, with proposals for administrative devolution with a committee system and proportionately distributed chairs. Two Lisburn Provisional Sinn Féin councillors who had received death threats the previous day were attacked by an Ulster Clubs picket as they tried to attend a council meeting in Hillsborough.

Thur. 28.1.88: The Court of Appeal in London rejected the new appeal of the Birmingham Six. The republic's government said Britain's failure to consult over the Stalker/Sampson affair had been a "breach of the Anglo-Irish Agreement".

Tues. 2.2.88: In pre-publication serialisation of his book, the former deputy chief constable of Greater Manchester, John Stalker, said that he had been suspended because of his Northern Ireland investigations, not because of his alleged associations with Manchester criminals.

Sun. 7.2.88: The UUP leader, James Molyneaux, said that the Anglo-Irish Agreement should be rewritten to cover the "totality of relationships" between the UK and the republic.

Tues. 9.2.88: The European Parliament called on Britain to reconsider its decision not to prosecute in the Stalker/Sampson affair.

Sat. 13.2.88: The Provisional Sinn Féin executive permitted Gerry Adams to resume talks with John Hume of the SDLP.

Sun. 14.2.88: The republic's government said Britain was persisting in sending extradition applications without evidence, despite the new requirements.

Mon. 15.2.88: The prime minister, Margaret Thatcher, met the taoiseach, Charles Haughey, at the EC summit in Brussels.

Wed. 17.2.88: The secretary of state, Tom King, announced two disciplinary inquiries arising from the Stalker/Sampson investigation.

Thur. 18.2.88: The Standing Advisory Commission on Human Rights called for three judges in Diplock courts. The secretary of state, Tom King, said he was not persuaded.

Sat. 20.2.88: The taoiseach, Charles Haughey, said that "the historic inability of Britain to comprehend Irish feelings and sensitivities still remains" and that he was willing to travel north to talk to unionists.

Sun. 21.2.88: Aidan McAnespie, who had earlier claimed to have been threatened by the security forces, was shot dead by a soldier at a border checkpoint at Aughnacloy, Co Tyrone. The army claimed the gun had gone off accidentally. The following day the republic's government appointed the Garda deputy commissioner, Eugene Crowley, to inquire into the killing.

Tues. 23.2.88: Pte Ian Thain was released from a life sentence for the murder of Thomas "Kidso" Reilly in west Belfast, after having served only 26 months, and returned to his regiment.

Wed. 24.2.88: Two part-time UDR men were killed by a Provisional IRA bomb in central Belfast. An 18-year-old Grenadier Guard was charged with the unlawful killing of Aidan McAnespie. The FEA said that whilst the Catholic share of employment in the public sector had increased this was not true of the private sector.

Thur. 25.2.88: The SDLP leader, John Hume, accepted an invitation from the secretary of state, Tom King, for talks about devolution.

Mon. 29.2.88: Two Provisional IRA men were killed by their own bomb near Crossmaglen, Co Armagh.

Tues. 1.3.88: The NIO minister of state, John Stanley, said in the Commons debate on the renewal of the Prevention of Terrorism Act that there were SAM-7 missiles "in the island of Ireland". Belfast councillors refused an invitation to join Dublin's millennium celebrations.

Sun. 6.3.88: Three unarmed Provisional IRA members, Mairead Farrell, Daniel McCann, and Sean Savage, were shot dead by the SAS on the streets of Gibraltar, while engaged, it is believed, on a reconnaissance for a bombing mission. There was rioting in west Belfast.

Mon. 7.3.88: The UDA commander, Andy Tyrie, found a bomb under his car at his home in east Belfast. The Provisional IRA denied responsibility.

Tues. 8.3.88: Spanish police found a car containing explosives at Marbella, apparently a bomb intended for use in Gibraltar. The taoiseach, Charles Haughey, said he was "gravely perturbed" over the shooting of unarmed people who could have been arrested.

Thur. 10.3.88: Sixty Labour MPs denounced the Gibraltar killings as "an act of terrorism . . . tantamount to capital punishment without trial". The SDLP asked the republic's government to press for low-level policing at the funerals of the victims.

Fri. 11.3.88: Andy Tyrie resigned as leader of the UDA after a vote of no-confidence by the organisation's inner council.

Mon. 14.3.88: The bodies of Mairead Farrell, Daniel McCann and Sean Savage were flown into Dublin and carried north in a funeral cortege. The army shot dead an armed Provisional IRA man, Kevin McCracken, in Turf Lodge in Belfast.

Wed. 16.3.88: A loyalist, Michael Stone, attacked mourners at the funerals in Milltown cemetery, Belfast, of the three Gibraltar dead, with grenades and a handgun. Three men were shot dead and several other people were injured.

Fri. 18.3.88: The Provisional IRA shot dead a Protestant woman, Gillian Johnston, near Belleek, Co Fermanagh, in mistake for her brother, who was thought to be (but was not) a member of the UDR.

Sat. 19.3.88: Two army corporals, Robert Howes and Derek Wood, were attacked by angry mourners—who thought they were loyalists—when they unaccountably drove into the funeral cortege of the Provisional IRA man Kevin McCracken in Andersonstown, west Belfast. They were stripped, beaten and later shot dead by the Provisional IRA.

Wed. 23.3.88: Following the killings at Milltown and Andersonstown in Belfast the RUC said it was re-examining its position on low-profile policing of paramilitary funerals. After resistance, and on legal advice, the BBC and ITN handed over untransmitted film of the attack on the two corporals to the RUC. The following day RTE became the third company to hand over footage without a court order.

Mon. 28.3.88: The Labour MP Tony Benn published a bill to end British rule in Northern Ireland by 1990.

Tues. 29.3.88: The SDLP presented a strategy for political progress to the secretary of state, Tom King.

Sat. 9.4.88: At the Alliance conference in

Belfast, David Steel, leader of the Social and Liberal Democrats, defended the demand by Amnesty International for an inquiry into the Gibraltar killings.

Mon. 11.4.88: The Libyan leader, Colonel Qaddafi, pledged his support for the Provisional IRA.

Tues. 12.4.88: The RUC chief constable's annual report said 1987 had been the most violent year since 1981.

Fri. 15.4.88: The RUC code of conduct was published for the first time.

Sat. 16.4.88: Proinsias de Rossa was elected president of the Workers' party, replacing Tomás Mac Giolla.

Fri. 22.4.88: Seven men were charged in Belfast in connection with the murders of the two corporals in Andersonstown on March 19th.

Tues. 26.4.88: The secretary of state, Tom King, met an SDLP delegation at Stormont.

Thur. 28.4.88: The foreign secretary, Sir Geoffrey Howe, described as "irresponsible" the decision by the Independent Broadcasting Authority to allow transmission of a Thames TV *This Week* programme, *Death on the Rock*, on the Gibraltar killings. In it, witnesses said that Farrell and McCann had been trying to surrender, that Savage had been shot in the back and that all three had been finished off at point-blank range. The secretary of state, Tom King, said the Anglo-Irish Agreement was "an end in itself" and not "part of a process sliding to something else".

Sun. 1.5.88: In separate Provisional IRA attacks in Holland, two RAF men were killed in an explosion, and one was shot dead and another injured in a machine-gun attack.

Tues. 3.5.88: Nigel Dodds of the DUP was elected mayor of Belfast.

Wed. 11.5.88: The attorneys general of the UK and the republic, Sir Patrick Mayhew and John Murray, met in Dublin to try to resolve the impasse over the republic's new extradition arrangements. The following day Sir Patrick announced his agreement to comply with the republic's new act, requiring a sufficiency of evidence to be demonstrated before extradition warrants would be backed.

Sun. 15.5.88: Three Catholic men were shot dead and six others were injured in a UVF machine-gun attack on the Avenue bar in central Belfast. The UUP leader, James Molyneaux, said his party was prepared to exchange position papers with the taoiseach, Charles Haughey.

Thur. 19.5.88: Thirteen people were injured when a Provisional IRA bomb exploded near the RUC stand at the Balmoral agricultural show in Belfast. Provisional Sinn Féin and the SDLP met in the latest round of their talks.

Mon. 23.5.88: The inquest into the shooting of three Provisional IRA members in Gibraltar, scheduled to start on June 27th, was postponed by the colony's coroner.

Tues. 24.5.88: A female UDR member and an army corporal were charged in Belfast with passing photographs of Provisional IRA suspects to loyalist paramilitaries.

Wed. 25.5.88: The British government white paper on fair employment was published. It

included compulsory monitoring of the religious composition of workforces and the establishment of a Fair Employment Commission to replace the FEA.

Thur. 26.5.88: The unionist leaders, James Molyneaux and Rev Ian Paisley, met the secretary of state, Tom King, for the last of their "talks about talks".

Wed. 1.6.88: Lieut-Gen John Waters replaced Lieut-Gen Sir Robert Pascoe as army GOC.

Tues. 7.6.88: Alan Wright, chair of the Northern Ireland Police Federation, called for internment north and south.

Fri. 10.6.88: A "model Conservative association" was launched in Bangor, Co Down, as part of the campaign to persuade British political parties to organise in Northern Ireland.

Mon. 13.6.88: The prime minister, Margaret Thatcher, expressed her "utter dismay" after Portlaoise District Court refused to extradite a republican suspect, Patrick McVeigh, because it was not satisfied by evidence of his identity.

Tues. 14.6.88: Christopher and Michael McGimpsey, both UUP members, began an action in the High Court in Dublin, claiming that the Anglo-Irish Agreement contravened articles two and three of the republic's constitution.

Wed. 15.6.88: Six off-duty soldiers were killed when a Provisional IRA bomb exploded under their minibus after they had taken part in a charity fun run in Lisburn, Co Antrim. Eleven bystanders were injured.

Thur. 16.6.88: The secretary of state, Tom King, refused to rule out the reintroduction of internment.

Wed. 22.6.88: The RUC chief constable, Sir John Hermon, announced that he would retire the following year. Northern Ireland's Catholic bishops attacked proposed changes in the education system, including greater support for integrated schooling.

Thur. 23.6.88: For the first time an army helicopter was shot down by the Provisional IRA, in Crossmaglen, Co Armagh.

Mon. 27.6.88: Amnesty International called for a judicial inquiry into disputed killings by the RUC and army since 1982.

Tues. 28.6.88: The prime minister, Margaret Thatcher, met the taoiseach, Charles Haughey, at the EC summit in Hanover and discussed security.

Wed. 29.6.88: The republic's government criticised the Police Authority decision, by a majority of one vote, not to inquire further into the role of the RUC chief constable and two senior officers in the 1982 "shoot to kill" cases investigated by John Stalker.

Thur. 30.6.88: The secretary of state, Tom King, said the new Police Authority included a "very substantial representation" of Catholics. A group of left-wing Labour MPs launched a Time To Go! charter, calling for British withdrawal from Northern Ireland.

Fri. 1.7.88: The Department of Economic Development said that the Belfast aerospace firm Shorts would "ultimately return to the private sector".

Mon. 4.7.88: The RUC chief constable, Sir John Hermon, said there would be disciplinary action against 20 policemen following the report of the Staffordshire chief constable, Charles Kelly, into the Stalker/Sampson inquiry. A Belfast City Council meeting was abandoned after unionist and Provisional Sinn Féin councillors came to blows.

Thur. 7.7.88: A man and a woman were killed and four people were injured outside Falls baths in west Belfast by a Provisional IRA bomb intended for the security forces.

Wed. 13.7.88: Two Provisional IRA bombs damaged an army base at Duisburg in West Germany.

Thur. 14.7.88: The NIO announced that the Criminal Justice Bill would allow samples of saliva and mouth swabs to be taken from those suspected of serious offences for genetic fingerprinting analysis.

Mon. 18.7.88: The attorneys general of the UK and the republic, Sir Patrick Mayhew and John Murray, met again to clarify procedural problems in extradition cases. It was announced that the Provisional Sinn Féin leader, Gerry Adams, had met the SDLP leader, John Hume, alone in west Belfast a week earlier.

Tues. 19.7.88: The British government announced a £10 million aid package for west Belfast.

Wed. 20.7.88: The UUP leader, James Molyneaux, rejected the suggestion of an Anglo-Irish inter-parliamentary tier.

Sat. 23.7.88: On the border near Newry, a 1,000lb Provisional IRA bomb, intended for Mr Justice Higgins, killed a Hillsborough family, Robert Hanna, his wife Maureen and their son David. The action brought to 17 the number of civilians killed in Provisional IRA "mistakes" since November 1987.

Thur. 28.7.88: The SDLP leader, John Hume, said all the Northern Ireland parties were agreed on their opposition to the privatisation of Harland and Wolff and Shorts.

Mon. 1.8.88: In the first Provisional IRA bomb attack in Britain since Brighton in 1984, a soldier was killed in Inglis Barracks in north London.

Thur. 4.8.88: Two elderly Protestant building workers who had been repairing the local RUC station were shot dead by the Provisional IRA in Belleek, Co Fermanagh.

Fri. 5.8.88: The UUP and the Police Federation called for the re-introduction of internment. Three soldiers and a civilian were injured by a Provisional IRA bomb at an army barracks in Düsseldorf, West Germany.

Mon. 8.8.88: Two Catholic men were shot dead by the PAF in Ardoyne, north Belfast. Mr Justice Brian Hutton succeeded Lord Lowry as lord chief justice.

Tues. 9.8.88: On the anniversary of the introduction of internment, vehicles were hijacked and 42 people were arrested in rioting in west Belfast.

Fri. 12.8.88: The Provisional IRA shot dead an army sergeant major in Ostend, Belgium. An IPLO proxy bomb exploded outside the law courts in Belfast.

Sun. 14.8.88: The leading Provisional Sinn Féin figure Martin McGuinness praised the "continental battalions" of the Provisional IRA.

Mon. 15.8.88: The SDLP leader, John Hume, defended his latest meeting with the Provisional Sinn Féin president, Gerry Adams.

Sat. 20.8.88: In the most serious attack on the army since Warrenpoint in 1979, eight soldiers were killed and many more were injured in a Provisional IRA bomb attack on a services bus near Ballygawley, Co Tyrone.

Sun. 21.8.88: The secretary of state, Tom King, announced a major security review.

Mon. 22.8.88: A Royal Navy recruiting officer was killed by a Provisional IRA bomb attached to his car in Belfast.

Tues. 23.8.88: Gerard O'Hare became the first person to be extradited north under the republic's new extradition arrangements. A massive Provisional IRA car bomb exploded in Belfast city centre.

Sat. 27.8.88: A Maze escaper, Robert Russell, who had lost his appeals against extradition, was successfully handed over to the RUC at the Killeen border crossing, near Newry. There was widespread rioting in west Belfast and Derry, which continued sporadically the following day.

Tues. 30.8.88: Three Provisional IRA men were shot dead by the SAS near Drumnakilly, Co Tyrone.

Wed. 31.8.88: Two pensioners inquiring after their neighbour in a block of flats in Derry were killed by a Provisional IRA booby-trap bomb meant for the security forces.

Mon. 5.9.88: The end of the SDLP/Provisional Sinn Féin dialogue was announced and papers were released by the parties. In the High Court in Belfast the NIO blocked an FEA investigation into Northern Ireland Electricity on grounds of national security.

Tues. 6.9.88: The Gibraltar inquest into the deaths of the Provisional IRA members Mairead Farrell, Daniel McCann and Sean Savage opened with the revelation that at least 27 shots had been fired at the three.

Wed. 7.9.88: The IPLO shot dead a leading UDA member, William Quee, outside his shop on the Oldpark Road in north Belfast.

Thur. 8.9.88: At the Gibraltar inquest, the Crown pathologist said that Sean Savage had died in a "frenzied attack" and that all three victims had been shot in the back and head.

Fri. 9.9.88: The Provisional IRA shot dead the treasurer of the Ulster Clubs, Colin Abernethy, on a commuter train on the outskirts of Belfast.

Tues. 20.9.88: The home secretary, Douglas Hurd, announced plans to restrict funds for paramilitary groups.

Wed. 21.9.88: A British Labour party document proposed north–south harmonisation of policies on the economy, security, the currency and social security, as a prelude to "unity by consent". In Gibraltar on this and the following two days, civilian witnesses said the SAS had fired without warning and had shot the victims as they lay on the ground.

Mon. 26.9.88: The DPP, Sir Barry Shaw, announced he would not proceed with charges

of manslaughter against a soldier in connection with the killing of Aidan McAnespie in Aughnacloy in February. In Gibraltar a policeman said he had heard warnings shouted before Farrell and McCann were shot.

Tues. 27.9.88: The NIO confirmed that army aircraft had been allowed to fly up to 200 metres into the republic for almost two years under a secret arrangement.

Wed. 28.9.88: The prime minister, Margaret Thatcher, visited Northern Ireland.

Thur. 29.9.88: The tánaiste and foreign minister, Brian Lenihan, told the United Nations (UN) that Britain and the republic were fully committed to the Anglo-Irish Agreement.

Fri. 30.9.88: After being directed by the coroner not to return an open verdict, the jury in the Gibraltar inquest decided by nine votes to two that the Provisional IRA members Mairead Farrell, Daniel McCann and Sean Savage had been lawfully killed by the SAS.

Sun. 2.10.88: Replying to a statement from the secretary of state, Tom King, that unionists had made no proposals for political development, the UUP leader, James Molyneaux, said it was up to Mr King to break the political stalemate. The BBC postponed a *Panorama* documentary on the role of the SAS in Northern Ireland.

Mon. 3.10.88: The Alliance party published a document, *Governing with Consensus*, advocating power-sharing devolved government with an equal input into a newly tripartite Anglo-Irish Conference.

Wed. 5.10.88: The education minister, Brian Mawhinney, announced reforms in line with Britain and said that his department now recognised a duty to promote integrated schools.

Fri. 7.10.88: Patrick McVeigh, whose extradition warrant had earlier collapsed, was rearrested by gardaí and later released. The Provisional Sinn Féin general secretary, Tom Hartley, rebutted SDLP claims that Britain was neutral on Irish unity as a result of the Anglo-Irish Agreement.

Sat. 8.10.88: A conference at Ballycastle, Co Antrim, organised by the Corrymeela Community, brought together the UUP MP Ken Maginnis and the SDLP MP Eddie McGrady to discuss devolution. In Derry the RUC kept apart a '68 Committee march to commemorate the original civil rights march there and a counter-demonstration organised by the DUP leader, Rev Ian Paisley.

Mon. 10.10.88: The UUP leader, James Molyneaux, again turned down an invitation from the secretary of state, Tom King, to talks on security.

Tues. 11.10.88: The DUP leader, Rev Ian Paisley, was thrown out of the European Parliament for continuously interrupting an address by Pope John Paul II. The secretary of state, Tom King, invited submissions to the review of the workings of the Intergovernmental Conference. The following day the joint unionist policy group rejected any involvement. Mgr Colm McCaughan, director of the Council for Maintained (Catholic) Schools, said Catholic parents who sent their children to integrated schools were breaking canon law.

Fri. 14.10.88: At the Conservative party conference in Brighton, the prime minister, Margaret Thatcher, praised the SAS action in Gibraltar.

Sat. 15.10.88: Jim Craig, a prominent UDA member, and Victor Rainey, a pensioner, were shot dead and four others were injured in a UFF gun attack in the Castle Inn in east Belfast.

Wed. 19.10.88: The home secretary, Douglas Hurd, announced a TV and radio ban on "direct statements" by representatives of paramilitary organisations, their political wings and their supporters.

Wed. 26.10.88: The European Court of Human Rights ruled that the republic's government must decriminalise homosexuality.

Fri. 28.10.88: At Winchester, three Irish defendants were found guilty, by a majority verdict, of conspiracy to murder Tom King and sentenced to 25 years' imprisonment.

Sat. 29.10.88: Thousands of Orangemen marched in Hillsborough against the Anglo-Irish Agreement. The UUP leader, James Molyneaux, said that the Intergovernmental Council agreed by the prime minister, Margaret Thatcher, and the taoiseach, Charles Haughey, in 1980 might provide an acceptable alternative to the agreement.

Wed. 2.11.88: The Intergovernmental Conference agreed to broaden the scope of its review.

Mon. 7.11.88: The British foreign secretary, Sir Geoffrey Howe, met the tánaiste and foreign minister, Brian Lenihan, to discuss sea-bed rights and the Anglo-Irish Agreement.

Tues. 8.11.88: A draft order allowing Northern Ireland courts to draw an adverse inference from a suspect's exercise of the right to silence was passed at Westminster.

Thur. 10.11.88: In Derry, an off-duty soldier was shot and seriously wounded by the army, in mistake for a Provisional IRA member.

Mon. 14.11.88: The inquest opened in Craigavon into the deaths of three Provisional IRA men shot by the RUC in Co Armagh in 1982, one of the cases investigated by John Stalker. The Friends of the Union published a proposed replacement for the Anglo-Irish Agreement. The following day the third anniversary of the agreement was marked by small unionist protests.

Wed. 16.11.88: The security forces uncovered a loyalist arms cache that included an RPG-7 rocket launcher, Kalashnikov rifles and red berets with the badge of Ulster Resistance—the organisation launched a year earlier at a rally led by the DUP leader, Rev Ian Paisley. The DUP later said it had severed all connections with Ulster Resistance some time previously.

Thur. 17.11.88: The Craigavon inquest was adjourned pending a High Court judicial review, seeking to compel the three RUC men involved to give evidence in person.

Sat. 19.11.88: The RUC chief constable, Sir John Hermon, announced the closure of 11 small RUC stations in an effort to save £2 million.

Tues. 22.11.88: The Queen's Speech proposed legislation requiring electoral candidates to eschew violence, making the Prevention of Terrorism Act permanent and reforming fair employment law. The prime minister, Margaret Thatcher, announced the cutting of remission for terrorist prisoners from one half to one third.

Wed. 23.11.88: A pensioner and his teenage granddaughter in a passing car were killed during a Provisional IRA bomb attack on an RUC station at Benburb, Co Tyrone. Eight others were injured.

Fri. 25.11.88: The Belgian government turned down a British application for the extradition of Fr Patrick Ryan to face charges of conspiracy to murder and to cause explosions. He was deported to the republic.

Tues. 29.11.88: The European Court of Human Rights ruled that Britain was in breach of the European Convention on Human Rights by detaining suspects without charge for more than four days. It was revealed that there had been inadequacies in British warrants seeking the extradition of Fr Patrick Ryan, both from Belgium and from the republic. The prime minister, Margaret Thatcher, was strongly critical of the Belgian and Irish handling of the cases. The following Thursday the taoiseach, Charles Haughey, rejected Mrs Thatcher's criticism and the republic's attorney general, John Murray, wrote to his British counterpart, Sir Patrick Mayhew, seeking further information on the case.

Sat. 3.12.88: Margaret Thatcher and Charles Haughey discussed the Fr Patrick Ryan extradition case at the Rhodes EC summit.

Sun. 4.12.88: More than 8,000 people took part in a peace rally in Belfast city centre, organised by the four main churches.

Tues. 6.12.88: The Dáil voted to make the 1987 Extradition Act permanent.

Fri. 9.12.88: EC justice ministers agreed to review extradition. Four UDA members were sentenced to from three to 10 years' imprisonment for blackmail and extorting money from builders, in a case which arose out of a TV investigation by the journalist Roger Cook.

Mon. 12.12.88: The Provisional Sinn Féin publicity director, Danny Morrison, left Belfast for a four-day visit to Belgium.

Tues. 13.12.88: The republic's attorney general, John Murray, ruled that Fr Patrick Ryan would not be extradited and suggested that Britain use the Criminal Law (Jurisdiction) Act. The prime minister, Margaret Thatcher, said the decision was an "insult to the British people".

Wed. 14.12.88: At an Intergovernmental Conference meeting in Belfast the main topic was extradition.

Thur. 15.12.88: The PLO formally denied any links with the Provisional IRA. The Fair Employment Bill was introduced in the Commons, proposing a Fair Employment Commission with twice the resources of the FEA and a range of new powers. A bomb was found in an army housing estate in Antrim, the first of a series of such attacks. The following day the Provisional IRA said the army had seven days to evacuate army families from Northern Ireland.

Mon. 19.12.88: The British Labour leader, Neil Kinnock, said on a visit to Northern Ireland that to evacuate army families would be to give in to the Provisional IRA.

Tues. 20.12.88: In Belfast the Court of Appeal ruled that members of the security forces could be compelled to attend inquests and ordered a fresh inquest into the RUC killings in Co Armagh in 1982.

Wed. 21.12.88: Police discovered by accident a Provisional IRA bomb factory in south London. The French company Montupet announced a £90 million investment, including substantial government assistance, based on the old De Lorean site in west Belfast.

Thur. 22.12.88: The home secretary, Douglas Hurd, said the government would derogate from the European Convention on Human Rights and retain seven-day detention under the Prevention of Terrorism Act.

Wed. 28.12.88: It was reported that senior Northern Ireland judges had informed the secretary of state, Tom King, of their disquiet over the erosion of the right to silence and over suggestions that they might be involved in extensions of detention under the Prevention of Terrorism Act.

Fri. 30.12.88: A Provisional IRA end-of-year message threatened British politicians and the royal family.

1989

Thur. 5.1.89: The UUP leader, James Molyneaux, said he accepted the government had no intention of suspending the Anglo-Irish Agreement.

Sun. 8.1.89: A Boeing 737 flight from London to Belfast crashed on the M1 in Leicestershire, killing 47 people and injuring 79 others, many from Northern Ireland.

Thur. 12.1.89: The secretary of state, Tom King, announced that suspects would now be cautioned that their silence "may be treated in court as supporting any evidence against them".

Sun. 15.1.89: A former RUC reservist, Harold Keyes, from Ballycassidy, Co Fermanagh, was shot dead by the Provisional IRA at Ballintra, Co Donegal. The following day the west Fermanagh brigade of the Provisional IRA claimed the killing, saying that Mr Keyes had been working covertly for the RUC.

Mon. 16.1.89: The home secretary, Douglas Hurd, announced he was referring the case of the Guildford Four to the Court of Appeal.

Tues. 17.1.89: During the committee stage of the new Prevention of Terrorism Bill, a junior Home Office minister, Douglas Hogg, claimed that "certain solicitors" in Northern Ireland were "unduly sympathetic" to terrorist organisations. The SDLP said it would be on his head if one was assassinated. The National Union of Journalists (NUJ) secured a judicial review of the home secretary's ban on interviews with supporters of terrorism. The Maze escaper, Robert Russell, who had been extradited from the republic, became the first defendant to be denied the right to silence.

Wed. 18.1.89: The Standing Advisory Commission on Human Rights claimed that the government's recent security package might be "eroding confidence in the impartiality of the Northern Ireland administration". The criticism was rejected by the secretary of state, Tom King.

Mon. 23.1.89: Republican sources claimed that they had "stood down and disarmed" the west Fermanagh Provisional IRA unit responsible for the killing of Harold Keyes a week before, saying they had been unhappy with it for some time.

Wed. 25.1.89: A massive car bomb exploded at Derry courthouse, causing extensive damage to St Columb's Cathedral and surrounding church property.

Thur. 26.1.89: An inquiry under Lord Windlesham into the Thames TV documentary *Death on the Rock* found it had not prejudiced the inquest into the deaths of the three Provisional IRA members shot in Gibraltar.

Sun. 29.1.89: At the Provisional Sinn Féin ard fheis in Dublin, the party president, Gerry Adams, said the Provisional IRA had to be "careful and careful again" in avoiding civilian casualties.

Wed. 1.2.89: The leaders of the UUP, DUP and SDLP met the secretary of state, Tom King, in London for talks about Harland and Wolff and Shorts, both facing privatisation.

Thur. 2.2.89: The BBC disclosed that representatives of the DUP, UUP, SDLP and Alliance had met in Duisburg, West Germany, in October, but claims of a "historic breakthrough" were discounted by party leaders. There followed days of dispute as to whether the SDLP had rejected a unionist formula involving a temporary cessation of meetings of the Intergovernmental Conference.

Sun. 12.2.89: One of Northern Ireland's leading solicitors, Patrick Finucane, was shot dead by the UFF in his north Belfast home. The shooting led to condemnation from many sources, including the republic's government, of the remarks by the junior minister Douglas Hogg a month earlier that certain solicitors were "unduly sympathetic" to terrorist organisations.

Tues. 14.2.89: A Magherafelt Provisional Sinn Féin councillor, John Davey, was shot dead by loyalist gunmen close to his Co Derry home. The secretary of state, Tom King, said that, in the light of the Duisburg talks and the unionist–SDLP delegation on Harland and Wolff and Shorts, he would sound out the parties on the scope for political progress.

Mon. 20.2.89: The trial began in Belfast of Michael Stone, the loyalist charged with the murder of three people at Milltown cemetery the previous March. He denied a total of 38 charges, including six of murder.

Tues. 21.2.89: The prime minister, Margaret Thatcher, attended a service in Belfast for the victims of the M1 air disaster.

Thur. 23.2.89: The Police Authority announced that Hugh Annesley, a Dublin-born Metropolitan Police assistant commissioner, would be the next RUC chief constable. The leaders of the UUP, DUP and SDLP met the prime minister, Margaret Thatcher, in London for talks about Harland and Wolff and Shorts.

Sat. 25.2.89: At the Fianna Fáil ard fheis, the

party leader, Charles Haughey, invited unionists to talk, saying their future lay with the republic in "a partnership of equals". Unionist reaction was hostile.

Thur. 2.3.89: Provisional Sinn Féin launched a document calling for a diplomatic offensive by nationalist parties to secure a British withdrawal from Ireland.

Fri. 3.3.89: At Belfast Crown Court, Michael Stone was sentenced to life imprisonment for murdering six people, including three mourners at the funeral of the Gibraltar Provisional IRA trio.

Sun. 5.3.89: The former Alliance leader, John Cushnahan, was selected as a Fine Gael Euro-candidate in Munster.

Tues. 7.3.89: Three Protestant men were shot dead in Coagh, Co Tyrone. Claiming the killings, the Provisional IRA said that one was a UVF member, a claim disputed by his family, but admitted that the two others, both pensioners, had no loyalist or security force connections.

Wed. 8.3.89: Two soldiers were killed and six others were injured by a Provisional IRA land mine in Derry. The home secretary, Douglas Hurd, warned that Britian was entering a period of "high-level IRA activity".

Tues. 14.3.89: Disciplinary hearings against 20 low-ranking RUC officers, which had arisen out of the Stalker/Sampson affair and were expected to last for weeks, ended on their second day with 18 reprimands and one caution. The RUC said "the matter is now finished with".

Fri. 17.3.89: In a St Patrick's Day meeting with the taoiseach, Charles Haughey, the US president, George Bush, pledged support for fair employment and further US investment in Northern Ireland.

Mon. 20.3.89: Two senior RUC officers, Chief Supt Harold Breen and Supt Robert Buchanan, were shot dead in a Provisional IRA ambush outside Jonesborough, Co Armagh, while returning from a meeting with gardaí in Dundalk.

Wed. 22.3.89: The British government announced that the Belfast shipyard Harland and Wolff was to be sold to a management/worker consortium.

Mon. 27.3.89: About 8,000 Apprentice Boys paraded through Belfast to commemorate the 300th anniversary of the siege of Derry.

Sun. 2.4.89: The Soviet leader, Mikhail Gorbachëv, discussed the north with the taoiseach, Charles Haughey, during a brief Irish stopover.

Wed. 5.4.89: At a meeting of the Intergovernmental Conference at Stormont, ministers agreed to "deepen and widen" its work.

Thur. 6.4.89: An NCCL report called for a judicial inquiry into the Gibraltar SAS killings. The call was rejected the following day by the prime minister, Margaret Thatcher.

Mon. 10.4.89: Alasdair Frazer replaced Sir Barry Shaw as Northern Ireland's DPP. At the launch of an appeal for Craigavon councillors surcharged for defying a court direction not to discriminate against the GAA, the UUP leader,

James Molyneaux, said the GAA had shown "a great deal of sympathy with terrorists".

Tues. 11.4.89: Reporting restrictions on Provisional Sinn Féin were lifted in the run-up to district council elections in the north.

Wed. 12.4.89: A 19-year-old woman was killed and 34 people were injured in Warrenpoint, Co Down, by a Provisional IRA van bomb intended for the RUC station.

Tues. 18.4.89: The prime minister, Margaret Thatcher, defended the media restrictions on Provisional Sinn Féin and others, saying that "terrorists . . . exploit freedom only to undermine it". Amnesty International published a report calling for a judicial inquiry into the Gibraltar killings. The government rejected it. The SDLP leader, John Hume, and the Presbyterian moderator, Dr Godfrey Brown, had a "frank and constructive" meeting in Belfast.

Thur. 20.4.89: FEA reports found that the University of Ulster had four times as many Protestant as Catholic employees and Queen's University Belfast more than three times as many.

Sat. 22.4.89: Three members of the Ulster Resistance were arrested with a US arms dealer and a South African diplomat in a flat in Paris in what was allegedly an attempt to trade arms for missile parts from the Belfast aerospace company Shorts. The following day the DUP repeated that it had severed links with Ulster Resistance some time previously. Shorts announced a security review.

Fri. 28.5.89: Fr Patrick Ryan announced he would stand for the Munster constituency in the European elections on an anti-extradition ticket.

Mon. 1.5.89: The secretary of state, Tom King, was in Washington to discuss the International Fund for Ireland and the Fair Employment Bill with the Friends of Ireland group in Congress.

Mon. 8.5.89: While still denying any connection with Ulster Resistance, the DUP leader, Rev Ian Paisley, said he intended to visit its three members held in Paris, as a minister of religion, following relatives' requests.

Thur. 11.5.89: A Cookstown Provisional Sinn Féin councillor, Christopher Neeson, was jailed for three years for possession of a loaded revolver.

Wed. 17.5.89: There was a low turnout in the local government elections in Northern Ireland. Seats won were as follows: UUP 187, DUP 114, Alliance 37, SDLP 121, Provisional Sinn Féin 43, Workers' party 4, reflecting a slump in DUP support.

Wed. 24.5.89: The review of the workings of the Intergovernmental Conference was published.

Thur. 25.5.89: The taoiseach, Charles Haughey, declared a general election for June 15th, the same day as the European election. In the Commons the secretary of state, Tom King, attacked the unionists' refusal to take part in the Intergovernmental Conference review, saying, "the door is open to come in from the cold". Also in the Commons, the Fair Employment Bill was passed, following around 80 amendments.

Fri. 26.5.89: The NUJ failed in its attempt at the High Court in London to have the media ban declared unlawful.

Sat. 27.5.89: Fine Gael and the PDs announced an electoral pact in the Dáil election.

Wed. 31.5.89: Sir John Hermon retired as RUC chief constable, and was succeeded by Hugh Annesley, who was sworn in the following day.

Thur. 1.6.89: Two Andersonstown men were jailed for life for abetting the murders of the two corporals at a Provisional IRA funeral in west Belfast in March 1988. Reg Empey (UUP) was elected mayor of Belfast.

Tues. 6.6.89: In the third attack in just over a year, the £60 million Castle Court shopping development in central Belfast was extensively damaged by a Provisional IRA bomb. The former taoiseach, Garret FitzGerald, described the British government's approach to Northern Ireland as "inept" and "stupid".

Wed. 7.6.89: The secretary of state, Tom King, announced the sale of the Belfast aerospace company Shorts to the French-Canadian firm Bombardier.

Tues. 13.6.89: It was revealed that plastic bullets were to be issued to the UDR. The education minister, Brian Mawhinney, announced the latest version of his reform proposals, including a government commitment to integrated education and designation of Irish as on a par with other European languages.

Thur. 15.6.89: The turnout was only 49 per cent in the north's European elections. In the republic's general election, Fianna Fáil remained the largest party but with fewer seats. In the European elections, Rev Ian Paisley (DUP), John Hume (SDLP) and James Nicholson (UUP) were elected in the north.

Mon. 19.6.89: The former Alliance leader, John Cushnahan, was deemed elected, after several counts, as Fine Gael MEP for Munster.

Tues. 20.6.89: A Provisional IRA bomb exploded near Finaghy railway station in Belfast.

Mon. 26.6.89: The taoiseach, Charles Haughey, and the prime minister, Margaret Thatcher, met for half an hour at the EC summit in Dublin.

Wed. 28.6.89: The families of the Gibraltar Provisional IRA trio issued civil actions against the Ministry of Defence, alleging unlawful killing.

Thur. 29.6.89: The Fianna Fáil leader, Charles Haughey, failed to be re-elected taoiseach and accepted he would have to resign.

Sun. 2.7.89: A corporal was killed and his wife and three children were injured in a Provisional IRA booby-trap bomb in Hanover, West Germany.

Mon. 3.7.89: A triple-bomb Provisional IRA attack on Belfast Harbour airport damaged two aircraft and a control tower. Two other bombs failed to detonate.

Wed. 12.7.89: Speaking at one of the 19 Twelfth venues in Northern Ireland, the UUP leader, James Molyneaux, said the Anglo-Irish Agreement was dying. The Fianna Fáil leader, Charles Haughey, was finally re-elected taoiseach after Fianna Fáil unprecedentedly entered a coalition, its partner being the PDs.

Sun. 16.7.89: The taoiseach, Charles Haughey, denied he was against devolution for Northern Ireland and repeated his call to northern political parties to talk to him.

Tues. 18.7.89: The body of John McAnulty, a Warrenpoint businessman, was found on the border near Crossmaglen, Co Armagh. He had been kidnapped by the Provisional IRA the previous day.

Mon. 24.7.89: In a cabinet reshuffle, the secretary of state, Tom King, was moved to the Ministry of Defence and replaced by the Conservative party chair, Peter Brooke. The following day Mr Brooke flew into Belfast to be briefed.

Wed. 26.7.89: The Fair Employment Bill passed its final stage in the Commons, without Labour party support.

Mon. 31.7.89: A laundry van containing a 1,000lb Provisional IRA bomb was allowed inside the precincts of the High Court in Belfast. The bomb caused extensive damage to the front of the building.

Tues. 1.8.89: In a Yorkshire TV documentary, soldiers of the Royal Anglian Regiment admitted to harassing civilians routinely in Northern Ireland.

Wed. 2.8.89: The chair of the working party for the Anglo-Irish Interparliamentary Body appealed to unionists to take up the two seats that would be allocated to them.

Thur. 3.8.89: It was revealed that "roulement" tours for army battalions in Northern Ireland would be extended from four months to six. A senior Foreign Office civil servant, Patrick Heseldine, was dismissed for writing a letter to the *Guardian* accusing the prime minister, Margaret Thatcher, of double standards over the Fr Patrick Ryan extradition affair.

Wed. 9.8.89: In an otherwise relatively quiet anniversary of the introduction of internment, a 15-year-old Catholic boy, Seamus Duffy, was killed in north Belfast by a plastic bullet. The RUC said it very much regretted his death, which brought protests from non-unionist politicians, the republic's government and the Catholic Church. The former secretary of state, Merlyn Rees, called for the suspension of the Anglo-Irish Agreement.

Sun. 13.8.89: Several thousand people marched along the Falls Road in Belfast to mark the 20th anniversary of the deployment of British troops. The RUC chief constable, Hugh Annesley, unexpectedly appeared to supervise policing of the event. The following day there was sporadic rioting in west Belfast and 5,000 people marched in Derry.

Mon. 14.8.89: The secretary of state, Peter Brooke, met the unionist leaders, James Molyneaux and the Rev Ian Paisley. The former Labour prime minister James Callaghan called for a conditional suspension of the Anglo-Irish Agreement. The West Midlands serious crimes squad, members of which had been involved in the interrogations of the Birmingham Six, was disbanded following allegations of the fabrication of evidence in more recent cases. It was revealed that the Apprentice Boys had applied for a grant from the International Fund for Ireland towards a £0.5 million cultural centre. The Orange Order and unionist leaders condemned the application.

Tues. 15.8.89: Following his meeting with unionist leaders, the secretary of state, Peter Brooke, said the government might consider replacing the Anglo-Irish Agreement with "alternative" arrangements under paragraph 29 of the Intergovernmental Conference review document—paragraph 29 contains no such reference. Martin Galvin, publicity director of Noraid, was arrested in Derry for breaking an exclusion order. He was subsequently deported.

Sat. 19.8.89: The Provisional Sinn Féin president, Gerry Adams, Fr Patrick Ryan, and the British Labour MP George Galloway led a 10,000-strong march in Dublin demanding withdrawal of British troops.

Wed. 23.8.89: The bishop of Down and Connor, Dr Cahal Daly, said he would endorse without qualification the decision of any Catholic to join the RUC.

Thur. 24.8.89: The Provisional IRA said it was not its intention to close the Belfast–Dublin rail link by its campaign of disruption but to attack troops sent to clear the line.

Fri. 25.8.89: A Catholic man, Loughlin Maginn, was shot dead at his home in Rathfriland, Co Down, by the UFF, which claimed he was a Provisional IRA "liaison officer". The NIO released 143 life prisoners for a short "summer home leave" following the success of a similar initiative the previous Christmas.

Tues. 29.8.89: Within hours of the funeral of the Rathfriland man Loughlin Maginn, the UFF showed a BBC reporter security-force documents and photographs that described Maginn as "heavily traced". Nationalist politicians condemned this collusion and the republic's government said it would seek clarification. The following day the NIO said security-force members who gave information to terrorists would be "prosecuted with the full severity of the law". The SDLP said there had been a breakdown in confidence in the RUC and army. The UUP security spokesperson, Ken Maginnis, called the leak "totally unacceptable". The Labour party called for an independent inquiry.

Sat. 2.9.89: Patrick McKenna, a Catholic from the Ardoyne area of Belfast, was shot dead by two UVF men on a motorcycle on the Crumlin Road. Minutes later one of the assailants was shot dead and the other injured by plain-clothes soldiers.

Sun. 3.9.89: The RUC seized documents from the UDA headquarters in east Belfast.

Mon. 4.9.89: It was revealed that a soldier, Cpl Cameron Hastie, who had been given an 18-month suspended sentence for passing information on republican suspects to the UVF, had returned to duty with his regiment. The SDLP called the decision "appalling", Alliance said it was "outrageous", Fine Gael found it "grossly offensive" and the UUP said it showed "a degree of contempt . . . for the entire community". The republic's government expressed "most serious concern". The following day the Ministry of Defence said Cpl Hastie would not serve in Northern Ireland again but described him as "a very fine soldier". The bishop of Down and Connor, Dr Cahal Daly, called for a public inquiry into collusion claims. The minister of defence, Tom King, was later described as being "incandescent with rage" over the army's decision to return Cpl Hastie to his regiment.

Thur. 7.9.89: Heidi Hazel, the West German wife of a British soldier, was shot dead by the Provisional IRA in her car in Dortmund.

Fri. 8.9.89: The British TUC called for the repeal of the Prevention of Terrorism Act and the removal of the broadcasting ban.

Mon. 11.9.89: Following the disappearance of a security document from Ballykinlar UDR base in Co Down, the SDLP called for the disbanding of the regiment. The republic's government said the next Intergovernmental Conference should be devoted exclusively to security. Two serving UDR soldiers were charged with the murder of Loughlin Maginn in Rathfriland on August 25th.

Tues. 12.9.89: During a visit to Northern Ireland, the prime minister, Margaret Thatcher, described the UDR as "a very, very, very brave group of men". The Irish National Congress, a product of Provisional Sinn Féin's "broad front" strategy, was launched in Dublin.

Wed. 13.9.89: The republic's foreign minister, Gerry Collins, met the home secretary, Douglas Hurd, in London for talks on the Birmingham Six. The secretary of state, Peter Brooke, said: "There can be no place in the security forces of Northern Ireland for those who betray their trust." Provisional Sinn Féin released a dossier of court cases indicating the UDR's "criminal and sectarian record". The DUP leader, Rev Ian Paisley, attacked "hysterical statements" on the regiment.

Thur. 14.9.89: The RUC admitted that a photomontage of republican suspects had disappeared from Dunmurry RUC station in Belfast. The chief constable, Hugh Annesley, appointed the deputy chief constable of Cambridgeshire, John Stevens, to investigate the theft as well as the Loughlin Maginn and Ballykinlar leaks. Mr Stevens arrived to begin his investigation on the 16th.

Fri. 15.9.89: The Intergovernmental Conference adjourned after meeting for seven hours in Dublin, the republic having put several demands about the UDR to which the British had promised to reply. The republic's foreign minister, Gerry Collins, spoke of the "total disillusionment" of nationalists and said the Anglo-Irish Agreement would be "held up to question".

Tues. 19.9.89: The SDLP released a photomontage allegedly leaked from a Belfast RUC station. RUC headquarters said it would be included in the Stevens inquiry and admitted that two photomontages and not one had gone missing from the RUC station in Dunmurry. The SDLP leader, John Hume, met the secretary of state, Peter Brooke, to discuss the leaks affair and the taoiseach, Charles Haughey, said the apparent collusion was "deeply disturbing".

Wed. 20.9.89: The SDLP deputy leader, Seamus Mallon, said three of his constituents in Newry had been sent a photocopy of a security-force document in which they had been named, accompanied by a UFF threat. Ulster Resistance said it had an "excellent" flow of information. The taoiseach, Charles Haughey, said an "appalling picture" was building up.

Thur. 21.9.89: Following a meeting with Charles Haughey, the republic's justice minister, Ray Burke, said his government was seeking "a justification from the British authorities of the very existence of the UDR".

Fri. 22.9.89: A Provisional IRA bomb exploded at the Royal Marines School of Music at Deal in Kent, killing 11 bandsmen and injuring 21 others. The taoiseach, Charles Haughey, sent a message to the prime minister, Margaret Thatcher, offering sympathy. The DUP leader, Rev Ian Paisley, blamed the Anglo-Irish Agreement. Provisional Sinn Féin said the British government should agree to peace talks.

Sat. 23.9.89: The *Independent* newspaper revealed that photographs of 60 republican suspects, 25 of them from the republic, had been delivered to its Belfast correspondent. The revelation prompted security-force and Justice Department meetings with the taoiseach, Charles Haughey, in the republic. The British Labour party said the broadcasting ban had been "extremely damaging" and would be removed by a future Labour government. It emerged that the Anglo-Irish Interparliamentary Body was to meet in secret for at least a year after its first meeting in February 1990.

Thur. 28.9.89: It was announced that the chair of the International Fund for Ireland, Charles Brett, was to be replaced at the end of his three-year term by the Ballymena businessman John McGuckian.

Fri. 29.9.89: At the UN General Assembly, the republic's foreign minister, Gerry Collins, again issued an invitation to unionists to talk to the taoiseach, Charles Haughey. The UUP leader, James Molyneaux, said there would be no discussions with the Anglo-Irish Agreement in place.

Tues. 3.10.89: The secretary of state, Peter Brooke, confirmed that the UDR would be issued with plastic bullets, subject to "very, very, very tight control". He said there was no need for fundamental reform of the UDR. The republic's government said Mr Brooke's remarks were "extremely unhelpful".

Thur. 5.10.89: An Intergovernmental Conference in London, discussing the UDR and the collusion affair, broke up after a record eight hours with the shortest ever communiqué. The republic's foreign minister, Gerry Collins, said a "big gap" remained between the two sides. After posting up pro-UDR posters in Dublin, the DUP leader, Rev Ian Paisley, launched a "Hands off the UDR" petition.

Sat. 7.10.89: Security forces foiled an ambitious attempted Provisional IRA escape from Crumlin Road prison in Belfast involving explosives inside the prison and a 500lb bomb, get-away cars and diversionary incidents outside.

Sun. 8.10.89: Twenty-eight UDR soldiers, 27 from 7/10 battalion in Belfast, were arrested in early-morning swoops by 300 RUC officers. Photomontages and ammunition were seized. The DUP called it a "publicity stunt". The SDLP asked, "Is this for the optics or is it for real?"

Tues. 10.10.89: The Conservative conference in Blackpool voted overwhelmingly to support party organisation in Northern Ireland.

Thur. 12.10.89: The republic's DPP said there was insufficient evidence to prosecute Fr Patrick Ryan under the Criminal Law (Jurisdiction) Act. The secretary of state, Peter Brooke, said he was disappointed.

Tues. 17.10.89: The British DPP, Alan Green, said it would be "wrong for the Crown to seek to sustain" the convictions of the Guildford Four.

Wed. 18.10.89: The Intergovernmental Conference met at Stormont for a record nine hours. The communiqué indicated that the British side would "not contemplate" any change in the role of the UDR but specified further controls and safeguards.

Thur. 19.10.89: The Guildford Four were released by the Court of Appeal in London, though one, Paul Hill, was rearrested to face an appeal in Belfast over a separate conviction. The lord chief justice, Lord Lane, said the police officers who interviewed the four "must have lied". The home secretary, Douglas Hurd, ordered a judicial inquiry.

Fri. 20.10.89: Paul Hill was released on bail at the Court of Appeal in Belfast. The republic's foreign minister, Gerry Collins, said the release of the Guildford Four had had "a very positive effect" on Anglo-Irish relations.

Sat. 21.10.89: At the UUP conference in Enniskillen, Co Fermanagh, the party leader, James Molyneaux, set out preconditions for political dialogue.

Mon. 23.10.89: The republic's foreign minister, Gerry Collins, requested an urgent meeting with the home secretary, Douglas Hurd, to press for a review of the Birmingham Six case.

Thur. 26.10.89: The Provisional IRA shot dead an RAF corporal and his six-month-old daughter in the family car near his base at Wildenrath, West Germany. The following day the Provisional IRA expressed its "profound regret" for the death of the child.

Sat. 28.10.89: About 800 people joined a "peace train" between Belfast and Dublin to protest against Provisional IRA attacks on the line. The return journey was halted by a bomb scare. The Provisional Sinn Féin president, Gerry Adams, attacked the bishop of Down and Connor, Dr Cahal Daly, as an "enthusiastic supporter of the RUC".

Fri. 3.11.89: In an interview for various media, the secretary of state, Peter Brooke, said the Provisional IRA could not be defeated militarily and he would not rule out talks with Provisional Sinn Féin if violence ended. In that eventuality he promised the government would be "imaginative". The statement was attacked by unionist leaders, but welcomed by the SDLP, by the taoiseach, Charles Haughey, and by the Provisional Sinn Féin president, Gerry Adams, who noted the "more moderate tone" of the remarks. Downing Street and the NIO said there had been no change in policy.

Tues. 7.11.89: The new home secretary, David Waddington, rejected an appeal by Birmingham church leaders to reopen the case of the Birmingham Six.

Fri. 10.11.89: The leader of the Northern Ireland Conservatives, Dr Laurence Kennedy, said their acceptance into the Tory fold would "make the Anglo-Irish Agreement pale into insignificance in due course".

Wed. 15.11.89: A unionist "human chain" to mark the fourth anniversary of the agreement drew only hundreds instead of the 300,000 predicted by its organiser, Rev Martin Smyth.

Thur. 16.11.89: Provisional Sinn Féin denied there was any debate within the republican movement about the "armed struggle", reiterated its full support for the Provisional IRA and called on the secretary of state, Peter Brooke, to enter talks without a ceasefire precondition.

Sat. 18.11.89: Three paratroopers were killed by a Provisional IRA land mine near Mayobridge, Co Down. A soldier and his wife were seriously injured in a Provisional IRA bomb attack on their car in Colchester, Essex.

Tues. 21.11.89: After a meeting with security advisers, the secretary of state, Peter Brooke, said the IRA would never be allowed to win.

Thur. 23.11.89: In the Commons, the SDLP deputy leader, Seamus Mallon, MP, praised Peter Brooke's earlier remarks about the possibility of talks with Sinn Féin and described him as "a man of courage and vision". The European Parliament voted to set up an inquiry into the convictions of the Birmingham Six.

Sat. 25.11.89: The Catholic primate, Cardinal Tomás Ó Fiaich, urged the British government to state that it would not stay in the north "for all time", causing a flurry of comment from political parties, churchmen and government in the following days.

Mon. 27.11.89: Two Provisional IRA bombs exploded at Shorts, destroying a light aircraft.

Wed. 29.11.89: Two men, one of whom had been convicted of Provisional IRA gun-running in New York in 1985, were shot dead by the UVF in a bar in Ardboe, Co Tyrone. The secretary of state, Peter Brooke, said the RUC would receive an additional £45 million in the next financial year.

Thur. 30.11.89: The Intergovernmental Conference met in Dublin and agreed to set a number of meetings in the coming year. The republic's foreign minister, Gerry Collins, said that though the Anglo-Irish Agreement would not be suspended he hoped unionists would make use of the two-month break before the next meeting to engage in talks. The DUP later said that two months would not be enough.

Wed. 6.12.89: Sixteen people were detained by the RUC in connection with the Stevens inquiry into collusion. One, Sam Duddy, a leading member of the UDA, was charged two days later with possessing a document containing information about an IRA suspect.

Thur. 7.12.89: Twenty-one people were injured by a 500lb Provisional IRA van bomb which caused extensive damage to Lisburn town centre. RUC figures showed there had been 155 punishment shootings in Northern Ireland in 1989 to date, compared with 66 for the previous year.

Sat. 9.12.89: The taoiseach, Charles Haughey, met the prime minister, Margaret Thatcher, at the EC summit in Strasbourg. He called for the Birmingham Six to be moved to open prisons.

Mon. 11.12.89: The Home Office said the Birmingham Six were to be redefined as "category B" prisoners, with fewer restrictions on visits.

Wed. 13.12.89: Two soldiers were killed and one was seriously injured in a Provisional IRA attack on a border checkpoint at Rosslea, Co Fermanagh.

Thur. 14.12.89: The UUP MP John Taylor said a gap in meetings of the Intergovernmental Conference would be enough to bring unionists to talks. The Education Reform Order, *inter alia* incorporating "cultural heritage" and "education for mutual understanding" into the school curriculum, and encouraging integrated education, completed its Commons stages.

Mon. 18.12.89: The RUC again raided the headquarters of the UDA in east Belfast in connection with the Stevens inquiry.

Wed. 20.12.89: The FEA report into Queen's University was published, showing that of locally born staff only 21 per cent were Catholic.

1990

Mon. 1.1.90: The new Fair Employment Act came into force, requiring all but small companies to monitor the religious make-up of their workforces, setting up a Fair Employment Commission and establishing a Fair Employment Tribunal.

Thur. 4.1.90: A new Community Relations Council was launched at Stormont by the education minister, Brian Mawhinney.

Fri. 5.1.90: The RUC said two guns had been stolen from military personnel in Lisburn but had been recovered. It was later reported that the incident appeared to be connected with the security-force killing of three men on January 13th.

Mon. 8.1.90: The Provisional Sinn Féin publicity director, Danny Morrison, was arrested with eight other men in a house in Lenadoon, west Belfast. The RUC also raided the party's offices in Andersonstown and on the Falls Road, seizing documents, discs and tapes. A further 22 loyalists were detained in connection with the Stevens inquiry.

Tues. 9.1.90: The secretary of state, Peter Brooke, said he had detected "common ground" between northern politicians about devolution. The government would operate the Anglo-Irish Agreement "sensitively", he said, calling for unionists to end their "internal exile". The statement brought praise from most parts of the political spectrum.

Wed. 10.1.90: Danny Morrison of Provisional Sinn Féin was charged with conspiracy to murder and membership of the IRA, in connection with the alleged imprisonment of an informer. Fire broke out at the Stevens inquiry office at Seapark, Co Antrim.

Thur. 11.1.90: Seven more loyalists, including the west Belfast UDA leader, Tommy Lyttle, were detained at the behest of the Stevens inquiry.

Fri. 12.1.90: Four men originally from Northern Ireland were charged in Florida with plotting to buy a Stinger anti-aircraft missile.

Sat. 13.1.90: Undercover soldiers shot dead three men, armed only with replica weapons, involved in an attempted robbery at a bookmaker's at the Whiterock Road/Falls Road junction in west Belfast. Local politicians called for an inquiry after eyewitnesses said the soldiers had fired repeatedly into the bodies of the men as they lay on the ground.

Thur. 18.1.90: Kevin Taylor, the Manchester businessman whose association with John Stalker led to the latter's removal from the "shoot to kill" inquiry, was acquitted of fraud. Mr Stalker claimed he had a document about a crucial meeting that led to his removal, with participants identified by initials. The following day he said he would produce it if the cabinet requested it.

Thur. 25.1.90: John Stalker presented his document to the Home Office. By the initials it appeared to name Douglas Hurd, then home secretary, and Tom King, then Northern Ireland secretary, among others. The Home Office said it showed that only the "appropriate police authorities" had been involved in removing Mr Stalker from his inquiry.

Sun. 28.1.90: Charles Love, a 16-year-old Provisional Sinn Féin member from Strabane, Co Tyrone, was killed in what the Provisional IRA described as a "freak accident" when he was hit by debris from a Provisional IRA blast at the Bloody Sunday commemoration in Derry.

Tues. 30.1.90: The armed forces minister, Archie Hamilton, contradicting years of denials, admitted that the former army press officer in Northern Ireland, Colin Wallace, had been engaged in "disinformation". Mr Hamilton announced a limited inquiry into Mr Wallace's dismissal. The following day a further Ministry of Defence inquiry was announced into how the relevant papers in Mr Wallace's case had gone missing. It emerged on May 17th that they had been destroyed in 1986.

Mon. 5.2.90: The secretary of state, Peter Brooke, said in a letter to the unionist leaders that there was "increased recognition that new arrangements are needed" and that unionist preconditions did not present "any insuperable obstacle" to talks.

Sat. 10.2.90: The RUC chief constable, Hugh Annesley, issued a force strategy document.

Sun. 11.2.90: Three soldiers were injured, one seriously, when the Provisional IRA forced down a helicopter with machine-gun fire near Clogher, Co Tyrone.

Mon. 12.2.90: The UUP MP for Upper Bann, Harold McCusker, died of cancer, aged 50.

Tues. 13.2.90: The Derry UDA commander, Cecil McKnight, was among four men detained in the city at the behest of the Stevens inquiry.

Sun. 18.2.90: Martin McGuinness, a leading Provisional Sinn Féin member, described Peter Brooke as the first secretary of state "with some understanding of Irish history" and urged him to spell out what he meant by "imaginative steps" in response to an abandonment of violence by the IRA.

Mon. 19.2.90: The unionist leaders, James Molyneaux and Rev Ian Paisley, met the secretary of state, Peter Brooke, at Stormont and gave him four weeks to say whether he would consider an alternative to the Anglo-Irish

Agreement. There was a flurry of comment from security-force commanders and politicians north and south after a BBC *Panorama* programme on the UDR, which reported that almost 200 members or ex-members had been convicted of serious offences. The UDR commander, Brig Charles Ritchie, admitted his patrols were not briefed on loyalist suspects.

Thur. 22.2.90: The leaders of Fine Gael, Alan Dukes and Peter Barry, met the secretary of state, Peter Brooke, at Stormont and said the UDR should be phased out.

Sat. 24.2.90: It was leaked that the taoiseach, Charles Haughey, was to attend an Institute of Directors conference on April 11th in Belfast.

Mon. 26.2.90: The 50-strong British–Irish Interparliamentary Body met for the first time in London, boycotted by unionist MPs.

Tues. 27.2.90: The *Irish Times* published what it believed to be the proposals presented in January 1988 by the unionist leaders to the then secretary of state, Tom King, for an alternative British–Irish agreement. The UUP leader, James Molyneaux, said the report was not completely authentic.

Thur. 1.3.90: The Supreme Court in Dublin rejected the appeal by the McGimpsey brothers that the Anglo-Irish Agreement contravened the republic's constitution. In so doing, the court defined the sovereignty claim in articles two and three as a "constitutional imperative".

Fri. 2.3.90: After a meeting of the Intergovernmental Conference in London, the republic's foreign minister, Gerry Collins, said RUC accompaniment of UDR patrols was "exceptionally important".

Tues. 6.3.90: The McGimpsey brothers and the UUP MP Ken Maginnis met the secretary of state, Peter Brooke, urging him to press the republic's government to seek to amend articles two and three of the constitution.

Thur. 8.3.90: The Law Lords, overturning a Northern Ireland Court of Appeal judgement, ruled that the RUC officers involved in the first of the "shoot to kill" inquests in Craigavon did not have to attend in person.

Tues. 13.3.90: The Supreme Court in Dublin upheld the appeal against extradition of two of the 1983 Maze escapers, James Clarke and Dermot Finucane, on the grounds of the risk to them from prison officers, none of whom had been disciplined for post-escape beatings. The Finucane judgement also reversed several years of judicial narrowing of the scope of the "political offence" exemption from extradition. The decision brought vociferous reaction from the British government and unionist politicians.

Wed. 21.3.90: The home secretary, David Waddington, announced a further inquiry into the Birmingham Six case.

Thur. 22.3.90: The Czech president, Václav Havel, claimed that the previous Stalinist regime had sold 1,000 tons of Semtex explosive to Libya.

Sun. 25.3.90: The Provisional IRA was adamant that it had shot dead two undercover soldiers in an attack at Cappagh, Co Tyrone, the previous evening. The incident was denied by the security forces but supported by some local evidence.

Wed. 28.3.90: A Granada TV drama-documentary named four people it alleged had carried out the Birmingham pub bombings of 1974. The prime minister, Margaret Thatcher, attacked it as "trial by television".

Sat. 31.3.90: The tánaiste, Brian Lenihan, said that as a result of the Intergovernmental Conference, the RUC was now "established as a professional police force holding the balance".

Thur. 5.4.90: The Stevens report into security-force/loyalist collusion was submitted to the RUC chief constable, Hugh Annesley.

Fri. 6.4.90: Following the precedent set in the Finucane case three weeks previously, the Supreme Court quashed an extradition order against the former Provisional Sinn Féin MP Owen Carron, again giving rise to strong criticism from the British government and unionist politicians.

Mon. 9.4.90: Four UDR soldiers were killed when their Land Rover passed over a Provisional IRA land mine outside Downpatrick, Co Down.

Wed. 11.4.90: Only about 400 loyalists joined a protest in Belfast against the presence of the taoiseach, Charles Haughey, at the Institute of Directors conference.

Thur. 19.4.90: The Intergovernmental Conference, meeting for over six hours in London, agreed that extradition should be reviewed. The conference reconvened for an hour the following day.

Fri. 20.4.90: The taoiseach, Charles Haughey, met the prime minister, Margaret Thatcher, in London and said afterwards that extradition had "hardly been touched on".

Thur. 26.4.90: Mary Robinson was selected as a Labour candidate for the republic's presidency.

Fri. 27.4.90: The Winchester Three had their convictions for conspiracy to murder the then secretary of state, Tom King, quashed by the Court of Appeal on the grounds that remarks by Mr King at the time of their trial had prejudiced their case. The three were rearrested and served with exclusion orders.

Sat. 28.4.90: The Workers' party leader, Proinsias de Rossa, called for the removal of articles two and three from the republic's constitution.

Fri. 4.5.90: In a letter to the unionist leaders, James Molyneaux and Rev Ian Paisley, the secretary of state, Peter Brooke, accepted their first precondition for talks, that he would consider proposals for an alternative to the Anglo-Irish Agreement.

Sun. 6.5.90: The UUP leader, James Molyneaux, reacting to Peter Brooke's letter, said the Intergovernmental Conference would have to be suspended and the Maryfield secretariat "closed down completely" before talks could take place. The Fine Gael spokesperson on Northern Ireland, Peter Barry, said Molyneaux was "moving the goalposts".

Tues. 8.5.90: The Catholic primate, Cardinal Tomás Ó Fiaich, died of heart failure in Lourdes.

Fri. 11.5.90: After over two hours, talks in London between the secretary of state, Peter Brooke, and the unionist leaders, James Molyneaux and Rev Ian Paisley, were "adjourned". There was agreement on the unionists' second precondition for talks—a predetermined gap between Intergovernmental Conferences—but Mr Paisley said: "The stumbling block is the secretariat, full stop."

Tues. 15.5.90: The funeral of the Catholic primate, Cardinal Tomás Ó Fiaich, took place in Armagh.

Wed. 16.5.90: A sergeant was killed and another soldier injured by a Provisional IRA bomb under their van outside an army recruiting office in Wembley in London.

Thur. 17.5.90: A summary was published of the Stevens inquiry report into security-force/loyalist collusion. It said collusion was "neither widespread nor institutionalised" but recommended tighter controls on documents and stricter UDR vetting.

Fri. 18.5.90: David Trimble of the UUP was declared winner of the Upper Bann by-election, called after the death of Harold McCusker. The first Conservative candidate in a Northern Ireland election, Colette Jones, lost her deposit.

Mon. 21.5.90: An inquiry under Sir John May into the convictions of the Maguire family and friends—seven people in all—implicated by the "confessions" of two of the Guildford Four, opened at the Old Bailey in London.

Tues. 22.5.90: It was reported that a Bank of Ireland study had found that the annual cost of the "troubles" to the British and Irish governments was £410 million. The unionist leaders, James Molyneaux and Rev Ian Paisley, had four hours of talks with the secretary of state, Peter Brooke, in London. After meeting the SDLP leader, John Hume, two days later, Mr Brooke said everyone had shown flexibility.

Sun. 27.5.90: The Provisional IRA shot dead two Australian lawyers in front of their partners in Roermond in Holland. The victims had a British-registered car and the Provisional IRA later said it "deeply regretted" their deaths.

Mon. 28.5.90: The secretary of state, Peter Brooke, met the taoiseach, Charles Haughey, and the republic's foreign minister, Gerry Collins, in Dublin, to report "steady progress" with his talks initiative.

Tues. 29.5.90: The new chair of the Northern Ireland Police Federation, Sam Beattie, called for selective internment.

Thur. 31.5.90: Ulster Television announced it would not be showing a two-part Yorkshire TV drama-documentary on the Stalker affair, *Shoot to Kill*, though it was to be broadcast in all other independent TV regions. The RUC said it contained "false and inaccurate information".

Fri. 1.6.90: The Provisional IRA shot dead a young soldier and injured two other recruits at Lichfield railway station in Staffordshire.

Sat. 2.6.90: The Provisional IRA shot dead an army major in Dortmund in Germany.

Tues. 5.6.90: The secretary of state, Peter Brooke, said talks on internal arrangements in Northern Ireland were a matter for the British government and the Ulster parties alone. Despite a call from Fine Gael for a contradiction, there was no response from the republic's government.

Wed. 6.6.90: A retired RUC reservist and his wife, James and Ellen Sefton, were killed and another elderly couple were injured by a Provisional IRA bomb attached to the Seftons' car in north Belfast.

Thur. 7.6.90: The deputy prime minister, Sir Geoffrey Howe, said there had never been a "shoot to kill policy".

Fri. 8.6.90: The Provisional Sinn Féin president, Gerry Adams, said the killing of the Seftons could not be condoned, and described his party's relationship to the Provisional IRA as "critical support".

Sat. 9.6.90: Seventeen people were injured by a Provisional IRA bomb at a birthday party at a Territorial Army company headquarters in Finsbury, north London.

Mon. 11.6.90: The secretary of state, Peter Brooke, and the republic's foreign minister, Gerry Collins, met for over three hours in London to discuss the talks initiative, in which Mr Brooke said there were still loose ends.

Wed. 13.6.90: Lord O'Neill—as Capt Terence O'Neill, Stormont prime minister from 1963 to 1969—died at his home in Hampshire, aged 75. The taoiseach, Charles Haughey, after a meeting in London with the prime minister, Margaret Thatcher, said they were "very satisfied" with the "very determined and sincere efforts" of the secretary of state, Peter Brooke, and his government would be "fully involved" in discussions about any arrangements transcending the Anglo-Irish Agreement.

Thur. 14.6.90: Counsel for the DPP told the May inquiry that the convictions in the Maguire family case were "unsafe and unsatisfactory". The home secretary, David Waddington, said their case would be referred back to the Court of Appeal.

Fri. 15.6.90: After meeting the secretary of state, Peter Brooke, the SDLP deputy leader, Seamus Mallon, said the Maryfield secretariat would remain in place "in its entirety". Mr Brooke said he was "astonished" by the progress so far and envisaged talks after the holidays.

Sat. 16.6.90: The DUP deputy leader, Peter Robinson, said suspension of the workings of the Maryfield secretariat would be necessary before talks. Donna Maguire, from Newry, who was acquitted in February in Dublin of carrying explosives and whose extradition had unsuccessfully been sought by Germany in connection with Provisional IRA attacks on British forces there, was arrested near an arms dump in Belgium. Gerard Harte, from Lurgan, was arrested across the Dutch border. Two days later Dutch police arrested a third member of the alleged Provisional IRA unit, Sean Hick, from Glengeary, Co Dublin, and the day after, a further member, Paul Hughes, from Newry, was arrested.

Wed. 20.6.90: With a judicial challenge imminent, the secretary of state, Peter Brooke, announced that the 1971 Payments for Debt (Emergency Provisions) Act would be repealed.

Thur. 21.6.90: Christopher Hanna, a former senior prison officer at the Maze, was jailed for life for aiding and abetting the Provisional IRA murder of the vice-chair of the Prison Officers'

Association in Belfast in 1988, by giving information to a female Provisional IRA intelligence officer with whom he had flirted. There were Provisional IRA bomb attacks in Cookstown and Dungannon, Co Tyrone, and at an RAF base in London.

Mon. 25.6.90: A Provisional IRA bomb at the Carlton Club in London, which has traditional Conservative associations, injured two patrons. The following day the Provisional IRA said it had "struck at the heart of Tory rule".

Tues. 26.6.90: At the European summit in Dublin, EC leaders expressed "categoric condemnation of all forms of terrorism".

Wed. 27.6.90: Four hours of talks in Dublin between the secretary of state, Peter Brooke, and the republic's foreign minister, Gerry Collins, failed to resolve the impasse over Dublin and SDLP opposition to the formula agreed by unionist leaders and London, that there be "substantial progress" in inter-party talks in the north before north–south talks began.

Thur. 28.6.90: The Provisional IRA said the aim of its campaign in Britain and Europe was "to hit the enemy on as many fronts as possible and to stretch their resources and nerves". An inquest jury into the killing of 15-year-old Seamus Duffy by a plastic bullet the previous August found he had not been rioting when he was killed. The two RUC officers involved had refused to appear.

Sat. 30.6.90: Two RUC constables were shot dead by the Provisional IRA in central Belfast.

Sun. 1.7.90: The freedom of the city of Dublin was conferred on Nelson Mandela, the African National Congress deputy president. Around 500,000 people thronged Dublin to welcome home the republic's World Cup soccer team.

Mon. 2.7.90: Nelson Mandela said there should be talks between the British government and the IRA, citing the "precedent" of Zimbabwe. The Provisional Sinn Féin president, Gerry Adams, demanded a "positive response" and urged the taoiseach, Charles Haughey, to endorse the call. Five RUC officers, three soldiers and two civilians were injured in a Provisional IRA RPG-7 rocket attack on Grosvenor Road police station in Belfast.

Tues. 3.7.90: In response to the comments by Nelson Mandela, the secretary of state, Peter Brooke, said everyone had a vote in Northern Ireland, which was not a colony.

Thur. 5.7.90: Despite intensive negotiations between London and Dublin and last-minute meetings with the unionist leaders and the SDLP, the secretary of state, Peter Brooke, was unable to report to the Commons that agreement had been reached on a schedule for talks. The stumbling block, he said, was at what point the republic's government would enter the discussions. The unionists blamed Dublin.

Sun. 8.7.90: The taoiseach, Charles Haughey, said his government was not to blame for the delay in political talks. All the talks had to take place "within an agreed time-frame", he said.

Wed. 11.7.90: A major review of the Emergency Provisions Act by Lord Colville recommended re-enactment in 1992 of the main powers but proposed various changes.

Thur. 12.7.90: Speaking at a Twelfth field, the UUP leader, James Molyneaux, said Ulster had come "close to a deliverance" the previous week until Dublin had prevented the secretary of state, Peter Brooke, making his Commons statement.

Fri. 13.7.90: A six-hour meeting in London between Peter Brooke and the republic's foreign minister, Gerry Collins, failed to resolve the talks impasse.

Mon. 16.7.90: A round of talks took place between Mr Brooke and the unionist leaders, Rev Ian Paisley and James Molyneaux; between the taoiseach, Charles Haughey, and John Hume and Seamus Mallon of the SDLP; and between Mr Brooke, Mr Hume and Mr Mallon. But the talks impasse remained.

Tues. 17.7.90: A five-hour meeting of the Intergovernmental Conference in Belfast again failed to bridge the gap on political talks between Dublin and London.

Fri. 20.7.90: A Provisional IRA bomb at the London Stock Exchange caused extensive damage but no casualties.

Tues. 24.7.90: A 1,000lb Provisional IRA bomb killed three RUC constables in a car outside Armagh. It also killed a nun and injured her passenger, a young social worker, in a passing car.

Wed. 25.7.90: The Independent Commission for Police Complaints report said that out of 803 complaints investigated in 1988–89 only two had resulted in officers being found guilty of a disciplinary offence.

Thur. 26.7.90: The secretary of state, Peter Brooke, said he had not yet secured agreement for talks but would renew his initiative in September.

Fri. 27.7.90: At the funeral in Middletown of Sr Catherine Dunne, one of the victims of the Provisional IRA bomb of the previous Tuesday, a message was read from the Pope condemning the "grievous injustice and futility" of violence.

Mon. 30.7.90: Ian Gow, Conservative MP for Eastbourne, was killed by a Provisional IRA bomb attached to his car outside his home in Hankham, Sussex. He had resigned as a junior Treasury minister in 1985 over the Anglo-Irish Agreement. Desmond Ellis had his appeal against extradition to Britain rejected in the High Court in Dublin.

Sun. 5.8.90: The Provisional IRA declared a week-long amnesty for members working secretly for the security forces.

Wed. 8.8.90: The secretary-general of the Norwegian Helsinki Committee on Human Rights, Bjorn Cato Funnemark, launched a report on Northern Ireland in Belfast and said that Britain's human rights record was "appalling".

Fri. 10.8.90: A conference, "Ireland—the Way Forward" was held at the Europa Hotel in central Belfast, attended by some 400 people, including many foreign commentators and republican activists.

Wed. 15.8.90: The UUP leader, James Molyneaux, said he was "pessimistic" about the talks initiative of the secretary of state, Peter Brooke.

Thur. 16.8.90: In a *Spectator* interview, the former Master of the Rolls, Lord Denning, said

he believed the Guildford Four were guilty and that if the Birmingham Six had been hanged "we shouldn't have all these campaigns to get them released".

Tues. 21.8.90: The SDLP celebrated its 20th anniversary. It was announced that Lieut-Gen John Wilsey was to succeed Lieut-Gen Sir John Waters as GOC.

Fri. 24.8.90: The Belfast teacher Brian Keenan was released in Damascus after 1,574 days in captivity in Beirut.

Sun. 26.8.90: After the SDLP had proposed making Brian Keenan a freeman of the city of Belfast, a political row erupted when the independent unionist councillor Frank Millar said Mr Keenan should stay with his "friend" the taoiseach, Charles Haughey.

Tues. 28.8.90: In the latest of a series of controversial "political vetting" cases, the NIO withdrew funding from the west Belfast branch of the Irish language body Glor na nGael, because of alleged paramilitary links.

Wed. 29.8.90: The home secretary, David Waddington, said the case of the Birmingham Six would be referred back to the Court of Appeal.

Mon. 3.9.90: The UUP said the talks initiative by the secretary of state, Peter Brooke, had "run into the sands" since his failure to deliver his intended statement to the Commons on July 5th.

Thur. 6.9.90: Austin Currie, formerly of the SDLP and now a Fine Gael TD for Dublin West, announced he would be standing in the presidential election in November.

Fri. 7.9.90: It was revealed that the DUP leader, Rev Ian Paisley, had been expelled and several clubs and individuals suspended from the Apprentice Boys, because of their protests against the order's application to the International Fund for Ireland. The secretary of state, Peter Brooke, relaunched his talks initiative with a speech in Ballymena, Co Antrim, warning that at some point he might have to "set the pace and show the way". The High Court in Belfast dismissed a Provisional Sinn Féin claim that the broadcasting ban was *ultra vires*. Meanwhile, it emerged that the Home Office had ruled that an Ulster Television schools series could not include the voices of Eamon de Valera and Sean MacBride, both in their day members of Sinn Féin and the IRA.

Thur. 13.9.90: The Calcutt inquiry found that the former army information officer Colin Wallace had been unfairly dismissed. The government agreed to its recommendation of £30,000 compensation. Opposition politicians called for a judicial inquiry into Mr Wallace's claims about attempts to smear politicians in the 1970s and the suppression of the Kincora scandal. It emerged that the SAS soldiers who killed eight Provisional IRA members in Loughgall in May 1987 had "declined" to attend the forthcoming inquest.

Fri. 14.9.90: The Intergovernmental Conference met in Dublin. The communiqué said the decision to withdraw funding from Glor na nGael could be reviewed.

Sat. 15.9.90: An RUC detective, Louis Robinson, was kidnapped on the border at Killeen, Co Armagh, by the Provisional IRA. He had been returning from a fishing holiday in

Kerry with five prison officers, two of whom were also taken and then released. The Provisional IRA said two days later that it had shot him. His body was recovered on the 18th. The Beirut hostage Brian Keenan was besieged by the media when he returned by train from Dublin to Belfast.

Mon. 17.9.90: Fianna Fáil nominated the tánaiste, Brian Lenihan, as its candidate in the presidential election.

Tues. 18.9.90: The governor of Gibraltar at the time of the SAS killings in 1988, Air Chief-Marshal Sir Peter Terry, was seriously wounded by the Provisional IRA at his home at Milford, Staffordshire.

Wed. 19.9.90: The prime minister, Margaret Thatcher, said the Provisional IRA was conducting "guerrilla warfare" against Britain. Labour's Northern Ireland spokesperson, Kevin McNamara, said it was "an easy slip from guerrilla warfare to freedom fighter". Provisional Sinn Féin said the remarks were a recognition that Mrs Thatcher's government was in a "war situation" and that she was "rattled".

Fri. 21.9.90: A protest group, Families Against Intimidation and Terror, was launched to oppose punishment shootings.

Sat. 29.9.90: Tens of thousands of Orangemen marched through Belfast, completing tercentenary celebrations of the Battle of the Boyne.

Sun. 30.9.90: Two teenage joyriders were shot dead in a stolen car in west Belfast by soldiers who claimed they had tried to crash through a checkpoint. Many eyewitnesses said there had been no checkpoint. There was widespread condemnation of the killings in west Belfast.

Mon. 1.10.90: The SDLP deputy leader, Seamus Mallon, said the secretary of state, Peter Brooke, should "tear up" his July talks proposals. There were no such things as the "internal affairs of Northern Ireland", he said.

Wed. 3.10.90: The bound body of William Crockett, a prominent Belfast loyalist, was found in a burnt-out hut in Antwerp, Belgium.

Fri. 5.10.90: More than 800 police and soldiers raided 65 republican homes and offices in Northern Ireland, including the Provisional Sinn Féin headquarters in Belfast. After the unionist leaders, James Molyneaux and Rev Ian Paisley, met the secretary of state, Peter Brooke, at Stormont, Mr Brooke said the differences between the parties, although "of substance", were not "huge".

Sun. 7.10.90: The SDLP leader, John Hume, endorsed the statement by his deputy, Seamus Mallon, the previous week that Peter Brooke should abandon his initiative in its present form.

Tues. 9.10.90: Two prominent Provisional IRA members, Desmond Grew and Martin McCaughey, a former Provisional Sinn Féin councillor, were shot dead by the SAS near Loughgall, Co Armagh. Three people were arrested and three rifles were recovered.

Wed. 10.10.90: The efficacy of the Stevens inquiry came into serious question when charges were dropped aginst five prominent members of the UDA at Belfast Magistrates' Court.

Desmond Ellis, facing extradition to Britain, began a hunger strike in Portlaoise prison.

Tues. 16.10.90: The Provisional IRA had to abort a bombing operation in Derry when the RUC sent a priest to the house it had commandeered.

Mon. 22.10.90: The secretary of state, Peter Brooke, rejected the appeal of the west Belfast branch of Glor na nGael against the withdrawal of its government funding. The Labour party said Mr Brooke was "handing the language back to the Provos".

Wed. 24.10.90: Six soldiers and a civilian were killed in simultaneous Provisional IRA proxy-bomb attacks on border checkpoints at Coshquin, near Derry, and Cloghoge, near Newry. Another attack at Omagh was unsuccessful. In all three attacks civilians whom the Provisional IRA claimed worked for the security forces were strapped into vehicles and told to drive with a bomb into the checkpoints. Five of the soldiers and the civilian were killed at Coshquin and the other soldier at Cloghoge.

Thur. 25.10.90: A political crisis erupted in the republic when a tape was released on which the tánaiste, Brian Lenihan, admitted to having rung the president in January 1982, when the Fine Gael/Labour coalition lost its Dáil majority, to urge him to have the Fianna Fáil leader, Charles Haughey, form an administration rather than accept a dissolution. A five-hour Intergovernmental Conference in London again failed to find a formula for talks.

Mon. 29.10.90: After over nine months on remand, the Provisional Sinn Féin publicity director, Danny Morrison, was committed for trial with eight others accused of IRA membership, unlawful imprisonment and conspiracy to murder an informer.

Wed. 31.10.90: Shortly before a no-confidence vote in the Dáil, the taoiseach, Charles Haughey, sacked the tánaiste, Brian Lenihan, to secure the support of the PDs and win the vote 83–80.

Thur. 1.11.90: The International Fund for Ireland offered the Apprentice Boys a 50 per cent grant towards a £0.5 million heritage centre in Derry.

Tues. 6.11.90: The bishop of Down and Connor, Dr Cahal Daly, was appointed archbishop of Armagh and Catholic primate.

Thur. 8.11.90: The new Northern Ireland (Emergency Provisions) Bill was published, proposing a new offence of "possession of items" intended for terrorist purposes and giving the RUC power to seize equipment used to reopen border crossings.

Fri. 9.11.90: Mary Robinson was elected president of the republic, after a second count when votes were transferred from the Fine Gael candidate, Austin Currie. Ms Robinson said her supporters had "stepped out from the faded flags of the civil war and voted for a new Ireland". The secretary of state, Peter Brooke, said in his Westminster constituency that Britain had no "selfish strategic or economic interest" in the Union, and that a non-violent republicanism could take its place with other political parties in Northern Ireland.

Sat. 10.11.90: Two RUC men and two civilians

were shot dead by the Provisional IRA at Castor Bay, near Lurgan, while out wildfowling.

Sun. 11.11.90: Seven people were detained after a raid on flats in Kilburn in London, when explosives, weapons, ammunition and documents were found in two cars. On the 19th three were charged with conspiracy to cause explosions and the other four were served with exclusion orders sending them back to Northern Ireland.

Tues. 13.11.90: The Fine Gael leader, Alan Dukes, resigned in advance of a no-confidence motion.

Wed. 14.11.90: The Dublin Supreme Court rejected the appeal against extradition by Desmond Ellis, who was flown to London and appeared at Bow Street Magistrates' Court on explosives charges. There were clashes in Dublin among English and Irish soccer supporters intermingled with extradition protesters. A BBC documentary on the Maze prison was previewed in Belfast, showing that the prison authorities unofficially recognised paramilitary hierarchies.

Thur. 15.11.90: Desmond Ellis, now in the medical wing of Brixton prison, ended his hunger strike.

Fri. 16.11.90: Responding to the speech by the secretary of state, Peter Brooke, on November 9th, the Provisional Sinn Féin president, Gerry Adams, issued a nine-page reply saying those who believed there was an alternative to the IRA's "armed struggle" should prove it and calling for talks without preconditions. Visiting the security forces in Co Fermanagh, the prime minister, Margaret Thatcher, sand "we must never, never, give in to terrorism, never".

Sat. 17.11.90: At the SDLP conference, the party leader, John Hume, quoted extensively from Peter Brooke's November 9th speech to show that Britain was now neutral on partition.

Tues. 20.11.90: The new Fine Gael leader, John Bruton, said articles two and three of the republic's constitution should be amended to make clear that Irish unity could only be secured by consent.

Thur. 22.11.90: Margaret Thatcher announced her resignation as Conservative leader and prime minister. It was reported that the NIO planned to close the Maze prison.

Fri. 23.11.90: The biggest ever Provisional IRA bomb, 3,500lbs, failed to explode after it had been driven into an army checkpoint near Rosslea, Co Fermanagh, by a "human bomb", a civilian whose family, the Provisional IRA claimed, had done work for the security forces.

Sat. 24.11.90: Because of fair employment conditions, the Apprentice Boys rejected a £0.25 million grant from the International Fund for Ireland towards a heritage centre in Derry.

Sun. 25.11.90: It was reported that the first secretary in the British embassy in the US, Sherard Cowper-Coles, had told a Boston conference that the biggest mistake Westminster ever made was letting Northern Ireland govern itself and that he had told the Fair Employment Commission that a few "sacrificial lambs" would be helpful.

Mon. 26.11.90: At the opening at Ballymaconnell, Co Cavan, of a cross-border waterway, the secretary of state, Peter Brooke, and the taoiseach, Charles Haughey, discussed a formula to break the talks impasse. The DUP leader, Rev Ian Paisley, said he would agree to Mr Brooke acting as impartial go-between, if he was "acting completely free of Dublin interference".

Tues. 27.11.90: John Major was declared Conservative party leader. Brig Angus Ramsey was declared the new head of the UDR.

Fri. 30.11.90: Five hundred extra troops were sent to Northern Ireland, bringing the total to 11,000. An Intergovernmental Conference in Belfast discussed the political talks initiative.

Mon. 3.12.90: Mary Robinson's presidential inauguration at Dublin Castle was attended by a wide range of religious and political leaders, including the UUP MP Ken Maginnis. President Robinson said she represented a new Ireland, open, tolerant and inclusive. As throughout her campaign, she offered to "extend the hand of friendship" to the north. To strong nationalist criticism, the RUC announced that four border-crossing points in Co Fermanagh were to be closed at night, in response to Provisional IRA attacks.

Tues. 4.12.90: The Workers' party introduced a bill in the Dáil to amend articles two and three of the constitution by the inclusion of a consent clause.

Wed. 5.12.90: After being held on remand for 11 months, the leading UDA figure Tommy Lyttle was returned for trial on 12 charges, including possession of documents of use to terrorists.

Thur. 6.12.90: The taoiseach, Charles Haughey, announced that there would be a white paper on marriage breakdown and that homosexuality would be decriminalised. Donna Maguire, along with three others arrested in June, was extradited from Belgium to Holland to face trial in connection with the murder of two Australians in Roermond in May.

Sat. 8.12.90: The RUC announced the closure of two more border crossing points in Fermanagh.

Tues. 11.12.90: The minister of state, Brian Mawhinney, said he understood the Official IRA to be still active. Three Irishmen were convicted in Florida of attempting to procure a Stinger anti-aircraft missile for the Provisional IRA.

Wed. 12.12.90: The republic's foreign minister, Gerry Collins, addressing the British–Irish Interparliamentary Body in Dublin, said that talks could lead to a "fundamental re-evaluation of all aspects of relationships within and between our islands" and that "everything and anything" would be on the table, including articles two and three of the constitution. The Workers' party bill to amend the articles was defeated in the Dáil by 74 votes to 66.

Thur. 13.12.90: The secretary of state, Peter Brooke, met the unionist leaders, James Molyneaux and Rev Ian Paisley, in London. Both sides later spoke of "useful progress".

Sun. 16.12.90: The installation in Armagh of Dr Cahal Daly as Catholic primate was attended by the president, Mary Robinson, the taoiseach, Charles Haughey, the secretary of state, Peter Brooke, and the UUP MP Ken Maginnis. Archbishop Daly said the IRA had no justification for its campaign and called for the release of the Birmingham Six.

Tues. 18.12.90: It emerged that the DPP had decided not to prosecute the undercover soldiers who had shot dead three robbers outside a bookmaker's in west Belfast the previous January. There was widespread nationalist and civil libertarian condemnation.

Wed. 19.12.90: Two dozen Provisional IRA bomb hoaxes threw Belfast traffic into chaos. The following day there was a further spate of hoaxes. The home secretary, Kenneth Baker, said the broadcasting ban would remain and be extended to include cable television and non-domestic satellite services.

Thur. 20.12.90: The Labour party leader, Neil Kinnock, visited Northern Ireland. A record number of prisoners, 434, were released on seven-day Christmas parole.

Sun. 23.12.90: For the first time in 14 years, the Provisional IRA announced a three-day Christmas ceasefire.

Thur. 27.12.90: Twenty minutes after the expiry of its ceasefire, the Provisional IRA attacked a border checkpoint at Annaghmartin, Co Fermanagh.

Sun. 30.12.90: A Provisional Sinn Féin member, Fergal Caraher, was shot dead and his brother Michael was seriously injured when soldiers opened fire on their car in Cullyhanna, Co Armagh, claiming they had failed to stop at a checkpoint and that two soldiers had been knocked down. Nationalist politicians condemned the shootings and the following day the republic's government expressed its concern. The toll for 1990 of deaths in Northern Ireland arising from the "troubles" was 76, up 15 on 1989, bringing the total since 1969 to 2,849.

NOTES ON CONTRIBUTORS

ROBERT BELL is supervisor of the Northern Ireland Political Collection at the Linen Hall Library, Belfast. His *Book of Ulster Surnames* was published by Blackstaff Press in 1988. He has had short stories published in the *Belfast Telegraph, Passages* and *The Blackstaff Book of Short Stories* (1988).

PAUL BEW is reader in politics at Queen's University Belfast, and author of several works on Irish history and politics, including, with Henry Patterson, *The British State and the Ulster Crisis* (Verso, 1985), and, with Patterson and Ellen Hazelkorn, *The Dynamics of Irish Politics* (Lawrence and Wishart, 1989). He is the current president of the Irish Association for Cultural, Economic and Social Relations.

KATHLEEN BOEHRINGER, originally from the United States, was a researcher in Belfast in the early 70s and is now a lecturer in law at Macquarie University, Sydney.

KEVIN BOYLE, originally from Newry, Co Down, is professor of law at Essex University. He has been co-author with Tom Hadden of various legal and political texts on the "troubles", including *Ireland: a positive proposal* (Penguin, 1985), *The Anglo-Irish Agreement: commentary, text and official review* (Sweet and Maxwell, 1989), and (with Paddy Hillyard) *Ten Years On in Northern Ireland: the legal control of political violence* (Cobden Trust, 1980).

KERRY CAMPBELL (now Goyer), former journalist and former editor of Blackstaff Press, lives in Cushendun, Co Antrim. She and Damian Gorman founded the *Belfast Review*.

SEÁN CORCORAN, from Drogheda, is a performer and collector of traditional music, of which he is archivist for the Arts Council of Northern Ireland.

JIM CUSACK is a former northern editor of the *Irish Times* and is currently security correspondent.

GERALD DAWE'S latest books are *How's the Poetry Going?* (essays, Lagan Press, 1991), and *Sunday School* (poems, Gallery Press, 1991). He edited *The New Younger Irish Poets* (Blackstaff Press, 1991). *See also* Edna Longley.

DOUGLAS DUNN is one of Scotland's leading poets and short story writers. His most recent collections are *Elegies* (Faber and Faber, 1985), which won the Whitbread Book of the Year award, and *Northlight* (Faber and Faber, 1988).

PAUL DURCAN'S latest book of poems, *Daddy, Daddy* (Blackstaff Press, 1990), won the 1990 Whitbread poetry prize. He is a member of Aosdána.

ANDREW ELLIOTT'S first poetry collection was *The Creationists* (Blackstaff Press, 1988). He now lives in London.

MICHAEL FOLEY'S poetry collections are *True Life Love Stories* (Blackstaff Press, 1976) and *The GO Situation* (Blackstaff Press, 1982). *Fortnight* published the revised version of *The Passion of Jamesie Coyle* (1984) in book form.

JACK FOSTER teaches at the University of British Columbia. His books include *Fictions of the Irish Literary Revival* (Gill and Macmillan, 1987) and *Forces and Themes in Ulster Fiction* (Gill and Macmillan, 1974).

GARRET FITZGERALD was minister for foreign affairs in the Fine Gael–Labour coalition government of 1973–77. He was leader of Fine Gael from 1977 to 1987, and taoiseach during the coalition administrations of 1981–82 and 1982–87.

PATRICK GALVIN was resident playwright at the Lyric theatre 1973–75. His latest poetry collection is *Folk Tales for the General* (Raven Arts Press, 1989).

ROBIN GLENDINNING teaches in Belfast. His plays, including *Culture Vultures* and *Mumbo Jumbo*, have been broadcast on BBC radio.

TOM HADDEN, the founder of *Fortnight* in 1970, was editor of the magazine until 1976 and in 1979–81. He is the secretary of Fortnight Publications and the company's principal shareholder. He is professor of law at Queen's University Belfast. *See also* Kevin Boyle.

TONY HARRISON is England's leading author of verse drama, notably for the National Theatre, and his long poems, such as *V*, have been filmed for television.

SEAMUS HEANEY, Ireland's most celebrated contemporary poet, is professor of poetry at Oxford University. He has also held the post of Boylston professor of rhetoric and oratory at Harvard University. His latest poetry collection is *Seeing Things* (Faber and Faber, 1991).

MARY HOLLAND, who began reporting on Northern Ireland for the *Observer* in 1968, now lives in Dublin where she is a columnist on Anglo-Irish affairs for the *Observer* and the *Irish Times*.

FRED JOHNSTON lives in the west of Ireland. He has published one novel and three collections of poetry, the most recent collection being *Song at the Edge of the World* (Salmon Publishing, 1988).

ROBERT JOHNSTONE, a former deputy editor of *Fortnight*, is currently on the magazine's editorial committee. He co-edits the *Honest Ulsterman* with Ruth Hooley. His latest books are *Eden to Edenderry* (poems, Blackstaff Press, 1989) and *Belfast: portraits of a city* (prose, Barrie and Jenkins, 1990).

SIOBHÁN KILFEATHER is an academic and literary critic now living in London.

JOHN LAMPEN, formerly head of a special school in Shropshire, has been a community worker in Derry since 1983.

MAURICE LEITCH'S novels include *Poor Lazarus* (re-issue, Blackstaff Press, 1985), *Stamping Ground* (Abacus, 1975), *The Liberty Lad* (re-issue, Blackstaff Press, 1985), *Silver's City* (Secker and Warburg, 1981) and *Chinese Whispers* (Hutchinson, 1987).

EDNA LONGLEY'S critical books include *Louis MacNeice: a study* (Faber and Faber, 1988), *Poetry in the Wars* (Bloodaxe Books, 1986) and *Across a Roaring Hill: the Protestant imagination in modern Ireland* (edited with Gerald Dawe, Blackstaff Press, 1985). *See also* James Simmons.

MICHAEL LONGLEY recently retired as combined arts director of the Arts Council of Northern Ireland. His poetry collections include *Poems 1963–1983* (Penguin, 1985) and, most recently, *Gorse Fires* (Secker and Warburg, 1991).

NELL MCCAFFERTY, originally from Derry, now lives in Dublin where she is a freelance journalist. Her publications include *A Woman to Blame* (Attic Press, 1985) and *The Best of Nell* (Attic Press, 1987).

ROY MCFADDEN at one time edited the magazines *Lagan* and *Rann*. His latest poetry collection is *After Seymour's Funeral* (Blackstaff Press, 1990).

MEDBH MCGUCKIAN, currently literary editor of *Fortnight*, was recently writer-in-residence at the University of California. Her poetry books include *Venus and the Rain* (Oxford University Press, 1984), *On Ballycastle Beach* (Oxford University Press, 1988) and *Two Women, Two Shores*, with Nuala Archer (New Poets Series, Baltimore, Maryland, 1989).

BERNARD MACLAVERTY now lives in Glasgow. Many of his short stories have been adapted for radio and television, and his novels, *Cal* and *Lamb*, have both been adapted for film.

ED MOLONEY, a former northern editor of the *Irish Times*, is currently northern editor of the *Sunday Tribune*. He is co-author with Andy Pollak of *Paisley* (Poolbeg, 1986).

JOHN MONTAGUE now lives in Cork. Amongst his books of poems are *The Rough Field* (Dolmen Press/ Blackstaff Press, 1972) and *The Dead Kingdom* (Dolmen Press/Blackstaff Press, 1984), *Mount Eagle* (Gallery Press, 1988) and *Selected Poems* (Dolmen Press, 1982).

JOHN MORROW'S short story collections are *Northern Myths* (Blackstaff Press, 1979) and *Sects* (Black Swan, 1987). His novels are *The Confessions of Proinsias O'Toole* (Blackstaff Press, 1977) and *The Essex Factor* (Blackstaff Press, 1982).

PAUL MULDOON, from the Moy, Co Tyrone, now teaches creative writing in the United States. His latest publication is *Madoc: A Mystery* (Faber and Faber, 1990).

SARAH NELSON, originally from Aberdeen, was editor of *Fortnight* in 1977. She is author of *Ulster's Uncertain Defenders* (Appletree, 1984) and of *Incest: fact and myth* (Stramullion, 1987), and is a freelance journalist in Edinburgh.

CIARAN O'DRISCOLL'S poetry collections are *Gog and Magog* (Salmon Publishing, 1987) and *The Poet and His Shadow* (Dedalus, 1990).

FRANK ORMSBY teaches in Belfast. His latest poetry collection is *A Northern Spring* (Secker and Warburg/ Gallery Press, 1986), and he has edited *Poets from the North of Ireland* (new edition, 1990), *Northern Windows: an anthology of Ulster autobiography* (1987), and *The Long Embrace: twentieth century Irish love poems* (1987), all published by Blackstaff Press.

STEWART PARKER died in 1988 at the age of 47. He wrote for television and the theatre. His stage plays *Northern Star*, *Pentecost* and *Heavenly Bodies* are collected in a single volume, published by Oberon Books in 1989.

GLENN PATTERSON'S first novel was *Burning Your Own* (Chatto and Windus, 1988).

HENRY PATTERSON is reader in politics at the University of Ulster at Jordanstown and author of several political and historical texts, including *The Politics of Illusion: republicanism and socialism in modern Ireland* (Radius, 1990). *See also* Paul Bew.

TOM PAULIN, a director of the Field Day Theatre Company, has written poetry, including *Fivemiletown* (Faber and Faber, 1987), verse drama, such as *Seize the Fire* (Faber and Faber, 1990), criticism, *Ireland and the English Crisis* (Bloodaxe Books, 1984), and has edited the Faber books of 'Vernacular' and 'Political' verse (Faber and Faber, 1986).

ANDY POLLAK was editor of *Fortnight* from 1981 to 1985. He is currently assistant news editor and religious affairs correspondent for the *Irish Times*. *See also* Ed Moloney.

GRAHAM REID has written many plays for stage and television, including *The Hidden Curriculum* (collected plays, Co-op Books, 1982) and *Too Late to Talk to Billy*, *A Matter of Choice for Billy* and *A Coming to Terms for Billy* (Faber and Faber, 1987).

BOB RODWELL is a freelance journalist for Fleet Street based in Belfast and covering Northern Ireland political affairs.

RAY ROSENFIELD has for many years been one of Belfast's leading critics on art. She and her late sister Judith were freelance journalists.

JAMES SIMMONS' books of poetry include *The Selected James Simmons*, edited by Edna Longley (Blackstaff Press, 1978), and *From the Irish* (Blackstaff Press, 1985). He founded the *Honest Ulsterman* in 1969, and currently runs 'The Poet's House', a creative writing centre in Islandmagee, Co Antrim.

JONATHAN STEPHENSON, originally from London, was editor of *Fortnight* in 1978. He is also a former editor of *Scope* magazine. He is currently press officer for the Northern Ireland Voluntary Trust.

MARTYN TURNER, originally from Essex, became assistant editor of *Fortnight* in 1971, was co-editor 1972–76, and has been a member of the editorial committee ever since. He is a political cartoonist for the *Irish Times* and several collections of his cartoons have been published, most recently *Heavy Weather* (Gill and Macmillan, 1989). He now lives in Co Kildare.

LESLIE VAN SLYKE, originally from Canada, was editor of *Fortnight* in 1986. She is a researcher for the Radio Ulster programme, *Talk Back*.

DERMOT WALSH, originally from Co Antrim, is a barrister and lecturer in law at University College Cork. He is author of *The Use and Abuse of Emergency Legislation in Northern Ireland* (Cobden Trust, 1983).

DICK WALSH is political editor of the *Irish Times*. He is author of *The Party* (Gill and Macmillan, 1986) and *Des O'Malley* (Brandon, 1986).

BARRY WHITE is political columnist of the *Belfast Telegraph*. He is author of *John Hume: statesman of the troubles* (Blackstaff Press, 1984).

PATRICK WILLIAMS lives in Belfast, where he was, for a time, poetry editor of the *Belfast Review*. His poetry collection *Trails* was published by Sidgwick and Jackson in 1981.

ROBIN WILSON has been editor of *Fortnight* since 1986.

FRANK WRIGHT is a lecturer in politics at Queen's University Belfast. He is author of *Northern Ireland: a comparative analysis* (Gill and Macmillan, 1987).

AUGUSTUS YOUNG now lives in London. He has translated from the Irish *Dánta Grádha* and, most recently, from Brazilian Portuguese.